D1426258

70001599046 3

GREATER LONDON

NICK BARRATT

GREATER LONDON

THE STORY OF THE SUBURBS

BOOKS

Published by Random House Books 2012

2 4 6 8 10 9 7 5 3 1

Copyright © Nick Barratt 2012

Nick Barratt has asserted his right under the Copyright, Designs
and Patents Act, 1988, to be identified as the author of this work

This book is sold subject to the condition that it shall not,
by way of trade or otherwise, be lent, resold, hired out, or otherwise
circulated without the publisher's prior consent in any form of binding
or cover other than that in which it is published and without
a similar condition, including this condition, being
imposed on the subsequent purchaser.

First published in Great Britain in 2012 by Random House Books
Random House, 20 Vauxhall Bridge Road,
London SW1V 2SA

www.randomhouse.co.uk

Addresses for companies within The Random House Group Limited can be found at:
www.randomhouse.co.uk/offices.htm

The Random House Group Limited Reg. No. 954009

A CIP catalogue record for this book
is available from the British Library

ISBN 9781847945327

The Random House Group Limited supports The Forest Stewardship
Council (FSC®), the leading international forest certification organisation.
Our books carrying the FSC label are printed on FSC® certified paper. FSC
is the only forest certification scheme endorsed by the leading environmental
organisations, including Greenpeace. Our paper procurement policy can be found at
www.randomhouse.co.uk/environment

Set in Ad[...]son by Palimpsest Book Production Limited, Falkirk, Stirlingshire
Printed and bound in Great Britain by Clays Ltd, St Ives plc

Haringey Libraries	
CC	
Askews & Holts	28-Nov-2012
942.1	
	HAOL17/8/12(2)

CONTENTS

PART IV:
THE MODERN CAPITAL

INTRODUCTION

It was while I was flying into London from Edinburgh, having just delivered a talk in Dundee the night before, that I was really struck for the first time by the sheer awesome scale of the city I call home. The plane was taking a route over the centre of London and towards Heathrow Airport, following the meandering path of the River Thames. It was easy enough to spot the central landmarks – skyscrapers, tourist attractions and railway termini – but as we flew over them I could see that the heart of London, seemingly so large when you cross it on foot, was completely dwarfed by the sprawl of the suburbs that embrace and encircle it. As far as the eye could see there stretched a dense swirl of terraces and housing estates, roads and railways, occasionally dotted with the green of a park or common.

Of course, I had always known that London was vast, but what brought the realisation so forcefully home to me on this particular occasion was the mental comparison I found myself making between the capital city I had just left behind and the one I was returning to. Edinburgh is not exactly negligible in scale, with its historic heart, its suburbs and its half-million inhabitants; but it's also clearly defined and contained. From the air at least, London seems to have no beginning and no end.

The aim of this book is both to explain how London got that way and to celebrate the suburbs that now dwarf its historic centre. However, I had better make two disclaimers at the outset. First of all, this is a history of the suburbs and the capital's relationship with them, not a broadly based history of London. London has been astonishingly fortunate in its biographers – from John Stow in the sixteenth century through to Peter Ackroyd more recently. Jerry White has written a brilliant trilogy about the capital's history from Georgian times to the present,[1] Jon E. Lewis has published his superb *London: The Autobiography*.[2] Many other historians and chroniclers have made invaluable contributions. I do not see the need to add to this weightily impressive body of literature.

Secondly, what follows is not a detailed history of each of London's suburbs. Tempting though it is, given their rich histories, to give a blow-by-blow account of the rise of Ealing, Hackney, Tottenham or Streatham, there is a real danger that not only would the resulting volume be impossibly bulky but it might well also be impenetrable. Instead I have set out to trace the steps by which a small settlement in the south-east corner of England became so vital to the national economy that it started to draw surrounding satellite towns and hinterland into its orbit, like a black hole sucking in planets and stars, and I have tried to explain how those satellite areas were transformed as a result. In the process, I have sought to explore various recurrent themes: the complicated relationship between central London, which supplied the jobs, and the outer areas which in the early days provided the centre with much of its food and vital supplies and, later on, with much of its workforce; the appeal of the suburbs as a place of refuge from the noise and bustle of inner London; the eastward pull of industry and the westward pull of wealth; the transformation wrought by changes to the capital's transport; the gradual exodus from central London to the suburbs from late Victorian times and the recovery of the inner suburbs more recently. I have also explored the ways in which generations of Londoners have struggled with the concept of 'London' and the long and bitter battle to establish a form of government that encompassed the capital's physical sprawl. To give a sense of how these broader themes have played out at a local level I have tried to include as many specific examples as possible, looking, for instance, at how Battersea developed in Victorian times and why Gospel Oak looks the way it does today.

I should also mention that what I mean by 'suburbs' is all of London that lies beyond the old City walls, that connects it with its twin city Westminster, and that surrounds both. In other words, I have chosen to interpret the word in its most literal and historical sense. It may seem strange to be asked to consider Covent Garden or Piccadilly as suburbs, but, of course, in their time they were and it is only as London has grown ever vaster that they have come to seem an inextricable part of its original self.

◆ ◆ ▶ ◀

London started to spill beyond its walls in the eleventh century, and very soon its chroniclers were taking an interest in what was happening beyond the City limits. Writing in the twelfth century, for example, William fitz Stephen observed:

Also up-stream to the West the Royal Palace rises high above the river, a building beyond compare, with an outwork of bastions, two miles from the City and joined thereto by a populous suburb. On all sides, beyond the houses, lie the gardens of the citizens that dwell in the suburbs, planted with trees, spacious and far, adjoining one another . . . There are also round about London in the Suburbs most excellent wells . . . among these Holywell, Clerkenwell and Saint Clement's Well are most famous.[3]

This description, brief as it is, nicely flags up those elements of the suburbs that made them so attractive to Londoners: as a source of the essentials of life, such as food and water, and as a quiet retreat from the hustle and bustle of a cramped and often filthy city. Over time, as London spilled ever further beyond its ancient boundaries and towards the separate entity of Westminster, so new chroniclers recorded the capital's expansion. The diary of Henry Machyn, citizen and merchant-taylor of London, noted many of the developments that took place during the reigns of Edward VI, Mary and early Elizabeth I.[4] More famously, John Stow produced his *Survey of London* in 1598[5] in which he explored the way in which the suburbs were continuing to march inexorably away from the City walls:

There was sometime in this suburb without Aldersgate an hospital for the poor . . . [and] there is at the farthest north corner of this suburb a windmill . . . [and] without Newgate lieth the west and by north suburb; on the right hand, or north side whereof, betwixt the said gate and the parish of St Sepulchre, turneth a way towards West Smithfield.

Stow's interest in the area beyond the City's square mile was shared by his successor John Strype, who chose, in his new edition of the *Survey* in 1720, to include a description of Westminster. Even so, he still regarded the City of London as a separate entity at a time when the whole of central London was expanding at a considerable rate.[6] Moreover, he had no concept at all of anything resembling a Greater London and no interest in what was going on in the capital's hinterland. No doubt this was in part because he regarded the areas away from London as obscure and unimportant, but his lack of interest was also a fair reflection of where he felt the focus of a London historian should really lie.

It was not until the very end of the eighteenth century that writers began to appreciate the extent to which the City of London and

Westminster were affecting the surrounding area, and how that surrounding area was becoming inextricably linked with the fortunes of the inner core. At the end of the eighteenth century, Daniel Lysons's *Environs of London* explored all the countryside within twelve miles of the city;[7] and it is at this point that we can start to see an awareness of a nascent metropolis, even if Lysons still preserved a strict separation between the largely rural and the wholly urban.

Within a century all that had changed. Walter Thornbury and Edward Walford's *Old and New London*, published towards the end of Queen Victoria's reign, accepted the seismic alterations that had taken place over the previous few decades and the stark contrasts to be seen between the 'old' and the 'new' identity of England's capital city. Edward Walford went even further with an independent project, tellingly entitled *Greater London* (1882), in which he enthusiastically explained that any book on London now had to embrace its suburban sprawl but also raised a question as to where this new giant of a city extended:

> 'Greater London!' What a vague and ill-defined term! We all know
> London proper, comprising the City and Westminster, and making up
> one metropolis. But 'Greater London!' What can the words mean? What
> and where are its limits? and how far afield will it carry us? Do you
> mean the area ruled over by the Metropolitan Board of Works, or by the
> authorities of the Census Department, or by the Metropolitan Police, or
> that which the Postmaster-General takes as the limits of his suburban
> deliveries of letters?[8]

If there is a year when Greater London came of age it is 1889 – just seven years after Edward Walford grappled with his definition of the Victorian metropolis. Today, mention of that date to most Londoners will elicit little more than a shrug, but 1889 was the year which saw the establishment of the London County Council, a body that was granted powers of local government over the suburbs and that therefore had built into its very being the idea that London was now not just a city but a metropolis.

The debates that informed the creation of the London County Council nicely point up the uncertainties about what London was and what it should become. Was there a case to be made for treating the whole area as one, or should it be regarded as an amalgam of villages, settlements and suburbs? How much authority should be wielded by a central body and how much should be left to those who for generations had run London's outlying regions? How far could London be said to stretch, and who should determine its limits? The same questions were to be asked over and over again throughout the twentieth century and the early years of the twenty-first.

The awareness of two Londons – a patchwork-village London and a unified Greater London – that shaped the set-up of the capital's government in 1889 is still deeply embedded in the capital's psyche. Ask Londoners in their home city where they live, and they will answer with the name of an old settlement: Clapham or Dalston or Willesden or Epping. Encounter any of those people away from the capital and ask them where they live, and they will respond, 'London.' At the same time they will be constantly alive to the nuances of different parts of the metropolis. North Londoners pity those who have to make do with life on the other side of the river, and vice versa; cockneys and mockneys regard each other with a raised eyebrow. Every area has its own identity and raises its own expectations, as Jack Rosenthal comically demonstrated in his 1984 film *The Chain*, where people shuffle on house-moving day between Hackney, Tufnell Park, Willesden, Hammersmith, Hampstead, Holland Park and Knightsbridge.

———————◆◆◆———————

'Don't waste time arguing about the accepted premises of life, of which one is that suburbans are dull,' Rose Macaulay wrote in her 1926 novel *Crewe Train*. In the following pages I hope to prove that the suburbs of London and the people who live there are very far indeed from being dull.

ACKNOWLEDGEMENTS

Knowing where to begin with all the expressions of gratitude to people who have made this book possible is an impossible task. What follows is not an exhaustive list; but without the following people's input, 'The Story of the Suburbs' would not have been told by me anytime soon. Heather Holden Brown and her wonderful team encouraged me to tackle this daunting subject; yet it was my commissioning editor, Nigel Wilcockson at Random House, who took the plunge (with I suspect a deep intake of breath) and said that he would publish it. We spent quite some time wrestling with the format; quite a bit longer struggling with the composition of the text; and eventually the book emerged in its final shape. But without his patience, extensive knowledge and encouragement I think I'd still be going round in circles, trying to make sense of the metropolis. And his team of picture researchers and map designers have brought the text to life, illustrating the various phases of suburban development with great clarity. My superb team of researchers tackled the mountain of primary and secondary material pertaining to Greater London, combing the libraries and archives for snippets of information, unusual stories and fascinating characters; Dr Jessica Lutkin, Charlotte Young, Sara Khan, Karen Averby and Genevieve Bovee have done a sterling job in this respect. I must also thank the various people who have read the draft manuscripts for errors, including London historian Fiona Rule who stepped in at the last moment. Any remaining mistakes that you may find are mine alone.

However, the book is dedicated to someone who has been constantly supportive throughout the writing of this book, and without whom it would not have been completed.

To Lydia, *dat significatum vitae.*

PART I

FOUNDATION

ONE

A TALE OF TWO CITIES

The Evolution of Roman and Saxon London

Great cities have an air of inevitability about them. They are so vast and so solid that it is impossible to imagine an alternative history in which they failed to thrive, or where they ended up being overtaken by some other town. When it comes to London, with its great urban sprawl covering some 607 square miles, the city's inexorable expansion from its centre on the north bank of the Thames seems a foregone conclusion.

As early as the twelfth century, London struck its inhabitants as unique. The chroniclers Geoffrey of Monmouth and William fitz Stephen went so far as to propose a pedigree for it that stretched back into the legendary past, attributing its foundation to the Trojan hero Brutus. His city of Trinovantum, or New Troy, they argued, was subsequently renamed in honour of an ancient King Lud, son of Heli, who fortified the city walls:

> A warrior and a generous feast-giver, he . . . always preferred
> Trinovantum . . . Later it was renamed Kaerlud, a name afterwards
> corrupted to Kaerlundein; as time passed and languages changed, it was
> called Lundene and then Lundres when foreigners landed and
> conquered the country.[1]

Yet London's significance was not a given, even in the twelfth century; and it was certainly not the 'inevitable' capital city of England. Before exploring its gradual spread and the complicated relationship between its heart and its suburbs, it's as well to consider the city's rather uncertain beginnings and look at the slow, faltering steps by which it was established.

Whatever Geoffrey of Monmouth and William fitz Stephen might have claimed – not to mention another legend that states that London was founded in 54 BC by the Roman Emperor Julius Caesar – it does seem from archaeological evidence that there were settlements in the

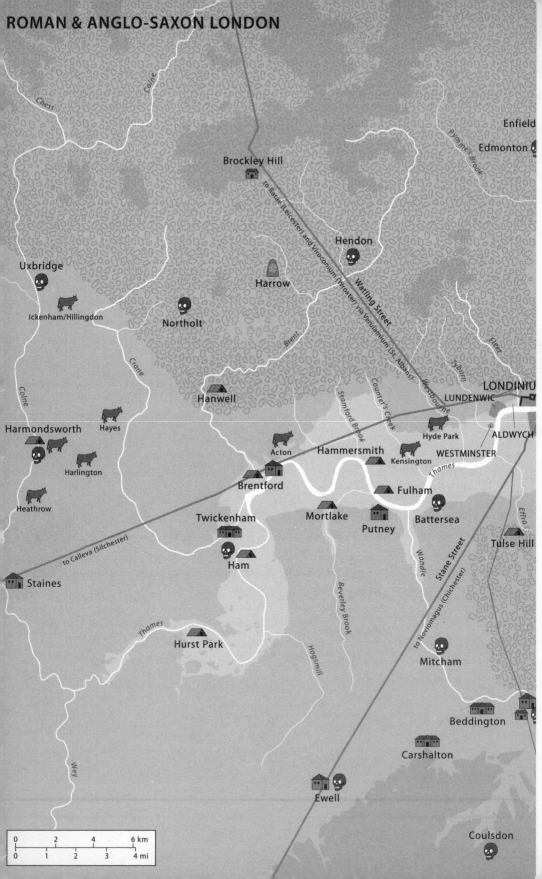

ROMAN & ANGLO-SAXON LONDON

Enfield
Edmonton

Brockley Hill

Hendon

Uxbridge

Harrow

Ickenham/Hillingdon

Northolt

to Ratae (Leicester) and Viroconium (Wroxeter) via Verulamium (St. Albans)

Watling Street

Westbourne

LONDINIU

LUNDENWIC

Colne

Chess

Colne

Crane

Brent

Stamford Brook

Counter's Creek

Tyburn

Fleet

ALDWYCH

Hanwell

Hyde Park

WESTMINSTER

Harmondsworth

Hayes

Acton

Hammersmith

Kensington

Thames

Harlington

Brentford

Fulham

Heathrow

Twickenham

Mortlake

Putney

Battersea

Effra

Tulse Hill

to Calleva (Silchester)

Ham

Wandle

Stane Street

Staines

Thames

Hurst Park

Beverley Brook

to Noviomagus (Chichester)

Mitcham

Hogsmill

Beddington

Carshalton

Wey

Ewell

Coulsdon

| 0 | 2 | 4 | 6 km |
| 0 | 1 | 2 | 3 | 4 mi |

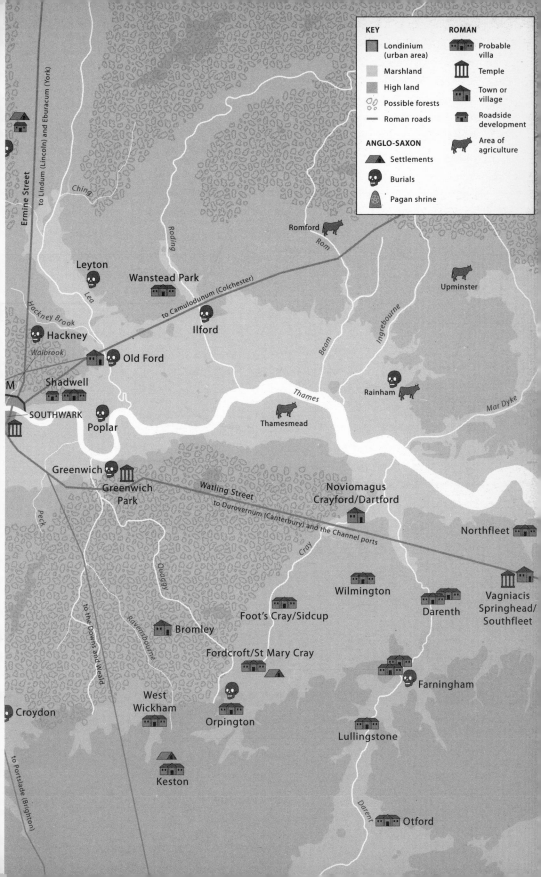

KEY

- Londinium (urban area)
- Marshland
- High land
- Possible forests
- Roman roads

ANGLO-SAXON

- Settlements
- Burials
- Pagan shrine

ROMAN

- Probable villa
- Temple
- Town or village
- Roadside development
- Area of agriculture

Ermine Street
to Lindum (Lincoln) and Eburacum (York)

Ching

Leyton

Wanstead Park

to Camulodunum (Colchester)

Roding

Lea

Hackney Brook

Hackney

Walbrook

Ilford

Old Ford

M

Shadwell

SOUTHWARK

Poplar

Greenwich

Greenwich Park

Peck

Watling Street
to Durovernum (Canterbury) and the Channel ports

Romford

Rom

Upminster

Beam

Ingrebourne

Thames

Thamesmead

Rainham

Mar Dyke

Noviomagus
Crayford/Dartford

Northfleet

Cray

Wilmington

Quaggy

Darenth

Vagniacis
Springhead/
Southfleet

Foot's Cray/Sidcup

Ravensbourne

Bromley

to the Downs and Weald

Fordcroft/St Mary Cray

Farningham

West
Wickham

Croydon

Orpington

Lullingstone

Keston

to Portslade (Brighton)

Darent

Otford

London area in the immediate pre-Roman period. At Brentford, for example, an Iron Age horn-cap was discovered, alongside Bronze Age flint and pottery items. A fine Bronze Age shield found in the Thames at Battersea and a wooden tankard discovered in the river at Kew both suggest that in the second and first century BC the Thames was a place of pilgrimage where ritual offerings were made. As for the names 'London' and 'Thames', these are clearly very ancient in origin, although their exact meanings have been much debated.

Any settlements that there might have been in 'central London', however, were largely eradicated or superseded by the building of a new settlement by the Roman general Plautius, within ten years of the Emperor Claudius' invasion of Britain in AD 43. The first recorded mention of the name 'Londinium' comes in the works of the historian Tacitus, in Book 14 of *The Annals*, when he was writing about the turbulent events that were to threaten the very existence of London in AD 61.

The siting of the Roman city was carefully judged: it was on a stretch of river that was narrow enough to allow the construction of a bridge but deep enough to enable sea-faring Roman vessels to dock. For those coming from such key settlements as Verulamium (St Albans) and Camulodunum (Colchester), this was the perfect place to cross the Thames; equally, for travellers to and from the Continent it was an excellent location to land and to do business. As for the precise location of the Roman settlement, the north bank was favoured over the south bank because it enjoyed certain natural advantages, notably the two tributaries of the Thames – later known as the Fleet and the Walbrook – that promised a plentiful supply of water to the whole settlement.

The early history of London after the Romans decided to settle there is fairly sketchy, and has to be inferred from archaeological rather than written evidence. It seems to have followed a layout typical of Roman settlements throughout Europe – based on a grid pattern and including various public buildings – but its physical appearance suggests haste and a certain lack of confidence, wood rather than stone being the main material used for constructing the various buildings. Its predominant purpose was as a trading post and supply depot, and the evidence suggests that the first residents were primarily civilian merchants.

The foundation of Roman London seems to have angered local tribes, most notably the Iceni from East Anglia under Queen Boudicca; and in the course of their revolt against Roman rule in AD 61, they sacked the city. Suetonius, the Roman governor, probably wisely decided not to risk defending the settlement with the few troops he had at his disposal, opting instead to take the difficult but strategic decision to abandon it to its fate and concentrate on saving the nascent province in which it was situated. In *The Annals* Tacitus states that:

> Unmoved by lamentations and appeals, Suetonius gave the signal for departure. The inhabitants were allowed to accompany him. But those who stayed because they were women, or old, or attached to the place, were slaughtered by the enemy.

After the sacking came retribution, and the Iceni were crushed in a typically ferocious Roman reprisal. In the aftermath of the rebellion London was rebuilt predominantly in stone rather than wood, and more thought and effort was devoted to its planning and layout as well as its defences. In addition to the development of the port and market to foster trade came the construction of such characteristic Roman civic buildings as a basilica, forum, temples, baths and an amphitheatre. Mindful of what

Various fragments still survive of the wall that once encircled the City. This bastion lies in the heart of the Barbican.

had happened to the previous settlement, a square fort was constructed. All embodied a clear statement of intent: from now on, London was to be a permanent fixture on the Roman map.

This statement was given even greater emphasis by the construction of the first stone defensive walls after AD 190. These may have been built in response to a southern incursion by the Picts in the 180s, or at the behest of the governor of Britain, Clodius Albinus, anxious to defend the city during a time when he was engaged in a bitter power struggle with the emperor Septimius Severus. Only fragments of the Roman wall survive today, but its overall course has been traced and would appear to have been used as the foundation for the medieval city wall. It started just east of what is now the Tower of London, running north towards Aldgate, round to Bishopsgate, then directly westwards towards Cripplegate, turning south-west to Aldersgate and Newgate, and then heading down towards the Thames along its tributary, the river Fleet.

In the ensuing decades London became a population magnet, attracting up to 60,000 people there at its height in AD 140, and still home to perhaps 30,000 in AD 250 after a period of political and economic instability had taken its toll. It was certainly the country's most significant town. By Roman standards, however, it remained a very small city in a largely rural setting – an outpost on the edge of the Roman Empire. Londinium's population never reached six figures; Rome, by comparison, could boast over a million residents.

London's walls not only gave the city a degree of security that enhanced its economic growth, they also fixed the boundaries of the settlement: anything constructed beyond them would eventually be defined as 'extra mural' or 'outside the walls' – in other words, not part of the city itself. Roman London, then, helped define the much later suburbs, and it therefore seems only appropriate that the word 'suburb' itself should have a Latin origin: in ancient Rome the wealthier people lived on the city's hills, while the poorer elements of the citizenry lived below, and so were deemed to be 'sub urbs' or 'under the city'. The word 'suburb' was first applied to settlements beyond the walls of London in the Middle Ages.

A trading base, a military outpost and a centre of local government, Roman London was also part of a closely integrated network of local settlements – a city-state supported by a hinterland, extending for about twelve miles in all directions, of villages, scattered farmsteads, villa estates

A statue of a Roman warrior, found in a bastion of the London walls.

and agricultural land supplying food and goods. Quite how many there actually were is hard to pinpoint accurately, thanks to the wholesale devastation that was wrought when the Romans left in the fifth century and to subsequent settlements that were built on top. It is clear, however, that most were situated to the south of the city; to the north the countryside remained largely wooded during the Roman occupation and was far more sparsely populated.

Roman villas, with their perimeter walls and often substantial complex of buildings within them, have perhaps left the clearest mark on the landscape. They were effectively self-sufficient little communities that also served as a hub of local commercial activity. The excavated villa at Keston in modern-day Orpington, Kent, is a good example. It began life as a farmstead, but over time started to make pottery and also undertook blacksmithing and bronze working: industrial pursuits that suggest that it stood at the centre of its own micro-economy. On a smaller scale, Beddington, to the south of London, was a villa estate that came complete with its own bath-house.

An illustration from the eighteenth-century Archaeologica, *showing recent Roman finds in London.*

Agriculture was, of course, key to this local economy. Traces of major Roman farms have been found at places such as Holloway to the north and Cranford to the west; and, a little further afield from the city, at Rainham (Moor Hall Farm) and Upminster (Hunts Hill Farm). Many would have supplied the city with such staples as grain. All were active right up until the end of the Roman occupation, though few south of the city survived the turmoil that came with the end of the Roman Empire to play a further role in London's development. Land was also cultivated as pasture for cattle and sheep, especially in the marshes and floodplains surrounding the Thames at places such as Erith, Rainham, the Lea Valley and Thamesmead.

Not only did London play a key role in the local economy, it also stood at the centre of a network of arterial roads that connected it to other important towns throughout the country, making it Roman Britain's main transport hub. People leaving London would first have passed rows of tombs lining the roads that led from the city. Then they would have encountered a 'ribbon development' of villages, trading centres and staging posts for travellers – both military and civilian. These were not suburban settlements as such, merely a collection of dwellings and retail outlets that hugged the roads and barely extended into the landscape beyond. Further out from the centre, travellers would have come across staging posts at roughly a day's travel, approximately eight Roman miles (about 12 km), from the centre. These were often substantial centres, combining places of accommodation with outlets that provided supplies and equipment for troops, as well as stores that sold more general goods. Notable among them were Enfield, situated on Ermine Street, which ran north to Lincoln and York; Crayford, on the stretch of Watling Street that connected London to the Channel ports via Canterbury; and Brockley Hill, on the part of the same road that emerged on the other side of the city and headed towards the north of England through St Albans. Ewell, located on Stane Street, and Staines, on the London to Silchester Road, are other examples.

The most important of these road-based settlements outside the walled city was Southwark. During the early years of the Roman occupation, it was probably a heavily fortified military site guarding the southern end of London Bridge. It then developed into a thriving place of trade in its own right, occupying a site that straddled the meeting point of two roads – Stane Street and Watling Street – as they approached London from the south. Other key settlements were ranged east and west along another main transport route – the Thames. Villages such as Brentford and Putney, where there were convenient natural places to ford the river, developed in size and importance through the Roman period, to the extent that it is likely that both were equipped with small docks for the further transport of goods and shipping to and from the main port of London.

All this came to an end in the early fifth century when the western Roman Empire entered a period of terminal decline and the outer provinces were abandoned, one by one, to the encroaching 'barbarian' hordes of Germanic tribes. In AD 410 Roman troops were withdrawn from Britain to fight elsewhere, and the Angles, Saxons, Jutes and Frisii, exploiting the country's poor defences, invaded in considerable numbers. This is a period in history about which we know very little – hence the sobriquet 'the Dark Ages' – and our lack of detailed knowledge extends to London. What is clear, however, is that when the Roman forces withdrew, the city was quickly abandoned and fell into disrepair. It became a ghost town, its stone buildings crumbling away even after the new arrivals began to abandon their itinerant lifestyles and look for places to set up organised settlements. Its fate was partly due to the temporary severance of trade routes with the Continent, which deprived London of its previous strategic importance; but it was also due to the reluctance among the Anglo-Saxon settlers to occupy or establish large towns or cities in their new lands: they were essentially warriors, and when they did settle their natural preference was for rural living, not town life. Consequently, they tended to occupy sites away from London, such as Greenwich, Mitcham and Croydon, all of which have yielded evidence of sixth- and seventh-century cemeteries and all of which, therefore, may well also have been settlements. The ready-made city with its stone defences was left derelict.

Many of the suburban names familiar to us today date from Anglo-Saxon times and give a very vivid sense both of the geography of the Thames Valley and the Anglo-Saxons' largely agricultural way of life. The marshy nature of the Thames is captured in such names as Bermondsey (Beornmund's island) and Battersea (Beaduric's island or patch of dry land). Local geography is evoked at Islington (Gisla's hill), Clapham (homestead or enclosure near a hill), Stockwell (stream by a tree stump) and Streatham (village or homestead on a Roman road). Farmland and settlements shape such names as Paddington (Padda's farmstead), Kennington (Cena's farmstead), Kensington (Cynesige's farmstead), Dalston (Deorlaf's farmstead), Wandsworth (Waendel's enclosed settlement) and Tooting (settlement of the family or followers of Tota). There are even hints of early trade at Chelsea (landing place for chalk or limestone), Lambeth (landing place for sheep) and Rotherhithe (landing place for cattle; though this particular name does not appear in written records before the early twelfth century).

Occasionally something more unusual or exotic is hinted at. Dulwich is the marshy area where dill grows. Chiswick is where cheese is made. Walthamstow is a holy place where strangers are welcome. Knightsbridge is the bridge of the young men (the bridge in question being across the river Westbourne). Brixton contains a stone – perhaps marking a meeting place – that belongs to a man called Beorhtsige. Walworth is an enclosed place where foreigners (i.e. Britons) live. Harrow is home to a heathen shrine.[2]

Whatever the appeal of these places to the Anglo-Saxons, the area centred on the Thames, with its navigable route to the sea, proved irresistible over time, and by the seventh century a new settlement had grown up on its banks. It was known as Lundenwic, or 'London trading town'. This new London, however, did not occupy the area covered by the old Roman city; instead it grew up a considerable distance to the west of the old stone walls. Nor could it really be described as a city. Excavations around the Strand and Covent Garden areas, which have revealed the presence of an Anglo-Saxon cemetery, suggest what to modern eyes would appear a large village, though the presence of later buildings makes archaeological excavation difficult and so it is impossible for us to know precisely how the village looked or how far it extended. At its largest it can have been no more than half the size of Roman London.

Furthermore the town of Lundenwic was very far from occupying the dominant position that its Roman predecessor had enjoyed. Because it stood on the boundaries of three of the seven main kingdoms of Anglo-Saxon England, it was not much more than a glorified – and disputed – outpost. At first it belonged to the middle Saxons (from whom the county name of Middlesex is derived). By the early seventh century it was nominally situated in the East Saxon kingdom that became Essex, but although it recognised the overlordship of the King of Kent, it felt an affinity to the East Anglian kingdom to the north and east which also claimed it as its own. The situation had become even more complicated by 670 when the kingdom of Mercia, whose lands stretched to the north, argued that London formed part of its territories. The death of the Mercian king Offa in 796 ushered in a period when London's ownership was vigorously disputed by neighbouring Anglo-Saxon kingdoms, leaving it wanted by all but governed by none.

It's perhaps therefore not surprising that when missionaries arrived in England from Rome in the late sixth and early seventh centuries, London didn't automatically become the centre for Christian worship in the country. The monk Mellitus, who arrived in 604, was made Bishop, not Archbishop, of London, and was later driven away by the pagan successors to his patron, King Saeberht of Kent. He went on to become Archbishop of Canterbury, which by the early 600s was firmly established as the seat of Roman Christianity in southern England.

London did, however, manage to re-establish a modicum of its former economic status thanks to the Thames, which facilitated trading links with the kingdom of Wessex as well as encouraging overseas trade; and slowly, commercial life returned to the walled city as French, Italian and German merchants established themselves in various districts. It is not clear when neighbouring Lundenwic declined, but certainly occupation gradually moved east again in the mid ninth century behind the security of the old walls. Yet easy access to the coast proved to be a source of vulnerability when the Vikings began to raid English shores in the same century. A major attack on London in 842 had left many residents and traders dead, and an even more ferocious assault nine years later saw the city and associated settlement on its outskirts in ruins. With the East Anglian kingdom to the north falling to Viking rule in 869 it was not long before London was overrun again, and in 871 it was used as the Viking fleet's winter quarters.

It was only the resistance of Wessex, under King Alfred, and the defeat of the Vikings at the Battle of Ethandun in 878 that turned the tide; yet it took until 886 to recapture London from the Danes. Alfred recognised its strategic importance as a defensive stronghold against further incursions into Wessex, and work began on rebuilding and revitalising the city and its defence. The *Anglo-Saxon Chronicle* recorded that:

> Alfred, King of the Anglo-Saxons, after the burning of the cities and
> the slaying of the people, honourably rebuilt the city of London, and
> made it again habitable. He gave it into the custody of his son-in-law,
> Aethelred, earl of Mercia.[3]

As part of the defensive measures put in place, the other main settlements around London moved within the old Roman walls, and these were incorporated into Alfred's system of fortified burghs, or forts. According to contemporary written sources, the city became known as Lundenburg – 'London fort' – while a second fortified settlement was constructed at Southwark, which translates literally as the 'southern defensive work'. The earlier Saxon settlement that had formed to the west of the Roman city became known as the *ealdwic*, or 'old settlement', which gives its name to Aldwych on the outskirts of the City today.

From the heart of the Roman administration to a trading outpost disputed by three kingdoms and a bulwark against Scandinavian raiding parties – at this point, the odds against London emerging as the capital of a unified kingdom of England must have seemed very long indeed.

Canterbury and York were the country's religious centres, and York also exercised considerable military and political authority. Winchester was the seat of government in Wessex – the Treasury was located there, for example – and any autonomy that Mercian London exercised under the rule of Aethelred I was lost after his death in 911, especially once Mercia was absorbed into Wessex in 918 and a single kingdom emerged in 927. Then, during the tenth century, there was Kingston, a town on the banks of the Thames eight miles upstream from London that almost upstaged both London and Winchester. Between 899 and 974 seven kings were reputedly crowned on its Coronation Stone, which still stands on display outside the current borough Guildhall complex. While it is a common misconception that the name Kingston is derived from 'King's Stone' (it is far more likely to have derived from King's *ton* or *tun*, a Saxon word that meant farmstead), the fact remains that for a brief period it was a powerful rival to London, offering many of the same attractions: a riverside setting, good transport routes up and downstream, and, quite probably, docks. Most importantly, it had a bridge – one of the few permanent ones built during this period that spanned the Thames downstream from London Bridge.

It was yet another wave of Danish invasions in the closing years of the tenth century and first decades of the eleventh that ended Kingston's brief period in the spotlight. As for London, it played a crucial strategic role in southern England's defence, most notably in 1014 during the Battle of London Bridge, when King Olaf of Norway helped the English King Aethelred II expel the Danes from the city – an event later recorded in Norse saga:

> On the other side of the river is a great trading place, which is called Sudvirke [Southwark]. There the Danes had raised a great work, dug large ditches, and within had built a bulwark of stone, timber, and turf, where they had stationed a strong army . . . King Olaf, and the Northmen's fleet with him, rowed quite up under the bridge, laid their cables around the piles which supported it, and then rowed off with all the ships as hard as they could down the stream . . . the bridge gave way; and a great part of the men upon it fell into the river, and all the others fled, some into the castle, some into Sudvirke. Thereafter Sudvirke was stormed and taken.[4]

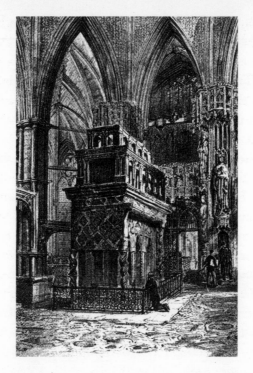

It was Edward the Confessor who transformed Thorney Island into the royal and religious centre of Westminster. This nineteenth-century engraving shows his shrine and chapel in Westminster Abbey.

It's scarcely surprising that no fewer than five churches in London were subsequently dedicated to 'St Olave'.

The respite may have only been temporary, as England finally fell to Danish rule in 1016, but London actually gained from the Viking raids this time round. Its defences made it attractive to settlers, and its population grew correspondingly. What's more, it established trading relations with many of the invaders. Consequently, when the Danish leader Cnut assumed power in 1016 after victory at the Battle of Ashingdon, London accepted his rule, his Anglo-Saxon rival King Edmund fleeing the city before Cnut's forces were able to encircle it. Cnut went on to be crowned in London on 6 January 1017. After nearly 600 years, London was again not just an important trading centre, but a politically significant one.

Even now, though, London was not self-evidently England's dominant city. The last of the Anglo-Saxon kings, Edward the Confessor, was crowned at Winchester in 1043, and when he elected to build himself a burial church he chose the site of St Peter's Abbey, located on Thorney Island – a mile and a half from London and separated from it by rivulets from the river Tyburn, which fed into the Thames. It had previously been renowned as a 'terrible place', though it was much improved by the start of the eleventh century. Edward spent his entire reign transforming the existing modest monastic house into his giant stone 'West Minster', and it was consecrated on 28 December 1065, just a week before his death.

At the same time that Westminster Abbey was rising above the banks of the Thames, Edward was constructing a royal palace on the same site, thus transforming this stretch of the riverbank to the west of the city into a major centre for royal administration. This naturally drew some of the prestige away from the old capital, Winchester, but it didn't automatically confer it upon London. The distance between the City of London and Westminster may not seem that significant today, but at a time when green fields divided the two settlements, they would have seemed entirely separate entities. Indeed Westminster must have increasingly appeared to have been a rival to London – a potentially much more powerful city on the banks of the Thames.

What gave London the upper hand over Winchester was a quirk of history. The death of Edward the Confessor in 1066 saw the Earl of Wessex, Harold Godwinson, seize power – prompting the invasions of

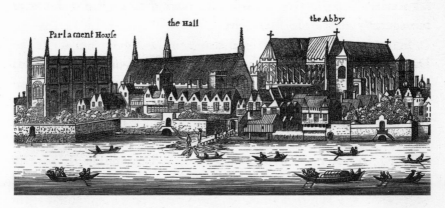

Wenceslas Hollar's 1647 engraving of Westminster, showing the royal chapel of St Stephen (home to the Commons by the mid sixteenth century), Westminster Hall and Westminster Abbey.

his embittered brother Tostig and the King of Norway, Harald Hardrada, to the north, and rival claimant to the throne William Duke of Normandy in the south. Had Harold emerged as ultimate victor, his Wessex dynasty would have remained intact, and Winchester might well have become entrenched as the nation's capital. There was even a moment after William's victory at the Battle of Hastings when it looked as though England might divide into two realms along a north-east, south-west axis, not too dissimilar to the state of affairs after the peace treaty agreed by King Alfred and the Danish leader Guthrum in 886 when the country was split between the independent English kingdoms and those under the new Danelaw. Now the southern area would be dominated by William, whose troops had slaughtered so many southern thegns, earls and housecarls from Harold's power-base in Wessex, while the northern area would be retained by the English. As it was, William managed to consolidate his victory and win the kingdom.

Even then his accession to the throne was not smooth. For two weeks after Hastings, William waited to be invited to take the throne by the Witenagemot – the Anglo-Saxon council of 'wise men' who traditionally met to advise the king but who, in the event of a power vacuum, could decide the successor. However, they proclaimed the surviving Anglo-Saxon blood prince, Edgar the Aetheling, as the next monarch – prompting William to march ominously towards London, which was then serving as the base for Edgar and his key supporters. William's advance was turned back at London Bridge, and he was forced to retreat – devastating Southwark in retribution – marching south and west of London to Wallingford, crossing the Thames there in early December having received the submission of Stigand, the Archbishop of Canterbury, and then reapproaching the city from the north-west. William's forces reached Berkhamsted a few days later, where Edgar formally relinquished his claim to the throne. It was at this point that William was finally offered the crown. His somewhat circuitous route from London Bridge to Wallingford and then up to Berkhamsted is quite telling. There were many places closer to London where he could have forded the Thames, and the fact that he avoided Surrey and Middlesex and travelled round the outskirts – beyond what is now the M25 motorway – suggests that London had an influence that extended well beyond its immediate boundaries.

Edward the Confessor had, of course, been crowned at Winchester. In contrast, William chose to hold his coronation in Westminster Abbey on

Christmas Day, 1066, less than a year after his rival Harold had been crowned there. This was not an arbitrary decision. Leaving aside the fact that the old royal centre of Winchester lay at the heart of what had been enemy territory, William was clearly anxious to emphasise the legitimacy of his claim to the English throne by linking himself to the resting place of his kinsman, Edward the Confessor. He also had more practical considerations in mind. If the new king was to keep an eye on affairs back in his home duchy of Normandy, he needed ready access to the coast, and it was, of course, much quicker and easier to cross the Channel from London and Westminster than from Winchester. His coronation did not go smoothly: the cheered acclaim when William was crowned so startled the Norman troops stationed outside that, convinced the abbey was under attack, they set fire to nearby houses, causing pandemonium. Nevertheless, it set the seal on Westminster's future importance, while William's decision to construct a fortress in London – the White Tower, now the heart of the Tower of London – consolidated London's position as a key city in the kingdom.

The Tower of London was established by William the Conqueror shortly after his victory at the Battle of Hastings in 1066. This early twentieth-century photograph shows the Chapel of St John the Evangelist, work on which began in the late 1070s.

London now became the fortified heart of Norman power, protecting a burgeoning commercial economy centred on the river and the developing port. It was the lynchpin that held together William's Anglo-Norman realm where cross-Channel connections to the Continent were more important than ever. At the same time, to the west of the ancient city Westminster became the religious and political heart of government, with the abbey and palace the focal points for royal administration. Together, these two centres of power broke Winchester's hold on England, although even then it took a further century before the Treasury was permanently moved from Winchester to London (where it was held in the Tower of London). Ironically, London's pre-eminence was achieved by invaders – first the Romans, then the Normans. Now it was in a position to dominate the national scene and to shape its immediate environment.

TWO

FROM THE BATTLE OF HASTINGS TO THE BATTLE OF BARNET

The Expansion of Medieval London

Some twenty years after William the Conqueror's less than auspicious coronation in Westminster Abbey, the king sent a team of assessors to travel the length and breadth of his new realm. According to the Anglo-Saxon chronicler, who followed events with a certain disapproval, the decision came in the wake of 'a very deep consultation' with his council and was formed by William's desire to know precisely who owned which areas of land and what dues they were meant to pay to the Crown – and consequently how much the throne of England was actually worth to him. 'So very narrowly, indeed, did he commission them to trace it out,' the chronicler recorded, 'that there was not one single hide, nor a yard of land, nay, moreover (it is shameful to tell, though he thought it no shame to do it), not even an ox, nor a cow, nor a swine was there left, that was not set down in his writ. And all the recorded particulars were afterwards brought to him.'[1]

The result was the Domesday Book: a vast survey of landholding originally known as the Winchester Roll because, until such key organs of government as the Treasury finally moved to London in the twelfth century, it was kept among other records in the former capital of Wessex. It is an extraordinary document, rich in detail, which allows us to peer back over nine centuries of history to gain a very accurate impression of English society in those first decades after the Conquest.

When it comes to London, however, Domesday is quite literally a blank. Two pages were allowed for the city, but they were never filled in. One can only assume that the complexities of ownership in London proved too much for the assessors, with their limited range of set questions

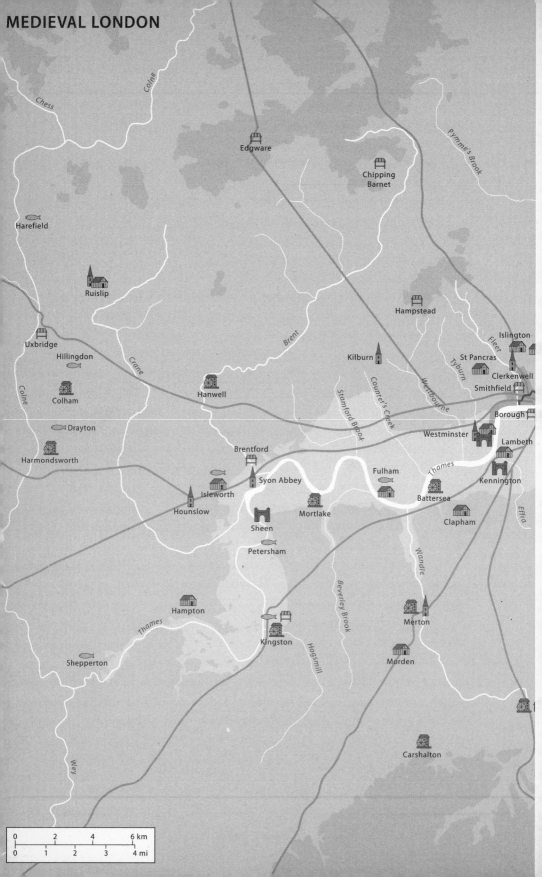

MEDIEVAL LONDON

Chess

Colne

Harefield

Ruislip

Uxbridge

Hillingdon

Crane

Colne

Colham

Drayton

Harmondsworth

Edgware

Chipping
Barnet

Pymme's Brook

Brent

Hampstead

Kilburn

Fleet

Islington

St Pancras

Tyburn

Clerkenwell

Smithfield

Westbourne

Hanwell

Stamford Brook

Counter's Creek

Borough

Westminster

Lambeth

Brentford

Syon Abbey

Fulham

Thames

Kennington

Isleworth

Battersea

Effra

Hounslow

Mortlake

Clapham

Sheen

Petersham

Thames

Wandle

Hampton

Beverley Brook

Merton

Kingston

Morden

Hogsmill

Shepperton

Carshalton

Wey

| 0 | | 2 | | 4 | | 6 km |
| 0 | 1 | 2 | | 3 | | 4 mi |

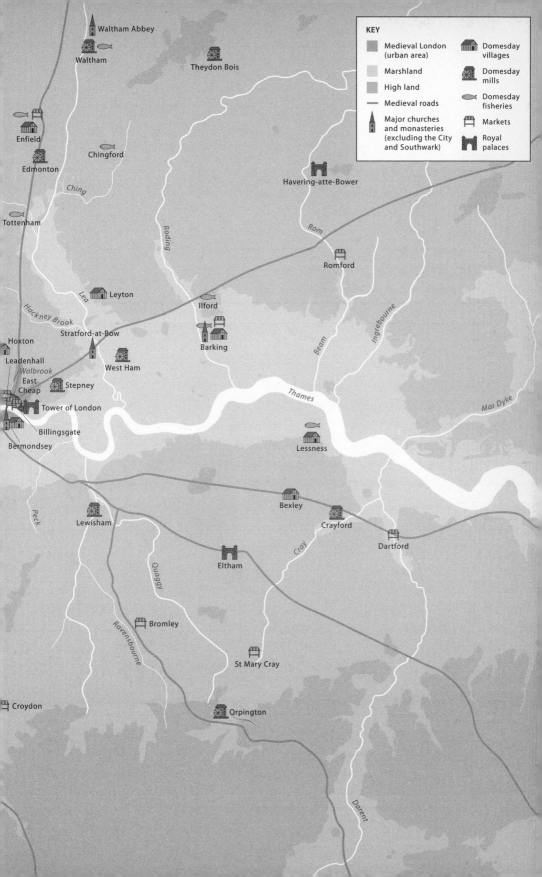

KEY

- Medieval London (urban area)
- Marshland
- High land
- Medieval roads
- Major churches and monasteries (excluding the City and Southwark)
- Domesday villages
- Domesday mills
- Domesday fisheries
- Markets
- Royal palaces

Waltham Abbey
Waltham
Theydon Bois
Enfield
Chingford
Edmonton
Ching
Havering-atte-Bower
Tottenham
Roding
Rom
Romford
Leyton
Lea
Ilford
Hackney Brook
Stratford-at-Bow
Barking
Beam
Ingrebourne
Hoxton
Leadenhall
Walbrook
West Ham
East Cheap
Stepney
Mar Dyke
Tower of London
Thames
Billingsgate
Bermondsey
Lessness
Peck
Bexley
Lewisham
Crayford
Croy
Dartford
Quaggy
Eltham
Ravensbourne
Bromley
St Mary Cray
Croydon
Orpington
Darent

focused on such issues as the amount of arable land in cultivation, the number of plough teams available for working it, the extent of meadows, woodland, pasture, fisheries, and other sources of revenue, and details about livestock and peasants associated with the land. Some other key urban areas proved similarly problematic: the Domesday Book is also silent about towns such as Winchester and Bristol.

We do know, though, that London at that time was already beginning to burst the bounds set by its Roman walls. The population may have been no more than around 18,000, but a geographical area of only one square mile, which also included houses, shops, industrial centres, docks and administrative buildings, was insufficient to hold them. For the purposes of its internal government, the City of London was divided into twenty-four wards. Each contained smaller ecclesiastical parishes, and elected aldermen to the City's governing council, presided over by

The medieval illustration on which this nineteenth-century engraving is based shows the Duke of Orléans, who was captured at the Battle of Agincourt in 1415, imprisoned in the Tower of London. It also gives a sense of how built up the medieval City was becoming.

the Lord Mayor of London. Drawing together all the householders and hired servants of each part of London, each 'ward-mote' constituted 'the basic unit of civic government' (in the words of the historian Caroline Barron).[2] Yet even at this early period, some of the wards covered an area that was partly inside and partly outside the City walls. This was particularly true of those situated near one of the seven historic Roman gates: (from east to west) Ludgate, Newgate, Aldersgate, Cripplegate, Moorgate, Bishopsgate and Aldgate. The parts of the wards that lay inside the walls acquired the suffix 'within', those outside were described as 'without'.

Farringdon is a particularly important case in point. It marked the westerly expansion of the City towards Westminster, and eventually became the largest of the wards, ultimately being divided into two portions separated by the City walls. It was in the Smithfield area of Farringdon beyond the walls that the famous encounter between the young King Richard II and the rebel leaders of the Peasants' Revolt took place in 1381, when Richard showed remarkable calm in a potentially very dangerous situation and the peasant leader Wat Tyler was stabbed by the Lord Mayor, William Walworth, and by one of the king's knights. When Loiset Lyedet came to illustrate the chronicler Jean Froissart's account of the event in the late fifteenth century, he showed an area packed with buildings. A degree of artistic licence may well have been in play here, but although Smithfield was an important livestock market in the later medieval period and still preserved its open spaces, it was clearly also becoming urbanised.

———— ◆·▸·➤ ————

London may have been a blank in the Domesday Book, but when it came to Westminster, the survey was a little more forthcoming:

> In the vill where lies the church of St Peter the abbot holds of this place 13 hides and a half. There is land for 11 plough teams . . . In all it is worth £10 . . . This Manor was and is in the demesne of the church of St Peter of Westminster.

These few terse words sum up an image of a simple 'vill' or village, only a mile and a half from the stone walls of the City, surrounded by enough open land to support eleven plough teams.

Even now, though, Westminster was starting to change. It already housed the newly constructed abbey and palace – the largest structures for miles around; and it was clearly finding favour with the new ruling dynasty. There was a practical reason for this: London was bursting at the seams, whereas Westminster had plenty of land available for building. But there was a political reason, too. London's various wards were very jealous of their identity and privileges, and they often conspired to close the City's gates in times of strife. Westminster, by contrast, was fully under the control of the Crown. It's scarcely surprising, therefore, that when the early Norman monarchs wanted to found an institution or expand an existing one, they looked not to London proper but to the royal district of Westminster. In the twelfth century, for example, the principal seat of royal justice, the King's Bench, was given a permanent home there. The Exchequer – first brought over from the Duchy of Normandy in the early 1100s to tackle the audit and collection of royal debts in the shires – acquired a physical building at Westminster by the midpoint of the century; and the Treasury arrived in around 1180.

Over the hundred or so years that ensued after the preparation of the Domesday Book, this growing assembly of government institutions around the abbey and palace increasingly attracted the professional classes: lawyers, advocates, clerks, royal officials and their entourages. At set times of the year, crowds of several hundred people would descend upon Westminster to conduct official business; there was, for example, the *adventus vice-comitum*, or coming of the sheriffs, to the Exchequer at Michaelmas and Easter, when the sheriffs would bring their payments and associated paperwork (or, to be strictly accurate, parchmentwork) to the Treasury, accompanied by their retinue of subordinates, associates, clerks and guards. Many would then stay for several weeks so that their annual accounts could be audited by the Exchequer officials. Permanent staff required housing; temporary visitors sought places to stay nearby. All required food, drink and the various items that went with the business of government: parchment, vellum, wax, quills and ink (rather later, in 1476, William Caxton would set up England's first printing press in a shop in the abbey grounds). As a result, a network of commercial and residential streets and roads sprang up in and around Westminster, extending down the Strand to the Inns of Court and beyond, quickly forming a suburb that connected Westminster to London. The twelfth-century commentator William fitz

Stephen, a resident of London, as well as a key administrator in Thomas Becket's household, duly acclaimed it:

> Also up-stream to the West the Royal Palace rises high above the river, a building beyond compare, with an outwork of bastions, two miles from the City and joined thereto by a populous suburb. On all sides, beyond the houses, lie the gardens of citizens that dwell in the suburbs, planted with trees, spacious and fair, adjoining one another.[3]

It wasn't just government officials who were attracted to this new suburb. The aristocracy and clerical elites wanted to be as close to the centre of royal power as possible, and established their homes and wardrobes (*garderobes*) not only in and around London to the east, but also in a secondary ring around the business district, which had Westminster situated at its heart. (Wardrobes, incidentally, were originally large storage facilities either within houses or standing independently of them, where rich merchants and their agents could conduct business; it was from this usage that the modern meaning – a piece of furniture to store clothes – was derived.) The properties they built were substantial ones, close enough to the centre of power to be convenient, but also attractively rural in feel – reminiscent of the nobility's country estates and houses. Many, complete with convenient river gates, lined the banks of the Thames, thus allowing their occupants to disembark directly from the river to their property. Those situated along the Strand included the Bishop of Exeter's Inn (built *c.*1310), home to the unfortunate Bishop Walter de Stapeldon, whose closeness to Edward II's favourites the Despensers made him a figure of such hate that he was set upon by a mob in Cheapside in 1326, lynched and decapitated with a bread knife. Then there was the Bishop of Bath's Inn (built before 1231 and later called Arundel House) and the Bishop of Carlisle's Inn (built before 1238).[4] Others started to spring up on the open fields to the north, including Ely Palace (late thirteenth century) and the Abbot of Malmsbury's Inn (mid fourteenth century), both in Holborn.

Perhaps the most magnificent of all was the Savoy Palace on the Strand, built first by Simon de Montfort, Earl of Leicester, in 1245 and taking its name from the uncle of Henry III's queen, Peter of Savoy, to whom it was granted shortly after it was built 'on condition of yielding yearly at the Exchequer three barbed arrows for all services'.[5] By the time that the

In the course of the Middle Ages, the commercial City and the royal centre at Westminster were gradually linked to one another by building development along the Strand. Of the various grand stone buildings that were erected, the Savoy Palace, established in the thirteenth century, was among the most magnificent. This seventeenth-century engraving shows it as it was when it was being used principally as a hospital.

palace came into the hands of the powerful John of Gaunt some hundred or so years later, it was a sprawling complex of buildings, stables, gardens and a Great Hall. Unfortunately, Gaunt's power made him a focus for discontent during the Peasant's Revolt. According to Froissart's *Chronicles*, a mob therefore descended on the Strand and razed the palace 'so that not an upright nor beam was left, but every single thing was burned', or, as the Tudor historian of London John Stow described events:

> They set fire on it round about, and made proclamation that none, on payne to loose his head, should convert to his own use any thing that there was, but that they should breake such plate and vessell of Gold and silver as was founde in that house (which was in great plentie) into small peeces, and throw the same into the river of Thames: Precious stones they should bruse in mortars, that the same might bee to no use, and so it was done by them: One of their companions they burned in the fire, because he minded to have reserved one goodly peece of plate.[6]

By Stow's time the Savoy was a hospital. All that is now left of the complex is the Savoy Chapel.

***

If the Domesday Book described an emerging hive of activity at Westminster, there is less evidence that areas further from the Thames were changing significantly. For much of the Middle Ages, the wider country around London and Westminster remained largely as it had been for centuries: great areas of forest and waste interspersed with small villages and farms. To the north and west was the Forest of Middlesex, a vast swathe of woodland that stretched northwards for over twenty miles from the City walls at Houndsditch, through which the old Roman road Watling Street cut a path. Today, north London contains only remnants of this woodland – Highgate Wood and Queen's Wood, for instance – but to William fitz Stephen in the twelfth century it was a 'vast forest, its copses dense with foliage concealing wild animals – stags, does, boars and wild bulls'[7]. Only in 1218 did the area start to be cleared of its woodland. Meanwhile, south of the Thames, there was the paradoxically named North Wood in Surrey, from which the later suburb of Norwood derived its name; it extended north from Croydon, parts of it surviving well into the nineteenth century. To the east of London was Waltham Forest – now known as Epping Forest – which covered the countryside from Forest Gate to Epping and along the road to Colchester. Marshland dominated the rest of the countryside to the east, as the Thames opened up to its estuary and was fed by other waterways such as the river Lea. It also dominated the immediate area south of the Thames, and patches of marsh were to be found in Kent and Surrey before the land became a mix of open countryside under cultivation and forest once more.

Among these forests, marshes and open countryside were the precursors of today's suburbs – generally small villages, each with a scattering of perhaps a few dozen wooden houses, maybe a grand manor house, one or two mills, a church, some barns, possibly a water mill or ponds, and a stretch of common land where cattle and sheep were grazed.[8] In St Pancras, to the north, for example, there was a good-sized estate containing thirty-five householders, though little in the way of plough-land. By contrast, Mortlake to the west was, according to the Domesday Book, a very large estate indeed, with 110 households, a fishery, a church and two mills. Camberwell to the south was a more modest affair with fewer households than St Pancras, although it did have a church and a large area of woodland given over to swine.

Scattered among these villages were boroughs. The word 'borough' derives from the old word 'burh' or 'burgh', originally meaning a hill fort and settlement, but, as already mentioned, developed by King Alfred in the ninth century into an extended system of walled stone towns established at strategic places across Wessex and designed to act as defensive strongholds to repulse invasions by the Danes. Because of the fragmented nature of communication – especially during times of invasion or attack – the burghs were granted a degree of self-government and semi-autonomous decision making, and they continued to enjoy a measure of independent authority even after the Norman Conquest. Indeed they were often granted charters by the Crown that set out or confirmed the degree to which they had the right to govern themselves. In Domesday, there are references to boroughs at Fulham and Staines in the section on Middlesex; in Essex they are mentioned at Barking, Thurrock and Waltham; and in Surrey at Banstead, Beddington, Bermondsey, Bletchingley, Chivington, Lambeth, Mortlake and Walkingstead. All would have been controlled by members ('burgesses') of a governing body, often formed into a borough council.

Boroughs, however, were the exception rather than the rule. Of the 112 boroughs and towns listed in the Domesday Book only a handful appear in the London area because London itself was the dominant borough. For the most part, the country around London was divided into manors, which served as the basic unit of local administration after the Norman Conquest. Each had its own lord and comprised land that was held by various types of tenant and that was usually divided into large fields which radiated out from the central village. The lord of the manor retained sufficient land for his own use – his demesne, which could be farmed in person but was often sub-let – while the remainder of the land was generally divided among the manorial tenants in smaller strips, often around half an acre in size, and scattered throughout the manor to ensure that no one person had either the most or least fertile land to till. In arable areas, land tended to be divided into three large fields, one for summer crops harvested in the autumn, one for winter crops to provide fodder for livestock and sustenance for the villagers until spring, one lying fallow; and crops would be rotated from one year to the next so that the soil in each field had an opportunity to recover its fertility.

This system of farming required a great deal of cooperation on the part of the manorial tenants, and those at the bottom of the heap – the peasants or serfs who held no land of their own – did little more than scrape by, working on their lord's land in return for shelter, some food and possibly a parcel of waste ground where they could try their luck growing a few crops of their own. Beasts of burden – usually oxen – were the preserve of wealthier farmers; most used hand tools and worked long hours in the fields. Over time, the more successful were able to aggregate strips closer together to improve productivity, and ultimately farming was to be transformed by improved techniques and by the gradual enclosure of common land. Nevertheless, in many parts of the Greater London area land usage stayed essentially the same for centuries, the fields worked by agricultural labourers in Roman times still continuing to yield crops or support livestock until the Victorian period and beyond. Many London place names reveal their agricultural roots. Chalk Farm in Camden not surprisingly recalls the farmland that survived there until the mid nineteenth century ('Chalk' is a distortion of the original Chaldecote, meaning 'cold cottage(s)'). Those place names ending in –ton (Alperton, Dalston) generally recall farmsteads and manors, and just occasionally something more specific is hinted at: pear trees once grew at Purley, just as Plumstead was once home to plum trees. Even that profoundly suburban name Surbiton betrays a deeply rural past: it was once a southerly grange or farm.

At the time of Domesday, there were only a few great tenants-in-chief controlling all this land, most of them the leading magnates who had accompanied William the Conqueror from Normandy when he made his bid for the English crown. Odo, Bishop of Bayeux, for example, was tenant-in-chief of Southwark, Peckham and Hatcham. Geoffrey de Mandeville was lord and tenant-in-chief of Ebury (the name now survives in only one or two street names in Pimlico). Count Robert of Mortain was tenant-in-chief of Bermondsey jointly with King William. Each of these powerful men would then grant parcels of the land they held to tenants and supporters.

The seal of Odo, Bishop of Bayeux, half-brother of William the Conqueror and the wealthiest landholder in England after the king. His estates around London included Southwark, Peckham and Hatcham.

The manor of Chelsea is typical of those listed in Domesday, though at £9 it was one of the more valuable holdings. In Anglo-Saxon times it had played host to various church synods and had been visited by King Offa of Mercia in the eighth century and King Alfred of Wessex in the ninth. Now it belonged to Edward of Salisbury. Meanwhile, the extensive manor of Stanwell was held by William fitz Other, constable of Windsor Castle. His descendants eventually took the name of Windsor, and were unusual in that they managed to hang on to Stanwell throughout the medieval period, despite the varying fortunes of war and dynastic accident that severed the ties of so many landowners from the property they inherited. Indeed the family built themselves a grand manor house, which in 1367 was described as having numerous chambers, a hall, a cellar, a solar (or upper private chamber) with a chimney, a garden, a bakehouse and kitchen, a dovecot, a well and pond, and a stable.[9] Unfortunately, it is clear that by the end of the century they were experiencing hard times: a surviving account suggests that the manor house fell into a state of considerable disrepair.

As William the Conqueror's holdings in Bermondsey demonstrate, the royal family were major landholders throughout the London area. In the thirteenth century, for example, Henry III's brother Richard owned substantial manor at Isleworth. According to the *Chronicles of the Mayors and Sheriffs of London*, this came under attack by Sir Hugh Despenser, keeper of the Tower of London, during the baronial revolt of 1264, and the account reveals one or two tantalising details of what Isleworth was like in the centuries after the Conquest:

> After this, Hugh le Despenser, the Justiciar, who then had charge of the Tower, with a countless multitude of Londoners, went forth from the City, following the standards of the aforesaid Constable and Marshal; none of them knowing wither they were going, or what they were to do. Being led however as far as Ystleworthe, they there laid waste and ravaged with fire the manor of the King of Almaine, and plundered all the property there found, and broke down and burned his mills and fish-preserves, observing no truce, at the very time that the said Parliament was in existence; And this was the beginning of woes, and the source of that deadly war, through which so many manors were committed to the flames, so many men, rich and poor, were plundered, and so many thousands of persons lost their lives.[10]

If the manor was the basis for the composition of most local communities, the manor court was the centre of authority, settling disputes between tenants, enforcing bye-laws, prosecuting offenders and ensuring the upkeep of roads. It was not, however, the only power in the countryside. Enforcing law at a higher level was the sheriff (literally 'shire reeve'), who held single or joint county shires, entrusted to him by the king, and who was backed by a retinue of officials and men at arms. Existing as a subdivision of the shire was the hundred – which dated from Saxon times and was originally based on a calculation of the area of land required to produce a hundred men at arms, or support one hundred homesteads – and the tithing, which was roughly one tenth of a hundred. Each had its own officials, such as the praepositus (sheriff's official).

◄ ♦ ► ►

The Domesday survey makes it clear that many of the networks of estates in and around London and Westminster were owned by the Crown or a handful of important magnates; but it simultaneously reveals just how powerful the Church was, too. The Bishop of London, for example, held great tracts of land in the region, including Fulham and Stepney. Fulham encompassed enough woodland to support 1,000 pigs, while Stepney had four mills: a useful source of revenue. Both estates contained over 150 households, which was a significant number for the period. As for the canons of St Paul's Cathedral, they held the rather smaller estate of Tottenham, valued at just £4 and with only eight households; but they also controlled other small estates around London, including Bishopsgate, and the rather larger ones of Islington and Hoxton. For its part Westminster Abbey held the small estate of Hampstead (where in Anglo-Saxon times the abbot engaged in the presumably unconnected activities of hunting and erecting a gallows) and the very large estate of Battersea. Nor were London ecclesiastical institutions the only ones to own land in the area; the somewhat marshy manor of Lambeth, with its central residence Lambeth House, was acquired by the Archbishop of Canterbury in the thirteenth century because its position on the south bank of the Thames placed it conveniently close to the heart of government at Westminster. Lambeth House soon became Lambeth Palace and the archbishop's principal London residence – even eclipsing Canterbury as a favourite haunt. The Archbishop of Canterbury also owned other property nearby, including the small estate of Walworth, only a mile from Lambeth Palace.

One of the most powerful of all medieval ecclesiastical establishments was Barking Abbey. The Domesday Survey reveals that as well as owning large parts of Essex, the abbey also possessed the manors of Tyburn and Marylebone in Middlesex, Slapton in Buckinghamshire, Lidlington in Bedfordshire, as well as lands in Thames Ditton, Weston Green and Wallington in Surrey. These manors would generally have been rented to tenants or let in return for a share of the profits. Not everything went the abbey's way during the Middle Ages; floods devastated many of its properties along the river Thames in 1377, hundreds of acres of valuable meadow and arable land, including Havering Park and Dagenham Marsh, being lost to cultivation. Nevertheless, the abbey's impressive property portfolio continued to expand inexorably. It also held a market charter for the town of Barking, giving it sole control of markets in the area and ensuring a nice steady stream of rent from traders. By the time of the Dissolution of the Monasteries under Henry VIII in the sixteenth century,

*The Domesday survey reveals that Barking Abbey, founded in the
seventh century, was a major landowner in the London area.
This nineteenth-century engraving shows the late medieval Curfew Tower,
the only complete building of the abbey complex to survive the
Dissolution of the Monasteries in 1539.*

the gross value of Barking's income stood at just over £1,000, making it
the third wealthiest abbey in England, behind Syon – also in the 'Greater
London' region – and Shaftesbury. Its growth was typical of many religious
foundations in the medieval period. They weren't prone to the dynastic
squabbles that sometimes beset the estates of laymen, nor could they be
divided among heirs. Furthermore, they were often the recipients of
generous donations by pious and wealthy people. In the decades after the
Black Death in the fourteenth century, for example, many relieved survivors gave thanks for their seemingly miraculous escape from pestilence
by making grants to the Church.

Comprised of a cluster of grand stone buildings that dwarfed nearby
houses and villages, a major abbey such as Barking would have dominated
the landscape for miles around. It evolved and grew over the centuries

to be far more than just a self-contained centre for religion, piety and education where the monks and nuns fulfilled their religious duties, as well as cooked and slept. This was a mini-village in its own right, with carefully laid-out kitchen gardens, dormitories for residents and guests, libraries and scholastic study centres, brew houses, barns and storage facilities, buildings for washing and bathing, as well as an imposing central place of worship. It might even have facilities that could be enjoyed by local people. One of the most notable features of the London Charterhouse, for example, which stood close to the City walls, was its revolutionary piped water system that provided fresh water to the neighbourhood via a system of lead pipes from a spring located in a meadow that it owned a mile to the north in Islington. On their way to the Charterhouse, the network of pipes happened to pass through land belonging to the Hospitallers of St John of Jerusalem and St Mary's Priory at Clerkenwell, and they too installed a conduit system to take advantage of the new technology. A plan of this collaborative system still exists, showing locations of the pipes, the taps, and the elaborate conduit house that the monastic houses constructed.

Religious foundations also played a vital part in the local economy. They offered employment opportunities, not just for new entrants to Holy Orders but to workmen maintaining the grounds and constructing or repairing the buildings, and were also focal points for the pilgrims whose patronage was so important to the local economy. Furthermore, the presence of an abbey stimulated the growth of local trade and commerce and helped keep the roads in reasonable repair. Sometimes its existence encouraged the establishment of a market town nearby, such as at Barking, Ruislip and Hounslow. Equally importantly, it acted as a hospital for the local sick or elderly. The origins of St Thomas's hospital in Southwark, for example, lie in an establishment set up by a mixed order of nuns and monks within the precinct of St Mary Overy in 1106 – just one of thirteen such infirmaries in the immediate suburbs. Its reputation later took a severe dip (in the early sixteenth century it was accused by parishioners of refusing to give charitable relief to the poor, allowing a pregnant woman to die at the church door, and taking payment from the destitute before they were allowed access to the hospital), but it nevertheless remained an integral part of the Southwark community. Indeed, the complaints levelled against it by its Tudor critics were prompted not by a desire to see it shut down but to see it improve. Ultimately it survived the dissolution of its parent religious foundation because, like so many hospitals that were similarly spared, it was simply too important to the local community to be abolished.

———◄ • ► ———

As London and Westminster grew in size in the centuries after the Norman Conquest, they inevitably acted as a magnet for aspiring artisans and professionals. Many moved within the cramped City walls, or took up residence in the suburbs abutting them or spreading westwards from Westminster. Some, by contrast, preferred to live in the open spaces well beyond the urban hustle and bustle. These were essentially the ancestors of the modern commuter, and one of the earliest we can trace with certainty is recorded in the Domesday Book. His name was Deormann of London, and he was a moneyer with an estate at Islington. According to Domesday he held 'Of the king half a hide in Islington. There is land for half a plough. There is 1 villein. The land is and was worth 10s.'

We know that Deormann travelled widely – there are records of him visiting Colchester and parts of Hertfordshire – but much of his business as a highly skilled maker of coins was conducted in London or with the royal court. His choice of Islington was clearly deliberate: he wanted to live in a rural area, but one that was in easy striking distance of the City, where his business was based. He was to be the first in a dynasty of moneyers, his social rise marked by the fact that one of his four sons was to become a canon at St Paul's. Incidentally, he has a claim to fame beyond being an early commuter, as he also played a role in establishing the standard of the twelve-inch English foot.

But while some Londoners chose to live outside the City and its immediate suburbs, many more elected to pack themselves in with an ever-growing number of fellow citizens. London and Westminster grew rapidly in the centuries that followed the Norman Conquest, reaching anywhere between 70,000 and 100,000 residents by 1300. The City became increasingly built up: Cheapside, its main trading street, contained somewhere in the region of 400 shops by the turn of the fourteenth century. As for the expanding population, they were accommodated in a haphazard sprawl of houses just beyond the City walls in places such as Southwark to the south and Tower Hamlets to the east. The rise in trade with the Continent also played its part, drawing ever more workers into the area around the Pool of London (the stretch of the Thames between London Bridge and Tower Bridge).

In general, these newcomers were drawn from a catchment area that extended about forty miles from London. Some inevitably fulfilled humdrum jobs; others were young and ambitious, seeking apprenticeship in one of the guilds or livery companies that professed expertise in a particular trade and became such an important element of London life from the late twelfth century – the Worshipful Companies of Mercers, Grocers, Drapers, Goldsmiths, Merchant Taylors, Skinners, Haberdashers, Salters, Ironmongers, Vintners, Clothworkers, Dyers and Brewers, to name just a few of the 108 that would eventually establish their halls in the City over the centuries. All required places to work, manufacture their goods, ply their trade and, of course, live and raise families. Starting as a humble apprentice, a particularly skilful and resourceful person could work his way to the top of his profession, finally acquiring apprentices and subordinates of his own.

The names of some, recorded in two early subsidy rolls, or tax docu-ments, from 1292 and 1319, show precisely where they originated. A certain Robert de Fulham, for example, is mentioned in the 1292 assessment for Bridge Ward. He was a fishmonger, and clearly a successful one since ten years later he is recorded as having his own establishment in St Magnus. Working in the same ward was Stephen de Totinham, who moved from Tottenham in Middlesex to run a butcher's shop. Meanwhile, in Cordwainer Street Ward in 1319 were two brothers originally from Barking – Stephen de Berkyngg and Richard de Berkyngg. Stephen was a hosier, while Richard was a draper who enjoyed such a successful career that he was ultimately to be elected sheriff of London in 1341. In Billingsgate Ward there was an Adam de Kyngestone, who arrived in London from Kingston in Surrey to serve as an apprentice to a fishmonger at the turn of the fourteenth century, and who died at the time of the Black Death.[11]

The arrival of the Black Death from the Continent in 1348 had a devastating impact on further expansion. A form of bubonic plague that wiped out up to one-third of the total population of England, it seems to have hit London particularly badly, spreading quickly among the City's crowded population. Its arrival was recorded by Robert of Avesbury, a secular clerk employed at the court of the Archbishop of Canterbury at Lambeth:

> It began in England in the county of Dorset, about the feast of St Peter in chains [1 August 1348], and immediately progressed without warning . . . The pestilence arrived in London at about the feast of All Saints [1 November 1348] and daily deprived many of life. It grew so powerful that, between Candlemas [2 February 1349] and Easter [12 April 1349], more than 200 corpses were buried every day in the new burial ground made next to Smithfield.[12]

At least 20,000 Londoners died in that first outbreak, the equivalent of the entire population of any of the other large cities in England at the time – Norwich, York, Lincoln or Bristol. Naturally enough, terrified people fled from the crowded city into the surrounding countryside, believing that in so doing they were escaping the putrid air that was wrongly believed by contemporaries to spread the disease. The abbot of Westminster, for example, sought refuge in Hampstead. However, so widely did the plague spread that its effects were almost as catastrophic in the outer regions as they were in the inner suburbs and City itself. It has been estimated that up to half of Barnet's residents died, and that Enfield's population was literally decimated, losing one in ten residents in a short period of only five months. In the small village of Brent, thirteen deaths were recorded during the pestilence, pushing it close to extinction as a functioning community. Southern Kingsbury, which had once been a village, became a church and a couple of virtually abandoned farms. As successive waves of pestilence struck, so communities dwindled further. In normal years, around 30 wills were enrolled in the City of London's Court of Husting; that number soared to 352 in 1349, and it reached 150 in the course of the next devastating plague year, 1361.

In the decades after those first virulent outbreaks of the plague, the population slowly recovered (though it was to be a century and a half before it was to reach pre-Black Death levels again). Building and rebuilding resumed almost at once, and by 1497 Andreas Franciscus, an Italian merchant, was able to say: 'The town itself stretches from East to

West, and is three miles in circumference. However, its suburbs are so large that they greatly increase its circuit.'[13]

As recovery took root, various well-to-do Londoners are recorded as purchasing property both in London proper and in the surrounding countryside – a sure sign of returning financial health and social aspiration. We know, for example, that the master mason Henry Yevele, who worked on Westminster Abbey and on John of Gaunt's Savoy Palace, and who owned various properties in London in addition to his own houses on Bridge Street near London Bridge, also bought estates elsewhere. According to his will, drawn up in 1400, he left lands and tenements in Wennington in Essex (now in the borough of Havering) to his wife Katherine for the term of her life.[14] Half a century later, his fellow mason John Comyn was also in a position to own property outside the city, even though his career scarcely hit the heady heights achieved by Yevele. Comyn left his daughter Katherine various lands and tenements in Yeading in the parish of Hayes, Middlesex. These holdings outside London were clearly not just intended to be investments. The fact that he also left a bequest to a certain John Godfrey of Hayes suggests that he enjoyed a social life both in London and in Middlesex.[15]

In fact, it does seem that many of those wealthier Londoners who owned property outside the City did so because they wanted somewhere to retreat to: a place of recreation within easy reach of London. Robert Amadas, a successful early Tudor goldsmith, had two properties outside the City, one in Barking and a small manor called 'Jenkyns' in Essex; we know that he and his family stayed in at least one of the Essex properties from time to time.[16] It is scarcely surprising, therefore, that throughout the later Middle Ages and early Tudor period a band of development started to grow up around the city, extending for perhaps twenty miles, that increasingly became home to the well-to-do and to retired Londoners – ex-mayors and aldermen, for example, who wanted to leave the hustle and bustle of City life behind them now that they were no longer part of the political scene. The legendary merchant and thrice-time mayor Dick Whittington (c.1350–1423) may have had few holdings outside the City, but his contemporary and business rival John Hende, who achieved the office of mayor twice, owned twelve manors and various other holdings in Essex and Kent.

*A late sixteenth-century depiction of Cheapside, the main trading street of
the medieval City of London.*

This band around the centre was, however, not just a refuge for
Londoners. It was also a vital source of supplies for a city whose population could not possibly have supported itself without outside help. We
know from the Domesday Book that manors within easy reach of London
provided the City's markets with fresh produce on a daily basis. Key
trading centres grew up, each with a particular speciality. There were meat
markets at East Cheap, Newgate Shambles and the Stocks; grain markets
at Queenhithe, Billingsgate, Newgate Pavement and Gracechurch Street;
fish markets at Bridge Street, Old Fish Street and the Stocks. More
general places of trade could be found at Cheapside, Newgate, Cornhill
and Leadenhall markets.

Because of the power and influence wielded by these central markets,
restrictions were placed over time on potential rivals close to the centre
that could have taken business away from them. Between 1175 and 1327
royal grants were awarded to Bromley, Chipping Barnet, Edgware,
Enfield, Romford and St Mary Cray; but in that latter year the Crown
specifically prohibited the establishment of new markets within a
seven-mile radius of the City.[17] The result was that whereas southern
counties with a strong agricultural base, such as Suffolk and
Hertfordshire, had roughly one market per 12,500 acres, Middlesex

and Surrey were limited to only one every 20,000 acres. London dominated the sale of food.

The Thames Valley proved to be a rich source of grain for the mouths of hungry Londoners. Its importance is nicely demonstrated by an argument that was advanced as late as 1632 that the cost of bread in London should be pegged to the cost of wheat in outlying markets as far away as Barking, Uxbridge, Brentford, Kingston, Hampstead, Croydon and Dartford (north-east Kent was a particularly important granary for the growing City). Towards the end of the Middle Ages there was a perceptible shift from arable to pastoral farming in the London area, as the City's demand for corn inevitably contracted after the Black Death and the price of wool rose, making it an increasingly attractive commercial proposition. Fresh livestock remained in demand, however, and a number of London butchers actually bought up manors near the City so that they could raise their own stock. Tottenham and Havering were among the areas favoured, as was the fertile grazing land of the Lea Valley.[18]

The restriction on markets close to the City encouraged the growth of several vital 'gateway' markets that had developed on its immediate outskirts. Borough Market, founded around the turn of the eleventh century, was one such. Smithfield, probably in existence in the tenth century, was another, its name soon synonymous with meat and livestock. It still functions today, while road names such as Cow Cross Street and Cock Lane preserve a memory of its former extent (a few others, such as Goose Alley, disappeared in the nineteenth century). Not that the London markets had it all their own way; the butchers of London, anxious to get the best deals they could, are known to have resorted to direct contact with graziers, and by the sixteenth century were also buying a large proportion of their supplies directly from Barnet cattle market to the north. The market men at Smithfield were far from happy with this, and made their discontent known.[19]

Certain areas became known for particular food stuffs. Enfield, for example, became famous for its meal and malt, though as it did not enjoy a monopoly, in time it came to face stiff competition from such places as Brentford, Kingston and Croydon.[20] Kent, Essex and Surrey acquired a reputation for their hop-grounds and orchards. Many manors employed a professional gardener and sold produce from their gardens to London and its merchants. The manor of Knightsbridge sold honey in the early fourteenth century; the manor of Laleham in Middlesex sold garden fruits to London merchant fruiterers in the fifteenth and sixteenth centuries; the manor of Holborn was prolific in its production of all varieties of fruit, vegetables and wine.

In time, market gardening became an important part of London's economy and market gardens an increasingly visible feature on its outskirts. The first mention of a guild of gardeners comes in 1345. In the early sixteenth century, Protestant refugees from the Netherlands were setting up market gardens in Kent and in such areas south of the Thames as Battersea and Wimbledon, where they cultivated novelties that included orange carrots. By the seventeenth century the suburban market gardeners were a force to be reckoned with, forming a company and receiving a royal charter of incorporation in 1605 that gave them jurisdiction over all gardening within six miles of London. This put the noses of the City authorities badly out of joint, though a report written by the City's aldermen in 1635 does give a grudging sense of the flourishing nature of market gardening among the husbandmen of Chelsea, Fulham and Kensington:

> They sowe seedes for parsnipps, turnopps, carriotts and the like in their Comon feildes whereof most of them they plough upp and others they digge upp with the spade . . . by this manner of Husbandry and ympoloyment of their groundes the Cittys of London and Westminster and places adiacent are furnished with above fower and twenty Thousand loades yearely of Roots as is credibly affirmed . . . some of them have belonging to their houses one two or three acres of ground in orchards and gardens which they ymploy and husband in setting forth and planting of Roses, Raspesses, strawberries, gooseberries, herbes for foode and Phisick which besides their owne necessary use they bring to the Marketts both of this Citty, the Citty of Westminster and other places adiacent'.[21]

Of course, it wasn't just food that London's neighbours were called upon to supply. Although manufacturing went on in the City itself – metalwork, clothes making and so on – some took place in important centres such as Kingston, and what was produced there (pottery, for example) often found its way to the City. Faggots for fuel and timbers for building also came in from the countryside around London. The heavily forested manors of Acton, Edgware and Hampstead (all in Middlesex) supplied around 3,000 to 4,000 faggots a year to the City in the early fourteenth century.[22] The royal manor of Havering also sold large quantities of wood to London for building and as fuel. Local specialists produced small bundles of firewood, called bavins, which proved particularly useful for the City's baking and brewing kilns. These came mainly from the manors of Hendon, Colham and Hyde in Middlesex.[23]

Heavier items tended to be carried by river, and so it is not surprising that the former royal centre of Kingston, with its stone bridge (still the only Thames crossing south of London Bridge) and its docks should have thrived in medieval times.[24] Kingston boasted its own market and a guildhall, not to mention its ancient church, mills and fisheries; and it was surrounded by rich farmland and woods, out of which various monarchs carved parklands and pleasure grounds. Just a couple of miles downstream in the early Tudor period, Cardinal Wolsey built his grand Hampton Court – and was then compelled to relinquish it to his difficult master, Henry VIII.

Southwark was also an important trading centre for London, but it enjoyed a rather freewheeling, if not an outright bawdy, reputation. Most of the area was held under the jurisdiction of the bishops of Winchester, who managed it very differently from the neighbouring City. It was here that tradesmen and craftsmen came if they wanted to sell their wares away from the prying eyes and scrutiny of the increasing number of livery companies in London, and it was also here that London's red-light district grew up, with the aptly and graphically named Gropecunt Lane and adjacent Popkirtle Lane, first recorded in the thirteenth century. It may seem surprising that prostitution should have been allowed by the Church, but it seems that the bishops of Winchester took a relaxed view of brothels, and realised that while there was no money in condemning them, there was certainly profit to be made out of controlling them. It was later claimed that the regulations under which they operated dated back to the time of Henry II. However, it was more likely that the specific rules governing brothels (or 'stews') were formalised in the fifteenth century, including the stipulations:

LAMBETH *Palais des Archevêques de* CANTORBERY

The southern bank of the Thames remained relatively undeveloped in the Middle Ages, apart from Southwark, Bermondsey and the Archbishop of Canterbury's residence at Lambeth. This eighteenth-century engraving of Lambeth Palace shows that, even several centuries later, the area retained a largely rural feel.

That no stewholder or his wife should let or stay any single woman to go and come freely at all times when they listed [liked] . . .

Not to keep open his doors upon the holy days . . .

No man to be drawn or enticed into any stewhouse . . .

No stewholder to keep any woman that has the perilous infirmity of burning [venereal disease].

Ordinances were passed whereby the river's boatmen were not allowed to carry passengers from Southwark to London after sunset and before sunrise. These, however, were not sufficient to remove temptation.

Inevitably, as London and Westminster expanded, they attracted and absorbed ever more power and authority. However, they weren't the only stage on which major events were played out in the Middle Ages. The big religious foundations, for example, with their substantial buildings and rich estates, were often host to the great and the good or became the setting for important gatherings. Barking Abbey was where William the Conqueror received the submission of the Saxon earls Edwin and Morcar. Lambeth Palace witnessed the signing of the Treaty of Lambeth between Louis of France and the regents of the young Henry III in 1217. In 1232 King Henry III ordered the mayor of London to rally an armed force to seize the royal justiciar Hugh de Burgh from his refuge in Merton Priory. If the chroniclers of the period are to be believed, the mayor duly obliged, surrounding the priory with some 20,000 men. Four years later, in January 1236, Merton was the venue for an even more important gathering, when Henry III convened a meeting to discuss various issues affecting the major landowners of the realm. In the normal run of events, such a meeting would almost certainly have been held at the Palace of Westminster. However, according to the historian John Stow in the sixteenth century, Westminster had been rendered uninhabitable by the severity of a winter that had caused the Thames to overflow its banks: 'And in the great Palace of Westminster men did row with wherries in the midst of the Hall, being forced to ride to their chambers.'[25] The meeting at Merton has been described as England's first 'Parliament', with the Statutes of Merton that emerged constituting the basis for large sections of English common law.

Henry's presence at Merton is a reminder that throughout the Middle Ages and beyond, the English monarchy was itinerant. Westminster may have been a major royal palace, but it certainly wasn't the only one. Henry III, for example, certainly spent time there, but he also owned palaces at Havering and Kennington. Indeed, as time went on, the royal family became increasingly fond of adding new palaces to their extensive property holdings; and since they sought to construct buildings that were far grander than anything owned by their subjects and also insisted on grand parks and forested areas around them, they had to look beyond London to the countryside for suitable sites. At the same time, though, they needed their palaces to be located within easy reach of Westminster, and this helps to explain why so many of

The monarchy remained itinerant throughout the Middle Ages, travelling widely through their kingdom and with palaces and residences scattered across the South East. In 1290 Edward I and his wife Eleanor were visiting Lincolnshire when the queen fell ill and died. Her body was brought back to Westminster, and a cross was erected at each place that it had rested on its journey, the final one being at Charing Cross. This nineteenth-century engraving shows the Eleanor Cross at Waltham Cross.

the fine buildings that sprang up in the later Middle Ages lay on or near the Thames: Bridewell, Elsynge, Greenwich, Richmond, Hampton Court and Nonsuch.

Richmond is a typical example. It started out life as a manor house in the village of Sheen, which Edward III enlarged and beautified, dying there in 1377, deserted by all (his mistress Alice Perrers even went so far as to prise the rings off his dead fingers). It was a favourite summer haunt of his grandson and successor Richard II, who entertained up to 10,000 guests there each day he was in residence. So devastated was he when his wife Anne of Bohemia died at Sheen in 1394 that he ordered the palace to be destroyed; but it nevertheless went on to be rebuilt by Henry V and used by his successors. After a fire in 1497 it was remodelled in stone and renamed Richmond after the family title of the new king, Henry VII. It remained a favourite royal residence throughout the sixteenth century and many lavish celebrations were held there.

Like other royal palaces on the Thames, Richmond transformed its locale. The royal household's constant demand for lavish food, drink, furnishings and fittings encouraged a vibrant regional economy. It also attracted aristocrats and other court hangers-on, many of whom built, bought or were granted property nearby (Elizabeth I, for example, gave Robert Dudley the conveniently located Kew House in the late sixteenth century). As a result, the small village which nestled close to Richmond Palace prospered and expanded; and over time, the Thames became a suburban corridor reaching out far to the west of London to Teddington, ribboned with grand houses, markets and fairs. In the late sixteenth and early seventeenth centuries this part of the river would give rise to Ham House, Syon Park and Kensington Palace.

At the other end of the social scale, certain areas of the open countryside around London proved convenient gathering points for unrest at various times in the Middle Ages. Pride of place here has to be given to Blackheath. During the Peasants' Revolt of 1381, for example, when groups of armed peasants set off from Essex and Kent to protest about the new poll tax, they congregated on this 'dark heathland', before heading towards London from the south. Having progressed to Southwark, they went on to attack the Duke of Lancaster's home, the Savoy Palace on the Strand, and marched to the Tower of London, where the hapless Archbishop of Canterbury and Sir Robert Hales were dragged out and summarily executed. Meanwhile, people from Middlesex marched into the city from the north. Some broke off to destroy the manor house at Highbury, while the residents of Chipping Barnet forced the abbot of St Albans to grant them a charter.

Blackheath proved a mustering ground again in 1450 during Jack Cade's rebellion against the inept government of Henry VI. This time the insurgents built defences of ditches and stakes there before marching on London via Southwark. They managed to take the city, but Cade was eventually defeated. He was then formally hanged, drawn and quartered, a portion of his mutilated body being sent for display at Blackheath as a warning to others. Later the king mustered his Lancastrian supporters at Blackheath as Richard, Duke of York – the leading critic of Henry's government – marched south with the intention of taking the capital, reaching Kingston before he was informed that the gates of the City would remain closed to him.

Perhaps Blackheath's most dramatic moment came some years after Henry VI's death, when a new royal dynasty under the Tudor Henry VII found himself facing the unlikely-sounding Cornish Rebellion in 1497. Over 15,000 armed protesters arrived at Guildford on 13 June, the same day that Henry VII's hastily recalled army of 8,000 troops, who had been heading north to Scotland, assembled on Hounslow Heath; and the two

Hadley Green, site of one of the most decisive battles of the Wars of the Roses, as it was in the nineteenth century.

sides skirmished outside Guildford the following day. When it became clear that the rebels had not gained the support of the men of Kent as they had hoped, they decided to head towards London from the south through Surrey via Banstead, eventually making their camp at Blackheath. The two armies clashed there on 17 June at what became known as the Battle of Deptford Bridge, where the rebels were ultimately crushed.

On the other side of the Thames, fields near the small town of Barnet were the setting for one of the decisive battles of the Wars of the Roses. Fought in thick fog on the morning of 14 April 1471, the Battle of Barnet culminated in the death of one of the most controversial figures of the fifteenth century, Richard, Earl of Warwick – the 'kingmaker' – and so allowed the Yorkist Edward IV to resume the throne that he had first seized from Henry VI in 1461.

PART II

EXPANSION

THREE

'THE MONSTROUS GROWTH'

The Tudor and Stuart Inner Suburbs

By the end of the Middle Ages the Thames Valley region was recovering from the ravages of the Black Death, and by 1550 the population of London had reached around 120,000. Most remained crammed behind the City walls. Many thousands more huddled in the crowded suburbs immediately outside. Upstream, London's twin city, Westminster, provided another suburban centre in what would later become the West End, a fair number of its population of around 3,500 coming from the aristocracy and the professional classes involved in one way or another with the governance of the nation. Areas further away from the centre continued to expand, though at a much slower rate – even in mid Tudor times the entire population of the county of Middlesex scarcely reached 40,000.

Already, though, there were the first signs of that accelerated expansion that was to become such a hallmark of the Greater London area over the ensuing centuries – indeed, even before the end of the sixteenth century the population of the City and the immediate area around it had grown by around two-thirds in the space of about a hundred years. London's ever-growing ascendancy as a trading centre was a crucial factor here. It was Tudor England's vibrant trading hub, taking goods – particularly woollen cloth – from East Anglia, the Cotswolds and elsewhere to sell locally and to export to the Continent. Ships loaded with cloth would regularly set out along the Thames for ports such as Antwerp. On their homeward voyage they would be loaded down with silks, wines, spices and iron which would then be traded in London's busy markets. The City's streets became increasingly packed with English and foreign merchants, with craftsmen and labourers, and with dock workers and sailors. It's scarcely surprising that London's population should have continued to rise.

THE TUDOR AND EARLY STUART INNER SUBURBS

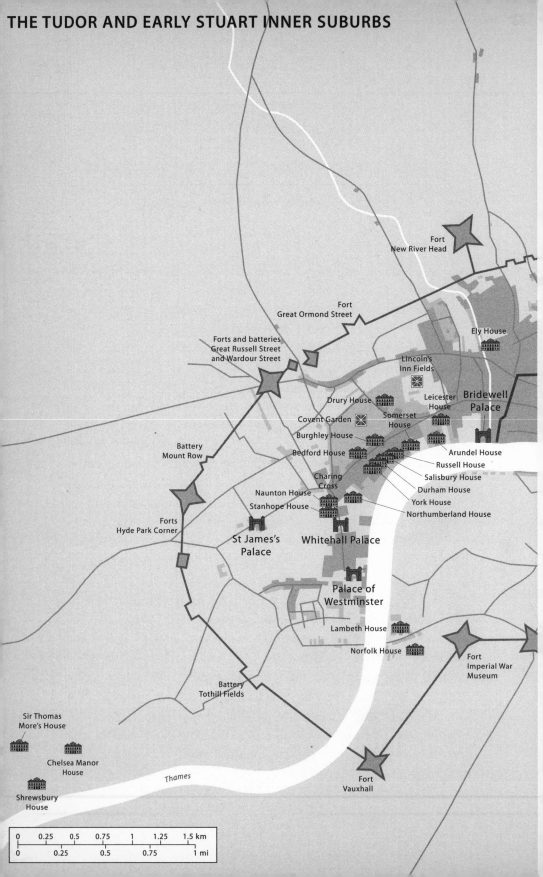

Fort
New River Head

Fort
Great Ormond Street

Forts and batteries
Great Russell Street
and Wardour Street

Ely House

Lincoln's
Inn Fields

Drury House

Leicester
House

Bridewell
Palace

Covent Garden

Somerset
House

Burghley House

Battery
Mount Row

Bedford House

Arundel House

Russell House

Salisbury House

Charing
Cross

Durham House

Naunton House

York House

Stanhope House

Northumberland House

Forts
Hyde Park Corner

St James's
Palace

Whitehall Palace

Palace of
Westminster

Lambeth House

Norfolk House

Fort
Imperial War
Museum

Battery
Tothill Fields

Sir Thomas
More's House

Chelsea Manor
House

Fort
Vauxhall

Shrewsbury
House

Thames

0	0.25	0.5	0.75	1	1.25	1.5 km
0		0.25	0.5		0.75	1 mi

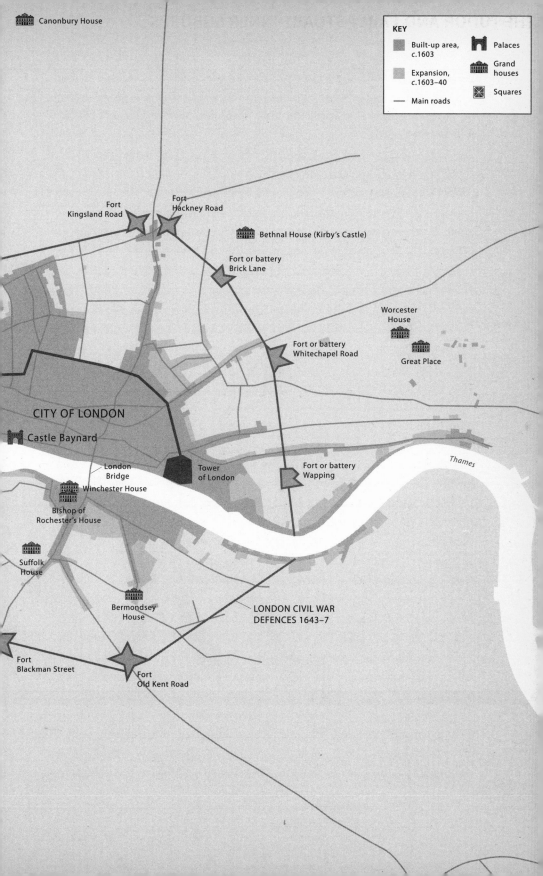

Canonbury House

KEY

	Built-up area, c.1603		Palaces
	Expansion, c.1603–40		Grand houses
—	Main roads		Squares

Fort Kingsland Road

Fort Hackney Road

Bethnal House (Kirby's Castle)

Fort or battery Brick Lane

Worcester House

Fort or battery Whitechapel Road

Great Place

CITY OF LONDON

Castle Baynard

London Bridge

Winchester House

Bishop of Rochester's House

Tower of London

Fort or battery Wapping

Thames

Suffolk House

Bermondsey House

LONDON CIVIL WAR DEFENCES 1643–7

Fort Blackman Street

Fort Old Kent Road

There was, however, another reason why the Greater London area was transformed in Tudor times, and it had less to do with the grand sweep of European trade than with the more local difficulty of Henry VIII, his first wife's inability to yield him a male heir, his insistence on a divorce, the row he had with Pope Clement VII as a result, and the break with the Church of Rome that ensued.

The Dissolution of the Monasteries that came in the wake of Henry's quarrel with Rome may superficially seem a largely political and religious affair, of interest to Church historians and lovers of old buildings, but of otherwise limited significance. However, the consequences for the London area, and indeed for the whole of England, went far beyond matters of government and faith. If London's growing importance as a trading centre gradually transformed its economy, the Dissolution of the Monasteries not only had an immediate impact on its economy, but also transformed its institutions, the nature of its population and even its physical appearance. Had Henry VIII not divorced Catherine of Aragon the London area today would look very different indeed.

Once Henry had decided to make the break with Rome, his right-hand man Thomas Cromwell assembled a team of assessors to visit every monastic house in the country – some 800 in all – value them and shut them down. In each case, the site and associated property was then seized by the Crown and either sold off by the newly created Augmentation Office, or leased out. To ensure that the monks did not return under the protective eyes of sympathetic new owners, the new possessors were required at the very least to remove the roof of the monastic buildings, though most went much further and demolished them altogether. At a stroke, a vast number of ancient, beautiful and majestic buildings – architectural wonders and works of art in their own right – were torn down for building material, and their lands disposed of. Some were left as ruins, spectral reminders of a lost way of life that still haunt our countryside today. The remnants of others are still to be found in masonry and brickwork that was taken from their walls and recycled to construct new buildings.

Of the forty-six religious houses that stood in early Tudor London, only a handful survived the cull. The buildings at Westminster Abbey were saved because they were turned over to the clergy (Westminster even acquired its own bishop briefly between 1540 and 1550). Those at

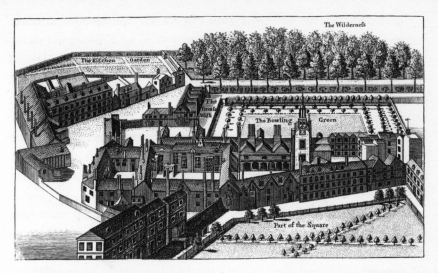

The look and nature of the London area was transformed by the Dissolution of the Monasteries put in train by Henry VIII. Charterhouse, shown here in an eighteenth-century engraving, put up a struggle; as a result its prior and several of his brethren were hanged, drawn and quartered at Tyburn.

Charterhouse and Greyfriars, by contrast, were much less fortunate. Charterhouse was used to store hunting tents, its wretched but stubborn prior, John Houghton, being hanged, drawn and quartered at Tyburn along with several of his brethren, for refusing to accept the newly imposed Act of Supremacy that proclaimed Henry VIII as Supreme Head of the Church of England. Greyfriars suffered the indignity of being used as a storehouse for war spoils taken from the French. Other City religious houses were likewise dissolved and dismantled, the Austin Friars, Holy Trinity Priory and the Crossed Friars among them. To the west of the City the hospitals of St Mary Rouncivall and the Savoy were lost. Further out, Merton Priory was swiftly demolished in 1538, and in April and May of that year some 3,600 tons of its stone were carted to Henry VIII's new pet building project, Nonsuch Palace at nearby Cheam. There, the intricately carved stone was used as rubble for the foundations, while plain stone was used to face the outer walls.[1] Barking Abbey was dissolved in 1539, its buildings – apart from the Curfew Tower – demolished and their materials sent to embellish royal properties at Dartford and Greenwich.

The Crown made a fortune. It has been estimated that the monastic land Henry VIII took into his hands was worth three times as much as the land he already possessed. Furthermore, he gained the right to collect the tithes that had formerly been due to the various religious foundations and he had first pick of their valuable moveable goods, including vast hoards of gold and silver ornaments. He wasted little time in exploiting his new-found possessions, keeping some, granting others to favoured courtiers and royal servants, and selling off yet more to ensure that the royal coffers were flush with hard cash.

The great and the good were swift to take advantage of the sales bonanza that ensued. Bermondsey Abbey, to the south of the City, was sold to Sir Robert Southwell, Master of the Rolls. The premises of the Crutched Friars in the City passed into the hands of Sir Thomas Wyatt, poet and alleged lover of Anne Boleyn. The king himself took possession of Syon Abbey. Indeed, some years later it was to be one of the places where his coffin rested on its journey to Windsor (ironically, it burst open during the night and the next morning dogs were discovered devouring some of the corpse). Ultimately, Syon ended up in the hands of Henry Percy, the ninth Earl of Northumberland, in 1594. He himself had only a few years in which to enjoy his grand estate before being compulsorily rehoused in the Tower of London under suspicion of involvement in the Gunpowder Plot against James I. His family, however, managed to retain Syon, keeping it in good repair before ultimately getting the architect Robert Adam to rebuild it for them after 1762 in the form we see today.

Close to the centre, much former monastic land went to speculators looking to build new houses for London's ever-growing population. The Carmelite Priory of the Whitefriars, for example, the remains of which still lie under the area south of Fleet Street, was demolished and replaced with taverns, tenements and shops. Further out, erstwhile monasteries were transformed into country estates, among them Stratford-at-Bow Priory, which ended up in the hands of Sir Ralph Sadler (one of Thomas Cromwell's henchmen), and Bermondsey Abbey, sold by Sir Robert Southwell to Sir Thomas Hope, founder of Trinity College, Oxford, who demolished it then replaced it with an impressive mansion, the stone from the old abbey being reused for buildings on Bermondsey Street.

This radical transformation of both landownership and the landscape went hand in hand with another Tudor development: the enclosure movement. Gradually, from the late Middle Ages onwards, the open fields of earlier times with their strips of land shared among local people started to give way to enclosed estates under the sole control of their owner. Traditional rights to graze livestock on communal land were withdrawn. Smallholders and migrant workers were forced off the land, and more profitable sheep often took their place. In the process, real hardship could be caused, as Thomas More described in his *Utopia* of 1516:

> . . . one covetous and unsatiable cormorant [greedy person] and very
> plague of his native country may compass about and inclose many thou-
> sand acres of ground together within one pale or hedge, the
> husbandmen be thrust out of their own, or else either by *coveyne*
> [dishonesty] and fraud, or by violent oppression they be put besides it,
> or by wrongs and injuries they be so wearied, that they be compelled to
> sell all: by one means therefore or by other, either by hook or crook they
> must needs depart away, poor, silly, wretched souls, men, women,
> husbands, wives, fatherless children, widows, woful mothers, with their
> young babes, and their whole household small in substance and much in
> number, as husbandry requireth many hands.[2]

A whole new class of itinerant rural poor were thus created during Henry VIII's reign, all in constant need of shelter and provision. Moreover, after the 1530s they were no longer able to call on the monasteries for help or make use of the services they had once offered. It is perhaps not entirely surprising, therefore, that some of London's religious houses associated with health care and poor relief were spared the fate suffered by so many other foundations. Bethlem (formerly St Mary Bethlehem), Christ Hospital (formerly the Greyfriars), St Thomas's and St Bartholomew's, for example, were all transformed to become the Royal Hospitals of London. Their role was charitable, though it is perhaps hard to discern a sympathetic note in the following rubric drawn up by St Bartholomew's, which explains that the hospital existed to deal with 'the myserable people lyeng in the streete, offendyng every clene person passyng by the way with theyre fylthye and nastye savors'.[3] Nor were health care and poor relief the only services that threatened to slip between the cracks after the Dissolution. Hospitality for travellers, a large proportion of road maintenance and aspects of local government were also undermined as the monasteries disappeared from the landscape.

———————◄•►———————

As employment prospects in the countryside dwindled, so a swarm of labourers swept into London, seeking a new life and the promise of new opportunities offered by a flourishing trading city. Soon the demand for cheap accommodation was outstripping available supply. The result, inevitably, was a building boom. Speculative builders quickly moved in to construct new houses, both legally and illegally; and before long a vast sprawl appeared in the 'liberties', or inner suburbs crowded around London's walls. Operating beyond the City's jurisdiction, they were densely packed, often poorly built and, because many were constructed from timber, a fire hazard. In a desperate attempt to control this dangerous suburban sprawl, an ordinance was passed in 1580 stipulating that in a band extending as far out as Tottenham to the north and Chiswick to the west, no new properties were to be built unless they stood in four acres of ground. The fact that further ordinances had to be passed in 1583, 1593 and 1605 suggests that this over-optimistic policy enjoyed little success. King James I was sufficiently alarmed by the rapid growth of housing across Spitalfields, to the east of the City, that in 1618 he passed yet another proclamation restricting further new developments. This was about as successful as its predecessors had been.

It has been estimated that around 80,000 people lived within the confines of the square mile by 1600, but 120,000 more were crammed into the new inner suburbs. Pressure to build on any available green space was intense, and fields rapidly disappeared under the weight of bricks and timber. Whitechapel was just one area to be transformed. By the end of the sixteenth century, and largely because it was beyond the jurisdiction of the City fathers, it was attracting the less fragrant industrial activities of the city, notably tanneries, slaughterhouses and foundries (such as the famous Whitechapel Bell Foundry, which later cast London's Big Ben). It also became something of a centre for brewing. As its industries grew, so more potential employees were attracted to the area, more houses were needed to accommodate them, and Whitechapel's once rural state was lost for ever.

In 1598 London's first biographer, John Stow, wrote a wonderfully evocative description of the ways in which London had developed in his time. Though the main focus of his *Survey of London* was on the City itself, with its venerable history, notable citizens and numerous churches, he recognised that it had long spilled beyond its walls and that the 'suburbs', as he called them, now seamlessly connected the City with Westminster, with nearby villages and hamlets to the north of the river, and, across London Bridge, with Southwark:

> Hog Lane stretcheth north to St Mary Spital without Bishopsgate, and
> within these forty years had on both sides fair hedge rows of elm trees,
> with bridges and easy stiles to pass over into the pleasant fields . . .
> which is now within a few years made a continual building throughout
> of garden-houses and small cottages; and the fields on either sides be
> turned into garden-plots, tenter yards [a yard or enclosure with tenters
> for stretching cloth], bowling alleys, and such like.[4]

There is an air of nostalgia here, and it is therefore scarcely surprising that his descriptions of the development outside the City walls were at times unflattering:

> Both sides of the streets be pestered with cottages and alleys, even up to
> Whitechapel Church, and almost half a mile beyond it, into the
> common field all which ought to be open and free for all men. But this
> common field, I say, being sometime the beauty of this city on that part,
> is so encroached upon by building of filthy cottages, and with other
> purpressors [legal or illegal enclosure of, or encroachment upon, land or
> property belonging to another or to the public], enclosures, and laystalls
> [a place for refuse and dung] (notwithstanding all proclamations and
> acts of parliament made to the contrary), that in some places it scarce
> remaineth a sufficient highway for the meeting of carriages and droves
> of cattle. Much less is there any fair, pleasant, or wholesome way for
> people to walk on foot; which is no small blemish to so famous a city to
> have so unsavoury and unseemly an entrance or passage thereunto.[5]

It says a lot for the power and influence wielded by the legal profession that they were able to prevent Lincoln's Inn Fields being developed in 1617. A memorandum in Privy Council notes that the open ground represented 'a small remainder of ayre' worth preserving, a poetic phrase that gives an indication of the oppressive and suffocating nature of the City buildings surrounding it – as well as the stench produced by such a large number of people living in such close proximity to one another. Various contemporaries felt that London was turning into some form of parasite, sucking away at the precious resources of the rest of the country and devouring its immediate vicinity. John Stow for his part found the whole idea of a 'Great Town' unpalatable:

> Great Towns in the body of a State are like the *Spleen* or *Melt* in the body natural; the monstrous growth of which impoverisheth all the rest of the Members, by drawing to it all the *animal* and *vital* spirits, which should give nourishment unto them.[6]

While many of the buildings going up around the commercial and industrial hub of the City were poorly constructed and squeezed closely in together, developments further west tended to be rather more gracious, as befitted an area that traditionally served the legal and political heart of Westminster. Just outside the City walls, in the area where Unilever House now stands, Henry VIII built a palace on the banks of the river Fleet on the former site of St Bride's Inn; a few years later, in 1531, it was leased to the French ambassador (in 1553 it was donated to the City of London to house homeless children and punish 'fallen women', before becoming the Bridewell prison, poor house and hospital until 1855). Then in 1530, after the fall from grace of his former favourite Cardinal Wolsey, Henry staked a claim to the other end of the Strand by taking over York Place, built in the fifteenth century, recently extended by the ill-fated cardinal and one of the finest private houses in London. The king quickly established it as his preferred London residence, rather than the rather antiquated Westminster Palace, lavishing money on it and adding a whole complex of buildings specifically designed for his own entertainment: a bowling green, a tennis court, a cock pit and tilt yard for jousting, all reminiscent of similar developments at Richmond and Hampton Court further downstream.

York Place, or Whitehall as Henry renamed it, clearly impressed contemporaries, not least the Moravian aristocrat Baron Waldstein, who declared in 1598:

*The social ascendancy of the West End was confirmed by
Henry VIII's decision to take over York Place on the Strand and
transform it into Whitehall Palace. This eighteenth-century engraving
shows what survived the fire of 1698.*

It is truly majestic, bounded on the one side by a park which adjoins
another palace which is called St James's, and on the other side by the
Thames, and it is a place which fills one with wonder, not so much
because of its great size as because of the magnificence of its bed-
chambers and living rooms which are furnished with the most gorgeous
splendour.[7]

The palace continued to develop throughout the seventeenth century,
increasing in size to form an irregular collection of buildings and offices,
reputedly the largest in the country by the time of the Civil War and
one of the largest in Europe by the end of the century. In Henry VIII's
time there could be over 1,000 members of the royal household there at
any given moment.

St James's Palace, which Baron Waldstein refers to, was another
lavish creation of Henry VIII's: a redbrick affair with four courts and
a park. Constructed on the site of a former leper colony between 1531
and 1536, it proved popular with both Henry and his successors. His
older daughter Mary Tudor stayed here on a regular basis and indeed
died in the palace in 1558; and it was from St James's that Henry's
younger daughter Elizabeth set out to address her troops at Tilbury

when the Spanish Armada threatened England's shores in 1588.

With all this royal activity at the western end of the Strand, it is scarcely surprising that members of the court were attracted to the area, and in the process the houses and lands that had once belonged to powerful prelates found their way into the hands of a new generation of ambitious aristocrats. During the reign of Henry VIII's son, Edward VI, for example, both Exeter House and Somerset House were constructed on the Strand for courtiers, the former for Sir Thomas Palmer, the latter for Edward's uncle Edward Seymour, Duke of Somerset. Neither man lived to enjoy his river view for very long. Sir Thomas was executed in 1553 for his support of Mary Tudor's rival, Lady Jane Grey (a few years later the house was given by Elizabeth I to her key adviser, William Cecil, Lord Burghley, before being replaced by Salisbury House in the seventeenth century). As for Edward Seymour, he started Edward's reign in virtual charge of the country but ended his life in disgrace on the executioner's block at Tower Hill. Such was his popularity with Londoners, though, that householders were ordered to stay in their houses until ten o'clock on the day of the execution in order to avoid the risk of civil unrest. John Stow was less impressed with him, complaining that in order to build his grand residence he was quite happy to resort to wholesale destruction of a series of fine old buildings.

One might have thought that the fates of Sir Thomas and the Duke of Somerset would have dissuaded other powerful men from wanting to set up home on the Strand, but this was not the case. During Elizabeth I's reign one of her favourites, Robert Dudley, Earl of Leicester, chose to move to and rebuild Essex House, former home of the ill-fated Bishop Walter de Stapeldon, who had been murdered by a London mob in 1326. Dudley himself survived the risks attendant on living in the Strand, but when he died in 1588 his stepson Robert Devereux, Earl of Essex, inherited it and sure enough, a few years later, was executed for treason. Only the Earl of Northampton who built Northampton (later Northumberland) House on the site of a former convent in the early seventeenth century seems to have outwitted fate, even though he was the son of Henry Howard, Earl of Surrey, whom Henry VIII had had executed many years before.

Among the most ambitious West End projects in the first half of the seventeenth century was Covent Garden. It had once been part of the

Northumberland House on the Strand, built in the early seventeenth century for the Earl of Northampton on the site of a former convent.

Fashionable Covent Garden, established by Francis Russell, Earl of Bedford in the 1630s. Later in the century, other aristocratic property speculators were also to make their mark on the West End.

estate owned by Westminster Abbey, and had consisted of fields and orchards before being walled off as the 'Abbey and Convent garden' (hence its later name). John Russell, the first Earl of Bedford, was granted the land by the Crown in 1552; and thirty or so years later, the third Earl built himself a house there to replace the old family mansion on the Strand. It was his successor, Francis Russell, who, anxious to make as much money for himself as possible, decided to license building land 'fitt for the habitacions of *Gentlemen* and men of ability'[8]. He called in Inigo Jones to design a grand square with a church (St Paul's) on one side and grand residential terraces on the other three, complete with an Italianate arcade. The development proved immediately popular, attracting wealthy tenants who were quite happy to splash out £150 a year to live there and who only started to move away as the central fruit and vegetable market grew in the 1650s and as the lure of points further west increased. The involvement of such a major architect as Inigo Jones in the project suggests a degree of royal interest, and it is therefore perhaps not surprising that two of the streets that sprang up on either side of Covent Garden acquired impressively lofty names: King Street and Henrietta Street (after Charles I's wife, Queen Henrietta Maria). Slightly further east at around the same time Lincoln's Inn Fields – that 'small remainder of ayre' that the lawyers had fought successfully to preserve in 1617 – succumbed to the attentions of the speculator William Newton. His one compromise was to concede a central area of greenery.

———————— ◆ ◆ ▶ ● ————————

Now that the growth of London's inner suburbs, both east and west, was taking on what seemed an almost unstoppable momentum, there was considerable confusion as to where the capital actually started or stopped. To talk about it in terms of its old walls was clearly becoming meaning-less; which areas were London and which areas were not? This may not perhaps have mattered on a day-to-day basis, but it was an issue that had to be addressed by the City's Parliamentary defenders during the English Civil War in the 1640s, and the decisions they arrived at are instructive. Faced with the threat of a royalist advance, they created earthworks that formed a ring stretching round the City and some of its suburbs. The defensive line began below the Tower of London, at the Thames. From there it ran northward towards Whitechapel Road, and then turned to the north-west, crossing the Hackney and Kingsland Roads, near Shoreditch. After that it headed south-west, crossing the end of St John Street and passing through Gray's Inn Lane, Bloomsbury and Oxford Road, near St Giles Pound. It then continued westward to Hyde Park Corner and Constitution Hill, and so on to Tothill Fields and back to the north bank of the Thames. On the other side of the river, the line started near Vauxhall and ran north-eastward to St George's Fields, before turning east and crossing the Borough Road at the end of Blackman Street. It then continued to the end of Kent Street on the Deptford Road. Finally, it inclined to the north-east, and joined the Thames nearly opposite to the point where it had begun on the north bank. This was London on a scale that would have been unthinkable to its medieval inhabitants.

Yet even this large defensive ring was not big enough to contain all of London's suburban sprawl, and many of the outer districts were left to their own devices, only the strategically important satellite town of Kingston further along the Thames being given its own garrison. This proved to be a sensible precaution, for it was from the west that 13,000

A redoubt at the end of Kent Street on the south bank of the Thames, built by the Parliamentarians to protect London from Royalist attack during the Civil War of the 1640s.

Royalist troops approached the capital in 1642, following the route of the river and the Great West Road before mustering at Hounslow Heath. Syon House was seized by the Royalist Colonel Thomas Blagge, who used its key position on the banks of the Thames to bombard Parliamentarian barges that were bringing supplies to the City from Kingston. On 12 November 1642 under the command of Prince Rupert, the Royalists stormed the Parliamentarian stronghold at Brentford before looting the town. With London under serious threat of capture, and the king expecting the submission of Parliament any day, the City's defenders mobilised their forces and assembled at Turnham Green, withdrawing troops from Kingston to swell their numbers to over 24,000. After some tentative skirmishing, the Royalists withdrew; it was the closest they ever got to London during the war. In time the headquarters of the Parliamentarians was established in Putney, ideally placed between Parliamentary London and Royalist Hampton Court, where Charles I was kept prisoner between August and November 1647. It was in Putney at the end of October and beginning of November of that year that soldiers and officers of Oliver Cromwell's New Model Army, along with some civilians, gathered to discuss the future direction of England's government.

As the inner districts around the City became increasingly built up and cramped, the more well-to-do moved further out, to be replaced by workers and artisans. Ultimately, though, there was a limit to just how far out most people could move if they needed ready access to the City and Westminster. The road network, still based on the system of Roman roads that radiated out from the old City gates, remained comparatively rudimentary throughout the Tudor and Stuart period; hence the heavy reliance on the river as a means of communication. Carriages (including the hackney carriages, first mentioned by the diarist Samuel Pepys in the 1660s) could be hired to take people around town, but they were cramped, dusty and dirty and had to compete with the carts of merchants and traders. Passenger coaches provided transport from provincial towns to London, but they were similarly uncomfortable, slow (it could take four

*A detail from Hollar's bird's-eye view of London as it was
in the mid seventeenth century.*

days to get from Dover to London) and expensive as well. Consequently, workers, businessmen and suppliers trying to make their way through the narrow and crowded streets of the city, aristocrats and diplomats requiring access to the royal court at Westminster, the army of clerks, officials, lawyers and accountants working for the institutions of government nearby – all had to have a base close enough to the centre that their daily commute was not too arduous.

Samuel Pepys is a case in point. Having lived for a while in Westminster (in Axe Yard, close to the present Downing Street), he moved to a house in the Navy Board's complex on Seething Lane in the City when he was appointed Clerk of the Acts there. Getting to the office each day, therefore, was scarcely a struggle, but getting around town was more challenging. In one typical week at the beginning of May 1663 he travelled on foot, by horse, in a coach and on water to carry out his work and conduct his social life. On 1 May he hired a horse to take his father to Bishopsgate Street to see him out of the City, and then had a troubled journey through the fields and on to Holborn and towards Hyde Park, 'whither all the world, I think, are going'. After a change of horse, he continued along the road by the park, changing horse again to get home as he could not get a coach. Three days later he decided he wanted to go to Woolwich by boat, but changed his mind when he realised that he would not be able to get home in time for dinner. Instead he went by coach to St James's Park and then walked to Whitehall, where he met the king. After that he travelled to White Friars by boat, before returning home by coach. Thursday 7 May involved a journey by boat to the New Exchange on the Strand with his wife (the New Exchange was a popular shopping centre), a journey by coach to visit Lord Crew, a further coach journey and then a return home by water. The distances involved were scarcely large, but the effort involved was clearly considerable.

Only those at the top of society could opt for the obvious compromise: a country seat and a London house. The Earls of Bedford, for example, who had owned Woburn Abbey in Bedfordshire since 1547 (when Edward VI had granted it to the first Earl), chose to make their family home there in 1619. However, they needed a London bolthole as well, and so made use of Bedford House (built around 1586), which was situated on the north side of the Strand where Southampton Street now runs. Contemporary records suggest that they scarcely had to slum it there. The house had stables and a large garden, and the family had the run of some forty-five rooms.

FOUR

THE INDUSTRIAL EAST, THE FASHIONABLE WEST

The Inner Suburbs after the Great Fire of London

As late as the 1660s the City of London still had a distinctly medieval feel, with its jumble of narrow streets, timbered houses, churches and markets. Its transformation almost overnight was the work of one man: Thomas Farriner. He was the king's baker, and it was his carelessness in the early morning of 2 September 1666 that led to a conflagration that raged for over four days and destroyed most of the old City. Around 13,000 homes for an estimated 100,000 people were consumed by the flames, as were numerous commercial sites along the river. The Great Fire even swept westwards into Fleet Street and towards the Strand. In effect, it destroyed the heart of London.

In the frenzy of rebuilding that followed the Great Fire, a slightly more considered approach to town planning was adopted than before, the random jumble of medieval houses and shops being replaced by homes that, in theory at least, were better constructed, interspersed with solid civic structures and places of trade and commerce. Building regulations stipulated that each house should be constructed from brick or stone and that it should not have wooden eaves; that the roof should be of slate or tile, never thatch, and should be pushed back behind a brick parapet; that wooden window frames should be reduced in scale (later they were recessed behind brick so that only a narrow edge of the wooden frame was exposed to possible fire); and that party walls between the house and its neighbours should be thick enough to withstand a two-hour fire.

A large number of people thought that the new City that emerged from the ashes of the old was not much of an improvement, and they had a point. The narrow, winding medieval street pattern was largely retained; despite all the regulations many houses were not much

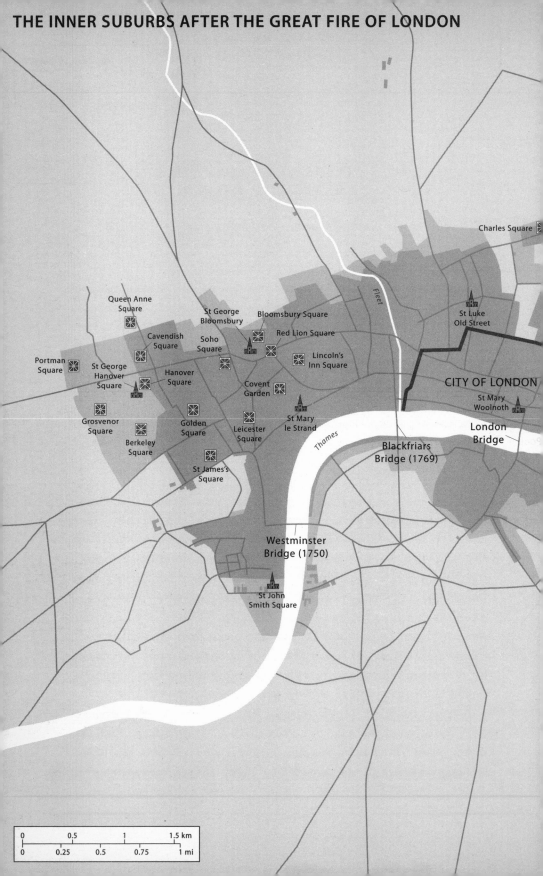

THE INNER SUBURBS AFTER THE GREAT FIRE OF LONDON

Charles Square

Fleet

Queen Anne
Square

St George
Bloomsbury

Bloomsbury Square

St Luke
Old Street

Cavendish
Square

Soho
Square

Red Lion Square

Portman
Square

St George
Hanover
Square

Hanover
Square

Lincoln's
Inn Square

CITY OF LONDON

St Mary
Woolnoth

Covent
Garden

Grosvenor
Square

Golden
Square

Leicester
Square

St Mary
le Strand

London
Bridge

Berkeley
Square

Thames

Blackfriars
Bridge (1769)

St James's
Square

Westminster
Bridge (1750)

St John
Smith Square

0		0.5		1		1.5 km

0	0.25	0.5	0.75	1 mi

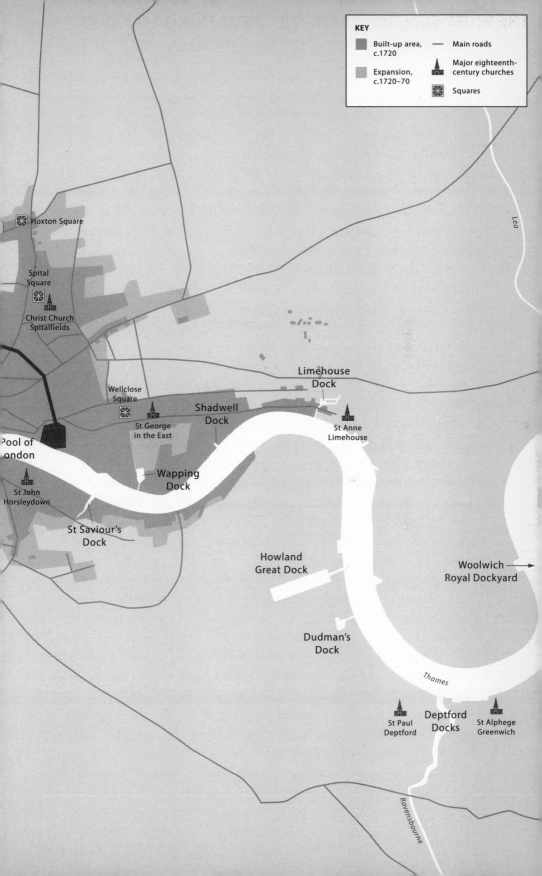

KEY

■ Built-up area, *c.*1720

■ Expansion, *c.*1720–70

— Main roads

⌗ Major eighteenth-century churches

⌗ Squares

Hoxton Square

Spital Square

Christ Church Spitalfields

Wellclose Square

St George in the East

Shadwell Dock

Limehouse Dock

St Anne Limehouse

Pool of London

Wapping Dock

St John Horsleydown

St Saviour's Dock

Howland Great Dock

Dudman's Dock

Woolwich Royal Dockyard →

Thames

St Paul Deptford

Deptford Docks

St Alphege Greenwich

Lea

Ravensbourne

better-built than the ones they replaced; but what is striking about the Great Fire is that while it destroyed the City, it did not devastate London. Most of the areas included within the Civil War defensive ring were untouched. The inner suburbs in the immediate vicinity of the City – essentially slums clustered around the walls and stretching towards Holborn in the west, Shoreditch to the east, and south of the river into Southwark – survived virtually intact. The West End was unaffected; indeed Pepys's diary entry for the first day of the fire, 2 September, implies that until he arrived at Whitehall people there were unaware of the devastation that it was wreaking.

Even so, the fire did have an impact beyond the area it destroyed. In its immediate aftermath, some of the City's inhabitants squatted amid the ashes of their former homes, but many more camped in the fields around the City. 'I then went towards Islington and Highgate,' John Evelyn recorded in his diary for 6 September (by which time the fire had largely burned out), 'where one might have seen 200,000 people of all ranks and degrees dispersed, and lying along by their heap of what they could save from the fire.' Before long, a large number of the poorer people among this throng were on the move again, but not back to the shattered City. Instead they flocked to the slums beyond its walls, which duly expanded to contain them, so continuing a swelling process that had begun some decades before in areas such as Wapping and Shadwell. Soon these new arrivals were joined by those brought in to put right the damage that the fire had caused; St Paul's Cathedral alone attracted a small army of masons, carpenters and others in the thirty-five years or so it took to rebuild from 1675. A further wave of new arrivals came to the East End over the next decades, as smallholders and seasonal workers, finding employment in the countryside an increasingly tough prospect, headed instead for the city, offering their skills as builders or craftsmen or their services as labourers and servants.

In the process, the East End was transformed. In came the poor and moderately prosperous; out went the nobility. Clerkenwell, once the fashionable abode of the aristocracy, including the Dukes of Northumberland, and a popular spa within walking distance of the City, lost its courtly appeal and became instead a major industrial centre, acquiring brewing, distilling, printing and clock making. Shoreditch was similarly transformed after the Fire. It, too, attracted industry and the workers to operate it, though these tended to be more affluent than their Clerkenwell brethren. Hoxton Square was laid out in the 1680s; Charles Square followed in the same decade.

Not all the accents that could be heard in the taverns and lodging houses of the East End were those of Londoners or of their country cousins from East Anglia, Essex and Kent. A significant Irish population started to build up, too; and then there were those from continental Europe. When Oliver Cromwell decided to allow a colony of Sephardi Jews to settle in England in 1656, many chose to establish themselves in and around Whitechapel. Spitalfields, meanwhile, proved popular with Huguenots escaping religious persecution, particularly after 1685 when Louis XIV revoked the Edict of Nantes, which had allowed French Protestants a degree of religious toleration. Both groups brought skills and vital connections with them. The Sephardi Jews were merchants, while the Huguenots were talented craftsmen, excelling at silk weaving, which became a major source of employment in the Spitalfields area over the following decades. In the process, Spitalfields was transformed. With its name derived from the medieval church and hospital of St Mary Spital ('spital' (related to hospital) means a charitable institution that serves the diseased), by the time of the Great Fire of London it was still a mass of fields and lanes. By 1669, however, it was home to the Truman's Brewery. In 1682 John Balch was granted a royal charter to hold a market on Thursdays and Saturdays in or near Spital Square. This gave the area a commercial edge that proved irresistible to the new Huguenot and Jewish communities. Within a matter of years, the old fields and lanes had gone.

London's East End was also a magnet for England's burgeoning international commercial activity. The establishment of the East India Company in 1600, which set up trading 'factories' at several sites on the subcontinent, laid the foundations for a period of growing commercial dominance that was to culminate in a worldwide empire in the nineteenth century. Equally, there were the growing English colonies in North America that proved such a vital link in the lucrative interlinked slave trade and sugar trade (which relied heavily on plantation slave labour in the West Indies). Bristol, Southampton and Portsmouth all rose to prominence in this period, followed a little later by Liverpool; but London enjoyed the lion's share of commerce. Ideally placed to link western trade routes with those in the east, it also continued to build upon its existing trading infrastructure – banking, insurance and stockbroking sectors – which helped fuel further growth. The Bank of England was established in 1694. Shortly afterwards the builder and speculator Nicholas Barbon founded the National Land Bank, aimed at raising funds secured on property. The scheme might have failed, but it is nevertheless significant – and inevitable – that it should have been launched in London in the decades following the Great Fire.

The Pool of London situated by the City, and Southwark to the south, continued to receive the bulk of trade during the sixteenth and early seventeenth centuries, but as ships became more substantial and the journey upriver correspondingly more problematic, docks closer to the coast sprang up. Deptford docks, which had been established by Henry VIII in 1513 to build vessels for the Royal Navy, became an invaluable mooring site for international vessels seeking to unload their goods, so cementing the relationship between the East End of London and the docklands, which today constitute parts of the modern boroughs of Southwark, Tower Hamlets, Newham and Greenwich – though for some time it remained a separate entity and self-contained community. The former fishing village of Poplar also benefited from its connection with the sea, and more specifically from the establishment by the East India Company of a shipbuilding yard at Blackwall in 1607; the company even went so far as to build almshouses and a chapel there to support the local community.

South of the river again, parliamentary permission was received to carve ten acres out of the rural landscape at Rotherhithe to create the Howland Great Dock, built between 1695 and 1699 on land previously donated to the Russell family by John Howland, a wealthy Streatham landowner, as part of his daughter Elizabeth's dowry. This created a secure environment for up to 120 ships at a time, primarily those of the East India Company, with which the Russell family retained a family link. The Howland Great Dock was never intended for the loading and unloading of cargo – the docks at nearby Deptford, and further upstream within the Pool of London, retained those functions – but it was an ideal place to carry out repairs and refits. As a result it was a commercial success and generated great wealth for its owners. That said, because its ambitions were limited, it did not develop into a sprawling industrial site – or, at least, not immediately. Engravings from the early eighteenth century show

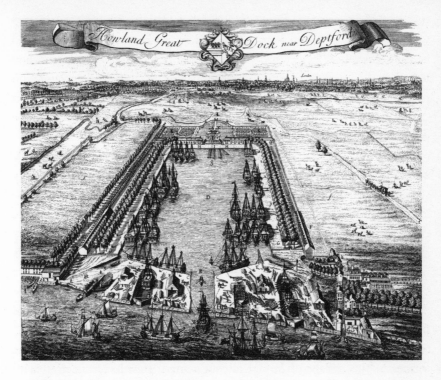

Howland Great Dock was carved out of the countryside at Rotherhithe in the 1690s. This slightly later engraving shows how rural the area nevertheless remained.

an area that was still predominantly rural, with trees lining the sides of the dock to act as a windbreak and the family mansion depicted in the background.

Hand in hand with commercial enterprise came military endeavour. Britain's pursuit of trade brought the country into conflict with other nations, first with the French and later the Dutch; and London dockyards inevitably played their part in the international arms race that ensued. Deptford was an important site; so, too, were Chatham in Kent on the river Medway, founded as a royal dockyard in 1567 (though the site had long been used as a refitting base), and Woolwich, founded in 1512 specifically for the purpose of building a warship for Henry VIII.

Woolwich's evolution was typical of other key settlements in the area. Founded in Anglo-Saxon times, it evolved into a small medieval town, probably connected with the wool trade. Its fortunes were then transformed

A nineteenth-century engraving of Woolwich Dockyard, founded in 1512 to build a warship for Henry VIII and a vital military site thereafter.

by the arrival of the royal dockyard, and the area soon grew into a site of national importance. The 'Woolwich warren' was created in 1671 as an ordnance storage depot, an experimental armament base was added in 1695 and then a gun foundry in 1717. By the mid eighteenth century the military site covered 100 acres (it was renamed the Royal Arsenal in 1806); and as Woolwich grew, so it attracted other industrial enterprises, from the early seventeenth century becoming a manufacturing centre for salt-glazed tinware and glassware. One of its most noteworthy features in the early eighteenth century was the long Ropewalk, home to many of the 400 rope makers working in the area.

Greenwich was similarly transformed by Britain's growing naval power. The old palace fell into a state of disrepair during the Civil War, and was converted into the Royal Hospital for Seamen by Sir Christopher Wren and Nicholas Hawksmoor from 1694. A few years earlier, in 1675, Charles II had decided to set up the Royal Observatory on the site. Given the close relationship between navigation and science, the decision was scarcely a surprising one. Yet as is so often the case with superficially similar places in London, while Woolwich shared a strong naval theme with Greenwich, in many other ways the two places could not have been more different from each other. Woolwich was exclusively an industrial centre. Greenwich,

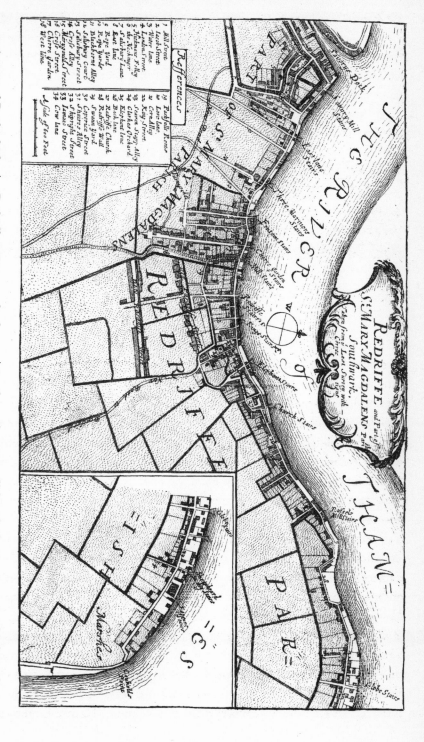

A map of Rotherhithe (or Redriffe as it was also known) in the early 1750s. Although the area remained relatively undeveloped, it had by now become notorious for overcrowding and poverty.

by contrast, retained the upmarket atmosphere it had acquired when Henry VIII had decided to make Greenwich Palace a favourite haunt in the sixteenth century. Two centuries later courtiers and civil servants set up house there, building the elegant Georgian buildings along Croom's Hill and Maze Hill.

As the docks strung along the Thames towards its estuary grew in importance and size, so did the communities around them. Wapping, Shadwell, Ratcliff and Limehouse all became home to seafaring folk, dock labourers, ships' craftsmen and cargo handlers. They also became home to alehouses, brothels, illegal pawnbrokers and dosshouses. Smugglers and other ne'er-do-wells lurked in the shadows of the great vessels; thugs pounced on unsuspecting passers-by and relieved them of their posses-sions, and possibly their lives too. Unsurprisingly, perhaps, as early as 1593 Deptford was the setting for a brawl in which the playwright Christopher Marlowe was fatally wounded by a certain Ingram Frizar at the house of Eleanor Bull.

In the century or so after Marlowe's death the population of the East End increased nearly fivefold: from around 21,000 in 1600 to 91,000 in 1700. There was dense development along the riverside and dock areas, with small villages transformed into sprawling urban parishes. Bethnal Green, for example, with its large central green and mansion where Pepys kept his diary during the Great Fire, was encroached upon by Spitalfields and, by the mid eighteenth century, had become miserably poor and overcrowded. The clergyman and founder of Methodism, John Wesley, was appalled by what he found there. 'I began visiting those of our society who lived in Bethnal Green hamlet,' he confided to his journal on 15 January 1777. 'Many of them I found in such poverty as few can conceive without seeing it. Oh, why do not all the rich that fear God constantly visit the poor!' Rotherhithe (or Redriffe, as it was known to Pepys) acquired a similarly dismal reputation, while one commentator, Arthur Young, observed of Gravesend in Kent in 1759: '[it] is a detestable exhibition of the worst out-skirts of London – it is Wapping in miniature'.[1]

Yet it would be wrong to describe all this suburban development in the East End in terms of unmitigated gloom and grime. While the areas close to the river could be pretty dire, those on the northern edge were quite the opposite. Bow, Hoxton, Hackney, Shacklewell and Stoke Newington – small villages in close proximity to the City, but far enough away from it to avoid being enveloped by suburban sprawl – all remained spacious and relatively affluent. And they remained rural enclaves for a considerable period. In his *Tour Through the Whole Island of Great Britain* (1726) Daniel Defoe noted both Hackney's expansion and its secluded appeal:

> This town is so remarkable for the retreat of wealthy citizens, that there is at this time near a hundred coaches kept in it; tho' I will not join with a certain satyrical author, who said of Hackney, that there were more coaches than Christians in it.[2]

As late as 1801 Hackney had a population of fewer than 13,000, while Bow was home to only 2,000.

If the new suburbs immediately east of the City were not always necessarily the most salubrious, those that sprang up to the west after the Great Fire were generally far more high-status. This western development continued a trend that stretched back at least a century, and it was, of course, intimately bound up with the presence of royal palaces in the West End. There was Whitehall, where Oliver Cromwell had lived during the Commonwealth Period and which was then frequented by Charles II – not least because he decided to stow two of his mistresses there. There was also St James's Palace, which became the principal royal residence in London after 1698 when a careless laundry woman at Whitehall managed to set fire to the complex, destroying all but the Banqueting House. Neighbouring it was St James's Park, little more than marshland fed by the river Tyburn when Henry VIII had bought it from Eton College in 1532 as part of his Whitehall scheme, but fashionable when Charles II decided to take constitutional walks around it and feed the ducks on the canal. As a result, aristocrats who in Elizabethan times might well have chosen to live in the City (the Earl of Essex, Sir Francis Walsingham) now invariably favoured the west over the east.

Not only did the wealthy want to live in the West End, many had a vested interest in its development. Large areas of freehold land had come into the hands of the aristocracy – often former church lands gained or purchased after the Dissolution of the Monasteries – and they were keen to exploit it and capitalise on their good fortune. As a rule, they would lease plots of land to building tradesmen or financial speculators, generally insisting that they should create high-status housing (at their own risk) which would secure the maximum in rental values. Some even took a close personal interest in the building schemes they unleashed. The Earl of St Albans, for example, was closely involved in the building of St James's Square in the 1670s. As a result a plethora of streets and squares, based in part on the earlier Covent Garden model, grew up: Bloomsbury Square after 1665 (on land owned by the Earl of Southampton); Leicester Square after 1671 (on land owned by the Earls of Leicester); Golden Square after the 1670s; Soho (originally King's) Square after 1681 (on land owned by the Earl of St Albans); and Red Lion Square (in the 1680s). Most soon acquired just the sort of tenants their aristocratic owners had hoped for: No. 5 St James's Square, for instance, was first occupied by

The gracious Soho (originally King's) Square in 1754. It was built in the mid seventeenth century on land owned by the Earl of St Albans.

Henry, second Earl of Clarendon; No. 20 went to Sir Allen Apsley, the Duke of York's treasurer of the household; and, no doubt for the purposes of convenience, the duke installed his mistress Arabella Churchill next door at No. 21 (she moved out three years later when their association ended).

The square may have seemed an aesthetic choice, but it had an economic rationale. By cramming tall, often four-storey houses next to each other, builders were able to shoehorn many in on quite small plots of land. They also managed to restrict the footprint of their houses by including basements, which were generally used as the kitchen and service area. Gardens were virtually non-existent; instead the central area of the square acted as its residents' recreational space. Sprouting off to the sides of the square were little side streets and mews for the supporting cast and tradesmen necessary to keep the grand households going.

Foremost among the building speculators who moved in on the West End was the remarkably named Nicholas If-Jesus-Christ-Had-Not-Died-For-Thee-Thou-Hadst-Been-Damned Barbon, founder of the previously mentioned Land Bank. Barbon was a self-made man. One of his first ventures in 1680–1 was an innovative fire insurance business that offered cover for around 5,000 households. After the Great Fire he acquired large tracts of land north of the Strand and in Bloomsbury and built numerous houses and commercial properties in the hope of making as fast a financial return as possible. It then emerged that not only was he a self-made man, he was a thoroughly unscrupulous one. In the pursuit of building profit he invariably disregarded objections from local residents, not to mention such trifling matters as bye-laws and existing buildings (those that stood in his way were prone to collapse mysteriously).

Dishonest and intimidating he may have been, but Barbon was the man who finally welded the City and Westminster together in a continuous and encompassing urban spread, brick by brick. On occasion the bricks came back in his direction: the lawyers of Gray's Inn, for example, were so angered by his plans to build Red Lion Square on some of their favourite recreational land that they engaged in pitched battles with his builders and exchanged brickbats with them. The fact that Red Lion Square nevertheless emerged was testament to Barbon's astonishingly thick skin and his skills as a wheeler-dealer. At the time of his death in 1698 or 1699 – the exact date is unknown – he was worth £200,000 and

St George's, Hanover Square, one of the new churches built in the West End following the passing of the Fifty New Churches Act of 1711.

had taken up residence in Osterley House (later Osterley Park) in the outer suburbs of west London. Small enclaves of his developments still survive – No. 12 Gerrard Street in Westminster, for example, and one or two houses along Bedford Row.

A recognition of just how much and how quickly west London was expanding came in 1711 with the passing of the Fifty New Churches Act, a piece of legislation that sought to ensure that the spreading of the Christian message kept pace with the spread of new building. Only twelve churches were actually built, but it is significant that while five of these were in the East End and the City, three were south of the river (in Greenwich, Deptford and Bermondsey) and four were to the west and north (St George's, Bloomsbury; St John's, Smith Square; St George's, Hanover Square; and St Mary le Strand). As the eighteenth century advanced, so did the line of houses. A speculative boom which culminated (as it usually does) in disaster with the bursting of the South Sea Bubble scheme in 1720 saw Hanover Square and the area around turned into a building site. The elegant Berkeley Square followed in the 1730s. Thereafter, much of the new building came at the behest of a small group of powerful individuals. In Bloomsbury the Russell Family (who owned, among other property, Southampton House – renamed Bedford House – in Bloomsbury Square) expanded on the development that had taken place there the previous century. In Mayfair, land acquired through marriage in 1677 by Sir Thomas Grosvenor (who also owned large tracts of Belgravia and Pimlico) was built upon after 1720. To the north of Oxford Road (today's Oxford Street), Portland Place and the Portman estate were laid out from the 1760s onwards, their respectability enhanced a couple of decades later when the rowdy hangings at Tyburn (near today's Marble Arch) ceased. People might have wanted to view public executions (and Tyburn attracted crowds in their thousands); that didn't necessarily mean, though, that they wanted to live next door to them.

The history of the Portman estate is typical of so many of that era. Acquired in 1532 by Sir William Portman, Lord Chief Justice to Henry VIII, it had remained largely undeveloped until the mid eighteenth century, home only to some pigs and 'night soil' (human excrement removed from privies and cesspools). However, its Georgian owner, William Portman, had ambitious plans for his estate, and started to realise them in the 1760s with the construction of Portman Square. Soon the area's manure-strewn history was forgotten as the square attracted elegant houses and elegant tenants. Setting the social seal on the area was the writer and literary hostess Elizabeth Montagu, who commissioned one of the leading architects of the day, James 'Athenian' Stuart, to build her a house in the north-west corner of the square. In the event, Stuart proved to be rather tardy: Elizabeth Montagu had hoped to move in during the spring of 1779 but had to chivvy him for another two years before the house was finished. However, it was worth the wait. Embellished by painters such as Angelica Kauffman and Biagio Rebecca, it was a mass of decorated ceilings and classical columns and even featured a large ballroom. As might be expected, however, it was merely Elizabeth Montagu's town house. She actually preferred to live at Sandleford in Berkshire.

Just how influential a small group of estate owners proved to be in the development of the West End is marked by the preservation of their names in so many of the area's streets and squares. Whereas the City had streets named after religious foundations (St Mary Axe, Amen Corner) and commercial enterprise (Poultry, Cornhill), the West End became awash with Leicesters, Southamptons, Grosvenors and Berkeleys. Gerrard

Street, a Barbon scheme built up after the 1670s, preserves the name of its landowner, Charles, Lord Gerrard. Lisle Street preserves the alternative name of the Earls of Leicester – Viscounts Lisle – who owned it. The second Duke of Buckingham perhaps represents the most extreme instance of this desire for immortality. When he agreed to allow Nicholas Barbon to redevelop York House on the Strand in the 1670s, it was on the condition that every element of his name should be preserved in the geography of the area; and so George (Street), Villiers (Street), Duke (Street), Of (Alley, now York Place), Buckingham (Street) came into being. Even Shepherd Market, which, had it been situated in the City might have suggested something to do with sheep, is actually named after a builder and architect.

Nevertheless, the built-up West End preserves some memories of its former self. Mayfair recalls the great annual fair held there between the late seventeenth and mid eighteenth centuries (by which time it had become so rowdy and disreputable that it had to be suppressed). Open fields and hunting are preserved in the name Soho (a word similar to 'tally-ho'). Pall Mall is named after the game of pall-mall or pallemaille played there in the seventeenth century, which involved hitting a ball with a mallet along an alley and through an iron ring.

The marked contrast between west and east was remarked on by contemporaries. Von Archenholz, for example, a Prussian who visited London in the late eighteenth century, noted that:

> . . . the East end, especially along the shores of the Thames, consists of old houses, the streets there are narrow, dark and ill-paved, inhabited by sailors and other workmen who are employed in the construction of ships and by a great part of the Jews. The contrast between this and the West end is astonishing; the houses here are mostly new and elegant; the squares are superb, the streets straight and open . . . If all London were as well built, there would be nothing in the world to compare it to.[3]

Typical of the grander sort of houses that were being built throughout the eighteenth century was No. 4 Grosvenor Square, erected in 1728 for the Earl of Malton, later first Marquess of Rockingham, and afterwards occupied by his son the second Marquess, prime minister in 1765–6 and 1782. According to an inventory from the time of the second Marquess,

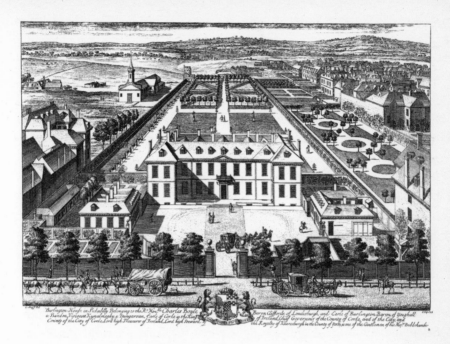

The eighteenth-century West End blend of town and country is nicely
captured in this engraving of the grand Burlington House.
Note the extent of undeveloped land to the north.

the house was a palatial affair with marble chimney pieces in the rooms
up to second-floor level and with 'Turkey' carpets, busts and bas-reliefs
in the more public rooms. The first-floor rooms were decorated in green
or green and white, with one rear room in red. The garret bedrooms
housed a footmen's room with four beds in it and a maids' room with
three beds, while the floor beneath (which contained one room decorated
in crimson) seems to have been occupied by the upper servants. Odds
and ends included 'an Iron Bar, taken from one of the Rioters in June
1780' (a reference to the anti-Catholic Gordon riots of that year), two
organs, and 'a White Flag taken from the French'. The establishment's
male servants alone ran to twenty-three.

Not all houses, of course, were on this scale, and not all were intended
for the aristocracy. Many were taken by the well-to-do middle class, of
whom there was no shortage in the late seventeenth and throughout the
eighteenth centuries. Britain's expanding commercial role on the world
stage generated vast fortunes for the shipowners, traders, merchants and

commodity brokers operating in the City, for those investing in the dockland economy via the infrastructure and support services associated with maritime trade, for lawyers and other professionals who regarded London as central to their business, and for writers, artists and musicians who appreciated that where there was money there were patrons and work. All wanted somewhere suitably upmarket to live, so that they could pursue their careers, hobnob with the people who mattered, and enjoy the balls, assemblies and theatrical entertainments that peppered the 'season' (generally October to April, after which the fashionable went to Bath and then to their country estates).

In time, the 'nouveau riche' who emerged from the ranks of the commercial entrepreneurs of the eighteenth century began to rival the old aristocracy, who traditionally owed their position in society to land, inherited wealth and position at court. New men wanted status and the trappings that went with it. They might or might not be able to afford a grand pile or a country estate, but they certainly wanted a substantial house in the right part of town – and ideally a country villa close to town as well. Increasingly, they desired the best of both worlds combined in one town house: conveniently placed for work but preserving some sort of illusion of rural life. Sometimes this was taken to ridiculous extremes, as when sheep were introduced to Cavendish Square in the 1750s and allowed to graze on the carefully tended lawns. The sense of countryside living in the West End was enhanced by the royal parks. St James's Park had first been laid out by James I, and in his reign even accommodated a menagerie of exotic animals, including an elephant. Charles II then developed the site further, adding an ornamental canal that was later converted to the lake we see today. He also opened the park to the public. Remaining close to the edge of built-up London throughout the eighteenth century, St James's Park preserved the atmosphere of a country estate. As the guidebook *London in Miniature* pointed out in 1755: 'In this park are stags and fallow deer that are so tame as to take gently out of your hand and [at] each end of the Mall there are stands of cows, from whence the company at small expence, may be supplied with warm milk.' Nearby, Green Park had a similar atmosphere. Originally swampy ground that had been enclosed in the reign of Henry VIII when it was owned by the Poultney family, it was transformed by Charles II to contain walks and even an icehouse to provide refreshments for guests.

The suburbs in which these parks stood were not purely residential, though. Right from the start, commercial enterprises went hand in hand with the gentrified enclaves, squares and villas that sprouted up. Covent Garden is a prime example. Inigo Jones may have designed a grand residential square, but a market for fruit and vegetables appeared as early in 1654 on the south side. In the course of the late seventeenth and eighteenth centuries newly fashionable coffee houses appeared, most notably the Bedford, which was patronised by many of the leading literary and artistic figures of the age, from Henry Fielding to William Hogarth. Theatres also sprang up in the surrounding streets, having migrated northwards and westwards from Southwark and Shoreditch where they had been established in Elizabethan times to avoid the licensing control of City authorities just over the river. The Theatre Royal, Drury Lane (1674), Haymarket Theatre (1720), and the old Lyceum off the Strand (1765) were early foundations in the West End; and while only authorised 'patent theatres' were theoretically permitted to perform drama from 1737 onwards, this did not stop many other music halls and playhouses opening

The frontispiece to the 1773 edition of Harris's List of Covent Garden Ladies. *It shows a prostitute in Covent Garden accepting money from a client.*

throughout the area (as well as towards the east of the City as well).

Theatre life had its less high-minded side: it became notorious for the rakes and prostitutes who gathered there, and other distinctly seedy concerns grew up, too – bagnios (or bathing houses), for example, and lodging houses that were little more than brothels. So notorious did the Covent Garden area become as a red-light district that it inspired *Harris's List of Covent Garden Ladies*, a catalogue of prostitutes and where to find them; priced at two shillings and sixpence, it sold over 250,000 copies between 1757 and 1795. Even the coffee houses were not necessarily that salubrious, as a description from the *London Spy* in 1700 suggests:

> There was a rabble going hither and thither, reminding me of a swarm of rats in a ruinous cheese-store. Some came, others went; some were scribbling, others were talking; some were drinking (coffee), some smoking, and some arguing; the whole place stank of tobacco like the cabin of a barge. On the corner of a long table, close by the armchair, was lying a Bible . . . Beside it were earthenware pitchers, long clay pipes, a little fire on the hearth, and over it the huge coffee-pot. Beneath a small book-shelf, on which were bottles, cups, and an advertisement for a beautifier to improve the complexion, was hanging a parliamentary ordinance against drinking and the use of bad language. The walls were decorated with gilt frames, much as a smithy is decorated with horse-shoes. In the frames were rarities; phials of a yellowish elixir, favourite pills and hair-tonics, packets of snuff, tooth-powder made of coffee-grounds, caramels and cough lozenges . . . Had not my friend told me that he had brought me to a coffee-house, I would have regarded the place as the big booth of a cheap-jack.[4]

In Covent Garden's case, as the bagnios and taverns moved in, so the middle classes moved out; but the pattern of high living and commerce was repeated elsewhere. Aristocratic Berkeley Square had its coffee house and admittedly very upmarket Gunter's Tea Shop, founded by an Italian pastry-cook, and purveyor of fine ices and sorbets. Residents of fashionable Mayfair were served by a range of local shops offering everything from fresh food to luxury goods. Even in the late eighteenth century, local butchers drove their livestock to their Mayfair shops for slaughter.

Crime was a problem in the West End just as it was in the City and the slums around it. The streets were full of pickpockets and ruffians. St James's and Green Park were dangerous places to walk in the eighteenth century, attracting robbers and acquiring the occasional highwayman. Horace Walpole was relieved of his possessions in Hyde Park and, proving that sometimes lightning does strike twice, was also robbed of money and a watch in a carriage there by the infamous highwayman James Maclaine in 1749. When the Earl of Chesterfield decided to build a mansion at Stanhope Gate, his friends were 'surprised at his having chosen so desolate a place, and he himself said that he required a house-dog, as he situated his house among thieves and murderers'.[5] Some of the streets around Mayfair had a sleazy reputation (Curzon Street, for example, was the site of a notorious unlicensed chapel that could arrange quick weddings for those in a hurry), and the parks offered opportunities for debauchery. The Earl of Rochester's poem 'A Ramble in St James's Park', written in the 1670s, describes scenes of sexual activity that were still taking place decades later:

> And nightly now beneath their shade
> Are buggeries, rapes and incests made.
> Unto this all-sin-sheltering grove
> Whores of the bulk and the alcove,
> Great ladies, chambermaids, and drudges,
> The ragpicker, and heiress, trudges,
> Carmen, divines, great lords, and tailors,
> Prentices, poets, pimps and jailors,
> Footmen, fine fops do here arrive
> And here promiscuously they swive.

To the east, meanwhile, commercial expansion continued apace. By the 1720s Howland Great Dock was increasingly being used by Greenland whalers, facilities ultimately being built to boil whale blubber for oil. So successful was this new enterprise that Howland Great Dock was renamed Greenland Dock. When the whale trade declined sharply at the end of the eighteenth century, the dock was converted for use in the timber trade. Then in 1806 it was sold to a Greenwich merchant called William

The opening of the West India Docks in 1802, shown here,
heralded a new influx of workers into East London.

Richie, who founded the Commercial Dock Company the following year. The same decade saw a proliferation of new docks: the West India Docks in 1802, the London Docks and East India Docks in 1805, and the Surrey Docks in 1807. All, of course, required a workforce, and so further pressure came both to squeeze dock workers and their families into existing accommodation and to find new housing for them. Even so, pockets of middle-class 'genteel' housing still remained, and the prosperous could still be found scattered in enclaves across the docklands area in the Georgian era. Wapping, for example, may have become a busy industrial centre, and possibly a heavy-drinking one if the twenty-six taverns in the High Street in 1750 are anything to go by, but it was also home to elegant houses at the Pier Head, occupied by customs officials.

As London expanded, so the old physical barriers between the City and the western suburbs began to seem somewhat anachronistic. The City gates were removed in 1760 to increase traffic flow into the suburbs and countryside beyond. At the end of the century and the beginning of the next, large areas of the old walls that had stood since Roman times finally came down. London was now a conurbation, at one with the suburbs that encircled the City at its heart and with the old royal centre of

Westminster. In his *Tour Thro' London*, written in 1725, Defoe guessed that the capital's perimeter must stretch for thirty-six miles, 'reaching from Black-Wall in the east, to Tot-Hill Fields in the west . . . and all the new buildings by, and beyond, Hanover Square . . . and how much farther it may spread, who knows?' He was particularly struck by developments in the West End:

> I passed an amazing Scene of new Foundations, not of Houses only, but as I might say of new Cities, New Towns, new Squares, and fine Buildings, the like of which no City, no Town, nay, no Place in the World can shew; nor is it possible to judge where or when, they will make an end or stop of Building . . . All the Way through this new Scene I saw the World full of Bricklayers and Labourers; who seem to have little else to do, but like Gardeners, to dig a Hole, put in a few Bricks, and presently there goes up a House.[6]

In the year he wrote this, more property deeds were registered in the Middlesex Land Register than in any other year until 1765 – an indication of just how much new building was going on.[7]

A few years later, Horace Walpole, fourth Earl of Oxford, author, politician and patron of the arts, marvelled at the fact that London was still growing, absorbing areas from Greenwich in the south, Marylebone in the north and Poplar in the east, to Knightsbridge and Chelsea in the west. In his time, expansion was greatly facilitated by the building of new bridges across the Thames to supplement the overused London Bridge (finally cleared of its houses between 1758 and 1762). The Company of Watermen had long resisted such projects: as early as 1670 they had had plans for new bridges at Lambeth and Putney thrown out on the grounds that such developments would destroy the livelihood of their 60,000 members who, for so many years, had ferried fare-paying passengers from one bank of the Thames to the other. However, their stranglehold was broken with the erection of Westminster Bridge in 1750 and Blackfriars Bridge in 1769. It seemed that the growth of the city was unstoppable and that, as Horace Walpole wrote to his close friend Mary Berry in 1791, 'there will soon be one street from London to Brentford . . . and from London to every village ten miles round!'[8]

FIVE

IN SEARCH OF 'HEALTHFUL AIR'

Escaping the Inner Suburbs

Dotted all around the growing central hub of London from Tudor to Georgian times were small villages and towns that helped supply the City with food, goods and services but increasingly became rural retreats for the more prosperous as well. Hackney is a typical example. A village that developed in the early medieval period, it became increasingly attractive to affluent Londoners as time went on. In its early days it would have featured thatched and half-timbered houses, a stone-built church and a scattering of inns. However, its oldest surviving residential property, Sutton House in Homerton High Street, belies these humble origins. It was built by Sir Ralph Sadler in 1535, and was originally quite a grand three-storeyed affair with a Great Hall and mullioned windows. Sadler himself clearly stayed there, but it was not his only residence: at the time the house was built he also had accommodation at Hampton Court, as well as at the palaces of Whitehall and Westminster.

Some years later, in 1600, the rectory at Hackney became home to John and Jane Daniell. They were retainers of the Earl of Essex and, again, people of some consequence, who no doubt wanted to partake of Hackney's 'healthful air', enjoy the company of gentlemen and merchants, and, with any luck, rub shoulders with the aristocracy (at that time Lord Oxford lived nearby at the King's Place, later Brooke House). In their particular case, though, social aspiration proved their undoing. John Daniell, the scion of a relatively wealthy gentrified Cheshire family, was desperate to become a member of the royal household, and when this elevation failed to materialise he very foolishly resorted to blackmailing the Earl and Countess of Essex over some compromising letters that the countess had handed over to him for safe keeping. The earl fell from grace in 1601 following an attempted coup, John's links with him were

The village of Hackney in the late eighteenth century, a place of refuge from the noise and bustle of London and home to many well-to-do people. It was also known for its farms and market gardens.

investigated, and he was fined, imprisoned and sentenced to the pillory beneath a notice which read 'A Wicked Forger and Imposter'. Hackney rectory passed to a certain Ferdinando Heybourne, a wealthy property owner who succeeded where John had failed, becoming a groom of the privy chamber in the royal household. John, by contrast, died intestate in lodgings in Westminster.

Chelsea proved similarly attractive to up-and-coming Londoners. A small village in the early sixteenth century, when it numbered only 190 adults and children, it achieved a measure of fame following Sir Thomas More's arrival in 1524 and its status survived his fall from grace a few years later and his subsequent execution in 1535 for opposing Henry VIII's actions against the Church of Rome. By the end of the century Chelsea was known – a little misleadingly, perhaps – as the 'Village of Palaces', home to a number of courtiers and royal officials who enjoyed both its seclusion and the fact that it was only a short boat's ride from Westminster.

ESCAPING THE INNER SUBURBS

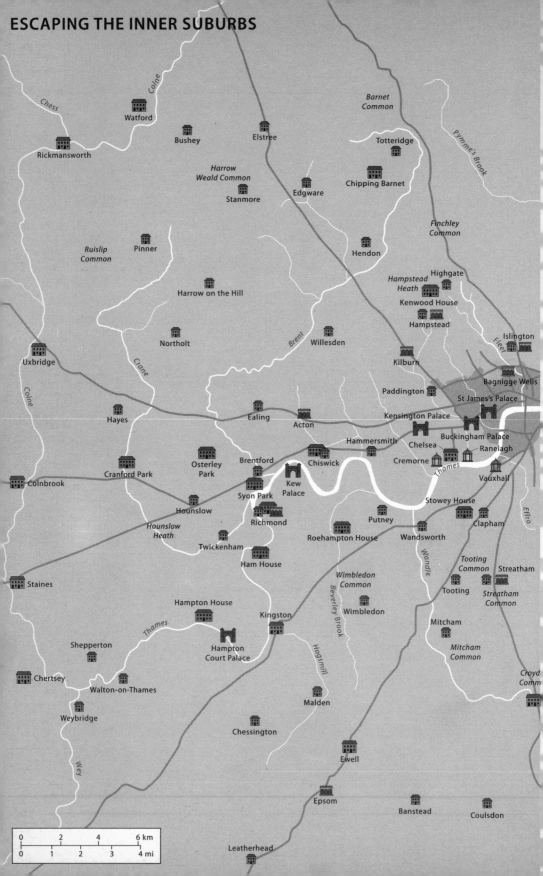

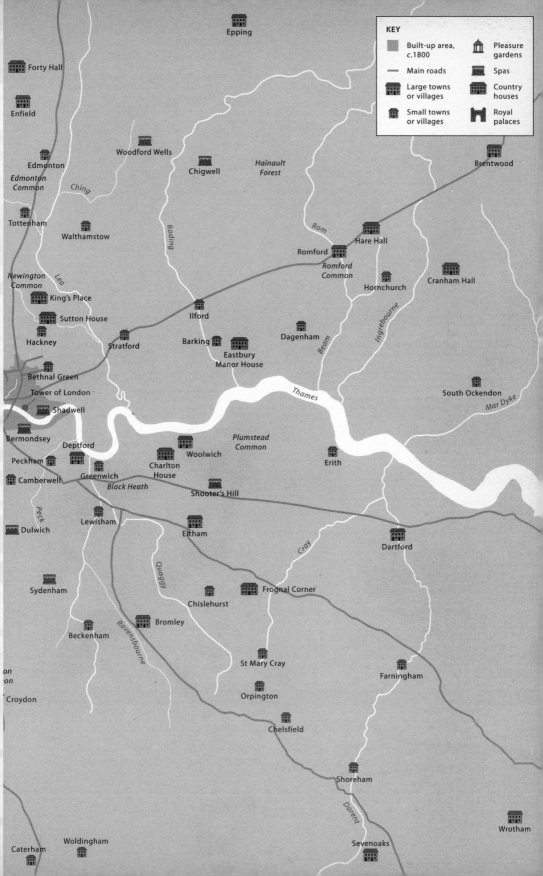

KEY

Built-up area, *c.*1800

Main roads

Large towns or villages

Small towns or villages

Pleasure gardens

Spas

Country houses

Royal palaces

Epping

Forty Hall

Enfield

Woodford Wells

Chigwell

Hainault Forest

Brentwood

Edmonton

Edmonton Common

Ching

Tottenham

Walthamstow

Roding

Rom

Romford

Hare Hall

Romford Common

Hornchurch

Cranham Hall

Newington Common

Lea

King's Place

Sutton House

Hackney

Stratford

Ilford

Barking

Dagenham

Beam

Ingrebourne

Bethnal Green

Tower of London

Shadwell

Eastbury Manor House

Thames

South Ockendon

Mar Dyke

Bermondsey

Peckham

Deptford

Greenwich

Black Heath

Charlton House

Woolwich

Plumstead Common

Erith

Camberwell

Peck

Dulwich

Lewisham

Shooter's Hill

Eltham

Cray

Dartford

Sydenham

Quaggy

Chislehurst

Frognal Corner

Beckenham

Ravensbourne

Bromley

St Mary Cray

Farningham

an on

Croydon

Orpington

Chelsfield

Shoreham

Caterham

Woldingham

Darent

Sevenoaks

Wrotham

A rare survival: the seventeenth-century Church Farm House in Hendon,
which stands amid a collection of typical village buildings –
a pub, a church and almshouses.

So great did the crush of powerful people at church services become that in 1621 Sir John Lawrence complained loudly that Viscount Wimbledon had resorted to the unthinkable, and invaded his pew.

At the same time, though, there was another Chelsea – a village of trades and local industries that included gravel extraction and brick making. It was also home to market gardeners, who became famed in the early seventeenth century for their root vegetables in much the same way that their neighbours in Fulham were esteemed for their carrots. Here again, Chelsea benefited from its proximity to the centre of London: each day, while it was exporting its wealthy residents to Westminster, it was also busy importing the capital's human waste and animal manure, spreading it liberally on its gardens to cultivate the crops.

Other villages that closely hugged the outer limits of London in the sixteenth and seventeenth centuries included Bethnal Green, Hoxton and Stoke Newington. Sir Walter Raleigh had a house in the manor of Islington, while Sir John Spencer, a merchant and lord mayor, seems to have preferred his house at Canonbury to the rather grand Crosby Place in Bishopsgate nearer town. South of the river it was a slightly different picture. Here the dearth of bridges across the Thames until the mid eighteenth century proved something of a barrier for those who needed easy access to Westminster and the City. Nevertheless, Lambeth and Camberwell proved popular, and when Putney Bridge was opened in 1729 a whole new area of south London became an attractive option for well-to-do commuters. Roehampton in particular acquired a certain cachet – and a number of stunning Georgian houses.

Contemporary references to Hackney's 'healthful air' point to one reason why so many well-to-do families increasingly wanted to live further away from London. The capital itself was a health hazard. Its water was of highly questionable quality. Its streets were filthy. Its houses, particularly in the poorer areas, were overcrowded. It was constantly ravaged by disease and, most terrifyingly, pestilence. There were outbreaks of the plague several times in the sixteenth and seventeenth centuries; the 1593 and 1603 epidemics were so serious that London theatres had to be closed, and the 1665 outbreak killed an estimated 100,000 people. Looking at the events of that latter year from the vantage point of 1725, Daniel Defoe described how someone living through those terrifying events would have viewed things:

> . . . the Inhabitants are quitting the old Noble Streets and Squares where they used to live, and are removing into the Fields for fear of Infection; so that, as the People are run away into the Country, the Houses seem to be running away too.[1]

Defoe's *Journal of the Plague Year*, which gives a compelling account of 1665, contrasts the low mortality rates around London with the very high ones within the capital, where up to 20 per cent of residents perished. Some villages (Walthamstow, for example) actually went so far as to ban refugees from London to avoid the risk of the plague spreading to their communities. Others, though, were prepared to help their suffering urban brethren and still managed to remain pestilence-free:

> The inhabitants of the villages adjacent would, in pity, carry them food and set it at a distance, that they might fetch it, if they were able; and sometimes they were not able, and the next time they went they should find the poor wretches lie dead and the food untouched.[2]

99

As for those Londoners who chose to stay during the worst of the plague in the seventeenth century and those who opted to flee, Defoe's observations nicely point up an overall distinction between the two groups:

> It is true a vast many people fled, as I have observed, yet they were chiefly from the west end of the town, and from that we call the heart of the city: that is to say, among the wealthiest of the people, and such people as were unencumbered with trades and business. But of the rest, the generality stayed, and seemed to abide the worst; so that in the place we call the Liberties, and in the suburbs, in Southwark, and in the east part, such as Wapping, Ratcliff, Stepney, Rotherhithe, and the like, the people generally stayed, except here and there a few wealthy families, who, as above, did not depend upon their business.[3]

Even when disease wasn't stalking the streets, there were plenty of other reasons for leaving town, as Matthew Bramble explains in Tobias Smollett's 1771 novel *Humphry Clinker*:

> I start every hour from my sleep, at the horrid noise of the watchmen bawling the hour through every street, and thundering at every door; a set of useless fellows, who serve no other purpose but that of disturbing the repose of the inhabitants; and by five o'clock I start out of bed, in consequence of the still more dreadful alarm made by the country carts, and noisy rustics bellowing green pease under my window. If I would drink water, I must quaff the maukish contents of an open aqueduct, exposed to all manner of defilement; or swallow that which comes from the river Thames . . . The bread I eat in London, is a deleterious paste, mixed up with chalk, alum, and bone-ashes; insipid to the taste, and destructive to the constitution . . . [The greens] are produced in an artificial soil, and taste of nothing but the dunghills, from whence they spring.[4]

Among the wealthier Londoners who retreated from town in the seventeenth and eighteenth centuries, the royal family was inevitably in the vanguard. The exodus had begun with Henry VIII's establishment of the palaces of Whitehall and St James in what were then the western fringes

*Rural living on a royal scale. Theobalds, near Cheshunt was built
in the sixteenth century by Lord Burghley, and later became one of
James I's favourite residences.*

of London. Over the next two centuries, however, these royal enclaves
were gradually surrounded by residential and commercial development,
and a further move westwards was felt desirable to escape this encroachment. In 1689 William III bought what became Kensington Palace to
flee the smoke and pollution of the town (he suffered badly from asthma).
At that time, Kensington was a village with a scattering of large mansions
and great swathes of market gardens to the south and arable land to the
north. In consequence it effectively became a country refuge for William,
who employed Sir Christopher Wren to transform Nottingham House
(as it then was) shortly after his accession. William even established a
private road, the Route de Roi – referred to now as Rotten Row – so
that carriages could take the royal party to Westminster via Hyde Park,
formerly Henry VIII's deer park where he had frequently hunted, but by
William's time a public park.

In the following century George III acquired Buckingham House
near St James's Park in 1761 as a private retreat (the house had originally

been built in 1702–5 for the Duke of Buckingham on land carved out of the ancient manor of Ebury). Much further west he bought Kew Palace, formerly known as the Dutch House, in 1781. It had been a favourite of his mother's and she, along with her husband Frederick, was responsible for laying out what would in time become the Royal Botanical Gardens. One contemporary puzzled why the Hanoverians should so clearly like what he regarded as a less than attractive site ('In a bog close to the Thames, and the principal object in its view is the dirty town of Brentford, on the opposite side of the river'), and reckoned that he had the answer, suggesting that it was 'a selection, it would seem, of *family* taste, for George II is known to have often said, when riding through Brentford, "I do like this place, it's so like Yarmany" [Germany]'.[5]

Where the monarchy built, others were swift to follow. Kew became an attractive village in Georgian times, with well-to-do houses grouped round a central green complete with a church, St Anne's (the land for which had been provided by another monarch, Queen Anne, earlier in the century). Further along the Thames, the royal palace at Richmond helped make the place socially desirable, while its subsequent demolition in the 1650s made the town's expansion possible; many of the grand town houses surrounding the green still proudly display some of the masonry that was recycled over the next century or so. Various of the great and the good of society lived there in the eighteenth and nineteenth centuries, including the banker and Lord Mayor of London Sir Charles Asgill. He spent weekends and the summer months in his grand Palladian house, built around 1760 on the site of the old palace brewery, and lived the rest of the time in his town house in Portman Square.

Back closer to town, royalty's desire for rural seclusion gradually became a self-defeating exercise. Kensington grew from a village of 1,000 and a scattering of grand courtiers' houses at the turn of the eighteenth century to a substantial community of nearly 9,000 a hundred years later. To its south, Chelsea was similarly transformed. While it continued to be separated from Westminster by fields, its old church and early eighteenth-century houses along Cheyne Walk gradually became surrounded by new development. Here the principal movers and shakers belonged to the Cadogan Estate, which had inherited a large parcel of land by marriage

*'A gentleman's seat' on Stockwell Common, c.1792. Stockwell
remained a village until well into the nineteenth century.*

from the wealthy scholar and physician Hans Sloane; hence the appearance of Cadogan, Sloane and Hans in local street names. And with the
development of Kensington and Chelsea it was clear that the farms of
Brompton, Earl's Court and Notting Hill would not remain under the
plough for ever.

Among the truly rich, grand country houses and estates were a means
to showcase wealth and good taste. The resplendent Roehampton House,
for example, was built in Wandsworth in 1710 by the architect Thomas
Archer for the wealthy merchant Thomas Cary. In Chiswick the third
Earl of Burlington, who had imbibed continental culture on the Grand
Tour in 1714–15 and had been inspired by Palladio's Villa Capra in Vicenza,
built Chiswick House in 1725, a highly innovative structure whose floor
plan replicated that of a Roman villa. Houses in the Palladian style became
de rigueur for a while; hence Manresa House in Wandsworth, constructed
for the Earl of Bessborough in 1750, and Syon House in Isleworth, redeveloped in the 1760s by the 'celebrity' designers of the day, Robert Adam
and Lancelot 'Capability' Brown. Often, such houses would have to be
remodelled a few years after they had been built to take account of
changing tastes or the latest architectural fashion. Holland House, originally called Cope Castle, was one such: built in Kensington in 1605, it

passed through many hands, every one of which put its own personal touches to the building and its interior.

Osterley Park near Syon offers a perfect example of this kind of aspirational living and the waves of redevelopment that it caused. Back in 1576, when Elizabeth I stayed there, it was owned by the wealthy London merchant Sir Thomas Gresham, founder of the Royal Exchange. Gresham famously had a wall built across the central courtyard in a single night when Elizabeth hinted one evening that such an edifice might improve the look of the place. In time Osterley passed to the notorious and seemingly inescapable building speculator Nicholas Barbon, and then in 1713 to the banker Francis Child. It was the Child family who in 1761 commissioned Robert Adam to remodel the house on a breathtaking scale, complete with a vast entrance hall and even an Etruscan-style dressing room. The family struggled to finance the monster they had created, and proper heating was not installed at Osterley until late in the twentieth century. Today it feels like a house that was designed to be displayed, not really to be lived in.

It wasn't just points west that witnessed this sort of rural aggrandisement. Throughout the seventeenth century, and especially in the eighteenth, grand houses and parks were built and rebuilt all over what would emerge as the outer suburbs: Frognal House in Sidcup (early eighteenth century), Stowey House in Clapham (seventeenth century), Danson House and Park in Bexley (1764–7), and Cranham Hall (early seventeenth century) and Hare Hall (1769–70) in Havering to name but a few. Even Mill Hill, largely cut off from central London by the northern heights of Hampstead until the coming of the railways, was home to three lord mayors between 1774 and 1808, one of whom, Sir John Anderson, was elevated to the status of first Baronet of Mill Hill.

The villages and towns such grand establishments nestled in, or were close to, also became fashionable as less elevated ranks of society from Barnet to Sydenham sought to ape their betters with more modest houses built in fashionable styles. To the north, places such as Kentish Town acquired a new cachet from the country houses that had been built there over the years. Approached via the road that ran past Camden's Mother Red Cap coaching inn (named after a notorious seventeenth-century fortune-teller), it became regarded as a healthy place, ideal for summer breaks and for genteel living; by the early 1790s Horace Walpole was warning his friend Sir Horace Mann that Lord Camden, who owned much of the area, was planning to develop it. Further on, Highgate, with its grand seventeenth-century houses, expanded further in the eighteenth century. Similarly, Muswell Hill, built up on land that had once belonged to the nuns of the St Mary's Priory, Clerkenwell, and formerly a place of pilgrimage for those taking the miraculous waters from its 'Mossy Well', acquired elegant modest villas and one substantial one, the Grove, which for a while belonged to the book collector and friend of Samuel Johnson, Topham Beauclerc. To the south, Streatham became popular with City merchants in the years after the Great Fire of London and then received a further boost a few years later with the establishment of a spa near Streatham Common, whose waters were supposed to have healing properties.

What made all this out-of-town living practicable was a gradual improvement in public transport and the transport network. The enclosed, four-wheeled stagecoach first arrived in London in Tudor times, and by the later seventeenth and eighteenth centuries regular coach services were operating between London and just about every point of the compass. The faster mail coaches, travelling at night, could reach speeds of up to seven or eight miles per hour (hence the expression 'post haste'); in 1784 a mail coach from London to Bristol managed to make the 120-mile journey in just seventeen hours. In the summer months when the roads were reasonably dry, someone living in Norwich could reach the City within about fifteen hours. It became increasingly possible, therefore, to commute daily from nearby suburbs or to commute weekly from ones further away, perhaps buying or renting a house in town to serve as accommodation during the week and finding one in the countryside to serve as a weekend or even summer retreat. The artist William Hogarth, for example, was able to own both a town house in Leicester Fields (now Leicester Square) and a country house in distant Chiswick. In his *Tour Through the Whole Island of Great Britain* (1726) Daniel Defoe noted the way in which places as far out as Tottenham and Edmonton were becoming quite sizable communities, appealing to 'the middle sort of mankind, grown wealthy by trade, and who still taste of London; some of them live both in the city, and in the country at the same time'.[6]

The busy traffic junction outside the old Elephant and Castle Inn, as depicted by Thomas Rowlandson in the early nineteenth century: a melée of horsemen, carriages and livestock.

In 1690 a stagecoach service was established that linked the newly popular Clapham and the City via the highwayman-strewn Clapham Common. A Leyton to Walthamstow route followed in 1707, then Ilford to London (1740), Stoke Newington to London (1760), Enfield to London (1783) and Holloway to London (1816), among many others. Each coach could accommodate up to eighteen passengers, although not all could fit inside; and travel was not cheap. In 1796 it cost one shilling to ride on the outside of the Camberwell to Charing Cross coach, and eighteen pence to sit inside. This was not transport for the poor. Despite the cramped conditions and general discomfort, it was a luxury that only the burgeoning middle classes could afford.

Nevertheless, by the mid eighteenth century the novelist Richard Graves was able to remark that 'every little clerk in office must have his villa, and every tradesman his country-house'.[7] Robert Lloyd's 1757 poem 'The City's Country Box' similarly commented on the commuter of the era:

> Some three or four miles out of town,
> (An hour's ride will bring you down),
> He fixes on his choice abode,
> Not half a furlong from the road:
> And so convenient does it lay,
> The stages pass it ev'ry day:
> And then so snugg, so mighty pretty,
> To have an house so near the city!'[8]

Inevitably the faster services offered by the stagecoaches required ever better road surfaces on which to travel. Early coach travel was dangerous, partly because of the risk of highway robbery (Hounslow Heath, Finchley Common and Shooters Hill were all notorious; in 1718 stage coaches from Hampstead were provided with guards), but more especially because of the risk of serious accident posed by rutted or poorly maintained roads. It was not unknown for coaches to overturn at great speed, killing driver and passengers alike. According to *Jackson's Oxford Journal*, for example, an accident that occurred to the night coach that set off from Oxford to London on 18 June 1779 caused the death of one passenger, broke the leg of another and badly bruised three more.

Some idea of just how bad the roads could be is given in this 1725 account of the roads leading to Hyde Park Corner:

Abraham Odell, of *Fulham*, Surgeon, said, That the Road between *Fulham* and *Knightsbridge* is very bad; and has seen Carts set between *Hyde Park Corner*, and the Stones End; and that there are Ruts in the Road 4 Foot deep.[9]

Even when the journey itself was safe, it was frequently bumpy and unpleasant, dust and dirt being constantly thrown up by the horses and carriages. As the coaches neared town, more and more passengers would join them, some of them clinging desperately to the outsides and risking their lives in the process.

Gradually, therefore, in response to growing pressure from visitors, commuters and tradesfolk, new and better roads were built. Following prompting from the inhabitants of St Marylebone, Paddington and Islington, London's first bypass, rather unimaginatively called the New Road, was constructed in the 1750s through fields to the north of the City, initially to help sheep and cattle drovers bring their livestock to Smithfield Market. The present-day Euston Road, which formed the central part of this new development, was opened in 1756. Around the same time some existing roads were improved in order to accommodate the new levels of traffic, including the old Roman road Ermine Street, which connected Stoke Newington to the City.

A major factor in the creation of these new roads and the improvement of existing ones was the introduction of the turnpike trust. Named after the defensive barrier that was used to defend against cavalry charges in battle, the turnpike was a gate erected across a stretch of highway that travellers had to pay to use. The trust associated with that particular stretch of road would then use the toll money raised for the upkeep of the road, ensuring that it was well surfaced, free from robbers and as attractive to travellers as possible; and they would be allowed to pocket any profit. Whereas roads had previously been the responsibility of local parishes or manors who had a vested interest in keeping only the more important ones passable (because of the cost of upkeep), it was now possible to attract private investors to help keep traffic moving.

Turnpike trusts were created by individual Acts of Parliament and proliferated throughout the eighteenth century. The Act that set up each trust determined the maximum toll rate, the extent of the trust – usually twenty miles of road – and the period of time that the trust would operate, normally twenty-one years. To manage the road repairs, make improvements and build toll houses, the trustees worked with the local parishes to recruit labourers in lieu of tolls, though in some places the placing of gates across the roads was fiercely resented by the local communities, who pointed out that hitherto they had been able to travel for free. Milestones were erected to show the distance between settlements from each major town; many of these can still be seen in London's suburbs today.

Some turnpikes proved to be hugely lucrative for their owners; the Tyburn turnpike, for example, which stood on the site of the old Tyburn gallows (at the junction of today's Edgware and Bayswater roads) charged carriages drawn by one or two horses the then considerable sum of ten pence. It is scarcely surprising, therefore, that toll roads should have sprouted up everywhere. By 1801, when John Cary published his map entitled a 'General Plan for Explaining the Different Trusts of the Turnpike Gates in the Vicinity of the Metropolis', they had become an intricate spider's web reaching towards the centre and connected to one another by radial routes. The main routes were the Kensington, Uxbridge and Marylebone roads to the west; the Hampstead and Highgate New and Old Roads, City Road, Old Street, Stamford Hill, Hackney, Shoreditch and Bethnal Green roads to the north; and Whitechapel road (along the Mile End Road) to the east. South of the Thames there were New Cross and Surrey New and Old Roads. Some of the toll gates are depicted on the maps, too, their names often redolent of what the area was like at the time: Kensington Gravel Pit Gate, for example, reminds us that the nearby area was being used as a de facto quarry; the Green Man Gate on the Deptford Road reminds us of the public house that stood there, satisfying the needs of travellers who wanted to rest before they continued their journey into or out of London. In total, twenty-two turnpike trusts were set up in Middlesex alone between the mid eighteenth and mid nineteenth centuries, with a further eleven trusts in Surrey. Rather fewer were established to the east to connect the parts of London that fell inside the borders of Kent and Essex; presumably the fact that there were no major arterial routes here, unlike those leading north, west and south to major ports and cities, made potential turnpike ventures less attractive to entrepreneurs.

New roads and improved old ones led to urban development around them. The Finchley Road, for example, which was established by Act of

Parliament in 1827 and which ran from St John's Wood to what is now the North Circular Road, stimulated the growth of Swiss Cottage – at first no more than a Swiss-style tavern built at one of the toll gates. The New Road, similarly, inspired urban expansion and by the 1830s was bordered by fashionable houses. By 1861 the London Road through Stoke Newington had attracted 132 houses on the west side of the road between Kingsland and Church Street – not to mention another 65 in courts and yards leading from the main road.

Improving transport routes did not just help Londoners to get to work; they helped Londoners play, too. As it became easier to reach outlying areas relatively speedily and therefore spend longer there – perhaps a whole morning or afternoon, or even a day trip – many attractions became more accessible. Spa towns sprang up around the capital from the late seventeenth century onwards, catering for urban dwellers who wanted to 'take the waters' and enjoy all that the countryside had to offer. Some of the earliest included Sydenham Wells, Richmond Wells, Kilburn and

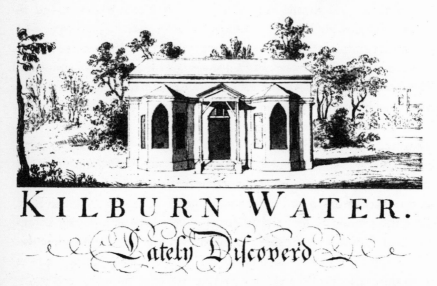

KILBURN WATER.
Lately Discover'd

Kilburn Wells was a popular spa resort for eighteenth-century Londoners. In the 1770s it was advertised as a 'happy spot equally celebrated for its rural situation and the acknowledged efficacy of its water'.

Epsom; later ones included Dulwich Spa after 1739 and Bermondsey Spa in the 1770s. Kilburn's fairly short-lived spa was typical, consisting of a great room ('particularly adapted to the use and amusement of the politest companies', according to the *Public Advertiser,* in 1773) and gardens. For its part, Dulwich Spa, near the corner of Dulwich Common and Lordship Lane, inspired the growth of what had been a small hamlet into the elegant Dulwich Village. Acton Wells flourished for a while until its charms were deemed to have been superseded by the delights of Tunbridge Wells and Bath.

Among the grander spas was Hampstead. Situated on the edge of Hampstead Heath and overlooking the City far below, Hampstead had since medieval times developed a reputation as a convenient bolt-hole for those seeking to escape pestilence in the capital, as well as the various floods that afflicted the outlying regions along the Thames (not that it was free from disease: people fleeing from the 1603 outbreak of the plague brought it with them to Hampstead, according to diplomat, administrator and local resident Sir William Waad, many dying under hedges 'whereof we have experience weekly here'). The village became a popular rural retreat. One visitor, the German Zacharias Conrad von Uffenbach, remarked in 1710 that 'many drive out of London and some spend all summer there';[10] the less charitable Daniel Defoe pointed out in 1724 that this meant that in winter Hampstead had nothing to recommend it.

From 1698 chalybeate waters from the heath were drawn at Hampstead Wells, and people started to come to sample their restorative powers. In due course, the village acquired a coffee room, a bowling green and, where Well Walk now stands, the substantial 'Great Room', comprising a pump room and an assembly room for dances and concerts. The village grew, from 200 or 300 small cottages and a couple of more substantial dwellings in the late seventeenth century, into a bustling place of some 600 families in 1730. Various grand new houses were built – for example, Church Row, the south side of which dates from 1720 – and inns and lodging houses appeared. By 1724 Hampstead 'had increased to that degree, that the town almost spreads the whole side of the hill'.[11] As the village grew, many of its wealthy residents began to move further out to colonise Upper Terrace, Littleworth and Frognal, clearing any existing small cottages to build their villas set in extensive grounds. By 1774 the heath was described as being adorned with many gentlemen's houses, the most spectacular of which was Kenwood House, built in the sixteenth century but extensively remodelled by Robert Adam in the 1760s and 1770s for the first Earl of Mansfield. It still survives, as do one or two earlier properties in the area, such as Burgh House in the heart of the old village and Fenton House on Windmill Hill.

By the end of the eighteenth century the Hampstead spa was in decline, outshone by other newly fashionable places, especially by Bagnigge Wells spa on the King's Cross Road. Nevertheless, while the village continued to retain its rural charm, still some way from the City that lay below, its population continued to rise. At the time of the 1811 census it contained over 800 inhabited houses and its residents were part of a 'select, amicable, respectable and opulent neighbourhood'.[12] It also proved popular with artists, writers and musicians – a popularity that it retained well into the twentieth century.

<hr />

Alongside the spas, pleasure gardens grew up around the outer reaches of London, the most popular and ambitious of these being on the south side of the river at Vauxhall, now a part of Kennington. Vauxhall at the

The Chinese pavilion at one of the great pleasure spots of
Georgian London: Vauxhall Gardens.

time was little more than a village. Indeed, it was regarded as sufficiently remote from London to be a suitable place to build polluting glassworks from the 1670s onwards. However, its open spaces made it ripe for new speculations, and the pleasure grounds that were laid out here just before the Restoration of Charles II in 1660 remained a landmark feature of London for 200 years, easily accessible by river or by coach.

The first mention of the gardens comes in a diary entry by Samuel Pepys for 28 May 1667:

> By water to Fox-hall, and there walked in the Spring Gardens [Vauxhall Gardens' original name]. A great deal of company, and the weather and garden pleasant; and it is very cheap going thither, for a man may spend what he will or nothing, all as one. But to hear the nightingale and the birds, and here fiddles and there a harp, and here a Jew's trump and there laughing, and there fine people walking, is mighty divertising.

This fairly humble series of gardens and walkways on the banks of the Thames, with a tavern for refreshments, was developed further by Sir Samuel Morland, but it was only when Jonathan Tyers took possession of the site around 1730 that it really took off as a popular attraction for fashionable society. Now a concerted effort was made to introduce various forms of entertainment for commercial profit, including public concerts and musical recitals in purpose-built pavilions:

> Mr. Tyers opened it with an advertisement of a *Ridotto al Fresco*, a term which the people of this country had till that time been strangers to. These entertainments were repeated in the course of the summer, and numbers resorted to partake of them. This encouraged the proprietor to make his garden a place of musical entertainment, for every evening during the summer season. To this end he was at great expense in deco-rating the gardens with paintings; he engaged a band of excellent musi-cians; he issued silver tickets at one guinea each for admission, and receiving great encouragement, he set up an organ in the orchestra, and, in a conspicuous part of the garden, erected a fine statue of Mr. Handel.[13]

Hot-air balloons became a regular feature, as well as fireworks, tightrope walkers and even military re-enactments. There was a rotunda and Turkish tent, decked out in rococo finery; supper boxes decorated with paintings of children's games and the contemporary theatre (designed by Francis Hayman at the St Martin's Lane Academy), a Chinese pavilion, fancy-dress balls and walkways lit by hundreds of lamps. Crowds of up to 20,000 at a time would congregate in the gardens, more if there was something particularly noteworthy in the offing. Dr Johnson's biographer and London enthusiast James Boswell captured something of the atmosphere of the gardens at their height:

> Vauxhall Gardens is peculiarly adapted to the taste of the English nation; there being a mixture of curious show – gay exhibition, music, vocal and instrumental, not too refined for the general ear – for all of which only a shilling is paid.[14]

There was also another side to Vauxhall, which this 1772 description hints at:

> These entertainments, which begin in the month of May, are continued every night. They bring together persons of all ranks and conditions; and amongst these, a considerable number of females, whose charms want only that cheerful air, which is the flower and quintessence of beauty. These places serve equally as a rendezvous either for business or intrigue.[15]

Away from the formality of polite society across the river, screened by bushes and trees, it wasn't just music that was made in the gardens at night.

In 1785 the Spring Gardens became Vauxhall Gardens, and a small admission fee was charged, which quickly rose from one shilling to four and sixpence by the early nineteenth century. Success continued into the first decades of the new century, but with the expansion of Kennington into a fashionable built-up neighbourhood, and fierce competition from other forms of attraction, the gardens finally closed in 1859.

Although the most successful of the public gardens, Vauxhall was not the only one offering entertainment: Ranelagh Gardens, situated in the grounds of Ranelagh House by the Royal Chelsea Hospital, was a major commercial rival between 1742 and 1803. Its centrepiece was a grand wooden rotunda, and it was particularly associated with music (Mozart performed here when he was nine years old). Further out, there were the Marylebone Gardens, set in the grounds of Marylebone's old manor house.

Ranelagh Gardens' grand wooden rotunda, where Mozart
performed as a child.

Originally their main appeal seems to have lain in such earthy pursuits
as bowling, gambling, cockfighting and boxing, but from 1738 music and
drama were also performed. To the east were the very popular Hackney
leisure gardens, the best known lying behind the Mermaid Inn on Church
Street, and near the inn where the diarist Samuel Pepys played shuffle-
board and ate cherries. Closer to the centre were Cuper's Gardens, which
existed from the 1680s until 1760, opposite Somerset House. Some idea
of this particular venue's nature in its declining years can be inferred from
the fact that in 1753 it failed to renew its licence under a new piece of
legislation that was entitled 'An Act for Better Preventing Thefts and
Robberies and for Regulating Places of Public Entertainment'. The
approaches to Waterloo Bridge now cover what was one of Georgian
London's great pleasure spots.

The open spaces around London offered opportunities for sport as well.
Back in medieval and Tudor times, kings, queens and nobles had enjoyed
the delights of the chase in Hainault Forest and in the royal parks. Their
humbler contemporaries had practised their archery skills in Moor Fields
and Finsbury. These pastimes had largely gone by Georgian times, but
others came to take their place. In Stoke Newington, for example, a
bowling green was leased to William Webb in the late eighteenth century,

tucked away behind the Weaver's Arms pub bordering Newington Common; another was established in Stoke Newington in 1783 at Abney House. Then there was cricket. Members of the precursor of the Marylebone Cricket Club started to play at White Conduit Fields, before instructing an employee, Thomas Lord, to find them a better site. He duly did so, and they moved to Dorset Square, playing there (at what became known as Lord's Old Ground) between 1787 and 1810. Their next home (Lord's Middle Ground) had to be surrendered in 1813 to make way for the Regent's Canal, at which point they moved to St John's Wood. Here, on 22 June 1814, they played their first match in their third and final home – against Hertfordshire. Since St John's Wood still retained much of its countryside charm, with its farms, gardens and meadows, it must have seemed an appropriately tranquil setting for a very rural game.

Gambling was a Georgian obsession (people frequently bet on cricket matches, for example), so it is scarcely surprising that many of the rougher forms of Georgian sport involved the giving and taking of cash. Horse

Bear-baiting, along with cock-fighting, were among the more brutal entertainments enjoyed by eighteenth-century Londoners.

racing was hugely popular, most notably at Hackney Marshes but also on Hampstead Heath in the 1730s and 1740s (before the local magistrates put a stop to it). Hackney also hosted boxing contests, while brutal bare-knuckle fighting could be found almost anywhere – in Barnet, Finchley and Kentish Town, for example. Cockfighting and bear-baiting were also popular fixtures, enjoyed both in town and away from it.

A love of violence was not the prerogative of any particular group. Rich and poor alike enjoyed sports that seem to us unsporting. However, one violent pastime did definitely have a class element to it: duelling. Technically illegal, it persisted throughout the eighteenth century; and while a duel could theoretically be fought anywhere, London's open spaces offered obvious attractions and fewer prying eyes. Hyde Park was a popular venue. John Wilkes fought Samuel Martin here in 1762, and ten years later the park was the setting for a fight between the playwright Richard Brinsley Sheridan and Captain Mathews (on this occasion, though, the protagonists found the park too crowded and so decided to reconvene their sword fight in Covent Garden). There was even an all-female match in 1792, when Lady Almeria Braddock, who felt that Mrs Elphinstone's speculations about her age amounted to an insult, challenged her to what became known as the 'petticoat duel'. However, as duelling became increasingly frowned upon, so it tended to move further out of town. When Prince Frederick was called out by Lieutenant-Colonel Charles Lennox in 1789, they took their quarrel to Wimbledon Common. Towards the close of the century, following a row in Parliament over proposals to change the Defence Act, William Pitt the Younger and George Tierney took their pistols to Putney Heath. Here, on 27 May 1798, the two men retreated twelve paces, turned and fired. Neither was hurt.

SIX

THE WELFARE OF THE PEOPLE

Local Government and Charity before the Victorians

Henry VIII's decision to dissolve the monasteries not only transformed the way the London area looked, it also transformed the way it was run. While the City retained its medieval instruments of government, with its wards, parishes, guilds, lord mayor and council of aldermen, local administration outside the walls changed. Up until the early sixteenth century the manor still held sway, its annual or semi-annual 'leet', or court, designed to uphold all the rules and regulations of the area within its jurisdiction, as well as a whole range of local bye-laws deemed insufficiently important to be the concern of itinerant royal judges. Such matters of local concern as the failure to keep the roads passable for general users, encroachment on manorial waste land and commons, grazing sheep or cattle on land without the permission of the lord, petty theft, land disputes, breaking the peace of the manor, and a host of other issues that affected regional life – all these were the responsibility of manorial leets from Richmond to Romford and every point on the compass in between.

With the Dissolution the secular manor gradually gave way to the ecclesiastical parish. This may seem somewhat paradoxical. After all, the Dissolution of the Monasteries was part and parcel of a wholesale onslaught on the authority of the Roman Catholic Church. However, Henry's minister Thomas Cromwell, while determined to remove the Pope's authority, was equally keen to buttress the power of the new Church of England, and he made the key decision that from now on the ecclesiastical parish should be put right at the centre of things. In 1538, for example, he introduced an innovative system of record-keeping that required every priest to make a note of each baptism, marriage and burial in his parish; the records were to be kept in the parish chest with a copy sent to the diocesan bishop each year. This may seem like a minor administrative change, but it made the parish priest the sole guardian and recorder of community life. From that point onwards, priests were required to undertake an ever greater range of tasks for society, including those that had previously been catered for by the monastic houses.

As parishes took on more responsibility, so the authority of the manorial leet declined. Local crown-appointed Justices of the Peace (who had begun holding quarter sessions four times a year from around the 1360s) were increasingly called on to enforce local bye-laws in the fifteenth and sixteenth centuries, and the manorial leet became effectively marginalised. By the eighteenth century it was predominantly being used to oversee land transfers and protect ancient manorial rights – in particular ensuring the retention of common land.

In outlying towns and boroughs this shift of authority had happened rather earlier, and in many of them manorial government had long been indistinguishable from civic government. Kingston upon Thames, for example, has a charter that dates from 1200 by which King John granted manorial rights – in other words, administrative powers – to the town's burgesses. In 1481 Kingston was granted borough status through a Charter of Incorporation which afforded an even greater degree of self-governance. Its authority even reached beyond its immediate town boundaries: as an ecclesiastical parish it also controlled the satellite hamlets of East Molesey, Ham, Hook, New Malden and Thames Ditton.

In established towns, then, authority tended to be wielded by the burgesses and the mercantile guilds. In small villages and settlements, local administration was increasingly handled not by the lord of the manor or his nominees but by parochial administrators drawn from the land-owning and professional classes who met on a regular basis as the parish vestry. The vestry was the equivalent of today's parish church council. Chaired by the parish priest, it included a number of churchwardens, various overseers of the poor and their assistants, and a clerk to record the minutes of each monthly Sunday meeting, held after divine service. Appointments were generally made annually at the vestry's Easter meeting, either by the borough council or guild (in towns), or by the patron or local landowner (in the countryside). The post of churchwarden was particularly significant because it carried with it responsibility for managing parish property and finances. Funds came from various rates which were levied on the owners and occupiers of land and property in the parish.

THE WELFARE OF THE PEOPLE

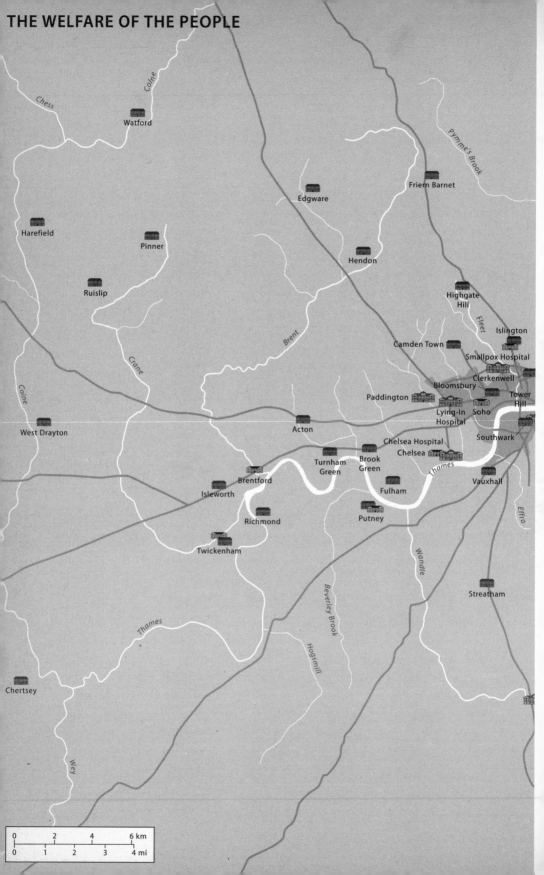

Watford

Chess
Colne

Harefield

Pinner

Ruislip

Colne

West Drayton

Edgware

Hendon

Brent

Crane

Acton

Brentford

Isleworth

Turnham
Green

Brook
Green

Fulham

Richmond

Twickenham

Putney

Thames

Beverley Brook

Hogsmill

Wandle

Chertsey

Wey

Friern Barnet

Pymme's Brook

Highgate
Hill

Camden Town

Paddington

Bloomsbury

Lying-In
Hospital

Chelsea Hospital

Chelsea

Fleet

Islington

Smallpox Hospital

Clerkenwell

Soho

Tower
Hill

Southwark

Vauxhall

Effra

Streatham

0   2   4   6 km
0 1 2 3 4 mi

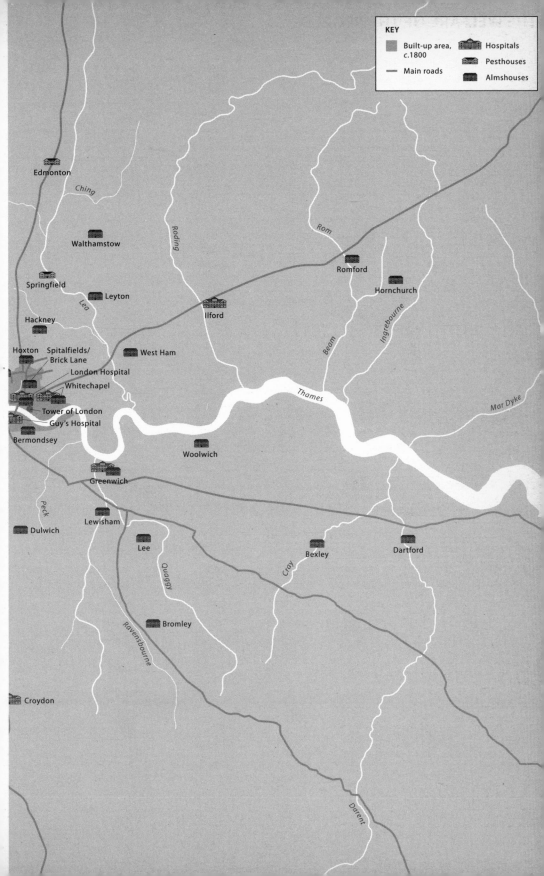

KEY

Built-up area, c.1800

— Main roads

Hospitals

Pesthouses

Almshouses

Edmonton

Ching

Walthamstow

Roding

Rom

Romford

Springfield

Hornchurch

Leyton

Lea

Hackney

Ilford

Ingrebourne

Hoxton

Spitalfields/ Brick Lane

West Ham

London Hospital

Beam

Whitechapel

Thames

Mar Dyke

Tower of London

Guy's Hospital

Bermondsey

Woolwich

Greenwich

Peck

Lewisham

Dulwich

Lee

Quaggy

Cray

Bexley

Dartford

Bromley

Ravensbourne

Croydon

Darent

By the start of the seventeenth century the vestry had responsibility not only for ecclesiastical affairs, but also for a whole range of social ones, from providing help for the poor and sick to dealing with such 'moral issues' as the welfare of single mothers with illegitimate children. In the opening years of the nineteenth century the parish vestry's duties expanded yet further. Now it oversaw graveyard and burial-ground maintenance and the upkeep of parish cottages, workhouses and almshouses. It also administered any other charities within the parish, including many early schools. In terms of law and order it was responsible for manning watch houses and administering such punishments as stocks, cages and whipping posts. Then there was a whole range of miscellaneous demands, from regulating weights and measures within the parish boundaries (particularly important in the market towns surrounding London), to overseeing the repair of roads and the maintenance of pumps and watercourses, to providing fire engines. The vestry was even responsible for exterminating vermin and setting the parish clocks. Some idea of the sheer diversity of its responsibilities comes across in the various sets of vestry minutes that survive. The Isleworth vestry minutes for 3 August 1674, for example, record that the officials agreed that £25 raised for church repairs should be used to 'rapaire & amend the causeway by the Church for the safety of travellers' and that John Salter the bricklayer should be employed to make the repairs. The following November, the vestry ordered that 'Goodman Ludgoll have 10 s[hillings] given him in full for the lodging dyet & nursing of Elizabeth How who breake her foote'; it also appointed one James Gerrard as a warder in the town 'to turne out all beggars & idle people'.

In short, each parish was a self-governing authority, providing for every aspect of local people's lives. Not every parish worked in quite the same way. Hackney, for example, had a very unusual form of government, instituted in 1613, which entailed dual administration by selected officials of the vestry and a coalition of parish officers and principal inhabitants of the parish, all of whom held open meetings every few months to assist with the planning of local affairs.[1] Waltham Forest also had its own unique system. Here a number of forest officials – known as 'verderers' – worked alongside local residents within the vestry – a leftover from medieval times when royal forests had their own system of administration.[2] Nevertheless, the basic principles were the same. Barking's history shows nicely how local government evolved over time. Here manorial leets were regularly held throughout the Middle Ages and early modern period but ceased to exist in the nineteenth century. Meanwhile, the vestry which had been set up in the sixteenth century eventually became the chief local authority in the parish.

What partly gave the church-related vestry body its civil authority was an assumption that everyone in the parish shared the same religious beliefs, that everyone attended the same church, and that the church was the central meeting place for parishioners. Inevitably, this assumption started to be challenged as Nonconformity became more prevalent in the eighteenth century, for example in areas such as Stepney and Stoke Newington – traditionally refuges beyond the City walls for dissenters and, later, areas settled by immigrants fleeing religious persecution. Nevertheless, the established church still held sway until the reforms of Victorian times.

Ilford hospital (shown here in a nineteenth-century engraving) was a medieval foundation, originally intended for thirteen 'lepers of the king's servants'. In 1572 Elizabeth I granted ownership of the hospital to one Thomas Fanshawe on the condition that he should supply a master, a chaplain and support for six poor men.

As London's population grew in the areas lying closest to the City, so parishes were increasingly divided into wards to make administration easier. Barking, for example, acquired four: Ilford, Chadwell, Ripple and Town (that is, Barking itself). A churchwarden represented each ward in the vestry, and each ward appointed its own constable and levied a separate poor rate. And as parishes grew up and became more complex, so it became necessary to set up markers to show where their boundaries lay. In the more rural areas these tended to be stone posts; in urban areas they might be plaques fixed to the walls of buildings with the initials of the neighbouring parishes denoted on them. Many from the late eighteenth and nineteenth centuries still survive: the letters 'SGB' that appear on some buildings in the West End, for example, denote the parish of St George Bloomsbury; the old parish of St Pancras has similarly left its mark on north London.

***

One of the main areas of responsibility for the parish vestry was the provision of poor relief, an endemic problem during Tudor times when it has been estimated that anything up to a third of the country's population lived in poverty, and a persistent one thereafter. England's poor lingered – often literally – on the doorstep of every hamlet, village, town and parish. In 1688 the Lancaster Herald in the College of Arms, Gregory King, estimated that there were in the region of 1.3 million cottagers and paupers in the country, at a time when the population of England and Wales was no more than 5.75 million. These were people living on average earnings of three shillings per week, a tiny sum given that a quartern (or 4lb) loaf of bread cost between four and six pence in London – rising to nine pence if there had been a bad harvest that year.

Poverty, then, was everywhere, and it was particularly visible in London because here it rubbed along beside such conspicuous wealth. Writing of eighteenth-century London, the historian Roy Porter observed:

> The dregs still festered too near the dukes for comfort. Piccadilly was
> just a stone's throw from the thieves' kitchen of Seven Dials.
> Bloomsbury bigwigs battled to boot Welsh cattle drovers, Smithfield-
> bound, off their elegant, wide leafy thoroughfares.[3]

Alleviation of poverty was not purely a parish affair. Individual acts of charity also played a very important role. Wills proved in the Prerogative Court of Canterbury from the sixteenth century onwards show that many rich people in and around London left annual sums to pay for bread or other goods for their struggling fellow citizens. In 1585, for example, Robert Rampston left the sum of twenty shillings to provide weekly bread for the poor of Leyton, a dole that was still being paid in the 1960s. In 1753 Jonathan Gurnell left the interest on a bequest of £200 to allow for coals to be purchased for the poor of Ealing so that they could heat their homes and cook their food. Robert Cromwell's will from 1720 granted sufficient lands to buy gowns for six poor women each year in Hayes.

In addition, rich local parishioners often also left provision in their wills for the construction and funding of almshouses, usually by establishing a trust fund that could draw on income from land or property rental. Almshouses were built in Clerkenwell in 1609, in Friern Barnet

In his will of 1682, the London merchant Robert Daniel made provision for the building of an almshouse within ten miles of the City for six men and four women of at least fifty years of age. The building was opened in Hendon in 1729, its benefactor commemorated on a plaque on the façade.

in 1612 and in Vauxhall in 1615, to name just three. Since such institutions were the result of individual charity, their rules had a tendency to reflect individual whim. There might be stipulations about appropriate conduct, the number of required attendances at church per week, what could be grown in the almshouse gardens, what clothes could be worn (some of those who lived in almshouses had to wear insignia that linked them to the establishment). There were also invariably selection criteria. Dr William Spurstowe built six almshouses in Hackney in 1666 specifically for widows. Three years later, Henry Monger's will established an equivalent number in the same parish for men aged sixty or over, along with thirty shillings each year by way of income.

Among the best-known almshouses still standing today are those on Kingsland Road in Hoxton, established in the early eighteenth century by Sir Robert Geffrye, former Lord Mayor of London and member of the Ironmongers' Company (they now form the Geffrye Museum). Geffrye accumulated a considerable fortune in the course of his career, and he left a generous legacy to the company in 1703–4 to buy land to provide homes 'for poor people of good character over the age of fifty-six'. The site chosen for fourteen small almshouses was on land to the north of the City, where open fields and market gardens could be guaranteed to provide healthy clean air for the residents (that said, even at this time there was light industry in the area in the form of clay pits and tile making). The plot was purchased in 1712 and construction began in 1715, the houses being built 'of oake or good yellow firr . . . [and] good plain tyles, with heart of oak lathes'. The windows were glazed with 'the best [New]castle glass' and each door was fitted with 'a stoute lock, key and a bolt and a latch with good hinges'. Residents were bound by the usual strict set of rules: they had to keep their rooms clean, return before the gates were locked at night, and avoid blaspheming, adultery and lewd behaviour. Nor could they keep chickens or poultry on the lawns at the front, though they were allowed to take on work in moderation to provide additional funds to supplement the small pensions that they were granted. If they failed to comply with the regulations, they ran the risk of being expelled.

In 1734 the Drapers' Company and Frameknitters' Company bought plots of land for almshouses nearby – their involvement in charitable work, like that of Geffrye's Ironmongers' Company, showing not just how important wealthy city institutions could be to the lives of the poor, but how far their reach extended. Moreover, not only did they set up institutions in and around London, they often became involved in existing ones. Sir Martin Bowes's almshouses in Woolwich, for example, were given into the care of the Goldsmiths' Company in the late sixteenth century. Lewisham Free Grammar School was placed in the trust of the Leathersellers' Company in 1633. A few years later, in the 1660s, the Leathersellers' Company also became trustees of Colfe's Almshouses in the same parish.

However, while individual and institutional charity certainly helped to alleviate poverty to an extent, the main burden of poor relief inevitably fell on local government. It was the Elizabethan Poor Law of 1601 that codified a national system centred on the parish. Thereafter, various additional pieces of legislation refined the system. The 1662 Poor Relief (Settlement and Removal) Act, for example, required that people leaving their parish should take a 'settlement certificate' with them to clarify where they had come from and therefore whose responsibility they were should they become destitute. The 1723 Workhouse Test Act, or Knatchbull's Act, sought to winnow out those claiming poor relief who were felt not to deserve it. Gilbert's Act of 1782 set out to create greater collaboration between local parishes caring for the 'deserving' poor. It included provisions for jointly funded workhouses to serve a wider community and boards of guardians to oversee their administration. It may not have been popular (only about a hundred 'Gilbert Unions' were formed, and very few of these were in the London area), but it laid the way for a more national approach to poverty in the following century.

Vestries were allowed to raise taxation from the local community through a system of rates, ranging from half a penny to six pence in the pound per week. The funds raised were then allocated to the poor, often in the form of 'outdoor' relief – small pension payments or subsidies to allow people to make essential purchases. What is striking, though, is how relatively few people actually received help in this way. Barking had approximately 60 pensioners but an overall population of around 2,000 in 1801. Ilford had only 78 pensioners in the same period. A successful claimant might receive somewhere in the region of fourteen to twenty shillings a month, but this wasn't much at a time when a new set of clothes for a poor woman cost fourteen shillings and a humble pair of shoes might cost two shillings and sixpence. The Barking vestry minutes show that some poor people received goods as well as meagre stipends. In 1742, for example, it was decided that the churchwarden should provide eight widows and six children of the parish each with a shift and a pair of shoes.

This sort of ad hoc outdoor relief, poorly funded as it was, could only deal with the tip of the problem. It was gradually recognised, therefore, that, despite the cost involved, purpose-built accommodation was required. The 'deserving' poor – those who were too old, ill or infirm to find full-time employment – found their way into workhouses. Those who were able-bodied, but who were regarded as 'undeserving', were sent to 'houses of industry', where they were expected to work for their supper. As for the 'idle' poor and the vagrant, they were dispatched to houses of correction or even to prison. Each parish was required to appoint between two and four Overseers of the Poor from among its principal ratepayers, whose task it was to regulate the system and decide which category each applicant for help belonged to. In many cases, this effectively gave them the power of life and death over the people they were assessing.

As the population of London's inner suburbs rose throughout the seventeenth and eighteenth centuries, and the cost of outdoor relief rose correspondingly, ever more individuals and families who had previously been sent to the parish vestry to apply for cash were handed over to the new network of workhouses for assessment and support. Knatchbull's Act of 1723 played an important role in this, and in the years after it was passed many new workhouses were built or suitable existing buildings rented. Towards the centre of London, for example, workhouses sprang up in the parishes of St George's Hanover Square (1725–6), St Mary's in Lambeth (1726) and St James's in Westminster (1728). At St Margaret, Westminster, the guardians of the poor hired a house and garden in 1726 which they subsequently expanded. Even today a handful of these former workhouses are still to be found: the workhouse for the parish of St Anne's in Soho, built in 1771, still survives as 14 Manette Street; further afield, eighteenth-century workhouses built at Upminster, at Harefield in Hillington and for Cudham parish in Bromley avoided later demolition to become private dwellings. Conditions varied from workhouse to work-house, much depending on the master who was appointed to manage day-to-day affairs, and who had total control over spending, discipline and intake. Those workhouses run by masters seeking to make a profit by cutting down on food supplies were grim indeed. Many inmates were consigned to an early grave. Child mortality often hit 90 per cent.

When it came to the numbers catered for by each of London's various vestries, this varied significantly from area to area and was very much shaped by the relative affluence of the parish in which the workhouse or workhouses stood. A parliamentary select committee report that looked at workhouses across the country in 1775–6 showed that wealthy Richmond had a workhouse for only 90 people, while neighbouring Kingston's could accommodate 288. Closer to town, the various parishes of Southwark combined to provide nearly 1,100 places, with a further 270 in Lambeth. As for Westminster, some 3,300 places were available in its various work-houses, including 300 for the poor of Covent Garden. To the east of the City, Whitechapel's workhouse catered for 600, Shadwell's held 350, Christchurch Spitalfields housed another 340 and Bethnal Green 400. To the north, beyond the old City walls, there were 600 places for the poor of St Marylebone, 300 in Clerkenwell and 350 in St Andrew's Holborn.

An account of 1732 from St Andrew's Holborn workhouse gives some idea of what life in the average poorhouse was like. Here, a property at 41 Shoe Lane had been leased in 1727 and was run by a management committee of sixteen gentlemen. A master and matron were in residence to assign work duties to the sixty-two inmates. Seven of the older residents (four of whom were in their eighties) were given the task of picking oakum (essentially recycling old and tarry ship's rope). Thirteen were dispatched to spin and knit yarn into sailor's caps. Various inmates under-took domestic chores such as cooking, cleaning and washing; and there were also twenty-one children, who were the responsibility of a school mistress.

All were bound by rules and regulations governing what they could wear, when they could come and go, what they could eat and what alco-holic beverages they were not allowed to drink. Their fare was sparse, basic and unappetising: milk pottage or water-gruel for breakfast during the week; broth, beef and beer, or rice, milk and beer, for lunch; and a dinner that alternated between bread and cheese or bread and butter, and beef, broth and beer. During the summer months a bell would sound at five in the morning to summon all inmates to work, and everyone would be in bed again by nine at night. In winter the waking hours were six

A young woman in the uniform of an inmate of the Magdalen House for 'penitent prostitutes' in Blackfriars Road. Many charitable institutions had strict rules about how those they were helping could behave and what they could and couldn't wear.

o'clock in the morning to eight in the evening. Anyone found smoking would be 'put in the dungeon of the house'. Accommodation was cramped, and space limited. In 1730 a second workhouse was opened on Saffron Hill.

———— ◄◄•► ————

Hand in hand with issues of poverty went issues of public health and sanitation, and these, too, became parish responsibilities. Prior to the Dissolution of the Monasteries, the care of the sick had been the remit of the monastic houses, whose role it had been to serve the community. However, only three monastic hospitals, all situated near the centre of London, survived the Dissolution: St Thomas's, St Bartholemew's and St

Mary's Bethlehem (the notorious Bedlam) – and even these were modest affairs, focusing for the most part on the treatment of minor complaints and discouraging those feverish patients whose ailments might spread to others. The involvement of the parish, therefore, was crucial. Since few poorer people could afford to pay for a visit from a doctor, their local vestry might well arrange for a surgeon to attend them. In Barking, for example, two practitioners, John Cocking and Robert Bayley, were paid to work alternate years for their local vestry from 1701. Nor was it unusual for a vestry to appoint an official apothecary or doctor to care for those who were both poor and ill. The sick and infirm might also on occasion be committed to the care of other parishioners who would be paid by the parish to house and care for them. Even so, it all remained somewhat hit or miss.

As with provision for the poor, provision for the sick by the parish authorities was also supplemented by individual charitable donations. John Whitgift, Archbishop of Canterbury, for example, founded the hospital of Holy Trinity in Croydon in 1594. Medical care was also provided through almshouses: Norfolk College, established at Greenwich in 1613 by Henry Howard, Earl of Northampton, supported a warden and twenty pensioners but also served as a hospital dedicated to the Holy Trinity. By the eighteenth century, however, it was becoming increasingly apparent that such health care as London had to offer was inadequate, and various steps were taken to establish new institutions. Some were given very

The Royal Hospital in Chelsea, founded by Charles II for veteran soldiers. In the eighteenth century Ranelagh Gardens stood immediately to the right of Sir Christopher Wren's grand building.

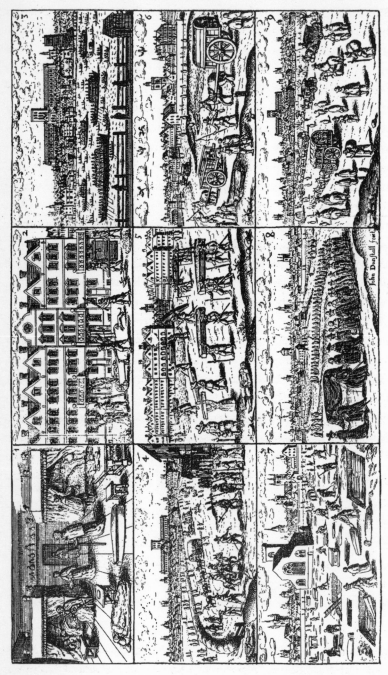

The 'Greatness of the Calamity and the Violence of the Distemper' are grimly shown in this depiction of the Great Plague of 1665. From left to right and top to bottom the artist shows the sick at home, shutting up the houses, leaving London by land, carrying coffins, carrying the dead in carts, burying the dead, a funeral procession, fleeing London by boat, and the return to town.

specific functions: a hospital for French Protestants was opened in Hackney in 1708 to serve the area's sizable Huguenot population; Thomas Coram's Foundling Hospital, established in Bloomsbury in 1739, was purpose-built for London's growing band of orphans and abandoned children; both the General Lying In Hospital in Lambeth (1767) and the Bayswater Queen Charlotte Lying In Hospital in Paddington (1773) were set up for expectant mothers; and an infirmary for sick pensioners was opened in Greenwich in 1763. Other hospitals had a wider remit: the Royal Hospital in Greenwich (1705), Guy's Hospital in Southwark (1721), the London Infirmary in Whitechapel (1740), the Middlesex hospital in Marylebone (1746) and the London Lock hospital in Paddington (1746). The widely scattered nature of these hospitals gives a good indication of key centres of population at the time, as well as showing how much open land there still was to build upon. For Coram's Foundling Hospital, for example, fifty-six acres of open land, known as Lamb's Conduit Fields, were bought from the Earl of Salisbury for £6,500.

Of the various health scourges of Tudor and Stuart times, bubonic plague was the most virulent and various pest-houses were set up to help deal with it. Infected patients – as well as anyone suspected of having been in contact with them – were placed in quarantine in the pest-house, where they were attended to by the local surgeon or apothecary, paid for out of parish funds. During the 1594 outbreak a pest-house was built in open fields in the parish of St Luke's, Islington. In 1665 more pest-houses were established in places on the city's outskirts such as Soho and Tothill Fields (Millbank), Chelsea and further out at Putney. The success of the Putney enterprise was later noted by Daniel Lysons in his *The Environs of London* from 1792:

> In the year 1625 twenty-five persons died of the plague here; in 1665 seventy-four; and in the ensuing year ten persons only. It may be observed, that its ravages were much less fatal here than at Mortlake, though the parish is more populous, and the communication with London must have been more frequent, Putney being a considerable thoroughfare.

At times of real crisis, any building could be pressed into service as a pest-house: at East Sheen, Sleigh's almshouses near Palewell Common were used by their trustees for this purpose in the 1660s.

It wasn't just the plague that pest-houses were expected to deal with. Outbreaks of tuberculosis and smallpox were dealt with in the same way. It wasn't until the cholera epidemics of the nineteenth century that the patchy nature of health care was recognised for what it was, and a more coordinated regional system was decided on to replace it.

⸻

While the precise causes of many diseases and epidemics remained a mystery until at least Victorian times, it was generally recognised that dirt and filth did not help; and London was notoriously filthy. Complaints about the stink and pollution went back to medieval times. The residents of Houndsditch used the moat surrounding the City walls as their rubbish dump, creating a noxious stench and suggesting to the Tudor historian John Stow why the area was so called: 'From that in old times, when the same lay open, much filth (conveyed forth of the City) especially dead dogges were there laid or cast.'⁴ In the eighteenth century, despite the elegance of so many city squares and houses in the West End, the smell of the place was much commented on. Jonathan Swift – never reticent in his descriptions of the less salubrious aspects of humanity – captured the worst of it in his 'Description of a City Shower' (1710):

> Now from all Parts the swelling Kennels [gutters] flow,
> And bear their Trophies with them as they go:
> Filth of all Hues and Odours seem to tell
> What Streets they sail'd from, by the Sight and Smell.
> They, as each Torrent drives, with rapid Force
> From Smithfield, or St Pulchre's shape their Course,
> And in huge Confluent join at Snow-Hill Ridge,
> Fall from the Conduit prone to Holborn-Bridge.
> Sweepings from Butchers Stalls, Dung, Guts, and Blood,
> Drown'd Puppies, stinking Sprats, all drench'd in Mud,
> Dead Cats and Turnips-Tops come tumbling down the Flood.

It's scarcely surprising that dysentery should have been such a constant problem – and not just in central London.

Vestries therefore became involved in the sanitary aspect of public health, too, though there was a limit to what they could do. Each house in London and the surrounding area had its own cesspit, which added to the stench caused by rotting vegetation and slops in the streets outside. Sewers were constructed on an ad hoc basis and were hard to get at or to control. It's true that in 1813 Barking vestry sanctioned the building of a sewer to alleviate the removal of human waste from the streets and water supply of the town, but many other parts of London either were not blessed with the same foresight, or simply felt they could not deal with a growing problem caused by thousands of people living close together. Each parish therefore made its own arrangements as best it could, and connected its network of pipes to the Thames or one of its tributaries, like the Fleet, where possible. There was, however, little cooperation between parishes. It was not until legislation was passed in 1855 that local councils made a more general effort to tackle the ageing sewer networks in their area.

Efforts to keep London's water fresh proved a constant challenge too, particularly as the suburbs started to swallow up the ancient wells. The Thames became ever more polluted and its main tributaries were either closed up and built upon or converted into the final sections of canals. The fate of the River Fleet is a case in point. A major watercourse in its own right in ancient times (the name comes from the Anglo-Saxon word for a creek or inlet), and with wharves along its banks as early as the thirteenth century, its main source lay in Hampstead, from where it flowed south through St Pancras and Clerkenwell to meet the Thames at Blackfriars. Flanking it was a string of wells. Sir Christopher Wren proposed widening the Fleet as part of his plans to remodel London following the Great Fire, but it was instead converted into the New Canal in 1680 and soon degenerated into an open sewer used by the expanding suburbs to the north. By 1728 Alexander Pope was distinctly unimpressed:

> . . . Fleet-ditch with disemboguing streams [streams emptying into it]
> Rolls the large tribute of dead dogs to Thames,
> The King of dykes! Than whom no sluice of mud
> With deeper sable blots the silver flood.[5]

Things were made worse by the decision, also taken in the seventeenth century, to dam the river's sources to create Hampstead Ponds. In 1737 the upper part of the New Canal from Holborn to Ludgate Circus was turned into a culvert, and the lower stretch was built over in 1769 during the construction of Blackfriars Bridge. By now the Fleet's days as a provider of drinking water were long forgotten.

Ultimately, providing fresh water lay beyond what vestries could achieve or what they regarded as their responsibility. Those people living away from the centre could rely on local rivers and wells – though often even these could not be trusted. Those in the centre and inner suburbs generally had to rely on public pumps set up in the streets or had to purchase their water. As late as the nineteenth century, water carriers went from house to house calling out 'Fresh and fair river water! None of your pipe sludge!' Gradually, though, public pumps and water carriers were supplemented by companies offering piped water. One of the earliest of these was the London Bridge Waterworks, set up in 1581 by one Peter Morris, who was granted a 500-year lease of the first arch of the northern end of old London Bridge to house a pump. He secured the rights to the second arch the following year. By the mid eighteenth century, the company he founded was operating five waterwheels installed in three arches, driving sixty-four pumps that extracted 1.5 million gallons of water a day; at the start of the nineteenth century, more leases were acquired and production was estimated to have reached 4 million gallons a day, supplying water to the City and large parts of Southwark.

By far the most ambitious project undertaken before Victorian times was the New River Project, set up to bring fresh drinking water into London from the River Lea and Amwell Springs. It was first proposed by Edmund Colthurst in 1602, who was rewarded with the grant of a royal charter two years later to carry out the work, but he quickly ran into financial problems. The responsibility for the project then fell to Sir Hugh Myddelton, under whose guidance the artificial river was successfully completed in 1613, despite construction problems and the opposition of some landowners who feared that the river would damage the value of their farmland and disrupt road transport. The route of the new waterway ran southwards from Ware to Great Amwell, Broxbourne and Cheshunt, then on to Enfield and Palmers Green, Wood Green, Hornsey, Harringay and Finsbury Park until its original point of termination at New River Head, near Clerkenwell. To cross some of the valleys on the outskirts of town, wooden aqueducts were constructed, for example at Harringay, hence local references to the 'boarded river'. To maintain the conduit, and

S. View of the New River Head.

Sir Hugh Myddelton's New River was the most ambitious of pre-Victorian schemes to bring fresh water to the centre of London.

manage the property portfolio it had acquired to fund the project, the New River Company was formed in 1619, and gradually acquired many of the other institutions that were founded to improve London's water supply, including Sir Edward Ford's Waterworks at Durham Yard on the Thames, as well as at Marylebone and Wapping, in 1667; later acquisitions were to include the London Bridge Waterworks Company and the York Buildings Waterworks Company.

As London expanded, so more water companies were set up. To the west of town, the Chelsea Waterworks Company was founded in 1723 'for the better supplying the City and Liberties of Westminster and parts adjacent with water', creating a number of substantial reservoirs and ponds in the tidal section of the Thames between Chelsea and Pimlico. To the east and north of London, similar waterworks were established at West Ham in 1743 and Lea Bridge by 1767 to cater for the needs of the growing docklands area. Some of the most significant foundations came in the later eighteenth century to the south of the City. The Borough Waterworks Company (1770), for example, covered the area between London and Southwark Bridges, adjacent to the London Bridge Waterworks Company.

Chelsea Waterworks in 1725, which supplied reservoirs in Hyde Park and St James's Park.

The Lambeth Waterworks Company was founded in 1785, near the current site of Hungerford Bridge, to supply water to south and west London. More companies came along in the opening decade or so of the next century. Within years of the Lambeth Waterworks Company expanding its remit to supply Kennington in 1802, the South London Waterworks Company was set up (1805), followed by the West Middlesex Waterworks Company and the East London Waterworks Company (1806), and the Grand Junction Waterworks Company (1811), the latter making use of the water brought by the Grand Junction Canal from the rivers Colne and Brent.

⸻

The level of involvement – and the effectiveness – of local government, then, presents a mixed picture. Vestries were able to raise funds to help the poor and sick, to an extent; they could run certain basic services and keep the main roads repaired. However, issues that really needed a more wide-ranging approach coordinated across parishes – such as the provision of fresh water – lay well beyond what they could do, and indeed what they saw as their duty to do; and it was this lack of co-ordination that hampered their efforts in one area that both they and their parishioners very clearly saw as part of their duty: dealing with crime.

London's rapid and haphazard expansion made it a dangerous city in which to live. The crowded city with its slums, its docks, its shifting population of sailors and soldiers, workmen and the unemployed (there were an estimated 12,000 beggars as early as 1594) was prey to robbery and violence and gangs of thugs. Wealthy areas rubbed shoulders with deprived ones; and genteel areas might well decline over a generation or so into tough neighbourhoods. Westminster provides a good example of this. It might have been the seat of government, but the fact that the abbey offered a safe haven to suspected criminals – the right of 'sanctuary' stretching back to medieval times and not abolished until the seventeenth century – meant that it also attracted a criminal element. During the eighteenth century, many of its open fields, gardens and courtyards were built over, creating a maze of narrow streets in the area around Old Pye Street, Great St Anne's Lane (now St Ann Street) and Duck Lane (St Matthew Street). Houses here were badly constructed from the cheapest available building materials, they had little or no drainage or sanitation, they were poorly maintained and they were badly lit. By Charles Dickens's time this enclave had become one of inner London's most dangerous suburbs, characterised by the novelist as 'The Devil's Acre'. Indeed, it was one of Dickens's contemporaries, Cardinal Wiseman, who, in describing the overcrowded, crime-infested streets of the area, helped to popularise the use of the word 'slum' to describe such inner-city squalor: 'Close under the Abbey of Westminster there lie concealed labyrinths of lanes and courts, and alleys and slums, nests of ignorance, vice, depravity, and crime, as well as of squalor, wretchedness, and disease.'

Criminal activity could happen anywhere, but it was a particular problem in the more densely populated regions of London. Yet there was no city-wide system for the prevention and prosecution of crime, and different areas had different – and sometimes confusingly overlapping – approaches and jurisdictions: Westminster, for example, had both vestries and a Court of Burgesses who fought with each other rather than with the criminals until parliamentary Acts in the mid eighteenth century empowered the vestries to establish their own small police forces and finance them through a new rate. Within the City of London, the wards, each subdivided into precincts, were the main structure for policing. Every year each ward elected a constable from among its householders to serve as the official keeper of the peace, assisted by paid officials from within the ward and marshals appointed by the City administration. Outside the confines of the City proper, parish vestries attempted to work with local magistrates to tackle the problem of crime, though they lacked the clear authority to establish or finance a fully fledged police force. It was not until the later eighteenth century that the Westminster approach to policing was more widely adopted.

Such officers of the law as existed were given the not inconsiderable task of preventing crime in their parish, and generally keeping the peace. A beadle would patrol during the days, and several watchmen would take over at night. The nightwatchmen would report to a watch house where a keeper was responsible not only for safeguarding their weapons but for guarding any prisoners apprehended during the night before they were sent before the local magistrates. In charge of the beadles and night-watchmen was the constable, who also had various other responsibilities:

London's nightwatchmen were proverbial for their ineffectiveness,
as this less than charitable depiction suggests.

he was, for example, expected to effect the removal from the parish of vagrants or other claimants on the poor rate who were not actual residents of the area; and he was expected to try to find the fathers of any single mothers who were claiming financial support from the parish for their illegitimate children in order to force them to pay up – an early form of Child Support Agency. In Georgian times he might also be called on to help combat the growing problem of body-snatching (as, for example, at St George's in Hanover Square in 1778), whereby corpses were exhumed from churchyards at night and sold to anatomists so that they could practise their medical skills – a problem made worse by the increasingly overcrowded nature of graveyards and the corresponding tendency for corpses not to be buried straightaway. The constable, or his nightwatchmen, would therefore stand guard in the graveyard, lantern in hand, to deter body-snatchers, or 'resurrection men' as they were known, from plying their trade. Watch houses were increasingly situated near graveyards. Two

Bridewell Prison where Moll Hackabout is sent in William Hogarth's sequence The Harlot's Progress. *Here Moll is obliged to beat hemp while the gaoler looks on.*

that still survive overlook the churchyards of St Matthew's in Bethnal Green and St Mary the Virgin at Rotherhithe, where a force of up to fourteen watchmen was stationed by the 1820s.

Parish constables had various punishments and deterrents they could call upon: a pillory, stocks, whipping posts, cages and small houses of correction. There were, however, few of these officers, and as their status sank with the rise of Justices of the Peace, the role of constable often became little more than an honorific position, paid deputies being taken on to do the real work. The science of detection was rarely brought to bear – though vestry accounts record how some parishes made payments to informers to help bring miscreants to justice.

Such a parish-based approach barely worked with local crime. It failed completely when the crime in question took place over a large area. Highway robbery is a case in point. It became more frequent in the seventeenth and eighteenth centuries as ever more gentry and rich merchants commuted to and from their suburban homes to the City, invariably carrying gold or silver coins rather than paper bills (which could have been more easily traced). Yet parish vestries were hardly in a position to tackle it. Consequently, any area in or around London where there were open spaces – notably those that the old manorial system had preserved – became a robbers' paradise. Turnham Green, Blackheath, Shooters Hill, Stoke Newington on the London Road and Paddington on the Uxbridge Road all became bywords for highway robbery. Hounslow Heath, to the west of town, offered easy pickings to robbers targeting the roads to Bath and Exeter, while Epping Forest became a legendary hiding place for violent criminals. So bad were things around Eltham, with robbers attacking travellers as they passed through the common on the Dover Road, that the local authorities went to the extreme of establishing two police stations.

Perhaps the worst of all – certainly in the eighteenth century – was Finchley Common to the north of town, an open expanse of 1,200 acres stretching between Hendon, Muswell Hill and Totteridge Lane in the north down to the area around what is now East Finchley tube station. In 1790 Sir Gilbert Elliott, Earl of Minto, wrote to his wife that he would not 'trust my throat on Finchley Common in the dark'. He was not the only one. While highway robbery may have acquired a romantic gloss in later times, mainly thanks to fictionalised accounts of the thug Dick

A nineteenth-century engraving of Ambresbury Banks in Epping Forest.
The area was notorious for its highwaymen, in particular Dick Turpin,
who lived for a while in Buckhurst Hill.

Turpin and his operations on Finchley Common, Hounslow Heath and elsewhere, for contemporaries it was a terrifying prospect. The criminals it attracted, both from London and from further afield, were violent men, not afraid to resort to murder, despite the erection of gibbets as a deterrent (on Finchley Common, for example, gibbets were erected at what is now Tally Ho Corner, East Finchley and elsewhere).

Ultimately, the taming of the commons was seen as a key goal of the enclosure movement that gradually brought London's open spaces to heel in the nineteenth century. As Sir John Sinclair, President of the Board of Agriculture, put it in 1803: 'Let us not be satisfied with the liberation of Egypt, or the subjugation of Malta, but let us subdue Finchley Common; let us conquer Hounslow Heath, let us compel Epping Forest to submit to the yoke of improvement.'

One early attempt at a more comprehensive solution to London's city-wide crime problem was the establishment of the Bow Street Runners (initially a mobile force of just six 'thief-takers') by the Bow Street magistrate – and author – Henry Fielding in 1749. The force was then expanded by Fielding's brother John after 1754. In 1785 William Pitt put forward a police bill, but failed to get it passed. In 1797 metropolitan police magistrate and pamphleteer Patrick Colquhoun wrote a treatise advocating the creation of a police force to regulate London's docks and associated docklands further to the east of the City. The result was the creation of the Thames River Police in 1799. Nevertheless, despite these various ventures, policing as a whole remained erratic. Even in the early nineteenth century the parishes of Kensington, Fulham and Deptford, for example, had virtually no police at all to control a rapidly growing population, which was to reach 55,000 at the time of the 1821 census.

What ultimately forced the authorities to think in terms of a more concerted approach to law and order were a number of outbreaks of civil disobedience during the later eighteenth and early nineteenth centuries. In itself sporadic rioting was, of course, nothing new: Londoners had been masters of the art for centuries. However, as Britain experienced periods of economic and political turbulence in the later Georgian period, so the sporadic became the more frequent. In 1765 and 1767 the weavers of Spitalfields, suffering a slump in trade, went on the rampage. In 1768 they rioted again, joined this time by the coal-heavers. In the same decade, followers of the populist politician John Wilkes also took to the street on several occasions.

However it was the anti-Catholic Gordon Riots of 1780 that proved the most effective wake-up call to those in charge, for this was urban unrest on a new scale. In an orgy of destruction extending over several days in early June, mobs attacked and burnt Catholic churches, foreign embassies, prisons and houses. They launched an assault on the Bank of England, virtually destroyed Sir John Fielding's house in Bow Street, and freed prisoners from Bridewell and New Prison in Clerkenwell, from Newgate, from the King's Bench and the Fleet, from the Clink in Southwark and from Surrey Bridewell. Up to 700 people were killed during the riots, of whom 21 are known to have been executed and 285 shot by troops called out to suppress the violence.

What struck contemporaries was the total inability of the civil forces of law and order to do anything about the riots; one spectator, Nathaniel Wraxall, even recalled how, as the mob tore through the streets, an old watchman wandered along 'calling the hour as if in time of profound tranquility'.[6] Moreover, the Gordon Riots did not just affect one small area. They started in Southwark and then spread to Westminster and the West End, to the City and eastwards to Spitalfields. Even Kenwood House, right on the edge of Hampstead Heath, was a target. Because the house was owned by the Lord Chief Justice, the Earl of Mansfield – an unpopular figure with protestors – a mob set out with the intention of burning it down. Fortunately for the earl, they stopped en route at the Spaniard's Inn nearby and were plied with such copious quantities of drink that they were all rendered insensible. They were then held there until troops could turn up to arrest them. It was a fortunate escape for Kenwood, but it had more to do with alcohol than with the authorities.

Ultimately, it was the memory of such events as this, and others elsewhere in England in the early nineteenth century (for example, Manchester's Peterloo Massacre of 1819), that prompted Parliament to look again at the issue of parish involvement in policing matters; and what was to be agreed upon would sweep away for ever the make-do-and-mend approach of previous generations.

PART III

THE NINETEENTH-CENTURY COLOSSUS

SEVEN

'THE MARCH OF BRICKS AND MORTAR'

The Birth of Victorian London

In 1795 the cartographer John Cary, whose company operated from premises on the Strand, prepared a 'New and Accurate Plan of London and Westminster'. At the time it appeared, the population of London and Westminster had nearly doubled from its half million at the beginning of the century. Yet what is striking about this elegant engraving, at least from a modern perspective, is how densely that million people were packed into the centre and just to what extent the countryside still reached into what we would now regard to be central London.

On the map the West End, with its squares and town houses, can be seen as clearly the most populous part of the suburbs away from the old City walls, but once it reaches the 'new road to Islington' on its northern flank – the modern-day Marylebone and Euston Roads – it becomes open fields. Piccadilly meanders to the edge of Hyde Park; after that lie the rural villages of Kensington, Brompton and Chelsea, separated from one another by Chelsea Common and by various market gardens. South of the river, Battersea is a collection of footpaths and fields dotted with a few windmills; Vauxhall only stands out because of its park and gardens. There is some development around Newington Butts, Walworth and Kennington, but only in the form of strips of houses and shops hugging the roads that run through them. The one obviously urban area south of the Thames is Southwark, its population clustered around Borough High Street and Great Surrey Street at the ends of London and Blackfriars bridges respectively. To the east of the City, narrow streets run beyond the Tower in an arc between Shoreditch and Whitechapel. Yet the docks are still surrounded by open fields. Bethnal Green is undeveloped, with fields and tree-lined lanes; and Stepney is little more than a village. To

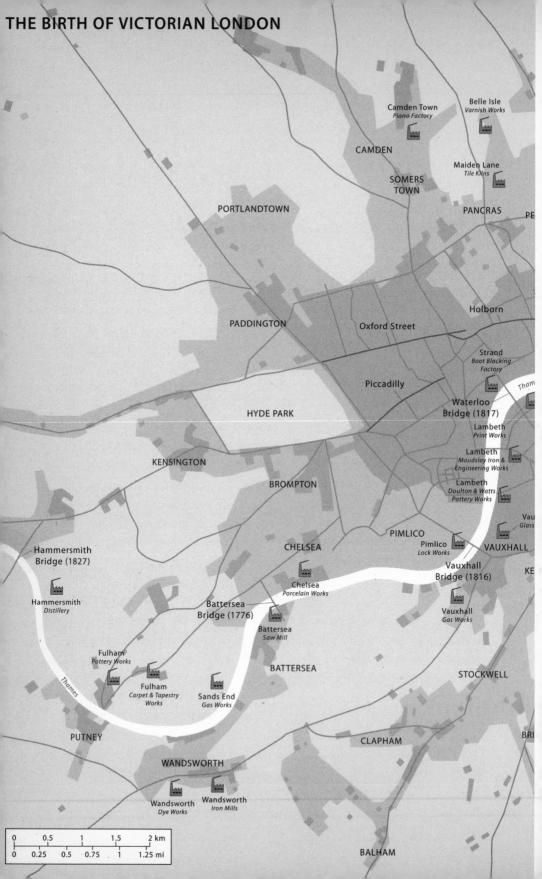

THE BIRTH OF VICTORIAN LONDON

Camden Town
Piano Factory

Belle Isle
Varnish Works

CAMDEN

Maiden Lane
Tile Kilns

SOMERS
TOWN

PANCRAS

PE

PORTLANDTOWN

Holborn

PADDINGTON

Oxford Street

Strand
*Boot Blacking
Factory*

Piccadilly

Waterloo
Bridge (1817)

Tham

Lambeth
Print Works

HYDE PARK

Lambeth
*Maudslay Iron &
Engineering Works*

KENSINGTON

Lambeth
*Doulton & Watts
Pottery Works*

BROMPTON

Vau
Glass

PIMLICO

Pimlico
Lock Works

VAUXHALL

Hammersmith
Bridge (1827)

CHELSEA

Vauxhall
Bridge (1816)

KE

Chelsea
Porcelain Works

Hammersmith
Distillery

Battersea
Bridge (1776)

Vauxhall
Gas Works

Battersea
Saw Mill

Fulham
Pottery Works

BATTERSEA

STOCKWELL

Fulham
*Carpet & Tapestry
Works*

Sands End
Gas Works

Thames

PUTNEY

CLAPHAM

BRI

WANDSWORTH

Wandsworth
Dye Works

Wandsworth
Iron Mills

BALHAM

0	0.5	1	1.5	2 km
0	0.25	0.5	0.75	1	1.25 mi

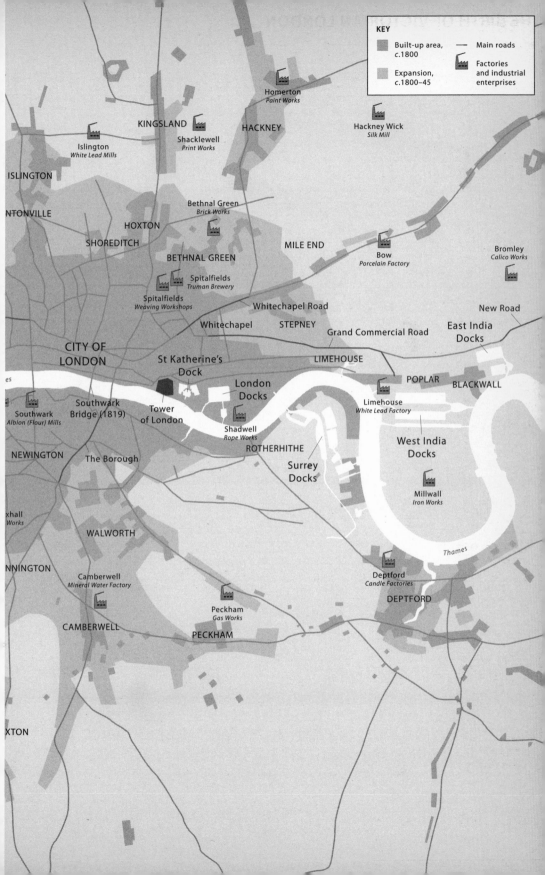

KEY

■ Built-up area, c.1800

■ Expansion, c.1800–45

— Main roads

🏭 Factories and industrial enterprises

ISLINGTON

NTONVILLE

Islington
White Lead Mills

KINGSLAND

Shacklewell
Print Works

HACKNEY

Homerton
Paint Works

Hackney Wick
Silk Mill

HOXTON

SHOREDITCH

Bethnal Green
Brick Works

BETHNAL GREEN

MILE END

Bow
Porcelain Factory

Bromley
Calico Works

Spitalfields
Truman Brewery

Spitalfields
Weaving Workshops

Whitechapel Road

Whitechapel

STEPNEY

Grand Commercial Road

New Road

East India
Docks

CITY OF
LONDON

St Katherine's
Dock

LIMEHOUSE

POPLAR

BLACKWALL

London
Docks

Limehouse
White Lead Factory

Southwark
Bridge (1819)

Tower
of London

Shadwell
Rope Works

ROTHERHITHE

West India
Docks

Southwark
Albion (Flour) Mills

NEWINGTON

The Borough

Surrey
Docks

Millwall
Iron Works

xhall
Works

WALWORTH

NNINGTON

Camberwell
Mineral Water Factory

Peckham
Gas Works

Thames

Deptford
Candle Factories

DEPTFORD

CAMBERWELL

PECKHAM

XTON

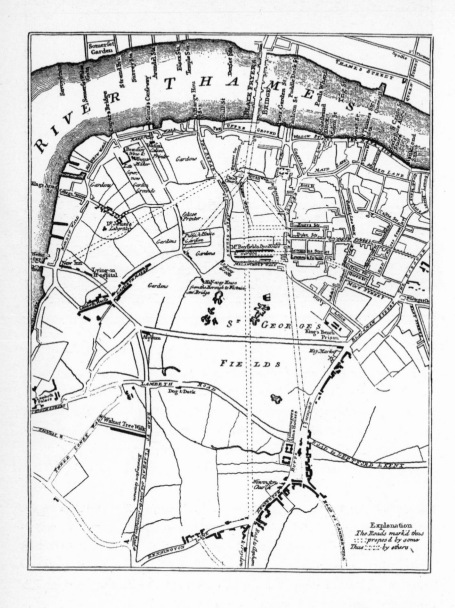

Development south of the Thames accelerated once new bridges were built.
This map shows the Lambeth area in around 1760 as Blackfriars Bridge and
its approach roads were being planned and constructed. Up until the
eighteenth century much of Lambeth was marshland and numerous
watercourses are marked on the map.

In the eighteenth century what is now the borough of Wandsworth comprised small villages and farmland. However, the construction of Putney and Battersea bridges made it increasingly attractive to the well-to-do, who built themselves houses of the sort shown in this engraving. Improved communications with the capital and also with the south coast simultaneously stimulated the local economy, and encouraged the establishment of inns and shops to serve travellers and Wandsworth's gradually increasing population.

the north of town, Hackney, Hoxton, St Pancras, Islington and Paddington are separated from London by fields and market gardens, not yet part of London proper – though signs of development can be seen in Somers Town, where, eleven years earlier, Lord Somers had leased farmland to a Frenchman, Jacob Leroux, for a gracious suburb that, in the event, rapidly descended into one of London's worst slums.

Beyond that ring is largely open countryside, dotted with villages. The Harrow Road towards what is now Westbourne Green appears largely empty except for the Red Lion pub. Kilburn Wells and its tea gardens are shown hugging the otherwise empty main road leading north to the

Midlands and Wales beyond. World's End in Chelsea is more or less as its name suggests, and at the map's eastern extremity Bancroft's Hospital and the Jews Burying Ground at Mile End are the last outposts on the road to Essex.

Had the map extended beyond these areas, it would have shown more of the same. To the north were the villages of Edgware, Hampstead, Highgate and Walthamstow, and the unenclosed Finchley Common. To the north-east were the forests of Epping and Hainault. A large expanse of marshland extended along the eastern stretch of the Thames from Plaistow to Dagenham and Hornchurch. A string of villages dotted the landscape south of the river from Eltham (which had grown up near the old medieval palace), through to Beckenham, Sydenham, Streatham and Tooting, all linked by a network of country lanes. Nearer the river was the large village of Wandsworth and beyond that the royal park at Richmond and the borough of Kingston, with some seven miles of fields, farms and hamlets separating the town from Chelsea. In west Middlesex the towns of Old and New Brentford sat on the Thames while the rural character of the area to the immediate north remained undisturbed.

This outermost part of the London area remained relatively untouched over the next few decades, and the number of residents there rose only slowly. Even as late as 1831 the combined population of Hillingdon, Harrow, Haringey, Ealing, Brent, Barnet, Enfield, Waltham Forest, Redbridge, Barking and Dagenham, Havering, Bexley, Bromley, Newham, Croydon, Sutton, Merton, Kingston upon Thames, Richmond upon Thames and Hounslow was less than a quarter of a million. In fact, more people were squeezed into the 7.5 square miles of Tower Hamlets at that time than were spread across the nearly 500 square miles of those outer reaches. Brent was home to just 3,000, while Barking and Dagenham, Harrow, Merton, Redbridge and Sutton had no more than between 6,000 and 7,000 residents each. Only Richmond could boast a population that could in any way be regarded as sizable, but even the 22,000 residents calculated to live there were spread across quite a large area – not just Richmond itself but neighbouring villages and settlements.

While the outer areas remained relatively static in the three decades or so between the first publication of Cary's map and the 1831 census, the same certainly wasn't true closer to the centre. Kensington and Chelsea, little more than villages in Cary's time and with a population of 18,000

While many villages around London were transformed in the nineteenth century, Dagenham was among those to remain largely untouched until the end of Queen Victoria's reign. This engraving shows a typical Essex village, comprising mostly fairly humble dwellings.

at the time of the first census in 1801, more than doubled to 46,000 by 1831. They now became the new 'front line' between the overcrowded and so less desirable inner suburbs – such as Westminster – and the countryside beyond. Brompton, for example, managed to retain an air of exclusivity that was attractive to City bankers and merchants moving ever westwards in their search for genteel living. As for the inner London region as a whole – an area of only 116 square miles comprising Hammersmith and Fulham, Kensington and Chelsea, Westminster, Camden, Islington, Hackney, Tower Hamlets, Greenwich, Lewisham, Southwark, Lambeth and Wandsworth – the number of people living here rose by nearly 700,000 to 1.65 million in the same thirty-year period. It was a staggering number to have to find homes for, and a particular challenge for those seven areas – Camden, Islington and Hackney to the north, Tower Hamlets to the east, Westminster to the west, and Lambeth and Southwark to the south – who bore the brunt of the population increase. Most doubled in size in thirty years; Lambeth tripled. By 1831 Westminster was home to over 340,000 inhabitants. Only the City itself saw a decline in numbers, as its appeal as a place to live was usurped by its suburbs.

Two complementary forces drove this escalation in numbers. One was growing poverty and unemployment in the English countryside of the mid to late eighteenth century. The other was increasing employment prospects in town. In the countryside, the late Georgian period saw a renewed wave of enclosures, partly designed to ensure the cultivation of more common land, but mainly to increase productivity and therefore profit for major landowners. In the process the last vestiges of the mano- rial system were swept away, large commercial farms were created, and thousands of agricultural labourers lost security of employment or were driven from the land altogether. In the towns, meanwhile, the Industrial Revolution was beginning to take hold. Although it is most associated with the Midlands and North-west, where factories and foundries rapidly sprang up to create new cities out of former villages, London too expe- rienced its own share of industrialisation and accordingly became a magnet for those from the countryside seeking new opportunities. London also had the additional benefit of being a leading global port at a time when Britain's empire was beginning to expand. For those with no future on the land it must have seemed irresistible. As the nineteenth-century civil servant and social researcher H. Llewellyn Smith put it:

> The contagion of numbers, the sense that something was going on . . . all, in short, that makes the difference between the Mile End fair on a Saturday night and a dark muddy land, with no glimmer of gas and nothing to do. Who could wonder that men are drawn into such a vortex?[1]

Not that industry was exactly unknown in London before this time. The weavers of Spitalfields had been active since the late seventeenth century, operating what was in effect a cottage enterprise on an industrial scale. They went through periods of real hardship in Georgian times, especially as cheaper textiles in the form of cotton started to arrive from India in the early eighteenth century, but, even so, population estimates for the area in 1831, provided for a House of Commons committee, suggest that of the roughly 100,000 people living in or around Spitalfields at that time, half were directly dependent on the industry, and most of the rest were indirectly employed in support services. Up to 17,000 looms were reckoned to be clattering away in garret rooms and elsewhere.

Slightly further afield, manufacture of other textiles was going on in eighteenth-century London. One of the earliest calico factories was opened in Merton Abbey in 1724; others were set up in Wandsworth. Fulham specialised in tapestries and carpets for the growing luxury end of the market. Bethnal Green was home to one of the region's first cotton factories in 1783. There was also pottery, produced in various locations around London since medieval times, and porcelain, introduced into the Southwark area in the late Tudor period by Dutch migrants. Mortlake became home to John Sanders's pottery in 1743, Chelsea housed the Chelsea Porcelain works after 1745, while the Bow Porcelain Factory was set up in Stratford in the 1740s. London was also home to the manufacture of chemicals in Georgian times, particularly those that could be used to kill people. Wandsworth had been the site of gunpowder mills since the seventeenth century: records show that the Royal Ordnance was purchasing supplies from James Lloyd of Wandsworth in 1671, for example. Crane Park, Whitton, was the site of a gunpowder mill from the sixteenth century until 1927 (hence Powder Mill Lane, which still survives today). Waltham Abbey near Enfield was another major production base in the seventeenth and eighteenth centuries, exploiting

A number of London's outer villages acquired industrial enterprises. Brickfields were a common sight, while Enfield was dominated by the Royal Small Arms Factory.

its position on the River Lea both to power its mills and to carry the end product down the navigable channel to the Thames. In many ways these were the blueprint for later industrial factories, the Waltham Abbey site in particular being developed as a one-stop-shop manufacturing plant. Described by local historian Thomas Fuller in 1735 as 'the largest and most complete works in Great Britain', in 1787 the whole complex was purchased by the Crown, so becoming one of its three Royal Gunpowder Mills.

At the more peaceful end of chemical manufacture, Lewis Steigenberger, a young German chemist from Frankfurt, came to London in 1760 and set up a small factory in Shadwell (under the more manageable name Lewis Berger) that produced paints, in particular 'Prussian Blue'. He was so successful that he was able to move to a larger site in Homerton in 1780. Here, as well as producing paint pigments, he began to offer such products as black lead and sulphur.

What transformed commercial enterprises towards the end of the century was the application of steam as a locomotive and mechanical source of power. Now London started to be home to heavy industry and factories, often sited on the Thames or other rivers where they could draw on water for their engines and for transport of the finished article. Perhaps the most famous of these, certainly London's first major factory, was Albion Mills, built in 1786 by Samuel Wyatt in Southwark on land that had become much more accessible for commerce with the construction of Blackfriars Bridge in 1769. Albion Mills ground flour, using a rotary steam-powered engine made by the leading designers of the age, Boulton and Watt, and with grinding gears constructed by John Rennie, the equally famous civil engineer, to produce 6,000 bushels a week. It dominated the skyline on the southern bank of the Thames for miles around, rivalling St Paul's Cathedral on the northern side, and it attracted hundreds of labourers who flooded into Lambeth, so creating an inner-city slum in a once green parish. Local millers, meanwhile, were driven out of business by the leviathan in their midst, their picturesque windmills torn down to make room for shanty houses. Albion Mills was devastated by fire in 1791 – Luddite arsonists were suspected – and though Rennie decided to rebuild the factory in 1798, his plans were never realised. Consequently, the site was redeveloped into houses and workshops in 1809, but not before the old mill passed into legend. The charred and blackened building made a striking silhouette against the backdrop of the hills of Hampstead and Highgate to the north, possibly inspiring one Lambeth resident to pen the lines:

> And did those feet in ancient time
> Walk upon England's mountains green:
> And was the holy Lamb of God,
> On England's pleasant pastures seen?
>
> And did the Countenance Divine,
> Shine forth upon our clouded hills?
> And was Jerusalem builded here,
> Among these dark Satanic mills?

Blake's *Jerusalem*, published in 1808 but probably dreamed up at least four years earlier, when Albion Mills still dominated Lambeth, can be seen in part as a yearning for an idealised rural world that was rapidly being eradicated by the march of industry.

Lambeth was transformed by industrialisation, its population leaping from 33,000 residents in 1801 to 99,000 in 1831 and its old agricultural land disappearing in the process. One major employer was Maudslay Ironworks and Engineering with its workshops in Westminster Road. A Royal Navy contractor, and a leading enterprise in the development of the screw propeller system of propulsion, it built the engine for Isambard Kingdom Brunel's transatlantic steamship, the SS *Great Western*, in 1838 and created the tunnelling shield that was used during the lengthy construction between 1824 and 1843 of the Thames Tunnel connecting Wapping with Rotherhithe. Such was its powerful influence on the area that other companies were attracted to Lambeth. William Cowes and Sons printing works arrived in 1825. Ten years later, Henry Doulton joined his father's small pottery Doulton & Watts on the high street in Lambeth, expanding the business the following decade to produce architectural terracotta, and eventually setting up a factory to manufacture the high-quality drainage pipes that were to prove so crucial in the battle to improve Victorian London's sanitation. In the 1860s the firm decided to embrace the elegant as well as the utilitarian through an association with the Lambeth School of Art, and in the 1880s, now trading as Doulton & Co, they began producing bone china. They received a royal warrant from Edward VII in 1901 and became Royal Doulton.

Some industry could be found to the west, too. Chelsea, for example, famed in Georgian times for its fine porcelain, became celebrated for porcelain of a different nature in Victorian times when Thomas Crapper established a water closet factory there in 1861 (it ultimately moved to 120 King's Road). Crapper's enterprise, and the various innovations he made, proved commercially very successful, winning the royal seal of approval in the 1880s when his company modernised the plumbing at Sandringham House in Norfolk for the Prince of Wales. However, for some, his decision to install plate-glass windows to show off his wares was an innovation too far: a number of people living in Chelsea complained that the sight of toilet pans would cause female passers-by to faint.

Generally speaking, heavier industrial concerns in London tended to be confined to the east, while lighter industry – breweries, factories, workshops for all varieties of household and luxury goods – were more widely spread through the capital. Certain areas became known for particular goods: bootmaking in the East End; furniture-making in the City, Shoreditch and the West End. The outer regions, by contrast, remained largely untouched by manufacturing in the nineteenth century – with one important exception. As London became ever more built up, so demand for building materials rose and so those regions that had gravel and brick earth deposits began to exploit them. Shortly after 1815, brick manufacturing started in largely rural Hillingdon, for example, its transport made possible by the earlier construction of the Grand Junction Canal (1805), which fed into the Thames at Brentford. By 1856 over 240 acres in Hillingdon were being devoted to brick making, and by the 1860s the industry had reached Harefield. In West Drayton a brickfield was established in 1845. It failed to delight everyone, a visitor in 1876 complaining that the charm of the area was being marred by the 'sulphurous and manury smells from brickfields'. Nevertheless, brick making spread to neighbouring parishes such as Hayes, and Ordnance Survey maps of the London area in Victorian times are sprinkled with brickfields and gravel pits.

Clapton and Ilford to the north-east of London, and Crayford and Lewisham south of the river, were just some of the places to host them.

———————— ◄ • ► ————————

The London area, however, did not become an industrial landscape in the way that cities further north did, nor would it be true to say that one particular raw product predominated in the way that cotton came to characterise Lancashire or steel defined Sheffield. It was always more of a distribution centre for finished goods than an originator for them. That said, its supremacy in this more middle-man role did bring with it one major manufacturing enterprise: shipbuilding.

Britain's increasing dominance of international maritime trade was dependent on its ability to build bigger, better and faster merchant ships that could carry cargo, passengers and troops around the globe, and bigger, better and faster warships and frigates that could defend the country's commercial interests and its growing international political influence. There were major shipbuilding works on the banks of the Clyde and the Tyne, and in Belfast at Harland and Wolff's. There's little doubt, though, that the capital played an absolutely central role in the early creation of a mechanised shipbuilding industry.

Inevitably, it was the areas to the east of the City that were transformed. As late as the eighteenth century the Isle of Dogs – the peninsula that bulges out into the Thames between Limehouse and West Ham – was essentially a mix of windswept marsh and pasture land dotted with wind-mills that ground corn and crushed oil seeds. Its mill wall held back the river along its western banks. Then in 1802 came the West India Docks, followed three years later by the City Canal, cut across the peninsula to create an island in the Thames. Millwall's significance as a centre for ship-ping was reinforced in 1824 by the establishment of the Millwall Iron Works, which served sailing ships and, increasingly in the course of the nineteenth century, developed the creation of iron ones. In the mid 1830s two engineers from Scotland, Sir William Fairbairn and David Napier, bought land on the isle and expanded the ironworks, Fairbairn going on to build more than a hundred ships at Millwall and winning contracts from the Admiralty and from abroad. Unfortunately demand did not automatically

The London Docks shortly after they were opened in 1805. One of a number of docks to be constructed in the early years of the nineteenth century they further transformed the economy and nature of the area.

mean profit, and by 1848 naval architect John Scott Russell had assumed control.

It was under John Scott Russell's watchful and nervous eye that the largest ship of the age was constructed and launched: Isambard Kingdom Brunel's *Great Eastern*. A nightmare project from its inception in 1852, it cost a fortune, caused endless rows – and because of its sheer scale had to be built not in Russell's own shipyard but in neighbouring Napier's Yard. Thousands gathered on the banks of the river on 3 November 1857 to watch the colossus's sideways launch into the Thames, but they had to wait until 31 January 1858 before the *Great Eastern* finally inched its way into the cold grey waters of the Thames, and a further year before the fitted-out ship headed out for testing in the English Channel.

The sorry tale of the *Great Eastern* mirrored the decline of the Millwall Iron Works. Scott Russell's financial embarrassment ultimately meant that ownership had to pass to a new company, the Millwall Iron Works, Ship Building and Graving Docks Company Ltd; but it was part and parcel of the area's rise to industrial power. The new company redeveloped the site and started to fit out a new generation of iron-clad naval vessels, employing in the region of 5,000 workers during its heyday. It even offered its workforce such amenities as a canteen, sports club and a works band before the banking crisis of 1866 brought it crashing down.

This whole area of the East End acquired a new vigour in the early decades of the nineteenth century; and as the opening of the West India Docks suggests, it wasn't just shipbuilding that brought new employment to the area. The West India Docks themselves handled sugar and other cargo from the Caribbean and beyond. In Wapping, St Katherine's Docks were opened in 1828 to support the neighbouring London Docks in the Pool of London – the two were merged in 1864 – dealing mainly with wool, tobacco and rubber. Others founded early in the century included the Surrey (1807) and West India South (1829). Later came the Royal Victoria Dock, situated on the Plaistow marshes and opened in 1855 (it was among the first to be specifically designed to cope with the new generation of steam ships), Millwall in 1868 and the even larger Royal Albert Docks in 1880. Alongside these commercial wet docks numerous dry docks offering repair services sprang up, the largest of these, at over 460 feet long, being Charles Lungley's Lower Dock at Deptford Green.

While their construction may have caused existing residents to be displaced, the docks and associated workshops brought in a flood of new people to the area of London that would come to be known as the Docklands: ship workers, dock workers, porters, lightermen to carry cargo between ships that was due to be re-exported, customs officials and others. New roads were driven through the expanding East End to link it and the City to the outer world. The Grand Commercial Road completed in 1810 connected the City's eastern extremity at Aldgate with Limehouse church and the new docks via the West India Dock and East India Dock Roads. The New Road (now Barking Road) reached out from the East India Docks to the Essex parishes of East Ham and Barking. The whole area became a network of thriving, tightly knit communities, each dock creating its own micro-economy and generating plenty of opportunities for skilled and unskilled labourers to find work. There was no central hiring system, and foremen would recruit workers at will, usually from known assembly points such as public houses. Life could be very tough indeed – not for nothing was the district known as Blood Alley, after the workers whose job it was to heave heavy sacks of sugar imported from the West Indies until their hands bled.

As the population expanded, so did the pressure on housing. Some new houses sprang up for the well-to-do, such as the fine terraces on Wapping Pierhead, built in 1811 for officials of the London Dock Company; but elsewhere former riverside hamlets became crowded shanty towns, filled with dock workers, sailors on leave and migrants from other parts of Britain. As a result, the riverside East End boroughs quickly became some of the least appealing residential areas in the London region with unplanned slums hugging the river. Silvertown in West Ham developed around the S.W. Silver & Co rubber works in the 1850s; north of Silvertown, the township of Hallsville, known later as Canning Town, was created in the same decade to house workers at the new Victoria Dock and the industries sited along Bow Creek at the parish's western extremity. An 1855 Board of Health report noted that this was a generally unhealthy area with poor-quality houses.

Only Cubitt Town on the Isle of Dogs proved an exception to the generally grim rule. Here, in the 1840s and 1850s, the future lord mayor William Cubitt sought to achieve something rather better than the norm. The crumbling river wall was replaced by an embankment and a new network of wharves. New roads were laid out, lined with houses for dock labourers and their families. Schools, places of worship and even a library were established. Cubitt Town became a near self-contained area, a small oasis amid swathes of destitution.

The fate of Bethnal Green perhaps best illustrates the worst consequences of rapid population increase in the East End in the early decades of the nineteenth century. It had long acted as an overflow destination for people drawn to Spitalfields in search of work, being transformed from a rural hamlet within the parish of Stepney to a crowded civil parish in its own right after 1743. In 1800, 'Globe Town' was established to provide additional accommodation as more people poured into the area in search of work. But it wasn't enough. Before long, inadequate houses were overcrowded to such an extent that the whole area became a slum (and was to get worse after 1860 when unemployed silk weavers from Spitalfields moved to Globe Town to seek new lines of work such as the leather trade and shoemaking). The spacious market gardens and large houses of the early eighteenth century now gave way to the grimmest of tenement housing, as the Fourth Report of the Commissioners appointed under the Poor Law Amendment Act made clear in 1838:

> The district of Bethnal Green contains upwards of 70,000 inhabitants; in the greater part of it the streets are not close, nor are the houses crowded. On the contrary, large open spaces of ground intervene between them; but in one part the population is as densely crowded as in the closest and most thickly populated parts of the city. I notice the places about to be described in the order in which I visited them . . .
>
> *Punderson's Gardens.* A long narrow street; the houses have no sunk area, and the ground floor is extremely damp. Along the centre of the street is an open, sunk gutter, in which filth of every kind is allowed to accumulate and putrefy. A mud bank on each side commonly keeps the contents of this gutter in their situation; but sometimes, and especially in wet weather, the gutter overflows; its contents are poured into the neighbouring houses, and the street is rendered nearly impassable. The privies are close upon the footpath of the street, being separated from it only by a parting of wood. The street is wholly without drainage of any kind. Fever constantly breaks out in it, and extends from house to house . . .

Alfred and Beckwith Rows consist of a number of buildings, each of which is divided into two houses, one back and the other front; each house is divided into two tenements, and each tenement is occupied by a different family. These habitations are surrounded by a broad open drain, in a filthy condition. Heaps of filth are accumulated in the spaces meant for gardens in front of the houses. The houses have common privies open, and in the most offensive condition. I entered several of the tenements. In one of them, I found 6 persons occupying a very small room, two in a bed, ill with fever. In this same room a woman was carrying on the process of silk-weaving. The window of the room is small, capable, if wide open, of ventilating the room but very imperfectly; yet this window is not only kept permanently closed, but is carefully pasted all round, so that not the slightest breath of air can enter. On remonstrating against this constant and total exclusion of air, I was told by the woman at work that they are obliged to stop up the window, to prevent the drying of the silk, which is always weighed out to them when they receive it, and they are expected to return the same weight.

The East End was not the only part of London to endure the more problematic consequences of a rapidly increasing population in the early part of the nineteenth century. Areas of Westminster, Camden, Lambeth and Southwark suffered as well, particularly during the economic turmoil of the 'Hungry Forties' when, as British farmers struggled to compete with cheap imports from North America and Russia following the repeal of the protectionist Corn Laws in 1846, yet more people abandoned the land for life in the city.

So far as many of the existing inner suburbs were concerned, this early part of the century saw changes to the social composition of neighbourhoods as poor incomers prompted wealthier inhabitants to move out. Soho is a good case in point. While the aristocratic residents who had once lived in Soho Square and the streets around it had long departed, in the early years of the nineteenth century it was still a relatively genteel area, popular with artists. By the mid-century point, however, it had

The notorious St Giles Rookery, later demolished to make way for New Oxford Street.

become one of the most densely packed areas of London, its houses endlessly subdivided into squalid tenements. Those affluent people who had remained, now fled the area once and for all after a terrible outbreak of cholera in 1854. Elsewhere the existence of gentrified suburbs to the west and restrictions on land that could be bought up for development in the inner suburbs meant that housing there was squashed and pushed upwards to contain ever more floors, with little thought for the provision of sanitation or fresh water. Westminster was just one area to suffer badly in this period, and working-class slums (often referred to as stews or rookeries) could also be found in places such as St Giles, Jacob's Island in Bermondsey and Old Nichol Street in the East End. Viewed as dens of filth, vice and criminality by such social reformers and commentators as Henry Mayhew and Edwin Chadwick in the mid nineteenth century, their grimness was well captured by Charles Dickens in his description of Jacob's Island in *Oliver Twist* (1838):

> . . . crazy wooden galleries common to the backs of half a dozen houses, with holes from which to look upon the slime beneath; windows, broken and patched, with poles thrust out, on which to dry the linen that is

never there; rooms so small, so filthy, so confined, that the air would seem to be too tainted even for the dirt and squalor which they shelter; wooden chambers thrusting themselves out above the mud and threatening to fall into it – as some have done; dirt-besmeared walls and decaying foundations, every repulsive lineament of poverty, every loathsome indication of filth, rot, and garbage: all these ornament the banks of Jacob's Island.[2]

In *Sketches by Boz* a couple of years earlier, Dickens described not only the slums but the people who lived in them:

Wretched houses with broken windows patched with rags and paper: every room let out to a different family, and in many instances to two or even three . . . filth everywhere – a gutter before the houses and a drain behind – clothes drying and slops emptying, from the windows; girls of fourteen or fifteen, with matted hair, walking about barefoot, and in white great-coats, almost their only covering; boys of all ages, in coats of all sizes and no coats at all; men and women, in every variety of scanty and dirty apparel, lounging, scolding, drinking, smoking, squabbling, fighting, and swearing.[3]

What particularly shocked contemporaries was that such squalor could exist in a city of such wealth. Friedrich Engels, for example, wrote in 1844:

London is unique, because it is a city in which one can roam for hours without leaving the built-up area and without seeing the slightest sign of the approach of open country. This enormous agglomeration of population on a single spot has multiplied a hundred-fold the economic strength of the two and a half million inhabitants concentrated there. This great population has made London the commercial capital of the world and has created the gigantic docks in which are assembled the thousands of ships which always cover the River Thames . . . It is only later that the traveller appreciates the human suffering which has made all this possible. He can only realise the price that has been paid for all this magnificence after he has tramped the pavements of the main streets of London for some days and has tired himself out by jostling his way through the crowds and by dodging the endless stream of coaches and carts which fill the streets. It is only when he has visited the slums of this great city that it dawns upon him that the inhabitants of modern London have had to sacrifice so much that is best in human nature.[4]

To make things even worse in the eyes of many, rich and poor on occasion lived virtually cheek by jowl. Poverty was bad enough, but it seemed even worse when set against a backdrop of affluence. A *Times* correspondent angrily noted on 12 October 1843 that even 'nigh the regal grandeur of St James's' hunger and disease also stalked 'in all their kindred horrors, consuming body by body, soul by soul', and he went to reproach his fellow citizens for their apparent indifference:

> . . . let all men, whether of theory or of practice, remember this – that within the most courtly precincts of the richest city on GOD'S earth, there may be found, night after night, winter after winter, women – young in years – old in sin and suffering – outcasts from society – ROTTING FROM FAMINE, FILTH AND DISEASE. Let them remember this . . .[5]

Not all squalor was packed into old developments. Agar Town (now covered by the approaches to St Pancras station), certainly one of the worst and most infamous slums of the early Victorian era, was actually of relatively recent origin. In the late eighteenth century it was still open fields. In 1810 it was leased by William Agar, and twenty or so years later, part of the estate was given over to building. Within a few years it had sprouted a shanty town into which the poorest of the poor – often Irish migrants – were forced to live. In an article entitled 'A Suburban Connemara', W. M. Thomas described it as:

> A new evil, which only began to come into existence about the time when Mr Chadwick's Report first brought before the public a picture of the filthy homes and habits of the labouring classes, and of the frightful amount of crime and misery resulting there from. In Agar Town we have, within a short walk of the City . . . a perfect reproduction of one of the worst towns in Ireland.[6]

As central parts of London acquired a greater number of poor residents in the early decades of the century, so more of the city's richer inhabitants fled further away, seeking new houses in previously undeveloped areas; and, as so often in the past, it was royalty who pointed the way.

King George III had led a relatively retiring life, particularly during his recurrent bouts of illness and madness. His son, the Prince Regent, however, was a man of a very different stamp, and one who was determined to leave his mark on the capital. A lover of architecture, as well as of flamboyant living, he decided that what London needed was some contemporary elegance, that he was the man to show the way, and that his favourite architect of the moment, John Nash, was the person to turn vision into reality. The area of town he chose to focus his creative energies on was that centred on Marylebone Park.

At that time the area north of the New Road (now Marylebone Road) was little more than open fields and farmland. Consequently, when the lease on the land expired in 1811, Nash was set the task of drawing up new plans for the area. The layout he duly evolved was gracious and eye-catching: there were to be terraces on the eastern and north-western sides and elegant villas dotted around the park, incorporating the recently

Regency elegance in Regent's Park. John Nash's development marked the move of polite society north of what is now the Marylebone Road.

planned Regent's Canal (which in turn linked to the Grand Union Canal). Like most things in which the Prince Regent was involved, the scheme was dogged with problems, not least financial, but enough of it was built to give us an idea of the scale of Nash's ambition for the area, and the rough and ready brickwork of the various places and terraces, particularly Cumberland Terrace, was sufficiently hidden under elegant stucco work not to put off the affluent. It certainly earned royal favour, and the Prince Regent was delighted to see the name Marylebone Park changed to Regent's Park; it was opened to the public in 1838.

The redevelopment around Marylebone Park was only part of the Prince Regent's vision for the West End. He also wanted a road that would link his opulent residence, Carlton House near St James's Park, to the new glories of Regent's Park. Whether in so doing he was also paying heed to a long-standing demand among Londoners for a good north–south road in Westminster is a moot point. At any rate, Nash obliged with Regent Street, an elegant array of houses and of superior shops around the sweeping curve of the Quadrant. The whole enterprise proved a hugely expensive and disruptive undertaking, but the impact it had on the West End went well beyond providing it with more neoclassical elegance. Essentially, Regent Street established a divide between the smart area around Piccadilly and points west, and the poorer areas to the east. It also marked the arrival of a new respectable area for those Londoners who could only countenance living amid refinement. Placing the cherry firmly on the cake, Nash designed Carlton House Terrace to the north-east of St James's Park in 1826, to replace the grand eighteenth-century Carlton House and extensive gardens that had stood there previously. George IV was Carlton House's last tenant, and he now moved to Buckingham Palace, on which he was to lavish hoards of taxpayers' money right up until his death in 1830. The palace was still scarcely finished, or habitable, when Queen Victoria came to the throne seven years later. Over the next few decades, the wealthy would gradually move in step with the royal family: the nineteenth-century census returns for Mayfair, for example, show a gradual decline in the number of its more aristocratic inhabitants as they were lured further west.

Setting the seal on this westward move of polite society was the creator of rather more substantially built houses than those around Regent's Park, Thomas Cubitt. Brother of William, of Cubitt's Town fame, he undertook various projects around town, of which perhaps the most notable and opulent were in Belgravia. There, in the 1820s, he agreed with Earl Grosvenor to redevelop nineteen acres of the 'Five Fields' which only the previous century had been home to footpads and highwaymen. Belgrave Square and Eaton Square were the result, and – fortunately for Cubitt – their grandeur immediately appealed to the wealthy types he had hoped to attract. Various titled individuals came to live in one or other of the large stuccoed houses on offer – the Earl of Essex, for example, at 9 Belgrave Square and the Duke of Bedford at No. 15 – while the enormous, detached Seaford House (built in 1842–6) went to Lord Sefton: old Etonian, military officer and ultimately inheritor of his father's title and stately home at Croxteth Hall near Liverpool. Cubitt went on to build further properties in the West End, not least two vast mansions at Albert Gate (1841), nicknamed 'Malta' and 'Gibraltar' because 'they would never be taken'. Given the scale of such houses, it's scarcely surprising that that year's census should list 170,000 domestic servants and 30,000 dressmakers and milliners living in London.

Some indication of just how grand life could be in the West End is given by Lady Eastlock's description of a social gathering in Piccadilly in 1850, held at Devonshire House, an opulent Georgian mansion (long since demolished), which the dukes of Devonshire remodelled in the nineteenth century:

Piccadilly in 1810, looking eastwards from the Hyde Park Corner turnpike.
Houses here were gracious and elegant.

There was an immense concourse of carriages in Piccadilly – a party at
Miss Coutts' and Lord Lansdowne's besides . . . We drew up under a
large portico, where, as it was raining, hundreds of servants were clustered. Then we entered a very large hall, with pillars in couples, looking
like the crypt of the whole building. This hall led to the grand staircase,
which encompasses a space big enough for billiard table, statues, etc.
Nothing could be more grand and princely than the *coup d'oeil* – groups
sitting and lounging about the billiard table, where the Duke of Argyll
and others were playing – crowds leaning over the stairs and looking
down from the landing above: the stairs themselves splendid, shallow
broad steps of the purest marble, with their weight of gorgeous crystal
balustrade from the wall; and such a blaze of intense yet soft light,
diffused round everything and everybody by a number of gas jets on the
walls. The apartments were perfect fairyland, marble, gilding-mirrors,
pictures and flowers; couches ranged round beds of geraniums and roses,
every rare and sweet oddity lying about in saucers, bouquets without
end, tiers of red and white camellias in gorgeous pyramids, two refreshment rooms spread with every delicacy in and out of season, music
swelling from some masterly instrumental performers, and the buzz of
voices from the gay crowd, which were moving to and fro without any
crush upon the smooth parquet. The [6th] Duke looks just fit for the
lord of such a mansion; he is tall and princely-looking with a face like a
Velasquez Spanish monarch.[7]

John Cary's revised London map of 1837 shows just how much the
West End had changed in those few decades since his 1795 edition.
Belgravia was now firmly ensconced, with Pimlico and Millbank emerging
as its slightly poorer relatives. Kensington and Chelsea were no longer
isolated villages, but parts of the suburbs. Kensington's Phillimore estate,
abutting Holland Park, was becoming increasingly built up with large
houses and elegant terraces. Chelsea Common had disappeared under a
network of new streets, and a proliferation of squares had appeared off
Sloane Street and the King's Road. When it came to that extra inch of
prestige, Kensington probably scored over Chelsea, which never quite
shook off its village image and the mixture of social classes that involved.
To that extent, it seems wholly appropriate that, later in the century,
Oscar Wilde should have lived among the artistic community of Chelsea's

*Chelsea contrasts. The rural Hans Place (above) and (below)
an omnibus in 1842 making its way through increasingly built-up streets.*

Tite Street – not too far from the nobility he mocked and adored, but scarcely in their midst, either. With Kensington and Chelsea now firmly on the map, developers were eyeing up the farms at Brompton, which accordingly embarked on its suburban journey.

People were moving north, too. The increasingly industrialised nature of Clerkenwell and Shoreditch drove outward expansion around Bloomsbury, Somers Town and beyond them Camden Town, breaching the erstwhile barrier of the New Road; and the Islington area witnessed a proliferation of fashionable and desirable property in planned estates such as Gordon Square (begun by the ubiquitous Cubitt in the 1820s) and Tavistock Square (started in 1803 and also completed by Cubitt in 1826). Other northern developments tried to hold on to the ideals of detached or semi-detached living, as opposed to tenement living, with elegant houses appearing in Canonbury Park, Highbury Crescent, Alwyne Road, Gloucester Crescent and elsewhere.

The Regent's Canal, which had proved so significant in the planning of Regent's Park, also had an influence on the gradual building up of the Paddington area. A branch of the Grand Junction Canal planned and built in the 1790s to link London and Birmingham, it ran – and still runs – from the Paddington Basin via Maida Vale, Camden and Islington to the Thames at Limehouse. When work began in 1812, much of the region was still countryside. The area later to be known as Maida Vale, for example, was the usual blend of pasture, woodland and farmland, though an Act of Parliament had been passed in 1795 to allow building on it. Gradually, however, houses appeared, if in a somewhat scattergun way. To the south, Bayswater acquired a rash of speculative builders and a mix of houses, some very grand, some less so. To the north, St John's Wood sprouted semi-detached villas for the professional middle class and upmarket courtesans. For its part Maida Vale (or Hill) grew with increasing rapidity from the 1820s, and by 1840 stuccoed villas were lining the Edgware Road. Some idea of the nature of its early inhabitants can be gauged from a perusal of the pages of *Boyle's Fashionable Court and Country Guide*. The 1857 edition, for example, includes among those living in Clifton Gardens two captains, one surgeon and the ex-Rajah of Coorg, deposed by the British some years before. This was scarcely Belgravia, but respectable nonetheless. Beyond that were north London's growing suburban villages. Hampstead in 1831, for example, was home to 356 'capitalists', bankers and professionals, and a large number of servants. By 1834 eight omnibuses were making twenty journeys a day from its centre to the City.

Some property speculations inevitably proved a street or so too far. Kensington in the early nineteenth century might have been a safe bet, but building in neighbouring Notting Hill was a more risky affair. Not that this was the view taken by the Ladbroke family, who owned an extensive estate in the area. They commissioned an architect to lay out a grand new development centred on what was to become Ladbroke Grove, with large houses set upon often curved roads, more than a little reminiscent of Nash's scheme at Regent's Park. Work started in the early 1820s, but it was too ambitious and Notting Hill too far from fashionable London to survive a building boom collapse later in the decade. For a while in the late 1830s the Hippodrome Racecourse was allowed to occupy part of the site, once a dispute had been settled with locals (described by the *Sunday Times* as 'filthy' and 'disgusting') who had objected to an early plan to allow the racecourse to lie across the public footpath between Kensington and Kensal Green. The Hippodrome was not a commercial success – the heavy clay soil of the area made the going slow – and it closed in 1841. Ultimately it was to take several decades for housing to inch its way to the Harrow Road end of Ladbroke Grove.

The story south of the Thames was similar to that north of the river. Here again ancient green spaces vanished in the opening decades of the nineteenth century to make way for the construction of planned developments and gentrified estates. By the 1820s and 1830s, Brixton, Stockwell and Kennington were all becoming suburban villages, their desirability enhanced by the building of a convenient new bridge over the Thames at Vauxhall (the first bridge over the Thames to be built out of iron), which made them more accessible from central London. Brixton, which for centuries had largely been waste land threaded through with winding country lanes, now started to acquire attractive detached and semi-detached villas around the turn of the century; the manor of Stockwell, sold off by auction and divided into plots in 1802, swiftly lost its resemblance to its name ('stream or spring by a tree stump'); and Kennington, once home to royalty, acquired new, attractive terraces along Kennington Park Road, Cleaver Square and elsewhere. The pattern was repeated in Clapham – where Cubitt struck once again with a new development of villas called Clapham Park, for wealthy clientele, near the green space of Clapham Common – and further south in Balham.

In places, development reached even further south. In Blackheath, the Wricklemarsh Estate was purchased in 1783 by a local timber merchant, John Cator, whose nephew went on to develop the land to provide exclusive and private accommodation for the professional classes. The construction of houses on the Cator Estate encouraged other speculators to take an interest in the area, leading to a rash of house building across Blackheath, Charlton and Kidbrooke. At first these tended to be spacious affairs, but as building land became scarcer, so more semi-detached and eventually terraced houses appeared. Parts of Lee Road, for example, which formed part of the Cator Estate, were quite grand, whereas those plots of land developed later tended to be more randomly sited and crowded.

This pattern of change – a combination of planned and unplanned – was repeated across the entire region as unconnected manors and parishes were converted into mini-towns. The increase in more densely packed housing in these outer areas was a sign of things to come. Indeed, much of the grander building of the late eighteenth and nineteenth centuries was to be short-lived: a substantial house built in the 1800s, with spacious gardens and perhaps some outbuildings, was more than likely to fall prey to a developer a few decades later, who could erect an entire terrace of houses on a site once thought appropriate for one. In fact, the buildings of this 'interim' period have left much less impact on the suburban landscape than their scale would suggest. Areas that remained attractive to the well-to-do – such as Regent's Park and Belgravia – generally retained their early nineteenth-century houses. Other areas such as Brixton and Clapham lost most of their grander houses and villas; much of Cubitt's Clapham Park was swept away with later developments; and in Brixton only a few survivals, such as 46 Acre Lane, a beautiful building from 1808, give a hint of its pre-Victorian elegance.

There were few restrictions to curb urban sprawl, and the sheer pace of change clearly bewildered contemporary commentators, who saw the quiet hamlets and villages of their childhood suddenly transformed. Between 1831 and 1851 the overall number of London residents jumped from 1.9 million to 2.65 million. Many of these were packed into previously built-up areas: in 1851 Westminster had 462,000 residents (double the population of 1801); Tower Hamlets was home to 377,000 folk (compared with 'only' 144,000 when the century opened); and the populations of Southwark and Camden were getting close to the 300,000 mark. Yet the populations of the outer parts of London were growing quickly, too. Kensington and Chelsea's population rose from 46,000 in 1831 to 88,000 twenty years later. In that latter year, Lambeth had 155,000 inhabitants and Hackney had 170,000.

In 1847 the social reformers Henry Mayhew and John Binny went up in a hot-air balloon to view the extent of the spread:

> The leviathan Metropolis, with a dense canopy of smoke hanging over it
> . . . It was impossible to tell where the monster city began or ended, for
> the buildings stretched not only to the horizon on either side, but far
> away into the distance . . .[8]

The use of the word 'Metropolis' is significant. People recognised that London was extraordinary, far greater in size and spread than one would expect a capital city to be. Indeed, there was a concern that it was becoming too big. The passing of the Chiswick Improvement Act in 1858, with its establishment of a board of commissioners to oversee such basic amenities as lighting and sewerage, shows that this part of London, for one, recognised that the old systems of local government were no longer sufficient.

In 1862, journalist George Rose Emerson observed from Primrose Hill:

> Sixty years ago even the hill was as secluded and rural, as completely
> removed from the hum and bustle of a great city, as any Sussex or
> Devonshire hillock . . . St John's Wood, spruce and trim, invades us on
> the right, and on the opposite side are huge railway stations, circular
> engine-factories, house upon house, and street upon street . . . and we
> willingly forget, that farther eastward, the once green slopes of Holloway
> are crowded with houses, and that castellated prisons rear their dismal
> and defiant towers.[9]

That mention of railway stations is more than a little significant. The railways may only have arrived in London in the 1830s, but their impact was already being felt. Over the next handful of decades they would transform the metropolis beyond recognition.

EIGHT

'THE RINGING GROOVES OF CHANGE'

The Victorian Transport Revolution

The railways came to London relatively late. While the Stockton and Darlington Railway opened in north-east England in 1825, London's first passenger venture, the London and Greenwich, which ran south-east from London Bridge, didn't open until eleven years later. There was an obvious practical reason for this: central London was so heavily built up that trying to buy land on which to construct a railway – or arrange compulsory purchase by Act of Parliament – was a slow and very expensive business. Nor was the London and Greenwich's answer to this – to elevate 3.5 miles of track on a viaduct consisting of 878 arches – an ideal solution; it certainly won few imitators around London. It's scarcely surprising that, although the service was soon carrying 1,500 passengers a day, and although a train leaving London Bridge station could reach Deptford via Spa Road only fourteen minutes later, the company failed to recoup its investment. It wasn't the most auspicious of starts.

Practical difficulties weren't the only initial obstacles. There was also considerable early scepticism. Railways might be working in other parts of the country, but London was felt to have so many existing modes of transport available that yet another one was deemed unnecessary. The *Quarterly Review*, for one, was very sniffy about the launch of the London and Greenwich line: 'Can anything be more palpably ridiculous than the prospect held out of locomotives travelling twice as fast as stage coaches . . . we will back Old Father Thames against the Greenwich railway for any sum.'[1] Nevertheless, despite engineering challenges and a palpable lack of confidence, railways did start to inch their way into town, their termini inevitably placed towards the edge of built-up London. The London and Birmingham opened at Euston in 1838; the Great Northern

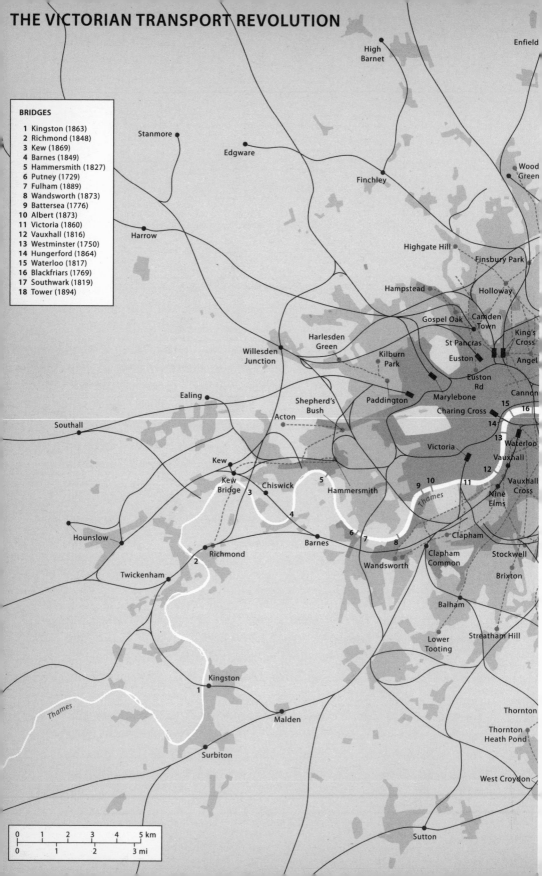

THE VICTORIAN TRANSPORT REVOLUTION

BRIDGES

1 Kingston (1863)
2 Richmond (1848)
3 Kew (1869)
4 Barnes (1849)
5 Hammersmith (1827)
6 Putney (1729)
7 Fulham (1889)
8 Wandsworth (1873)
9 Battersea (1776)
10 Albert (1873)
11 Victoria (1860)
12 Vauxhall (1816)
13 Westminster (1750)
14 Hungerford (1864)
15 Waterloo (1817)
16 Blackfriars (1769)
17 Southwark (1819)
18 Tower (1894)

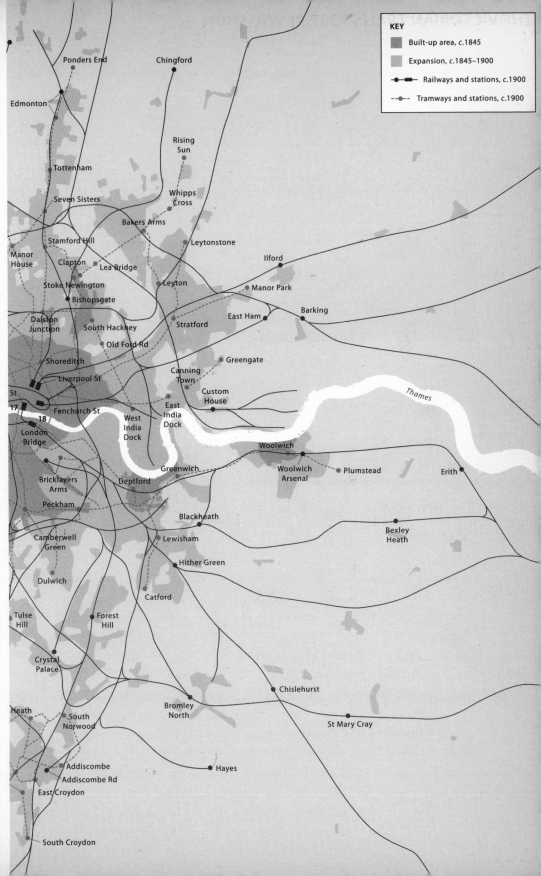

KEY

■ Built-up area, *c.*1845

■ Expansion, *c.*1845–1900

●—■— Railways and stations, *c.*1900

●--●-- Tramways and stations, *c.*1900

Ponders End

Chingford

Edmonton

Rising
Sun

Tottenham

Whipps
Cross

Seven Sisters

Bakers Arms

Leytonstone

Stamford Hill

Ilford

Manor
House

Clapton

Lea Bridge

Manor Park

Stoke Newington

Leyton

Bishopsgate

East Ham

Barking

Dalston
Junction

South Hackney

Stratford

Old Ford Rd

Shoreditch

Greengate

Liverpool St

Canning
Town

St

Custom
House

Thames

17

Fenchurch St

18

West
India
Dock

East
India
Dock

London
Bridge

Woolwich

Bricklayers
Arms

Deptford

Greenwich

Woolwich
Arsenal

Plumstead

Erith

Peckham

Blackheath

Bexley
Heath

Camberwell
Green

Lewisham

Dulwich

Hither Green

Tulse
Hill

Catford

Forest
Hill

Crystal
Palace

Chislehurst

Heath

South
Norwood

Bromley
North

St Mary Cray

Addiscombe

Hayes

Addiscombe Rd

East Croydon

South Croydon

The arrival of the railway: the Doric arch of Euston station, built in 1838. Over the next few decades, the ever-growing railway network was to transform London's suburbs.

opened at King's Cross in 1852; the rival London, Brighton and South Coast Railway and the London, Chatham and Dover Railway each brought their lines to a halt at London Bridge station in the 1840s before deciding in the 1850s to extend to Victoria, their mutual hostility enshrined in the fact that each established its own station there. The year 1854 saw the opening of Paddington station, the terminus of Isambard Kingdom Brunel's ambitious Great Western Railway, which linked London with the west of England via the increasingly important port of Bristol (and hence a link in a route designed to extend to the New World with the aid of vast transatlantic steamships). On the other side of town, Liverpool Street station was built by 1875 on the site of the ancient Bethlehem Royal Hospital, commonly known by this date as Bedlam, to replace an earlier terminus for the Great Eastern Railway at Shoreditch.

Even though the stations were at the edge of town, however, constructing them and building the hotels and hostelries that went with them proved a hugely disruptive business. London's northern boundary had pushed further outwards in the early 1830s, which meant that as those early lines approached the centre they had to negotiate ramshackle houses and slums

– or more likely have them forcibly cleared. Camden was one of the areas hardest hit. Largely rural until the 1790s, it had acquired its first genera-tion of houses when a stretch of the Regent's Canal was built in the area, bringing with it coal wharves and small-scale industry. These houses, however, were brutally removed to make way for first the London and Birmingham and later the Midland Railways. In *Dombey and Son* (1846–8) Charles Dickens gave a vivid description of the havoc that was wrought:

> Houses were knocked down; streets broken through and stopped; deep
> pits and trenches dug in the ground; enormous heaps of earth and clay
> thrown up; buildings that were undermined and shaking propped by
> great beams of wood . . . Everywhere were bridges that led nowhere;
> thorough-fares that were wholly impassable.[2]

Nor was Camden the only area to suffer. During the construction of St Pancras station in the 1860s over 4,000 houses were torn down not only in the slums of Camden but in those of Somers Town and Agar Town, too, leaving 32,000 people homeless. It cost £19,500 to compensate local landowners – and £200 to pay for the actual demolition of the houses. Even the dead weren't safe: the remains lying in the old St Pancras and Islington graveyard, which lay in the path of the new route, had to be exhumed and moved – by, among others, the young Thomas Hardy, not yet an author but a junior architect on the project. The Hardy Tree, in St Pancras churchyard, with its surrounding cluster of old gravestones, commemorates his endeavours. It has been calculated that by the end of the nineteenth century over 100,000 people in central and inner London had, one way or another, been displaced by the railway lines.

What most of these displaced people had in common was poverty; they therefore had neither voice nor influence. Rather different rules applied to the rich; indeed, it was wealthy landowners who were largely responsible for the siting of the Euston terminus in the first place. The original plan had been for the route of the London and Birmingham Railway to pass further north and end where King's Cross station now stands, but since this would have affected various of the vocal moneyed class, the route was altered to pass via Watford and Harrow to Euston. Similarly Brunel, who had originally wanted the terminus of his Great Western Railway to be at Vauxhall Bridge, had to bow to the wishes of local landowners and accept Paddington instead; and allegedly it was because Lord Southampton had a say in the Act of Parliament that authorised the building of the Euston to Birmingham service that trains had to be cable-hauled uphill to Cámden by a stationary steam engine until 1844 rather than find an easier route through his lands.

Each terminus proved to be a grand affair, attracting some of the best architects of the time. Euston station, with its 420-foot-long platforms and its accompanying hotels (one on either side of the portico), was designed by the Duke of Wellington's favourite architect, Philip Hardwick, in collaboration with his son Philip Charles Hardwick. King's Cross, built on the site of a former smallpox hospital, was the work of Lewis Cubitt, brother of the famous Thomas and William Cubitt. St Pancras, arguably the most magnificent of them all, and commissioned by the Midland Railway in 1863, ended up with the flamboyantly Gothic Midland Grand Hotel designed by George Gilbert Scott. The project was a heroic task taking nearly ten years to complete, and was dogged by difficulties, not least an outbreak of cholera among the workforce that required the nearby River Fleet to be encased in an iron pipe, and the hazards caused by human remains occasionally falling into the excavated tunnels from the graveyard above. Further south, the eminent Sir John Hawkshaw's designs for Charing Cross were brought to completion in 1864, and his Cannon Street project was concluded two years later.

The ambitions of these early railway companies is nicely summarised in the prospectus drawn up by the London and Birmingham Company to promote their scheme, the first part of which, operating between Euston and Boxmoor, Hemel Hempstead, was opened on 20 July 1837:

> First, the opening of new and distant sources of supply of provisions to
> the metropolis; Second, easy, cheap and expeditious travelling; Third, the
> rapid and economical interchange of the great articles of consumption
> and of commerce, both internal and external; and Lastly, the connexion
> by railways, of London with Liverpool, the rich pastures of the centre of
> England, and the greatest manufacturing districts; and, through the port
> of Liverpool, to afford a most expeditious communication with Ireland.[3]

It's no chance affair that passenger travel should be ranked second here. The early railway companies weren't thinking particularly in terms of cheap travel for the masses; indeed, early fares were pegged at a level that was out of the reach of all but the most affluent. To travel from London

Canonbury station, c.1905.

to Birmingham in 1838 would set you back £1.10s if you travelled first class and £1 if you went second class – sums of money well beyond the budget of most at the time. Nor were the early railway companies particularly planning for short-distance commuter travel; their ambition was to connect cities, not suburbs. When the London and Birmingham line opened, the first station on the outskirts of London was Harrow, but thereafter there was nothing in between until the terminus at Euston.

Trains were not an overnight commuter success. At the start of the 1850s far more people travelled along the Thames in boats than sat in railway carriages. A decade later, only 27,000 commuters made their daily way into town by train, the remaining 90 per cent opting to walk or use other forms of public transport such as the omnibus. Nevertheless, the railway boom of the 1850s and 1860s created ever more sets of track snaking their way to all points of the compass and increasing numbers of stations opened. Moreover, aware that trains tended to be used for long-distance travel or for leisure excursions by the better off, the government sought to broaden their use by passing new legislation in 1844 that stipulated that all railway companies must provide at least one cheap service each way every day. In 1863 the House of Lords went even further, ruling that all future railway bills must allow for workmen's trains, particularly in those cases where the construction of a new line would involve wholesale demolition of existing houses and the displacement of poorer families. Even so, many railways dragged their feet.

Precisely which routes were established when is a topic of almost labyrinthine complexity. North of the Thames, broadly speaking, the early services tended to be long distance (in 1838 the first stop on the Great Western Railway from Paddington to Maidenhead was West Drayton, some thirteen miles from the London terminus; the London and North Western Rail Company had its stations similarly placed far apart in the London area). In time, though, passenger services grew to connect Willesden on the north-western outskirts of the city with destinations south and west of the river including Kew, Kingston and Clapham Junction. In the north-east, the outer reaches of London were rather better served early on, with the North and Eastern line from Stratford to Tottenham and Edmonton opening in 1840 and extending to Enfield at the end of the decade. By the late 1860s a number of lines ran through Finsbury Park and Seven Sisters, serving Hornsey, Highgate, Barnet and Edgware. In 1870 a service opened between Crouch Hill and Moorgate.

To the east, various rail links connected dock developments with points north and south of the Thames, while the Eastern Counties Railway in its various manifestations constructed lines from Shoreditch and Mile End to Stratford, Loughton and Ongar. South of the river the corridor between London and North-west Kent became well developed. The London to Greenwich suburban line, which had begun operating in 1836, opened extensions to Lewisham, Woolwich and Erith by 1849. Beckenham was connected to central London in 1855, and Croydon in 1862. Meanwhile, the London, Chatham and Dover Railway connected the City with Crystal Palace and Peckham Rye, taking in Brixton, Herne Hill and Denmark Hill along the way. To the south-west, Sutton, Wimbledon, Richmond, Kingston and Epsom all became connected to the London termini at either Victoria or Waterloo.

In this network of railways and railway companies, cheap services for the poor could certainly be found but they were not consistently spread out or necessarily used. In 1892 the London County Council bemoaned the lack of workmen's trains in the west and north-west where in any case there was little appropriate housing. Southern railway companies did operate cheaper services, but many of their passengers were the more prosperous middle class. It was really north-east London that had most to offer working-class travellers and that had the most working-class travellers to offer their services to. Here the network that became the Great Eastern Railway was described as 'the workman's London railway – the one above all others which appears to welcome him as a desirable customer'. When the Great Eastern opened its services at Liverpool Street station in 1875 it allowed for special early morning workmen's trains from Edmonton and Walthamstow that charged only twopence for a return journey. It was now theoretically possible, therefore, for poorer people to work in central London but live up to eleven miles away.

Bringing railway lines right into the centre proved both problematic and contentious. For some time, the only City station was Fenchurch Street, opened in 1841 by the London and Blackwall Railway and, until 1849, a strangely steamless one that relied on a combination of gravity and cables to convey the trains between the termini. However, the City posed major problems for would-be railway builders: it was too heavily developed, there were too many important civic buildings, places of worship and places of commerce, and perhaps most importantly there was a lot of antagonistic and powerful vested interest. The logical solution – to go underground – offered its own share of difficulties. Many commentators, understandably, feared that houses and streets might collapse into the excavated tunnels. A few suggested that such a project was contrary to God's will, and that tunnels might accidentally break their way into hell. A handful, notably the Duke of Wellington, entertained the quixotic worry that one day a French army would arrive in central London without anyone knowing it had even set off.

Charles Pearson, who held the position of Solicitor to the City of London from the 1830s until his death in 1862, didn't agree, and argued the case strongly for 'cheap railway accommodation to enable working classes to reside in their adjacent country districts'.[4] An 1846 royal commission strengthened his case by refusing to grant approval for any more construction applications for lines or stations closer to the centre than already existed (except for Waterloo station) and so effectively ruling out an overground option. In 1853, therefore, the Metropolitan Railway Company was formed, and in 1860 it started to construct a network of tunnels under the crowded streets between Paddington and Farringdon Street via King's Cross, using the 'cut and cover' method – that is, digging deep railway cuttings below street level, and then covering them up afterwards.

Despite this fairly rudimentary form of construction, the scheme proved disruptive, particularly in the St Pancras and King's Cross area, where many buildings had to be demolished to make room for the new railway line. It also brought the railway into conflict with Joseph Bazalgette and his Fleet Ditch Sewer scheme, in an early manifestation of that phenomenon that irritates so many Londoners today: different workforces on different projects failing to coordinate the disruption they unleash. Things came to a head in 1862, when the railway and the new sewer came into rather closer contact than either of their planners had intended. Furious letters flew back and forth between Bazalgette and the chief engineer for the railway John Fowler, each trying to blame the other for what had gone wrong:

16 June 1862

Dear Sir

I beg to direct your immediate attention to the fact of a portion of the Fleet Sewer, in Victoria Street, having fallen in yesterday, in consequence of the works to the Metropolitan Railway, now in progress at that spot, and to request that you will at once take the necessary steps for reinstating the sewer to our satisfaction, and guard against the recurrence of any similar accident for the future.

Joseph Bazalgette

17 June 1862

Dear Sir

At the moment when I received your letter of yesterday's date respecting the falling in of the Fleet Sewer in Victoria Street, I was preparing to write to you to call attention to the same fact, and to request you to take all necessary precautions to prevent injury to the Metropolitan Railway works, which are placed somewhat in peril by the occurrence, but have clearly nothing to do with causing it.

You will find on examination the works of the Metropolitan Railway are unmoved, and, therefore, incapable of even assisting to cause the falling in, and you will also find what a narrow escape we had from our works being flooded. I hope you will lose no time in reinstating the work in a substantial manner.

John Fowler[5]

Despite such teething problems, the new railway was opened on 10 January 1863 and was an immediate success, carrying nearly 40,000 passengers on its first day. In fact, it was such a success that another London phenomenon was created on the same day – overcrowding: 'At this point, during the morning, the crowds were immense, and the constant cry, as the trains arrived, of "No room", appeared to have a very depressing effect upon those assembled.'[6]

Early commuters would have found travelling underground a less than ideal experience, particularly as the gas lighting that was installed in each carriage had a tendency to flicker badly when the train was in motion. Smokers would have been frustrated by the fact that smoking was initially banned (though, owing to public demand, smoking carriages were introduced in 1874). The service was less egalitarian than perhaps Pearson had hoped for: trains were divided between first- and second-class carriages, and fares for working men were established on only two early morning trains. On the Metropolitan Railway the normal return fare was nine pence, but for workmen it was three pence. Nevertheless the underground was an overnight success.

Buoyed by the achievement of the first line, the Metropolitan Railway was quick to expand its routes out into the suburbs, launching the Hammersmith and City Railway in 1864, and four years later embarking on an extension towards Middlesex, Hertfordshire and Buckinghamshire by creating a branch line from Baker Street to Swiss Cottage. This was extended ever further outwards in the 1880s and 1890s to Rickmansworth and Pinner. However, a subterranean rival appeared in the form of the Metropolitan District Railway, which opened a service between South Kensington and Westminster on Christmas Eve 1868 and then extended it east towards both Aldgate and Whitechapel in 1884, and to the south and west via Earl's Court to Richmond in 1877 and Ealing in 1879, before arriving in Wimbledon via Putney in 1889. In effect, the two companies created what we know today as the Circle line, grudgingly sharing the responsibility of running

Edwardian workers excavating a new tube tunnel.

trains on the track. By 1880 over 40 million passengers were being carried by the Metropolitan line alone.

Nor were these the only underground companies to get in on the act. The City and South London Railway opened a line from King William station in the City to Stockwell in 1890, and in 1900 the line was extended south to Clapham Common. Also opening in 1890 was the Central London Railway from Bank to Shepherd's Bush, so providing a west–east line through the city centre. Four years later the mainline London and South Western Railway opened a small underground branch – the Waterloo and City line – to connect its passenger terminus at Waterloo with the City and financial institutions at Bank. More ambitious underground projects soon followed. The Great Northern and City Railway from Finsbury Park to Moorgate opened in 1904; the Baker Street and Waterloo Railway (Bakerloo) started a service from Baker Street to Elephant and Castle via Waterloo in 1906 (extended to Edgware Road in 1907); the Great Northern, Piccadilly and Brompton Railway, cutting diagonally across London and connecting Finsbury Park to Hammersmith, opened at the end of 1906; and the Charing Cross, Euston and Hampstead Railway from the Strand to Hampstead was opened by the president of the Board of Trade David Lloyd George on 22 June 1907.

Complexity could have led to confusion, but instead it gave way to improvements and streamlining. Electrified trains had started to replace steam engines in 1890 (initially for the City and South London Railway between Stockwell and King William Street), ensuring a much cleaner journey. Then, in the early years of the twentieth century, the bewildering plethora of underground companies were slowly amalgamated into one by the American tycoon Charles Yerkes, who had made and lost a fortune in the US stock exchanges trading corn and who arrived in London in 1900. His Metropolitan District Electric Traction Company, which in 1902 became the more English-sounding Underground Electric Railways Company of London, systematically went about buying up rival organisations that had secured the right to build lines through London, and proceeded to resurrect construction programmes that had lain dormant for many years through lack of funds. Yerkes died in 1905, but by this time the modern underground system was well on its way. In 1908, more integrated maps of stations appeared and the railways within the network jointly adopted the name 'Underground' to promote themselves. Another proposed name was 'Tube', which had previously featured on signs at the entrance to some stations. It stuck with the general public but failed to find official recognition. In 1913 the distinctive emblem of the disc and bar was introduced, evolving into the logo that is now so familiar.

The transformation wrought by London's underground and suburban railways can be readily traced in the literature of the period. When Charles Dickens published *The Pickwick Papers* in 1836–7 the world he evoked was eighteenth century, one of pedestrians and coach travel. Even a late novel such as *Great Expectations*, published in 1860–1 but seemingly harking back to a slightly earlier time, could move its characters around without a train in sight: Pip gets from his guardian's office in Little Britain near Smithfield to his guardian's clerk's house in Walworth on foot; he travels from his childhood home in the Kent marshes to London by four-horse stagecoach in a journey that takes five hours; he travels from his accommodation in Barnard's Inn to the Pocket family's house in Hammersmith ('west of London') by coach; and he and his would-be love Estella make their way to Richmond in the same way. However, *Dombey and Son* (1846–8) acknowledges that things are changing:

> Crowds of people and mountains of goods, departing and arriving scores upon scores of times in every four-and-twenty hours, produced a fermentation in the place that was always in action. The very houses seemed disposed to pack up and take trips. Wonderful Members of Parliament, who, little more than twenty years before, had made themselves merry with the wild railroad theories of engineers, and given them the liveliest rubs in cross-examination, went down into the north with their watches in their hands, and sent on messages before by the electric telegraph, to say that they were coming. Night and day the conquering engines rumbled at their distant work, or, advancing smoothly to their journey's end, and gliding like tame dragons into the allotted corners grooved out to the inch for their reception, stood bubbling and trembling there, making the walls quake, as if they were dilating with the secret knowledge of great powers yet unsuspected in them, and strong purposes not yet achieved.[7]

When it comes to Dickens's contemporary Wilkie Collins, railways are omnipresent. Indeed the pace of a novel such as *The Woman in White* (1859–60) would be impossible unless his characters could find their way into and out of London – to Fulham, to St John's Wood – via train. By the time that Conan Doyle wrote his Sherlock Holmes story 'The Adventure of the Bruce Partington Plans', set in 1895, the train could even become part of the plot. The victim, a clerk at the Woolwich Arsenal, having taken a train from Woolwich Station to London Bridge, makes his way to Gloucester Road where he is murdered and his body placed on the roof of an underground train. The corpse eventually falls off the carriage at the points beyond Aldgate.

＊＊＊

It wasn't just that people could travel more quickly and more cheaply by the second half of the nineteenth century. The spread of suburban rail networks, linking what had been satellite towns and villages to metropolitan London, encouraged new building and development on an awe-inspiring scale. The outer suburbs ceased to be the preserve of the affluent, and in consequence the villas and rural estates of the few were supplemented or gave way to terraces and speculative building for the many. Areas around railway junctions and network interchanges underwent particularly radical change. Wimbledon, for example, was a quiet village on a hill, with a cluster of buildings dating back to medieval times, until the London and Southampton Railway arrived in 1838. The first station was situated on lower ground, about half a mile away from the village, but as more lines were added in the 1850s and Wimbledon became a key junction, new streets of semi-detached houses transformed it into a railway suburb. Willesden Junction in Harlesden developed from several smaller stations into a major communication hub that generated a housing boom in the area. Yet perhaps the greatest suburban transformation occurred with the creation of Clapham Junction. Railway lines were driven through the area from the 1840s, and once a station was sited there in 1863, suburban housing duly followed. Strictly speaking, Clapham Junction should have been called Battersea Junction, but early developers, aware that Clapham was rather more genteel than Battersea at the time, opted for the more salubrious name.

The easiest and most telling way to show what happened is through statistics. In 1851 the Greater London area contained 2.65 million people; by the end of the century this figure stood at 6.5 million. Some population expansion occurred close to the centre – notably in Southwark and Tower Hamlets – but it was really the outer suburbs that made the greatest contribution. Hammersmith and Fulham, and Kensington and Chelsea, both grew to 250,000 from 30,000 and 70,000 respectively, while Wandsworth jumped from 36,000 in 1851 to over 310,000 fifty years later. In few places, though, was the growth as rapid as in Tottenham, where the population doubled in just one decade between 1871 and 1881. The percentage increases were even more marked in what had been the comparatively empty outer regions. In 1851 there were only 288,000 people living in all the outer boroughs combined – half the figure crammed into Westminster – but by 1901 there were nearly 2 million, a staggering rise of 585 per cent. Places such as East and West Ham, Highgate, Bromley and Croydon suddenly experienced sharp population rises; villages like Sydenham and Norwood that had hitherto been immune to the population and housing boom suddenly found themselves part of the new commuter belt.

Not that development was immediate or evenly spread; there were periods of relative quiet followed by periods of frenetic activity. Furthermore, the appearance of a railway station did not automatically mean immediate suburban expansion. James Thorne's *Handbook of the Environs of London*, first published in 1876 on the cusp of the late 1880s and 1890s boom in railway construction, shows this nicely. Each of his alphabetically arranged gazetteer entries starts with a note of the nearest railway and railway station, but many of the villages he mentions as having a railway station are still that: villages. He notes, for example, that Willesden, with stations at Willesden Junction, 'Dudding Hill' and Harrow Road ('for the new district called Stonebridge Park') has become built up: 'The builder has invaded the once tranquil meadows; field-paths (and fields also) are disappearing; and the lanes are for the most part green no longer.' However, 'Neasdon', only a quarter of a mile from Dudding Hill station, is 'a small collection of scattered cottages, with a considerable sprinkling of good houses, some in large grounds'; and 'Sherrick Green' near Dollis Green

Not every Victorian village that lay close to a railway station was automatically transformed as a result. Heston was served by nearby stations at Hounslow and Southall, but apart from brickmaking it remained a largely agricultural community, growing wheat, vegetables and fruit for the London market.

is 'pleasant, peaceful, and secluded'. As for those areas that have become built up, some come in for Thorne's disapproval (Harlesden has been 'utterly spoiled by the builder'), while more upmarket developments tend to win plaudits. Brondesbury is 'a new district of genteel villas', and Stonebridge Park 'is a cluster of 60 or 80 smart new villas for City men'.

The same pattern endlessly repeats itself elsewhere. To the east, for example, Thorne finds Leyton under threat, 'but much land is still under culture as market gardens and nursery grounds, and large quantities of roots and flowers are grown for Covent Garden Market', while Leytonstone is largely untouched, 'with a few older and better houses standing apart in their well-timbered grounds'. Wanstead is a 'little rambling village', though Wanstead Flats, formerly 'a bright breezy expanse of furze and bramble, heath and fern', is now home to brick fields, farms and new houses 'wherever land could be obtained'. Snaresbrook is just about holding

In the eighteenth century Tooting was rather overshadowed by neighbouring Streatham, which, among other things, boasted a finer water supply (the residents of Tooting eventually sank an artesian well at their own expense in the 1820s). However, it grew slowly in the early decades of the nineteenth century and then rapidly after the 1870s, by which time it was served by the Tooting, Merton and Wimbledon Railway. This Edwardian photograph shows old cottages in Merton Road, with newer buildings behind.

its own, but it has lost its woods and is starting to acquire 'smart new villas and cottages'. To the west, Hammersmith has lost many of its earlier houses, and its orchards and dairy farms have gone, but while 'modern villas and cottages of the semi-detached class' are crowding in on Ealing, the area around Ealing Common retains many of its old mansions. To the south, Clapham is 'daily becoming more a part of London', having lost the area formerly known as Bleak Hill but now as Clapham Park to Thomas Cubitt's 'capacious detached villas'. Tooting, by contrast, 'is a region of villas and nursery gardens, very pleasant, and, except the Common, very commonplace'.

For those already living in these rural spots, the arrival of the railway was often a cause for hand-wringing as the old, quiet way of life gave way to suburban bustle. The Revd B. J. Armstrong, whose father decided to move to Southall in 1830, described vividly in his diary what this area, then west of London, was like during his childhood before the coming of the railways:

> It was thought advisable to take some small place in the country for the benefit of our health . . . He took a very pretty and rather commodious residence at Southall Green, Middlesex, about a mile out of the high road to Uxbridge and exactly 10 miles from Tyburn Gate. Our intention was to reside half the year at Southall, and the remainder in London . . . My delight at everything I saw was beyond bounds – gardens were allotted my sister and self – there was the canal to fish in – a pony to ride – besides animals of different kinds . . . Having been long pent up in town, Annie and myself viewed Southall as a second Paradise . . .

Eight years later the main line from Paddington to the West was opened, and the following year – 1839 – stations sprouted up at Ealing, Hanwell and Southall. The Revd Armstrong recorded what happened:

> A remarkable change for the worse took place about this time in the hitherto retired neighbourhood of Southall Green. The railway spread dissatisfaction and immorality among the poor, the place being inundated with worthless and overpaid navigators [navvies]; the very appearance of the country was altered, some families left, and the rusticity of the village gave place to a London-out-of-town character. Moss-grown cottages retired before new ones with bright red tiles, picturesque hedgerows were succeeded by prim iron railings, and the village inn, once a

pretty cottage with a swinging sign, is transmogrified to the 'Railway Tavern' with an intimation gaudily set forth that 'London porter' [a dark type of beer] and other luxuries hitherto unknown to the aborigines were to be procured within.[8]

This, of course, raises the question of who precisely moved into these new suburbs. The Victorians had a tendency to lump all the suburbs in together and disapprove of them equally. Some worried that 'the higher class suburbs [were] being brought down to the levels of the poorer districts'.[9] Those who made any distinction at all tended to note the polite suburbs (often described as being the homes of 'city men'), the dreary, cramped ones (home to a class known vaguely as 'clerks') and the impoverished ones (home to the 'working classes').

In fact, the social composition of the suburbs was complex and reflected London's kaleidoscopic job market. Those of Edmonton, Enfield and Tottenham, for example, were an eclectic mix of clerks, typists, shop assistants, teachers, petty officials and skilled labourers such as craftsmen, cabinetmakers, train drivers, mechanical engineers and machine builders. By contrast, Willesden started out as a predominantly working-class suburb, home to a large number of railway workers around the junction and rail yards. Finsbury, Harringay, Hornsey, Crouch End, Muswell Hill, Kilburn and West Kensington were all firmly middle class. The sprawling suburb of Hampstead contained, according to the 1861 census, 92 solicitors, 46 barristers, 132 merchants, 23 stockbrokers, 147 gardeners and 2,559 female servants. It was also home to 102 coachmen and 56 grooms or horse keepers, a group of individuals who were soon to become an endangered species as well-to-do Hampstead dwellers increasingly came to favour trains and omnibuses over travel in private – and expensive – carriages; by the 1880s ever fewer Hampstead houses were being built with stables or mews, a pattern repeated elsewhere in London. It was the social group known as the 'clerks' that seemed to cause so much of the hand-wringing – and not a little sneering. George Bernard Shaw, for example, described how his uncle, a doctor, had been devastated by the arrival of the lower middle class in Leyton:

The country houses of his patients were demolished and replaced by rowls of little brick boxes inhabited by clerks, supporting families on incomes scaling down to fifteen shillings a week. This ruined him.[10]

Much of the humour of George and Weedon Grossmith's *Diary of a Nobody*, first published in 1892, derives from their gentle mockery of the clerkly social pretensions of Mr Pooter. Working for a company in the City, he has recently moved to 'The Laurels', Brickfield Terrace, Holloway ('a nice six-roomed residence, not counting basement, with a front break-fast-parlour', which backs on to the railway line). Ultimately, all comes right for him, but he remains a figure of fun.

———— ◆·▸· ————

As these diverse workers flooded into new areas, the communities that had been there before started to wane or were forced to transform themselves. Among the first to be hit were those whose livelihood had depended on the coaches and the coach roads that connected London with other towns and cities. In Hounslow, twelve miles from the centre, up to 2,000 horses had been kept at the various inns during the heyday of coach travel. By 1842, however, a local paper reported that in the 'formerly flourishing village of Hounslow . . . so great is the general depreciation of property on account of the transfer of traffic to the railway that at one of the chief inns there was an inscription "new milk and cream sold here"'.[11] A measure of the transformation in people's lives can be seen rather further out of London in the major coaching centre of Guildford. Here, in the early nineteenth century, twenty-eight coach services carrying 200 passengers apiece operated daily and there were associated coaching inns to cater for the passengers. In 1842 the last mail coach ran. Seven years later, coaching in the town ceased altogether.

Some long-standing businesses associated with the pre-train form of life managed to transform themselves. The carriers Pickfords, who had warehouses in Paddington, Brentford and elsewhere, with branches throughout the country, continued in the business they had established in the seventeenth century, in part by linking up with the London and North Western Railway in 1847. Other enterprises tried to accommodate themselves to the brave new world of railways. Two of London's leading coach firms, Chaplin and Horne, joined together and threw in their lot with the railway operators who had recently encroached on their area of operations, and in 1840 became the London collection and delivery agents for the Grand Junction Railway. Inevitably, though, some businesses could not adapt. In Walthamstow the Wragg family, who had been coach masters since 1764, running 'short-stage coaches' from the Nag's Head at Church End eight times a day (eighteen passengers maximum) into the city, bowed to the inevitable and closed their doors for business in 1870.

Farming communities were affected, too, and not just because so much land previously under the plough ended up being buried under bricks and mortar. For centuries, farms and market gardens in and around London had been essential to keep the city fed. However, as it became easier and cheaper to bring fresh food into the centre from relatively far away by train, the need for these local farms began to diminish. Now a broader variety of fresh food products could be sped into the city from farms as far away as Lincolnshire and Yorkshire. Fish was brought down from Scotland on the London and North Eastern Railway, and oysters from the Channel were brought by steamer to Brighton and by rail to Billingsgate fish market. By 1870 half of London's milk was coming by train, as was a profuse variety of fruit and vegetables. In some cases the railways even set up railhead markets to sell the products they delivered to the metropolis. London and North Eastern Railway Company set up a potato market at King's Cross in 1865, and Great Midland built the Somers Town Market to sell vegetables next to the St Pancras terminus.

Some farms in the Greater London area kept going – there was still a farm at Broadwater in Tottenham until well into the twentieth century – and people continued to keep cows and livestock, but the old imperative to have them near at hand was gone. Slowly but inexorably, they started to dwindle and die, their fields greedily eyed by property developers who would then sweep in at the whiff of a possible sale and, once successful, cover them with terraces and small gardens. Such was the fate of Hyde Farm in Balham in south London. Throughout the medieval period the land it came to occupy had been a single large field of sixty acres called The Hyde, or Hydefield. It was then sold in the 1500s to Emmanuel College, Cambridge, which built Hyde Farm and rented it out to tenant farmers until the nineteenth century. Over time, as farming in the suburbs became less economically attractive, some of the fields of Hyde Farm were let out for sport and recreation, while others were turned over to pig breeding. By the end of the nineteenth century the college was thinking long and hard about what to do with the farm, and eventually decided to allow building to take place on it. Hydethorpe Road came first in 1896, and by 1916 most of the old farmland had disappeared. In the process Balham – situated on high ground and once renowned for its healthy atmosphere – went from being a village surrounded by fields to a crowded suburb.

Even those communities that had acted as middlemen in the agricultural economy found themselves squeezed. It no longer made sense to walk cattle and sheep into town, wasting food on fattening them after their long journey; it was much better to bring them in by train. When the Eastern Counties Railway opened, a Norfolk farmer could get his cattle to Smithfield in twelve hours by train rather than the fortnight it had taken on foot along narrow, crowded roads. The cattle dealers of Southall therefore found themselves struggling in a market where their buyers claimed to be able to obtain cattle more cheaply elsewhere. The village of East End in north London (later to be known as East Finchley) also found things tough. In the eighteenth century it had been home to the largest pig market in Middlesex, and had held market days every Wednesday and Thursday. By the 1840s the market was being held only on Mondays and it was abandoned a few decades later.

The arrival of a suburb did not always mean the extinction of the old community and old buildings – both Hendon and Walthamstow, for example, preserve fragments of their former selves. Nevertheless, many villages which acquired a network of outlying suburban roads and houses were ultimately redeveloped or swallowed up. There's no sign today of the medieval village centre of Streatham or Leyton that was there in the 1850s and 1860s. Where the old did survive it tended to be in affluent areas whose inhabitants had absolutely no intention of making way for new developments and who often joined forces to resist change. Highgate village managed to hold back the encroachment of Archway, and even today contains a fine collection of seventeenth- and eighteenth-century buildings. Hampstead resisted the westward march of Camden and Kentish Town. Dulwich, Bexley and Ham all retain their old village cores. Pinner has a well-preserved Tudor high street. But they are the exceptions rather than the rule.

It wasn't just trains that helped transform open land into new towns. Throughout the nineteenth century there was an expansion – and improvement – in road travel too, notably in the realm of public transport.

*A tram on the corner of Pentonville Road and Islington
High Street c.1890. The lettering on the front reads 'Archway Tavern,
Highgate and Moorgate St'.*

Omnibuses, for example, made their first appearance in 1829 when, inspired
by what he had seen in Paris, the coach builder George Shillibeer created
a service to run between Paddington Green and Bank. The typical two-
horse omnibus that evolved could carry twenty-two passengers, a dozen
or so inside and the rest on top. By the 1850s it still wasn't cheap at
sixpence for a typical fare, but it was well within the budget of middle-
class travellers and had accordingly become popular. Various companies
sprang up, many of them ultimately amalgamated into the London General
Omnibus Company in 1855, which by 1856 was running three-quarters of
the estimated 800 omnibuses in and around London (a decade later there
were 1,300). Omnibuses were colour-coded and ran to all points of the
compass: termini sent green ones from Bayswater, red from Brentford,
purple from Chelsea, white from Richmond and chocolate-coloured from
Westminster. While they did seem to get involved in accidents on an
alarmingly regular basis, they were also astonishingly convenient – particularly for those who wanted to travel only fairly short distances. As for

Shillibeer, his various enterprises and underhand financial dealings ultimately landed him in the Fleet prison, and he got into further trouble
when 130 gallons of smuggled brandy were found in premises he owned
in Camden Town. All this seems to have darkened his view of life, and
he spent his last years patenting a new form of funeral carriage and
operating as an undertaker in the City Road.

In time the omnibus fused with the train to produce the horse-drawn
tram, introduced by the rather aptly named George Francis Train, who
laid his first iron rails (along Victoria Street, Westminster) in 1860. Early
tram tracks were clumsy affairs, and on one occasion Train was arrested
for 'breaking and injuring' the roadway on the Uxbridge Road. However,
once the tracks were sunk into the road surface, objections disappeared,
and tram routes established themselves across London, with lines (in the
early 1870s) linking Blackheath and Vauxhall (with a branch from Brixton),
Whitechapel and Bow, and Kensington and Oxford Street. A brief experiment with steam trams in 1873 did not amount to much, and until the
arrival of electrified routes in 1903, the horse remained the preferred source
of power. This brought its own set of problems. It has been estimated

Brixton Road in Edwardian times, complete with tramlines.

that by the end of the century 50,000 horses were being employed to keep London moving one way or another, and they made a rather dirty mark on the metropolis. One correspondent in *The Times* in 1894 worried that soon all London's streets would be buried under several feet of horse manure. Quite a business sprang up dealing in equine dung, much of it being taken out to the fields of outer London to be spread as fertiliser. Dirthouse Wood (now Cherry Tree Wood), north of Highgate, acquired its name because for many years it was where night soil and horse manure were brought from central London before being liberally applied to hayfields.

Perhaps the defining transport image of the era was the hansom cab, designed and patented by the Yorkshire architect Joseph Hansom in 1834, two years after the Stage Carriages Act had done away with the monopoly previously enjoyed by hackney carriages. A highly manoeuvrable two-wheel vehicle, the hansom cab was drawn by a single horse – and so was relatively cheap to run and to hire. Not surprisingly, therefore, it proved hugely popular. In their *Street Life in London* (1877), J. Thomson and Adolphe Smith estimated that there were over 4,000 hansom cabs operating in London and a more or less equal number of four-wheel cabs. Incidentally, while the authors thought that hansom cab drivers were prone to overcharge, they also thought they were otherwise pretty honest, pointing out that in 1875 they handed over 15,584 items left behind in their cabs to the Lost Property Office. Their main focus of operation was in the City and West End, but they also carried passengers much further afield. Mr Pooter is described as regularly taking a hansom cab around town. One of the hansom's greatest fans, Arthur Conan Doyle, has Sherlock Holmes travelling from Baker Street to the Brixton Road by cab in order to investigate the murderous goings on there in *A Study in Scarlet* (1887).

───────◆◆▶───────

The constantly increasing level of transport put huge pressure on the roads themselves, and by the early decades of the century London threatened to grind to a halt. In Georgian times, turnpikes had seemed a good makeshift solution to road building and maintenance, but under the new onslaught they buckled. Roads became increasingly crowded. The resources of the smaller turnpike trusts were put under pressure as companies found themselves having to repair the damage caused by carts, horses, carriages and thousands of pairs of feet. Travellers became frustrated. Those making a journey of any length at all found themselves constantly having to negotiate the toll gates of different trusts. They also found that the interests of the many trusts did not necessarily coincide with their own, and that there was no strategic coordination at all. The roads ran where they traditionally ran; but there was no guarantee that they ran where they were needed.

By the 1820s the problem had become a crisis, and so a single Metropolitan Trust was created by Act of Parliament in 1826 to administer the key roads to the north of the City. Fourteen trusts were amalgamated: Brentford, Camden Town, City Road, Hackney, Harrow, Highgate, Hampstead Old and New Roads, Isleworth, Kensington, Kilburn, Lea-Bridge, Mary-le-Bone, Old Street and Uxbridge. The new network, created under the control of a single authority – admittedly with a restricted remit – brought a degree of standardisation to nearly 130 miles of road. It was also symbolically significant, the first instance of a coordinated approach to transport. Responsibility was placed in the overall control of

The lucrative Tyburn turnpike (near today's Marble Arch) in 1813. By the mid nineteenth century turnpikes seemed increasingly anachronistic and the last ones were abolished in the 1870s.

the 'General Surveyor of the Metropolis Roads North of the Thames', Sir James Nicoll McAdam – son of the John Loudon McAdam who had invented the road-surfacing technique known as 'macadam'.

Granted further powers in 1829, the trust set about managing existing turnpike routes, and building new roads where required. The existing ones were reorganised into sixteen districts, each with a different scale of tolls that raised the vast sum of £83,000 in 1838 alone. Some of the toll revenues raised went to pay for a road from Stamford Hill to Camden Town (now known as the Seven Sisters Road); a new route for the Hertford Road at Enfield Highway; and a road from Lea Bridge Road, Walthamstow, to the main Epping road (today, the Woodford New Road).

However, with the coming of the railways, toll revenues started to fall, and toll operators understandably became concerned. To add insult to injury, they also found themselves coming under increasing attack from frustrated London travellers who regarded the whole idea of turnpikes as anachronistic and unfair. Lobbying groups sprang into action; in 1855 a parliamentary committee was established to investigate the whole issue, and a heated debate ensued that spilled over into the newspapers. An article published in the *Illustrated London News* in June 1857 took a distinctly jaundiced view of the turnpike system. It pointed out that, even in its reformed guise, it was costly to run and that the number of tollgates had actually risen rather than fallen over the previous twenty or so years. There were now 87 gates and bars within four miles of Charing Cross, sixteen more than when the more centralised approach had been adopted. Indeed, whereas there had been 71 gates in total across the network in 1830, there were now 117 over the 123 miles covered by the entire Metropolitan Turnpike Trust in the mid 1850s. Furthermore, the whole system was inconsistent. Sixteen different tariffs were in operation. Some suburbs had numerous gates and bars, while Westminster contained only one gate and the City of London none at all. If you lived in Notting Hill and wanted to walk the short distance to Kensington (within the same parish) you had to pay two tolls. If you lived in Kilburn you were surrounded by gates and bars, and it was no good fleeing to, say, the Hackney Road, because things were just as bad there. Yet it was often the untolled roads that were most heavily used and therefore most expensive to maintain:

The 11 miles untolled are situate in the heavy traffic districts, such as Knightsbridge, St. Margaret's, Westminster, Paddington, Marylebone, &c., but the 112 miles are situated in such places as Kentish town, Holloway, Hackney, Kingsland, Stamford hill &c. Thus the suburban districts, after paying for their own suburban roads at the rate of £340 per mile, are taxed for the repair of roads, at the rate of £1400 per mile, in the crowded thoroughfares near Belgravia and Tyburnia; a double injustice.[12]

What's more, the wrong people got hit with charges. Producers of agricultural goods who used the turnpikes, for example, had to pay money they could often ill afford and then pass on those charges to their customers, who might also live in impoverished circumstances. An additional source of frustration was the army of tollgate keepers and other officials who were required to operate the system, taking their fees from the tolls that they raised. The whole system seemed grossly unfair and wasteful.

An ingenious social argument was made, too:

Wherever a toll-gate is erected within the limits of this fast-growing metropolis, it depreciates existing property, and prevents the extension of building. Those who remember Tyburn-gate, close to the spot where the Marble Arch now stands, will recognise the extent of the evil. Respectable London may be said to have ended at the corner of the Edgware-road. Westward of that point – where now stands rows of palaces, and some of the finest squares, crescents, and streets in the world – were to be found either corn-fields or vegetable crofts, or build-ings of the most inferior description; mean public-houses and squalid tea-gardens, the resort only of those who could walk to them, and never frequented by any one rich enough to ride his own horse or sit in his own vehicle. But, when the bar was removed, Tyburnia – the noblest and most magnificent suburb of London – speedily arose beyond its boundary. Many other examples might be cited, but this will suffice for our purpose.[13]

... The operation of the system of toll-gates is in every way most injurious, particularly in the depreciation of property outside the toll-gates. The contrast between the value of houses within the bars, as compared with those outside, is obvious and entails serious loss.

Toll-gates have the injurious effect of causing the erection of stables, cowhouses, cattle-sheds, and slaughter houses, within the gates, to save the expense of tolls, thus causing great injury to the health of the inhabitants inside the gates.[14]

Such was the level of public discontent that action was eventually taken. In 1863 the Metropolis Amendment Act was passed and the hated toll gates were removed, the responsibility for the upkeep of roads and the associated taxation being handed over to the Metropolitan Board of Works or the various vestries and district boards created in 1855 by the Metropolis Management Act. The only roads left under the administration of the Metropolitan Turnpike Trust were the arterial routes outside the extent of the Metropolitan Board of Works, including the Great Western Road from Hammersmith to Isleworth; the section of the Harrow Road from Hampstead to Harrow; the stretch of the Seven Sisters Road beyond Islington; and the Lea Bridge Road from Hackney to Snaresbrook. The final death knell for the last of the metropolitan turnpikes came in 1872 when the commission was finally abolished, and maintenance reverted to the vestries and district boards. Only traces remain today of the old system: the eighteenth-century toll house at the Spaniards Inn in Hampstead, for example; a plaque on a pub wall on East End Road in Finchley; and toll houses on Mill Hill Road, Barnes, on the road to Beckenham, Kent, and the Dulwich Toll House, College Road. Turnpike Lane in Haringey recalls the Turnpike Road established there by 1813.

The abolition of the turnpikes is not just an interesting footnote in London's history. Up until the point they disappeared, the failings of the city's road system acted as a break on outward expansion. It simply wasn't practical to live too far from town given the cost of travel, and the delay to journeys that tollgates involved. Once the turnpikes were done away with, and the railway network started to expand, so people were granted much more freedom to live where they wanted.

⬤—◄·▸—⬤

One barrier that both roads and trains had to contend with was the Thames. For centuries it had served to keep north and south London well apart, and acted as a brake on southern expansion. Crossing the river by boat had, of course, long been an option and the Thames watermen were a powerful contingent for many centuries. A few ferries operated – for example, from Woolwich, where after 1810 an army ferry service ran from Woolwich Arsenal to Duvals Wharf, and in 1811 the Woolwich 'western ferry' was introduced (although some sort of ferry service seems to have been in existence in Woolwich since medieval times). Then there was the steamboat service introduced in 1816 to run between Chelsea and the City. Generally speaking, river travel appealed most to those who lived further up the Thames corridor – in Gravesend, Margate and Ramsgate nearer the coast, or Greenwich and Woolwich closer to the centre. In the mid 1850s around 15,000 people used the river each day to travel to work.

River travel, however, was a slow and expensive affair. Crossing the river by bridge was infinitely preferable; but one of the striking things about London is how late so many of the bridges we take for granted today were constructed. In fact, for most of the capital's history its only major crossing was London Bridge, connecting the City to Southwark (the 'Old' London Bridge, designed in 1176 by clergyman Peter de Colechurch and soon crowded with houses, was eventually demolished in 1824 to be replaced by a stronger, wider structure). It is remarkable to think that prior to 1729 (when Putney Bridge was constructed) the nearest crossing upstream from London Bridge was Kingston Bridge, some twenty-four miles away.

Things started to change in the eighteenth century. A new bridge was constructed at Westminster in 1750, followed in quick succession by Blackfriars Bridge in 1769 and Battersea Bridge in 1776 – evidence of the pull of London's western suburbs. Like the turnpikes, these bridges operated tolls to pay for their construction, and consequently they weren't always that heavily used. It would also be fair to say that the quality of London's new bridges didn't impress all who saw them. Louis Simond, a French-American merchant who travelled around Britain in the early nineteenth century, for example, offered a distinctly sniffy view of them in 1810:

The bridge opposite Somerset House [Waterloo Bridge] is just begun; it will be only the fourth bridge, and not enough for this overgrown town. Paris has six or seven bridges. Blackfriars Bridge is decaying rapidly. The

A nineteenth-century view of Blackfriars Bridge (as rebuilt in the 1860s) with the cast-iron Southwark Bridge (replaced in the 1920s) beyond. Victorian road and railway bridges firmly bound north and south London together.

stones are too soft, and scale off near the water's edge. The ornamental columns at each pier will not stand many years. It is a very handsome bridge . . . Nothing can well be uglier than London bridge; every arch is of a size different from its next neighbour; there are more solid than open parts; it is in fact like a thick wall, pierced with small unequal holes here and there, through which the current, dammed up by this clumsy fabric, rushes with great velocity, and in fact takes a leap, the difference between high and low water being upwards of 15 feet . . . Below London Bridge, the Thames begins to assume the appearance of a sea port. You see shipping at anchor on both sides; many Dutch, Danes, and Swedes, with licences, I suppose, and many Americans; two or three seventy-fours on the stocks, and some East Indiamen.[15]

With the dawn of a new century, a rash of bridge building broke out. Vauxhall Bridge appeared in 1816, Southwark in 1819 and Hammersmith in 1825. At a stroke the north and south banks of a large stretch of the Thames from Hammersmith to the City became more accessible, while many existing bridges were substantially refurbished or reconstructed: London Bridge (again, but this time designed by John Rennie) in 1831, and Blackfriars in 1869. The godfather of London bridges was surely Joseph Bazalgette, the doyen of the Metropolitan Board of Works. During the last years of the organisation, from 1884 to 1890, he either designed, built or rebuilt four bridges, namely Albert, Putney, Hammersmith and Battersea, as well as modifying large sections of the river by creating the Thames Embankment between Battersea and Blackfriars bridges, and the smaller Albert Embankment – in effect reclaiming the marshy banks that were prone to flooding so that they could be used for civil engineering projects. Further out west, bridges were erected at Richmond in 1848, Barnes in 1849, Kew in 1869, Kingston in 1863 and Fulham in 1889.

East of the City, where the Thames was home to scores of tall ships making their way to and from the docks, bridges were scarcely a practical option. Various attempts were therefore made after 1799 to dig a tunnel under the river, including one by Cornish miners led by Richard Trevithick; all failed. Finally, in 1825 the engineers Marc Brunel and Thomas Cochrane, using revolutionary tunnelling shields and with financial backing from, among others, the Duke of Wellington (making his comments about the French secretly invading via underground railway all the more

An artist's impression of the walled Roman city of Londinium.

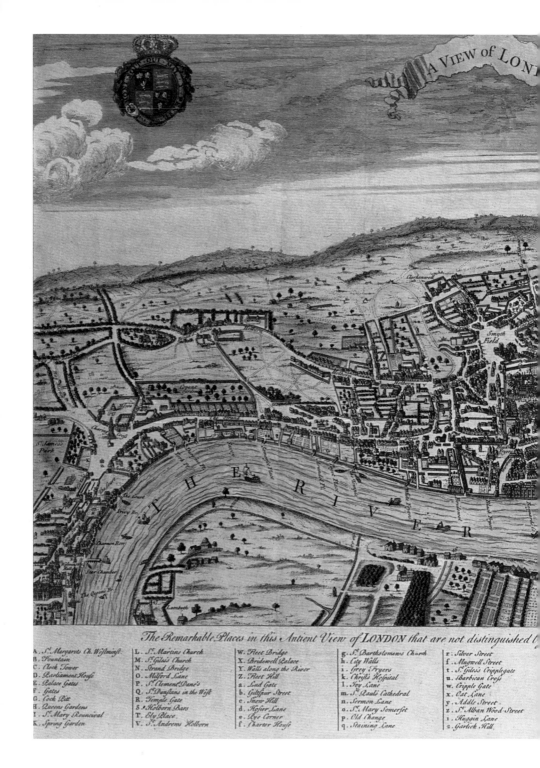

The Remarkable Places in this Antient View of LONDON that are not distinguished b...

A. St Margarets Ch. Westminst:	L. St Martins Church	W. Fleet Bridge	g. St Bartholomews Church	r. Silver Street
B. Fountain	M. St Giles's Church	X. Bridewell Palace	h. City Walls	f. Maguell Street
C. Clock Tower	N. Strand Bridge	Y. Walls along the River	i. Grey Fryers	s. St Giless Cripplegate
D. Parliament House	O. Milford Lane	Z. Fleet Hill	k. Christs Hospital	u. Barbican Cross
E. Palace Gates	P. St Clements Dane's	a. Lud Gate	l. Ivy Lane	w. Cripple Gate
F. Gates	Q. St Dunstans in the West	b. Giltspur Street	m. St Pauls Cathedral	x. Oat Lane
G. Cock Pitt	R. Temple Gate	c. Snew Hill	n. Sermon Lane	y. Addle Street
H. Queens Gardens	S. Holborn Bars	d. Hosier Lane	o. St Mary Somerset	z. St Alban Wood-Street
I. St Mary Rouncival	T. Ely Place	e. Pye Corner	p. Old Change	1. Huggin Lane
K. Spring Garden	V. St Andrews Holborn	f. Charter House	q. Staining Lane	2. Garlick Hill

A bird's-eye view of Tudor London.

N about the Year 1560.

ts in the Body thereof; are referr'd to by Letters and Figures, as hereunder specified.

ntington's College	13. Bush Lane	23. Love Lane	33. Woodroof Lane	43. St Mary Overys Church
Lythes Lane	14. Eastcheap	24. St Dunstan's E. Ch. & Hill	34. Seething Lane	44. St Tooley's Church
aying Hall	15. Burchin Lane	25. St Andrew Undershaft	35. Tower Hill	45. Winchester Place
uld Hall	16. St Anthony's Church	26. Bishops Gate	36. Tower hill Postern	46. Paris Garden
oeks Market	17. Allhallows in the Wall	27. Spittle Fields	37. Minories Cross	47. Lambeth House
llbrooke Church	18. St Augustine's Ch.	28. Cree Church	38. Abby of Grace	
artholomew Lane	19. St Helen's Church	29. Ald Gate	39. St Katherines Tower	
ndon Stone	20. St Dennis's Church	30. St Botolph's Aldgate	40. Tower Bridge	
earbinder Lane	21. Fen Church	31. St Katherine Coleman	41. Barkin Church	
Mary Botolph Lane	22. St Margaret's Church	32. Hart Street	42. Nonsuch House	

Eighteenth-century contrasts: the Royal Hospital at
Greenwich, a reminder of the crucial role that the sea and
maritime trade played in London's relentless expansion.

Elegance and trade in Covent Garden, *c.*1725.

Wealth and rural seclusion at Osterley Park.

A spa was established at Kilburn Wells in Georgian times. This mid nineteenth-century painting shows it in its final days.

The mouth of the River Fleet in Georgian times.
Constantly abused by Londoners, who dumped their
refuse in it, the river was ultimately covered over.

Industrial Lambeth: an 1813 view of Watt's Shot Tower
(for producing shot balls for firearms). Somerset House
can be seen in the background.

The coming of the canals: Paddington Basin
on the Grand Junction Canal, 1801.

The coming of the railways:
Euston station in 1831.

A Victorian picnic in Epping Forest, courtesy of
Huntley & Palmer's, *c.*1880.

unfathomable), began the construction of a tunnel between Rotherhithe and Wapping:

> The mode in which this great excavation was accomplished was by
> means of a powerful apparatus termed a shield, consisting of twelve
> great frames, lying close to each other like as many volumes on the shelf
> of a book-case, and divided into three stages or stories, thus presenting
> 36 chambers of cells, each for one workman, and open to the rear, but
> closed in the front with moveable boards. The front was placed against
> the earth to be removed, and the workman, having removed one board,
> excavated the earth behind it to the depth directed, and placed the
> board against the new surface exposed. The board was then in advance
> of the cell, and was kept in its place by props; and having thus
> proceeded with all the boards, each cell was advanced by two screws, one
> at its head and the other at its foot, which, resting against the finished
> brickwork and turned, impelled it forward into the vacant space. The
> other set of divisions then advanced. As the miners worked at one end
> of the cell, so the bricklayers formed at the other the top, sides and
> bottom . . .[16]

The project was beset by problems. The tunnel was flooded on a number of occasions, several men died in accidents, and the evil-smelling Thames water caused illness among many of the workers, including Marc Brunel himself.

However, the Thames Tunnel project was finally opened in 1843 and was acclaimed an engineering wonder of the age:

> It consists of two beautiful Arches, extending to the opposite side of the
> river. These Arches contain each a roadstead, fourteen feet wide and
> twenty-two feet high, and pathways for pedestrians, three feet wide. The
> Tunnel appears to be well ventilated, as the air seemed neither damp nor
> close. The partition between these Arches, running the whole length of
> the Tunnel, is cut into transverse arches, leading through from one road-
> stead to the other. There may be fifty of them in all, and these are
> finished into fancy and toy shops in the richest manner – with polished
> marble counters, tapestry linings, gilded shelves, and mirrors that make
> everything appear double. Ladies, in fashionable dresses and with
> smiling faces, wait within and allow no gentleman to pass without

giving him an opportunity to purchase some pretty thing to carry home as a remembrancer of the Thames Tunnel. The Arches are lighted with gas burners, that make it as bright as the sun; and the avenues are always crowded with a moving throng of men, women and children, examining the structure of the Tunnel, or inspecting the fancy wares, toys, &c., displayed by the arch-looking girls of these arches . . . It is impossible to pass through without purchasing some curiosity. Most of the articles are labelled – 'Bought in the Thames Tunnel'.[17]

The problem with the new tunnel, though, was that it was only suitable for pedestrians and so offered no relief at all to the traffic congestion that built up to the east of London Bridge; horses, carts and carriages all might have to wait up to several hours for their turn to cross to the other bank, with the certain knowledge that they would face another lengthy delay on their return. In a way it was less significant for what it achieved than for the engineering possibilities it offered the later London Underground system. It was only when the City of London's architect, Horace Jones, working with John Wolfe Barry, came up with the idea of a combined suspension and bascule bridge in 1884 which could be raised to allow ships to pass that East London's river-crossing problem was solved. Tower Bridge was opened in 1894, and at a stroke the eastern suburbs were fully connected to the rest of the metropolis. It was the final link needed to draw north and south London inextricably together.

— ◄ ♦ ► —

By 1900, London sprawled over a hundred square miles. Virtually continuous suburbs stretched to Putney, Acton and Hammersmith in the west; to Hampstead and Hornsey in the north; to Walthamstow and Stratford in the east; and to Streatham, Camberwell and Blackheath in the south. Beyond those were the nascent suburban centres of Hounslow, Finchley, Barking, Bromley and Merton. All these accommodated a population that was continuing to increase, as London attracted yet more people from others parts of Britain and from overseas. The capital had become a city of commuters – some 200,000 of them travelling from the suburbs to the centre each day by 1900. Moreover it was a city whose new outer core was starting to draw people from the centre, attracting them away from often antiquated and cramped housing in long-built-up areas to new homes in leafier ones. As the population of the outer suburbs continued to rise, so that of some of the inner suburbs started to decline. Between 1851 and 1901 the population of the City of London fell from 128,000 to 27,000. Between 1871 and 1901 the population of Westminster slipped from 524,000 residents to 460,000. It was the first sign of a move that would become an exodus in the following century.

NINE

A TALE OF SEVERAL SUBURBS

The Creation of Victorian London

To many contemporaries, suburbs were unwelcome intrusions that all looked the same. The children's writer E. Nesbit, who had known Brixton when it was a pretty little country village and who moved with her husband to Eltham when it was still surrounded by fields and country lanes, was so horrified by what she saw happening around her that she established a strange anti-suburb ceremony. According to the novelist E. M. Forster, each evening she would produce models of factories and suburban villas made out of brown paper and cardboard and then ritually set fire to them. Her views were at one with the correspondent in *The Times* in 1904 who warned that to surround London with so much suburban housing:

> . . . is to produce a district of appalling monotony, ugliness and dullness.
> And every suburban extension makes existing suburbs less desirable.
> Fifty years ago Brixton and Clapham were on the edge of the country; a
> walk could take one into lanes and meadows. Now London stretches to
> Croydon. It is no longer possible to escape the dull suburbs into
> unspoiled country.[1]

Most Londoners today wouldn't agree. Someone who lives in, say, Kilburn knows that Kilburn High Road looks and feels different from nearby, more 'upmarket' Brondesbury; and that Brondesbury, in turn, has a different atmosphere from Queen's Park with its desirable late nineteenth-century houses. They also know that if they travel east a little, they will leave behind terraces and encounter instead the solid late Victorian and early Edwardian mansion blocks of West Hampstead. All this architectural diversity can be viewed in the course of a brisk walk along a few streets. Even within a single street there can be huge variety: West End Lane, for example, which runs through West Hampstead, contains along its winding route not only mansion blocks but terraces with shops and restaurants beneath, three railway stations (including the tube) and some modern development. It was laid out over many years by different developers and then revisited by later ones.

The fact is that while the suburbs were created by broadly the same social and economic forces, no two developed in quite the same manner. Some, such as Maida Vale or Warwick Avenue, were intended for the more well-to-do from the start and stayed that way. Others, like Notting Hill Gate or Ladbroke Grove, began life as relatively grand developments, and then suffered a period of decline before climbing back up the social ladder. Others again, including Battersea, Poplar and West Ham, mixed industry with housing. All were shaped by small accidents of history, by the people who built them or lived in them, and by what was there before. The only way to appreciate the numerous and subtle forces at work is to look at a handful in a little more detail.

Battersea, just south of the river, is a good example of a small community transformed twice in the nineteenth century, first slowly by suburban sprawl, then rapidly by the coming of the railways. For centuries it had been little more than a village next to the Thames, connected to the north bank since 1771 by a rickety wooden bridge carrying foot and carriage traffic. St Mary's church, mentioned in the Domesday Book and rebuilt in 1777, catered for the spiritual needs of the few thousand people who lived there, clustered around one or two streets by the river and the bridge. Such houses as there were tended to be small, though in Georgian times there was a manor house and the beautiful Old Battersea House, built the previous century and still standing today. What dominated the landscape was Battersea Fields: common land comprising 'an entirely open space, a good deal of it given up to corn and the rest grazing fields, which were inhabited by an enormous herd of cows'.[2] These fields extended south from the banks of the Thames and were criss-crossed by footpaths and bridleways that led to the nearby villages of Wandsworth, Balham, Stockwell and Clapham. Large parts of Wandsworth and Clapham Commons also fell within the parish of Battersea. Much of its open land was given over to farms and market gardens – some 300 acres in all, in the hands of about twenty people. Specialist 'crops' included lavender (hence Lavender Hill today), and asparagus, sold as 'Battersea bundles'. The market gardeners were also famed for their fine cabbages.

By the later eighteenth century, large suburban villas were appearing, particularly to the north of the parish in Battersea Rise, 'it being a spot much admired for its pleasant situation, and fine prospect' according to Daniel Lysons's *Environs of London* published in 1792. There was also quite a lot of industry, some of it dating back to the seventeenth century. Mills, potteries, candle factories, starch works, silk producers, breweries and a large number of chemical works all abutted the river, drawing upon its water for power, and wharfs and jetties were built to allow the goods they produced to be shipped elsewhere. Many of the factories survived well into the twentieth century. The Patent Plumbago Crucible Company, for example, was set up in 1856 to make graphite crucibles. Renamed the Morgan Crucible Company, it only finally moved away from Battersea in the 1970s.

The farms and market gardens of Battersea appear to have relied upon seasonal workers from other parts of the country such as Shropshire and Wales. Industry, on the other hand, needed a regular workforce, and it was Battersea's industrial concerns that led to a slow increase in population in the early nineteenth century. A series of residential streets known

A late eighteenth-century view of Battersea from the river.

as Battersea New Town were built on land to the east of Battersea Fields towards Vauxhall and Nine Elms, and a new church was erected.

In the early 1840s, then, there were two Batterseas: an industrial one by the river and a rural one. Thereafter things changed rapidly. In part this was due to a decision made by the Commissioners of Works in 1846, supported by Thomas Cubitt, to purchase 320 acres of land at Battersea Fields and build a royal park there. The idea received enthusiastic backing from the vicar of St Mary's, Battersea, who disliked the raucous Sunday fairs traditionally held on Battersea Fields ('the resort of the roughest and most vicious characters in the neighbourhood')[3], and work duly started in 1855. The park was opened three years later by Queen Victoria and ultimately boasted walks, gardens, an ornamental lake and sports facilities.

One would be forgiven for assuming that the creation of a park would have held back suburban development, but in fact the opposite proved to be the case. Now that common land was lost to gentrified parkland, the agricultural base of the parish was severely undermined. What's more, a hundred acres or so of the land had been sold off by the commissioners as building plots. Far from preserving green spaces, therefore, the creation of Battersea Park actually hastened their demise.

Then came the railways. Nine Elms was established in 1838 as the terminus for trains arriving from Southampton (the line running through the parish can clearly be seen on Cary's map), and over the next two decades four more companies drove lines through the area. The decision was therefore taken to establish a major interchange to the south of the parish, and Clapham Junction duly opened in 1863. Within a decade the market gardens to the north had gone, to be replaced by residential streets in what would become the Winstanley Estate. Houses for railway workers and others spread rapidly. In 1872, for example, the Shaftesbury Park Estate to the east of the station near Lavender Hill was founded by the Artizans (*sic*), Labourers and General Dwelling Company. It involved the construction of 1,200 two-storey houses, complete with small gardens but lacking bathrooms except in a few exclusive cases. Now Battersea had two new identities: 'old Battersea' by the bridge, with its industrial enterprises on the river; and 'new Battersea', centred on the railway lines and station to the south.

By the end of the nineteenth century, practically all the land in the area had been built over, and substantial development had spread around

7232.

Town Hall & Shakespere Theatre, Battersea.

S.S.Series.

Battersea transformed: the town hall and Shakespeare Theatre on Lavender Hill. The theatre was built in 1896 and survived until the 1950s. Its site is now occupied by an office block.

the surviving stretches of Wandsworth and Clapham Common. Battersea was now a suburb. Its population, which in 1861 had stood at 19,600 people, reached 107,000 by 1881.

With new houses came new social demands, and new institutions to cater for them. John Erskine Clarke, who was vicar of St Mary's church for forty years after 1872, oversaw the construction of additional churches to serve his enlarged congregation and encouraged the building of new schools, such as the Vicarage School for Girls and Battersea Grammar School (both subsequently moved out of the area). A workhouse for the poor had been built between 1838 and 1840 in open fields on St John's Hill, but as the population continued to spiral and social problems grew, a new, much larger workhouse was built at Garratt Lane, Wandsworth, in 1885.

Industry and services continued to come to the area, encouraged by the presence of a larger potential workforce. The Southwark and Vauxhall Water Company Works and the London Gasworks sprang up on the east side of Chelsea Bridge near the Nine Elms railway complex. Later on, in 1937, Battersea Power Station would be constructed here. Other businesses grew up to cater for local people. Arding and Hobbs, for example, founded its celebrated department store on the corner of Lavender Hill and St John's Road in 1885. Civic buildings were constructed, too, such as a police station and town hall. Numerous pubs were established.

Battersea even acquired a huge music hall – the Grand – which opened in 1900, playing to capacity crowds of up to 3,000 at a time. In this, it was typical of many later Victorian inner suburbs. While the West End may have retained its dominance as a theatrical centre for Londoners, many other areas of the capital also wanted to get in on the act (so to speak). By the late 1880s the venerable, often Georgian, foundations around Drury Lane, Haymarket and Covent Garden had been joined by the Royal Court Theatre in Sloane Square, and by the turn of the century by the Borough Theatre in Stratford, the Alexandra Theatre in Stoke Newington, the Grand Theatre in Fulham, the latest incarnation of the Richmond Theatre and Opera House, the Royal Duchess Theatre in Balham and the King's Theatre in Hammersmith. Islington's determination to be entertained at all costs is shown by its dogged rebuilding of theatres that seemed to have an unerring knack of burning to the ground: one Frank Mitcham creation after another succumbed to the flames in the 1880s and 1890s and it was not until he built the Islington Empire that his run of bad luck came to an end. The Grand in Battersea proved to be more flame-retardant. Opened by the hugely popular Dan Leno, who lived nearby, it survived intact for a number of years before going through the inevitable twentieth-century progression from theatre to cinema to bingo hall to nightclub.

Battersea was not immune to self-improvement either. Concerns about the plight of the urban poor, and in particular worries about the links between poverty and alcohol, were common throughout the nineteenth century, and various groups advocated creating local establishments that would remove people from the temptations of drink and offer them something more intellectually intoxicating in its place. Francis Place, for example, the social reformer who was involved with the London Working Men's Association, strongly supported the notion of the library rather than the pub as a social gathering point in the evidence he presented to an 1830s parliamentary select committee looking at the issue of drunkenness. Vigorous campaigning eventually won the day and in 1850 the Public Libraries Act was passed, seeking to create lending libraries in every borough by allowing for a small rise in local rates. Battersea, therefore, not only had its musical hall, it acquired a library as well. Nor was it alone. By the end of the nineteenth century a large number of public lending libraries had opened across London and the suburbs, including Southgate and Clapham (1889), Croydon, Chiswick and Streatham (1890), Brixton and Canning Town (1893), Willesden Green (1894), Hendon (1895), Brentford (1896), Balham (1898), Stanmore (1899), Lewisham (1900), Sydenham (1904), Hounslow and Manor Park (1905), and Twickenham (1907).

While Battersea's story is unique in its details, aspects of its development are typical of the river-based suburbs close to the centre of London. West Ham, for example, may look very different indeed from Battersea, but it too was an early industrial area that then grew rapidly after the 1840s. However, West Ham's transformation had less to do with the railways than the passing of the 1844 Metropolitan Building Act, which placed restrictions on where dangerous industries could be located. Because lands to the east of the River Lea were excluded from the provisions of the Act, West Ham found itself almost overnight in possession of chemical factories and other manufacturing plants, either established there for the first time or relocated from somewhere else. It came to be known as 'London over the border', *The Times* of 1886 recording its rise to industrial might:

> Factory over factory was erected on the marshy wastes of Stratford and Plaistow, and it only required the construction at Canning Town of the Victoria and Albert Docks to make the once desolate parish of West Ham a manufacturing and commercial centre of the first importance and to bring upon it a teeming and an industrious population.[4]

In 1851 the population of West Ham was 9,000. Fifty years later it had reached 267,000.

Completely different forces were at work in Victorian Finchley, eight miles north of the City of London as the crow flies, and right on the Middlesex border with Hertfordshire. This was never an industrial area. For centuries the parish of Finchley was little more than a collection of rural hamlets abutting the Bishop of London's park to the south and surrounded by arable land and commons, through which the Great North Road passed. Leaving aside Whetstone to the extreme north of the parish, which was to develop its own identity, the main settlements that today constitute Finchley grew up in North End, Church End and East End, along with a scattering of dwellings at Woodside and Fallow Corner. All of them are now swallowed by suburbia, but the original settlements are marked by nearby tube stations at Finchley Central (Church End), East Finchley (East End) and Woodside Park. At the turn of the nineteenth century the area was best known for its fine hog market at East End and for producing good-quality hay; and there were no more than 1,500 people living there. In some ways its claim to fame was more that it was an area to be driven through than visited. The Great North Road was a busy one. By 1835 nearly a hundred long-distance coaches passed along it each day. Its claim to notoriety was Finchley Common, long a centre of operations for highwaymen.

A few fine brick houses went up in Finchley throughout the eighteenth century (for example the Manor House on East End Road, built in around 1723 and now a centre for Judaism), but the area was never as popular with merchants and the aspiring middle classes as its southern neighbour, Hampstead. As late as the 1790s it was described by one visitor as little more than a straggling village, small but respectable: weatherboard cottages interspersed with a few detached brick and stuccoed houses.

The first change to Finchley's fortunes came with the enclosure award of 1811, which saw Finchley Common divided into various plots five years later. One hundred and twenty acres were sold to Regent's Canal, who wanted to create a reservoir to serve their growing network. However, the scheme was abandoned in 1820 – the reservoir being created further west on the Brent River – and the land drained and sold to James Frost, an enterprising cement manufacturer. He went on to build houses to demonstrate the fire resistant qualities of the building materials he espoused. One, Hawthorne Dean (1826), still stands, awkwardly squeezed up against the slip road from the North Circular to East Finchley.

More important than the taming of Finchley Common, however, was the transformation of Finchley's roads, which involved improvements to the Great North Road and the construction from 1826 of a new turnpike route – Regent's Park Road – to connect Marylebone to the Great North Road at Tallyho Corner, North End. At a stroke, traffic in the area increased, and coach services started to operate from Finchley to Bank in the City, among them morning services from the Torrington Arms and the Queen's Head at Church End. Local shops, businesses and stables sprang up – rather unusually the local blacksmith in 1839 was a woman, Elizabeth Humphreys. Moreover, omnibuses started to run into town as well, with three a day from the Five Bells to Charing Cross in 1845, and three more from Church End by the 1860s. The traffic through Finchley became heavier by the year: nineteen coaches passed through en route from Birmingham alone each day. As Finchley became, as it were, ever closer to London (no more than a couple of hours' coach journey by the 1860s), so it became more attractive to wealthy commuters. Various new houses appeared in the 1840s and 1850s, generally detached villas 'so much in request by merchants and professional gentlemen preferring a location distant from London, undisturbed by railway excitement'.[5]

Paradoxically, at a time when the railways were starting to transform other parts of London, it was the lack of railways in Finchley that was proving appealing. There were plenty of people in Victorian England who wanted rural peace, charm and good old-fashioned transport by road.

Grand living in Finchley: Avenue House on East End Road.
Dating from the late 1850s, it was acquired in 1874 by the
ink magnate Henry Stephens.

They might have complained about levels of road tolls in Finchley – among the heaviest on all routes into London – but they still came to live there. Such, for example, seems to have been the appeal of Finchley to the immensely wealthy Henry Charles ('Inky') Stephens, son of the man who invented Stephens' blue-black ink, who bought Avenue House on East End Road in 1874 and went on to establish magnificent landscaped gardens and an arboretum there.

The next change to Finchley's fortunes had to do with the dead, rather than the living. By the mid nineteenth century London's cemeteries were bursting at the seams. Built to serve a much smaller city, they simply couldn't cope with the new demands placed on them. The city therefore turned to the countryside, and Finchley came to house not just one but two major new cemeteries in 1854 on what until 1816 had been common land: the St Marylebone (now East Finchley), established at Newmarket Farm; and St Pancras and Islington on Horseshoe Farm. The latter was one of the largest in London, and the first to be publicly owned. Over the next decades, thousands of people were buried there, and Finchley became familiar to successions of mourners visiting the cemetery chapels and the graves of their departed relatives.

Finally, the railways came. In 1867 the Great Northern Railway opened a line to Mill Hill and Edgware, with a station at East Finchley, and another at Church End called Finchley and Hendon (now Finchley Central). Five years later a branch line was run to High Barnet with stations at Woodside Park, and Totteridge and Whetstone. Journey times into town fell to half an hour. From the 1890s, 'workers' trains' offered fifty services a day, at four pence a time. Omnibuses increased their number of services to compete with the railways, running both into town and out to Barnet. Trams arrived in 1905, with a major depot constructed near Tallyho Corner three years later, to connect the towns scattered around outer Middlesex and Hertfordshire. From being a rural backwater, Finchley had become a transport hub.

Population statistics, as ever, are revealing. While Finchley may not have seen the stratospheric increases that marked Battersea or West Ham, it did nevertheless expand at an extraordinary rate. In 1861 there were just under 5,000 people living in Finchley; forty years later this figure had risen to over 22,000; and by 1911, when the trams were well and truly in place, nearly 39,500 people lived there. From the 1870s and 1880s, new roads were laid out around the stations and were quickly built upon. Modest terraced housing appeared around East Finchley, built along the straight roads running parallel to each other characteristic of so many of the Victorian suburbs and appealing to working-class and lower-middle-class people.

The average Finchley Victorian terraced house – like that in every London suburb – might have two, three or, at a pinch, four bedrooms. The earlier and humbler ones lacked a bathroom, so that people would have to make use of basins and ewers, and a portable bath for which the water would have to be specially heated. If a water closet was built at all, it would invariably be located outside the house or at the back of the scullery, which meant that chamber pots were ubiquitous and essential, kept under the bed or in a washstand. Downstairs there would be a back room for eating and family leisure, and a more lavishly furnished front room for entertaining. The kitchen would have its coal-fired cooking range and perhaps a scullery. For much of the century, piped water, if it was laid on, was rarely available twenty-four hours a day, seven days a week;

The typical clutter of a parlour in a well-to-do Victorian house.

in fact, as late as 1874, only 10.3 per cent of London households got a constant supply. Cisterns were therefore essential.[6]

The later part of the century did, however, see some improvements. By the 1870s, hot-water pipes were beginning to appear in middle-class houses, and landlords in the 1880s were installing bathrooms even in quite modest properties in order to enhance their appeal and rental value. Around the same time, gas lighting made its way into people's homes, to be followed after 1900 by electricity. That said, even the new and improved terraced house was hard work. It's not surprising, therefore, that those who could afford it hired a servant to cook and clean. The 1871 census reveals that 35 per cent of London's population employed one servant; 25 per cent employed two; and the remaining 40 per cent either had more or none at all. In Finchley, the larger properties in North End were rather more likely to see a bustle of servants than the humbler ones in East Finchley, though even North End was not immune to the encroachment of servant-poor cottages and terraced housing near the station.

*Suburban living in Finchley: an Edwardian postcard showing
North Finchley's High Street.*

Meanwhile, in the main streets around Finchley's burgeoning terraces,
gas lighting arrived in 1883, and whole parades of shops sprang up; and
over the next forty years, the three old parts of Finchley became ever
more connected to one another by a ribbon of houses, shops and places
of work. Slowly but inexorably, North Finchley, East Finchley and Finchley
Central merged as distinct suburbs. Agriculture continued to be a source
of employment: College Farm in East Finchley, for example, was supplying
milk at twopence a pint throughout London in the 1890s, delivered by a
team of 130 horses and miscellaneous carts. However, the rural way of
life was fast disappearing. By the early twentieth century, you were more
likely to get a local job in a shop or one of Finchley's new small industrial concerns than one on the land.

As in Battersea, a new suburban population needed public amenities.
Although some of the old, large houses in Finchley had been converted to
schools earlier in the century, those in authority clearly remained worried
about the minds of the young of Finchley: as early as 1813 concerns had
been raised that 'no parish within 300 miles of London had a greater proportion of its inhabitants in a more deplorable state of ignorance'.[7] The response
then had been to open a National School, with space for a hundred pupils,
at Church End. By 1846, however, this was deemed to be no longer sufficient

for the parish, and both East End and North End were given schools as well, in 1847 and 1869 respectively. As for the souls of local people, Finchley's parish church, St Mary's, had served their needs in Church End (logically enough) since medieval times, but by the later nineteenth century a single church was felt to be insufficient for the burgeoning parish. Consequently, Holy Trinity was built in 1846 to provide for the 'godless' hamlet of East End, and a second church, All Saints, was opened nearby in 1891. Christ church in North Finchley owed its origin in part to a mission sent in 1864 to offer spiritual sustenance to the sometimes worryingly religion-free navvies working on the railways. Various Nonconformist and Roman Catholic places of worship also appeared, reflecting the social diversity of newcomers to the area. To complete the community, a voluntary library was opened in North Finchley High Street in 1896; and a small cottage hospital with eighteen beds opened in 1908. For other key institutions – workhouse, infirmary, and so on – people had to step over the border into nearby Barnet.

Finchley's development then was as much shaped by a pre-railway as by a post-railway era. For a long time in the nineteenth century it was a rural retreat – a place for a smattering of wealthier Londoners, for legions of London's dead, or for smallpox victims from St Pancras seeking shelter in temporary tents during an outbreak in 1881. Its transport routes also pulled it further out towards Barnet as much as into central London. In its late adoption of the railway, it was not unlike a whole swathe of settlements in the outer boroughs – Croydon, Richmond, Sutton, Bromley, Barking and Harrow, to name a few – some of which actively fought against the encroaching tracks. Kingston was just one town that resisted railways, fearing (correctly) that they would damage coach travel through the town. Consequently, when a railway station was finally built in 1838, it was placed not near Kingston but down the road at Surbiton instead, generating steady suburban growth there over the next eight decades: a new high street, middle-class tenement dwellings, new schools, health care and working-class estates.

If Battersea embraced the railway and Finchley grudgingly accepted it, Walthamstow actively demanded its arrival. This was a settlement with a long history. Back in medieval times it had been home to a few hundred people living in the village centre at Church End and neighbouring scattered hamlets. By the seventeenth century the area was favoured by London merchants and officials, who built large houses among the fields and marshland. An estate map of the area drawn up as late as 1820 shows a Walthamstow that comprised little more than open fields, grand villas and a single high street. Then transformation came, and by the time the late Victorian Ordnance Survey maps of the area were prepared the village had been virtually smothered by grids of streets and terraced housing – and a station. Given what happened in Battersea, it's tempting to assume that this pattern of development, so characteristic of so much of London's suburban growth, was brought about by that station and the railway that led to it. In fact, the truth is very different.

In 1849, social reformers set up the National Freehold Land Society, also known as the National Permanent Mutual Benefit Society, to help people of limited means to acquire sufficient freehold land to gain them the right to vote – the franchise at this stage being largely restricted to property holders of freehold land above the value of forty shillings. The intention, of course, was to counter the undue influence of the then small number of legally registered voters who had a tendency to return MPs pretty much like themselves – in other words, Tory landowners – to the House of Commons. Large parcels of land were purchased by the society, and broken down into smaller plots – worth a minimum of forty shillings each – and houses duly built, in the expectation that their first inhabitants would be more likely to vote for the predominantly 'middle-class' Whig party than the 'patrician' Tories.

Walthamstow became a centre of activity for the society, and various quite well-spaced semi-detached and terraced houses were built. However, the village's new residents needed to be able to travel into town to work. They therefore made clear their desire for better transport connections, supported by local landowners who could foresee a rise in the value of their holdings were there to be a local railway boom.

The railway therefore duly arrived. With that in place, the next phase of the area's development began with the rapid construction of cheaper, working-class dwellings that enveloped the middle-class enclave.

Walthamstow's story was to be repeated elsewhere across the eastern region. First the large estates would be broken up to create middle-class housing. Then artisans' houses would join them. In Leyton and Leytonstone, for example, small villages gave way to the large, comfortable suburban buildings of Woodgrange Park and the Gurney Estate between the 1870s and 1890s, which were soon joined by humbler dwellings.

◆ ◆ ◆

If Walthamstow's origins as a suburb were somewhat earnest, Sydenham's were rather more light-hearted. Sydenham Hill had once been part of the Great North Wood (preserved in the Norwood name) and a regular site of gypsy encampments (hence Gypsy Hill). In previous eras, Londoners had trekked southwards to have their fortunes read, as Samuel Pepys recalls in his diary for 11 August 1668: 'This afternoon, my wife and Mercer and Deb went with Pelling to see the gipsies at Lambeth and have their fortunes told, but what they did, I did not enquire.' Then, in 1854, the huge edifice that had housed the Great Exhibition of 1851 in Hyde Park was moved to a new park in Penge Place Estate on Sydenham Hill, formerly owned by Leo Schuster, a director of the London, Brighton and South Coast Railway. It was one of the highest points in London, and the rebuilt palace could be seen for miles around. Visitors flocked to it, enticed by the mystique of the original exhibition

An aerial view of the Crystal Palace in Sydenham. A popular tourist attraction, it was destroyed by fire in 1936.

and by the new venue, with its majestic fountains and concrete model dinosaurs (the wonders of the age). A School of Music and Art found its home there, as did a School of Forestry and Engineering. The grounds were used for fairs, temporary exhibitions and music concerts of the highest order. In short, Sydenham became one of Victorian London's greatest tourist attractions.

Such was Sydenham's drawing power that it ended up with not one railway station but two. The first was built at the foot of the hill by the London, Brighton and South Coast Railway as Crystal Palace Low Level station, complete just a little too late for the grand opening of the site in 1854. The second, Crystal Palace High Level, opened a year later following complaints that the walk to the park from the first station was too long and too arduous; visitors may have liked their recreation but not, apparently, if it involved effort on their part. Over the next thirty years, in excess of 2 million visitors came. To serve them and to accommodate all the workers who maintained the palace, railways, shops and associated businesses, houses sprouted up around the park and Sydenham quickly became a residential suburb.

———— ◄ • ► ————

Those contemporaries who disliked suburbs came from both ends of the political spectrum. On the right, there were people such as T. W. H. Crosland, whose *The Suburbans* of 1908 is an attack on the 'low, inferior species' of suburbanites with their 'idiotic free libraries' and love of tinned salmon. On the left, there were people such as the Fabian socialist E. Nesbit, who hated what the suburbs had done to the countryside of her childhood. Both mindsets were shaped by a desire for a return to a neverland of rural bliss.

Nostalgic stirrings helped inspire such major figures of the period as William Morris. Many of his passions could be regarded as profoundly anti-suburban. He loathed what was happening to the Walthamstow of his childhood, describing it as 'terribly cockneyfied', and in 1877 founded the Society for the Protection of Ancient Buildings. The Arts and Crafts movement (of which he was a major proponent) was a reaction against the 'improvements' of the Victorian era. His Red House in Bexleyheath, designed in 1859, was a celebration of natural materials and a rejection of mass production: fireplaces bore medieval mottoes; the hall was decorated with murals by Burne-Jones, and the garden, with its separate 'rooms', was designed to be an extension of the house; Morris was devastated when money problems forced him to sell up in 1866. Yet despite all this, and despite all Morris's active and eloquent campaigns against modern urban sprawl, the values that he espoused helped inspire the building of one of London's most prestigious developments: Hampstead Garden Suburb.

The suburb was a product of the Garden City movement, championed by Ebenezer Howard, founder of Letchworth Garden City. Howard was born in Fore Street in the City and understood well the 'harsh existence experienced by so many residents of London'. In 1898 he published *Garden Cities of Tomorrow* in which he argued that the answer to England's overcrowded and unhealthy industrial cities was a new generation of more rural, green and attractive towns. His ideas proved influential and certainly made their mark on Hampstead Garden Suburb. Where the new suburb differed from the Howard model, however, was that it was intended to be part of a city, not a town in its own right; in other words, there were no plans to incorporate the factories, workshops and businesses to be found in a garden city. To that extent it belonged to a more long-standing tradition of philanthropic nineteenth-century schemes such as Port Sunlight on the Wirral and Bournville near Birmingham, built by benevolent employers for the workforce.

In Hampstead's case, its moving spirit was not so much an employer as a social reformer, Dame Henrietta Barnett. Disturbed by her experiences of the squalor of the East End and horrified by the onward march of 'rows of ugly villas such as disfigure Willesden and most of the suburbs of London',[8] her initial involvement in the Hampstead area came about from a fear that development might soon encroach on Hampstead Heath (where she lived at St Jude's Cottage on the heath's fringes) and so cause the 'ruin of the sylvan restfulness of that portion of the most beautiful open space near London'. As a result, she and her husband Samuel campaigned, through the formation of the Hampstead Heath Extension Council, to save eighty acres of land. They then went on to plan an ambitious and philanthropic project that would provide planned social housing in the north of the capital

In 1906 a trust was established with the aim of buying up land in the

Rural charm in Hampstead Garden Suburb.

Hampstead area. Two hundred and forty-three acres were purchased from Eton College, and further parcels of land were acquired over the next two decades. Raymond Unwin was appointed as architect and surveyor and with his partner, Barry Parker, and the renowned Edwin Lutyens as Consulting Architect laid out a scheme and designed many of the principal buildings. Plenty of space was deemed essential and was enshrined in the private bill that was passed in Parliament to allow work to begin:

> There shall not be built in the Garden Suburb on the average throughout a greater proportion of houses to the acre than eight.
>
> On every road in the Garden Suburb (whatever the width of the said road) there shall be between any two houses standing on opposite sides of the road a space not less than fifty feet free of any buildings except walls, fences or gates.

It wasn't just space that the champions of the suburb wanted to create; they also wanted to bring together all classes of society. This was to be a utopian village where hedges not walls separated houses, where trees lined the streets, where woods and public spaces were incorporated into the overall design rather than built over. Larger houses for the better off in the south of the suburb were complemented by smaller artisans' houses to the north, and there was a grand square in the middle with two churches.

With its attractive curved roads – very different from the ramrod straight ones of Victorian speculative developers – and a variety of architectural styles for the houses (some brick-built, some rough-cast, a few half-timbered, a few clad with tiles), Hampstead Garden Suburb certainly looked more picturesque and 'rural' than other suburbs of the same period. Perhaps the high-minded decision not to include shops was a mistake: the central square, though grand, can seem rather forbidding and the two vast churches there suggest a degree of moral finger-wagging. Nevertheless, the suburb proved popular from the start and a major extension was built in 1911–12. Where it failed was in its ambition to bring different social classes together. The Hampstead Garden Suburb Trust Ltd, which owned the land, worked in partnership with development companies that actually built the houses, and people who wanted to participate had to purchase a share in the scheme. The initial investment of £5 was well beyond most

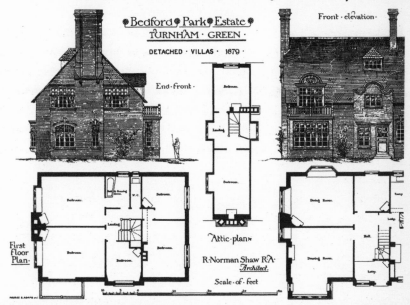

A detail from Norman Shaw's 1879 plans for a detached villa on the Bedford Park Estate in west London. This particular one is quite a grand affair, with five bedrooms, a bathroom and separate toilet and, downstairs, a dining room, drawing room, pantry, scullery, kitchen and toilet.

working-class people, and so from the start they were effectively excluded. Today it's one of the most expensive areas to live in the whole of London.

Hampstead Garden Suburb is probably the most famous of its type, but it was not the only garden suburb in London, nor indeed the earliest. That accolade goes to Bedford Park, in Acton, begun in 1876. Bedford Park was the work of speculative builder Jonathan T. Carr, who developed open land north of the District line at Turnham Green. His aim was to create comfortable dwellings a short journey from the City for the new, educated middle classes at an affordable price; and he employed a number of architects to create houses that were innovative and convenient, yet inexpensive. Quality of life was an important consideration. Instead of crowding the maximum number of houses on to his land, the new dwellings were set back from road and given space. The development included churches, shops, a club and even tennis courts, all designed to encourage a sense of community.

After Bedford Park came Brentham Garden Suburb near Pitshanger in Ealing. In 1901 Ealing became a municipal borough. Technically, it lay outside the metropolis (though within Middlesex), but so dramatic had its transformation been from largely rural to largely built-up that it was fast becoming part of London's spread, complete with new industry and excellent railway connections. Yet one stretch of land between Castlebar Hill and Hanger Hill remained undeveloped, and in the same year that Ealing achieved municipal borough status the land was chosen as the site for a social housing scheme under the auspices of the cooperative movement. Building was undertaken by Ebenezer Howard's cooperative building firm General Builders Ltd, a branch of which was located at Ealing. Members bought up land (to build the first nine houses) and a tenants' association, Ealing Tenants, was formed to continue the purchase process. By 1907 over 100 houses had been completed; and at the outbreak of the First World War in 1914 this had grown to over 600 houses, providing accommodation for 2,000 people. It was typical of nineteenth-century London – and of the Victorian mind – that such utopian schemes should exist alongside less carefully planned speculative ones built purely for profit.

All these new suburbs created their own life and momentum. They might have sprawled into one another, but they retained a certain village atmosphere, with their shops, small businesses, churches, chapels, libraries and places of entertainment. That said, many of their inhabitants preserved a relationship with the centre that went beyond the daily commute. You might shop locally most of the time, for example, but when it came to something a bit grander or more unusual the emporia of central London were the places to go. The shops of the West End continued to thrive, whether they were drapers such as D. H. Evans in Oxford Street (1879), or the trend-setting Liberty and Co. in Regent Street (1875) or the long-established Fortnum and Mason in Piccadilly or, just a few doors down, Hatchard's booksellers.

Central London also retained its magnetic power as the place to be entertained. West End theatres boomed, as did restaurants, clubs and bars and the nightlife that went with them. At a more exalted intellectual level, public museums and art galleries flourished in the middle of Victorian London. The British Museum, created in 1753 to accommodate the collection of physician, naturalist and Chelsea estate owner Sir Hans Sloane, and rebuilt on its Bloomsbury site after 1823, proved a popular draw. So, too, were the various museums founded in South Kensington in the years after the Great Exhibition of 1851; the Natural History Museum, for example, which was opened to the public in 1881, was so anxious that the working classes should come and view the amazing objects it possessed that it even took the then radical step of labelling the displays. The Museums Act of 1845 might have sought to establish a museum in every borough with a population of over 10,000, but its effect was limited. There were certainly museums and art galleries to be found in the suburbs – the Dulwich Picture Gallery, for example, established in 1811 – but they remained comparatively few and far between. If you wanted to see extensive collections you had to come to Bloomsbury, or South Kensington, or Pimlico (where the former Millbank Prison was demolished to make way for the Tate Gallery), or Trafalgar Square (where the National Gallery was established in 1838). Thanks to the wonders of modern transport, all were readily accessible.

That said, central London did not have it all its own way. Department stores, offering a range of different goods under one roof, started to sprout up in the mid-Victorian suburbs, appealing to people who wanted to do all their shopping in one place but who did not necessarily want to go all the way to Oxford Street. Westbourne Grove became home to William

Recreation in the suburbs: the Great Wheel at Earl's Court, c.1900.

Whiteley Limited in 1863, a great sprawling giant that boasted that it could supply everything 'from a pin to an elephant at short notice'. William Pearce Jones opened a shop in Holloway that by 1885 was selling everything from clothes to fancy goods to china and glass. Charles Harrod, the son of a tea merchant, took over a grocer's shop in Knightsbridge in 1849 and thought it might be a good idea to name it after himself. Kensington High Street became a shopper's paradise. Open-air entertainment was to be had in London's central parks, but it could also be found in the suburbs. Vauxhall Gardens may have finally succumbed to building developers in 1859 and Cremorne Gardens might have closed in the late 1870s (ultimately to be replaced by Lots Road power station), but towards the end of the century Earl's Court had its brief moment in the sun. The area had already been transformed by the arrival of the District line, when in 1887 the derelict land between the railway lines at Earl's Court came up for grabs, and the decision taken by J. R. Whitely was to transform it into an entertainment ground. The attractions he offered included a big wheel and helter-skelter, and he also engaged such spectaculars as Buffalo Bill's Wild West Show. All proved popular and so, like most popular things, inevitably won criticism from those who felt that the tone of the neighbourhood was under threat:

> [24 January 1899] These [exhibitions] have brought numbers of undesirable characters to the neighbourhood at night – the good people have gone & the lodging-house keepers come in their stead.[9]

Disapproval even extended to the 'Large number of foreigners employed & of their fondness for gambling, dancing & drinking after their work is done. They form clubs at once & are not particular about the admission of non-members.'[10]

The fairground continued to operate until the beginning of the First World War, the site ultimately being redeveloped as the Earl's Court Exhibition Centre in the 1930s. In many ways its appeal to the late Victorians and Edwardians aped that of Vauxhall Gardens and Cremorne Gardens decades before. However, there was a difference between the enterprises that encapsulated just how much London had changed in a very short period. Vauxhall and Cremorne Gardens had both been established in largely open countryside. Earl's Court enjoyed its glory days amid houses, shops and railway lines. Its visitors came not only from the immediate area or from central London but from all over the suburbs, drawn by the appeal of its big wheel and fairground attractions and brought by train or omnibus.

TEN

FEELING THE STRAIN
The Victorian Inner Suburbs

While London's burgeoning outer suburbs took some pressure off the centre, the inner suburbs nevertheless creaked under the strain of ever greater numbers. The populations of the City and Westminster may have declined in the course of the nineteenth century, but areas close to them continued to grow. Lambeth expanded from 34,135 people in 1801 to just over 131,000 in 1841, and reached 295,637 by 1881. Islington's numbers increased from 65,721 in 1801 to 162,717 in 1841 and 368,850 in 1881. Poplar similarly saw a jump in its population from 8,278 in 1801 to 31,122 in 1841 and 156,510 in 1881. Even the affluent twin villages of Kensington and Chelsea doubled from 22,088 in 1801 to 46,807 by 1841, reaching an extraordinary 247,725 by 1881.

When contemporary commentators talked about the worst of London, it was the worst of the inner suburbs that they invariably had in mind. Districts such as Shoreditch, Hackney, Lambeth and Bermondsey, all of which had once had their share of elegant houses and prosperous inhabitants, had since degenerated into grim slums. Bermondsey's Jacob's Island and Old Nichol Street in the East End had become notorious rookeries, riddled with poverty and crime. Saffron Hill, north of Holborn, was perhaps one of the worst. Once home to Elizabeth I's favourite Sir Christopher Hatton, who built himself a fine residence here, by the mid nineteenth century it was one of the most deprived areas in the capital. In Charles Dickens's *Oliver Twist* (1838) it is where Fagin's gang have their headquarters, in a decaying house where the staircase is broken and the walls and ceilings are black with age.

Various piecemeal attempts were made to deal with the worst of the slums. In the same year that *Oliver Twist* appeared, for example, the second report of the Select Committee on Metropolis Improvements recommended driving new streets through the worst areas:

> There are some districts in this vast city through which no great thor-
> oughfares pass, and which being wholly occupied by a dense population,
> composed of the lowest class of labourers, entirely secluded from the
> observation and influence of wealthier and better educated neighbours,
> exhibit a state of moral and physical degradation deeply to be deplored.[1]

The result of this was the construction of a new road, New Oxford Street, through Holborn and the St Giles rookery. At the same time the committee recommended taking in hand the Rose Lane and Essex Street area of Spitalfields and the 'Devil's Acre' behind Westminster Abbey.

The issue, however, was that such brutal redevelopment rarely did much to solve the problem; it simply moved it elsewhere. Those uprooted by the demolition of the St Giles rookery relocated a few streets away and crammed themselves into an even smaller area. By the late 1840s in nearby Church Lane up to eight people shared each room. Much disruption had been caused; little or no improvement had been effected. Slum clearance might have produced straighter streets, but it hadn't addressed the basic problem it had set out to solve.

Alongside these brutal schemes to demolish the slums, therefore, ones sprang up that had the more helpful aim of actually providing new houses

A typical Victorian slum.

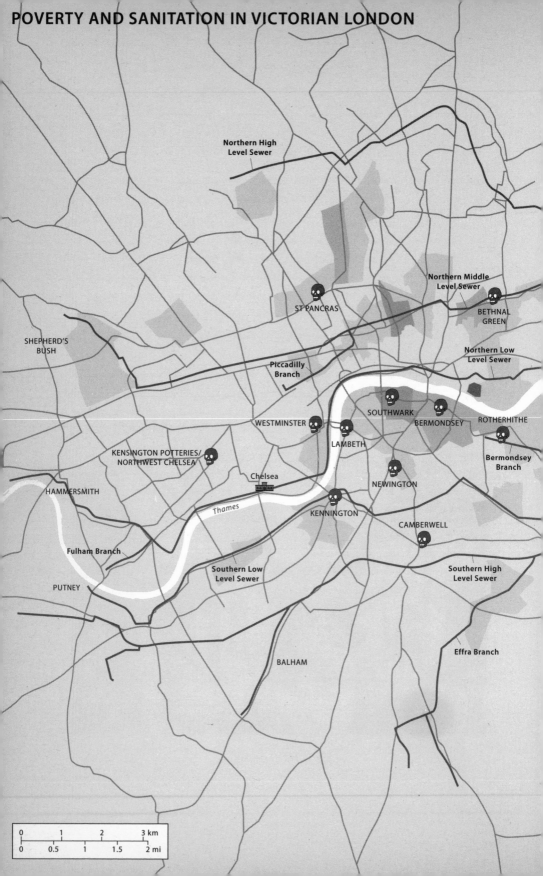

POVERTY AND SANITATION IN VICTORIAN LONDON

Northern High
Level Sewer

Northern Middle
Level Sewer

ST PANCRAS

BETHNAL
GREEN

SHEPHERD'S
BUSH

Northern Low
Level Sewer

Piccadilly
Branch

SOUTHWARK

WESTMINSTER

BERMONDSEY

ROTHERHITHE

LAMBETH

KENSINGTON POTTERIES/
NORTHWEST CHELSEA

Bermondsey
Branch

Chelsea

NEWINGTON

HAMMERSMITH

Thames

CAMBERWELL

Kennington

Fulham Branch

Southern Low
Level Sewer

Southern High
Level Sewer

PUTNEY

Effra Branch

BALHAM

| 0 | 1 | 2 | 3 km |

| 0 | 0.5 | 1 | 1.5 | 2 mi |

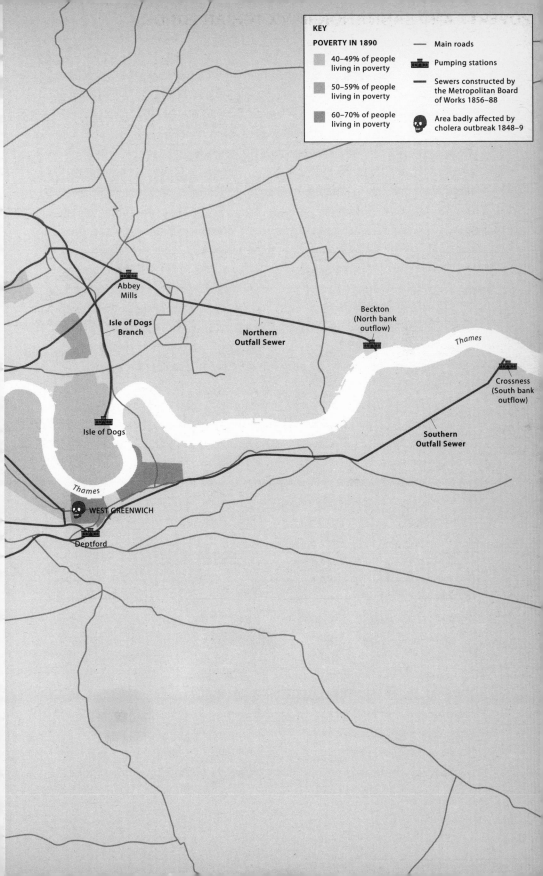

KEY

POVERTY IN 1890

40–49% of people living in poverty

50–59% of people living in poverty

60–70% of people living in poverty

Main roads

Pumping stations

Sewers constructed by the Metropolitan Board of Works 1856–88

Area badly affected by cholera outbreak 1848–9

Abbey Mills

Isle of Dogs Branch

Northern Outfall Sewer

Beckton (North bank outflow)

Thames

Crossness (South bank outflow)

Isle of Dogs

Southern Outfall Sewer

Thames

WEST GREENWICH

Deptford

for the poor. The first of these, backed by a whole army of Victorian luminaries, was set up by the Metropolitan Association for Improving the Dwellings of the Industrious Classes, formed in 1841. The Metropolitan Buildings in King's Cross was an impressive five-storey apartment block (now demolished) containing 121 flats, built under the supervision of the architect Henry Roberts (who went on to patent cheap, hollow bricks). Completed in 1848, it attracted visits from Dickens, William Gladstone and the Duke of Wellington, among others, and it proved so popular that shortly afterwards a second development was opened in Mile End New Town: this time a block of family flats, a lodging house for single men, and four terraces of cottages. Henry Roberts also designed buildings for the Society for Improving the Condition of the Labouring Classes, founded in 1844 with Prince Albert as its president, notably Streatham Street Buildings, now known as Parnell House, in Streatham Street, Bloomsbury, just to the north of New Oxford Street. Here again a five-storey block of flats went up in 1849, with balcony access built around a courtyard.

Individual philanthropists also became involved in providing housing for the poor. Of these, Sydney Waterlow was perhaps one of the most remarkable. The son of a small-scale stationer, he had followed in his father's footsteps and also become a printer, his great break coming towards the end of his apprenticeship when he was put in charge of printing for the Foreign Office. Thereafter his rise was swift. He took on various official posts (he was, for example, closely involved in the 1851 Great Exhibition), became an MP and was Mayor of London in 1872–3. Towards the end of his life he presented Lauderdale House in Highgate and its estate to the London County Council. In the midst of all this activity, he built at his own expense a block of working-class tenements for eighty families in Finsbury (1862), and the following year started the Improved Industrial Dwellings Company Ltd, remaining chairman until his death in 1907. The company went on to build a large number of model dwellings in Camden (including Derby Buildings and Stanley Buildings) and Poplar (Leopold Buildings, Tower Buildings), as well as in Camberwell and Westminster, and by the early twentieth century could claim to own 6,000 tenements and to have housed some 30,000 people. In the same period, the Artizans, Labourers and General Dwellings Company founded by William Austin in 1867 was similarly active on both sides of the Thames,

George Peabody was an American philanthropist who established a fund to finance the building of model dwellings for the London poor. This engraving shows the development in Peabody Square, Blackfriars Road.

in Streatham and Battersea to the south, and Kilburn, Wood Green and Pinner to the north.

However, the largest, and today best-known, enterprise was the Peabody Trust, set up in 1862 by American banker George Peabody. His ambition was, as he explained in a letter to *The Times*, to 'ameliorate the condition of the poor and needy of this great metropolis, and to promote their comfort and happiness' and he set out to achieve this with an initial gift of £150,000 – worth at least £7 million in today's money – to the Peabody Donation Fund. By the time he died in 1869 he had added another £350,000 to the trust's nest egg. With these considerable sums of money under its control, the Peabody Trust (as it came to be known) was able to create model dwellings throughout London, starting with the construction of property in Commercial Street, Spitalfields, in 1864 and moving on to multi-storey blocks in the poorer districts of Chelsea and Islington, in Bermondsey, Poplar, Stepney, Whitechapel and Westminster, and in various other inner London boroughs. By 1882 it had housed nearly 15,000 people in 3,500 buildings. As with other similar enterprises, it imposed a strict code of conduct on aspiring tenants. They were expected to be of good moral character. Paupers who would not work were excluded, and drunkenness was prohibited. Even the decor of the flats was regulated: tenants were not allowed to bang nails into the walls or hang wallpaper in case it encouraged or harboured vermin. A superintendent resided in each building to ensure the rules were kept.

Inevitably, however, these philanthropic enterprises, welcome though they were, were partial and scattergun. The problems faced by some areas of London – particularly the East End – were on such a scale that the occasional housing scheme was never going to be sufficient to address them. Tredegar Square to the north of Bow Road was helped a little by a scheme in the 1830s, for example, but the benefits didn't spread very far. It wasn't really until the 1880s and the foundation of the East End Dwellings Company in 1882 that the East End started to change; their first block of dwellings designed to be let by the room, Lolesworth Buildings, was completed in 1886–7. East European immigrants to the area were also helped a little by the establishment by Lord Rothschild in 1885 of the Four Per Cent Jewish Industrial Dwellings Company.

Towards the latter part of the century, therefore, the government, accepting that local and charitable endeavours were insufficient, felt obliged to step in. Its first major piece of legislation was the Artisans' and Labourers' Dwellings Act (1875), which authorised local authorities to purchase and demolish unfit housing – and also made sure that they then rehoused the former residents. Fifteen years later came the Housing for the Working Classes Act, which empowered the new London County Council and, after 1900, the metropolitan boroughs to sweep away the worst slums and create new housing schemes: tenements and newfangled blocks of flats that offered the maximum accommodation on the minimum amount of land. The Boundary Estate in Bethnal Green was one of the earliest council estates built under the terms of the Act, replacing the notorious Friars Mount slum, also known as the Old Nichol Street rookery.

Without doubt Friars Mount was one of the worst places in England, with appalling mortality rates and some 6,000 people crammed into a handful of streets, its grimness memorably captured by the journalist and novelist Arthur Morrison in *A Child of the Jago* (Jago being the name he

Photo Press.

Poverty was endemic in Victorian and Edwardian London.
Here, a group of needy people gathers outside a Salvation Army soup kitchen.

gave the slum), his 1896 novel about a child who lives and dies miserably there. At the time, some of Morrison's critics thought that he had made things up, or at the very least exaggerated how bad the slums were. 'The original of the Jago has, it is admitted, ceased to exist,' wrote the satirist Henry Duff Traill. 'But I will make bold to say that as described by Mr Morrison, it never did exist.'[2] Morrison, however, knew exactly what he was talking about. Although he lived in leafy Loughton in Essex, he had once been clerk to the Beaumont Trustees, a charitable trust that administered the People's Palace, an educational and cultural centre in Mile End. His fictionalised depiction of Friars Mount may be melodramatic, but the squalor and poverty it describes were all too real. Even today *A Child of the Jago* retains its power to shock:

> What was too vile for Kate Street, Seven Dials, and Ratcliffe Highway in its worst day, what was too useless, incapable and corrupt – all that teemed on the Old Jago . . .
>
> On the pavement some writhed wearily, longing for sleep; others, despairing of it, sat and lolled, and a few talked. They were not there for

lack of shelter, but because in this weather repose was less unlikely in the street than within doors: and the lodgings of the few who nevertheless abode at home were marked here and there by the lights visible from the windows. For in this place none ever slept without a light, because of three kinds of vermin that light in some sort keeps at bay: vermin which added to existence here a terror not to be guessed by the unafflicted: who object to being told of it. For on them that lay writhen and gasping on the pavement; on them that sat among them; on them that rolled and blasphemed in the lighted rooms; on every moving creature in this, the Old Jago, day and night, sleeping and walking, the third plague of Egypt [i.e. lice], and more, lay unceasing.[3]

Demolition of the rookery began in 1890, and ten years later the new buildings – providing accommodation for a number equivalent to that of the population of the old slum – were opened by the Prince of Wales. By that time, many of those for whom the new development had been intended had migrated further into the East End towards Dalston, their place taken by new arrivals from overseas, in particular thousands of Jewish immigrants fleeing persecution in Eastern Europe. Many of those who had remained behind found the rents on the new flats too high for their budgets, and so went off to find slum accommodation elsewhere.

That bad housing and poverty remained major problems in late Victorian London is immediately apparent in Charles Booth's seminal and ambitious *Inquiry into the Life and Labour of the People in London*, undertaken between 1886 and 1903. Written at a time when people were starting to adopt a more scientific approach to social research, it was based on evidence compiled by an army of researchers: volunteers from Toynbee Hall (a champion of social reform situated in the East End), policemen on the beat, School Board visitors, and others. Famously, it used colour-coded maps to show the relative poverty – or affluence – of different parts of London. Black represented:

> . . . the lowest class which consists of some occasional labourers, street sellers, loafers, criminals and semi-criminals. Their life is the life of savages, with vicissitudes of extreme hardship and their only luxury drink.

Red, by contrast, represented:

> . . . the lower middle class; shopkeepers and small employers, clerks and
> subordinate professional men; a hardworking sober, energetic class.[4]

Moreover, as today, what the maps revealed was that wealth and poverty
often existed cheek by jowl. Streets in Hoxton and between the West
India Dock Road and Gill Street in Limehouse, for example, were classed
as among the poorest in London, yet West India Dock Road itself was
deemed to be lower middle class. Moreover, as today, the fortunes of an
area were subject to fluctuation:

> [18 October 1898] Blackheath Village has changed . . . during the past 10
> or 12 years from a sleepy little village to a busy . . . centre. The few
> working people living here are persons dependent on the large houses or
> shops and are a local colony – gardeners etc. Except a couple of laun-
> dries in Blackheath Vale and a few livery stables there are few centres of
> employment.[5]

> [June 1899] The story of Lambeth in the last 10 years is a story of
> worsement. The fairly comfortable have left & are leaving. The poor
> remain & additional poor are coming in. The effect of cheap trams &
> cheap railway fares is most marked in this area. Brixton & Stockwell
> have claimed the mechanic & artisan, while the labourer remains here &
> his ranks are reinforced by displacements in Westminster across the
> river.[6]

Islington was another case in point. A desirable area in the eighteenth
century, with its tea gardens and fine houses, it started to slide as the
railways brought ever more industry and ever greater numbers of people
to the area. Elegant eighteenth-century houses gradually became ramshackle,
multi-occupation nineteenth-century homes. In George Gissing's novel
about literary London, *New Grub Street* (1891), a move to Islington even
manages to precipitate the end of a marriage. The aspiring novelist Edwin
Reardon, who starts out in a garret near Tottenham Court Road, achieves
a small measure of success that allows him to move into a top-floor flat
(eight flights of stairs up) in the Marylebone area when he marries:

> A sitting-room, a bedroom, a kitchen. But the kitchen was called
> dining-room, or even parlour at need; for the cooking-range lent itself

to concealment behind an ornamental screen, the walls displayed pictures
and bookcases, and a tiny scullery which lay apart sufficed for the
coarser domestic operations.

When things start to go wrong, however, he realises that he and his wife,
Amy, will have to move, and in one of the most painful chapters in the
novel he tells her that he has decided on Islington:

> . . . for the present we are poor people, and must live in a poor way. If
> our friends like to come and see us, they must put aside all snobbish-
> ness, and take us as we are. If they prefer not to come, there'll be an
> excuse in our remoteness.[7]

Amy is horrified, and even more outraged when Edwin threatens
Whitechapel as an alternative. She refuses to go with him and their
relationship collapses.

Although the local pattern is complex, it is possible to make some
generalisations about the relative location of wealth and poverty in the
inner suburbs. As a rule the West End was generally home to wealthier
white-collar workers. By contrast, Stepney, Whitechapel, Limehouse and
Wapping in the East End, and Bermondsey and Southwark across the
river, were among London's poorest inner suburbs. Camberwell, for
example, once a farming village with a green, an August fair (suppressed
in 1855) and a sprinkling of fine Georgian houses, was also home to
grinding poverty. Describing it in 1912, Walter Besant did not pull his
punches:

> This neighbourhood has always had a bad reputation, the murderer
> Greenacre [who murdered a washerwoman, cut her up and disposed of
> her remains around London] having lived here in 1836, and to-day the
> streets off Crown Street are crowded with the vicious and poverty-
> stricken classes. Costers, hawkers, and labourers herd together in dirty
> streets which swarm with neglected children.[8]

———— ◄ • ► ————

A Child of the Jago isolates the three things that went hand in hand with
poverty in Victorian London: filth, disease and crime. Of these it was
filth, and the disease that went with it, that proved most deadly. Moreover,

both problems were on such a scale that they extended well beyond the slums. Poor-quality water was to be found throughout the inner suburbs. As for London's sewage systems, they were totally inadequate to cope with the demands of what was by now an imperial capital. The drainage network ultimately dated back to the time of the Roman empire, and made use of the area's natural watercourses: Stamford Brook, the Westbourne, the Tyburn and the Fleet to the north of the Thames; and the Wandle, Ravensbourne and Effra to the south. As the centuries passed, these open streams were gradually covered over, becoming filthy in the process and prone to harbouring disease. Just how dangerous they could be is demonstrated by a disaster that occurred during a violent storm on the afternoon of Saturday, 1 August 1846, when fetid gases from the Fleet built up to such an extent that they caused an explosion of sewage that swept away three houses in Clerkenwell. A contemporary account vividly describes what happened:

> The Fleet ditch, which was then carried to the second arch of
> Blackfriars Bridge through a drain formed of strong iron plates, blew up
> with a tremendous explosion . . . [and] being surcharged flowed into
> most of the cellars and underground apartments on the west side of
> Farringdon Street, and a linen-draper had upwards of £3000 worth of
> goods destroyed or damaged. In the lower parts of Clerkenwell, where
> the sewer was open, the effects of the flood were of most disastrous
> character. In the valley formed by the descent of Brook-hill and the
> opposite acclivity of Vine Street, great damage occurred. In Bull's Head
> Court, Peter Street, the water rose five feet, completely filling the under-
> ground rooms, and sweeping cattle and furniture away. Three houses in
> Round Court, Brook-hill, inhabited by many poor families, were partly
> carried away, and with great difficulty the inmate escaped. A warehouse
> belonging to a dry salter had one front washed away. The house of
> correction was under water to a depth of several feet; and the entire
> space at Acton Place, Bagnigge Wells Road, to King's Cross, was
> flooded to a depth that prevented the inhabitants leaving or entering
> their dwellings . . .[9]

The fact is that nineteenth-century London was drowning in human waste. The city's natural streams apart, all that the city had to offer were drains, culverts and clay pipes, often dating back to medieval times.

Among the most squalid – and dangerous – occupations open to the London poor was that of the tosher, who scoured the sewers for items of value.

However, they had been designed to receive surface water and discharge it safely into the Thames, not cope with foul-smelling, thick sewage. Other sanitary measures had been taken over the centuries, but none was sufficient to deal with the sheer quantity of excrement that Victorian Londoners produced.

The most widely adopted approach to waste was to store it in local cesspools, of which there were up to 200,000 in London by 1800. These would be emptied from time to time by 'rakers', 'night soil men' or 'gong fermors', who would then sell the waste to farmers in the outlying areas of London to fertilise their fields. However, cesspools brought with them their own set of problems: they were generally badly maintained and they frequently leaked. Edwin Chadwick's *Report on the Sanitary Condition of the Labouring Population of Great Britain* (1842) was just one report that sought to highlight their deficiencies, describing how overflowing sewage often seeped into the streets. Moreover, as London expanded, and farmland became built over, rakers were forced to travel further afield to find a market for their raw sewage. Their prices for emptying cesspools rose accordingly, and cesspool clearing became a luxury rather than a necessity. Rising costs highlighted a class element when it came to the disposal of London's filth. The rich of the West End, in their spacious houses, could afford to be parted from their waste; the poor of the East End, crammed together and with no means of disposal, had to live with theirs. Soon sewage began to accumulate in the streets, while cesspools overflowed or were dug so deep that their contents leaked into the underground water supply. To make matters worse, under pressure from water companies and residents alike, local authorities removed statutory prohibition on dumping effluent into the sewers or into the Thames.

Ironically, the gradual introduction after 1810 of the water closet, which removed the need for cesspools altogether, actually made a bad situation much worse. Because water closets were connected directly to the sewer network, raw sewage increasingly made its way straight into London's water system. By 1855 a correspondent in the *Lancet* was painting a very grim picture indeed:

> The waters are swollen with the feculence of the myriads of living beings that dwell upon the banks, and with the waste of every manufacture that is too foul for utilisation. Wheresoever we go, whatsoever we eat or drink within the circle of London, we find tainted with the Thames . . . No one having eyes, nose or taste, can look upon the Thames and not be convinced that its waters are, year by year, and day by day, getting fouler and more pestilential . . . The abominations, the corruptions we pour into the Thames, are not, as some falsely say, carried away into the sea. The sea rejects the loathsome tribute, and heaves it back again with every flow. Here, in the heart of the doomed city, it accumulates and destroys.[10]

It's scarcely surprising that whereas London in earlier times was characterised by the plague, London in the nineteenth century was characterised by cholera. Arriving from India in 1831, the first outbreak devastated East London during the winter of 1831–2, and then returned several times in the 1840s on a regular basis, killing thousands across the metropolis. The riverside suburbs of Southwark and Vauxhall were

among the worst affected areas, but cholera proved fairly undiscrimi-
nating about where it chose to break out. One hundred and fifty boys
at a pauper establishment in Tooting died from the disease in 1845. In
1846 the district medical officer for Hammersmith noted that cholera
was rife in the poorer slums in the district. In 1847 there was an outbreak
in leafy Harrow, and the 'Piggeries and Potteries' of Notting Dale in
Kensington were affected the following year. In 1849, cholera raged
from Uxbridge in the west to Ilford in the east. Indeed, the devastation
of the outbreak in Ilford was so great that an orphanage had to be
established in distant Richmond, while the citizens of Uxbridge were
so horrified by the pestilence that had hit their town that they became
the first to petition Parliament for an inquiry into the causes of the
disease.

Some idea of just how appalling the 1848–9 outbreak was – and just
how bad the conditions that engendered it could be – is provided in a
report prepared for the General Board of Health. In this passage, the
researcher describes what they saw when they visited Christopher Court,
Rosemary Lane, in Whitechapel:

Limehouse, one of the poorest areas of
Victorian London, in the 1870s.

The court is a cul-de-sac; the entrance is narrow, and covered over by the houses in Rosemary Lane; at the upper end is a large dust hole, full of filth of every description. Out of the inhabitants, 60 in number, 13, or 21%, were attached with cholera. There were, on the first floor of one house, 8 cases of cholera, of which 3 were fatal; the door at the foot of the stairs was shut, and on opening it I was repeatedly driven back by the horrid odour and stench from a privy down stairs. This was one of the dirtiest places which human beings ever visited; the stench, the horrible stench which polluted the place, seemed to be closed in hermetically among the people; not a breath of fresh air reached them, all was abominable. After getting up stairs my head reeled in the sickening atmosphere; and on reaching the top, and surrounded by the dead and dying, I was compelled to rush to the window and open it. I threw off the contents of my stomach, and supported myself on the miserable, rotten straw bed . . . In the same court, on the opposite side, were several cases of cholera. In one house, on the ground floor, were three cases; the smell from the privy down stairs was fearful, and it required some courage to go down and search for the plague spot. I found the privy overflowing directly below the beds of sick persons, and the cellar containing an immense quantity of excrement, bones, urine and straw. The worst sewer in London could not have been more dangerous to life.[11]

Making the connection between cholera and polluted water took time and, as ever in the history of London reform, involved not just research but politics. Powerful interest groups existed to argue for the status quo, not least London's water companies, who were outraged that anyone should think the problem lay with them. When, for example, in 1828 a parliamentary committee investigating pollution in the Thames called in Dr Pearson to given evidence on behalf of the Grand Union Junction, they came up against an impressively worded denial of blame:

It will be easily imaginable, that the impregnating ingredients of the Thames' water are as perfectly harmless as any spring water of the purest kind used in common life, indeed, there is probably not a spring, with the exception of Malvern, and one or two more, which are so pure as the Thames' water.[12]

As the problem grew worse, so did some semblance of a sense of urgency, but so, too, did the endless infighting. The social reformer Edwin Chadwick, who joined the newly formed Metropolitan Commission of Sewers for London in 1848, had very clear ideas about what was causing the problem ('miasma') and what to do about it (install self-flushing earthenware pipes that, ideally, would convey waste straight to farmers' fields). His plans, however, antagonised many engineers; he had a nervous breakdown in 1849, and had to be removed from the commission. Others had equally strong ideas, which were equally misguided. It was not until five years later that Dr John Snow correctly identified the link between cholera and a polluted water supply when he noted that those suffering from an outbreak of the disease in Broad Street, Soho, had all bottled and drunk water from one particular public water pump – and that the outbreak stopped when he persuaded the local authorities to remove the handle from the pump. Even so, he had a battle on his hands before his arguments carried the day.

The commission was finally disbanded in 1854, and the following year saw the passing of a major piece of legislation, the Metropolis Management Act. This effectively paved the way for the creation of London-wide government for the inner and outer suburbs and the City, establishing a second tier of local government to undertake public service works based on the civil parish vestry system, with some parishes merged into district boards. In total some thirty-nine vestries or districts were created in parts of Middlesex, Surrey and Kent to cover the inner suburbs, each sending at least one representative to serve on the newly constituted Metropolitan Board of Works. The Metropolitan Board was also granted the power to raise funds to improve sanitation across the metropolis through local taxation in the form of sewer rates (some of the money being used to build a headquarters in Spring Gardens).

That ought to have been that, but inevitably skulduggery and political manoeuvring dogged the early days of the Metropolitan Board of Works. Its engineer, Joseph Bazalgette, was confident that he knew what needed to be done, but his efforts were constantly thwarted by Sir Benjamin Hall, the government's chief commissioner of works, who twice got him to modify his plans for a new sewage network and then called in various rival engineers to make counter-suggestions. New Year's Day 1858 dawned, and still nothing had been agreed upon.

It was the Thames itself that finally broke the deadlock, achieving a level of pollution in the summer of that year that no one could ignore and that led Charles Dickens to write:

I have to cross Waterloo or London Bridge to get to the railroad when I come down here, and I can certify that the offensive smells, even in that short whiff, have been of a most head-and-stomach-distending nature.[13]

This was the year of 'The Great Stink' when Parliament, sitting in the newly rebuilt Palace of Westminster, and having failed to block out the smell with curtains coated with slaked lime, decided that the only option was to suspend itself. It was therefore also the year when Parliament decided to break the impasse between Sir Benjamin Hall and Joseph Bazalgette and to award the funds necessary to bring the plans of the Metropolitan Board's engineer to fruition.

Bazalgette's plan was both astonishingly ambitious and very simple. He designed a sewer network that ran on either side of and parallel to

Perhaps the greatest achievement of the Metropolitan Board of Works was the creation of a new system of sewers for London. Shown here is the pumping station at Abbey Mills, designed with an elegance that belies its function.

the Thames, flowing from Shepherd's Bush and Hammersmith on the north side of the river and Putney and Balham on the south side to northern and southern outfall sewers, which carried London's waste eastward and ultimately discharged their contents into the river. The Northern Outfall was constructed at Beckton, on the west side of Barking Creek, while on the south bank the Southern Outfall was placed at Crossness, near Plumstead. Both were located well away from the City and the main suburbs. Those who lived in London were delighted; those who lived near the outfalls were probably less so, though there were benefits as well as drawbacks: at Beckton, local farmer Joe Morton took up where the old 'night soil men' had left off and began processing the new, plentiful sewage into manure, turning a handy profit in the process and proving that where there's muck, there's brass.

Construction work on the sewers was dangerous to residents and workers alike. Many of the tunnels disrupted street foundations, causing houses to collapse; and flooding was a constant menace. Accidents were commonplace, such as the one reported here in *The Times* from 28 April 1863:

> Yesterday morning a fatal accident happened at the main drainage works now in progress at Deptford. A deep cutting for the sewer nearly 50ft in depth, passes near the Deptford railway station, through some gardens between Griffin Street and the south side of the Greenwich line. The work had proceeded to within a few yards of Church Street, and a number of navigators were employed in the cutting at a depth of 35ft. About 7 o'clock, without the least warning, some of the soil at the back of the cutting began to slip, which causing an unequal pressure on the side supports, the timbers gave way, and great masses of earth fell from the two sides and front of the excavations right down upon 8 men who were at work beneath. Two of them escaped unhurt; 3 were injured, though not seriously. The remaining 3 were covered under the mass of timber and earth.

Once the disruption was out of the way, though, the new system transformed the health of Londoners as well as the look of London. Bazalgette's Victoria and Albert Embankments, constructed to house the interceptor sewers and channel the flow of the Thames more effectively, changed the flow of the river for ever, narrowing it and allowing new parks, roads and even underground stations to be planned and built along its new banks. The Metropolitan Board of Works' remit also included the maintenance and management of streets and bridges, and it took steps to remove tolls from the bridges across the Thames as well as rebuilding four of them: Putney Bridge, Battersea Bridge, Waterloo Bridge and Hammersmith Bridge. The Board also actively engaged in a partial slum clearance programme, and drove new streets through the centre of town – Charing Cross Road, Garrick Street, Northumberland Avenue and Shaftesbury Avenue, among them – in an attempt to ease traffic congestion.

As what came out of human bodies was more safely disposed of, so what went in was greatly improved. At the time London awoke to the perils of its polluted river, the supply of fresh water was in the hands of nine private water companies, each with a geographical monopoly. Regulation, however, was tightened and standards were more rigidly imposed under the terms of the 1852 Metropolis Water Act. This forbade any water to be taken from the tidal reaches of the Thames, and demanded that drinking water should be properly filtered. The result was a further transformation in London's landscape, as companies set about founding reservoirs and filtration plants in the outer river-based suburbs. The Southwark and Vauxhall Water Company, for example, established a reservoir at Hampton (now the Sunnyside Reservoir); the Chelsea Waterworks Company built a water treatment plant at Seething Wells near Surbiton; and the East London Waterworks Company constructed a string of reservoirs around Walthamstow, in the Lea Valley.

Another physical reminder of the way in which Victorian London finally got to grips with its water supply is the fountains and the drinking troughs for horses and cattle still scattered all over London, put there by the Metropolitan Drinking Fountain and Cattle Trough Association. Founded in 1859 as the Metropolitan Free Drinking Association by the MP Samuel Gurney, the aim of the organisation was 'that no fountain be erected or promoted by the Association which shall not be so constructed as to ensure by filters, or other suitable means, the perfect purity and coldness of the water'. Its achievement was to provide

*Attempts to improve London's water supply included the provision
of fountains and cattle troughs. This photograph was taken in
Barnet High Street around 1900.*

drinkable water for free. The first fountain was opened on Holborn Hill,
and soon over 7,000 people were using it each day. By the late 1870s
most places had a drinking fountain, prompting Charles Dickens Jnr
to write in 1879:

> Until the last few years London was ill-provided with public drinking
> fountains and cattle troughs. This matter is now well looked after by the
> Metropolitan Drinking Fountain and Cattle Trough Association, which
> has erected and is now maintaining nearly 800 fountains and troughs, at
> which an enormous quantity of water is consumed daily. It is estimated
> that 300,000 people take advantage of the fountains on a summer's day,
> and a single trough has supplied the wants of 1,800 horses in one period
> of 24 hours.[14]

Examples of these fountains can be seen today in Wilmington Square in Clerkenwell, in Sloane Square, Finsbury Circus and Surrey Quays, and many other places. Cattle troughs, too, are to be found as far apart as North Street in Horsham and Lauriston Road in Hackney, though they no longer serve their original purpose and are more likely today to be filled with flowers. All tell us that if Victorian London could be grim, it also espoused good causes, urban improvement and philanthropy. They also demonstrate that the Victorians were waking up to the fact that areas of southern England which had once seemed quite separate from each other now needed to be regarded as a single entity.

ELEVEN

ESSENTIAL SERVICES

Victorian Londoners from Cradle to Grave

Until late in the Victorian era the impact of local and central government on the lives of Londoners was intermittent and partial, and often based far more on the principle of the stick than the carrot. There were institutions for apprehending and punishing criminals and discouraging the poor from being poor. There were stocks and lock-ups in which convicted felons could be subjected to public ridicule, and gibbets on which the corpses of the executed could be exposed to public gaze. Health care, on the other hand, was piecemeal, education of the metropolis's children erratic, and help for those genuinely in need patchy.

Change – in attitudes to social issues and in views about how best to tackle social problems – was slow in coming. When it did come, however, it took a similar course in each area of Londoners' lives. Local approaches gradually gave way to more centralised and considered ones, and in the process London came to be viewed, not as a few square miles centred on the Thames, but as a vast metropolitan entity of city streets and suburban sprawl.

What happened to education in Victorian London is perhaps the most remarkable case in point. At the beginning of Victoria's reign the capital and the villages around it contained a ramshackle network of private, church and charity schools, both good and bad. By the end of the century, however, something approaching a centrally driven educational system for all was starting to emerge. Moreover, it was a system which, under the auspices of the London School Board, had a very broad geographical remit indeed.

For much of Queen Victoria's reign, education was a prerogative of the better off, as indeed it had been for centuries. Furthermore, it was a largely male preserve. One of the commissioners involved in a government inquiry in the 1860s made it clear that, in his view, boys were educated for the world and girls for the drawing room. Boys, in other words, were expected to train for jobs, and girls for marriage:

> Parents who have daughters will always look to their being provided for
> in marriage, will always believe that the gentler graces and winning
> qualities of character will be their best passports to marriage, and will
> always expect their husbands to take on themselves the intellectual toil
> and the active exertions needed for the support of the family.[1]

Middle- and upper-class London girls tended to be educated at home by governesses until they were ten, might then go to a day school for a few years, and could even end up at a boarding school or finishing school, leaving at seventeen. Lower-middle-class girls would probably complete their education by fifteen. For both groups the emphasis was as much on domestic 'accomplishments' as academic achievement. Middle- and upper-class boys, by contrast, received a more thoroughgoing education and, for the well-to-do, there were a number of schools in and around Victorian London that they might attend. Harrow is among the best known. Founded by a wealthy farmer during Elizabeth I's reign, it was originally designed to provide free education for local boys. Increasingly, however, it took on fee-paying 'foreigners' (boys from outside the parish), who by the mid Victorian era greatly outnumbered the local children. The novelist Anthony Trollope, whose father lived near the school and who was therefore able to gain a free place, later recalled the snobbery displayed by those whose parents paid to those whose parents did not:

> My two elder brothers had been sent as day-boarders to Harrow School
> from the bigger house, and may probably have been received among the
> aristocratic crowd, – not on equal terms, because a day-boarder at
> Harrow in those days was never so received, – but at any rate as other
> day-boarders. I do not suppose that they were well treated, but I doubt
> whether they were subjected to the ignominy which I endured. I was
> only seven, and I think that boys at seven are now spared among their
> more considerate seniors. I was never spared; and was not even allowed

VICTORIAN LONDONERS FROM CRADLE TO GRAVE

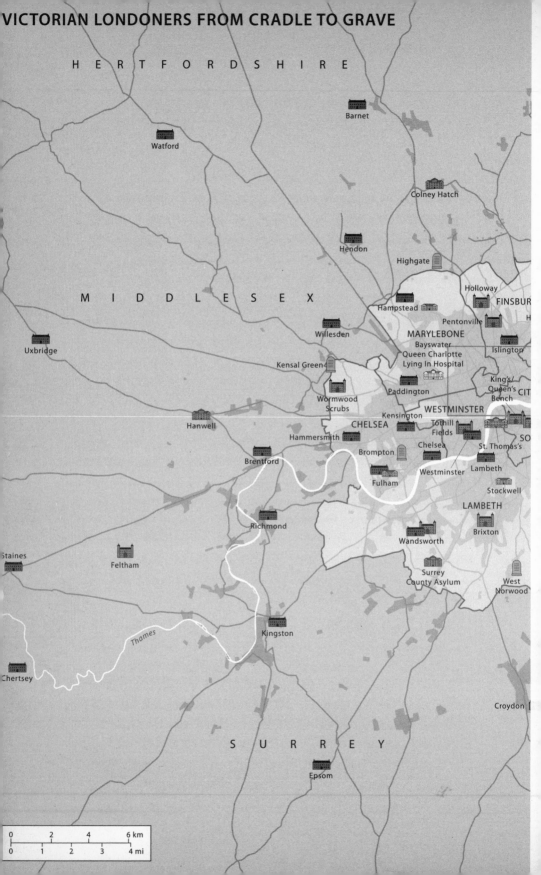

HERTFORDSHIRE

Barnet

Watford

Colney Hatch

Hendon

Highgate

MIDDLESEX

Holloway

Hampstead

FINSBUR

Pentonville

Willesden

Uxbridge

Bayswater

MARYLEBONE

Islington

Kensal Green

Queen Charlotte
Lying In Hospital

Paddington

King's/
Queen's
Bench

CIT

Wormwood
Scrubs

WESTMINSTER

SO

Hanwell

Kensington

WESTMINSTER

Tothill
Fields

CHELSEA

Hammersmith

Chelsea

St. Thomas's

Brompton

Lambeth

Brentford

Westminster

Fulham

Stockwell

LAMBETH

Richmond

Wandsworth

Brixton

Feltham

Staines

Surrey
County Asylum

West
Norwood

Kingston

Thames

Chertsey

Croydon

SURREY

Epsom

0	2	4	6 km
0	1	2	3	4 mi

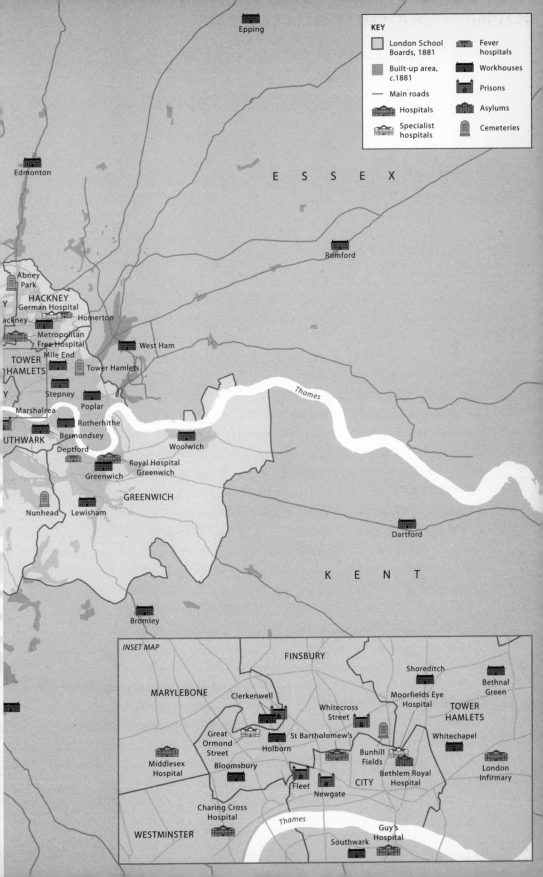

KEY

London School Boards, 1881	Fever hospitals
Built-up area, c.1881	Workhouses
Main roads	Prisons
Hospitals	Asylums
Specialist hospitals	Cemeteries

Epping

ESSEX

Romford

Edmonton

Abney Park

HACKNEY
German Hospital
Hackney Homerton
Metropolitan Free Hospital
Mile End
TOWER HAMLETS
Tower Hamlets
Stepney
Marshalsea
Poplar
Rotherhithe
Bermondsey
SOUTHWARK
Deptford
Woolwich

West Ham

Thames

Royal Hospital Greenwich
Greenwich
GREENWICH
Nunhead Lewisham

Dartford

KENT

Bromley

INSET MAP

FINSBURY

MARYLEBONE
Clerkenwell
Shoreditch
Moorfields Eye Hospital
Bethnal Green
TOWER HAMLETS
Whitecross Street
Great Ormond Street
Holborn
St Bartholomew's
Whitechapel
Middlesex Hospital
Bloomsbury
Fleet
Newgate
Bunhill Fields
CITY
Bethlem Royal Hospital
London Infirmary
Charing Cross Hospital
WESTMINSTER
Thames
Southwark
Guy's Hospital

to run to and fro between our house and the school without a daily purgatory. No doubt my appearance was against me. I remember well, when I was still the junior boy in the school, Dr. Butler, the head-master, stopping me in the street, and asking me, with all the clouds of Jove upon his brow and the thunder in his voice, whether it was possible that Harrow School was disgraced by so disreputably dirty a boy as I! Oh, what I felt at that moment! But I could not look my feelings. I do not doubt that I was dirty; – but I think that he was cruel. He must have known me had he seen me as he was wont to see me, for he was in the habit of flogging me constantly. Perhaps he did not recognise me by my face.[2]

Other schools similarly offered free places to able students: Westminster School, for example, held an open competition for Queen's Scholars in June and July each year. Yet even these schemes involved an element of cost for the parents of would-be pupils. The fixed expenses for a Queen's Scholar, for example, were some £30 in the late nineteenth century, according to Charles Dickens Jnr's *London Guide* of 1888 – a sum sufficient to deter anyone who did not have access to quite a little spare cash.

For the children of all but the most affluent or most fortunate Londoners, therefore, such well-known establishments as Harrow, Dulwich and Westminster would be out of the question. So, too, most likely, would be the numerous schools run by entrepreneurs and educa-tionalists, such as the progressive Bruce Castle School in Tottenham, set up by the founder of the Penny Post, Rowland Hill, in 1827, or the private school in Sunbury where Anthony Trollope was sent by his father when he left Harrow. Instead, education for those of middle-class birth and below, if it was available at all, was a far more hit-and-miss affair. Those whose parents could afford it might be sent in their early years to a dame school, of which there were perhaps 3,000 operating in London by 1819, but these were little more than childminding services operated in their own homes by women who might or might not have had some formal education themselves and who might or might not therefore be able to teach basic reading, writing and arithmetic, as well as such practical skills as sewing and knitting. Otherwise, the education of the moderately well off relied on small private schools of often dubious quality (as the novels of Charles Dickens testify), while the education of the poor depended heavily on acts of charity, offered by those with deeply held religious beliefs.

The Hornsey-born Samuel Wilderspin was one such man. In 1820 he and his wife were invited to run an infants' school for two- to six-year-olds in Spitalfields, and there he wrote his work *On the Importance of Educating the Infant Children of the Poor*, in which he upheld education as a means of helping the poor and preventing crime. He brought an evangelical zeal to what he regarded as an essentially Christian mission, teaching some 165 children, many of whom came to school unfed, dirty and without shoes. In Walthamstow, meanwhile, the Revd William Wilson was similarly inspired to found the Walthamstow Infants' School, run on similar lines. Other similarly high-minded individuals were to be found scattered across nineteenth-century London.

Christian ideals also underpinned the Ragged Schools, designed for the poorest of the poor and supported by such leading evangelicals as the Earl of Shaftesbury, who chaired the London Ragged School Union. Their grand ambition was to 'rescue from vice, and misery, and crime in this world, and from ruin in the world to come, those who have no parents',[3] and their work therefore involved taking abandoned and home-less children from the streets, feeding and clothing them, and then providing them with basic education. By 1850 there were some eighty-two of these schools, located in some of the grimmest areas of London: Pye

*A Ragged School in Smithfield as depicted by
George Cruikshank in 1844.*

Street, near Westminster Abbey; Thrawl Street in Spitalfields; and Lisson Grove in Marylebone. All were well attended and all won plaudits from contemporaries, not least Charles Dickens, who, despite his innate suspicion of Christian do-gooders, was impressed by the dedication shown by their staff, describing his visit to Field Lane Ragged School, near Holborn, in September 1843 in the following admiring terms:

> The school is miserably poor, you may believe, and is almost entirely supported by the teachers themselves. If they could get a better room (the house they are in, is like an ugly dream); above all, if they could provide some convenience for washing; it would be an immense advantage. The moral courage of the teachers is beyond all praise. They are surrounded by every possible adversity, and every disheartening circumstance that can be imagined. Their office is worthy of the apostles.[4]

Field Lane not only had a Ragged School, but also contained a linked industrial school, which provided training for sixty destitute boys under the age of fourteen (the school was eventually demolished by the Metropolitan Board of Works in 1877 to make way for its 'improvements' to the area). Another significant Ragged School in a tough area was the one founded in 1877 by Thomas Barnardo in three former canal-side buildings on Copperfield Road near the Grand Union Canal at Mile End. For the next thirty or so years, until it closed in 1908, the school catered for thousands of children. Today it houses the Ragged School Museum.

Both the extent and the limitations of such charitable endeavours are reflected in the pages of Henry Mayhew's huge survey *London Labour and the London Poor*, published in 1851. On the one hand, he was able to track down a fair number of children who were spending perhaps a couple of hours a week at a Ragged School and were picking up just enough to be able to read and write a little. As Mayhew noted, they might still be frighteningly ignorant about the wider world, but they were often smart – and very good at any mental arithmetic that involved money. What's more, thanks to the Ragged Schools, there were many more of these comparatively educated street children than there had been a decade or so before:

Perhaps it may be sufficiently correct to say that among a given number of street children, where, a dozen years ago, you met twenty who could read, you will now meet upwards of thirty. Of sixteen children, none apparently fifteen years of age, whom I questioned on the subject, nine admitted that they could not read; the other seven declared that they could, but three annexed to the avowal the qualifying words – 'a little'. Ten were boys and six were girls, and I spoke to them promiscuously as I met them in the street. Two were Irish lads, who were 'working' oranges in company, and the bigger answered – 'Shure, thin, we can rade [read], your honour, sir.' I have little doubt that they could, but in all probability, had either of those urchins thought he would be a penny the better by it, he would have professed, to a perfect stranger, that he had a knowledge of algebra. 'Yis, sir, I do, thin,' would very likely be his response to any such inquiry; and when told he could not possibly know anything about it, he would answer, 'Arrah, thin, but I didn't understand your honour.'[5]

On the other hand, there were still children who slipped through every safety net in sight. One such that Mayhew interviewed was a fatherless and shoeless nine-year-old mudlark, who searched the filth along the Thames's banks looking for discarded items he might be able to sell. He told Mayhew that although he had once been to school he couldn't remember anything about it. He certainly couldn't read or write. He knew that he lived in London but wasn't sure where England was – perhaps it was in London?

Just as the Ragged Schools were religiously motivated, so more formal education for the less well off was largely spearheaded by the Church of England. In 1811, for example, the National Society for Promoting Religious Education was formed – or more precisely, the National Society for Promoting the Education of the Poor in the Principles of the Established Church in England and Wales. Its religious and moral ambition was more than summed up in its name; its practical ambition was to set up a school in every parish, usually close to the church and adopting the principles of Dr Andrew Bell's 'monitorial' system – whereby a schoolmaster taught older, more able children, who then acted as tutors for younger children. The London region soon became dotted with new school buildings that offered the chance for people from lower classes of society to receive a basic education – reading, writing and arithmetic. Inevitably they didn't find favour with everyone. Many poor parents required their children to bring in money, not to absorb learning. Many higher up the social scale shared their view, fearing that education might give the children of the working classes ideas above their station.

By the middle years of the century, however, the view was increasingly being taken that the existing approach to education – partial, piecemeal and scattergun – was scarcely fitting for the most powerful nation on earth. That there could be children in Henry Mayhew's London who were clearly puzzled by the notion of 'England' was shocking. That, a few years later, and with the Reform Act of 1867 on the statute books, there could be people actually eligible to vote who could scarcely read or write was truly appalling. Clearly, the time had come to make sweeping changes.

Parliament duly debated the issue, and the result of their deliberations was the 1870 Education Act. This was a landmark piece of legislation. For the first time, provision was made for funded education for children

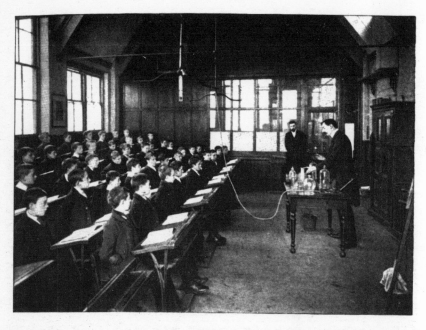

Teaching a class in a London board school. There is a marked contrast between this Edwardian photograph of a well-appointed classroom and Cruikshank's evocation of the distinctly makeshift Ragged School.

between the ages of five and twelve (extended to thirteen by a bye-law in 1871). Moreover, the practical means to achieve this were put in place. From now on, local education boards were empowered to raise funds through rates to run 'board schools', alongside existing church ones. In addition, the Act facilitated the construction of new school buildings via loans from central government.

The significance of the Act for London lay not just in its scope, but in the way it was applied. Whereas the rest of country was covered by a network of local boards, London was given a single School Board, covering the same area as the recently formed Metropolitan Board of Works, which oversaw so many of the capital's great building projects. In other words, as with the Board of Works, the 1870 Education Act recognised that the sprawling city on the Thames was a single entity, comprising (for the purposes of administration) ten divisions returning their own elected officials: City, Southwark, Chelsea, Greenwich, Lambeth, Tower Hamlets, Hackney, Westminster, Finsbury and Marylebone.

The Act was a critical stepping stone along the path towards universal, compulsory education, and in its wake there followed an ambitious building programme in the inner and outer suburbs. Over 400 schools

The imposing exterior of a London board school.

were constructed in the London area in the course of the next few decades. Three-quarters of them were designed by the London School Board's architect Edward Robert Robson, who came up with large, imposing, often three-storey edifices, invariably built with colourful brickwork, terracotta detailing and ornate gables. They had separate playgrounds and entrances for boys and girls, and often individual classrooms that fed off a central schoolroom. Even today, there is scarcely a London suburb that doesn't contain a building with the monogram 'SLB' (School Board for London) proudly and prominently displayed. 'Lighthouses! Beacons of the future! Capsules, with hundreds of bright little seeds in each, out of which will spring the wiser, better England of the future.' So Sherlock Holmes describes them as he heads into Clapham Junction by train in 'The Naval Treaty' (1894).

***

If education for many early Victorian Londoners was a hit-and-miss affair, so too was health care. Mortality rates could be terrifyingly high, particularly in the earlier years of the century. A London baby born in the 1830s, for example, had an average life expectancy of twenty-nine years. Even towards the end of Queen Victoria's reign a child born in the impoverished parts of Notting Dale, where poor Irish settlers scratched a living from pig keeping, brick making and street peddling, had only a 50 per cent chance of reaching its first birthday.

Health difficulties were not left behind once the risks of early childhood receded. There were smallpox epidemics in 1837–40, 1871–2 and 1881. There was the ill health that accompanied poor housing and bad sanitation that manifested itself in the periodic outbreaks of cholera. There were also the health hazards that went with particular jobs – from the 'phossy jaw' suffered by those who worked with phosphorus in the match factories, to the illnesses picked up by those who scavenged dog excrement to sell to tanners, to the frequent accidents experienced by those working on the docks and in the factories.

The tendency of many Londoners to drink heavily also brought its own set of health problems. Overindulgence in itself, of course, could be a killer; but in a more insidious way, alcohol went hand in hand with unhealthy living: poverty prompted people to drink, and drink could lead to poverty. In the view of the poet and columnist George Sims in his book *Horrible London* (1889), some poor people spent up to a quarter of their earnings in pubs and gin-palaces. Any pub on a Saturday night, he argued, would be crammed with 'artisans and labourers drinking away the wages that ought to clothe their little ones' and 'women squandering the money that would purchase food, for the lack of which the children are dying'.[6] It was concerns about alcohol abuse that led to the foundation of the National Temperance League, and concerns about the prevalence of alcohol in hospitals across the capital prompted the league to found its own hospital on Gower Street in 1873 (it moved to Hampstead Road in 1885).

The problem, particularly earlier in the century, was that although London was demonstrably not a healthy place, the facilities people could call upon were both sparse and rudimentary. A small number of medieval and Tudor hospitals still survived, and had been joined in the eighteenth century by a number of new charitable institutions set up by concerned citizens, but the rate of their foundation had never kept pace with the

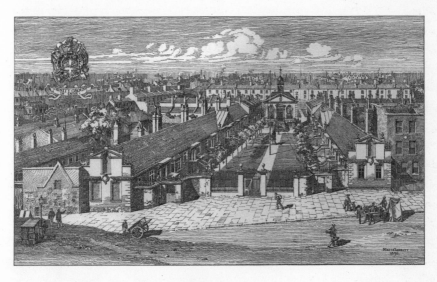

Private and institutional philanthropy remained a powerful force throughout the nineteenth century. This late nineteenth-century engraving shows the Trinity Almshouses in Mile End Road. Trinity House had for centuries cared for retired sailors and their spouses, and also took responsibility for the building of lighthouses.

rate of population increase. In 1861, for example, there were only 1,300 beds in south London's two hospitals – St Thomas's and Guy's – to provide for the three-quarters of a million or so people who lived in the fifty square miles that extended to Greenwich; and that was to reckon without the people in parts of Surrey and Kent who also made use of the same two hospitals. North of the Thames it was a slightly better picture, but still a far from ideal one.

New hospitals were certainly set up in the early nineteenth century: the London Fever Hospital (1802), Moorfields Eye Hospital (1805) and the Charing Cross Hospital (1818) among them. Since, however, they were invariably philanthropic concerns, they appeared in a piecemeal way and were of only limited effectiveness. Funding could be a problem. The Metropolitan Free Hospital, established in East London in 1836 to treat patients 'whose only recommendations are poverty, destitution and disease', received various charitable donations from the very beginning, but found that they were insufficient and had to drop the word 'free' from its name when it instituted a subscription scheme.

That this was a wholly unsatisfactory way to organise health care in the nation's capital became increasingly obvious in the course of Queen Victoria's reign, as London's population entered an extended period of rapid growth. Some doctors took matters into their own hands, founding both general and specialist establishments. The children's hospital at Great Ormond Street, for example, was set up by Charles West, a physician and paediatrician who in the late 1840s personally petitioned every London physician for support and who in 1851 managed to raise sufficient funds to buy 49 Great Ormond Street and turn it into a hospital. Public campaigns were also launched, championed by the likes of Florence Nightingale and Charles Dickens, all insisting on a new approach. Florence Nightingale even went so far as to lobby politicians herself, drawing up a detailed proposal for health-care reforms in which she argued the case for special- ised institutions for children, the sick, the insane and the incurable; for a single authority to control London's medical care; and for effective financing via a general levy.[7]

As with the campaigns to bring greater central control of London's infrastructure and its education system, so the campaign to improve the capital's health caught the mood of the times, and in 1867 the Metropolitan

Poor Act was passed. This not only established a central authority – the Metropolitan Asylums Board – but also ensured that its work was funded via the rates and gave it authority for non-private hospitals throughout the London area. In other words, it created an authority that had teeth and was able to use them.

The Asylums Board moved quickly, establishing hospitals in Hampstead, Homerton and Stockwell just in time to help deal with the smallpox outbreak of 1871–2, and then two further hospitals, in Deptford and Fulham, a few years later (all served by horse-drawn ambulances). However, the process was not without incident. While the plan may have been to ensure that the new hospitals were away from the crowded middle, it wasn't possible or desirable to set them up in the middle of nowhere, and inevitably those living close to the new establishments were less than delighted. Hampstead residents, including the now ex-teacher and renowned postal reformer Rowland Hill, campaigned against their new neighbour. The citizens of Fulham applied for an injunction to stop smallpox cases being brought to Fulham Hospital. Newspapers suggested a plausible link between the pres-ence of hospitals and nearby cases of smallpox. Eventually compromises were agreed upon. The Hampstead hospital, for example, agreed to cut down the number of patients and move its main entrance (its continued presence, though, made the area around Haverstock Hill so unpopular that by the 1890s only the poorest would live there). Later in the century, new hospitals were opened in Tottenham, Tooting, Shooters Hill and Hither Green.

Care of the mentally ill, too, was transformed in the course of the nineteenth century. For hundreds of years, people suffering from any form of mental affliction had been dismissed as 'imbeciles' or 'lunatics'. Some had even been shackled or put on public display – the Bethlehem Royal Hospital, or Bedlam, for example, had opened its doors to the curious early in the seventeenth century. However, by the first decades of the nineteenth century a different spirit was beginning to prevail, in part because the recurrent mental illness of George III had awoken both public interest and sympathy. In 1807 a government report recommended the setting up of new asylums, each to be situated in 'an airy and healthy situation, with a good supply of water, and which may afford the probability of the vicinity of constant medical assistance'. It was also suggested that while asylums should be large enough to offer economies of scale, none should contain more than 300 inmates.[8] A year later, the County Asylums Act passed into law.

The first London asylum to be built within the terms of the Act was at Hanwell in Middlesex in 1831. Here the deeply religious superintendent William Charles Ellis established a gentler, more caring regime than many of his forebears had thought fit to provide. Emphasis was placed on cure rather than control. Patients were, wherever possible, given work to do – weaving, perhaps, or painting or bricklaying – Ellis believing strongly that work had a therapeutic power. Twenty years later an even larger establishment was founded at Colney Hatch in Friern Barnet. With its separate wings for male and female patients, and large grounds where they could work and rest until they were ready to face the world again, it encapsulated the notion of an asylum as a place of safety and refuge rather than as a prison. As in other areas of health care, private philanthropy still played its part: the patent medicine manufacturer Thomas Holloway, for example, created a sanatorium at Virginia Water between 1873 and 1885 on the very edge of the London region. Nevertheless, central supervision continued to gain ground,

The little hamlet of Colney Hatch where a large mental hospital was built in 1851.

hospitals for the 'insane' being made part of the remit of the Metropolitan Asylums Board when it was established in 1867.

Crime was another key area of nineteenth-century London life to be brought under closer central scrutiny and control over time. Quite how much of it there was in the Victorian capital at any given point, however, is hard to say. Contemporary statistics were often partial or incomplete, and because the way they were calculated changed over time it's very difficult indeed to make comparisons. Much ink, for example, has been spilled over the simple question of whether and to what extent overall levels went up, down or stayed the same over the course of the century.

What the records do show us, though, is which crimes were most common; and, hardly suprisingly perhaps, most seem to have been fairly mundane. People brought before the Old Bailey (which dealt with felony crimes in the City of London and County of Middlesex) were more often than not accused of 'breaking the peace', a rather vague term that included assault, rioting, threatening behaviour, libel and barratry – the offence of causing quarrels by spreading malicious rumour (hence the surname 'Barratt'). In many cases, casual violence seems to have been involved. Domestic disputes and fights with neighbours litter the court records, the one sometimes leading to the other, as this case from 1851 shows:

DANIEL HARRINGTON. I am eleven years old, and live with my father and mother, in Spring-gardens, Mile-end New Town. On 27th June, about 9 o'clock at night, I was going home – there was a great crowd – I saw the prisoner up at his window, the third pair – they said he had *chucked* his wife out of [the] window – he *chucked* a brick out at me, and knocked me down – I did not see him *chuck* it, the people said so – it struck me on the side of the head, and I do not remember anything else.

CHARLES DUKE. I am house-surgeon, at the London Hospital. The boy was brought there – he was in a confused state, from the effects of the blow – there was a contused lacerated wound of the scalp, on the left side of the head, above the temple, a little more than an inch long – it might have been done by a brick – he was three weeks under my treatment, and is quite recovered now.

PETER WILLIAM DUNNAWAY (*policeman, H 129*). I was sent for on the night of 27th June, and took the prisoner – I told him he must go to the station with me, that he was charged with assaulting two little boys, who had gone to the Hospital, one I believed had died – two boys were hurt, but only one appeared before the Magistrate – on the way to the station, he said he should not have done it if they had not thrown at him – there was a very great mob – we found it difficult to get him from the house, the people were so much excited at what he had done – I found him concealed in a hole, between the ceiling and the tiles.

Prisoner's Defence. GEORGE SMITH. This afternoon I was out along with my wife; I had a little drop to drink, and we had a few words; my little boy went into the court; I ran to the window to call him, and accidentally knocked a brick off the sill; it was not *heaved*.[9]

Smith was sentenced to twelve months in prison.

Prostitution was also a widespread problem, as it had been since medieval and particularly Georgian times. Some experts have estimated that up to 80,000 prostitutes were working in London by the middle decades of the nineteenth century. During the frantic police hunt for Jack the Ripper in 1888 it emerged that in the immediate area where he had attacked and killed five or more prostitutes, some 1,200 were working in sixty-two rookery-based brothels. Elsewhere in the East End, Ratcliff Highway, Frederick Street, Brunswick Street and Shadwell High Street were all well-known red-light districts, their pubs – such as the Half Moon and Seven Stars, the Ship and Shears, and the Duke of York in Shadwell High Street – all notorious pick-up points.

The West End similarly continued with a tradition that had existed virtually since its first buildings had appeared. Prostitutes in Haymarket, according to novelist Fyodor Dostoevsky, swarmed by night in 'their thousands'. Soho, Drury Lane, Piccadilly Circus and Leicester Square similarly had their vice-ridden side. Particular establishments became virtually synonymous with prostitution, notably Kate Hamilton's Café Royal in Princess Street, and the very lively Argyll Rooms by Windmill Street.

It wasn't just the poorer areas and the centres of nightlife that attracted prostitution. The grand establishments of upmarket Tyburnia, now the eastern end of Bayswater below Sussex Gardens, became notorious in the

1840s and 1850s as houses of ill repute. As for St John's Wood, it became almost a byword for upmarket prostitution, its elegant early nineteenth-century villas home to various ladies of various degrees of notoriety. A snippet of conversation in Robert Hichens's 1898 novel *The Londoners* hints at the reputation that the area had even at the end of the century:

'I'm so glad you are back from St John's Wood, Mrs Verulam. You were
so difficult to get at there – even by omnibus.'
　'It was rather far out.'
　'And then the neighbourhood is hardly –'

London's major problem, however, was not so much prostitution or violence (the evidence suggests roughly forty-five murders a year towards the end of the century), as theft and robbery. Throughout the course of the eighteenth century, an average of 418 prosecutions were brought before the courts each year; by 1825 that figure was 1,035; by 1850 it had reached 2,100. The Old Bailey alone heard 53,000 cases relating to theft between 1826 and 1850. 'Swell mobs' of elite, well-dressed street pickpockets relieved unsuspecting passers-by of their possessions; and we know from Dickens's *Oliver Twist* that armies of children roamed the streets, slipping their deft fingers into people's pockets. Watches and purses vanished, as did hand-kerchiefs; the records of the Old Bailey suggest that between 1825 and 1875, half of all thefts involved a handkerchief changing hands illegally.

Gangs broke into houses, they stole from shops and they appeared everywhere. Sir Joseph Bazalgette, for example, was burgled in Wimbledon Park in 1877, losing in the process a cash box and a silver trowel presented to him by the Board of Works in commemoration of the laying of the first stone of the Thames Embankment. Some robberies were rather more ambitious. In Lewisham in March 1844, thieves raided the premises of Mr Lindsay, keeper of the Lewisham Post Office, and, having opened and torn up various letters, got away with banknotes, silver, gold and a quantity of plate worth around £300. In 1850 a 'daring' attempted burglary at the mansion of a J. Holford in Regent's Park excited 'an extraordinary sensation amongst the gentry residing in the vicinity and the villas in the northern suburbs of the metropolis', according to the *Morning Chronicle* for 21 October. At the more thuggish end of things, a mob of 200 descended on West End Fair in Hampstead in 1819 and stripped and robbed every person who came their way.

Criminals were mobile, too. In *Oliver Twist*, Fagin's gang generally sticks to London's teeming streets, but on one occasion the brutal Bill Sikes forces Oliver to accompany him on an expedition that takes him from the East End to Hyde Park by foot, and then by cart through Kensington, Hammersmith, Chiswick, Kew Bridge and onwards to Brentford, where they proceed on foot again to burgle a house near Chertsey. A few years later, Edmund Yates's one-act play *A Night at Notting Hill* (first performed in 1857) made a joke of the fact that an area nicely situated away from the centre had become so prone to crime that it was necessary to turn houses into virtual fortresses protected by patented anti-theft devices. 'Now,' says Alderman Syllabub, '. . . when I've closed the shutters for the night, I fasten this cord to the bolt, and when the robber puts his jemmy through, this box will blow the roof of the house off, and we can all escape in the confusion.' As transport improved, so criminals got around even faster. By the 1850s, Bill Sikes's successors were able to reach the scene of crime – and leave it swiftly – by train or omnibus. Now London's 'swell mobs' could rush off at will to any area where crowds were gathering – a race meeting, perhaps, or a fair.

Squaring up to these villains in the first quarter of the century was a ragtag army of city police, and hopelessly ineffectual watchmen. In the parish of St Pancras alone there were eighteen different night watches in operation, each with its own patch to keep an eye on, and each generally ignoring the crimes happening on another's turf – even if that happened to be the other side of the same street. After 1805 the Bow Street Horse and Foot patrols were there to keep a nightly watch over the outer highways and inner streets (in the process virtually eliminating the centuries-old problem of highway robbery), and from 1821 a new dismounted patrol numbering a hundred men were introduced to cover the nearer suburbs at night (a day patrol of twenty-seven men operated throughout the central region by day from 1822). Yet the random nature of local policing at this time is illustrated by the fact that Kensington, Fulham and Deptford – with over 55,000 inhabitants between them in 1821 – had no night watch at all.

It's scarcely surprising that local groups of crime-fighters sprang up to defend themselves both against home-grown criminals and ones who were commuting from inner London: the Chiswick Association for the Protection of Persons and Property, and the Harrow on the Hill

Association for the Protection of Property and the Prosecution of Robbers among them. Some areas even created their own independent police forces, as in Wandsworth, where one operated between 1819 and 1840. Criminals, however, had an irritating tendency not to observe parish boundaries when carrying out their crimes. As a result, the local approach, even early in the nineteenth century, seemed totally inadequate. Something more ambitious was required.

The idea of a metropolitan police force had been mooted on a number of occasions since the 1790s, but it was finally brought to fruition by the Home Secretary, Sir Robert Peel, in 1829. His original plan had been to bring the whole of London under one authority, but he had known from the outset that the City would be strongly opposed to seeing a single, unified force, and he made it clear that he was prepared to agree to a compromise whereby the City police continued to operate under their own authority provided he could have his metropolitan force. It was an adroit political move. By looking as though he was bowing to the power of the City, he was able to get his way where it really mattered. As for the new metropolitan force, this was placed under the jurisdiction of the Home Office and given responsibility for a rather ragbag collection of inner and outer suburbs that comprised Westminster, Holborn, Finsbury,

Police quelling a riot in 1844. Established in 1829, the Metropolitan Police initially met with considerable suspicion and hostility from Londoners.

the Tower, Kensington, New Brentford, the Inns of Court, the liberty of Ely Palace, the parishes of St Paul and St Nicholas, Deptford, Greenwich, Bermondsey, Camberwell, Clapham, Lambeth, Stoke Newington, Putney, Rotherhithe, Streatham, Tooting, Wandsworth, Christchurch, Southwark, the liberty of the Clink, and Hatcham. Its headquarters were established at Scotland Yard, with local police stations in each of its seventeen local divisions (lettered A to V).

The new force – only a thousand strong in the early days – initially had to co-exist alongside such long-standing entities as the Bow Street Runners, the Horse and Foot Patrols, and the Thames Marine River Police. A degree of inevitable confusion ensued, but this was resolved in 1839 when the runners and other detectives were pensioned off, and the Horse Patrol and Thames Marine River Police were absorbed into the Metropolitan Police. Even so, there was no detective branch until 1842, and the number of detectives on the force remained under twenty until the late 1860s. Moreover, while the early police force might occasionally have become caught up in outbreaks of civil disorder, strictly speaking keeping the peace on this scale remained the responsibility of the militia; nor did it help that the police were initially unpopular and regarded with considerable suspicion by great swathes of London's population. Nevertheless, over the next few decades the force grew in numbers (16,000 men by 1900), in authority (with the setting up of Special Branch in the 1880s, for example – initially to deal with Irish terrorism) and in jurisdiction. By 1840 the Metropolitan Police District was extended to include Leyton, Richmond, East Ham, Uxbridge, Hillingdon and West Drayton. Two years later, Stanmore and Hackney followed suit. Three new divisions – Clapham, Willesden and Holloway – were added in 1865. In the process the London bobby, with his truncheon (and cutlass in an emergency), his reinforced top hat and minimum height of five foot seven went from being resented to being broadly accepted and even, sometimes, welcomed.

Although it's dangerous to generalise about Victorian crime, it does seem to be the case that in the period after about 1850 the authorities began to get the problem under greater control. Felonies involving property reported to the police fell from 21,000 a year in the 1860s to around 18,000 in the 1870s, and although this rose again to around 20,000 in the following decade, it decreased dramatically to 16,000 by the 1890s (by which time London's population had grown yet again). Londoners may not have felt particularly safe – they rarely do – and much crime may well have gone unreported – as it always does – but the metropolitan area as a whole seems to have been a more tranquil place in 1900 than it had been, say, sixty years earlier.

When it came to punishment of convicted criminals, petty offences remained within the remit of Justices of the Peace and local magistrates, as they had since the early eighteenth century, and the penalties handed out generally involved time in the local lock-up, or a fine. More serious cases were referred to the criminal sessions held at the Old Bailey, and here retribution could be savage. Some 3,210 people received the death penalty in the first quarter of the nineteenth century, their crimes often amounting to no more than theft or burglary. Twenty-year-old James Parish from North Mimms, for example, was indicted in April 1830:

> . . . for feloniously breaking and entering the dwelling-house of Henry
> Pitham, on the 10th of February [1830], at South Mimms, and stealing
> therein 56lbs. of pork, value 1l. 15s.; 8lbs. of beef, value 4s. 8d.; 6 knives,

A hanging outside Newgate Prison.
The last public hanging here was in 1868.

value 3s.; 6 forks, value 3s.; 2 pairs of shoes, value 1l.; 1 coat, value 8s.; 3 live tame pigeons, value 6s.; 1 hat, value 10s.; 1 handkerchief, value 2s., and 1 bag, value 1s.[10]

Convicted largely on the evidence that he often wore a red hat similar to the one found at the scene of the crime, he was sentenced to death, though this was later commuted to transportation for life.

Age was no barrier to the death penalty, as this case from 1833 shows:

NICHOLAS WHITE was indicted for feloniously breaking and entering into the dwelling-house of Thomas Batchelor, on the 19th of April, at St. Matthew, Bethnal Green, and stealing therein, 15 pieces of paint, value 2d., his property.

THOMAS BATCHELOR. I keep a house and shop in the parish of St. Matthew, Bethnal Green. A pane of glass in my shop window had been damaged – it had been broken by a knife, or something, and had been mended by a piece of glass being put over it and stuck on with putty; it was quite safe until Friday evening, the 19th of April, between 6 and 7 o'clock, when I was at work backwards, and this happened – my son alarmed me – I know nothing of it myself.

GEORGE DAVIS. I am 9 years old, and am the son of William Davis who lives in the Hackney-road. I was one of the boys who went into Batchelor's shop on Friday evening, and told him what I had seen – I saw the prisoner put a stick through the window with a point at the end of it; it was straight; he shoved it through the window and the piece of glass fell in, and then he said he would give me half if I would not tell; but I went in and told Mr. Batchelor, and he came out – I saw the prisoner take out some paints when he said he would give me half – I did not know him before – I took notice of his face and dress; he was dressed all in cord – Mr. Batchelor told us to go and look after the prisoner – I went and saw him again about five minutes after looking into a snuff-shop in Shoreditch; he was looking in at the window at the snuff-boxes – I then went back to Batchelor's and told him I had seen him – I met a policeman, and he took him into custody.

GUILTY – DEATH Aged 9[11]

Those who escaped the death penalty in the early years of the nine-teenth century were often transported to one of the penal colonies in

Australia for the fixed terms of seven or fourteen years, while those whose death sentence was commuted, as in the case of James Parish, were transported for life. Many transportees were first held in 'hulks', or old prison vessels, moored at Woolwich, Deptford and further downstream at Chatham, before departing for the colonies. Of the 160,000 people transported between 1787 when the First Fleeters left and 1868 when transportation ended, some 27,930 had first been tried at the Old Bailey. Those sentenced to transportation for life, but who dared to return, faced the death penalty – as Dickens's convict Abel Magwitch knew only too well in *Great Expectations*. In fact, by the time Dickens was writing, most who dared to return were simply sent back. Earlier in the century they might not have been so lucky: Edward James, a 31-year-old glasscutter, was executed in 1812 for returning from transportation before his allotted time. His original crime had been to steal a silk handkerchief.

In the course of the nineteenth century, however, the more draconian punishments meted out to sinners gradually declined in ferocity and frequency. Most of those 27,930 people sentenced to transportation at the Old Bailey before the punishment was suspended in 1868 were actually sentenced before 1825. Similarly, far more people were sentenced to death there in the first half of the century than in the second: after 1850 perhaps five people a year faced the hangman's noose. Whereas 9,000 people were given custodial sentences at the Old Bailey between 1801 and 1825, some 30,000 were sent to prison over the next quarter of a century.

This posed an inevitable practical problem. London's prisons had been built for a smaller population and they certainly had not been built to take account of a policy that involved awarding a greater number of custodial sentences. In the early years of the nineteenth century there were nineteen principal prisons in the capital, made up of debtors' prisons, bridewells (a colloquial term derived from the prison on the north bank of the Thames which had been used as a place of punishment for petty offenders and disorderly women) and comptors (the gaols of the sheriffs of London). Many dated back to the Middle Ages; all showed their age. Moreover, they had very limited capacities. The four debtors' prisons, for example – the Fleet, the Marshalsea, the King's (later the Queen's) Bench in Southwark, and Whitecross Street – held only about 1,700 prisoners between them. And they were sitting on valuable land ripe for more profitable or uplifting redevelopment: the Tothill Fields House of

The Marshalsea Prison in Southwark, closed in 1842.

Correction, for example, was demolished in 1884 to make way for Westminster Cathedral, while Whitecross Street was replaced in 1877 by a railway goods depot on the site of what is now the Barbican development. The old prisons were not only bursting at the seams, but were also being knocked down.

Over time new, larger prisons were constructed, and they were built, unlike their predecessors, far from the centre. Millbank in Pimlico came first in 1816 (it was demolished towards the end of the century to make way for what is now Tate Britain). Clerkenwell was rebuilt in 1818 (and again in 1847), to be joined by Brixton in 1820, Pentonville in 1840, Wandsworth in 1851, Holloway in 1852, Feltham in 1854 and Wormwood Scrubs between 1874 and 1890. All were placed on open land well beyond the sulphurous fogs of the town and surrounded – initially, at least – by greenery. The early Brixton prison, for example, stood in one of the most rural spots in the southern suburbs of London, while Wormwood Scrubs, as its name suggests, had, long before, been a 'snake-infested thicket or wood'[12] and more recently farmland.

As a rule, these new prisons were cleaner and better run than their predecessors. They were nevertheless forbidding places, where prisoners were given menial labour (picking oakum or sewing mailbags) or deliberately pointless tasks (such as endlessly climbing a treadmill or winding a handle that was not connected to anything). At Pentonville it was decided that a form of solitary confinement was best, and prisoners were

An Edwardian photograph showing prisoners going to dinner in Wormwood Scrubs prison. It was one of a number of nineteenth-century London prisons to be set up well away from the centre of the capital.

locked in admittedly comfortable cells for hours at a time. Some went mad; others committed suicide. Nevertheless, Pentonville was considered a marvel of its day, an article in the *Illustrated London News* of 13 August 1842 painting the following admiring picture:

> We believe the whole principle of the erection resolves itself into a greater uniformity of plan and purpose than has yet been exhibited in prison architecture. A more decided facility for the perfect classification of prisoners, and a total impossibility of any means of escape from the fact of a perpetual surveillance having been contrived to operate along the walls from every angle of the building. Their exterior is less repulsive than that of many edifices of the kind; but what we have principally to hope for the benefit of society, is, that the interior may be little and as seldom tenanted, so that it may be set up less as a symbol of punishment, than as a sign of the diminution of crime.

If the authorities started to get a handle on education, health and crime in Victorian London, their record with the capital's poor remained unimpressive. Towards the end of the century the social investigator Charles Booth estimated that up to a third of Londoners were living to a greater or lesser extent in poverty. Some were poor immigrant communities (Irish and Jewish settlers, for example), others struggled in low-paid jobs, many failed to find jobs at all, while some were their own worst enemies – heavy drinkers or criminal or idle. The elderly were among the hardest hit. Generally speaking, poverty was not a fixed condition. You might be a poor agricultural labourer one day, struggling to make ends meet, but a reasonably well-paid factory worker tomorrow; or you might be prosperous today, with a good job and pleasant living conditions, but be ruined the next by illness or unemployment. One thing was fairly certain, though: unless you were extraordinarily prosperous or extraordinarily lucky, you would almost certain encounter poverty in old age. Once you could no longer work, you were in trouble.

The problem throughout the century, however, was that the authorities had a strong suspicion that much poverty was self-inflicted. They might acknowledge that there was a distinction to be made between the 'deserving poor' and the 'undeserving poor' but in practice they often struggled to find it. Their view, therefore, tended to be that any steps taken to alleviate it, or rather to deal with it, should be designed as much to discourage as to help. The Poor Law Amendment Act of 1834 is a case in point. In administrative terms, it took the principle of cross-parish cooperation enshrined in Gilbert's Act of the previous century to the next level, obliging neighbouring parishes to combine into larger administrative units and construct a workhouse for each new Poor Law Union. In practical terms, this meant the erection of grim institutions throughout the London area into which the poor were herded and cared for in a manner designed to encourage them to seek work instead. The workhouses that were built after 1834 tended to follow a similar plan: a cruciform layout, with four buildings joined at the centre, exercise yards between each, and the entirety surrounded by a high perimeter wall. They looked like prisons, and they extended across London's Poor Law Unions: from Woolwich and Poplar

A late nineteenth-century view of the Wandsworth and Clapham Union Workhouse in Garratt Lane. Built in what was then still largely open countryside, it offered accommodation to 650 men and women, with the two sexes kept carefully separated from one another. Inmates were divided into four classes: aged, able-bodied of good character, and two classes of able-bodied of bad character.

in the east to Hammersmith and Wandsworth in the west; though only as far south as Clapham and as far north as Hampstead.

Later in the century the Metropolitan Poor Act of 1867 took a few practical steps to alleviate the worst of poverty – particularly in its setting up of hospitals – but the problem did not go away, and the 1880s and 1890s were dotted with workhouse scandals and tales of appalling neglect. It was to be left to a new century and the government at Westminster to come to grips with London's poor. In the meantime, there were many, such as Betty Higden in Charles Dickens's *Our Mutual Friend* (1864–5), who struggled with their poverty and prayed that they would not end up in the workhouse:

> Old Betty Higden fared upon her pilgrimage as many ruggedly honest creatures, women and men, fare on their toiling way along the roads of life. Patiently to earn a spare bare living, and quietly to die, untouched by workhouse hands – this was her highest sublunary hope.[13]

Ultimately, of course, all Londoners, whether rich or poor, met the same fate; but even in death there was little equality. The better off found their final resting places in church vaults and in churchyards; the poor had to squeeze in where they could in any remaining space around their more affluent companions. The problem here was an entirely practical one. Burials in a Christian country had to take place in consecrated ground. Religious dissenters might be exempted (hence, for example, the establishment of a burial ground at Bunhill Fields in City Road, Islington), but for the rest, only at times of pestilence – as in the 1340s and again in the seventeenth century – could burial elsewhere be countenanced. In 1665, for example, the authorities sanctioned the digging of pits, lined with quicklime, in various places north of the City wall – in Moorfields, Finsbury Fields, Goswell Street, Bishopsgate, Shoreditch and Stepney – their horror captured by Daniel Defoe in his *Journal of the Plague Year* (1722):

> There was a strict order to prevent people coming to those pits, and that was only to prevent infection. But after some time that order was more necessary, for people that were infected and near their end, and delirious also, would run to those pits, wrapt in blankets or rugs, and throw

themselves in, and, as they said, bury themselves. I cannot say that the officers suffered any willingly to lie there; but I have heard that in a great pit in Finsbury, in the parish of Cripplegate, it lying open then to the fields, for it was not then walled about, [many] came and threw themselves in, and expired there, before they threw any earth upon them; and that when they came to bury others and found them there, they were quite dead, though not cold.[14]

By the nineteenth century the condition of many London churchyards resembled the horror of the plague pits. Quite simply, there was no longer the space to cater for the dead of the metropolis. St Martin-in-the-Fields, in Westminster, which in 1841 catered for a parish of around 24,500 people, had a churchyard 200 feet square (60 square metres) that was estimated by the end of decade to contain 60,000 to 70,000 bodies – and St Martin's was scarcely unique. In the same decade Hector Gavin surveyed Bethnal Green, in the East End, and published his findings in 1848 under the rather unwieldy title *Sanitary Ramblings, Being Sketches and Illustrations of Bethnal Green: A Type of the Condition of the Metropolis and Other Large Towns*. His calculations suggested that the burial ground of St Matthew's church, opened only a century previously in 1746, was 2,400 square yards (2,000 square metres) and contained 50,000 bodies. These had once arrived at an average of 500 a year, but in 1847 there had been 800 interments: 765 in the ground and 25 in vaults. In a display of human closeness that was not necessarily apparent in life, there were now twelve people to each grave plot, and an average of 240 burials per acre. It's scarcely surprising that an article in *Punch* in 1849 should have compared the forced intimacy of London burials to the forced intimacy of London transport:

> Mr Walker, speaking of the St Giles' Churchyard in London, says, 'in less than 2 acres it contains 48,000 bodies.' A London churchyard is very like a London omnibus. It can be made to carry any number. If there is no room inside – no matter, there is always plenty of accommodation outside. The same with a London churchyard – number is the last consideration.[15]

Gavin's investigation into the problem went into some detail, and his account of the practicalities of graveyards in *Sanitary Ramblings* makes for grim reading:

In Shoreditch and in St. Matthew's the ground has been very considerably raised by the numerous bodies which have been interred. I regret to state, that at no very great distance of time it was the practice to burn the coffins in one of the church-yards; it would be needless to inquire what became of the corpses. It would be greatly to the credit and advantage of the Christians, if they would follow the practice of the Hebrews, who *never*, upon any account, reopen a grave, or inter more than one in it. They bury at a depth of four feet below the surface, and when the ground has been fully occupied, they cover the whole surface with a fresh layer of earth, to a height of four feet, in which they again bury as before. This process has been twice followed in the Jews' burying-ground, so that three persons are interred in every 21 feet (3 feet by 7 feet), at a depth of 4, 8, and 12 feet below the surface. This practice is to be preferred to sinking a deep grave, as is the custom in some grave-yards, burying in it, filling it up a few feet, and leaving the grave open for the next occupant, when the same process is carried on, till the last coffin reaches a few feet sometimes a few inches from the surface.

It wasn't just a practical or aesthetic problem. Overcrowded graveyards posed a health problem, too. Each body released noxious gases and fluids post mortem that seeped into the soil and could reach the water table beneath. It could take anything up to a year for a body buried in a wooden coffin to reduce down to a dry skeleton, and active decomposition – with the generation of fluids and gases – was still occurring between three weeks and two months after burial. Yet corpses were arriving at such a pace that they were being buried before the previous corpses had had an opportunity to rot down. Many churchyards were a seething mass of decomposition. In *Bell's Life in London and Sporting Chronicle* for 9 September 1838 it was reported that a man digging a grave in Aldgate churchyard had been so overcome by fumes that he had collapsed and died at the bottom of a twenty-foot pit. A ladder was procured to retrieve the corpse, but the volunteer who agreed to descend, on reaching the bottom, 'appeared as if struck with a cannon-ball, and fell back with his head in a different direction to his fellow sufferer, and appeared instantly to expire'. A witness at the coroner's inquest reported that:

> ... the grave was a pauper's grave, and added that 'such graves as those were kept open until there were 17 or 18 bodies interred in them. It was

not the custom to put any earth between the coffins in those graves, except in cases where the persons died of contagious diseases, and in that case some slacked lime and a thin layer of earth were put down to separate them. Sometimes the gravediggers would not go down a grave, owing to the foulness of the air; but were in the habit of burning straw, and using other means to dispel the impure air.

Not surprisingly, the more unscrupulous tried to find new ways to store old bodies. They might bury them under the floorboards of a chapel, or, as Richard Kelsey, Surveyor to the Commissioner of Sewers for the City of London, testified in a parliamentary report of 1845, they might stow them in drains and sewers. In one case, he said, a sewer passing under a churchyard had been broken into and bodies placed there – presumably by the sexton.

On occasion, the corpses didn't even make it as far as burial, however superficial. Resurrection men had been making use of graveyards to supply medical schools since the eighteenth century, but they became more active in the early 1800s as demand rose and as the alternative supply of executed criminals declined (thanks to a reduction in the number of capital offences on the statute book). One Bethnal Green gang confessed to having stolen and sold somewhere between 500 and 1,000 bodies over a twelve-year period before they were arrested in 1831. John Bishop, Thomas Williams and James May were all convicted, two of them were hanged at Newgate Prison, and then in an unsavoury exhibition of poetic justice, both were handed over to the Theatre of Anatomy for viewing and dissection. In an attempt to free up the legitimate market, the Anatomy Act was passed in 1832, legalising the dissection of corpses other than those of executed felons.

Cramming, concealing and dissection could only deal with so many corpses, and by the time Kelsey was submitting his evidence the first proper attempts had been made to deal with the problem. Since inner London was now full, it was decided that burials would have to be carried out in the empty, outlying districts; and in 1832 a parliamentary bill was passed to establish privately owned cemeteries outside the City of London. This provided the necessary spur to the entrepreneurially minded, and a series of large, grand out-of-town cemeteries duly appeared over the next few decades, the principal ones amounting to a 'Magnificent Seven' (as

Hugh Meller, documenter of London's cemeteries, described them in 1981). First, in 1832, came Kensal Green cemetery, straddling the borders of Hammersmith and Fulham, and Kensington and Chelsea, and designed to serve the west of London. It was followed in 1837 by West Norwood (or South Metropolitan) cemetery in Lambeth, and three years later by Nunhead cemetery in Southwark, which catered for the needs of the south. In the north, Highgate cemetery was laid out in Camden in 1839, followed by Abney Park in Hackney the following year. The east was served by Tower Hamlets (or Bow) cemetery from 1841 and the west by Brompton cemetery, sandwiched today between Old Brompton Road to the north and the Fulham Road to the south, and opened in 1840.

Kensal Green cemetery, developed along the north bank of the Paddington branch of the Grand Junction Canal, established the look and layout for the other cemeteries that were to follow: walkways and processional routes amid landscaped grounds and with an Anglican chapel at the centre. While the cemetery may have fallen on hard times later in the twentieth century, in its early days it enjoyed considerable cachet (which transferred to the surrounding area), and it was regarded as the height of fashion to be buried there. Many of the great and the good of the Victorian age found their final resting place in Kensal Green: the mathematician Charles Babbage, the academic George Birkbeck, the engineer Isambard Kingdom Brunel and the writer William Makepeace Thackeray among them. Nor was it regarded as beneath the dignity of royalty to be seen there – at least in a deceased state – and Kensal Green also came to house Prince Augustus Frederick, son of George III. He made his choice for a touching reason: he wanted to be buried somewhere where his wife would be able to join him in due course; because he had married outside the terms of the Royal Marriages Act, he knew that she would never be given burial at Windsor, and so he decided on Kensal Green.

After Kensal Green cemetery opened, a request was made to establish a Catholic cemetery next door. An extensive report was prepared, whose details show just how much careful planning went into these early cemeteries. Proposed situation and proximity to housing; vehicular and pedestrian approaches to the site; the quality of the soil and, more importantly, drainage; the size of the proposed plot of land in relation to population density and mortality rates: all these were carefully examined, as were assessments of the growing railway network in the area and planned new housing that criss-crossed the area, as well as suggested new roads for housing development. Once approved, preparation of the site went ahead, and St Mary's cemetery opened in 1858. It became the final resting place for many of the Irish immigrants who had come to London to escape the potato famine of the 1840s.

Yet not even these new cemeteries could completely solve the problem of a rising tide of London dead. Furthermore, they were only really accessible to the more affluent, who could afford the expenditure required to be buried in such places: the middle and upper classes, administrators, politicians, men of the cloth and the military. In death, as in life, these people competed with each other, building themselves ever more elaborate monuments, mausoleums and tombs and leaving us with some of the finest examples of Victorian architecture to be found anywhere. The chairman of the Highgate Cemetery Company boasted that his new venue would provide 'most interesting ornaments to the suburbs of this great metropolis and be an honour to the country', and with its catacombs, Egyptian Avenue and stunning mausoleums it certainly did that. Perhaps

*The picturesque Highgate cemetery, as it appeared in the 1850s.
Note the swathes of open countryside beyond.*

most spectacular of all was the mausoleum (based on the original at Halicarnassus) built for Julius Beer, who was born in poverty in Germany but died immensely wealthy in London, having become both a financier and proprietor of the *Observer*.

For the less fortunate in society, parish churchyards continued to supply a parcel of ground where they could go to their final rest, but in 1845 a pressure group called the National Society for the Abolition of Burial in Towns was formed to lobby for the closure of urban graveyards; and their efforts, combined with new attempts to create extra-parochial places of burial, led to the decline of the parish churchyard. Finally, the Metropolitan Interments Act of 1850 and the Burial Act of 1852 created the legislative framework for the closure of all town churchyards and the establishment of municipal cemeteries around London and the suburbs. The preamble to the Act contains a long list of parishes and hamlets that were included, from Hammersmith and Barnes in the west to Bow and Plumstead in the east, and from Marylebone, Hampstead and Stoke Newington in the north to Streatham and Tooting in the south.

Over the next few decades even these new cemeteries, placed in hitherto open space, were surrounded by further development and then swallowed up by suburban housing. As a result, sites yet further out became necessary, culminating in Brookwood cemetery (1854), near Woking in Surrey – some twenty-five miles from the centre of London and beyond even today's suburbs. Created with the intention of serving London's

An Edwardian military funeral in the Brompton cemetery.

needs for the next 500 years, it was set in 2,000 acres of grounds, of which 500 were extravagantly landscaped. Guilds, organisations and parishes could all lay claim to particular plots, and individuals were given considerable leeway in planning their particular resting places. A special train service, the Brookwood Necropolis Railway, was created to run a funeral train service on the London and South Western line, with a private terminus next to Waterloo station. On arrival at Brookwood on the main line, the funeral train would then reverse on to the cemetery's private railway line, first to the North station, which served the Nonconformist section of the cemetery, and then on to the South station, where the Anglicans were to be found.

Over time, however, even Brookwood proved insufficient to absorb all London's dead, and a more efficient if radical complementary approach was adopted: cremation. In its early days it was very definitely controversial. The citizens of Roman London might have burned their dead, but by Victorian times it was regarded as an unpleasantly foreign and 'heathen' idea. People wanted to meet their maker whole, not in the form of ashes. Nevertheless, Sir Henry Thompson, Fellow of the Royal College of Surgeons, bravely proposed in his 1874 work *The Treatment of the Body after Death* that cremation should be regarded as a practical and a humane way to lay corpses to rest. The Cremation Society was duly formed, and four years later bought land near Woking on which to build a crematorium. Their first successful cremation – of a horse – took place in 1879, despite the inevitable local protests. Six years later the first human, Jeanette Pickersgill, was consigned to the flames here. However, it was not until 1902 that an Act of Parliament gave the Home Secretary the powers to regulate the practice of cremation, and that crematoria therefore started to appear more widely around London. Golders Green crematorium, opened by Sir Henry Thompson in the same year, is perhaps the best known and was to become the final resting place for such twentieth-century luminaries as Rudyard Kipling, Sigmund Freud and George Bernard Shaw. Golders Green, and other crematoria like it, helped to solve what otherwise would yet again have become an unmanageable problem for London's suburbs.

TWELVE

A GOVERNMENT FOR THE METROPOLIS

The Creation of the London County Council

By the late Victorian era it was becoming only too apparent that piece-meal and local approaches to London's needs were totally inadequate. It was also becoming accepted that 'London' could no longer be said just to cover a small area around the Thames. This marked a major shift in perception. Back in 1819, when the poet Percy Bysshe Shelley wrote his wistful fantasy about the cataclysm he hoped would overtake the city, he thought in terms of its centre, longing for a time:

> . . . when London shall be an habitation of bitterns; when St. Paul's and Westminster Abbey shall stand, shapeless and nameless ruins, in the midst of an unpeopled marsh; when the piers of Waterloo Bridge shall become the nuclei of islets and reeds and osiers, and cast the jagged shadows of their broken arches on the solitary stream.[1]

But when biographer and historian Edward Walford considered what 'London' was some sixty years later, he came to the conclusion that it was much more than this small heartland:

> But in truth, when we speak of 'London', we do not mean so much a city as a collection or gathering together of cities. Not only is our metropolis many-handed, like Briareus, and many-headed, like Cerberus: it is manifold. It is no longer singular, but plural; it consists no longer of one city, but of many. It has engulfed gradually many cities, towns, villages and separate jurisdictions. Its present surface, as already inti-mated, includes large portions of four commonwealths, or kingdoms, those of the Middle Saxons, of the East Saxons, of the 'South Rie' (Surrey) fold, and of the men of Kent. Taken in its wider acceptation, as

shown above, London – or rather the district which is under the rule of the Metropolitan Police – now embraces, not only the entire cities of London and Westminster, but the entire county of Middlesex, all the boroughs of Southwark and Greenwich, the towns of Woolwich and Wandsworth, the watering places of Hampstead, Highgate, Islington, Acton, and Kilburn, the fishing town of Barking, the once secluded and ancient villages of Hanwell, Cheshunt, Harrow, Croydon, Finchley, Twickenham, Teddington, Chigwell, Sutton, Addington, and many others. It will be seen, therefore, that there is some truth in the witty definition which has been given of London, namely – 'That world of stucco which is bounded by Barnet on the north and Croydon on the south; which touches Woolwich in the far east, and Richmond and Twickenham in the far west.'[2]

Consequently, as mid and late Victorian reformers sought to grapple with social problems – poverty, disease, illness and other needs of society, such as housing, utilities, transport – they increasingly came to the conclusion that not only were more effective public bodies required, but also that these bodies should operate on a metropolitan-wide, as opposed to just a city-wide, basis.

For much of the nineteenth century, however, that was impossible. There were simply too many groups with vested interests, and too many fragmented organs of local government, from parishes to vestries (and not forgetting the powerful City of London), to allow even a semblance of a coordinated approach to any of these issues. True, central government had managed to create a metropolitan police force under the control of the Home Secretary, but even that had been a struggle and the new body had scarcely been popular, at least at the outset. So disliked were policemen in the early days that when one was killed by a mob during the Clerkenwell riots of 1831, the coroner's jury brought in a verdict of 'Justifiable homicide'. An annual banquet was held for several years afterwards to commemorate the event. It was hardly a ringing endorsement for central planning.

Yet the problem wouldn't go away. As the social reformer John Stuart Mill pointed out in 1861, London was inadequately governed by the wrong people:

The subdivision of London into six or seven independent districts, each with its separate arrangements for local business (several of them

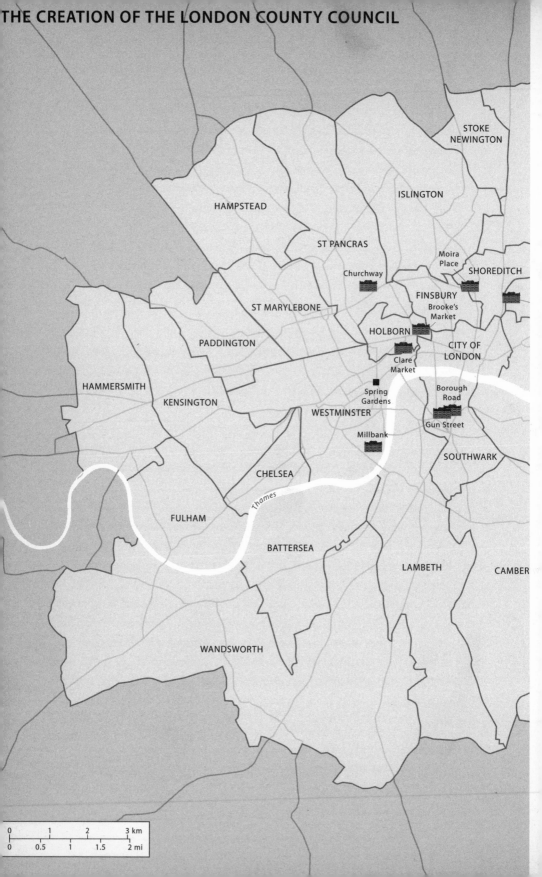

THE CREATION OF THE LONDON COUNTY COUNCIL

STOKE NEWINGTON

ISLINGTON

HAMPSTEAD

ST PANCRAS

Moira Place

SHOREDITCH

Churchway

FINSBURY

ST MARYLEBONE

Brooke's Market

HOLBORN

CITY OF LONDON

PADDINGTON

Clare Market

HAMMERSMITH

Spring Gardens

Borough Road

KENSINGTON

WESTMINSTER

Gun Street

Millbank

SOUTHWARK

CHELSEA

FULHAM

Thames

BATTERSEA

LAMBETH

CAMBER

WANDSWORTH

0   1   2   3 km
0   0.5   1   1.5   2 mi

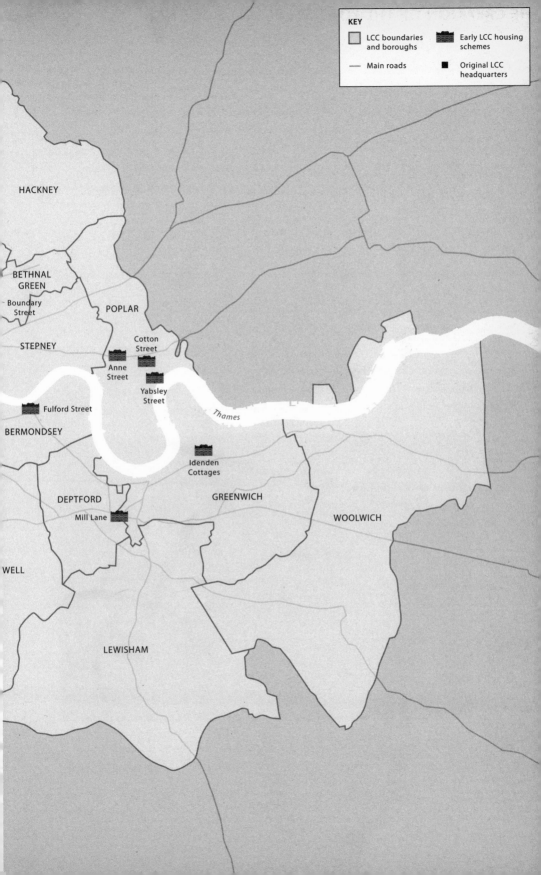

KEY

LCC boundaries and boroughs

Main roads

Early LCC housing schemes

Original LCC headquarters

HACKNEY

BETHNAL GREEN

Boundary Street

STEPNEY

POPLAR

Cotton Street

Anne Street

Yabsley Street

Fulford Street

BERMONDSEY

Thames

Idenden Cottages

DEPTFORD

Mill Lane

GREENWICH

WOOLWICH

WELL

LEWISHAM

without unity of administration even within themselves), prevents the possibility of consecutive or well-regulated cooperation for common objects, precludes any uniform principle for the discharge of local duties, compels the general government to take things on itself which would best be left to local authorities, if there were any whose authority extended to the entire metropolis, and answers no purpose but to keep up the fantastical trappings of that union of modern jobbing and antiquated foppery – the Corporation of the City of London.[3]

At the time he wrote this, such a view would still have seemed very radical. Even so, because London and its problems were growing so fast, few could ignore the need to do something; the difficulty was that nobody could agree what that something might be.

Earlier periods had witnessed some attempts at more concerted action: street lighting, for example, was introduced from the late seventeenth century, while the Westminster Paving Act of 1762 sought to coordinate and improve the capital's road surfaces and gutters; but these initiatives were few and far between, and it wasn't really until 1848 and the establishment of the Metropolitan Sewer Commission at the height of the cholera

Keeping London clean has always been a constant battle.
Here a group of street sweepers are doing their best in Covent Garden.

crisis that the first real step was taken towards running the metropolis in a more coordinated way. The commission's remit included Westminster, Southwark, all areas previously under the control of a local sewer commission, and:

> Any such other place in the counties of Middlesex, Surrey, Essex and Kent or any of them being not more than twelve miles distant in a straight line from St Paul's Cathedral, but not being in the City of London or the liberties thereof.

That said, if the intention behind the commission was noble, the outcome was dispiriting. Scheme after scheme was placed before the commissioners, but they were so busy fighting each other that they didn't have time to tackle the sewage problem. By 1855, when the commission was laid to rest, only a few miles of sewers had been constructed.

However, in 1853, while the commissioners were still busy attacking each other, a Royal Commission on the Corporation of the City of London was set up to look into a wide range of management issues affecting the City and the metropolitan area. Three commissioners were appointed – Henry Labouchère, Sir John Patteson and George Cornewall Lewis – and in 1854 they submitted a report to the Home Office with thirty-two recommendations. Quite a few of these were specifically to do with the City (the granting of a new charter, altering election methods for the lord mayor and aldermen, amending ancient administrative tools). However, the last five proposals they made were potentially far more wide-reaching:

> The remainder of the metropolis should be divided into districts for municipal purposes. The boundaries of the districts should correspond with the seven metropolitan parliamentary boroughs: Finsbury, Greenwich, Lambeth, Marylebone, Southwark, Tower Hamlets and Westminster. The districts would be governed by 'municipal bodies'.

> A Metropolitan Board of Works should be established consisting of a number of members deputed from the 'municipal bodies' and the Common Council (of the corporation of London).

> The coal duties of the corporation of London should be transferred to the Metropolitan Board.

The Metropolitan Board should be empowered to levy a rate for public works of 'general metropolitan utility'.

No works should be performed by the Metropolitan Board without the sanction of the Privy Council.

In the event, the call for the creation of municipal boroughs was rejected. It seemed just a bit too radical, even though other cities in England had been setting up their own versions since 1835. However, the proposal for a Metropolitan Board of Works did find favour. In 1855 the Metropolis Management Act was passed to sanction its creation, and it was formally constituted on 1 January 1856. Its remit was broad: forty-five members elected from parish vestries and district boards were to oversee the sewage crisis, and tackle issues such as slum clearance, new street planning, bridge construction and the building of the Thames embankments. A few years later, in 1865, the Board also took over responsibility for the Metropolitan Fire Brigade.

There's no doubt that in certain key areas the Metropolitan Board of Works, under the auspices of its chief engineer Joseph Bazalgette, was highly successful. It created a superb London-wide system of sewers, many of which are still there today. It built grand thoroughfares that greatly eased congestion in central London, cleared some of the city's slums and, operating alongside philanthropic housing associations such as the Peabody Trust, built new estates for the poor and labouring classes. A prime example is the Whitechapel Peabody Estate. Here the Metropolitan Board of Works cleared a maze of slums around Glasshouse Street between 1879 and 1881, and sold the land to the Trust, which built nine five-storey blocks to house nearly 1,400 people.

However, the Metropolitan Board of Works was controversial and not always popular. Some objected to its power to levy rates to fund its actions, and to the disruption that its schemes caused. At the other extreme, there were those who thought it had too narrow a remit, and argued that it should tackle other areas of metropolitan government beyond construction projects. An 1854 commission suggested creating a central body with wider powers, and a select parliamentary committee suggested in 1867 that the Metropolitan Board of Works should simply change its name to the Municipal Council of London and take on greater responsibilities. Three years later, two bills were proposed in Parliament that went even further

Building London's infrastructure: this photograph shows the laying of a new water main by the Southwark and Vauxhall Water Company.

in their attempt to bring London's cumbersome and disparate administration into some semblance of order. The County of London Bill proposed that the metropolis be made into its own administrative county – the County of London – while the Municipal Boroughs (Metropolitan) Bill attempted to reform the existing status quo by proposing ten municipal corporations that would accord with the metropolis's parliamentary boroughs. Neither proposal found much favour and both were resisted by, among others, the Corporation of London, which saw in the bills a less than veiled attack on its ancient liberties.

Yet further administrative coordination wasn't entirely stymied and the early 1870s did see a little progress, particularly in the area of education. The 1870 Education Act, as already mentioned, allowed for a School Board for London to oversee the improvement of existing facilities, the building of new schools and the provision of school places for all poor children in the city. Its significance lay not only in the fact that it was allowed to exist as an independent body in the first place, but that it was constituted in a similar way to the Metropolitan Board of Works: it shared the same boundaries and it used the same method of secret ballot and cumulative voting by London's ratepayers to elect its members. In other words, it seemed to embody a new consensus on how organisations with a wide remit should be constituted.

All this sounds high-minded and promising. It was as though London was inevitably evolving a better form of self-government. Local muddle required central supervision. However, as so often was the case with civic government, what actually brought about a real transformation in London's administration was not principle or the inexorable march of best practice but scandal. For some time the Metropolitan Board of Works had been accused of corruption and malpractice. Indeed, Board members were so widely believed to be feathering their own nests at London's expense that their organisation was known in some quarters as the 'Metropolitan Board of Perks'. Then, in 1886, a real public storm broke.

The particular circumstances that led to the outcry were several years in the making and of Machiavellian deviousness and complexity. Back in 1879 a proposal was put forward that the old Pavilion music hall in Piccadilly Circus should be purchased so that it could be torn down to make way for the construction of Shaftesbury Avenue, one of the Board's flagship new road schemes. However, until the work actually began, the site was granted a temporary stay of execution and was leased to the music-hall proprietor R. E. Villiers, who paid the Board a regular sum for the use of the site. He also paid an additional sum to F. W. Goddard, the Board's chief valuer, to ensure he got favourable treatment. When it seemed likely in 1883 that the redevelopment scheme would go ahead, Villiers met with Goddard and his assistant Thomas James Robertson to discuss how he could secure a lease to build a new theatre on the site once the road scheme was completed. In return for his building lease, Villiers agreed to allocate one corner of the site to a certain W. W. Grey (who just happened to be Robertson's brother), so that he could build a public house there.

In November 1884 the original lease on the site officially came up for renewal and Villiers promptly offered £2,700. The Board quite rightly requested an official valuation, but made the mistake of asking their ageing superintending architect, George Vulliamy, to carry out the work, not quite appreciating that he would delegate the task to his subordinates – who just happened to be Goddard and Robertson. They valued the site at £3,000, Villiers quickly sealed the deal, and a higher bid of £4,000 from another interested party somehow never got considered. The following year the area was redeveloped, with the completion of Shaftesbury Avenue, the reshaping of Piccadilly Circus and the erection of a new Pavilion Theatre. In December 1886 Villiers sold off his new establishment, having made such a handsome return on his investment that he was able to hand over £1,000 in cash and £5,000 in debentures to Goddard.

All this was exposed by the press in late 1886, and the Board felt obliged to conduct an internal investigation. Not for the first time, nor indeed the last, the internal investigation failed to find evidence of any wrongdoing by its officials. Unsurprisingly the public were less than impressed; and then, inevitably, the official body set up to look into the whole affair discovered that the Piccadilly scandal was only the tip of the iceberg. When the 1888 Royal Commission that looked into the management of the Board reported back, it concluded that various officials had been guilty of taking bribes from site owners and lessees, and that lucrative projects had effectively been sold to favoured architects. The inspector of theatres, John Hebb, had even gone so far as to suggest to managers whose establishments faced upcoming inspections that their best chance of getting a favourable report might be to send him free tickets. Most had complied, though Hebb increasingly found that his free ticket placed him at the back of the auditorium or behind a rather large pillar.

While the scandal was still brewing, various campaigns were waged to improve London's administration, including one by the London Municipal Reform League, founded in 1881 by a group of idealists and supported by such luminaries as the radical MP Sir Charles Dilke; retired judge and social reformer Sir Arthur (Lord) Hobhouse; Lord Shuttleworth, who had previously championed municipal reform in Parliament; and the vocal young MP for Tower Hamlets and Poplar, Sydney Buxton. However, these campaigns came to nothing, and it was not until well into Gladstone's second Liberal administration of 1880–5 that someone with the desire to see reform was given the authority to push it through: the Home Secretary Sir William Harcourt.

Harcourt was one of the Liberal party's heavyweights, with a particular interest in the capital, and while he had much else to contend with (not least a bombing campaign by Irish nationalists in England), he was determined to deal once and for all with the Metropolitan Board of Works and the creaking inadequacies of the parish vestries. Soon he was drafting reforming legislation, and by 1884 the task had become an all-consuming passion. 'I am buried up to my eyes day and night on the London Government Bill,' he wrote to his son, 'and see and hear of nothing else.'[4]

Harcourt's proposal for the metropolis was radical and simple. He conceived of London as a single unit, administered by one council rather than by a collection of separate boroughs, and with the City Corporation at its head – a canny recognition of its power. The Metropolitan Board of Works and the parish vestries would be swept away; and local district councils, controlled directly by the central council, would deal with regional administration. Even Harcourt realised that he could only push his ideas for unification so far. He did not suggest, for example, that there should be a single police force – rather a system whereby the City Police would report to the central council, and the Metropolitan Police would remain under the control of the Home Office. A degree of pragmatism was, however, accompanied by a sprinkling of populism; he argued that the current system was responsible for many of the City's evils, and that London was a place 'where wealth accumulates and men decay'. When he presented the bill to Parliament in 1884, a crowd of up to 120,000 people gathered in Hyde Park to voice their support.

Harcourt unwisely made little attempt to mask his contempt for the organisations he was seeking to abolish; these, he said, 'would not rise to the dignity of turtle soup – they would hardly rise to the dignity of conger'.[5] There is no doubt, however, that even had he not so openly antagonised vested interests he would have had a fight on his hands. Certainly, he was under no illusions about the challenges he faced. 'I approach the task,' he said, 'with the feelings of a navigator who enters a sea strewn with many wrecks, and whose shores are whitened with the bones of many previous adventurers.'[6] He can scarcely have been surprised, then, that in the event anyone who could oppose him did so quickly and vociferously: the Conservative Party, the City Corporation, the Metropolitan Board of Works and the parish vestries.

This was not an easy time for the Liberal administration. Ireland was in turmoil; the hugely popular General Gordon was hemmed in by the forces of the Mahdi in Khartoum, facing annihilation. The London Bill would have been controversial at the best of times, but the political climate now was about as unfavourable as it could be. Harcourt sensed that he had an unwinnable battle on his hands, bowed to the inevitable and finally wrote to Prime Minister Gladstone to admit defeat: 'It is too kind of you to offer to throw your shield over the London Bill. It will at all events give it euthanasia and throw a halo over its setting sun.'[7]

Harcourt's bill may have failed, but it aired a crucial issue and further galvanised the activities of such organisations as the London Municipal Reform League. Consequently when the 1886 general election produced a Conservative government without an overall majority, and so reliant on the Liberal Unionists for support, part of the price that the Conservatives had to pay for Commons support was a local government bill that recognised the need for greater administrative powers away from the centre. Over sixty boroughs throughout the country were to be removed from the jurisdiction of the historic counties and made county boroughs, while those parts of Middlesex, Kent and Surrey that formed the metropolis were to be united in a new County of London. The queen was to appoint a sheriff for the new county and grant a commission of the peace and court of quarter sessions.

Championing the creation of the new county councils was Charles Ritchie, the president of the Local Government Board, a key post that had previously been held by one of the supporters of the London Municipal Reform League, Sir Charles Dilke. Just a few short years before, Ritchie had been a vociferous opponent of Harcourt's Bill, but with the unblinking smoothness of a seasoned politician, he now claimed: 'I never denied for a moment that great alterations ought to be made in the administration of the municipal affairs of the Metropolis.' He also accepted that the Metropolitan Board of Works was no longer fit for purpose:

> I cannot shut my eyes to the fact that there does exist in London at the present time an authority which has the weight and power which an authority proposing to speak in the name of so great a centre as London ought to have. A great deal has been said of late about the Metropolitan Board of Works and about its administration. I am not going to refer to any of those statements beyond begging the House to accept my assurance that our proposals with reference to London have nothing whatever to do with any recent acts of administration by the Metropolitan Board of Works.[8]

The Act was duly passed, and on 21 January 1889 elections were held for the new London County Council.

———— ◄•►► ————

It's important to point out the things that the Local Government Act of 1888 didn't cover, as well as the areas that it did. This was not a radical piece of legislation. For a start, even though London was still expanding, for the purposes of the Act its limits were deemed to be those of the Metropolitan Board of Works as defined in 1856. The parish vestries and district boards were left intact, having retained all their powers while shedding the burden of the cost of repairs to main roads and some of the expenses of maintaining minor streets and footpaths. Nor did the Local Government Act bring the functions of various other institutions, such as the School Board of London, the Metropolitan Asylums Board and the guardians of the Poor Law, under the control of the London County Council. The Metropolitan Police force also remained outside its remit. Most importantly, the Act did very little to challenge or to change the long-standing autonomy of the City of London. The Act may have brought the City into the new County of London for 'administrative' purposes, but the City still controlled its own planning and transport, and retained its own police and judicial institutions.

The Fabian socialist Sidney Webb for one was disappointed by what had been achieved, and in 1889 published a tract entitled *Facts for Londoners*, laying out proposals for further reform that he thought London still needed:

> The capital of the empire has at last got its directly elected central
> municipal body of 118 elected members (with 19 co-opted aldermen!)
> under the name of County Council; but so much still remains to be
> done before London attains the freedom and social activity of the
> provincial cities . . . Notwithstanding their mismanagement and neglect
> of duty, the Vestries and District Boards are exceedingly costly.[9]

Nor was the London County Council greeted with ecstatic acclaim by the press or by the electorate. It seemed a grey, bureaucratic organisation with none of the pomp or ceremony one might hope for in the governing body of the most powerful city in the world. An editorial in *The Times* on 18 January 1889 reflected the general mood of indifference:

> It is, we are afraid, undeniable that the election of the County Council for London did not evoke yesterday the earnestness, not to say the enthusiastic zeal, which might have been looked for on such an occasion among the inhabitants of the greatest city in the world. In few districts were there signs which even the least eventful of parliamentary contests is wont to arouse. The polls, so far as they have been hitherto declared, were comparatively light.

The poor turnout and the view expressed by some that those elected to the council were 'mere vestrymen' certainly depressed Lord Rosebery, the inaugural chairman of the council, who remarked somewhat gloomily: 'Though we have worked hard, there has been a dead set against us by the public and in the majority of the Press.'[10]

For some the only positive thing that could be said about the council was that at least it wasn't the Board of Works. This discredited body limped on for a few transitional months and then expired the way it had lived, granting large pensions to those due to retire and huge salaries to those transferring to the council. Even in its dying moments it managed to cause an unseemly fuss when it insisted on making decisions on such key matters as the award of a contract to build the Blackwall Tunnel, despite written appeals from the council to leave matters to them. In the event it took the intervention of central government to resolve the row by abolishing the Board of Works earlier than planned, and allowing the council to take up the reins of power on 21 March 1889. The Board's epitaph was written by *Punch*, which praised the consistent way in which it had demonstrated 'how jobbery may be elevated to the highest level'.

If the London County Council was not exactly welcomed with open arms, and if its remit was comparatively limited, it nevertheless marked a major step forward. It did not simply inherit the powers of the Metropolitan Board of Works, it acquired new ones as well, ranging from responsibility for river embankments and flood prevention, to administering commons, main drainage, main roads and tramways, and the fire brigade. Now London had a central authority that held sway over an area that extended for some 117 square miles. Charles Ritchie's statement to the House of Commons when introducing the bill showed just what London now meant and how far it was officially deemed to extend:

> We propose to take London as defined under the Metropolis
> Management Act out of the counties of Middlesex, Surrey and Kent,
> and we propose to create it a county of London by itself with a lord
> lieutenant, a bench of magistrates and a county council of its own . . .
> We propose that the council shall be directly elected by the ratepayers as
> in all other counties and boroughs . . . It will take over the licensing
> powers and all the duties of the Metropolitan Board of Works, which
> will cease to exist . . .

To that extent it is quite understandable why the London Municipal Reform League should have been so ecstatic: 'Our victory had come, none the less valued, by a stroke of good fortune and without raising a finger. The apple had fallen from the tree into our lap!'[11]

Even Sidney Webb recognised that at least something had been achieved. He initially likened the new council to a medieval 'commune' – in other words, a self-governing community. Laurence Gomme, appointed as the council's clerk in 1900, and a driving force behind both the ambitious *Survey of London* and the blue plaque commemorative scheme, went even further. He viewed the London County Council as 'the reincarnation of the democratic spirit of the medieval charters, and traditions of citizenship as ancient as the Saxon and Roman origins of the city'. More recently, the historian Roy Porter described the creation of the LCC as 'perhaps the first unified government the settlement had enjoyed since it had been Londinium'.[12]

<hr />

The first elections to the council, using the mechanism of existing parliamentary constituency boundaries, took place on 21 January 1889. One hundred and eighteen councillors were voted in for three years, and they in turn voted for nineteen aldermen to serve for a period of six years. This first council was scarcely a radical body. Many of the old vestrymen were returned as councillors, and only a handful of people who could be said to represent working-class interests – John Burns (Battersea), the docker's leader, for example. Women fared even worse. As it happened, two were elected as councillors, and another selected as an alderman, but all three were then subjected to a furious campaign by disgruntled men. The suffragist Lady Sandhurst, who was returned as member for Brixton, was unseated in May when her disappointed male opponent Beresford Hope managed to get a ruling that while women might be allowed to vote in municipal elections, they certainly could not serve as councillors. Miss Cobden and Miss Cons then suffered a similar fate. It was to be another twenty years before women were allowed to sit on county and borough councils.

Even though the first LCC only partially represented the people it was supposed to serve, it did display a more progressive spirit than the Board of Works it superseded. This was a period of growing trade union activity, and of the Bryant & May match girls' and the dock workers' strikes. The Labour Party was beginning to emerge as a political force, its first MP, Keir Hardie, being returned as MP for Newham in 1892. In 1898 the socialists won the municipal elections in West Ham. The LCC may have been slow to see Labour councillors appear among its ranks, but the more old-fashioned Progressives, who allied themselves with the Liberal Party, did nevertheless dominate for the best part of two decades, leaving the Moderates (also called the Municipal Reform Party) to side with the Conservatives.

Soon the new body was making its influence felt. It took on all the responsibilities previously held by the Metropolitan Board of Works, including the management of the Metropolitan Fire Brigade, and quickly expanded its remit to include education, city planning and the provision of new housing. Slum clearance in the inner suburbs was an early responsibility, and public housing schemes a goal. Grand construction schemes, such as the building of Aldwych (1905) to link Holborn and the Strand, were also masterminded. In addition, the council tackled the demands of London's transport network, completing the Blackwall Tunnel in 1897 and acquiring tram companies from 1891 onwards; by 1899 it ran all of London's trams and it began electrifying the routes four years later. In 1892 the LCC was given powers to provide technical training and education in London. When the School Board for London was disbanded in 1903, its functions passed to the council.

The new authority soon decided that it needed a new home. At first it moved into the offices of the old Metropolitan Board of Works in

The headquarters of the Metropolitan Board of Works in Spring Gardens, taken over by the London County Council in 1889.

Spring Gardens (Trafalgar Square), but the building was soon bursting at the seams with councillors and aldermen, and by 1893 it was proving necessary to acquire various new properties to deal with the overspill. Some felt that a new purpose-built headquarters should be erected in Parliament Street near the seat of national government, but that idea came to nothing. Eventually, in 1905, the decision was made to purchase a site on the south side of the river in Lambeth. Proponents of the plan argued that this 'would brighten up a dull place, sweeten a sour spot and for the first time bring the south of London into a dignified and beautiful frontage on the River Thames'. Opponents argued that Lambeth was 'on the wrong side of the river . . . in a very squalid neighbourhood . . . and quite unworthy of the dignity of a body like the council'.[13] Work began six years later, and the LCC building – County Hall as it was to become known – was finally completed in 1922.

With their dominant position in the LCC – seventy-two councillors and eighteen aldermen in the 1889–92 administration – the Progressives, under the leadership of the first chairman Lord Rosebery, fought for more powers. In particular, they wanted a fully integrated system of local government, with the LCC very clearly in charge. As Rosebery argued in 1892:

> The present arrangement by which a comparatively small district in the centre of London is detached from London and held aloof cannot be maintained. The object of parliament and of reformers must be that the city should be united with London as soon as possible and with as little friction as possible. Of all London reforms I lay infinitely the most stress on this, because each can supply what the other lacks, because so many reforms are contingent on it, and because you cannot have a complete municipality without it.[14]

In the national and local elections of that year, the Progressives and the Liberals won the day. Rosebery found himself firstly Foreign Secretary in Gladstone's new administration, and then Prime Minister in 1894 on Gladstone's retirement. In 1892, that other proponent of local government, Sir William Harcourt, became Chancellor of the Exchequer. With such staunch supporters at the head of national government, the Progressives at the LCC felt emboldened to demand:

> The unification of London, by the removal of the division of the juris- diction between city and county, which now hampers every reform, but especially the great questions of the public services, such as water, gas, markets &c?[15]

The result was an inevitable royal commission with a five-man committee invited to 'consider the proper conditions under which the amalgamation of the City and County of London can be effected, and to make specific and practical proposals for that purpose'.[16]

Scarcely surprisingly, the City of London was not exactly delighted. Here was a commission that wasn't even being asked to consider whether amalgamation was a good idea; that view seemed to be taken for granted as part of its terms of reference. Instead, all the commission was being asked to do was to sign the execution form and sort out the practical details. The City responded by dragging its feet. Its special committee even advised that no further evidence should be furnished to the commissioners. Amalgamation, in its view, was 'a thing that should not be done and that the creation of a monster municipality is a thing to be utterly avoided, and the annihilation of the City equally to be avoided'.[17] The commission nevertheless proceeded on its way, publishing its final report on 29 September 1894. No one in the City could have been very surprised by the conclusions. The commission recommended a two-tier authority for London: a central body that brought together the LCC and the City of London Corporation and then a number of local authorities under its remit. The new central body would be called the Corporation of London, it would comprise 122 councillors and 20 aldermen, and it would run most of the services that the LCC already had under its control: bridges, water supply, street improvements, metropolitan markets, the management of open spaces and so on. Any remaining municipal duties would be passed to the new local authorities, and to those groups with particular remits, such as responsibility for public libraries, or for wash houses and baths, or for certain types of poor relief.

The London Liberal and Radical Union met to discuss the commission's report on 15 October 1894 and were joined in their deliberations by three Members of Parliament representing London constituencies, including Britain's first Asian MP, Dadabhai Naoroji (Finsbury Central). Their conclusion was that the commission didn't go far enough, and that even more powers should be granted to the proposed new body, including responsibility for the Metropolitan Police and the Metropolitan Asylums Board. The City and the Conservatives took a rather different view. The patrician Lord Salisbury railed against the evils of centralisation and described the commissioners as 'about the worst men' to be allowed to consider the whole issue. He took a pretty dim view of the LCC, too – ironically so, given that he was involved in setting it up – pointing out that at the last election the turnout had been only 40 per cent and that those who had bothered to vote were 'people with strong feelings . . . cranks and crocheteers [politically perverse people]' motivated by 'their special, limited fanatical views, or by their partisan or class antipathies'. As far as he was concerned, the LCC was 'the place where Collectivist and Socialistic experiments are tried. It is the place where a new revolutionary spirit finds its instruments and collects its arms.' Not only did he not support the commission's findings, he actually proposed decentralising power back to municipal authorities – in other words, back to the days before the Metropolitan Board of Works.

The Liberal administration accepted the recommendations of the commission, and a bill was duly drafted in June 1895. However, that was as far as things got. A new political wind was blowing which in March wiped out the Progressives' majority in the LCC and in June returned Lord Salisbury's Conservatives to power in the general election. The Progressives continued to fight a rearguard action, but decentralisation, not centralisation, was now the watchword. A new London Government Bill was drafted, brought before Parliament on 1 March 1899 and passed, receiving the royal assent on 13 July. Council and City would now never be brought together. Instead they stood in splendid isolation from one another, while twenty-eight new metropolitan boroughs were created, each with its own council comprising a mayor, councillors and aldermen, and each absorbing the old vestries and district boards. These metropolitan boroughs were granted some new powers, including shared responsibility for the demolition of buildings, regulation of water companies, power to acquire land, housing of the working classes and the ability to pass bye-laws. In the words of *The Times*, the legislation 'had probably brought to its last stage the long controversy as to the form of government best suited to the needs of London'.[18]

On 1 November 1900 the new metropolitan boroughs finally appeared: Westminster, Holborn, Finsbury, Shoreditch, Bethnal Green, Stepney, Bermondsey, Southwark, Camberwell, Deptford, Lewisham, Woolwich, Greenwich, Poplar, Hackney, Stoke Newington, Islington, St Pancras, Hampstead, St Marylebone, Paddington, Kensington, Hammersmith, Fulham, Wandsworth, Lambeth, Battersea and Chelsea. Slowly, the nature of the LCC started to change. Although the Progressives regained and indeed increased their control over the LCC in 1898, their days were numbered. In their place was a nascent Labour Party, who gained their first alderman in 1898 and returned councillors from 1907 onwards. Labour were even more successful in the boroughs, controlling eleven of the twenty-eight borough councils by 1919, the same number as the Municipal Reform Party – who were forced to form alliances with the remnants of the Progressives in the other six to keep Labour out. As for the Municipal

Reform Party, formed in 1906, they were essentially the London arm of the Conservatives. In 1907 they ousted the Progressives from power and so embarked on a Punch and Judy battle with Labour that was to continue throughout the new century.

THIRTEEN

'BREATHING PLACES FOR THE METROPOLIS'

The Fight for London's Open Spaces

For centuries, Londoners had been eating away at the landscape in which they lived, clearing forests, draining marshes and building on what remained. Street and place names frequently pinpoint the moment when the natural world was invaded by humans: Barnet, for example, which literally means 'burnt', refers to the clearing of forest by early medieval settlers in Middlesex; Cheam records the foundation of a medieval village among tree stumps; Woodridings, in Pinner, means the clearing in the woodland.

For us today the greater contrast is between what the street and place names literally mean, and what we can see in front of us. Acton was once an estate among oak trees. Up until the 1860s it was still largely agricultural. By 1901 38,000 people lived there and, thanks to its soft water, it was famed for its laundries. By the time of the 2001 census it was home to over 50,000 living in a tightly packed network of streets. Charlton similarly went from being a peasants' farmstead to an attractive Georgian village, before becoming subsumed into London. Peckham was once a hill (peak) village. Wembley was a meadow or grove belonging to a certain Wemba. All witnessed, sooner or later, the substitution of buildings for vegetation.

Up until the late eighteenth century the erosion of London's green spaces happened quite slowly. The outer villages and settlements remained generally small. If forest or scrub was cleared, it was generally to turn it into farmland rather than building land. Contemporaries sometimes lamented the growth of the city and the evils it contained, but few commented on the complementary changes that took place in the landscape. John Stow in the sixteenth century was a rare exception; so, too, was John Evelyn some

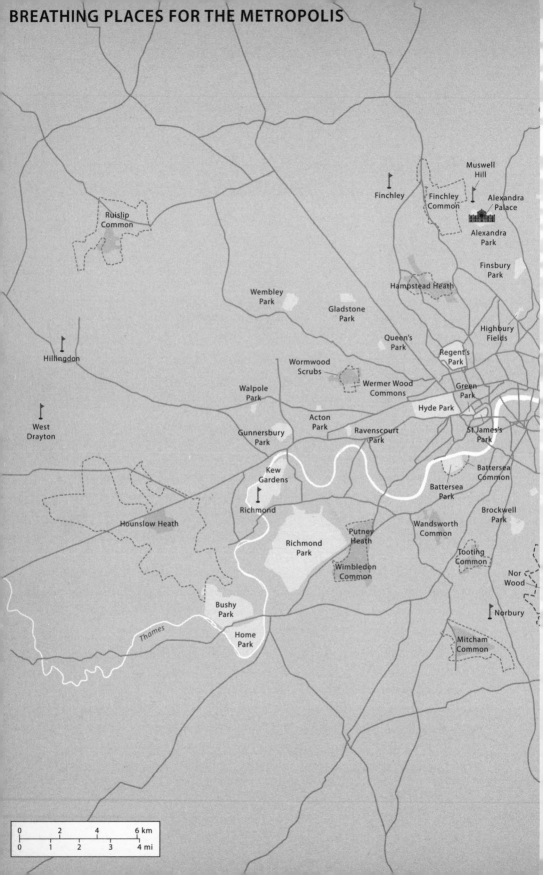

BREATHING PLACES FOR THE METROPOLIS

Finchley

Muswell Hill

Finchley Common

Alexandra Palace

Alexandra Park

Ruislip Common

Finsbury Park

Hampstead Heath

Wembley Park

Gladstone Park

Highbury Fields

Queen's Park

Regent's Park

Hillingdon

Wormwood Scrubs

Wermer Wood Commons

Green Park

West Drayton

Walpole Park

Acton Park

Hyde Park

Gunnersbury Park

Ravenscourt Park

St James's Park

Battersea Common

Kew Gardens

Battersea Park

Richmond

Brockwell Park

Hounslow Heath

Richmond Park

Putney Heath

Wandsworth Common

Tooting Common

Nor Wood

Wimbledon Common

Bushy Park

Norbury

Home Park

Thames

Mitcham Common

0   2   4   6 km

0   1   2   3   4 mi

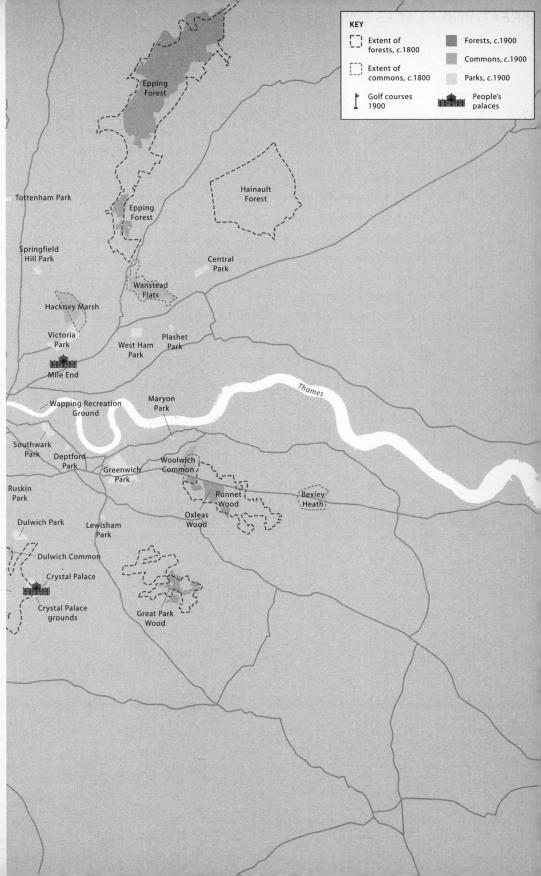

KEY

☐ Extent of forests, *c.*1800

☐ Extent of commons, *c.*1800

⚑ Golf courses 1900

■ Forests, *c.*1900

■ Commons, *c.*1900

■ Parks, *c.*1900

🏛 People's palaces

Epping Forest

Hainault Forest

Tottenham Park

Epping Forest

Springfield Hill Park

Central Park

Wanstead Flats

Hackney Marsh

Victoria Park

West Ham Park

Plashet Park

Mile End

Thames

Wapping Recreation Ground

Maryon Park

Southwark Park

Deptford Park

Greenwich Park

Woolwich Common

Ruskin Park

Runnet Wood

Bexley Heath

Dulwich Park

Lewisham Park

Oxleas Wood

Dulwich Common

Crystal Palace

Crystal Palace grounds

Great Park Wood

150 years later. In addition to decrying London's polluted air in *Fumifugium* (1661), he railed against the loss of London's (and England's) forests to industry and to house- and shipbuilders, and noted how woodland was being stripped bare and not replaced. His 1664 work *Sylva, or A Discourse of Forest Trees*, laments the decline of many trees, including the chestnut ('one of the most sought after by the carpenter and joyner'), of which he notes:

> It hath formerly built a good part of our ancient houses in the city of London, as does yet appear. I had once a very large barn near the city, fram'd intirely of this timber: And certainly they grew not far off; probably in some woods near the town: For in that description of London, written by Fitz-Stephens, in the reign of Hen. II. he speaks of a very noble and large forest which grew on the Boreal [north] part of it.

Certainly, quite a lot of London's woodlands appear to have disappeared in the course of the seventeenth century, and particularly during the English Civil War and Commonwealth period. This, for example, seems to be the time when the Crown-owned wooded estate at St John's Wood was stripped of its trees. They were never to be replanted. The first encroachments on Southgate's woodland took place even earlier: timber was being cut down there in Tudor times for use as firewood and to be converted into charcoal.

However, both in Evelyn's time and for the best part of a century afterwards this erosion continued in quite a slow and piecemeal manner. It wasn't until the late eighteenth century that London's open countryside, and particularly its wastes and forests, really started to come under pressure. Much of this was to do with the inexorable rise in the region's population. More specifically, though, it was hastened by the final stages of the enclosure movement, which continued to sweep away the traditional system of open field farming in England, stripping local people of their rights over common land, pasture and woodland in the process. In the two centuries between 1700 and 1900, nearly 7 million acres of land were enclosed across England, of which 2.5 million acres had been common land, or waste (generally deemed unsuitable for arable farming or pasturing). In many cases, enclosure was achieved by private agreement between the owners of the land and their tenants. In other instances, landowners sought approval from Parliament to remove rights of common

A somewhat impressionistic view of the rural idyll that was
Harrow in Victorian times.

over their land so that they could reserve it for their own use. Such land
might then well be given over to cultivation or, more often around London,
be leased to builders and speculators.

In his *View of the Agriculture of Middlesex* (1798) John Middleton made
a meticulous record of precisely which areas of common land were still in
existence in the county, and calculated that in total there were around 17,000
acres ripe for development and improvement, ranging from the very extensive (Hounslow Heath, Sunbury, Finchley, Harrow and Bushey, and Ruislip
Commons) to parcels of land under 100 acres (Hampstead Heath, Pinner
Common and 'Wormwood-shrubs'). His comments on Hounslow Heath
display his zeal to do something about land that he regarded as being wasted:

> Such parts of this tract of land as lie within the parishes of
> Twickenham, Teddington, and Hanworth, in case they were inclosed,
> would lett for very high rents. The rest of Hounslow-heath is land of
> such good quality, that it is disgraceful to the country, and insulting to
> the inhabitants of the metropolis, that it should remain in its present
> unproductive state . . .[1]

This particular observation suggests that for the most part Middleton viewed the commons as potential farmland, but elsewhere in his survey he was alive to the potential for covering them with houses:

> . . . from Muswell-hill, the south-east corner of this common, there is a most enchanting prospect over Hornsey, Clapton, London, and the beautiful river Thames. There are many points in this situation, that as much deserve to be adorned with elegant villas as any other spot in this, in many respects highly favoured county.[2]

By the 1820s, alarm bells were beginning to ring. So much land was now disappearing under piles of bricks and mortar that it seemed to some as though one day London would be an endless procession of streets and squares, denuded of trees and bereft of parks. The prospect clearly alarmed the Scottish-born landscape gardener John Claudius Loudon, who had taken up residence in London in the early 1800s, and who experienced life both as a town dweller in Porchester Terrace, Bayswater (the house he designed there still stands), and as a countryman in Pinner. In 1829, prompted in part by a proposal to enclose Hampstead Heath, he published his utopian view of the London of the future: *Hints on Breathing Places for the Metropolis, and for Country Towns and Villages, on Fixed Principles* – a plea for a greener capital city. 'Our plan,' he said, 'is very simple':

> that of surrounding London, as it already exists, with a zone of open country, at the distance of say one mile, or one mile and a half, from what may be considered the centre, say from St. Paul's. This zone of country may be half a mile broad, and may contain, as the figure shows, part of Hyde Park, the Regent's Park, Islington, Bethnal Green, the Commercial Docks, Camberwell, Lambeth, and Pimlico; and maybe succeeded by a zone of town one mile broad, containing Kensington, Bayswater, Paddington, Kentish Town, Clapton, Lime House, Deptford, Clapham, and Chelsea; and thus the metropolis may be extended in alternate mile zones of buildings, with half mile zones of country or gardens, till one of the zones touched the sea. To render the plan complete, it would be necessary to have a circle of turf and gravel in the centre of the city, around St. Paul's, half a mile in diameter. In this circle ought to be situated all the government offices, and central depots connected with the administration of the affairs of the metropolis. That

being accomplished, whatever might eventually become the extent of London, or of any large town laid out on the same plan and in the same proportions, there could never be an inhabitant who would be farther than half a mile from an open airy situation, in which he was free to walk or ride, and in which he could find every mode of amusement, recreation, entertainment, and instruction.[3]

Loudon was realistic enough to realise that his plan could never be realised in full: too much building had already occurred to allow for his first two green zones. His argument, though, was that if the government acted quickly enough it could establish zones further out from the centre that would come into their own 'during two centuries' as the pell-mell of building and expansion continued. In an impressive demonstration of foresight, he also suggested that key public services, such as sewers and cemeteries, should be placed outside the inner ring of development, and that there should be a coordinated radial transport network for commuters and for the delivery of goods.

When it came to the form that London's future open spaces should take, he was quite specific:

In the country zones . . . we would lay out [remaining space] as park and pleasure-ground scenery, and introduce in it all the plants, trees, and shrubs which would grow in the open air, with innumerable seats, covered and uncovered, in the sun and in the shade. We would also introduce pieces of water, under certain circumstances (especially if there were no danger of it producing malaria), rocks, quarries, stones, wild places in imitation of heaths and caverns, grottoes, dells, dingles, ravines, hills, valleys, and other natural-looking scenes, with walks and roads, straight and winding, shady and open; and, to complete the whole, there should be certain bands of music to perambulate the zones, so as at certain hours to be at certain places every day in the year.

Wherever a country town is likely to extend beyond a diameter of half a mile, we think a zone of breathing ground should be marked out as not to be built on, for the sake of the health of the poorer part of the inhabitants . . . It is much to be regretted, we think, that in the numerous enclosure acts which have been passed during the last fifty years, provision was not made for a public green, playground, or garden, for every village in the parishes in which such enclosures took place.[4]

Even allowing for a degree of pragmatism on his part, Loudon's vision for London was far too ambitious ever to be realised. However, in one superficially unpromising area of town planning, his views were shared by his immediate contemporaries; and this was to do with the arrangement and design of cemeteries.

The inspiration here came from the Continent, where landscaped public cemeteries had been popular for some time. Loudon was particularly impressed by the Père Lachaise cemetery in Paris, which first opened for business in 1804. Consequently, when plans were mooted and then passed for establishing London's new out-of-town cemeteries, he was an enthusiastic supporter, writing to the *Morning Advertiser* on 14 May 1840:

> Observing by the reports from the Commons House in this day's paper, that the above subject is likely to soon undergo discussion, allow me to suggest that there should be several burial grounds, all, as far as practicable, equidistant from each other, and from what may be considered the centre of the metropolis; that they be regularly laid out and planted with every sort of hardy trees and shrubs; and that in interring the ground be used on a plan similar to that adopted in the burial-ground of Munich, and not left to chance like Pere la Chaise. These and every other burial-ground in the country, might be made, at no expense whatever, botanic gardens; for, were nurserymen and gardeners invited, I am certain they would supply, everyone to his own parish, gratis, as many hardy trees and shrubs, and herbaceous plants, as room could be found for. It would be for the clergy and the vestries to be at the expense of rearing these trees if they choose, which I think they ought to do, if they get them for nothing.
>
> The burial places of the metropolis ought to be made sufficiently large to serve at the same time as breathing places, and most churchyards in the country are now too small for the increasing population. To accomplish the above and other metropolitan improvements properly, there ought to be a standing commission, for the purpose of taking into consideration whatever might be suggested for the general improvement, not only of London, but of the environs.

Loudon was particularly delighted by what happened at Abney Park, where the cemetery, opened in 1840, was liberally planted with trees and shrubs – 'one of the most complete arboretums in the neighbourhood of

London', he wrote in 1843. Cemeteries, clearly, in his view were not only for the grieving but for the pleasure-seeking, too. Unfortunately, he had little opportunity to practise what he preached. The only Loudon-designed cemetery to be seen through to completion turned out not to be in London, but in Cambridge, where his Histon Road cemetery still survives. In 1843, the same year that he published *On the Laying Out, Planting and Managing of Cemeteries*, he died and was buried at Kensal Green cemetery.

Cemeteries apart, more or less the only other areas of London guaranteed to be both free from development and open to the public were the royal parks, among them Regent's Park, St James's Park and Hyde Park in what was now the centre of the capital, and Bushy Park and Richmond Park further out. Many of these were landscaped, with attractive walks to be enjoyed on fine days. Some offered additional delights. London Zoo opened in 1828 in the northern corner of Regent's Park. Kew Gardens, which was handed to the nation in 1841, boasted classical temples, an orangery, a pagoda and a cluster of glass houses.

However, many of the other open spaces were either reserved for the few (for example, the gardens that were often placed in the middle of exclusive London squares) or potentially at risk of development. Of all these, it is Hampstead Heath that perhaps best demonstrates both the precarious status of much of London's greenery in the early nineteenth century and the sheer bloody-minded determination of many Londoners to keep it intact.

The villain of the battle for Hampstead Heath was Sir Thomas Maryon-Wilson, eighth Baronet of Eastbourne, nicely described by the *Oxford Dictionary of National Biography* as 'landowner and thwarted urban developer'. Owner of the manor of Hampstead and its accompanying estate of 416 acres, he made a series of attempts from the 1820s onwards to carve out long-term building leases from his land, even though he was restricted from doing so by the terms of his inheritance. It didn't assist his case that he had earlier opposed the construction of what was to become the Finchley Road on the grounds that it would disturb the peace and quiet of his Hampstead estate; nor did it help that his opponents included his powerful Hampstead neighbour Lord Mansfield, who didn't want his view from Kenwood spoilt by suburban villas. A further stumbling block for his scheme was the opening of Hampstead Heath station in 1860 and the consequent growing popularity of the area as a leisure spot for

*Holidaymakers on Hampstead Heath in 1871 – the same year that the future
of this large area of North London greenery was guaranteed.*

Londoners. Public opinion turned ever more forcefully against him.
Undeterred, between 1829 and his death in 1869 Sir Thomas brought a
dozen private estate bills before Parliament, becoming increasingly irascible
as each was rejected.

Eventually, in 1871, two years after he had gone to meet his maker in
a state of considerable irritation, his heirs agreed to sell their rights as
lord of the manor of Hampstead to the Metropolitan Board of Works
for the not inconsiderable sum of £47,000. Later in the century, a
committee, which included the formidable Baroness Burdett-Coutts and
Octavia Hill, raised some £300,000 to add the Maryon-Wilsons' East
(Heath) Park and Lord Mansfield's Parliament Hill Fields to the core of
Hampstead Heath. By this time the Maryon-Wilsons needed that extra
infusion of cash: they had just spent a fortune on a grand building scheme
that was to feature exclusive villas and a magnificent boulevard (later
Fitzjohn's Avenue).

The Hampstead Heath affair caused a huge and very public rumpus,
and it was in part thanks to the storm of protest which met every attempt
by Sir Thomas to drive through his scheme for redevelopment that a
ginger group was formed by, among others, the philosopher John Stuart
Mill, the author of *Tom Brown's Schooldays* Thomas Hughes and the

ubiquitous Octavia Hill. Their Commons Preservation Society (1865) vociferously campaigned to stop common land being dug up, over-grazed or built upon; and they also raised the alarm over former market gardens being sold off to the highest bidder. Their efforts paid off. A year after the group had been founded, Parliament passed a landmark piece of protective legislation: the Metropolitan Commons Act (1866). This covered the whole area encompassed by the Metropolitan Police District and, as its preamble stated, was:

> A scheme for the establishment of local management with a view to the expenditure of money on the drainage, levelling, and improvement of a metropolitan common, and to the making of byelaws and regulations for the prevention of nuisances and the preservation of order thereon.

In effect, the Act empowered local authorities to protect surviving commons. It could not strip landowners of all their rights of enclosure, but it did ensure that the interests of the public were taken into account.

What this meant in practice can be seen in a late Victorian account of Blackheath which describes what the common was like before the Act and what it became afterwards:

> From the early part of the present century, down to the year 1865, a considerable part of the surface of Blackheath has been greatly disturbed and cut up, owing to the Crown having let, for a rental of £56, the right to excavate an unlimited quantity of gravel. All these and other such encroachments, however, were brought to an end by the Metropolitan Commons Act of 1866, when Blackheath was secured to the public as a place of healthful recreation. During the summer months the heath is largely resorted to by holiday-makers, and, like Hampstead Heath, it is much infested with donkeys; but owing to the stringent bye-laws that have been passed of late years, the donkey drivers are not the nuisance that once they were. Cricket matches take place here in the summer; the Royal Blackheath Golf Club also use the heath as their play-ground, and in winter a well-contested match at foot-ball may often be witnessed here.[5]

The 1866 Act, then, helped ensure that many of London's open spaces were safeguarded for posterity. Without it, it's doubtful that names such as Hounslow Heath, Clapham Common, Wimbledon Common and Putney Heath would be anything more than a distant memory.

In addition to saving London's commons, the Act also helped protect much of the metropolis's surviving woodland. Like the commons, forests and woods had been under assault for centuries. Their trees had been felled and not replaced, and parcels of woodland had gradually been cordoned off and sold. Like the open areas, the forests had endured their own struggles to survive, the most public of which was the battle for Epping Forest.

The eventual victory at Epping Forest actually started with a defeat. In 1851 the Commissioners of Woods, who were agents for the Crown, decided to sell off the adjoining ancient tract of forest known as the King's Wood at Hainault. Two years later the steam tractors moved in, and within six weeks 3,000 acres of what had been royal forest since the time of Edward the Confessor were transformed into fields, roads and three large farms. The commissioners were delighted and eagerly awaited a flow of profits, calculated at £3,500 a year.

What they hadn't reckoned upon was a storm of public fury. 'Let not our rulers take from us a source of so much good, merely for the grati-

A Victorian picnic in Epping Forest around the Fairlop Oak.

fication of a few selfish members of the community,' thundered one of many letters of outrage to *The Times*. Articles were written, and protests loudly made. In the case of Hainault Forest, of course, it was all too late, but it didn't augur well for the commissioners' next campaign: to redevelop neighbouring Epping Forest. Sure enough, when the plans were announced in the early 1860s an almighty row erupted. Battle lines were swiftly drawn. On one side were ranged the Commissioners of Woods and the Maitland family, Loughton's lords of the manor; on the other were the Commons Preservation Society and a group of local people, led by the elderly Thomas Willingale, whose families had for centuries enjoyed lopping rights in the forest (that is, the right to collect wood for fuel provided that it was higher than six feet off the ground). In the conflict that followed, one side took 'trespassers' to court, the other tore down enclosing fences.

As with the battle of Hampstead Heath, the preservationists fought a rearguard action until the passing of the 1866 Metropolitan Open Spaces Act. Even then, the war wasn't definitively won until nearly a decade later. By that time the Corporation of London, who owned land in the area and thus technically had certain commons rights within the forest, had decided to take legal action against those landowners who had been busy enclosing areas of the forest; and in a landmark case they emerged as victors. In 1882 Queen Victoria came to Epping Forest to declare to cheering crowds: 'It gives me the greatest satisfaction to dedicate this beautiful Forest to the use and enjoyment of my people.'

The preservation of London's open spaces did not automatically mean the preservation of all the leisure activities they had once offered Londoners. The annual Epping hunt, for example, which over the years had become an excuse for heavy drinking by an assorted mixture of locals, finally came to an end around the time that Queen Victoria made her visit to the forest. No doubt those high-minded Victorians who had campaigned so furiously to keep the forest intact hadn't envisaged preserving it for such raucous activity. Similarly, many of London's traditional fairs were done away with in the course of the century, their working-class pleasures unappreciated by new suburban settlers. Greenwich Fair was one such victim of a new, more prudish era. Back in the 1830s, when it was attracting up to 200,000 people, it had been celebrated by Dickens in *Sketches by Boz* as a place where:

Whitsun revelries at Greenwich Park. The Victorians tended to take a dim view of the more raucous traditional London fairs, and many were suppressed.

*Charlton Horn Fair. Hugely popular in the seventeenth century,
the last one was held in 1872.*

The principal amusement is to drag young ladies up the steep hill which
leads to the Observatory, and then drag them down again, at the very
top of their speed, greatly to the derangement of their curls and bonnet-
caps, and much to the edification of lookers-on from below.[6]

Many locals, however, were not amused, and petitioned the Home
Secretary to close it down in 1857. Fifteen years later Charlton Horn Fair,
which had seen its heyday in Charles II's reign, went the same way. So,
too, did Blackheath's fair, as Edward Walford noted in 1878:

Blackheath Fair lasted, till a very recent date, as a 'hog and pleasure' fair
– being held on the 12th of May and 11th of October – till the year 1872,
when it was suppressed by order of the Government; and the swings,
roundabouts, spiced gingerbread, penny trumpets, and halfpenny rattles
have now become things of the past.[7]

By 1900 the vast majority of London's fairs had been suppressed.

Nevertheless, even if many fairs and their associated flagrant jollity disappeared, the open spaces continued to offer other, more sedate, pastimes. Even before the arrival of the railways, Epping Forest was popular with working-class visitors from the inner city who would come there by carriage on a Sunday to walk for miles around High Beach. Once Loughton and Chingford stations opened (in 1856 and 1870 respectively), up to 50,000 visited at a time, and on Whit Monday 1880 it was estimated that nearly 400,000 made the trip by train to spend a day in the forest.

Writing in 1885, and while lamenting some of the things that had befallen London, Edward Walford could also claim:

> With all this, there are happily many places round London still unbuilt upon . . . to which the cockney holiday maker may take a day's excursion, where he will find the fields still green, the hedgerows fresh, and the forest-trees in summer-time in full leaf, and waving bravely in the breeze . . . near London there are Wimbledon Common and Putney Heath, Wandsworth and Clapham Commons, Streatham, Tooting and Kennington Commons – in all, nearly 2,000 acres. Further afield are Bagshot Heath, Epsom, Leatherhead, Ashtead, Weybridge, Epping Forest, and other open spots.[8]

Once the preservation battles had been fought and won, the Victorians left Epping Forest and many of the larger green spaces more or less as nature intended them. Elsewhere, however, they couldn't resist reshaping and remodelling wherever possible. Parks and recreation grounds within the city were carefully landscaped, planted with trees and shrubs and furnished with various amenities and entertainments for the city's populace. One of the first was Victoria Park in east London, which opened in 1845. The plan drawn up by the surveyor of the Crown Estates, James Pennethorne, included a boating lake, sports pitches and a pagoda brought over from Hyde Park. Some years later, in 1864, the Metropolitan Board of Works went even further in laying out Southwark Park at Rotherhithe, installing ornate cast-iron gas lamps and building an impressively grand bandstand. Water featured prominently: there were ornamental lakes, an open-air swimming pool and drinking fountains. Wapping Recreation Ground came a little later, in 1875, on land reclaimed through slum clearance, while in 1886 the thirty-acre Queen's Park between Kensal Green and Kilburn was laid out by the city authorities. The following year the Metropolitan Board purchased the mansion house and grounds at Ravenscourt Park and created not just a green space there but a place of recreation for residents on the western side of the city, complete with a refreshment house and bandstand where performances were given twice a week during the season.

Some green spaces acquired a somewhat didactic air, inspired by the huge success of the 1851 Great Exhibition 'of the Works and Industry of All Nations', held in Hyde Park. The original Great Exhibition attracted some 6 million visitors from all social classes to see nearly 19,000 displays and exhibits housed in Joseph Paxton's Crystal Palace. 'Whatever human industry has created,' Charlotte Brontë wrote, 'you find there, from the great compartments filled with railway engines and boilers, with mill machinery in full work . . . and the carefully guarded caskets full of real diamonds and pearls worth hundreds of thousands of pounds . . . It seems as if only magic could have gathered this mass of wealth from all the ends of the earth . . .'[9] Given its huge popularity, it's scarcely surprising that when the Exhibition ended, the Crystal Palace was not demolished but moved lock, stock and barrel to Sydenham, where it became the centre piece of an amusement park, housing a concert hall, theatre, menagerie and exhibitions. It continued to attract visitors until 1936 when it was destroyed by fire.

Sydenham's rival to the north was Alexandra Palace, built using materials from the 1862 International Exhibition in South Kensington, and situated in a dominating position in a large park on what had once been farmland. Like the Crystal Palace in Sydenham, it offered a blend of entertainment and high-mindedness, with music festivals and a reading room inside, and archery, cricket and racing on offer outside. Like the Crystal Palace, too, it was consumed by flames, but whereas Sydenham managed to stave off its final catastrophe for eighty years, Alexandra Palace avoided conflagration for only sixteen days after it was opened in May 1873, at which point a fire in the dome devastated the complex. It was rebuilt, but was never the great commercial success that the Crystal

Alexandra Palace offered a blend of entertainment and high-minded instruction, but was never the commercial success that its promoters had hoped for.

Palace proved to be. It limped on until the First World War, when it was used to house German prisoners of war and, because of its position high above the London skyline, part of it was then taken over by the BBC for its early television broadcasts from 1936. Sadly, it managed to catch fire again in 1980.

The air of worthiness, and emphasis on self-improvement and education, that hung over such grand Victorian projects reached its apogee with the People's Palace in Stepney. Here was Alexandra Palace and the Crystal Palace rolled into one – but this time without the surrounding parkland. Championed by Edward Robert Robson, the architect who was instrumental in designing and building board schools throughout the metropolitan area from 1870, it was comprehensively aimed at working-class self-improvement, though it did offer general entertainment as well. It owed its origins in part to a trust fund set up before his death in 1840 by John Thomas Barber Beaumont (founder of the Beaumont Philosophical Institution in Beaumont Square on Mile End Road) 'for the mental and moral improvements of the inhabitants of the said Square, and the surrounding neighbourhood'. It was also inspired by Walter Besant's fictional *All Sorts and Conditions of Men*, published in 1882, which describes a 'palace of delight' that brings concerts, picture galleries and art to the inhabitants of the East End.

With funds in place, work duly began on a five-acre site on the Mile End Road, and the main hall, named 'Queen's Hall', was opened by Queen Victoria herself in 1887. The complex as a whole was completed five years later, and housed a library and reading room, gymnasium, exhibition halls, technical schools funded by the Drapers' Company, glass-enclosed winter gardens and swimming baths. It proved hugely popular, enticing thousands of people to take advantage of its facilities, and to visit the various shows that were put on – including animal fairs, poultry and pigeon displays, and even a chrysanthemum exhibition. Today, the site forms part of Queen Mary College, University of London.

For those looking to entertain themselves, rather than be entertained or 'improved' by others, London's green spaces had plenty to offer. There was the pleasure of a ramble in Highgate Woods, or a stroll on Clapham Common, or the prospect of feeding the ducks in St James's Park (a popular Victorian and Edwardian pastime). Alternatively, for the more energetic

A Sunday in Hyde Park.

there was sport. Sportsmen had, of course, always been part of the London scene, from the archers of seventeenth-century Finsbury to the gentlemen cricketers of the Marylebone Cricket Club in the late eighteenth century. Yet there's no doubt that sport – certainly organised sport – started to become much more prevalent in Victoria's reign. Golf is a good case in point. Thanks to the accession of the Edinburgh-born James I in 1603, who took up residence at the royal palace in Greenwich, it was being played in Blackheath in the early seventeenth century, but widespread popularity had to await Queen Victoria and her love for all things Scottish. Towards the end of the century various golf clubs opened on the outer fringes of London, including Richmond (1891), Finchley and Hillingdon (1892), Muswell Hill (1894), West Drayton (1895) and Norbury (1898).

A sport of rather more recent creation that became a virtual craze in late Victorian London was cycling. By the 1890s, bicycles were technically sophisticated and relatively cheap – certainly within the budget of most upper-working-class and lower-middle-class Londoners. The hero of H. G. Wells's *The Wheels of Chance* (1895), Mr Hoopdriver, for example, is only a lowly draper's assistant in Putney, but he can nevertheless afford a bicycle and spends his annual holiday cycling around the south coast in those final halcyon days before the arrival of the motor car. Cycling parties and clubs became briefly hugely popular in and around the metropolis. Uxbridge Cycling Club, formed in 1892, was only one of many examples. In Catford a cycling track was opened in 1895, though it lasted only five years. Putney even boasted a velodrome between 1892 and 1906.

In a handful of cases, whole suburbs became inextricably linked with particular sports. Kensal Green became famous for its National Athletics Grounds, which were laid out in 1890. Wimbledon became home to the All England Croquet and Lawn Tennis Club, a seemingly unlikely combination today, but a reflection of the popularity that croquet enjoyed in the 1860s and that lawn tennis eclipsed a decade later. In 1877 the first men's tennis singles championship was played, and the first women's championship was held a few years later in 1884. Twenty or so years later a ten-acre market garden in Twickenham, previously used to grow cabbages, was transformed into the home of English rugby (yet another nineteenth-century sport that grew tremendously in popularity). The first game there, between Harlequins and Richmond, took place on 2 October 1909.

However, of all athletic pastimes, it was football that came to dominate the sports played in London's open spaces. Enjoyed in villages and towns for centuries, it was left to the Victorians to remove most of the arbitrary violence and to codify the game, establishing representative bodies, leagues and competitions; and with their commercial pragmatism, to transform it from a local pastime into a paying national sport.

By the 1860s there was a small network of London clubs in existence, and in 1863 a number of them came together to discuss creating an official set of rules for the game: Barnes, Bucks FC (High Wycombe), Civil Service, Crusaders, Forest of Leytonstone (later Wanderers), No Names Club Kilburn, Crystal Palace, Blackheath, Kensington School, Perceval House (Blackheath), Surbiton, Blackheath Proprietary School and Charterhouse. Out of the meetings they held, the Football Association emerged (though not all the teams agreed to join), and the inaugural game under the new rules between Barnes and Richmond was held at Mortlake late the same year (it was a goalless draw). Nearly a decade later came the first FA Cup competition, which for most of its early years was dominated by the London-based clubs. Wanderers won the first final in 1872, playing in front of a crowd of 2,000 at the Oval, and went on to win four more times in the early years. Clapham were victors in 1880. The 1890s were not good for London football as northern professional teams started to make their impact felt, and it wasn't until 1901 that Tottenham Hotspur were able to bring the trophy back to the capital. Such was the popularity of the sport by now that some 110,000 people gathered at Crystal Palace to watch the final.

The London clubs had strong local affiliations, and – public schools aside – were often rooted in the workplace. Millwall football club, originally Millwall Rovers, was, for example, founded by the workers of J. T. Morton, a cannery and food processing plant at Millwall docks. By the end of the century a popular day out might involve watching Millwall and indulging in some heavy drinking, as the district inspector of police told one of Charles Booth's researchers:

> [28 May 1897] Occasional licence is no longer granted to supply beer on
> the athletic ground during football matches. This has diminished
> drinking on match days as there are many more people who would
> drink than can be supplied on the premises.[10]

Organised sport became a hallmark of the Victorian age.
This 1894 photograph shows the Woolwich Arsenal team.

Millwall's arch-rivals to the east were Thames Ironworks FC, formed in 1895 by the owner of the Thames Ironworks and Shipbuilding Company (they became West Ham United in 1900). Since both Thames Ironworks and Millwall's J. T. Morton often found themselves competing for contracts, it's scarcely surprising that rivalry spread to the players and supporters; nor is it surprising that West Ham are still known as 'The Irons' as well as 'The Hammers', while Millwall were popularly called 'The Dockers' up until 1910, when they moved to grounds in New Cross.

Woolwich Arsenal football club was similarly formed by workers, in this case workers employed at the Dial Square workshop in the Royal Arsenal at Woolwich. They turned professional in 1891 – an unpopular move to some, who therefore went off to form a breakaway team, the Royal Ordnance Factories (it folded five years later). Some measure of the level of support for Woolwich Arsenal is shown by another of the reports put together for Charles Booth:

[28 May 1900] Arsenal Football Ground with a grandstand and surrounded by a wooden paling; crowded in winter; 'sometimes 25,000 onlookers of a Saturday' said [Police Constable] Clyne; boys paid 3d and men 6d and 1/-; different gates for each price.[11]

As fan bases grew, London teams acquired open spaces to play. Tottenham Hotspur, for example, transferred in time from Tottenham Marshes to White Hart Lane, the former site of Charrington Brewery. Unlike Millwall and Woolwich Arsenal, they were not a works team, their players being originally drawn from grammar-school boys attending the Bible class at All Hallows church. Millwall played at various grounds on the Isle of Dogs in their early years before pressures of space forced them to move south of the river. Fulham (founded by worshippers at St Andrew's church) similarly played at a number of locations before settling on Craven Cottage – formerly, as its name suggests, a cottage built by Lord Craven in the late eighteenth century and, until football arrived, surrounded by woodland. As for Woolwich Arsenal, they wandered a long way from their original home: having started out on the muddy fields of Plumstead, they ended up in Highbury in 1913 and, logically enough, decided to drop the 'Woolwich' part of their name the following year.

When it came to national and international events, London's great opportunity came at Italy's expense when Mount Vesuvius erupted in 1906, and funds that had been reserved for the fourth Olympiad due to be held in Rome two years later were diverted instead to Naples. London beat off competing offers from Munich and Berlin to host the Olympics, and in an extraordinary feat of civil engineering, a purpose-built stadium was constructed in only ten months: the White City Stadium, built on farmland in Shepherd's Bush. Not all events were held there: clay pigeon shooting, for example, was held at the Lancaster Shooting Club at Uxendon Farm.

The 1908 marathon, which started within sight of the nursery window at Windsor Castle at the specific request of Princess Mary, nicely linked together London's western suburbs, passing in an arc through Uxbridge and Harrow before making its way to White City Stadium. Scandal and excitement surrounded the event. The American marathon runner and flag-carrier Ralph Rose won considerable notoriety at the opening ceremony when he refused to dip the Stars and Stripes before the Royal Box as he passed by. Fortunately, for royalists, he did not win. That honour went to his compatriot Johnny Hayes, but not before it was decided that the Italian Dorando Pietri should be disqualified because in his exhausted estate he had actually been helped across the line by two well-intentioned officials.

The ultimate fate of the White City Stadium, however, showed the continuing precariousness of London's open spaces. Where parks, commons and open ground were protected by law, they remained safe from further development. Where they lacked protection, they would always be under threat. Most of the grounds surrounding the White City Stadium were acquired by the London County Council in 1936 and covered with housing. The stadium itself was demolished in 1985 to make way for BBC buildings.

PART IV

THE MODERN CAPITAL

FOURTEEN

FROM METROPOLIS TO METROLAND

London, 1889–1939

In the half-century between 1889 and the outbreak of the Second World War the suburbs came to dominate London. Not only did they continue to expand over previously open countryside to the north and south of the Thames, but they also lured and enticed the population from the centre to such an extent that by the eve of war in 1939, more people were living outside the middle (4.6 million) than within it (4 million). When Hitler's blitz on the capital began in 1940, the City itself – London's heart – was home to only 9,000 people. The City's old rival – Westminster – was in decline. So, too, were Wandsworth, Tower Hamlets, Lambeth, Islington and Camden. By contrast, such once seemingly remote areas as Brent, Harrow, Havering, Hillingdon, Merton, Redbridge and Sutton were on the rise, their terraced streets, shops, workshops and factories snaking their way to meet up with earlier established suburbs. It was London's final great growth spurt.

Part of the reason for this extraordinary migration outwards was that from late Victorian and Edwardian times onwards, there were ever fewer places to live in the centre. By 1900, London was not just the capital city of a nation, but of a great empire, and it was felt that it needed the grand civic edifices of an imperial city. Whitehall and the surrounding area became packed with government buildings. The Foreign Office and the India Office south of Downing Street were completed in 1868; the new Colonial and Home Offices in 1878; and a whole complex of buildings that included the Cabinet and War Offices were constructed between 1900 and 1915. From 1851 to 1901 the number of civil servants required to man these various offices more than doubled from just over 19,000 to 49,000. Elsewhere, great financial buildings sprang up: the Baltic Exchange

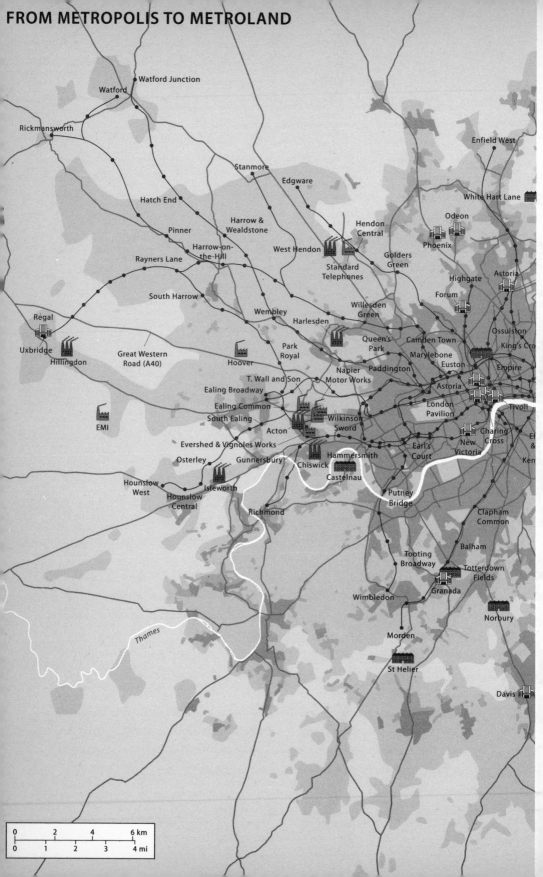

FROM METROPOLIS TO METROLAND

KEY

- Built-up area, *c*.1900
- Expansion, *c*.1900–14
- Expansion, *c*.1914–39
- Main roads
- Underground lines and stations
- Factories
- Industrial centres
- Council estates
- Cinemas

Lea Valley

British Xylonite Co

Gestetner Works

Finsbury Park

A12

Upminster

Becontree

Stratford

A12

Plaistow

Upton Park

West Ham

West Ham/Beckton

Ford Motor Co

Liverpool St

Whitechapel

Aldgate East

Bank

Waterloo

ephant Castle

nington

Thames

Woolwich Arsenal

Siemens

GEC

New Cross Gate

Page

Downham

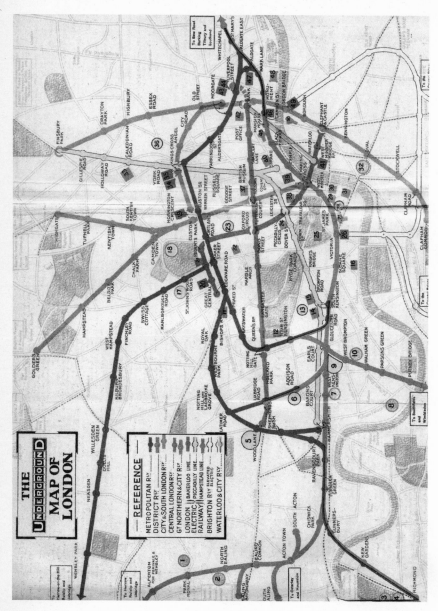

The London Underground network in 1911.

in 1903, opulent headquarters for the Prudential Assurance Company in Holborn (1899–1906) and a clutch of new banks in Gracechurch Street just before the First World War. In the West End, magnificent hotels, restaurants and shops arose around Piccadilly and Oxford Street, including the Ritz (1903–6), the Regent Palace Hotel (1912–15) and the department store built by the extravagant and ultimately near-bankrupt American Gordon Selfridge (1906–9). All these involved massive redevelopment, and in the process many houses were lost: Holborn's early Edwardian development, for example, spelled the end for the slum dwellings that had once surrounded Saffron Hill.

However, it wasn't just that there were fewer houses to be found in central London; outer London seemed ever more reachable and, more importantly, desirable and affordable. Thanks to the wheeler-dealer Charles Yerkes, the London Underground was being transformed into a unified and highly efficient system. Not only did he integrate what was already there, he also paved the way for a series of new lines. The early history of what was to become the Bakerloo line perfectly illustrates his galvanising influence. Construction of the line was actually started back in 1898 by the Baker Street and Waterloo Railway. Unfortunately, in 1904 its leading light, Whitaker Wright, was convicted of fraud and, rather than face the music, opted for cyanide instead. Yerkes therefore stepped in. Sadly, he did not live to see the project's conclusion, but shortly after his death in 1905 the Bakerloo line (a nickname coined by a journalist and regarded as vulgar by many) was opened on 10 March 1906 between Baker Street and Kennington Road. In the same year another one of Yerkes's companies, the Great Northern, Piccadilly and Brompton Railway, established a railway between Baron's Court and Finsbury Park. It was rapidly followed by the Hampstead (later Northern) line from Charing Cross to Golders Green and Highgate, opened with considerable fanfare by David Lloyd George in June 1907. This was also the decade when lines were increasingly electrified and steam trains abandoned.

The tram system was similarly being overhauled. As with the Underground, lines were electrified throughout the early Edwardian period, while the London County Council moved in to buy and integrate many of the routes previously run by the London Streetways Company, and the North Metropolitan Tramways Company. In 1908 a link was forged between the northern and southern networks when the Kingsway

347

Westbourne Grove around the turn of the twentieth century.

Subway was opened, and by 1909 the LCC was operating over a hundred miles of track. Meanwhile, small, independent tram companies continued to operate elsewhere (though both the City and the West End proved very sniffy about trams on their roads) and in the process came to transform the lives of people in places such as West Ham, Leyton and Dartford to the east, and Richmond, Twickenham, Hampton, Hounslow and Chiswick to the west. During the same period motorised omnibuses were introduced (1902), increasingly under the single authority of the London General Omnibus Company after 1912.

Electric trams and motorised omnibuses spelled the end of the great days of the horse. They were still pulling carts – particularly milk carts – well into the 1930s and, in a few cases, until after the Second World War, but they were increasingly to become the exception rather than the rule. The last horse-drawn omnibus trotted its way out of London history on 25 October 1911, ending a relationship between horses and Londoners that stretched back two millennia. Meanwhile, travel on more modern forms of public transport continued to rise inexorably, nearly doubling in the Greater London area between 1901 and 1911, to 250 journeys per head of population per year.

Then, as now, public transport was not without its problems. For a start it could be quite dangerous. Over 25,000 people were killed on London streets in 1913, motor buses being principally responsible for the carnage. Trains and buses were often dirty and overcrowded, and full of the smoke of cigarettes and pipes. Fellow passengers had an unpleasant tendency to spit on the floor. Yet, if all that could be tolerated, the rewards of public transport were considerable. In a matter of a few minutes the commuter could be transported from the grime and smog of central London to the leafy suburbs. The decision to leave the centre behind was, for many, an easy one to make.

The great surge in suburb-building occurred in two waves. The first reached a peak towards the end of Queen Victoria's reign before subsiding, to be brutally cut off short by the outbreak of the First World War. The second wave started in the mid 1920s and was again curtailed by global conflict. That second wave certainly outstripped the Edwardian one, but the former was nevertheless substantial. To the north, areas such as Tottenham, Wood Green and Edmonton completed their process of suburbanisation by the second decade of the twentieth century, and new developments appeared in Palmers Green, Winchmore Hill and New Southgate. Hendon expanded rapidly, as did Golders Green. To the west, Wembley and Ruislip experienced their first suburban stirrings, while Willesden and Acton completed a process that had begun with the arrival of their railway junctions the previous century, and middle-class housing spread across Ealing, Hanwell, Southall, Heston and Isleworth. South of the river, Balham, Tooting and Streatham all became increasingly linked to one another by an expanding web of streets, shops and houses. The populations of Merton and Morden rose sharply, and Raynes Park became south-west London's new frontier. Even further out, suburbs sprang up wherever there was a convenient railway station: Epsom, Wallington, Carshalton, Sutton, Cheam and Croydon, Beckenham and Bromley, Chislehurst and Sidcup, East and West Ham. The number of people living in Ilford nearly doubled in the ten years between 1901 and 1911.[1]

A fair number of the late Victorian and Edwardian suburbs sprang up to serve London's burgeoning lower middle class: the clerks, teachers and shopworkers who helped to keep the metropolis ticking. These were increasingly affluent people, whose wages might even run to hiring a maid to take on the household chores that came with owning a suburban property. Other new suburbs were created to house skilled workers in London's factories and service industries. In Beckton the establishment of a gasworks before the First World War attracted workers to the area, accommodated in small cottages constructed by the gas company. Many are still standing today. Upton Park and Plashet, formerly the north end of East Ham parish, similarly saw the development of new estates of 'long terraces of small but well-built dwellings for clerks and skilled workers',[2] their appeal enhanced by the good transport links provided by the Eastern Companies Railway and by the extension of the District line to the area in 1902.

Some late Victorian and Edwardian development was carefully planned: Hampstead Garden Suburb, for example, LCC housing, a few cooperative projects, and some projects funded by individual companies. Most, however, were created by the speculative builders whose ancestors had built so much of earlier London. As in previous eras, an area of land would be purchased and sliced up into building plots. An individual builder might

The suburban dream fulfilled: a family gathering outside a house in Dulwich, c.1910.

then take over six or so plots on which to build houses, and generally come up with the unsurprising terraced house with its best parlour and scullery. Ordnance Survey maps of the period reveal just how piecemeal most local development was. Typically, the first map in the chronological sequence will show a small settlement – perhaps a church, a few cottages, a handful of larger houses standing in extensive grounds, a main road and some footpaths, an expanse of fields – and a railway station. By the time of the next map, a grid of new streets has often appeared, generally running parallel to one another, with intersecting roads cutting through them. All are neatly divided up into building plots; some already marked with the clear outline of houses on them – either virtually block-like or square, with a back extension. Fast forward to the subsequent map, and all (or virtually all) of the plots have been filled, and any green space that had previously lain just next to them has started to disappear under the next network of streets and houses.

The Ordnance Survey maps of East Finchley in north London show this pattern of development nicely. The detailed 1894 map shows a number of new roads laid out near the station, running at right angles to the High Road – once the old coach road out of north London, and by 1894 lined with shops. All the new roads are shown divided up into building plots, but houses are shown continuously only on those roads closest to the station. The 1911 Ordnance Survey, by contrast, shows almost contin-uous development along all the streets, though there are a few vacant plots to be seen. Because the houses were built by different builders over a period of years, these East Finchley roads lack the majestic sweep of the grand early nineteenth-century inner-London terraces. Here terraces start and stop after a few houses; and although all are brick-built, they are also subtly different from one another, reflecting the particular tastes and budgets of their builders. Some have elaborate front porches, some have front bay windows, most are resolutely rectangular and a few display the flamboyant arched features of high Victorian Gothic.

In more expensive parts of town, where land was at a premium and the potential for profit therefore that much greater, new speculations from the 1870s onwards often took the form of mansion blocks. The early ones constituted quite a gamble. Most Londoners assumed that only poorer people (or foreigners) shared buildings, so the idea that the more pros-perous might want to do the same must initially have seemed very strange indeed. It is perhaps for that reason that the early developers so eagerly stuck the word 'mansions' after the name of the block they were building, as though that elevated word could disguise what was going on inside.

Nevertheless, there were compelling reasons for creating middle-class blocks of flats that went well beyond their financial attractiveness to their creators. Many people – single men, young couples, the elderly and retired – simply didn't need or want a house or the expense that went with it, but they did want to be close to town. What's more, they might want a servant, but they didn't want the small army that larger establishments required, particularly at a time when, because a limited pool of hired help was becoming shared among an ever-growing number of middle-class Londoners, servants' wages were going up.

Mansion blocks, then, made sense, and after a slow, uncertain start they started to spread. Queen Anne's Mansions, built in Westminster in the 1870s and long demolished, were among the first. They were followed in due course by Albert Hall Mansions in Kensington: three six-storey blocks designed by Norman Shaw in the 1880s and featuring bathrooms, wine cellars and even lifts. Soon mansion blocks could be found in locations from Kensington to St John's Wood and Belsize Park, from

Mansion blocks increasingly became a feature of the London landscape from late Victorian times. This block stands in West Hampstead.

Marylebone to Maida Vale, and from Battersea to Fulham and Chiswick. The less ambitious involved flights of stairs for their tenants. The grander ones offered every modern convenience: lifts, bathrooms and lavatories, electric lights and a room (usually off the kitchen) for the maid. Their developers were keen to keep them exclusive – the bill of sale for the land in West Hampstead that came to be occupied by Yale Court in Honeybourne Road, for example, made it quite clear that any new housing was not to be of the variety in which 'artisans' would live; and in that they seem to have been successful. The 1901 census returns for Ashworth Mansions in Maida Vale (which boasted uniformed porters) show it to have been home to three engineers, a couple of journalists, a theatrical manager, a barrister and an architect, among others. For its part, Kensington Mansions in Earl's Court was occupied by a number of people living on private means. Inevitably, the fact that mansion blocks could as readily house single young ladies as bachelors gave them, in some parts of town at least, a somewhat louche reputation. In the early years of the twentieth century Maida Vale for some was what St John's Wood had been just a few decades before. Nevertheless, by 1900 middle-class flat-living was firmly ensconced in the capital.

When it came to choosing street names for the new roads in which they were planting their mansion blocks and terraces, developers looked near and far for inspiration. Frequently, the name had a strong local association: possibly the name of the previous owner of the now terrace-strewn estate, perhaps reflecting the farm or large house that had once stood there, or recalling a local celebrity or former landmark. The great and good of Victorian and Edwardian times also frequently lent their names to suburban development. Victoria was quite a popular choice (as was 'Jubilee', particularly in commemoration of the Diamond Jubilee of 1897); so, too, were such leading statesmen as Palmerston, Gladstone and Disraeli; and figures from the worlds of art and science, both ancient (Chaucer, Shakespeare, Newton) and modern (Tennyson and Darwin). In Mill Hill a small late Victorian development on what had previously been fields managed not only to come up with Victoria and Albert Roads alongside one another, but Shakespeare, Milton and Tennyson in a row, and Byron at right angles. Elsewhere in London these might be leavened by references to great moments in imperial history. The Boer War, for example, contributed a small rash of Ladysmiths and Mafekings. In that peculiarly British way, great disasters were commemorated, too: the death of General Gordon at Khartoum in 1885 duly left its mark on the London map.

Occasionally, imaginative desperation seems to have set in, and roads and streets ended up being numbered or lettered rather than named. The London A–Z shows a whole sequence of streets following the 'first avenue' model. When the Artizans, Labourers and General Dwellings Company had their new development laid out in Queen's Park in north-west London in the late 1870s, they lettered their streets from A to P. It wasn't a popular choice, and the streets were soon renamed.

Often, of course, the way a speculator's house looked precisely reflected the sort of people who were going to end up living in it. Two-bedroom cottages were likely to be occupied by poorer people. Large houses in posh areas, perhaps detached or built in pairs, were more often than not going to be popular with the prosperous. In *The Railway Children*, for example, written by that suburban sceptic E. Nesbit in 1906, it's clear from the opening that this is a book about middle-class people:

> They were not railway children to begin with. I don't suppose they had ever thought about railways except as a means of getting to Maskelyne and Cook's [a magic act that often performed at the Egyptian Hall in Piccadilly], the Pantomime, Zoological Gardens, and Madame Tussaud's. They were just ordinary suburban children, and they lived with their Father and Mother in an ordinary red-brick-fronted villa, with coloured glass in the front door, a tiled passage that was called a hall, a bathroom with hot and cold water, electric bells, french windows, and a good deal of white paint, and 'every modern convenience', as the house-agents say.[3]

It comes as no surprise to learn in the ensuing pages that whatever servant crisis may have been affecting other Edwardians, the occupants of Edgecombe Villa are not affected: the railway children's father is able to employ a cook, a nursemaid, a housemaid and a parlourmaid.

That said, because the bulk of new suburban streets and the houses they contained were created speculatively, it didn't automatically follow that they would be taken by the sort of people the builder had in mind for them, or indeed be filled right away. A perusal of the detailed returns from the 1911 census reveals again and again that houses seemingly built for a single family ended up being sublet to a number of tenants. Hatherley

Road in Sidcup offers a good example of this sort of residential pattern, and also serves as a reminder of just how mixed and varied London suburbs could be. Most of the people living here could be described as middle class, but there was a quite a difference in status between those who lived in the spacious houses at the top of the road, and those at the other end who were crammed into flats in buildings that had clearly originally been designed as individual houses for single families. Number 32, which contained nine rooms, was home to the relatively prosperous architect Charles Canning Winmill, his wife and daughter, and their two servants. Number 61, by contrast, was split into two flats. One, containing three rooms, was home to Amelia Wright, a 57-year-old spinster, and her two boarders, Charles Algernon Wooderidge, a 37-year-old printer master, and 26-year-old Maurice Booty, employed as a schoolmaster; the other, again with three rooms, was where the wine merchant's clerk Frank Wright and his new wife Melissa Wright lived. A more unusual note was sounded by numbers 2–5, which were occupied by St Joseph's Convent, home to seven nuns, their Mother Superior Felicité Cronillard and, on the day the census was conducted, six boarders.

The fact that apparently quite well-to-do houses could end up with numerous tenants makes it very difficult to guess the relative affluence of a Victorian or Edwardian house from its physical appearance. There were all sorts of gradations in a single street like Hatherley Road, and further ones between one street and the next. Moreover, then as now, the social status of an area could change, sometimes very swiftly. Some wealthy suburbs such as St John's Wood or Richmond might retain their status from year to year, but other once relatively affluent areas might well decline as their middle-class owners moved out and poorer tenants moved in. Fulham, Hammersmith and north Kensington, Camden and Islington, Hackney and areas of Bermondsey all witnessed an exodus of the well-to-do and their replacement by the badly off in the late nineteenth and early twentieth centuries. Even parts of Hampstead suffered a decline as a new generation of middle-class families from the 1880s and 1890s onwards turned up their noses at the large houses of Belsize Park and Rosslyn Park, opting instead for smaller homes with modern bathrooms elsewhere. Some of these formerly grand Hampstead edifices were turned into small schools, but others became boarding-houses or were divided into flats and bed-sits, moving 'down market' in the process.

Islington is perhaps among the most extreme examples of a previously genteel area fallen on hard times. When it was still separated from town by fields, it was a popular suburban retreat for well-heeled city workers. Nearby Canonbury and Barnsbury were home to bankers and stockbrokers, and Holloway to humbler but nevertheless 'respectable' clerks. The area, however, started to decline in the 1870s as the more well-to-do took advantage of improved railway links to move further out and the poor from the inner suburbs moved in. Previously elegant Georgian houses were subdivided. New cramped terraces and estates were built on such open ground as remained. By the time George Gissing wrote his novel *New Grub Street* in the 1890s, Islington was well on its way down, home to hawkers and sweat shops, and things continued to get worse through the early years of the twentieth century. In Edwardian times Islington was notorious for having some of the poorest housing in the capital. Three-quarters of the people who lived there did not have ready access to running water, an inside lavatory or a bath.

The First World War brought all development to a temporary halt, as London's energies were turned to defeating the Germans, its young men went off to serve at the front, and those at home faced increasing shortages as enemy U-boats sank ever greater tonnages of British ships.

In physical terms the war had comparatively little effect. Zeppelins and, later, squadrons of German aeroplanes may have brought terror to the capital, but their destructive power was limited. On 31 May 1915 Zeppelin airship LZ-38 bombed the docks and the East End of the capital, killing seven people, but its impact was more psychological than physical:

> London watched the inadequate defences go into action. The searchlights lanced the skies but were unable to pick up the raider. The ineffective pom-poms grunted and growled but only showered the suburbs with jagged shrapnel. A few Home Defence flyers took off to do battle, but as usual nothing happened. The warning sirens shrieked and died down. The pungent smoke pall seeped across the Thames, and hurriedly organized rescue teams clambered through the wreckage, cursing a government that had failed to anticipate this form of warfare.[4]

In all, some 670 Londoners died in bomb raids between 1914 and 1918.

Yet if the war had a limited effect on London at the time, its aftermath transformed the metropolis. In the period of euphoria that followed the silencing of the guns on 11 November 1918, a utopian desire to see a better and brighter England – and London – took root. The existing city, with its slums and tenements, seemed wholly inadequate in a post-war world; too many people were crammed into too little space. This was not how the capital city of Europe's imperial colossus should be. Prime Minister David Lloyd George declared his determination to create a 'land fit for heroes', and that required a capital city fit for heroes, too; and while the fruits of this publicly expressed desire sound superficially very mundane – the passing of a new Housing and Town Planning Act in 1919 – the impact was to prove seismic.

The Act was the result of an investigation in 1917 into the state of the nation's housing and health, prompted by the revelation that so many conscripts in the First World War had deep-rooted health problems (similar revelations had been made during the Boer War a few years before). In essence, the new legislation promised government subsidies to help finance the construction of new dwellings, and gave local authorities the task of creating housing and rented accommodation for those working people who required it. In theory, 500,000 houses were supposed to be built across the country in three years. In practice, because of Britain's worsening economic situation in the early 1920s, only 213,000 were completed. This was nevertheless a substantial achievement, and laid the way open for further pieces of legislation that, in 1924 for example, provided local authorities with substantial grants and in 1930 obliged them to clear all remaining slums in their area. By 1939, local councils across England had built 1.1 million new homes.

In London itself, the LCC bulldozed their way through slum after slum in the inner suburbs in the 1920s, flattening the houses of some 127,000 Londoners and creating thousands of jobs in the construction trade in the process. The metropolitan boroughs for their part had to find new accommodation for the 55,000 people they similarly made homeless through slum clearance. Hackney and the East End, and the southern Thames-side boroughs of Battersea, Lambeth and Southwark, were particularly affected, their eighteenth- and nineteenth-century houses – often declared 'unfit for habitation' – giving way to neat modern flats or

*The vast Becontree Estate in Barking and Dagenham
under construction in 1924.*

commercial developments. Some third of all new houses built in London between 1920 and 1931, in fact, were created by the LCC and the boroughs.[5]

The biggest of the interwar council estates was the Becontree Estate in Barking and Dagenham, where, by the time work was completed in 1938, some 27,000 homes had been built for 120,000 people. To achieve this, over 300 acres of farmland and scattered houses and cottages were compulsorily purchased, to be replaced by cottage-style houses set amid gardens, parks and green spaces. The whole site was designed in part with former slum dwellers in mind, but its attractive layout, and accommodation that included gas and electricity, inside toilets and fitted baths, made it appealing to the more well-to-do manual blue-collar workers who were making their money in factories and the transport industry. In fact a constant issue for council housing was that the rentals due on new developments were often higher than could be afforded by those who were supposed to be helped by them.

Not that Becontree was a flawless idea, perfectly executed. It had poor transport links, little in the way of local employment opportunities (until Ford opened their plant at Dagenham in the late 1920s), no hospital, relatively few doctors and little to offer in the way of social recreation (there were, for example, only six pubs – one per 20,000 people). It could therefore be quite a lonely place to live. When the social research organisation, Mass Observation, talked to people living in council estates in the 1930s, loneliness and a sense of isolation were not uncommon complaints. People might have hated their former houses, but they felt that at least the streets they had once lived in had some sense of community. On the other hand, Becontree did at least offer its inhabitants houses. In an unheeded warning for the future, many of those who talked to Mass Observation before the Second World War made it clear that they liked houses with gardens where they could grow things and let their children play, not remote flats that were far separated from the wider life of the community.

A similarly ambitious plan to that at Becontree was mooted in 1937 for the site of the former White City exhibition and Olympics ground. Here, it was boasted:

> All dwellings will be 5 storeys high and the total accommodation will be 2,286 dwellings containing 7,290 rooms. The desirability of a reasonable provision in respect of social services has been recognised and sites have been reserved for 14 shops, an administrative building and possible schools, medical clinic, reading rooms etc and children's playgrounds.[6]

Work started in 1939, came to a grinding halt when war broke out later in the same year, and was not substantially completed until 1953.

Other estates were built in outlying parts of London where relatively undeveloped land was still to be had. The Roehampton Estate, for example, replaced the estates of two large houses, Dover House and Putney Park. Largely rural Morden was transformed by the opening of Morden Underground station in 1926 and the consequent construction of the 825-acre St Helier Estate between 1928 and 1936, designed for former inner-city slum dwellers. Then there was the Norbury Estate in Croydon, the Bellingham Estate in Lewisham and the Castelnau Estate in Barnes. Borough councils got in on the act, too; for example, Woolwich was responsible for the Page Estate in Eltham Green, as well as the Middle Park and Horn Park estates constructed in the 1930s on the site of the former hunting grounds of Eltham Palace. All in all, some quarter of a million people were rehoused south of the Thames in this way between 1919 and 1939.

Not all council estates were grandly ambitious affairs constructed on previously wide open spaces. Many were squeezed into already built-up areas, and this not infrequently led to a degree of class tension, with working-class incomers being resented by their more affluent neighbours. In *London in the Twentieth Century*, Jerry White describes how in 1927 a developer built a wall across a road to prevent council tenants in the Downham Estate on the Lewisham–Bromley borders from taking a short cut through a private housing estate to reach local shops and buses. The wall was not demolished until 1946. There was a general and depressing tendency on the part of people in privately owned or rented houses to take a condescending view of their council-estate neighbours.

The situation of the council-house dwellers' more prosperous neighbours between the wars was, given the nation's overall condition, a surprisingly positive one. Britain faced real economic problems through the later 1920s and much of the 1930s. The Wall Street Crash of 1929 had a devastating impact on the country's financial health, industry struggled and by 1931 nearly 3 million people were unemployed. Hunger marches became a defining image of the time. London, however, was relatively unaffected by the country's economic woes. Unlike the Midlands and the North, it didn't rely principally on heavy industry to pay its way. Instead, it could offer men relatively recession-proof jobs in central and local government, in banks, in offices and shops, and in the leisure industries. What's more, because the widespread employment of women to do men's jobs during the First World War had broken down many of the old prejudices and restrictions, the post-war London woman (who now had the vote for the first time) could also pursue a career. The professions tended to remain male bastions, but secretarial jobs for women boomed, and their numbers in the civil service rose from 33,000 in 1911 to 102,000 by 1921. Single women now didn't have to be domestic servants to support themselves, and as a result the servant class started to disappear from the census returns. Married women, particularly in working-class families, could help with the bread-winning. Assisted by the low interest rates that followed Britain's decision to abandon the Gold Standard in 1931, for the first time many families found themselves in a position to get a mortgage and buy a house.

This was the period when the suburbs finally conquered Middlesex, whose population expanded at five times the average rate for the rest of England and Wales between 1921 and 1931. South and east of the river, modernisation of the Dartford Loop Line and the opening of such new stations as Albany Park in 1935 brought a wave of settlement around Bexley. To the east, the electrification of the track that would become the District line in 1933, and the creation of new stations at Elm Park and Upminster Bridge, similarly led to an influx of fresh commuters. Dagenham's Ford Motor plant attracted new working-class housing to supplement the late nineteenth- and early twentieth-century garden suburbs of Emerson Park and Gidea Park.

In both inner and outer suburbs, the newly relatively affluent and the rehoused slum dwellers often benefited from the post-war financial woes of old landed families. Death duties had been introduced in 1894 and rose first to 40 per cent by 1919 and then to 50 per cent by 1930. Long-established estates therefore went under the auctioneer's hammer, to be rapidly replaced by neat streets and equally neat houses. Not even Mayfair was sacrosanct: most of its great mansions disappeared after the war, including Chesterfield House in South Audley Street. Built for the Earl of Chesterfield in the 1740s on a then remote site at the edge of Westminster and within earshot of the jeering crowds at Tyburn, it was torn down in the 1930s, to be replaced by flats. Such transformations prompted the novelist E. M. Forster to complain: 'Greed moulds the landscape of London.'

Flats, in fact, became something of a motif of the 1930s as mansion blocks continued to enjoy the popularity they had achieved in late Victorian and Edwardian times. Soon they were cropping up everywhere, both in prestigious central London locations and in more suburban areas. Bayswater acquired its Albion Gate, Pimlico its massive Dolphin Square development and Baker Street its Dorset House in the years before the Second World War, and similar developments took place in St John's Wood, Hampstead and other desirable neighbourhoods close to the centre. In Highgate, Berthold Lubetkin and Tecton came up with Highpoint I and II (1933–5 and 1938), commissioned by Sigmund Gestetner, who had originally thought in terms of creating housing for the employees in his factory at Tottenham Hale, but who ended up building two ultra-modern high-rise blocks of flats with eight flats per floor, a winter garden, a

The modernist mansion block: Highpoint Two in Highgate.

tearoom – and small rooms for maids on the ground floor. Further out was the wonderfully flamboyant art deco Lichfield Court in Richmond, Du Cane Court in Balham and Taymount Grange in Forest Hill, all of which boasted their own social clubs, restaurants and concierge services. 'The servant problem solved,' declared advertisements for Taymount Grange, which also offered its residents a swimming pool and tennis courts – all for rents that ranged from £115 to £150 a year. As for Chiltern Court, built over Baker Street station by the Metropolitan Railway in the late 1920s, this sought to offer the best of town and country living: it was a luxury development in what by now was the heart of London, with shops, a restaurant, 180 flats, 30 maids' rooms and every modern convenience you could think of; at the same time it was perfectly located for the Londoner who wanted to hop on a train at the weekend and wander in the countryside or play golf at one of the various golf clubs that now dotted Middlesex. No wonder that it included among its early tenants the writer H. G. Wells, who loved and hated the modern world and the modern city in almost equal measure.

Of all the areas of 1920s and 1930s expansion, the most characteristic is Metroland, that swathe of suburbia built on great areas of previously largely untouched north-west Middlesex where the Metropolitan line snakes ever outwards towards Rickmansworth and Amersham, and where the Metropolitan Railway created new branches (to Watford and to Stanmore) before the Second World War. The railway company itself promoted the suburban idyll to be enjoyed here, its annual guide, *Metro-land*, published between 1915 and 1932, extolling the virtues of Harrow, Neasden, Ruislip, Hillingdon and Wembley as rural paradises that just happened to have plenty of new houses available. Since it was a major landowner in the area, its motives were not exactly altruistic. The company itself, or rather its subsidiary, the Metropolitan Railway Country Estates Limited, built houses in places such as Kingsbury, Neasden, Wembley Park and Cecil Park in Pinner, while also encouraging other developers to get involved.

Villages now turned into towns. Harrow Weald grew from a village of only 1,500 residents in 1901 into a town of 11,000 thirty years later. Pinner's

The art deco mansion block: this example is in Baron's Court.

Metroland comes to Pinner. The engraving (above) shows the little village of Pinner as it was in the nineteenth century. The photograph (below) shows a fair in Pinner in the 1930s.

trajectory was even more pronounced. Taking its name from an early Anglo-Saxon settler (Pinna's riverbank) it had long been an important settlement, boasting a chapel by AD 793 and a weekly market and two fairs a year by the middle of the fourteenth century. Until the 1920s and 1930s, however, it was still essentially a village, with attractive timbered houses (some of which still survive) and a parish church. In the mid nineteenth century a good proportion of its inhabitants worked on local farms, though many of them moved into domestic service as the farms increasingly turned their attention to the less-labour-intensive production of milk (for London's people) and hay (for London's horses). The arrival of the Metropolitan Railway in 1885 turned Pinner into a commuter town, but its population in 1901 was still only 3,000 or so. Then came Metroland; almost overnight, Pinner found itself with 23,000 mouths to feed.

John Betjeman's name is for ever associated with Metroland, his famous 1973 documentary displaying that love–hate relationship that so many people have with an area they've known all their lives – loving what it was, hating what it had become. E. Nesbit and George Bernard Shaw's generation lamented the arrival of the first wave of suburbs. Betjeman and his contemporaries, who associated these suburbs with their childhoods and so loved them, reserved their disdain for the second wave:

> The trees are down. An Odeon flashes fire
> Where stood their villa by the murmuring fir.[7]

T. R. Fyvel, writer and a 'child of Metro-land', later recalled:

> I distinctly remember that when I was a schoolboy in North-West London, there were still batches of fields around Wembley. It grew between the wars, the creation of the speculative builder; street upon street of box-like, semi-detached houses sprung into full existence, indistinguishable from those of other London suburbs. There they all are; 'Chatsworth' beside 'Knole', 'Blenheim' next to 'Balmoral'; the tiny front gates, the back gardens with patches of lawn and scarlet runners and pink Alexandra roses; brick and mortar of English suburb-life – a life where the youthful hero of the local tennis club or amateur dramatic group seems far too early changed to the captured young family man

showing snapshots of his offspring on the 8.42 to London, and, almost before he knows, to 'Dad', middle-aged, working in the garden and worrying over insurance instalments and school bills.[8]

These new suburbs adopted a new pattern of building. Straight Victorian roads were out of fashion; in their place came cul-de-sacs, avenues and closes. The heavy red-brick Victorian terraced house no longer found favour. In its place came the semi-detached house. Typically, this would have two living rooms and a kitchen downstairs, three bedrooms upstairs and – an exciting and relatively recent feature – an internal bathroom. There would be a neat front garden with perhaps a hedge and a formal flower bed, and a back garden with its own vegetable plot. Building styles harked back to bygone days: mock-Tudor houses with exposed wood beams on the outside and period metalwork details inside, or red-brick and clay tiles reminiscent of Jacobean times, or a pebbledash finish that gave the house a cottagey, stippled look. For the more adventurous there was the art deco house, with its sleek curves, use of concrete and love of a flat roof. It's fascinating today to compare the first generation of Arts-and-Crafts-inspired houses in Hampstead Garden Suburb with their white modernist nearby neighbours.

Inside a typical 1930s house.

Much as some commentators sneered at these new houses, and the social aspirations of those who lived there, there's no doubt that they offered people a standard of living that few had enjoyed before. For a start, they had piped, clean water. Huge strides forward had been taken since the low point of the mid nineteenth century, notably the 1902 foundation of the Metropolitan Water Board – a new authority that covered not just the county of London but also parts of Essex, Kent, Surrey, Middlesex and Hertfordshire. Now, for the first time, the supply of water to places as far afield as Cheshunt, Loughton, Dartford and Surbiton was all the responsibility of the same group of people.

Kitchens were improving, too. Many now had gas cookers (by the Second World War three-quarters of the population had them), and some had fridges. Thanks to thriving local shops, the housewife had easy access to good quality food – not just meat and bread but fresh fruit, vegetables and dairy produce. What's more, although she might no longer have a household servant to help her as her mother might have done (the servant class dwindled after the First World War), the weekly shop was costing rather less: in the mid 1930s, people earning between £250 and £500 a year (about one in five of the population) were in a position to spend less than a third of their weekly pay packet on food.

Phones were also becoming more widespread. When the United Telephone Company had been established back in 1880, the phone had been very much the plaything of the few. With the arrival of the National Telephone Company, however, the network spread wider to the point where it became a monopoly; it was subsequently nationalised and transferred to the Post Office under the terms of the 1911 Telephone Transfer Act. Improved technology played its part, too. The introduction of automated exchanges by the late 1920s, and the use of direct-dial handsets for private consumers, made phone calls easier and cheaper. By 1928 over a billion phone calls were being made each year in the UK. Ten years later, this figure had doubled.

The other novelty for many of the new suburban class was electricity. London's first generating station had opened as long ago as 1882 in Holborn Viaduct, but it was only really after the First World War that an integrated electricity network developed across the region, bringing rationalisation to the previously ramshackle system of small local power stations. Nineteen twenty-five proved a key year when ten smaller independent companies merged to form the London Power Company. They set out to build a series of very large power stations, the first of which (Deptford) was started in 1925, and the most famous of which was Battersea Power Station. Designed by Sir Giles Gilbert Scott, who also created the iconic shape of London's red telephone boxes, Battersea Power Station was opened in 1935, and a second station was constructed on the site just after the Second World War. Various other power stations were also developed before the war (including one at Barking), with yet more coming on tap in the immediate post-war period, most notably – at least, from the point of view of the London skyline – Bankside, which was commissioned in 1947.

The other point to make about the houses that sprang up in the late 1920s and 1930s was that they were affordable. Rents were not high, and for those who wanted to buy their home, mortgages were relatively easy to obtain. Whereas today the average cost of a three-bedroom house is 6.5 times the average salary, in the 1930s it was closer to 1.5 times. A middle-ranking banker or insurance official earning between £300 and £600 a year could, in 1938, buy a house in Brook Avenue, Edgware, for £835.

Not all of London enjoyed relative prosperity in the interwar period. The docks, in particular, found things quite tough. Fierce and bitter competition between the various docks in the Pool of London and new ones constructed at Tilbury in 1886 by the East and West India Docks Company had been resolved by the creation of the Port of London Authority in 1909, which opened the last great docklands construction project, the King George V Docks, in 1921. However, this proved to be the final throw of the dice. Britain's international supremacy was beginning to wane. The full impact might not have been felt until after the Second World War, but the telltale signs were there in the interwar period. Significantly, the population of Tower Hamlets actually declined during the period – a sure sign that the docks jobs market was no longer as buoyant as it had once been.

However, elsewhere the picture was rather brighter. Because more Londoners than ever before found themselves with disposable incomes in the 1920s, they wanted more newfangled consumer goods. This demand in turn required the building of more factories; and these factories often ended up in the suburbs, where there was still land to be had, where

Industry became an important feature of many London suburbs in the interwar period. This 1937 photograph shows workers leaving the Ford Motor Works at Dagenham.

communications were good, and where the generally light nature of the industry meant that the usual paraphernalia of docks and train-marshalling yards wasn't required. West London in particular found itself playing host to such enterprises as H. Bronnley and Co (soap), Evershed and Vignoles (electrical equipment), T. Wall and Son (Wall's sausages and Wall's ice cream) and Wilkinson Sword (razors). Hillingdon, Harlesden, Chiswick and Acton all became mini industrial centres. The Great West Road attracted American investment: Hoover built a fantas-tical art deco factory there in 1932; nearby, a few years later, the Gillette Company constructed their European headquarters, replete with glowing four-faced clock tower. This was also the period that saw the first of the supermarkets. Jack Cohen, who had started with a market stall in Hackney, opened a string of shops throughout London's suburbs in the 1920s and 1930s, combining his name with that of his tea supplier, T. E. Stockwell, to create Tesco. Acton's grocery partnership of Waite, Rose and Taylor, founded in 1904, went on to become Waitrose. In fact, more than three-quarters of all new factories built in London between 1900 and 1939 were placed in the suburbs, and their scope ranged from the traditional to electrical engineering. The Gramophone (EMI) Company complex in Hayes, Siemens of Woolwich, Standard Telephones of Hendon, and the General Electric Company (GEC) of Erith and Wembley all represented the white heat of the latest technology

Not all industry was light in nature. Acton became a hub of the new car industry, boasting such companies as Napier Motor Works in Acton Vale after 1903 and Du Cros, which started out as a garage and repair shop in 1908. The Great West Road came to house the Firestone tyre factory in 1924, and Dagenham became a production site for the Ford Motor Company in the same year. The importance of these factories, and the many smaller businesses that grew up to supply them, is, as ever, reflected in population figures. In 1911 Barking and Dagenham combined could muster 39,000 residents; by 1939, with the motor industry in full swing, there were 184,000 people living there.

———— ◄ • ► ————

The rise of car manufacturing implies, of course, the rise of cars, and there's no doubt that in the interwar period car ownership blossomed. The number of car licences issued to London addresses, which back in the early 1920s had stood at around 100,000, had leapt to 260,000 by the early 1930s. By the Second World War, many new suburban houses were being built with a garage.

Out in the country, cars had the road to themselves for much of the interwar period. In town it was a different picture, and as early as 1924 a London and Home Counties Traffic Advisory Committee was set up to make recommendations to the Minister of Transport about how best to deal with traffic issues in the London area. The fact that other consultative bodies had to be established, and plans put forward, one after the other, in the ensuing decades shows that roads were to be one area of London planning where no apparent solution was ever right for long. In 1938 the Highway Development Survey, overseen by Sir Charles Bressey and Sir Edwin Lutyens, recommended miles of new roads and junctions, including a series of orbital routes around the capital. In the

The classic Victorian semi-detached house, *c.*1890,
complete with a maid servant at the door.

A detail from Booth's poverty map, showing the Bow and Mile End area.
The colour coding ranges from black and dark blue to denote the poorest
families to red for the well-to-do and yellow for the wealthy.

A 1922 poster extols the virtue of a new housing scheme in Greenwich and promotes the London County Council's issuing of housing bonds to fund it.

Industry in the west London suburbs: the magnificent art deco Hoover building in Perivale.

SOUTH LONDON FOR THE BEST VALUE IN MODERN LUXURY FLATS

DU CANE COURT

BALHAM HIGH ROAD, LONDON, S.W.17

9 Minutes from Victoria, 19 Minutes from Bank, 21 Minutes from Piccadilly. Within 1 Minute of Balham Tube Station and Balham and Upper Tooting Station (Southern Railway)

READY FOR OCCUPATION BEFORE JUNE, 1936

INCLUSIVE RENTALS

from £60 per annum, or 23/1 per week

provide for Rates and Taxes, service of porters, electric passenger and service lifts, central heating and constant hot water

RENTALS FOR UNFURNISHED FLATS AND MAISONETTES

	Per Annum £ s. d.	Per Week		Per Annum £ s. d.	Per Week
One roomed Flats, each with Bathroom and Kitchenette - - - - - from	70 0 0	26/11	Five roomed Flats - - - - from	190 0 0	73/1
Two roomed Flats - - - - "	90 0 0	34/8	Three roomed Maisonettes - - - "	130 0 0	50/-
Three roomed Flats - - - - "	130 0 0	50/-	Four roomed Maisonettes - - - "	170 0 0	65/5
Four roomed Flats - - - - "	170 0 0	65/5	Five roomed Maisonettes - - - "	195 0 0	75/-

One roomed (Shared Bathroom) Flats, each with separate Kitchenette. Per Annum, £60. Per Week, 23/1

Mansion blocks became very much part of the London landscape from late Victorian times. This advertisement for Du Cane Court in Balham dates from 1935.

METRO-LAND

PRICE TWO-PENCE

A 1926 issue of *Metro-Land* evokes the rural idyll to be enjoyed in the new suburbs of north-west London.

Suburban variety:
Georgian terrace, Hampstead.

Nineteenth-century terrace,
Baron's Court.

Late Victorian terrace, Finchley.

Interwar terrace, Collier's Wood.

Interwar housing, Muswell Hill.

Modern housing, Bow.

London as far as the eye can see.

1940s the County of London Plan proposed, again, a series of ring roads, excitingly labelled A to E, to help with congestion in the centre. Neither came to anything.

Instead, as so often in London before and since, the actions that were taken were hesitant, constrained both by tight budgets and what was already there. It was all very well proposing A to E ring roads, for example, but even if someone had come up with more enticing names for them, no one could have claimed that such a plan would have meant anything less than the wholesale demolition of existing housing and the devastation of green spaces. The big road-building projects of the 1920s and 1930s, therefore, were piecemeal, intermittent and did not form part of some overall grand design. Western Avenue, also known as the Great West Road, or more prosaically as the A40, was constructed through the western boroughs in the early 1920s. The A12, which heads out into Essex and beyond into East Anglia, was formed in 1922 and initially led from Stratford to Gallows Corner along what is now the A118, and onwards into the countryside.

The one major contribution that the pre-war period did make to urban planning was the London Passenger Transport Board. This was set up in 1933, its remit to coordinate rail, tram and omnibus networks over an area that extended approximately thirty miles from Charing Cross – far beyond what would ultimately become Greater London, and stretching from Baldock to Horsham, and Brentwood to High Wycombe. Among its achievements were the extension of the Underground network to Archway, High Barnet and Mill Hill East, incorporating the last of several old rail suburban branch lines that had been unable to compete with the Underground; and the gradual phasing out of trams – not a popular move, especially south of the river, which was less well served than the north by the Underground network, but inevitable as tram routes increasingly failed to keep up with new suburban development and new estates. The last London tram ran in 1952. The London Passenger Transport Board also brought a degree of standardisation to what had previously been a mixed bag of branding and scheduling. From now on, buses, trams and Underground trains were painted red, while buses and coaches serving districts lying further from the centre were painted green. Accidents remained a problem, though. The fatality rate nationally in the 1920s topped 5,000 a year – a horrifying figure when one considers that in 2007 (by which time virtually everyone had a car) fewer than 3,000 died in motor-related accidents.

Meanwhile, creeping up on the periphery of London were new aerodromes to serve the newly emerging business of air travel. Heathrow may be the best-known London airport now, but in the early days it was Croydon that ruled supreme. Formed in 1920 when aerodromes at Beddington and neighbouring Waddon merged, Croydon Aerodrome handled most of the early international flights, particularly those run by Imperial Airways Limited. A crash in 1924 necessitated a major redevelopment and four years later, at a cost of £267,000, a new aerodrome opened with sizable new hangars, a purpose-built passenger terminal and even a purpose-built hotel on Purley Way. Not surprisingly, the village of Purley boomed over the following years. Penshurst Airfield also appeared in 1916, as did Heston Aerodrome to the north of town, which operated from 1929 to 1947 and doubled up as a major aircraft manufacturing centre as well. In the same year it was formed, a small airfield was set up to the west of London on farmland near a village called Heathrow. It would come into its own as a military base in the Second World War.

———— ◄ • ► ————

Contemporary views of London suburbia before the war were, as previously noted, not always flattering. Writers bemoaned the sprawl, the 'ordinariness' of the houses, and what they saw as the limited aspirations of those who lived there. Even the generally benign comic writer P. G. Wodehouse occasionally took a gentle swipe at the suburbs, as in his short story 'Uncle Fred Flits By' (1936), where Lord Ickenham proposes to revisit the area where he was brought up:

> 'The neighbourhood is now suburban, true. It is many years since the meadows where I sported as a child were sold and cut up into building lots. But when I was a boy Mitching Hill was open country. It was a vast, rolling estate belonging to your great-uncle Marmaduke, a man with whiskers of a nature which you with your pure mind would scarcely credit, and I have long felt a sentimental urge to see what the hell the old place looks like now. Perfectly foul, I expect.' [. . .]

> Alighting from the bus ... you found yourself in the middle of rows and rows of semi-detached villas, all looking exactly alike, and you went on and you came to more semi-detached villas, and those all looked exactly alike, too.[9]

Mitching Hill is clearly based on Dulwich, where Wodehouse had gone to school.

J. B. Priestley was similarly underwhelmed by the suburbs in his *English Journey* (1934):

> This is the England of arterial and bypass roads, of filling stations and factories that look like exhibition buildings, of giant cinemas and dance-halls and cafés, bungalows with tiny garages, cocktail bars, Woolworths, motor coaches, wireless, hiking, factory girls looking like actresses, grey-hound racing and dirt tracks, swimming pools, and everything given away for cigarette coupons. If the fog had lifted I knew that I would have seen this England all round me at that northern entrance to London, where the smooth wide road passes between miles of semi-detached bungalows, all with their little garages, their wireless sets, their periodicals about film stars, their swimming costumes and tennis rackets and dancing shoes.[10]

Priestley's account, however, mentions precisely those things that people liked about the suburbs in the 1930s: comfortable houses and the opportunity for leisure. At home you could potter in the garden or listen to the radio. If you wanted to go out but didn't want to venture all the way into town you had the pick of local attractions, from pubs to lidos. Purpose-built cinemas swept across London from the early part of the century onwards (what is now the Phoenix in East Finchley is the oldest surviving one in London, dating from 1912), and by the late 1930s almost every suburb boasted a grand art deco edifice where people would go several times a week to see the latest films. There was the Astoria in Finsbury Park (1930), the Granada in Tooting and the Regal in Uxbridge (both 1931), the Forum in Kentish Town (1934), the Odeon in Muswell Hill (1936), and many more. Complete with coffee lounges, mirrored powdered rooms and plush seating, they seemed both ultra modern and ultra chic. For the sports-minded there was football at Wembley Stadium. Although it was not officially opened until 1924 for the British Empire

Suburban entertainment: the elegant Odeon cinema in Muswell Hill.

Exhibition, it hosted its first FA Cup final the previous year, when it drew a crowd of around a quarter of a million (possibly even as many as 300,000; the FA failed to ticket the game). There was also greyhound racing, a sport with a long pedigree but transformed after 1926 by the introduction (from America) of the artificial hare and the subsequent adaptation of existing stadiums (Wembley from 1927, Stamford Bridge from 1932) and the building of new venues in places such as West Ham (opened 1928), Dagenham (1930), Walthamstow (1931) and, perhaps above all, White City (1938).

Life, then, for many suburban Londoners in the 1930s offered a rich-ness and level of comfort on a scale previously unknown; but not for all Londoners. Poverty, though not as prevalent or as grinding as it had been before the First World War, still stalked the streets of the inner suburbs – and those of some of the outer suburbs, too. One estimate suggests that in 1929 perhaps 1.3 million citizens lacked what could reasonably be called the basic requirements of life.[11] London, then as now, could also be a friendless place to live; it's no coincidence that the journalist Alfred Barrett should have launched his lonely hearts publication *Link* in the capital in 1915. Indeed, isolation – that sense of being alone among millions of other

A family having toast and tea for elevenses at their home in Wellard Street near Lambeth Walk. The date is 31 December 1938.

people – became something of a theme of the interwar period, explored by journalists, novelists and poets, some of whom also meditated darkly on just how many millions there were: 'I had not thought death had undone so many,' wrote T. S. Eliot in *The Waste Land* (1922) of the crowds surging across London Bridge.

For his part, George Orwell depicted London's down-at-heel quality, its ordinariness and the dullness that he felt all too often went with the search for respectability. His 1936 novel *Keep the Aspidistra Flying* gives deeply unflattering portraits of Hampstead ('dingy and depressing'), the Lambeth area ('a huge graceless wilderness') and the Edgware Road ('a dull quarter'). All this, of course, is seen through the jaundiced eyes of the struggling writer Gordon Comstock, but in his description of Gordon's bedsit in Lambeth Cut, Orwell describes a way of living that must have been familiar to many:

> His bed-sitting-room was eight shillings a week and was just under the roof . . . There was a large, low, broken-backed bed with a ragged patch-work quilt and sheets that were changed once fortnightly; a deal table ringed by dynasties of teapots; a rickety kitchen chair; a tin basin for washing in; a gas-ring in the fender. The bare floorboards had never

been stained but were dark with dirt. In the cracks in the pink wallpaper dwelt multitudes of bugs; however, this was winter and they were torpid unless you over-warmed the room. You were expected to make your own bed. Mrs Meaking, the landlady, theoretically 'did out' the rooms daily, but four days out of five she found the stairs too much for her. Nearly all the lodgers cooked their own squalid meals in their bedrooms. There was no gas-stove, of course; just the gas-ring in the fender, and, down two flights of stairs, a large evil-smelling sink which was common to the whole house.[12]

Gordon's bedsit in Lambeth Cut was as much a part of the suburbs between the wars as the brand-new three-bedroom house and garden in Edgware.

FIFTEEN

WARTIME DESTRUCTION, PEACETIME RECONSTRUCTION

London, 1939–70

Although London had been relatively unaffected by Zeppelin raids in the First World War, planners in the 1930s were less optimistic about what might happen were there to be another major European conflict. Prime Minister Stanley Baldwin's gloomy view in 1932 that 'the bomber will always get through', and an official estimate that 58,000 might die in a first bombing wave, suggested that in the increasingly likely event of a Second World War, London could well be reduced to smouldering fragments, its population either destroyed or dispersed.

That such a doomsday view could be expressed so openly by the British premier serves to explain why civil defence planning for the next war began well before hostilities were actually declared on 3 September 1939, and well before Britain's mollifying 'appeasement' policy towards Hitler's Germany was formally abandoned. Indeed, in 1935 Baldwin himself produced a pamphlet entitled *Air Raid Precautions* that invited local authorities to make plans for civil defence in the eventuality of war. Measures subsequently taken included plans to regulate control of fire and ambulance services and coordinate volunteer first-aid posts, stretcher parties, gas decontamination and light rescue parties; and to establish an Air Raid Wardens' service, with one warden per 500 head of the population. London, it was decided, was to be number five of twelve Civil Defence Regions, divided into Inner London and Outer London zones. The inner group was further divided into five, while the outer group contained four subgroups arranged by county. The inner Group 2, for example, contained Hampstead, St Marylebone, Paddington, St Pancras, Islington and Stoke Newington, while the outer Group 6D comprised Feltham, Heston and Isleworth, Hayes and

WARTIME DESTRUCTION,
PEACETIME RECONSTRUCTION

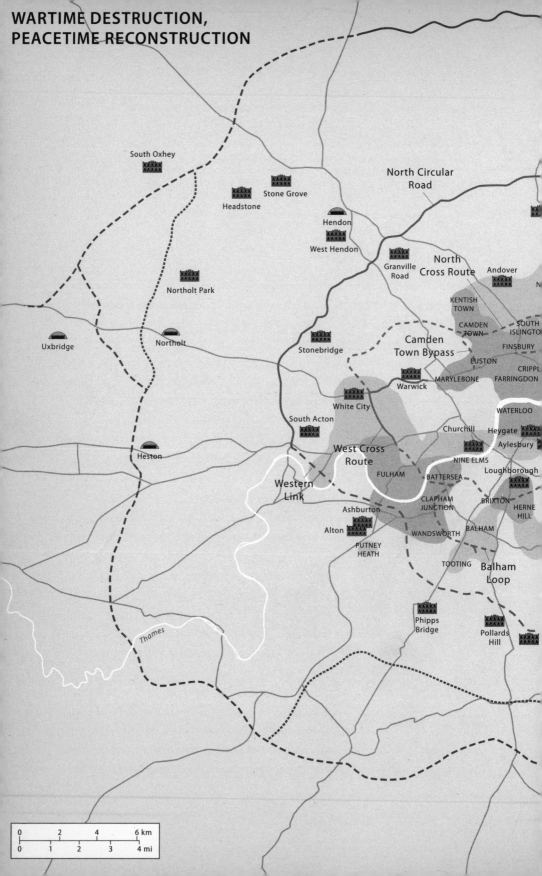

South Oxhey

Stone Grove

Headstone

Hendon

West Hendon

North Circular Road

Granville Road

North Cross Route

Andover

Northolt Park

KENTISH TOWN

CAMDEN TOWN

SOUTH ISLINGTO

Uxbridge

Northolt

Stonebridge

Camden Town Bypass

FINSBURY

EUSTON

CRIPPL

FARRINGDON

MARYLEBONE

Warwick

White City

WATERLOO

South Acton

Churchill

Heygate

Aylesbury

Heston

West Cross Route

FULHAM

NINE ELMS

Loughborough

Western Link

BATTERSEA

BRIXTON

HERNE HILL

Ashburton

CLAPHAM JUNCTION

Alton

WANDSWORTH

BALHAM

PUTNEY HEATH

TOOTING

Balham Loop

Thames

Phipps Bridge

Pollards Hill

0		2		4		6 km
0	1	2	3	4 mi		

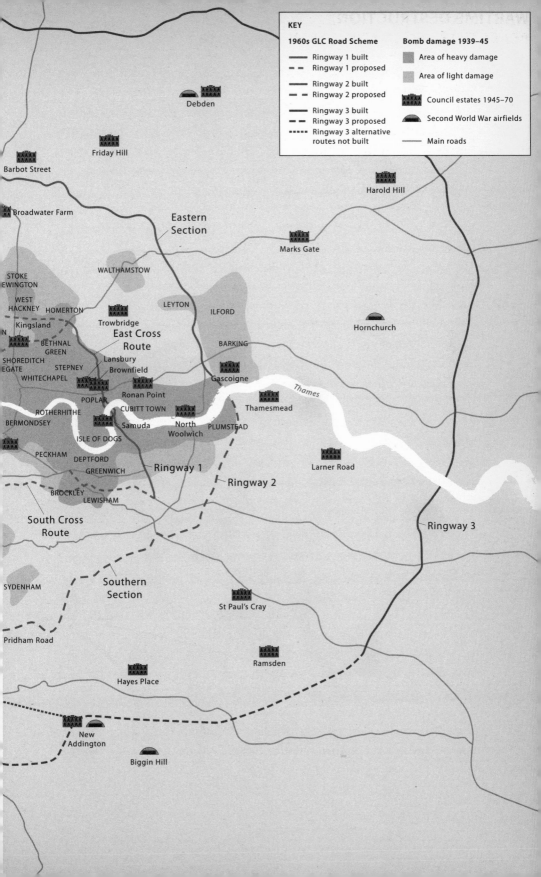

KEY

1960s GLC Road Scheme

— Ringway 1 built

-- Ringway 1 proposed

— Ringway 2 built

-- Ringway 2 proposed

— Ringway 3 built

-- Ringway 3 proposed

···· Ringway 3 alternative routes not built

Bomb damage 1939–45

◼ Area of heavy damage

◻ Area of light damage

🏛 Council estates 1945–70

◗ Second World War airfields

— Main roads

Debden

Friday Hill

Barbot Street

Broadwater Farm

Harold Hill

Eastern Section

Marks Gate

STOKE EWINGTON

WEST HACKNEY

HOMERTON

WALTHAMSTOW

LEYTON

ILFORD

Hornchurch

Kingsland

Trowbridge

East Cross Route

BETHNAL GREEN

SHOREDITCH EGATE

STEPNEY

WHITECHAPEL

Lansbury Brownfield

BARKING

Gascoigne

Thames

Ronan Point

POPLAR

CUBITT TOWN

Thamesmead

ROTHERHITHE

BERMONDSEY

Samuda

ISLE OF DOGS

North Woolwich

PLUMSTEAD

Larner Road

PECKHAM

DEPTFORD

GREENWICH

Ringway 1

BROCKLEY

LEWISHAM

Ringway 2

South Cross Route

Ringway 3

SYDENHAM

Southern Section

St Paul's Cray

Pridham Road

Ramsden

Hayes Place

New Addington

Biggin Hill

Harlington, Yiewsley and West Drayton, Twickenham, Staines and Sunbury on Thames.

Initially, it was proposed that children, mothers with infants and the infirm should be evacuated from the inner zone only; but after a hastily convened conference in August 1939, it was agreed that this was insufficient and that the evacuation programme should be extended to the outer zone as well. Consequently, provision was made for some 1,423,000 people to leave their homes in London for relocation in safer areas of the country, along with nearly 200,000 residents of the neighbouring parts of Surrey, Kent and Sussex.

In the event, many of the 660,000 women and children estimated to have been evacuated in September 1939 by the London County Council came from inner London. A fair number of them then drifted back to the capital during the 'Phoney War' that preceded the German onslaught on France. The figure of 660,000, however, has to be treated with a degree of circumspection. Such was the level of upheaval at the time, and the attendant confusion, that it's very difficult to know for sure precisely how many people were moved and how many resolutely decided to stay in their homes. Moreover, the official numbers do not take account of the exodus by those who made a voluntary decision to leave the capital – perhaps 800,000 in the early months of the war. These came from all over London and from all social classes. Some went wherever there was space to stay; others joined relatives living well away from the big cities. My own mother and grandmother, for example, left Norwood Green for the safety of a farm on the Holkham Estate in Norfolk at the insistence of my grandfather, who was away in India at the time. One way or another, it's clear that the population of London as a whole declined sharply in the early years of the war. If those who were away fighting in the armed forces are included in the overall figures, then inner London lost well over 40 per cent of its population by 1941, declining to a mere 2.3 million. Bethnal Green, for example, home to an estimated 90,000 or so people in 1939, was left with only 47,000 two years later. A further wave of evacuations took place in the summer of 1944 when V1 bombs started to rain down on London.

Londoners' experience of evacuation varied wildly. For those who knew where they were going and whom they were joining, it could be an enjoyable adventure. My mother still speaks fondly of her time in the Norfolk countryside, of the small village school where she was sent and of the experience of walking through fields, rather than streets, every day. For others, though, there was an inevitable sense of trepidation as the unknown beckoned. Here, for example, one North London schoolgirl describes the day she left home in London for Dunstable:

> We stood on the station platform for about twenty minutes feeling rather subdued and wishing that our rucksacks were not quite so heavy. At last the train came and we bundled in. Only the engine driver knew our destination. However, we kept our spirits up, for it was rather an adventure and we were all in it together. We did crossword puzzles, munched sweets, sang, and a member of staff even produced a wireless. The train stopped at St Albans and our hearts sank, for after all, we wanted to go somewhere new and interesting, and St Albans was too near home. But to our relief the train started off again, and finally stopped at Luton, which to most of us was an unknown quantity. Somebody yelled to us to get out, and out we came. It began to drizzle as we walked down to Dunstable Road School, and the adventure began rather to pall.[1]

Once in the countryside, many children settled in straightaway and were kindly treated. Some then acquired a love of a life spent in the open that was to help determine whereabouts they chose to live as adults. Inevitably, though, there were those who found the move a huge culture shock, and who then had a miserable time trying to settle in – ill at ease with their new surroundings and often regarded with suspicion or disdain by those who were supposed to be their hosts. In a few cases they were abused and exploited.

***

Hitler's initial plan was to focus the attention of his bombers on the East End and particularly on the docks, and that is precisely what happened during the first attack on 7 September 1940. The impact was devastating, as one eighteen-year-old living in Poplar vividly recalled:

> Then the real impetus came, in so far as the suction and the compression from the high explosive blasts just pulled you and pushed you, and

the whole of this atmosphere was turbulating so hard that, after an explosion of a nearby bomb, you could actually feel your eyeballs being sucked out. I was holding my eyes to try and stop them going. And the suction was so vast it ripped my shirt away, and ripped my trousers. Then I couldn't get my breath, the smoke was like acid and everything round me was black and yellow. And these bombers just kept on and on, the whole road was moving, rising and falling.[2]

In the weeks and months that followed, this central area was hit again and again. Docks, factories, warehouses, offices and houses were constantly pounded or bombed into oblivion. On the worst night of the Blitz, 10–11 May 1941, 100,000 incendiary bombs were dropped over London, damaging the Houses of Parliament, hitting Waterloo station and destroying the Queen's Hall in Langham Place. It wasn't only central London and the East End that suffered, however: aerial bombardment was scarcely an exact science, and when the bombs rained down they could land anywhere, particularly once the Luftwaffe switched from daytime to night-time raids in October 1940. Moreover, in the early phase of the Battle of Britain it was actually the outlying parts of London that were at most risk, since these were home to the RAF bases that the Luftwaffe targeted in August and early September before it switched to its blitz on the capital. Biggin Hill, now in the London borough of Bromley, was attacked six times in three days and its operations room destroyed; between 30 August and 4 September 1940 some seventy ground staff were killed or injured. A single entry in the RAF's campaign diary for 18 August 1940 gives some sense of the ferocity of German attacks:

Biggin Hill Aerodrome was attacked at 1330 hours with HE and several DA bombs which went off periodically but caused no interference with routine.

Kenley Aerodrome was bombed at 1400 hours and serious damage was done [to] hangars and buildings by blast and fires, one of which was still burning at 1800 hours. Twelve Service deaths were caused and many injuries. The pumping station and waterworks were also hit and temporarily put out of action.

Serious fires were caused when Croydon Airport was attacked at 1330 hours, and major damage was done to Purley Way and gas mains in the area. The Rollason Works was hit again.

During the attacks, neigbouring areas were often hit. New Addington, near the Croydon, Biggin Hill and Kenley RAF bases, suffered quite extensive damage and sustained civilian casualties. Some sense not just of the level of damage done, but of the area over which it was spread, is contained in these two entries from the RAF diaries. The first is particularly telling because it actually pre-dates the principal German offensive. On the night of 24–5 August 1940, whether by accident or design:

> London and suburbs were attacked in the early hours and the following districts are reported as having been bombed: Canonbury Park, Tottenham, Highbury Park, Leyton, Wood Green, Stepney, Islington, Enfield, Hampton Court, Millwall and others. A large fire was started at Fore Street spreading to London Wall. Neill Warehouse, West India Dock, was badly damaged by fire, and Warehouse Nos 3 and 4 are now reported to be ablaze. At 0240 hours, it was reported that the Imperial Tobacco Factory and Carter Patterson's Works in Goswell Road were on fire but only slight damage has since been reported.
>
> The following places were also bombed: Malden, Coulsdon, Feltham, Kingston, Banstead and Epsom.

On the night of 10–11 September, when the Blitz was well underway, the RAF diary recorded further widespread devastation across London:

> The major damage in the London area caused by bombs during this night, is reported to be St Katherine's Dock where a raging fire is reported to be out of control, at Islington, in the City (Golden Lane and Aldgate Avenue) at Shadwell where East End Maternity Hospital set on fire, at Stepney a major fire in Cable Street, at London Docks (2 large warehouses on fire), at Millwall (Hydraulic Mains burst), in the Mile End Road a major fire at Durrell's Timber Yard, at Paddington, St Marylebone and Bayswater Road.
>
> At Brentwood over 1,000 incendiary bombs are reported to have been dropped and serious fires were started at a Convent and a Woolworth's Store.[3]

Destruction and damage could be wholesale or it could be strangely specific – obliterating one house while leaving its next-door neighbour more or less intact. Virginia Woolf recalled in her diary how a raid on

10 September 1940 caused devastation in Bloomsbury, where she lived, and yet allowed her own house to emerge unscathed:

> The house about 30 yards from ours struck at one this morning by a bomb. Completely ruined. Another bomb in the square [Bloomsbury Square] still unexploded. We walked round the back. Stood by Jane Harrison's house. The house was still smouldering. That is a great pile of bricks . . . Our house undamaged . . . it's coming very near. I had thought myself a coward for suggesting that we should not sleep 2 nights at 37. I was greatly relieved when Miss P. telephoned advising us not to stay.[4]

The ceaseless pounding of heavy bombing largely came to an end after May 1941, but occasional raids continued to take place, causing appalling isolated tragedies. On 10 January 1943 a school in Catford was hit, killing thirty-eight and injuring seventy-four. Towards the end of that year, on 7 November, a dance hall in Putney was destroyed. A further seventy-four people lost their lives.

The aftermath of a V1 attack in Kentish Town, June 1944.

A new phase of German bombing began in the summer of 1944 when the first flying bombs were sent over. These were avowedly *Vergeltungswaffe* – 'Vengeance weapons': not strategic but designed to instil fear into civilians – and since they were pilotless, they hit the capital more or less at random. The first V1, launched on 13 June 1944, only days after the D-Day landings, struck a railway bridge in Grove Road, Hackney, damaging it, destroying several neighbouring houses and killing six people. By the end of the month, V1s were hitting London at a rate of seventy to a hundred a day. As the Senior Regional Commissioner wrote:

> As many as 15 [V1s] have been known to land in the London Region almost simultaneously . . . the largest number to fall in any 24 hours was 98 on 2/3 August . . . not one of the 95 Local Authority areas in the Region has escaped.[5]

No area of London was safe. One hundred and forty-one people were killed when a V1 hit the Guards Chapel in St James's Park on 18 June. On 28 July fifty-nine people died in Lewisham Market and forty-five in Kensington High Street. On 2 August a restaurant in Beckenham was hit and forty-four perished. Over 50,000 houses in Croydon were damaged to a greater or lesser extent by V1s.

For war-weary Londoners this was a new and very real terror:

> These Robot Planes go on after daybreak, which the old raids never did. I could hear the wretched thing travelling overhead at 6am. They did not fall on us – but they fell on someone. Our guns barked out and spat and fussed until they had gone. They travel quickly and on Thursday night were low over Kensington. In fact every one of us was perfectly convinced the thing was exactly three inches off the roof.[6]

By 31 August 1944 over 5,000 Londoners had been killed in V1 attacks, and three times as many had been injured.

There was a brief let-up in the late summer of 1944. By now, tactics had been successfully developed to destroy V1s in the air as they came over the Channel, their number falling in any case as launch sites on the Continent were overrun by invading allied troops. However, in September came the first of the V2 rockets. These were if anything more terrifying for Londoners. Unlike V1s, whose low droning noise warned of their imminent arrival, V2s were silent: you didn't know one had

landed until you heard the explosion. In their indiscriminate and destructive nature, though, they were not that different from the V1s. Some 500
hit London before the end of the war, and – along with the V1s –
accounted for the deaths of nearly 9,000 people. South and east London
were worst affected, Woolwich, Ilford, Barking, Greenwich and West
Ham each being hit over twenty times. Yet the V2s could strike anywhere.
The first, which hit Staveley Road in Chiswick on 8 September 1944,
killed three; another hit Calton Road in Barnet on 20 January 1945,
leaving only one house standing and killing over a dozen people. Others
landed as far away as Waltham Abbey, Enfield and Mitcham. Perhaps
the worst single incident came on 25 November 1944, when a V2 landed
in New Cross, killing 268 people. As late as 27 March 1945 one V2 hit
Orpington while another struck a block of flats in Valance Road, Stepney,
killing 130 residents.

Early assumptions that London's population would be virtually wiped
out by air raids proved to be very wide of the mark, though the casualty
figures were nevertheless grim. Up to and including July 1941, just under
20,000 were killed in air raids. By the end of the war that figure had
reached nearly 30,000. Westminster, Bermondsey, Chelsea, Shoreditch,
Holborn, Poplar and Southwark were hardest hit, but no part of London
emerged unaffected: 144 people died in Twickenham; 372 in Willesden.
If injury figures are included with fatalities, one person in twenty-five in
wartime London was a casualty of war. It was a grim statistic.

That the level of casualties wasn't greater was partly due to the fact
that so much hostile attention was focused on precisely those areas where
the fewest civilians actually lived: the docks. It also had much to do with
the fact that, certainly in the more prosperous parts of London, many
houses were actually empty during the war years, their owners choosing
to live well away from the capital. As Edward R. Murrow, correspondent
for the US network CBS, noted:

> In the fashionable residential districts I could read the TO LET signs on
> the front of big houses in the light of the bright moon. Those houses
> have big basements underneath – good shelters, but they're not being
> used. Many people think they should be.[7]

The relative effectiveness of civil defence also played a major role in saving
lives. Tens of thousands of private air raid shelters – in particular Anderson

shelters designed in 1938 – were built in suburban gardens (my own grandfather Lewis Miller constructed his unique brick and corrugated steel panel hybrid known locally as Miller's Folly in his backyard in Norwood Green). Inside, Morrison shelters – rigid steel cages – provided protection against all but a direct hit. Time and time again, a suburban street would be bombed so extensively that it must have seemed that no one could have survived; and yet once the all clear had been sounded, its residents – shaken and Blitz-stained as they were – would emerge relatively or wholly unscathed from the wreckage.

Public shelters were slow in coming. At first the authorities resisted the use of the Underground as a place of refuge because they felt it should be kept clear to move troops around and because they feared the potentially deadly consequences of mass panics and stampedes amid the Underground's narrow passageways and exits. There were also concerns that the network might flood should a tunnel under the Thames be hit; and there was an anxiety that a 'shelter mentality' might descend that would keep people cowering underground rather than helping with the war effort.

*Sheltering from air raids at Bounds Green
Underground station in 1940.*

However, as the public increasingly took things into their own hands and started to troop into Underground stations each afternoon, the government accepted a fait accompli, and on 21 September 1940 officially sanctioned the nightly transformation of the Tube into makeshift billets, complete with bunks and basic provisions. It also authorised the construction of eight deep-level shelters specifically for the defence of the civilian population at Belsize Park, Camden, Goodge Street, Chancery Lane, Stockwell and Clapham Common, North and South stations.

Not even an Underground station or any other official air raid shelter could necessarily survive a direct hit. On 14 October 1940, a bomb fell on the road above Balham tube station and in the blast that followed sixty-eight people perished. Dozens were killed at the public trench shelters dug in Kennington Park when a fifty-pound bomb fell. Most appalling of all were the events at Bethnal Green station on 8 March 1943. Around 1,500 people were sheltering there when a salvo of anti-aircraft rockets were launched in nearby Victoria Park, causing mass panic. In the ensuing stampede and crush, 173 were killed, tragically realising the fears of those who back in 1940 had voiced their concerns about the use of the Underground as a place of refuge.

One way or another, between 1940 and 1945 London sustained 101 daylight and 253 night attacks, not to mention the V1 and V2 strikes towards the end of the war. In the process the fabric of London was devastated. 50,000 houses were lost in the inner boroughs and a further 16,000 in the outer ones, while nearly 2.3 million suffered some degree of damage. No house on the Isle of Dogs emerged undamaged; West Ham lost a third of its residential properties; and Barking was hit by no fewer than 38 rockets, 28 mines, 200 antipersonnel bombs, 500 high explosive devices and thousands of incendiary devices. Barnes may have got away fairly unscathed (only one or two houses actually appear to have been completely destroyed), but leafy Putney recorded around 1,000 bombing incidents. Public buildings all over London inevitably suffered, too. Canon Street station was left a skeletal ruin, while a fire at the Great Hall of the Gray's Inn and Inner Temple Library saw 120,000 books go up in smoke. The John Lewis department store on Oxford Street was lost to bombs, and Holland House in Kensington, built in the early seventeenth century, was obliterated when twenty-two incendiary bombs fell on it on the night of 27–8 September 1940.

Finally, peace came in the summer of 1945:

We walked arm in arm into the middle of Piccadilly Circus which was brilliantly illuminated with arc lamps. Here the crowds were yelling, singing and laughing. They were orderly and good-humoured. All the English virtues were on the surface. We watched individuals climb the lampposts, and plant flags on the top amidst tumultuous applause from bystanders. We walked down Piccadilly towards the Ritz. In the Green Park there was a huge bonfire under the trees, and too near one poor tree which caught fire.[8]

VE day, 8 May 1945, may not have been celebrated with the fervour of Armistice Day 1918 when total strangers are said to have copulated in the streets, but there was certainly a sense of euphoria; and as in 1918 there was a new idealism and utopianism evident both in official circles and in society as a whole. Labour's surprise victory at the 1945 general election signalled a determination to break with the past: voters may have cheered Winston Churchill in the streets for his indomitable spirit as wartime leader, but at the ballot box they supported Clement Attlee and his very different vision of a future Britain; and when it came to London, there was a widespread view that the capital – and its people – needed renewal. What's more, there was a conviction that this time everything would be better.

In 1919 the result of utopian deliberations had been the new Housing and Town Planning Act. In 1944 there was the Abercrombie Plan. This had its roots in a 1943 scheme, the County of London Plan, drawn up at the behest of the London County Council by its architect John Forshaw and by the architect and consultant Patrick Abercrombie. Looking ahead to a now foreseeable post-war period, the LCC wanted to see if it could tackle once and for all the problems that had plagued London for so long: traffic congestion, inadequate and slum housing, poorly distributed green spaces and the constant uneasy juxtaposition of heavy industry and houses. The scheme Abercrombie worked on, however, was soon complemented by and expanded upon by his Greater London Plan, a grander project conceived by the standing conference on London regional planning. The two would become known as the Abercrombie Plan.

Whether or not Abercrombie was the right man to take on this work is a moot point. He wasn't himself a Londoner – he actually came from

Altrincham – and he had that love of neatness and beautiful shapes on maps that is endemic in planners but that sadly rarely takes account of what is already there, or what people actually want. In London's case, while Abercrombie declared himself to be anxious to preserve the 'village' structure of the metropolis, his fingers itched to demolish and rebuild large swathes of the urban landscape. His grand vision may never have been formally adopted, but many of its precepts found their way into the post-war rebuilding of the capital.

The Greater London Plan was simple and, to that extent, elegant. It envisaged four concentric rings: an inner core, a suburban ring, a green belt (reminiscent of Loudon's work over a century before) and a country ring. The green belt would start at the point where built-up London stopped in 1939. It would limit the further spread of suburbs and offer Londoners a recreational band formed from existing open spaces and land that had been converted to food production during the war. In his precise statistical way, Abercrombie wanted to ensure that there were at least four acres of open space per thousand inhabitants. The three inner rings would be connected by American-style landscaped parkways for traffic that would run alongside the existing roads. Beyond them would be the outer country ring, with its agriculture and a string of ten new satellite towns that would absorb displaced Londoners from the crowded centre and allow for future population growth. Decentralisation was everything: 'The numbers in the centre will decrease, those in the outer areas will grow,' Abercrombie declared. Industry would be banned from inner London. Only the docks would be left to remind people of the city's trading past. Two specific tasks of urban regeneration would be undertaken. The West End would be redeveloped so that 'inexpensive flats' would offset the luxury apartments built there before the war, while the decaying industry of the South Bank would be replaced by 'a great cultural centre, embracing amongst other features a modern theatre, a large concert hall and the headquarters of various organisations'. The 'bad and ugly things', as he put it in an interview, would go.

In immediate practical terms a lot of patching up needed to be done. The London Repair Executive, established by the Ministry of Works in 1944 and in operation until June 1945, was just one of many organisations given the massive task of rebuilding and reconstructing the shattered City: its houses, its businesses and its transport network. The LCC for its part rebuilt nearly 3,000 war-damaged homes and constructed over 32,500 more. Eight thousand of these were temporary prefabs, erected in places such as Martin Street in Southwark, Excalibur Street in Catford, Lordship Lane in Dulwich, Highams Park in Waltham Forest, Fore Street in Enfield and St John's Avenue in Putney.

However, this was just scratching the surface; London, after all, had an estimated 350,000 damaged properties that awaited repair. Moreover, even those houses that had survived the German onslaught were often scarcely fit for a post-war world. Many had been flimsily constructed and lacked basic amenities. They had also all too often been poorly maintained over the decades – sometimes centuries – since they had been built. This was particularly the case in poorer areas where tenants had lived for years crammed into spaces not designed for so many, and where landlords had elected to spend as little as possible on keeping them in a fit state.

Notting Hill was a notorious example of a nineteenth-century suburb gone wrong: dotted with cheap lodging houses, bedsits and flats 'crawling with rats and rubbish'.[9] Films and photos of the period give a good

Urban decay in Notting Hill, 1953. This view is of Rillington Place, where the notorious serial killer John Christie lived.

indication of just how grim it had become by the early post-war period. Mid-Victorian terraces that today gleam with freshly painted stucco walls were then dingy affairs with badly chipped front pillars and broken windows. No. 10 Rillington Place, where the notorious serial killer John Christie lived, was a case in point. One of what once had been quite an elegant terrace of three-storey houses built in the 1860s, it had been divided into flats by the time Christie moved there in December 1938. The second-floor flat had no kitchen, there were no bathrooms and occupants had to share an outside lavatory. The sheer grimness of the terrace was memorably captured in the film *10 Rillington Place*, made in 1971 shortly before the terrace was demolished to make way for the new houses of Bartle Road.

Notting Hill's other villain, Peter Rachman, made money from the area's distress. Exploiting the housing shortage in immediate post-war London, he bought up slums in North Kensington and Paddington, used bully boys to throw out existing tenants and then 'sweated' the houses, stuffing them with new tenants (often Caribbean immigrants) or leasing them to brothel or club owners. It was estimated that at one point he was making £10,000 in rent a year for a house that had cost him £1,500. Remarkably, he was never prosecuted, being claimed by the grim reaper in 1962 before more earthly authorities could feel his collar.

If Notting Hill was bad, then Kensal New Town to the north was arguably even worse. Sandwiched between the Paddington branch of the Grand Junction Canal and the Great Western Railway, it had become progressively more built-up through the 1860s and 1870s, many of its early residents being either railway workers or poor migrants from central London whose previous slum lodging houses had been demolished. When Charles Booth surveyed the area in the early 1900s he calculated that more than half the residents were living in poverty. Thereafter, things went further downhill. By 1923, 2,500 people were crammed into the 140 narrow Victorian houses in and around Southam Street – most without ready access to running water – and while some improvements were made in the 1930s, the area declined again during the Second World War. By the late 1950s Kensal New Town was a dangerous mix of slum housing, poor white residents and poor Afro-Caribbean new arrivals, attracted – if that is the right word – to the area by its cheapness, and shunned in more salubrious areas because of the colour of their skin. Southam Street acquired further notoriety on 17 May 1959 when Kelso Cochrane, a 32-year-old carpenter from Antigua, was set upon by a gang of white youths and stabbed through the heart with a stiletto knife. More than 1,200 people, both black and white, attended his funeral. No one, however, was convicted of his murder.

Notting Hill was not unique in its fall from grace. Islington, and especially the Canonbury area, could be a grim place to live in the years after the Second World War. So, too, were Camden Town, Brixton, Camberwell and Denmark Hill. Lynne Reid Banks's novel of 1960, *The L-Shaped Room*, captures Fulham as it was at its lowest ebb. The heroine of the book – pregnant and unmarried – has to move there when she is thrown out of her father's home, and ends up in a bug-infested flat in a house occupied by other London 'outcasts'.

When it came to rebuilding London after the war, therefore, it was clear that far more needed to be done than simply patching up bomb damage. Although much of the capital was less than a hundred years old, it looked tired, old and run-down, its air filled with smoke from coal fires and steam trains, its buildings dirty and poorly maintained. Inspired by the zeal of the Abercrombie generation, and sharing many of the ideals put forward in the Abercrombie Plan (though never adopting it as it stood), urban developers therefore opted to level huge areas of the capital, sweeping away Georgian and Victorian terraced houses and slums and old street patterns. In their place they put confidently modern blocks of medium- and high-rise flats, standing in landscaped green parks or amid trees and shrubs.

One early and very ambitious result of this kind of thinking is the Alton Estate in Roehampton. Here, in the late 1940s, the LCC bought Roehampton Park and three Georgian country estates and transformed them into the Alton East Estate (originally the Portsmouth Road Estate) and the Alton West Estate (originally known as the Roehampton Lane Estate). Alton East, influenced by Scandinavian design, was a mixed development of flats and houses, designed to accommodate 100 persons per acre (Abercrombie recommended a density of 200 per acre in the centre of town and 70 at the periphery). Alton West, a far more monumental affair, was inspired in part by the work of the French architect Le Corbusier and consisted of a mix of buildings (including bungalows for the elderly) dominated by five substantial tower blocks raised on stilts

LANSBURY NEIGHBOURHOOD

MAP REVIEW 134,
JUNE 16, 1951

Many of our towns and cities suffer from the drab congestion of the Industrial Revolution on the inside and the sprawl of the jerry-builder on the outside. In the last few decades we have tried various incomplete remedies: 'slum-clearance' for the former, 'garden cities' for the latter. Neither really worked, and the planners, who have been made to try rebuilding after the destruction by bombing have taken a new form: neighbourhood planning.

A sense of community, of neighbourly responsibility, satisfies an essential human need. People do not just reside in a place, they live in it: they need schools, pubs, shops, markets, churches, public buildings, parks, theatres and places to work, within easy range. Different

kinds of families, too, need different kinds of houses—flats and houses both large and small, for big families, old people, single people, and so on. A 'neighbourhood', if it is to live, needs all these, and they should be related to one another in situation and design.

The County of London Plan published in 1943 works on the principle of creating 'neighbourhoods'. In this Plan the whole of Stepney and Poplar (three square miles) was to be rebuilt in the form of eleven new neighbourhoods. Part of the first of these, Lansbury in Poplar, is now being built as the Live Architecture exhibition of the Festival of Britain. Visitors will be able to see the site being built while the people already living there go about their daily life.

Schools

Homes

Shopping Centre

Post-war utopianism: plans for the Lansbury Estate in Poplar, published in 1951. The photographs are beaded 'schools', 'homes', 'shopping centre' and 'Trinity congregational church' and seek to show how the estate will become a 'neighbourhood'.

over parkland. Flat roofs and an extensive use of concrete helped give the scheme its sense of optimistic modernity. The original plan was that the tower blocks should be placed and orientated in such a way as to give as many residents as possible views over Richmond Park. The Minister for Housing, Harold Macmillan, however, worried that this would create a virtual continuous high wall overlooking a royal park, and the plans therefore had to be changed.

The post-war tower block was seen – at least in the early days – as an urban panacea and a Londoner's paradise. The Lansbury Estate in Poplar, for example, begun in 1950 and only completed in 1982 – and one of the largest to be built in the heart of the Docklands area – was intended to incorporate a series of distinct neighbourhoods, each one a self-contained community. Different types of flat were provided to suit different types of tenant, and the development also included schools, shopping areas, churches, public houses and open spaces: an aerial version of a garden suburb community. In 1953, renowned American architecture critic Lewis Mumford praised the development:

> Its design has been based not solely on abstract aesthetic principles, or on the economics of commercial construction, or on the techniques of mass production, but on the social constitution of the community itself, with its diversity of human interests and human needs. Thus the architects and planners have avoided not only the clichés of 'high rise' building but the dreary prisonlike order that results from forgetting the very purpose of housing and the necessities of neighbourhood living.[10]

Leading architects became involved in planning many of these new cities in the sky. Ernö Goldfinger, for example – arch-modernist and arch-enemy of James Bond creator Ian Fleming – was responsible for the 27-storey Balfron Tower in Poplar, built between 1965 and 1967. Here he carefully separated living spaces from service spaces, creating a separate tower that housed the lifts and also the laundry rooms and rubbish chutes. Goldfinger went on to design the not dissimilar 31-storey Trellick Tower in North Kensington on the bulldozed remains of the notorious Southam Street.

It has been estimated that by 1983, when the first national survey of local-authority-owned high-rise housing was conducted, 1,799 blocks of flats had been constructed in Greater London of six storeys and more, and that nearly one-fifth were twenty or more storeys high. Since it was

The iconic Trellick Tower in North Kensington, viewed from the streets of Kensal Rise.

inner London that tended to have the worst housing problems and the least space to solve them, it is not surprising that most of these new tower blocks were close to the centre of the capital. Newham led the way with 125 tower blocks, closely followed by Tower Hamlets, Wandsworth and Southwark. That said, tower blocks could be found as far away as Barnet, Bromley, Willesden and Brent. Kensington and Chelsea alone had seventy-seven.

Not every major post-war building project was high-rise. Some local councils such as Islington, for example, often opted for high-density, low-rise development. A maze of interlocking estates grew up to the west of the Caledonian Road in an area where bombing had destroyed many houses; building began in 1947, much of which was the responsibility of the LCC. Others went for the sort of mixed development that Abercrombie favoured. Churchill Gardens in Pimlico is a classic example. Designed in 1946, the estate combined ten-storey blocks of flats with four-storey maisonettes and some three-storey terraced houses. The design

High-rise flats proved hugely popular with post-war developers. The block in the background here is one of three built in the 'old village' of East Finchley, which had been devastated by a German bomb in November 1940.

included three new schools, shops and a community centre. Meanwhile, the area in south London around Lambeth Road and Hercules Road – where, strangely enough, the classic film comedy *Passport to Pimlico* was filmed in 1949 – developed in a similar fashion, with residential neighbourhoods intersected by pedestrian routes and interconnected by roads. As for Thamesmead, built in the 1960s on the Woolwich and Erith marshes, this provided housing for 60,000 residents in a mix of medium-rise tower blocks and low-rise blocks, arranged around a twisting spine of pedestrian walkways. In one form or another, local authority housing went from 21 per cent of the total in 1961 to 46 per cent by 1981.

For many, the move from pre-war slums to post-war flats couldn't come soon enough. They welcomed the fact that houses that had been rotting away for years or had been damaged by enemy bombing were being swept away. They liked the fact that they were going to be rehoused in smart, bright new homes. They were excited at the prospect of the properly appointed kitchens and bathrooms that so much of the older housing stock lacked. On the surface, at least, a Trellick Tower must have seemed to offer so much more than a Southam Street and the grim poverty that went with it.

———◄•►———

As part of his grand decentralised view of London, Abercrombie had been keen to move industry away from the centre, and to an extent this process was already underway when he was drawing up his plans. While the docks could scarcely be transported somewhere else to avoid German bombing, other industrial concerns could, and many of them chose not to return when the bombing had stopped. Their decision marked the first steps along the way to an industrial decline that would become increasingly precipitous over the ensuing decades, and that, along with the various urban regeneration schemes of the 1950s and early 1960s, would push people ever further from the centre. In 1931 the population of Greater London stood at 8.1 million, 4.9 million of whom lived in the inner city. By 1951 those figures had become 8.2 million and 3.5 million respectively, and by 1981 they were 6.8 million and 2.5 million.

That latter figure shows just how many people were choosing to live a very long way out indeed. Abercrombie's dream of a ring of new towns beyond his planned green belt had largely come true. Stevenage was designated a new town in 1946; the following year Crawley, Hemel Hempstead and Harlow followed suit; in 1948 came Hatfield and Welwyn (building on the garden city that was already there); and in 1949 Basildon and Bracknell. By 1961 over 130,000 new homeowners were living in these new towns, and around and beyond them there stretched a commuter belt that now extended well into Kent in the south-east, to Essex in the north-east, to the Home Counties of Hertfordshire, Bedfordshire and Buckinghamshire north of the river, and to Berkshire, Surrey and Sussex to the south. This Greater London Urban Area, as it became known, encompassed in its clockwise sweep a swathe of towns that included Wycombe, Luton, Chelmsford and Southend, Tonbridge and Maidstone, Crawley, Guildford, Woking, Bracknell and Reading. It marked the final triumph of the longer-distance commuter.

Given this gravitational pull outwards, it's scarcely surprising that

Abercrombie and his ilk should have regarded transport as such an important part of their vision of a post-war London. Given the ever-growing popularity of the car, it follows that they should have turned their planning attention to roads rather than railways. Not that railways were ignored completely in the post-war period; the Victoria and Jubilee lines were both constructed in the 1960s and 1970s, not only to improve travel around the middle of the network, but also to serve commuters out towards Stanmore in one direction and Walthamstow in another. Nevertheless, railways played second fiddle, subject to endless rethinks and budget cuts.

Roads, by contrast, won more enthusiastic support among developers. For a start, there was recognition that London's existing road network was becoming increasingly inadequate. As already mentioned, as early as 1938, the Ministry of Transport published *The Highway Development Survey, 1937*, based on research conducted by civil engineer and road specialist Sir Charles Bressey, and the renowned architect Sir Edwin Lutyens. The report concluded both that more roads in general were needed, and that a series of concentric ring routes were required to serve the burgeoning outer suburbs (the outermost north and south orbital routes of the plan largely anticipated the route later taken by the M25). Since road widening was clearly impractical in many places, the suggestion was that some roads might follow railway routes, and that flyovers could be pressed into service in places to carry cars above them. Since the war intervened the following year, the report was stillborn, but Abercrombie took up the baton again in 1943 and 1944 and came up with five ring roads for London, somewhat unimaginatively labelled A to E: an inner route for the central area (A); four arterial routes linking Earl's Court, the Isle of Dogs, Islington and Dulwich (B); a ring that connected the North and South Circular roads (C); an express arterial outside London's built-up area (D); and a final ring that would comprise north and south orbital routes (E).

Such an ambitious scheme was bound never to get further than the drawing board. It would have involved massive disruption, and it would have cost a fortune – a fortune that austerity Britain of the 1940s and 1950s did not possess. Consequently, in 1955 the LCC stated in its Development Plan that:

... it is not yet possible to contemplate a drastic re-arrangement, including motorways, of the main road system. It is therefore the Council's intention that the main highway structure of the Administrative County shall be based on the existing road network of principal traffic roads, improved where practical by reconstructed inter-sections, widening roads or construction of new sections of routes on a comprehensive and co-ordinated basis.[11]

Two years later, in 1957, the Herbert Commission, which was set up to look once again at the perennial issue of how best to govern London, again investigated the thorny issue of London roads, again made recom-mendations, and again proposed ring roads. This time, according to reports published in 1966 and 1967, there were to be two: Ringway 1 and Ringway 2. The inner Ringway 1 described four sides of a box – a North Cross Route from Harlesden to Hackney Wick, an East Cross Route from Hackney Wick to Kidbrooke, a South Cross Route from Kidbrooke to Battersea, and a West Cross Route from Battersea to Harlesden. The outer Ringway 2 was intended to improve the existing North and South Circular routes, which at that stage were little more than suburban roads meandering their way round London in a gentle fashion, but with some faster stretches constructed in the 1940s and 1950s. Under the new plans, the northern section was to become a motorway, labelled the M15. Work duly began on the East Cross Route – now the A2 and A12 – and the West Cross Route, linking Shepherd's Bush and North Kensington to Paddington via an elevated section of the A40 called the Westway.

———— ◄ ► ————

It had always been passionately believed by post-war planners that in this brave new world of council estates and ring roads, London needed its green spaces; and the quid pro quo for all the new development was not just landscaped parks and gardens in and around council estates, but a green belt around the capital. This had actually been initiated back in 1935 by the LCC, which had embarked on a buying spree of farmland to preserve it from the developer. Abercrombie had, of course, incorporated the Green Belt in his own plans, and in 1950 it formally came into being when specific boundaries for its extent were drawn up. It wasn't always adhered to – the LCC itself built estates on the Green Belt in Oxhey (Watford), Debden (Loughton) and elsewhere in the late 1940s – but as an overall barrier to further development its effectiveness was marked.

A further transformation of Londoners' lives came with the passing of the Clean Air Acts of 1956 and 1968. Pollution had, of course, long been a problem in the capital. As early as 1661 in his *Fumifugium, or the Inconvenience of the Air and Smoke of London Dissipated,* John Evelyn had described in his prefatory dedication to Charles II how:

> It was one day, as I was walking in your majesty's palace at White Hall (where I have sometimes the honour to refresh my self with the sight of your illustrious presence, which is the joy of your people's hearts) that a presumptuous smoke issuing from one or two tunnels near Northumberland House, and not far from Scotland-yard did so invade the Court; that all the rooms, galleries, and places about it were fill'd and infested with it, and that to such a degree, as men could hardly discern one another for the cloud, and none could support without manifest inconveniency.[12]

After Evelyn's time, things got worse rather than better. An increasing population using ever more wood and coal fires, along with London's various factories and industries, all combined to produce smoke-exacerbated fogs, or pea-soupers, in which visibility shrank to zero. The great wake-up call finally came in 1952. On Friday 5 December of that year, dense penetrating smog descended on London. Roads ground to a halt, while railway stations and airports were forced to close. At Sadler's Wells a performance of *La Traviata* had to be abandoned because the audience couldn't see the stage. By the time the smog lifted four days later, well over 4,000 people (some estimates suggested as many as 12,000) had died from bronchitis and other breathing-related conditions. The Clean Air Acts that came in the wake of this disaster banished pea-soupers from London for good, legislating for smokeless fuels and encouraging the development of power stations away from the centre. Even back-garden bonfires were discouraged.

A clean city, with an extensive green belt, carefully thought-through urban planning that reduced overcrowding, and modern houses and better roads. It sounds idyllic. However . . .

SIXTEEN

SECOND THOUGHTS

The Capital after 1970

It was 5.45 on the morning of Thursday, 16 May 1968. Miss Ivy Hodge, a 56-year-old cake decorator, was in the kitchen of her one-bedroom flat on the eighteenth floor of her tower block, making herself breakfast. She filled the kettle, placed it on the cooker, turned on the gas and lit a match. The explosion that followed blew out the external walls of the flat. Simultaneously it fatally weakened the entire building's structure. Within seconds the whole south-east corner was collapsing like a pack of cards. Remarkably, Miss Hodge survived. Four other people, however, were crushed to death.

If there was a moment when the drawbacks of the brave new world of post-war London were revealed, this was it; for the disaster at Ronan Point in Canning Town was a very public demonstration of the way in which the utopian dream of the late 1940s was, only twenty years later, running the risk of becoming an urban nightmare. As the inquiry that was launched after the explosion showed only too clearly, Ronan Point had been poorly constructed: crucial joints within the structure had been filled with newspaper rather than concrete; the walls rested on levelling bolts rather than on a solid foundation; and poorly fitted external panels had gradually taken in rainwater, fatally weakening the whole structure in the process. Completed in the spring of 1968, the building had survived barely two months. Today, the remains of Ronan Point form the hardcore under the runway of London City Airport.

The problem was that Ronan Point was not unique. In the flurry of rebuilding and redevelopment that had followed the Second World War, standards had become compromised. Cash-strapped councils, an LCC (and then GLC) keen to see its vision realised as quickly as possible, and successive governments who wanted Britain's housing problem 'solved'

Ronan Point in Canning Town after the gas explosion that devastated
it on 16 May 1968. A subsequent inquiry revealed that it had been
very poorly constructed.

overnight, had encouraged a climate of cost-cutting and they had tended
to turn a blind eye to the reduction in quality that inevitably accompanied
it. Many tower blocks scattered across London had problems with damp,
poorly fitting windows and lifts that constantly broke down. Many were
simply built too high, thanks in part to the misguided 1956 Housing
Subsidy Act which offered local authorities a bigger subsidy the higher
they were prepared to build.

Even the better-constructed tower blocks had their share of problems.
One thing that post-war urban planners hadn't taken into account was
the sense of isolation that high-rise living could cause and that the Mass
Observation surveys of the 1930s had warned of. Taking an old terraced
community and piling it vertically sounded like common sense, but the
social results could sometimes be disastrous: pulling people together at
random, and calling them a community, was rarely a recipe for success.
Moreover, even though all housing requires expensive maintenance, it

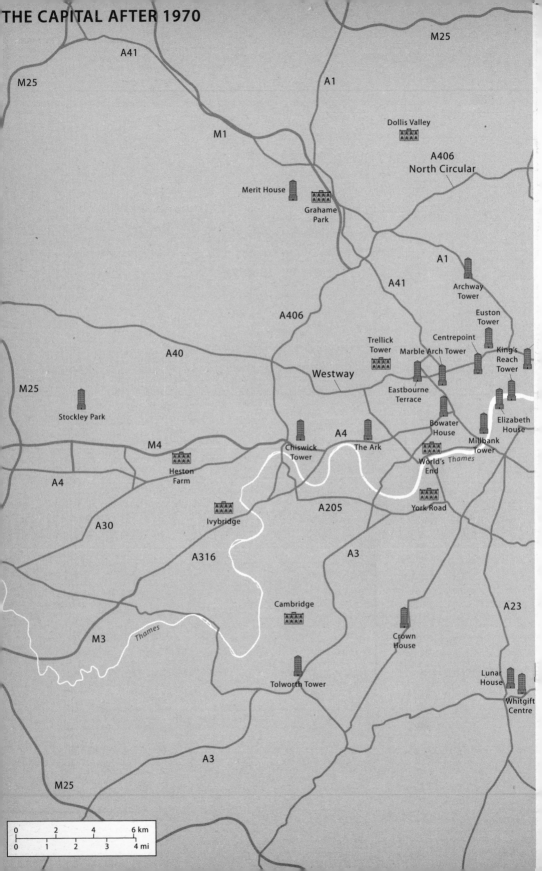

THE CAPITAL AFTER 1970

M25

A41

A1

M25

M1

Dollis Valley

A406
North Circular

Merit House

Grahame
Park

A1

A41

Archway
Tower

Euston
Tower

A406

Centrepoint

King's
Reach
Tower

Trellick
Tower

Marble Arch Tower

A40

Westway

Eastbourne
Terrace

M25

Bowater
House

Elizabeth
House

Stockley Park

Chiswick
Tower

A4

The Ark

Millbank
Tower

M4

World's
End

Thames

Heston
Farm

A4

A205

York Road

A30

Ivybridge

A316

A3

Cambridge

A23

M3

Thames

Crown
House

Lunar
House

Tolworth Tower

Whitgift
Centre

A3

M25

| 0 | | 2 | | 4 | | 6 km |
| 0 | 1 | 2 | 3 | 4 mi |

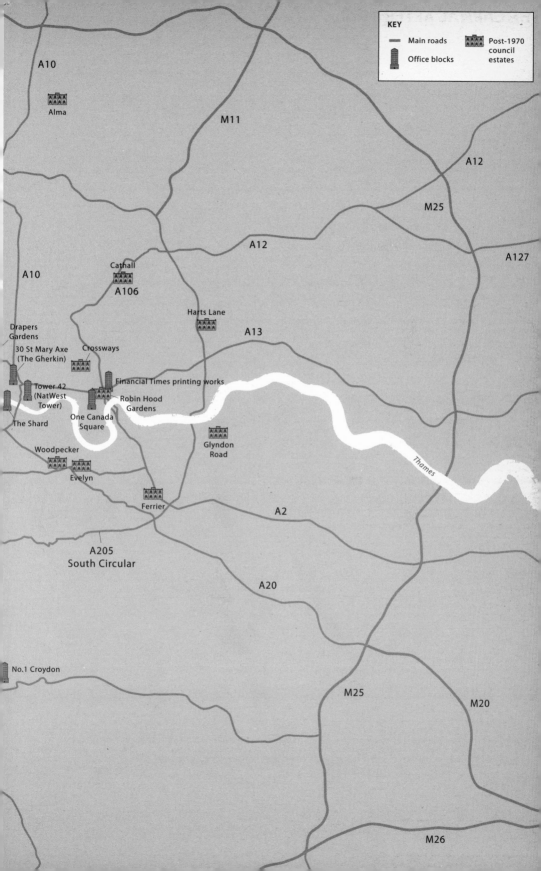

KEY

— Main roads

Office blocks

Post-1970 council estates

A10

Alma

M11

A12

M25

A12

A127

A10

Cathall

A106

Harts Lane

A13

Drapers Gardens

30 St Mary Axe (The Gherkin)

Crossways

Financial Times printing works

Tower 42 (NatWest Tower)

Robin Hood Gardens

One Canada Square

The Shard

Glyndon Road

Woodpecker

Evelyn

Ferrier

Thames

A2

A205 South Circular

A20

No.1 Croydon

M25

M20

M26

seemed to be assumed that, once built, post-war council estates could look after themselves. Trellick Tower in North Kensington, started the year of the Ronan Point disaster, was by the 1980s popularly known as 'the tower of terror'. Newspapers carried stories of drug addicts attacking children on the estate, of women being raped in the lifts and of arsonists setting fire to flats. There was even an urban myth in circulation that the architect had become so overcome by guilt at the monster he had created that he had thrown himself from the roof. The nineteenth-century houses of Kensal Town that Trellick Tower replaced had taken many years to decline into slums; Trellick Tower had done it in barely a decade.

Trellick Tower was not alone. The 1960s Aylesbury Estate in Walworth and the predominantly 1970s Ferrier Estate in Kidbrooke, both intended to accommodate some of the poorest of the local community, were, within a few years of their completion, showing the classic signs of inner-city decay: tensions between residents and a rapidly increasing crime rate. The same was true to greater and lesser degrees of Ashburton Estate (Putney), Ivybridge Estate (Isleworth), New Cambridge Estate (Norbiton) and many others. London became dotted with pockets of deep unhappiness and daily struggle, where residents were forced to live in poor accommodation served by lifts that often did not work and where antisocial behaviour and crime was a constant presence.

Perhaps the most notorious of all the post-war estates was Broadwater Farm in Tottenham. Here the construction of 1,063 flats on what had previously been boggy farmland began in 1967, with walkways linking the blocks at first-floor level. All were occupied by 1973, but within three years major design faults had become apparent. It also became clear that insufficient thought had gone into making the estate an attractive place to live: it was a long way from the nearest tube station and it was managed from a housing office over two miles away. A grim and forbidding place, it proved so unpopular that 53 per cent of council tenants refused offers of accommodation there, and many existing residents begged to be housed elsewhere. In her book *Estates: An Intimate History*, Lynsey Hanley graphically chronicles the estate's decline:

> According to its tenants, the years between 1979 and 1981 were the worst time to live on the estate. Its very future was in doubt, and the all-white

tenants' association was vastly unrepresentative of an estate population that comprised nearly half from ethnic minorities. Many residents could not even move around the estate, both for fear of robbery and burglary and because the walkways were often flooded due to inadequate draining.[1]

Improvements were made in the ensuing years, and a very successful youth association was set up, but the inhabitants of the estate continued to struggle against poverty (unemployment at Broadwater Farm stood at 42 per cent), poorly maintained buildings and racism. Things spiralled out of control in 1985, when tensions between the youth of the estate and the police spilled over into a riot following the death of Broadwater Farm resident Cynthia Jarrett during a police search of her flat. Petrol bombs were hurled; shots were fired; and in the mayhem PC Keith Blakelock was hacked to death – the first officer to be killed while on riot duty since 1833.

As scepticism about one cornerstone of the Abercrombie generation's vision of urban dwelling increased, so opposition to another started to make its voice heard. Abercrombie had argued that new arterial roads were

The aftermath of the Broadwater Farm riot of 1985.

essential in a city where so many people would be living ever further away from the centre – in the suburbs and across the new satellite towns on the outskirts. His views continued to carry weight with town planners in the 1950s and 1960s; and in September 1969 the LCC's successor, the Greater London Council (GLC), published its plan for three concentric ringways that would deal with traffic congestion in the capital once and for all. 'London needs better organizing,' it declared, 'not meaning more busy-bodying and interference with individual freedom, but basic planning.'

Even the GLC recognised that there were some practical difficulties here: 'Everyone regrets the disturbance of private property which this road planning involves,' the report admitted. The problem was that the word 'disturbance' was something of an understatement. To create the inner ring road, or box, would have meant punching multi-lane highways through the Victorian terraces of Kensington, Battersea, Hackney and Camden, involving the demolition of some 30,000 homes and the bisection of whole communities by motorways. Hampstead and Belsize Park would have been transformed by a cut-and-cover tunnel that would have required bulldozing on a major scale – and the loss of Sigmund Freud's house on Maresfield Gardens (now a museum). Whole swathes of Brixton would have vanished under tarmac; to add insult to injury, since there were no plans to provide an interchange in the area, the residents of Brixton would have been the recipients of a road not only that they did not want but to which they had no access.

A vision of the future was provided by the opening of the Westway in 1970. Raised on thick concrete stilts, and passing in places within feet of people's bedrooms, it aroused furious local protest in the planning stages. The residents may have lost on this occasion, but opposition to the GLC's Greater London Development Plan became ever more widespread and increasingly hostile, even leading to the creation of a group calling themselves 'Homes before Roads'. Set up in the same year that the Westway was opened, they went on to put up eighty-five candidates in the Greater London elections.

The official review and inquiry set up to look at the GLC's new road schemes was conducted by Frank Layfield and lasted 237 days between July 1970 and May 1972. In that time the panel heard over 28,000 objections, many of them focusing on the deterioration in the quality of Londoner's lives that the scheme would almost certainly involve. The panel itself had various criticisms to make. It felt that the plan was 'distinctly half-hearted' in its supposed commitment to the recreational use of green-belt land, that it did too little to make provision for the rehabilitation of derelict land and that insufficient attention had been paid to the polluting effects of new roads. 'London has not got enough public open space,' it argued. It concluded that work on the controversial Ringway One to relieve congestion in central London should begin, but that other aspects of the plan needed a rethink.

The Layfield Panel's findings, coupled with the economic woes Britain suffered in the 1970s, meant that the GLC Plan was only realised in part. The outer ringway did indeed go ahead in 1973, and was duly opened in 1986 as the M25 orbital motorway. An extension to the M11 in east London was also constructed. However, the era of the grand scheme was passing and it seemed increasingly unlikely that any new major road scheme would ever be approved. On the plus side, this left the capital on a much more human scale than it might otherwise have been. On the minus side, London was left with its eternal traffic problem unsolved. By the time the M25 opened it already seemed out of date, unable to cope with the flood of cars that had come on to Britain's roads since it was first mooted. Soon it had become synonymous with congestion and frustration, the inspiration for Chris Rea's 1989 track 'The Road to Hell'. In this context, other attempts to speed up the flow of traffic – including road widening and improvements to the Dartford Crossing in 1963 and 1980 (in the form of tunnels) and again in 1991 (the Queen Elizabeth II Bridge) – looked like tinkering.

The final vestiges of the GLC's road plans for London were effectively killed off in the 1980s, by which time public opposition had become a given. Indeed, when plans were advanced to widen the Archway Road in north London in the 1980s, the government inspector appointed to run the inquiry was so intimidated by the fury the scheme unleashed that he felt compelled to resign. The Minister for Transport, Nicholas Ridley, reported to the House of Commons on 28 February 1984:

> In his letter of resignation he describes how for several months he has
> been plagued with telephone calls, how callers have sought various
> means of speaking to his wife, the receipt of hundreds of letters at his
> private home, some addressed to his wife, two deputations at the house
> over Christmas, the receipt of a parcel of excreta, trespassers in his
> garden and the breaking of a window.[2]

*A 1994 photograph of activists seeking to halt plans to extend the M11.
They resisted street by street and house by house, but the new road
nevertheless went ahead.*

As for the M11 extension, it went ahead only after years of rearguard
action by protestors. Here whole streets were occupied by activist squatters who were forced into yielding them one at a time as the bailiffs
moved in. The optimistic republics of 'Wanstonia', 'Leytonstonia' and
'Euphoria' were established: a symbolic 'two fingers' to those in authority.
Wanstonia even went so far as to ask the UN for official recognition and
created its own national flag, the Union Jill. It was invaded and occupied
by the police and bailiffs in 1994. Arguably, though, if Wanstonia lost the
battle, it did win the war.

———◄◆►———

By the early 1970s, opposition to new development was going hand in
hand with complementary campaigns to preserve what was left of old
London. There was nothing very novel here; since the days of William

Morris and Octavia Hill, people had been drawing up petitions and creating organisations to deflect the demolition ball. However, the scale of post-war development and the radical dislocation it was causing between the old and the new prompted a much wider – and more vociferous – response. The Georgian Group, for example, which had been founded in 1937 when the magnificent Adelphi Terrace between the Strand and the Thames had been demolished, was active in areas such as Spitalfields and Islington. When the grand Euston Arch outside Euston station came under threat in 1960, a positive alliance of ultimately unsuccessful preservationists came together: John Betjeman and the art historian Nikolaus Pevsner; the Society for the Protection of Ancient Buildings; and the Victorian Society (of which Betjeman was vice chairman).

It wasn't just London's grand buildings that the preservationists increasingly fought to keep. By the 1960s they were also campaigning to save more everyday Victorian houses that only a generation before would doubtless have encountered sneers of disdain. In Islington, for example – home to so much gracious Georgian architecture – people also tried to safeguard the 1860s houses of Packington Square, once elegant, now overcrowded and unmodernised. Islington Council bought the square in 1963 and announced their intention to demolish it as part of their redevelopment plans for the area, not without the expression of misgivings by members of its own housing committee. Soon the press had taken up the story and even the politicians at Westminster became embroiled in the battle between those who argued for demolition and replacement and those who believed in preservation and refurbishment. In this particular case the preservationists lost and the new Packington Estate went ahead (opening in 1970); but it was a sign of the times that the battle should have been so bitterly and fiercely fought.

Away from the public limelight there were many from the 1950s onwards who chose to preserve London's past by living in it. The Marxist sociologist Ruth Glass, who published several books and articles on London's post-war housing problem, pinpointed (and lamented) this phenomenon in 1962 when she came up with the term 'gentrification' to describe what was starting to happen in areas as far apart as Islington, Notting Hill, Camberwell and Kennington. Long neglected, often slum-ridden, these deeply unfashionable suburbs were, she noted, now beginning to attract middle-class buyers, enchanted by their Georgian and nineteenth-century

faded elegance and excited by the prospect of living, not in the 'respectable' outer suburbs, but in the 'bohemian' inner ones. There were also more
practical considerations that helped them: eviction of long-term tenants
was greatly facilitated by the 1957 Rent Act; and from the late 1950s
onwards it became ever easier for aspiring home owners with perhaps
only a little disposable cash in their pockets to get a mortgage.

Moreover, these inner-suburb houses were astonishingly numerous and
temptingly cheap. To an extent, their shabbiness was part of their appeal.
Indeed, the famous 1960s estate agent Roy Brooks made a virtue of
emphasising the problems that came with so many of the houses he
sought to sell. 'Do not be misled by the trim exterior of this modest
period res with its dirty broken windows,' he wrote of a house in Chelsea;
'all is not well with the inside. The decor of the nine rooms, some of
which hangs inelegantly from the walls, is revolting. Not entirely devoid
of plumbing, there is a pathetic kitchen and one cold tap. No bathroom,
of course . . . Sacrifice [£]6,750.'

Some sense of the benefits that could accrue to the adventurous is
contained in an advertisement he placed for a house in Pimlico:

Wanted: Someone with taste, means and a stomach strong enough to
buy this erstwhile house of ill-repute in Pimlico. It is untouched by the
20th century as far as conveniences for even the basic human decencies
are concerned. Although it reeks of damp or worse, the plaster is coming
off the walls and daylight peeps through a hole in the roof, it is still
habitable judging by the bed of rags, fag ends and empty bottles in one
corner. Plenty of scope for the socially aspiring to express their decora-
tive taste and get their abode in The Glossy, and nothing to stop them
putting Westminster on their notepaper. Comprises 10 rather unpleasant
rooms with slimy back yard, [£]4,650 Freehold. Tarted up, these houses
make [£]15,000.[3]

Gradually, gentrification spread. The decayed old houses of Kensington,
both big and small, were eagerly snapped up. In Camden, Primrose Hill,
Hammersmith, Fulham, Ealing, Kilburn, Clapham and Stockwell, nineteenth-century terraces went almost overnight from decay to glory; and
in the process, prices began to rise. In Islington a Georgian house that
might have cost only £6,000 in the mid 1960s was fetching £130,000
barely a decade later; it would be worth ten or so times that figure today.

As one area became gentrified and expensive, so colonisers moved on to the next. 'Up and coming' was the epithet increasingly attached to house details by a new generation of estate agents who no longer saw the need to resort to Roy Brooks's humour and candour.

━━━━━━━◄•►━━━━━━━

The backlash against redevelopment caused something of a crisis of confidence in official circles in the closing decades of the century. It was only too clear that council estates were not necessarily a universal panacea; that balancing the need for moderately efficient roads with the wishes of local residents had to involve the sort of messy compromise that neither side would ever be happy with; and that other grand projects weren't going down too well either.

The Barbican is a good case in point. Here in the heart of historic London was a City development designed to return residents to the centre after centuries of population decline. Two thousand housing units were constructed, in an urban landscape punctuated by high-density high-rise tower blocks clothed in reinforced concrete and connected by secure, if rather bleak, walkways. Its intentions were laudable, and it has understandably gained architectural plaudits (it is now Grade II listed), but when it was opened in 1982 many found it strangely cut off from its surroundings, forbiddingly fortress-like, and bafflingly complicated to negotiate. It became the butt of jokes, the 1985 BBC nuclear thriller *Edge of Darkness*, for example, mocking its impenetrability in a chase scene that ends with the hero getting away and the pursuing police hopelessly lost in the Barbican labyrinth. The Elephant and Castle scheme (London's first enclosed shopping centre) was also considered a failure: opened in 1965, it was soon dismissed as a brutal development trapped on a large traffic island. Croydon's ambitious 1960s and 1970s redevelopments involved the creation of a rash of office and retail units which many local people similarly struggled to warm to.

The growing scepticism about utopian schemes was rooted in social and aesthetic concerns. What actually killed them, though, was the rather more practical matter of a lack of cash. Much of the rebuilding of the 1950s and early 1960s had been made possible by a short-lived post-war economic boom. After that, however, everything seemed to go wrong.

Part of the reason Britain had been able to bounce back so quickly after 1945 was that its manufacturing base had survived wartime bombing largely intact. Twenty years later, though, that manufacturing base was looking increasingly antiquated in comparison to the brand-new factories springing up in Europe and elsewhere. In the same period the special trading advantages imperial Britain had once been able to exploit were slipping away as the empire was dismantled; and to compound the misery, renewed Arab–Israeli conflict in the Middle East in the mid 1970s led to an oil crisis that threatened to cripple Britain's economy.

London's traditional industrial base was eviscerated in the late 1960s and 1970s. Clothes-making industries migrated from the East End to Stoke Newington and Hackney, and then abroad. Furniture-making in east and north London staggered and then stalled, the workforce plummeting from 16,390 in 1960 to a mere 1,320 in 1984. Brewing suffered a similar fate: Cannon's Brewery and Nicholson's Distillery in Finsbury went by the end of the 1960s; Watney Mann's Albion Brewery in Whitechapel closed in 1979. Among the casualties inevitably were some of the capital's oldest enterprises. Whitefriars Glass factory, for example, founded in 1680 on the site of the former Whitefriars monastery just off Fleet Street and resident in Wealdstone near Harrow since 1923, abandoned its production of stained glass in 1973 and finally closed its doors altogether in 1980.

No area was spared. That beacon of 1930s industrial might, the Great West Road's 'golden mile', lost its sheen. Brentford and Isleworth were both badly hit in the 1970s and 1980s as the Firestone factory, Hoover, and United Biscuits all went. Hounslow is estimated to have shed 23,000 manufacturing jobs between 1973 and 1988. Hammersmith and Fulham, home to nearly 400 factories in the late 1960s, had lost most of their industrial legacy by the end of the century. Dagenham's car industry shed nearly half of its 28,000 workforce between the mid 1970s and 1984. Virtually every sector was devastated, from heavy industry (Woolwich, Greenwich), to specialist wiring and electrics (Edmonton), to sweet manufacturing (Hackney, Wood Green, Hayes).

Coal and gas power stations were similarly decimated, their fate finally sealed by the discovery of gas in the North Sea in the mid 1960s and oil a decade later, which removed the provision of raw power from London for ever. In 1959, London had nine gasworks and seventeen electricity generating stations, with a further three power stations under construction. In 1969, however, Beckton Gasworks was closed (the disused site taken over by the London Docklands Development Corporation). In 1976 the East Greenwich Gasworks followed suit (part of the site is now the Millennium Dome), as did Southall (in 1973) and the Imperial at Sands End in Fulham (1978). Elsewhere, many of the electricity-generating power stations built in the 1930s and expanded after the war also fell victim to the supply of cheap oil and gas in the 1970s, with Battersea closing in 1983 – its fate still to be determined nearly three decades later.

There is no doubt, however, that it was the docks that were most dramatically hit. Devastated by bombing during the Second World War, notorious for their appalling labour relations, and facing increasing competition from more modern and better-run European ports (Hamburg, Rotterdam, Dunkirk), by the early 1960s they were beginning to feel the strain. First to go were the East India Docks in 1967. The St Katherine Docks followed in 1968, the same year that a container port opened downstream at Tilbury, sucking what business remained much further east. The Surrey and London Docks went in 1969, and the royal docks and those on the Isle of Dogs were shut by 1981. In total, over 10,000 jobs were lost between 1966 and 1976, and a further 8,000 over the next five years, hitting Stepney, Poplar, Limehouse, Wapping, Southwark, Bermondsey, Rotherhithe and Deptford particularly hard. Entire communities, and a way of life going back centuries, were destroyed.

One of the very few growth areas after the war was aviation or, more particularly, Heathrow; and since this could be described as a 'grand project' it is scarcely surprising to find Patrick Abercrombie's fingerprints all over it. It was he who recommended that a wartime airbase for long-distance bombers should be transformed into an international airport. In the process he greatly irritated the then owner of Heathrow, Sir Richard Fairley, who rejected a compensation offer that valued the 230-acre site at £10 per acre, in no uncertain terms:

> It is manifestly so much easier for the Civil Aviation authorities to look over the airports near London, that the foresight of private companies has made available, and then using government backing forcibly to acquire them, than to go to the infinite trouble that we had in making an aerial survey to find the site, buying the land from different owners,

and then building up a fine airfield from what was market-gardening land. And why the haste to proceed? I cannot escape the thought that the hurry is not uninspired by the fact that a post-war government might not be armed with the power or even be willing to take action that is now being rushed through at the expense of the war effort.[4]

This was, however, the early days of the 1940s 'brave new world' mentality. Consequently, even though the scheme was opposed by Winston Churchill, the Ministry of Agriculture, Middlesex County Council and many others, the Undersecretary of State for Air, Harold Balfour, was able to push through a compulsory purchase order, only later admitting that his claim that the scheme was necessary for military reasons had been a ruse to avoid a lengthy and costly public inquiry once the war was over. Fairley sued and the court case dragged on until 1964. In the meantime, Balfour got both a peerage and his hands on around twenty farms and smallhold-ings, along with numerous houses and roads around the airfield. Thirteen hundred acres in all were requisitioned and plans were also announced to extend further into the villages of Sibson and Harlington. On 1 January 1946 the Ministry for Civil Aviation took control of the site and the airport was officially opened just under three months later on 25 March.

The area was transformed. Villages became service centres; Harlington, Harmondsworth, Longford, Cranford, Hounslow, Hatton, Bedfont, Stanwell, and even Colnbrook (situated just outside Greater London), all started to sprawl into one another, several of them now connected to central London via the Piccadilly line. Southall, already the home of Associated Equipment Company (AEC), who produced chassis for trucks and buses, enjoyed a mini industrial boom. Kingston acquired British Aerospace. In time, Hillingdon became the headquarters for British Airways and a regional office for British Midland International. Hotels sprang up along the Bath Road, and when the growth in global air travel exceeded Heathrow's capacity (62,000 planes took off there in 1953), Gatwick was expanded (in 1958), followed by Stansted (redeveloped from 1984) and Luton (rebranded in 1990 as London Luton). Heathrow itself remodelled its runways over time and acquired a fourth terminal in 1986, followed by a fifth terminal in 2008.

Aviation, however, was very much the exception to the rule of London's industrial decline. At the end of the 1950s, one in three of all London's workers was employed in a factory or workshop; between 1961 and 1977, half a million manufacturing jobs were lost; and by 1997, fewer than one in 10 people remained in the manufacturing sector. London was no longer a workshop.

———◄•►———

The 1970s and 1980s were not happy times for London and, in particular, its inner suburbs. Industry was disappearing faster than jobs could be created elsewhere, the population was declining (in the 1980s, inner London contained fewer people than it had in 1851), and poverty was on the rise. The early 1970s were dominated by industrial unrest that led to power blackouts, food shortages and the imposition of the 'three-day week'; at the end of the decade, during the bitterly cold 'winter of discontent' of 1978–9 when the country was lashed by strike after strike, the capital's ills seemed symbolised by the uncollected rubbish piled ever higher in Leicester Square. There were riots in Southall (1979), Brixton (1981 and 1985), Peckham (1985) and Tottenham (1985). Recorded crime levels rose, and, to compound the grief, it became clear that some of those crimes were actually being committed by the police – Operation Countryman, an investigation into police corruption conducted between 1978 and 1984, resulted in over 400 Met officers losing their jobs (though none was ever charged). To make a bad situation even worse, Londoners had to endure a sustained IRA bombing campaign that began in 1973, reached a peak over the next couple of years and then continued sporadically through the next two decades.

Behind the scenes, though, the capital was being fundamentally remodelled. Manufacturing may have been waning fast, but another sector was on the ascendant: the office. There was, of course, a long tradition to be upheld here: London had been the country's administrative centre since medieval times, and its financial heart since at least the Tudor and Stuart era. Nevertheless, the transformation that took place from the 1950s onwards was extraordinary both in its scale and in the seismic effect it had on the look of the capital, on the nature of the employment it had to offer and therefore on the nature of Londoners themselves. During the Second World War the City of London had lost a third of its floor space to bombing. Within scarcely more than a decade, however, all that had been recovered, and by 1962 there was actually 6.1 million square feet more of it than there had been in 1939. Nor was the City the only part of London to undergo rapid change; increasingly, from the 1950s onwards, new offices sprang up all over central London. The property speculator Joe Levy built block after block along the Euston Road. Between 1963 and 1967 another developer, Henry Hyams, constructed Centrepoint on New Oxford Street (it remained empty for many years, Hyams holding out for a single tenant to occupy the entire 32-floor edifice). The heavily squat Bowater House appeared in 1958, punctuated by a hole through its middle to allow access to Hyde Park (it was demolished in 2007). The 118-metre Millbank Tower sprang up in 1963 in the shadow of the Palace of Westminster. The 1960s Elizabeth House, designed by the infamous John Poulson who was later to be jailed for corruption, came to straddle Waterloo station.

These office blocks served many different purposes. Some housed Britain's growing government departments and civil service, estimated to employ around 78,300 civil servants in 2011.[5] Some attracted the advertising, media and entertainment industries (hence, for example, the South Bank Television Studios, with its distinctive black and white twenty-one-storey tower). Far more, though, became home to London's burgeoning commercial and financial sector. Here the starting pistol had been fired in 1958 when London became the first European capital to relax exchange controls. By 1973, when Britain joined the Common Market, London was the financial capital of Europe and after further deregulation in the 1980s vied with New York to be the financial capital of the world. In the twenty years after the 'Big Bang' of 27 October 1986 when the City moved to electronic trading and scrapped the old division between stockbrokers and stockjobbers, jobs in the financial services increased by a third (around 280,000 people worked in London's financial sector in 2009), and yet more employment was created in those sectors whose work supported the City, from accountancy to insurance to the legal profession. Today in the City of London there are 1,760 solicitors to every 1,000 residents.[6]

The office boom wasn't a purely central London phenomenon. Since the capital's workforce was so mobile and office rents in the suburbs invariably cheaper than in the centre, it often made sense to locate somewhere a little leafier. Gunnersbury station was completely rebuilt in 1966 to accommodate an eighteen-storey office block for IBM (now renamed Chiswick Tower). Putney acquired high-rise offices between East Putney station and Putney Hill around St Mary's church. In the Paddington area the Church Commissioners decided to reorganise their estate in 1954, and the result was a rash of new offices, including Eastbourne Terrace (1957–9). That most American of companies, McDonald's, placed its headquarters not in central London, but in East Finchley. The Great West Road perhaps most neatly shows the shift in London's priorities. Home to so much industry in the 1930s, and to so much industrial dereliction by the 1970s, from the 1980s onwards it witnessed the creation of business parks and offices. Today the borough of Hounslow can boast over 200 companies on or near its stretch of the road, including the world headquarters of GlaxoSmithKline in Brentford. Local government, too, required local office space from which to administer its services and employees (8,500 of them in Camden alone in 2010–11, for example).

Much recent commercial development has been relatively low-rise: Chiswick Business Park (2000), for example, the Ark at Hammersmith (1992), or Stockley Park between Hayes and West Drayton. However, the notion of the office block created in the 1950s retained its appeal, long after the housing block had gone out of fashion. Tolworth Tower (1964) in the borough of Kingston upon Thames, which provides offices for local government departments and private sector companies, continues to dominate the south London landscape for miles around. The Post Office Tower, completed two years later, was London's tallest building until it was eclipsed by the Nat West Tower ten years later, and the Nat West Tower was itself overtaken in due course by One Canada Square in Canary Wharf (1991) and by the Shard in 2012. Many of these buildings have worn well; some are outstanding. A few – Centrepoint, for example – are arguably the right buildings in the wrong place; indeed quite a few of the more ambitious schemes in central London look awkwardly squeezed into the space available and ill-at-ease with their low-rise neighbours. Inevitably, some developments might be viewed as the wrong buildings in the wrong places. It's hard to imagine, for example, that the 1960s grey, seventeen-storey Archway House in North London that looms forbiddingly over the tube station can ever have had that many fans.

High-rise office blocks are most closely associated with central London, but for every Centrepoint (above) there is also an Archway House (below).

Although landmark office buildings continue to be built, however, for the most part the general pattern of development since the 1980s has been quieter and more piecemeal. When the 1951 Festival of Britain was envisaged, it was agreed that a whole swathe of the South Bank should be cleared; but when the Tate decided to open a new modern gallery in the late 1990s, it opted to renovate and redevelop Bankside Power Station, which had closed in 1981 (the refurbished site opened in 2000). The power stations at Kingston upon Thames, Barking (Creekmouth site) and Acton Lane were decommissioned in 1980, 1981 and 1983 respectively, and were later demolished; but when Croydon B Power Station was demolished in 1991 its chimneys were retained to serve as a local landmark. London's Docklands area, redeveloped after 1981 by the London Docklands Development Corporation (LDDC), is a mix of the confidently, sometimes aggressively, new and the restored past: old warehouses, far from being demolished, were increasingly refurbished and pushed into service as flats and shops. It is all a far cry from the heady days of the Barbican.

In the residential suburbs, it's still possible to trace the points at which the bulldozers ground to a halt and the refurbishers stepped in or where

Back from the brink: these Georgian houses in the Tachbrook Triangle in Pimlico were earmarked for demolition and were boarded up for a number of years. They have now been fully restored.

the self-confident developers of the 1960s and 1970s yielded their place to the gentler ones of the 1980s and 1990s. In Pimlico, for example, the Tachbrook Triangle, a tiny enclave of Georgian shops and houses amid post-war redevelopment, was threatened with demolition by the local council who wanted to see it replaced by commercial redevelopment; but while the shops were indeed demolished in 2001, the Georgian Group and Save Britain's Heritage lobbied successfully to get the derelict 1820s terrace Grade II listed, and they are now homes once again.

In Gospel Oak in the borough of Camden changes of mind and attitude are even more evident. In the 1950s much of the local Victorian housing was earmarked for demolition, and several ambitious new housing schemes emerged as a result – among them the ten-storey Barrington Court (1954) and the extensive 1960s and 1970s redevelopment around Mansfield Road and Lismore Circus. Carlton Chapel House, by contrast, built that little bit later in 1984, while sleekly white and modern, is also a modest three-storey block of flats with an old-fashioned gable that sits easily alongside the Victorian survivals in the next street, and in the same decade quite a few local Victorian houses were reprieved and revived. Within a few streets, today's Gospel Oak therefore presents a succinct architectural history of London over the past 150 years. There are the 1850s and 1860s St Pancras Almshouses, originally built as 'an asylum for decayed and deserving ratepayers of the parish' and now home to Camden residents over the age of fifty-five. There are Victorian terraces, the Gothic extravagance of St Martin's church and then those strange isolated survivals that are so often to be found in London suburbs – in Gospel Oak's case two gate piers that were left when the Alexandra House orphanage of 1847 was demolished. From the 1930s come blocks of flats around Maitland Park, and then there are the estates, flats and town houses built from every decade from the 1950s to the present – the earlier ones often assertively confident, the later ones more self-deprecating.

There was much to be said for the gentler approaches to urban planning that were gradually adopted through central and suburban London. Historic areas that might otherwise well have succumbed to the bulldozer were saved for new generations of Londoners to enjoy. One only has to look at photographs of Chelsea in the 1950s, Barnsbury in the 1960s, Spitalfields in the 1970s, Bermondsey in the 1980s or Hoxton in the early 1990s to appreciate just how much was saved and then enhanced. Local

Two views of Gospel Oak: postwar redevelopment (above) and preservation (below). The two photographs were taken within a few yards of one another.

councils' establishment of conservation areas similarly helped. In Haringey, for example, not only were Bruce Castle and Highgate unsurprisingly deemed worthy of preservation, but so too were the attractive but perhaps less remarkable Edwardian Rookfield Estate and parts of Victorian Crouch End. Most boroughs came in time to establish carefully controlled conservation areas: fifty-four in Westminster, seventy-two in Richmond upon Thames and sixteen in Barnet. In the process much of what was left of London's historical suburbs was safeguarded. Inner suburbs that had witnessed decades of population decline started to recover, creating new communities in the process.

However, there was a price to be paid, and it was not one that was asked of the people who benefited from the new spirit of preservation. As houses were done up and sold on, so they moved beyond the reach of the less prosperous. Those who might have lived in the area for years increasingly found themselves pushed out of the way by the relentless force of well-to-do buyers; and as they were marginalised, so their voices became increasingly stifled. By the late 1990s, and with London property prices at an all-time high, the capital had become a place where many could work but only the more fortunate could afford to live. Gentrification was not an unmixed blessing.

The battle over Spitalfields exemplifies the problem very starkly. By the early 1970s one of London's great social melting pots had become badly run-down, its once-elegant eighteenth-century houses neglected and in many cases derelict. A group of activists, shocked by proposals to bulldoze the area, formed the Spitalfields Trust and successfully prised many of the houses away from their owners. As Spitalfields was rescued, however, so it began to draw wealthier buyers, attracted to the area by its proximity to the City and by its new 'chic' image. It was not long before those who had saved the area found themselves in that strange – and now not uncommon – position of owning houses that they couldn't possibly afford to buy. Towards the end of the century the Spitalfields Market extension built in 1926 was redeveloped – not particularly sympathetically to some eyes – to accommodate restaurants, shops and an arts and crafts market that enhanced the area's appeal without having much to offer to those who might have wanted to live there but now found it intimidatingly expensive. Significantly, recent plans to redevelop the Fruit and Wool Exchange contained provision for an office and shopping complex, but no houses. The redevelopment of the Docklands tells a similar story.

———————◄ ◆ ► ◆ ►———————

As the twentieth century drew to a close, less prosperous Londoners felt increasingly squeezed out. The areas in which they may have grown up or in which people like them may once have lived were out of reach. What's more, they were provided with ever fewer choices as to where to live. Back in the 1950s, Harold Macmillan had given local authorities the option to sell off their council houses and some transactions had duly followed. Then, in December 1979, Margaret Thatcher made tenants' right to buy a central plank of Conservative policy, her argument being that ownership bred a sense of responsibility, the incentive that she offered being that tenants could now buy their houses at a substantial discount. The scheme was wildly popular. Between 1980 and 1996 over 2.2 million homes across the country were bought by their former tenants, many of them in Greater London. In Barking and Dagenham alone, transactions were occurring at the rate of 2,000 a year by 1982. Whereas 42 per cent of the population relied on their local councils to provide them with accommodation in 1979, by 2008 that figure had plummeted to 12 per cent, with a further 6 per cent renting from housing associations and cooperatives.

For those who bought their council houses, the benefits were obvious. For those who could not, the problems they faced seemed intractable; and they grew more so over time. A sting in the tail of the Conservative legislation was that local authorities were not allowed to use the proceeds from council-house sales to build or acquire new homes. Instead they were obliged to use the windfall from the sale of council houses to pay off any existing budgetary debts. As a result the supply of social housing quickly fell behind demand, creating massive waiting lists that by 2008 had reached the staggering national figure of 4 million. At the same time as the more economically active ex-council-house dwellers moved on, so some estates declined ever further.

Various attempts were made to address the problem of 'sink estates' (an expression that dates from the 1970s), either prompted or part-funded by Westminster; and some progress was and is still being made. The

Cathall Road Estate in Walthamstow, for example, with its two twenty-one-storey tower blocks built between 1966 and 1972 became London's first Housing Action Trust in 1991; in the following years the old blocks were demolished and most of the estate rebuilt as low-rise terraced housing. Chalkhill Estate in Brent (originally built 1966–70) was similarly replanned and renewed, and the problematic Ocean Estate in Stepney was earmarked for redevelopment. London's successful 2005 Olympic bid included a pledge to regenerate areas of the East End, notably Stratford and Newham, a project that will involve the creation of parkland, shops and thousands of new homes after 2012.

Nevertheless, poverty and unemployment continue to stalk London's suburbs. A report compiled in late 2011, *London's Poverty Profile*, suggested that 220,000 households in the capital lived in overcrowded accommodation, that 400,000 Londoners were unemployed and that 50 per cent of young adults were paid less than the London Living Wage. At the other end of the scale the affluence of the better off in the capital seems ever more apparent. Ten per cent of London's population controls 65 per cent of its financial wealth. Conspicuous consumption can be indulged in expensive West End shops or in such super-shopping malls as Bluewater, and the two Westfield centres at White City and Stratford. Restaurants are ubiquitous. Relative levels of wealth are reflected in relative health levels. According to *London's Poverty Profile*, 'Babies born in Southwark, Croydon, Haringey and Harrow are twice as likely to die before their 1st birthday as those born in Bromley, Kingston and Richmond. Adults in Hackney are twice as likely to die before the age of 65 as those in Kensington & Chelsea.' For some, such very visible contrasts are among the reasons for the rioting that took place in several areas of London in August 2011.

Other statistics, however, point to an underlying vigour. The 2011 census revealed that after several decades of decline, London's population was recovering. On the eve of the Second World War, 8.6 million people lived in the capital, the majority in the outer boroughs. Each decade after 1951 that figure fell, reaching 6.4 million in 1991 as people left the inner suburbs and some of those who had once lived in the outer suburbs were attracted further away to the ring of satellite towns outside the confines of the M25. By 2001, however, London's population had risen to 7.1 million, and in 2011 to 8 million. Every borough except Hammersmith and Fulham witnessed an influx of new residents, the population of Tower Hamlets rising by 26.6 per cent in a decade, that of Newham increasing by 23.5 per cent, and Islington becoming the country's most densely populated area, at 13,873 people per square kilometre. London was increasingly justifying its reputation as a city of commuters: on an average day in 2007, 23.8 million trips were being made in, to or from London. The suburbs were justifying their existence afresh.

SEVENTEEN

WHO IS IN CHARGE?

The Rise, Fall and Rise Again of London Government

For much of the twentieth century there was a general acceptance that London needed strong leadership; and it was also widely agreed that any central authority should have a broad range of responsibilities, from the management of sewerage and drainage, to the building of bridges and tunnels, to the maintaining of parks and open spaces. In the case of the London County Council there was even a consensus that here was a body that was performing the task of governing the capital better than anything that had gone before (not in itself a difficult achievement, perhaps, given the dismal record of the Metropolitan Board of Works). It's scarcely surprising therefore that over time the LCC was granted additional responsibilities. The Education (London) Act of 1903, for example, transferred responsibility for schools from the School Board to the LCC. London's water was municipalised in the same year. The LCC became ever more involved in town planning and the establishment of new housing estates. It looked to be on an ever-upwards trajectory, taking control of more and more areas of Londoners' lives.

There is a complicating factor to be taken into account, however. London in the twentieth century had not one but three sets of rule makers: the LCC (later the GLC and then the GLA); the local borough councils; and central government. Given that politicians were involved, the relationship between the three was never likely to be a wholly comfortable one; and given that determining the future direction of the nation's capital was at stake, it frequently wasn't. Westminster in particular was a constant critic of London's local government and worried endlessly about what it was up to. In fact, as previously mentioned, within years of the foundation of the LCC in 1889, central government was already tinkering with it. Alarmed by the way in which the Progressives had dominated the LCC from its inception, Lord Salisbury's government sought to counterbalance their influence by creating twenty-eight new metropolitan borough councils in 1899, strengthening the powers that local district councils had retained in 1889, and also establishing a mayor and aldermen for each borough council. These new, more powerful borough councils were given an important say in the implementation of central government policy, while the City simultaneously was left well alone, emphasising its independence from the LCC.

The Progressive Party's domination of the LCC came to an end in 1907. Many Londoners had been antagonised by the cost of LCC's ambitious plans for housing, by the expense of municipalising the capital's water, and by the increase in the rates charged to householders to pay for them. At the March elections, the Progressives were swept away by a Conservative landslide that was to last until 1934. Cost-cutting now became the order of the day (though an attempt to do away with free school meals lasted only a year); nevertheless, the LCC under the Conservatives continued to support ambitious social programmes, not least the Becontree and Dagenham housing schemes of the 1920s and 1930s.

Ironically, however, Salisbury's decision to handicap the Progressives by creating the metropolitan borough councils came back to haunt a later generation of Conservatives. By 1918 the old-fashioned radicalism that the Progressives espoused was giving way to the politics of the trade unions and the working class. In the process, the Liberal/Progressive political movement withered, to be replaced by the Labour Party. And this gave rise to a turn of events that Salisbury could never have predicted. Back in 1899 the metropolitan boroughs had been created to curb the 'extremism' of the LCC. In 1921, by contrast, the precise opposite occurred: an 'extreme' metropolitan borough challenged the conservatism of the LCC in what became known as the Battle of Poplar.

Although Labour were very much still the coming power in national politics in 1919 (the first Labour administration was to serve briefly in 1924), at a local level in London they had arrived somewhat earlier. By 1914 Labour controlled West Ham, Woolwich and Poplar and had a foothold in a number of other boroughs. In 1919, buoyed in part by the growth in trade union membership in London during the war years, Labour trebled its pre-war vote to win fifteen seats on the LCC. A few months later in the municipal by-elections, the party gained outright

GOVERNING LONDON

HERTFORDSHIRE

ENF

BARNET

HARROW

HARINGEY

BRENT

CAMDEN

ISLINGTON

HILLINGDON

EALING

CITY OF
WESTMINSTER

CIT

HAMMERSMITH
& FULHAM

KENSINGTON
& CHELSEA

SOU

Thames

HOUNSLOW

LAMBETH

WANDSWORTH

RICHMOND
UPON THAMES

Thames

MERTON

KINGSTON
UPON THAMES

SUTTON

SURREY

| 0 | | 2 | | 4 | | 6 km |
| 0 | 1 | 2 | 3 | | 4 mi | |

KEY

GLA boundaries
and boroughs

Motorways

Main roads

ELD

E S S E X

WALTHAM
FOREST

REDBRIDGE

HAVERING

HACKNEY

BARKING &
DAGENHAM

NEWHAM

TOWER
HAMLETS

Thames

Y

THWARK

GREENWICH

BEXLEY

LEWISHAM

KENT

BROMLEY

CROYDON

control of twelve out of twenty-eight borough councils. It was a seismic shift in the political landscape.

In Poplar, Labour was led by the former MP George Lansbury – the son of a railway timekeeper – and before long he and his colleagues were at loggerheads with the LCC over the ever-vexed issue of local rates. Poplar in the early 1920s was not an attractive place to live. It was riddled with slums and populated by a largely unskilled working force. Furthermore, its economic reliance on the docks meant that its fortunes were always uneasily dependent on the state of world trade. When there was a slump – as there was in 1920–1 – Poplar was bound to be badly hit. Things became so grim, in fact, that the Poplar Board of Guardians felt obliged to raise the poor rate to help out those who were suffering most. At the same time, however, they were under pressure from the LCC to raise more from the local rates to support LCC projects. This would have involved a double-hit on the poor of Poplar; and Lansbury and his colleagues refused to be party to it. In March 1921, Poplar Council resolved

Councillor Baker of Poplar holding his two daughters, with George Lansbury just visible behind, during the Battle of Poplar, August 1921.

not to collect the levies due to the LCC so that they could keep the overall level of the rates down. The LCC were furious, and in July thirty-six councillors from Poplar were taken to court. Popular demonstrations ensued, but in September five women councillors (including the six-month-pregnant Nellie Cressall) were carted off to Holloway Prison while twenty-five men, including the 62-year-old George Lansbury, ended up in Brixton Prison.

The Battle of Poplar was both a victory and a defeat for Labour. Faced with a full-blown rebellion, the London County Council backed down, the prisoners were released and the government was forced to introduce the Local Authorities (Financial Provision) Act to create a more equitable common fund to administer poor relief. At the same time, though, Labour emerged from the battle as a divided party, and in the 1922 metropolitan borough council elections they were torn to shreds. Labour retained Deptford, Poplar and Woolwich, and were the largest party in Bethnal Green, but they lost control of Islington, Camberwell, St Pancras, Stepney, Fulham, Hackney, Southwark and Greenwich and – in outer London – Erith, Edmonton and Enfield. At a national level Labour went on to take power after the 1924 election, but they had acquired an (undeserved) reputation for extremism that the Battle of Poplar seemed to confirm, and at the first whiff of scandal (a false allegation that they were in bed with the Communists of the Soviet Union) they fell from power.

Meanwhile, the splintered nature of London politics that the Battle of Poplar revealed was confirmed in the deliberations of yet another royal commission set up to look at the best way to govern the capital. In fact, there had been moves afoot since 1919 to review the administration of transport and utilities (particularly electricity), but events in Poplar gave the process a new urgency and a sense that any investigating committee needed to be given a wider remit. Viscount Ullswater was therefore invited to chair a commission that would:

> Inquire and report what, if any, alterations are needed in the local
> government of the administrative county of London and the
> surrounding districts, with a view to securing greater efficiency and
> economy in the administration of local government services and to
> reducing any inequalities which may exist in the distribution of local
> burdens as between different parts of the whole area.[1]

Evidence was invited from a wide range of witnesses, and an inevitably wide range of opinions was the result. The LCC's view was a simple one: Westminster needed to give them more power over the 'whole continuous urban area . . . together with such a surrounding belt that was likely to become of an urban character within a short time'.[2] They were supported by the Labour Party and by the Ministry of Health, whose representative pointed out that the current system was a mess, not least because there were ninety-two separate but overlapping authorities within the County of London, each making demands on the ratepayers.

Neighbouring county councils, however, were not so sure. Representatives of the County of Middlesex were at pains to point out that they governed their area rather better than the LCC governed its own. Those from Surrey County Council took up a classic negotiating stance: yes, the boundaries of London should indeed be increased – only not in their direction. Most borough councils felt that their powers should be increased. West Ham Borough Council, by contrast, made a nuanced case for autonomous county boroughs around the County of London that would act as an independent buffer and pointed out that the interests of the poor were generally best served by smaller authorities. The City of London, of course, opposed everything on principle.

The outcome of all the witness testimony and wrangling was not one but three reports in 1923. There was an official 'majority' report signed by four commissioners which recommended changing very little, while at the same time recognising that there were problems with the current system – especially in the unequal imposition of rates. Then there were two 'minority' reports, each supported by two commissioners and both arguing that the recommendations of the majority report did not go far enough. Messrs E. H. Hilley and G. J. Talbot proposed dividing the metropolis into a number of substantial units, equal in status to county boroughs (like those created across the country in 1889) and overseen by a principal authority that would handle the administration of a few major city-wide services such as water supply and tramways. Sir Robert Donald and Mr Stephen Walsh argued for a directly elected central authority with jurisdiction over an enlarged County of London and with wide-ranging powers but with shared responsibility with district councils for many services. It was the sort of mess that only a royal commission could be and, in the end, its single tangible achievement was to lay the way open for the introduction of a London Transport

Bill, which would create a London and Home Counties Traffic Advisory Committee – not much of a return on the time invested.

Labour's divisions over Poplar were not healed by the passing of time. With its heady mix of traditional middle-class radicals and socialists, working-class activists and trade unionists and a leavening of Communists it was never going to be the quietest of parties to belong to. The 1926 General Strike, prompted by a national call to support the mineworkers faced with wage cuts, certainly revealed deep divisions. Many trade unionists and London Labour Party members supported the strikers, bringing London to a standstill for the first few days of the strike and engaging in running battles with the police in New Cross, Deptford and the ever-radical Poplar. There were those, however, who worried about the more extreme edges of the party and, in particular, its Communist agitators. By 1929 the national Labour Party had expelled fifteen London parties.

A food convoy proceeds along India Dock Road during the General Strike of 1926.

Even so, Labour's fortunes were on the rise in London, particularly as economic clouds over Britain began to grow in the early 1930s. On 27 October 1932 a crowd of some 100,000 protestors converged on Hyde Park from all parts of London, sparking confrontations with the police:

> Inside the park one could hear the roar of the crowd as they fought tenaciously around the Marble Arch and along Oxford Street. At one juncture a plain-clothes detective stepped forward to speak to a chief inspector; as he did so a zealous special constable struck him down with a terrific blow on the head with a staff.[3]

Two years later, Labour took majority control of the LCC for the first time, dominating the east and the north of the capital, while the Conservatives held on, for the most part, to the west and south. It set a pattern for the next three decades; until the mid 1960s there was to be no Conservative administration in London.

In those final twilight years before the Second World War, Labour proved itself to be very active. It built schools and embarked on new housing projects. It became more involved in the running of hospitals (following legislation in 1930) and helped the unemployed, scrapping the grim 'general mixed workhouse' and paying out poor relief. It established the Green Belt and replaced Waterloo Bridge.

Labour's record during the Second World War was mixed, though. London had never been put under such intense pressure before, and inevitably certain services buckled under the strain. Hospitals, the fire brigade and rescue services operated astonishingly well in the circumstances; on the other hand, despite pre-war anticipation of aerial assault, local government in London had made little provision for those likely to be made homeless by bombing raids, and local services in the event were overwhelmed by the sheer scale of the problem they faced. Some 1.4 million Londoners were bombed out of their homes between September 1940 and May 1941.

———— ◂ ◦ ▸ ————

The post-war period was the period of 'The Grand Plan' – the Greater London Plan put forward by Patrick Abercrombie in 1944 and, when that proved too rich for people's stomachs, a succession of other plans. In the wake of the 1947 Town and Country Planning Act, which required each authority to create its own regeneration scheme, came the 1951 London Development Plan, prepared by the LCC. Nine areas, all within inner London and victims of the worst of the bombing raids, were identified as Areas of Comprehensive Development, and plans were outlined to reduce London's overall population density and to substitute cross routes based on existing roads for Abercrombie's ambitious ring roads.

This new development plan had to be mothballed for two years due to lack of funds, but four years later in 1957 a royal commission, led by Sir Edwin Herbert, was set up to:

> Examine the present system and working of Local Government in the Greater London area; to recommend whether any, and if so what, changes in local government structure and the distribution of local government functions in the area, or any part of it, would better secure effective and convenient local government.[4]

Not only were London and Middlesex included within the remit of the commission, but also parts of Essex, Hertfordshire, Kent and Surrey, as were the county boroughs of Croydon, East Ham and West Ham. Over the next three years the commission held over a hundred meetings, and asked 16,000 questions of politicians, civil servants, experts and various groups with vested interests, finally publishing a report in 1960 that contained some suggestions for change that were both radical and simple.

The commission's fundamental conclusion was that the existing County of London was 'inhuman' and 'monolithic'. Instead, it argued, responsibility for many local and day-to-day services should be given to the boroughs, while a new 'Council for Greater London' should be created that would focus on such London-wide services as overall planning, fire, education and traffic. Only one thing alone should not be allowed to change: the City Corporation should be left as it was.

It wouldn't have been London politics if there hadn't been both objections to the commission's findings and vigorous subsequent horse-trading. The commission had wanted fifty-two boroughs covering the old counties of London and Middlesex and parts of Kent, Surrey, Hertfordshire and Essex. By 1961 this had been whittled down to thirty-four boroughs, and by August 1962 to thirty-two. Some areas outside the old LCC area desperately wanted to be included in Greater London; while others just as desperately wanted to be left out (including Carshalton, Coulsdon and Purley, Feltham, Yiewsley and West Drayton, Barnet and Romford). A few had no say at all in what happened to them. The Minister of Housing and Local Government, for example, decreed that Banstead, Caterham and Warlingham, and Walton and Weybridge were to stay out, a concession made to Surrey County Council, which was already facing the loss of a whole string of places formerly in its control, including Kingston, Richmond, Barnes, Mitcham and Morden. Cheshunt, Chigwell, Esher, Potter's Bar, Staines and Sunbury on Thames were similarly denied the right to decide their own fate (since Middlesex would no longer exist under the new plans, the latter three were assigned to different counties). Epsom and Ewell for their part danced the political hokey-cokey: the northern part of the borough wanted to stay in; Epsom was determined to stay out. In the end, to avoid utter confusion, both were omitted.

With the unveiling of the final proposal for thirty-two boroughs in 1962 came a redrawing of the London map. Wanstead and Woodford, which might have become part of Waltham Forest, instead joined Ilford, as well as parts of Dagenham and Chigwell, to form the borough of Redbridge. Clapham and Streatham were taken out of Wandsworth and assigned to Lambeth. Part of Wandsworth was moved over to Battersea. Chislehurst and Sidcup were split from one another along the lines of the A20, and were assigned to the new boroughs of Bromley and Bexley. The reshuffling seemed endless.

Even the names of the boroughs were hotly debated. When the parliamentary bill was originally drawn up, this contentious issue was neatly sidestepped by assigning a number to each proposed new regional grouping, along with a list of the areas or councils that were to be merged together to create it. However, then the nettle had to be grasped. Harrow, Westminster, Tower Hamlets, Camden, Croydon, Kingston upon Thames and Ealing were all settled without fuss. After that it was something of a free-for-all, as local pride challenged municipal neatness, and a series of gladiatorial contests were staged. In the end, Twickenham lost to Richmond, Fulham lost to Hammersmith (the compromise suggestions of Riverside and Olympia having been rejected). Wembley and Willesden fought each other to a standstill, and compromised on the name of the local river, Brent. Various authorities in north London considered Northgate or Northern Heights before settling for Barnet. Just occasionally, a rematch was allowed. Uxbridge, for example, started out as Uxbridge in the 1963 plan but became Hillingdon a year later; the Royal Borough of Charlton became Greenwich; and Morden ultimately ended up as Merton. The early ban on double-barrelled names was relaxed to allow for the preservation of Kensington and Chelsea, and with that principle established, one or two areas that had lost the battle earlier went on to reclaim their historic identity. The Local Government Act of 1972 reinstated Fulham alongside Hammersmith, while Barking became Barking and Dagenham.

The proposed reorganisation created two distinct rings – the inner London boroughs of Camden, Greenwich, Hackney, Hammersmith, Islington, Kensington and Chelsea, Lambeth, Lewisham, Southwark, Tower Hamlets, Wandsworth and Westminster, which roughly corresponded to the old County of London – and twenty outer boroughs. Once approved in 1963, the London Government Act laid the way open for elections to the new Greater London Council on 9 April 1964, at which point the London County Council passed into history.

The new authority was both more and less than the body it replaced. It covered a far greater area of the south-east region, but its remit was in many ways more restricted. Some services – notably health – had been removed from local control altogether some years before when the National Health Service was established in 1948; while electricity was nationalised in 1947. Responsibility for education was transferred to the London Education Authority (for the inner boroughs) in 1965 and to local education authorities for the outer boroughs. The GLC was solely in charge of the fire service, emergency planning, flood prevention and waste disposal, but shared the running of most other services with the boroughs.

The formation of the GLC may have an air of inevitability to it: after a century or so of wrangling it formalised an acceptance that London had become Greater London. Yet behind-the-scenes machinations show London politics at its most involved and fractious. Back in the 1930s it had been Labour who had pushed for reform of the way in which London was governed. By the late 1940s, though, as its hold over the LCC began to weaken, it became less enthusiastic. Indeed, one of the most outspoken critics of plans for the GLC was the previous head of the LCC, Herbert Morrison. The Conservatives, meanwhile, had become more enthusiastic about reform, hoping that by adding outer boroughs to the new London mix, the traditional Labour areas of inner London would be diluted.

In the event, the Conservatives were to be disappointed – at least in the short term. The new body that sat for the first time on the rather unfortunate date of 1 April 1965 comprised sixty-four Labour councillors and thirty-six Conservatives. It was this body under the leadership of Bill Fiske that was given the task of drawing up a Greater London Development Plan. The new GLC might have had to cede control of many services to the boroughs and other authorities, but it was nevertheless expected to come up with a master plan for everything from population and employment, to housing, transport, utilities and open spaces.

In the ensuing years the GLC, like the old Metropolitan Board of Works, was certainly able to instigate some grand projects of its own. Most notable perhaps was the Thames Barrier, which stretches between New Charlton and Silvertown. Built to safeguard against the sort of flooding that in 1928 had caused the deaths of fourteen people and disrupted business, it cost £534 million and took eight years between 1974 and 1982 to complete. At the time, some regarded it as a GLC vanity project, but rising sea levels have changed people's minds. The barrier was used thirty-five times in the 1990s; in the first decade of the twenty-first century it was raised seventy-five times.

It has to be said, though, that overall there were probably as many failures as there were successes. The GLC's ambitious motorway road scheme for central London was finally killed off by central government in 1973, following fierce criticism from the thousands of Londoners who would have been affected. The GLC also dithered over the challenge of redeveloping the now-defunct London docks, proving adept at drawing up reports and feasibility studies but weak at implementing them. The 1976 London Docklands Strategic Plan – which called for the building of council houses in the area and the establishment of manufacturing jobs – was stillborn, not least because it had no suggestions of how the vast sums of money that would have been required to transform vision into reality would be raised. Given that Britain was in dire economic straits at the time, and had just had to negotiate a loan from the International Monetary Fund, this failure to address adequately the issue of funding was a rather serious one. For many, the shortcomings of the GLC were symbolised by the Covent Garden debacle. The GLC wanted to flatten

The GLC's plans to redevelop Covent Garden became mired in controversy and were ultimately shelved. This photograph shows the market as it was c.1961.

what had once been London's best-known fruit and vegetable market and replace it with a national conference hall, hotels, new houses and shops and the inevitable new roads. Locals were opposed; preservationists were horrified. Many thought that the debate represented high-handed officials at their worst. The redevelopment did not go ahead.

What ultimately killed the GLC, however, was not disillusionment with the failings of its grand schemes, but considerations of a more overtly political nature. Throughout its comparatively short lifetime it was always dominated by whichever political party happened at that particular moment to be in opposition at Westminster. To that extent it served as a barometer of public opinion either mid-term or just prior to a general election, reflecting the disappointment most people felt when promises made in opposition failed to materialise in government. In 1967, with an unpopular Labour administration in power that only a year before had imposed a pay and wages freeze, the Conservatives enjoyed a landslide victory, winning eighty-two seats to Labour's eighteen. In 1970, at the tail end of Harold Wilson's Labour government, the Conservatives managed to retain control of the GLC under Desmond Plummer. The Conservatives won the 1970 general election, so not too surprisingly in 1973 a Labour administration under Reg Goodwin was returned to County Hall, helped in part by opposition to the previous council's transport plans for London. In 1974 Labour were back in power nationally, but the economic woes they endured, and spiralling expenditure in London, guaranteed that the Tories under Horace Cutler dominated the 1977 GLC elections, winning sixty-four seats to Labour's twenty-eight (the number of councillors had been reduced from a hundred to ninety-two in 1973). When the Conservatives won in 1979 and Margaret Thatcher moved into Downing Street, Labour council-lors must have started measuring for curtains in County Hall. If so, it is to be hoped that they rented rather than bought them.

GLC leader Ken Livingstone, with colleagues Val Wise, Charlie Rossi, John McDonnell and Michael Ward outside County Hall for the unveiling of a 75-foot-long sign announcing London's unemployment figures in January 1982. Their actions did not exactly endear them to Mrs Thatcher's Conservative government.

Labour did indeed secure a narrow majority in the 1981 elections for the GLC, gaining fifty seats. The day after the results were announced on 7 May, however, there was a palace coup. Labour's GLC leader Andrew McIntosh, who had taken the party to victory, was deposed by Labour councillors in favour of a young left-wing radical, Ken Livingstone, who had lost out to McIntosh in a leadership contest the year before. Livingstone was a larger-than-life populist and it was under his leadership that the GLC embarked on a collision course with the Conservative government and more particularly the inflexible Prime Minister, Margaret Thatcher. Facing each other across the Thames, one in County Hall, the other in Westminster, they infuriated and antagonised each other. Livingstone even went so far as to post giant billboards on County Hall criticising the Conservatives by pointedly proclaiming the country's growing unemployment figures. So far as Londoners at large were concerned, some of his enterprises – to combat racism, to tackle London's eternal traffic problems, to encourage the arts – won general plaudits; others, such as his constant goading of the government and his support for radical political causes that had nothing to do with London, may have ensured headlines but won him opprobrium in certain quarters.

Abolition of the GLC had been mooted before, and an 'Abolish the GLC' party had even fielded candidates at the 1981 elections, though it hadn't enjoyed much success. Faced with Livingstone, however, Margaret Thatcher decided that abolition was the only way forward, and it was duly included in the Conservative manifesto for the 1983 general election. There was to be no way out for the GLC. Although opinion polls showed increasing support for it (helped by the popularity of the subsidised fares it offered on London Transport), and although there were many Conservatives who argued for its retention, the GLC elections scheduled for 1985 were cancelled. On 31 March 1986 it went out in a blaze of farewell fireworks.

With the demise of the GLC, London was left without a central governing body for the first time in virtually a century. Key services were gradually hived off or privatised. The Thames Water Authority became Thames Water Utilities Ltd in 1989, its regulatory and river management responsibilities passing to the National Rivers Authority. The Inner London Education Authority disappeared in 1990, its role and remit passing to the boroughs. The London Underground became the responsibility of London Regional Transport, which in turn was the responsibility of the Ministry of Transport – a strange instance of effectively renationalising a service at a time when favoured policy was privatisation. The Labour government that came to power in 1997 then introduced a public private partnership (PPP) scheme that involved breaking the London Underground into a publicly owned operator and three private infrastructure companies – a scheme of such fiendish complexity that it cost £500 million just to draw up the contracts.

London's experiment in living without a central authority was, however, short-lived. As early as 1990 the Labour MP for Newham North West, Tony Banks, mooted a plan to resurrect local government, and with devolution in the air at the time of the 1997 election and the ensuing establishment of the National Assembly for Wales in 1998 and the Scottish Executive the following year, the setting up of a new authority for the capital seemed ever more likely.

The Greater London Authority that took office in July 2000 after elections two months previously is effectively a scaled-down version of the Greater London Council, and comprises twenty-five members. The outer boroughs are represented by eight constituencies: Barnet and Camden; Brent and Harrow; Ealing and Hillingdon; South West

City Hall, headquarters of the GLA.

(Hounslow, Kingston and Richmond); Croydon and Sutton; Bexley and Bromley; Havering and Redbridge; and Enfield and Haringey. The inner ring consists of six constituencies: West Central (Hammersmith and Fulham, Kensington and Chelsea, Westminster); Merton and Wandsworth; Lambeth and Southwark; Greenwich and Lewisham; City and East (Barking and Dagenham, City of London, Newham, Tower Hamlets); and North East (Hackney, Islington and Waltham Forest). The balance of eleven delegates is decided by an 'additional member system' that takes account of the overall pattern of party voting across the region. Overseeing the authority is an elected mayor, who is invested with considerable powers. Much to the annoyance of the mainstream Labour Party, Ken Livingstone not only stood for election in 2000 but won. He began his term of office with the words 'As I was saying before I was so rudely interrupted fourteen years ago . . .' He was to win one further election. As to whether the GLA is a power for visionary genius, an administrative white elephant or indeed largely irrelevant in any area except traffic control, it's too early to tell. A decade or so, after all, doesn't count for much in the history of Greater London.

EIGHTEEN

THE PEOPLE OF THE SUBURBS
London's Changing Population

When I consider this great city in its several quarters and divisions, I look upon it as an aggregate of various nations distinguished from each other by their respective customs, manners, and interests. The courts of two countries do not so much differ from one another, as the court and city, in their peculiar ways of life and conversation. In short, the inhabitants of St James's, notwithstanding they live under the same laws, and speak the same language, are a distinct people from those of Cheapside, who are likewise removed from those of the Temple on one side, and those of Smithfield on the other, by several climates and degrees in their ways of thinking and conversing together.[1]

Joseph Addison made these observations in 1712 when London's expansion was both comparatively limited and quite new. Today, his comments have acquired an extra weight, for modern London is an astonishingly diverse city – far more diverse than Addison can ever have imagined. Each area is different from its neighbour, each has its own look and feel, each is constantly evolving.

It's not even possible to make absolutely hard and fast rules about the prosperity of an area. While it's true to say that people in Barnet are generally better off than those in Brent, or that Hammersmith is more affluent than Camden, or that Croydon experiences less poverty than Merton, once each of those areas is examined in detail a far more complex picture emerges. Barnet has one of the richest roads in Britain – the Bishop's Avenue near Kenwood – and over 70 per cent of the borough's population own their own house, but there are also pockets of deprivation, particularly in the west. Even the Bishop's Avenue is not an entirely straightforward proposition. Described in the relevant volume of the

Buildings of England series as 'a by-word for opulence and vulgarity', it has also played host in recent years to dereliction and squatters.[2] The royal borough of Kensington and Chelsea routinely emerges from surveys as among the most expensive places to live in Britain, but there is real poverty there too, particularly in its northern reaches.

Even a single street can contain an astonishingly rich mix of social groups: well-to-do newcomers attracted by those elegant early nineteenth-century terraced houses will rub shoulders with people who remember the road in the days before it was deemed trendy. Housing association flats stand next to multi-million-pound private homes. Even when there is superficial coherence, there are nevertheless subtle social differences. Belgravia has always been home to the wealthy, but among the rich who live there today there will be some who have inherited their money and others who made a fortune in the City, some whose families have lived in London for generations and others – Russian billionaires, perhaps – who have arrived within the last twenty years. All will be as aware of the differences between them as of the things they have in common – an awareness that stretches right back to the earliest days of Belgravia when the super-rich bought the largest houses and the merely very rich squashed in where they could. 'The unfashionable side. I knew there was something,' says Lady Bracknell in *The Importance of Being Earnest* (1895) on learning that her prospective son-in-law has a house at 149 Belgrave Square.

––––––◆◆►––––––

Londoners' different levels of prosperity, however, have not historically been the only reasons for the capital's diversity. Variety has also stemmed from the fact that the capital has always been a melting pot for people from elsewhere – from other parts of England, from Ireland (hence the London Irish RFC), from Scotland (hence the London Scottish Regiment) and from Wales (hence the London Welsh Centre on Gray's Inn Road). Before the Second World War around a third of the capital's citizens at any one time had actually been born outside it, and then as now the population was endlessly shifting, some moving to the area to become Londoners, others moving away and losing their Londoner status in the process. Different areas experienced varying degrees of toing and froing: in that pre-war period, some inner-city areas such as Bethnal Green and

THE PEOPLE OF THE SUBURBS

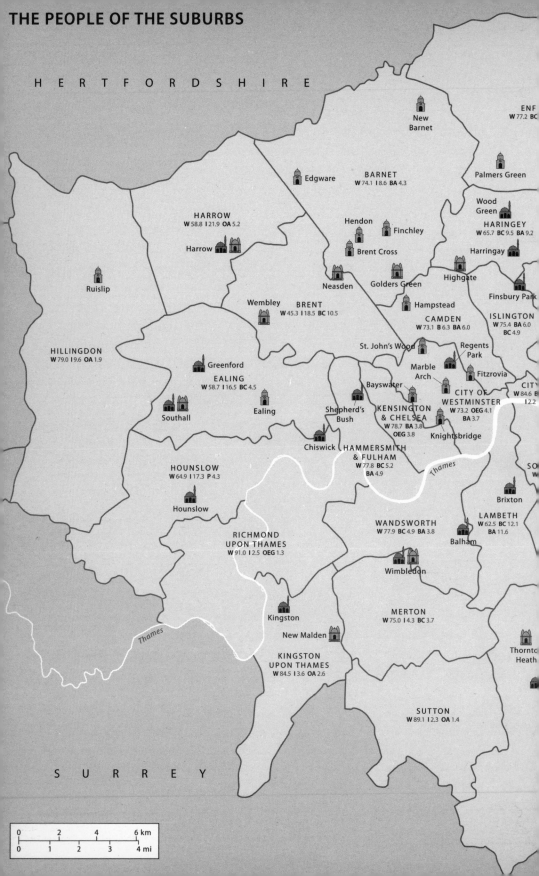

H E R T F O R D S H I R E

ENF
W 77.2 BC

New
Barnet

Edgware

Palmers Green

BARNET
W 74.1 I 8.6 BA 4.3

Wood
Green

HARROW
W 58.8 I 21.9 OA 5.2

Hendon

Finchley

HARINGEY
W 65.7 I 9.5 BA 9.2

Harrow

Brent Cross

Harringay

Ruislip

Neasden

Golders Green

Highgate

Finsbury Park

Wembley

BRENT
W 45.3 I 18.5 BC 10.5

Hampstead

ISLINGTON
W 75.4 BA 6.0
BC 4.9

HILLINGDON
W 79.0 I 9.6 OA 1.9

Greenford

CAMDEN
W 73.1 B 6.3 BA 6.0

Regents
Park

St. John's Wood

EALING
W 58.7 I 16.5 BC 4.5

Marble
Arch

Fitzrovia

Southall

Ealing

Bayswater

CITY
W 84.6 B
I 2.2

Shepherd's
Bush

KENSINGTON
& CHELSEA
W 78.7 BA 3.8
OEG 3.8

CITY OF
WESTMINSTER
W 73.2 OEG 4.1
BA 3.7

Knightsbridge

Chiswick

HAMMERSMITH
& FULHAM
W 77.8 BC 5.2
BA 4.9

Thames

Brixton

HOUNSLOW
W 64.9 I 17.3 P 4.3

LAMBETH
W 62.5 BC 12.1
BA 11.6

Hounslow

WANDSWORTH
W 77.9 BC 4.9 BA 3.8

Balham

RICHMOND
UPON THAMES
W 91.0 I 2.5 OEG 1.3

Wimbledon

SO

Thames

Kingston

MERTON
W 75.0 I 4.3 BC 3.7

New Malden

Thornto
Heath

KINGSTON
UPON THAMES
W 84.5 I 3.6 OA 2.6

SUTTON
W 89.1 I 2.3 OA 1.4

S U R R E Y

| 0 | 2 | 4 | 6 km |
| 0 | 1 | 2 | 3 | 4 mi |

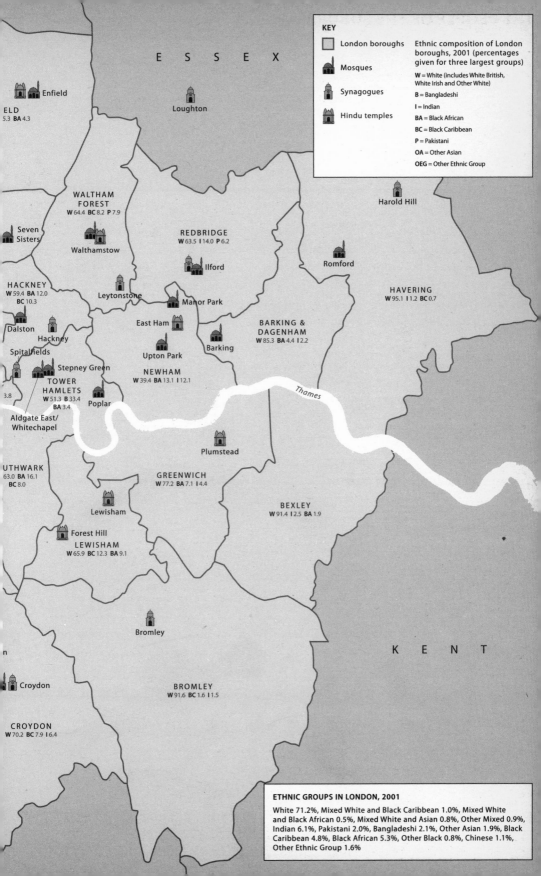

E S S E X

KEY

☐ London boroughs

🕌 Mosques

🏛 Synagogues

🛕 Hindu temples

Ethnic composition of London boroughs, 2001 (percentages given for three largest groups)

W = White (includes White British, White Irish and Other White)

B = Bangladeshi

I = Indian

BA = Black African

BC = Black Caribbean

P = Pakistani

OA = Other Asian

OEG = Other Ethnic Group

Enfield

Loughton

ELD
5.3 BA 4.3

Harold Hill

WALTHAM
FOREST
W 64.4 BC 8.2 P 7.9

REDBRIDGE
W 63.5 I 14.0 P 6.2

Romford

Seven
Sisters

Walthamstow

Ilford

HACKNEY
W 59.4 BA 12.0
BC 10.3

Leytonstone

Manor Park

HAVERING
W 95.1 I 1.2 BC 0.7

Dalston

East Ham

BARKING &
DAGENHAM
W 85.3 BA 4.4 I 2.2

Hackney

Spitalfields

Upton Park

Barking

Stepney Green

NEWHAM
W 39.4 BA 13.1 I 12.1

TOWER
HAMLETS
W 51.3 B 33.4
BA 3.4

Poplar

3.8

Aldgate East/
Whitechapel

Thames

Plumstead

UTHWARK
63.0 BA 16.1
BC 8.0

GREENWICH
W 77.2 BA 7.1 I 4.4

Lewisham

BEXLEY
W 91.4 I 2.5 BA 1.9

Forest Hill

LEWISHAM
W 65.9 BC 12.3 BA 9.1

K E N T

Bromley

Croydon

BROMLEY
W 91.6 BC 1.6 I 1.5

CROYDON
W 70.2 BC 7.9 I 6.4

ETHNIC GROUPS IN LONDON, 2001

White 71.2%, Mixed White and Black Caribbean 1.0%, Mixed White and Black African 0.5%, Mixed White and Asian 0.8%, Other Mixed 0.9%, Indian 6.1%, Pakistani 2.0%, Bangladeshi 2.1%, Other Asian 1.9%, Black Caribbean 4.8%, Black African 5.3%, Other Black 0.8%, Chinese 1.1%, Other Ethnic Group 1.6%

Bermondsey tended to retain their long-standing population; others, such as Paddington and Hampstead, were far more fluid. London also has a history of foreign migration that stretches right back to the earliest days of the city. There was a strong Jewish presence in the City until Edward I expelled England's Jews in 1290. At the beginning of the fourteenth century, Spanish and French merchants were congregating around Dowgate in the City, while German merchants could be found in the Steelyard in Thames Street. A hundred years later, brewers and craftsmen from Flanders and Holland could be found in Southwark and Westminster; they were collectively and indiscriminately known as 'the Dutch'. Italian bankers also constituted a significant community from the later twelfth century onwards, their importance to the City symbolised by a change in the name of the street where they were centred from Langburnestrate to Lumbardstret – today's Lombard Street. Jewish and Huguenot settlers arrived in the capital in the seventeenth century, Chinese settlers in the nineteenth, Afro-Caribbean, African and Asian settlers in the mid twentieth century and Eastern Europeans in the early twenty-first century.

The appeal of London to the non-native born has always been twofold: as a place of refuge for those fleeing persecution or unrest, and as a city of possibilities for those seeking a new or more affluent life. The Polish community in London exemplifies both factors at work at different times. In the 1940s, tens of thousands of Poles left their homeland in the wake of the Nazi invasion of 1939 to join their government in exile and to sign up with the British army or the RAF. These people were then joined by others fleeing post-war communist rule to settle in places like Brixton, Lewisham or Earl's Court. Then, after Poland's accession to the EU in 2004, a new wave of Polish migrants arrived, their motivation this time economic and their dispersal far wider. In fact there is scarcely a London suburb today that is not home to Polish native speakers or to a Polish shop or to a Catholic church where Poles are among the worshippers. In west London there's a Polish Social and Cultural Centre in King Street, Hammersmith; there are Polish enclaves in Balham and Streatham to the south, Willesden Green and Haringey to the north and Stratford to the east.

A similar pattern emerges with the large Turkish and Greek Cypriot communities in London. Some of the handful of early settlers, who came when the island was declared a British protectorate in 1878, were economic migrants. So, too, were the many Turkish Cypriots who, a century later, came to London when the international community's refusal to recognise the Turkish Republic of Northern Cyprus in 1983 led to the region's stagnation. However, between those two points was a long period after the Second World War when internal conflict drove members of both communities abroad. The ugly and messy end of British rule in Cyprus was accompanied by an exodus that peaked in 1960, and was followed by a further one in 1974 when Turkish forces invaded the island. By the end of the century there were Greek and Turkish Cypriots scattered across north London, sometimes even sharing suburbs – notably Wood Green, Palmers Green and Edmonton.

In 1911 there were 176,000 foreign-born Londoners, just 4 per cent of the capital's population; by 2006 there were 2.3 million, or 31 per cent of the total number of London residents. Today the city is home to people who speak 300 different languages and to fifty non-indigenous groups whose population exceeds 10,000. It contains two boroughs – Newham and Brent – with non-white majorities. It is France's sixth biggest city (more French people live in London than in Bordeaux), has an Australian population spread across west London from Earl's Court to Hammersmith, and its skyline is dotted with Orthodox churches, Hindu temples, mosques and synagogues. Every London suburb contains people who were not born there or whose families originate from outside the London area, and all provide case histories of the way in which the precise mix of the area's population helps give it its particular feel and flavour. Just a handful, though, are perhaps sufficient to demonstrate London's endless variety: Golders Green to the north, Southall to the west, Soho in the centre and Brixton to the south.

Golders Green, or Goldhurst Green or even Groles Green as it has been known at various points of its history, exchanged its ancient woodland for farms in the eighteenth century. It remained a village until the arrival of the Northern line in the early 1900s and then expanded rapidly, acquiring new grids of streets and even a hippodrome. Soon it was becoming home to its first Jewish families. Their numbers remained relatively small before the First World War, but then grew in the 1920s, in part because Golders

Green lay in Middlesex and not within the boundaries of the LCC so that it was exempt from the LCC's policy of forbidding 'aliens' to move into local council housing. Golders Green's first synagogue opened in Dunstan Road in 1922, the same year that the area acquired its first kosher butcher, and further synagogues opened in the 1930s.

Most of the community originally came from the East End, and their migration northwards is typical of the path trodden by so many immigrant communities: an early focus in particular areas followed by wider dispersal through the capital. Not that it was quite that neat in terms of London's earlier Jewish population: some lived in the City when Cromwell readmitted Jews to England in 1655; in the early eighteenth century Daniel Defoe recorded a Jewish presence in Hampstead; in the nineteenth century Jewish Londoners lived as far apart as Stamford Hill, Bayswater and Brondesbury, many of them quite prosperous, a few very wealthy. Nevertheless, it was the East End that proved a particularly powerful magnet for the Jewish community in Victorian London.

The Jewish East End: a coffee shop near Jubilee Street in 1902.

The pivotal moment in the history of Britain's Jews came with the assassination of the Russian Tsar Alexander II on 13 March 1881. Convinced that 'the Jews' were in some way responsible, the Russian authorities unleashed a wave of pogroms that drove Jewish communities out of their country, towards relatively safe havens in America and Britain. What followed was an extreme version of what has so often happened with immigrant communities. The newcomers were inevitably attracted to places that were already home to Jews – notably Spitalfields and Whitechapel – not least because these were poor regions of London that they could just about afford to live in. However, their sheer weight of numbers (the existing Jewish community quadrupled virtually overnight) upset the area's delicate ethnic balance. Many locals were displaced, including large numbers of Huguenot weavers who had already suffered economic decline. Tensions rose with the large contingent of Irish people living in the area.

The newly enlarged Jewish community – 100,000 strong in the East End by the end of Queen Victoria's reign and spread across Whitechapel, Bethnal Green and Stepney – remade the locale in its own image. New synagogues appeared; new cuisine was introduced (the fried fish component of fish and chips almost certainly has a Jewish ancestry, and was established in London by the mid nineteenth century); and new words, such as kosher, chutzpah and kvetch, were introduced into the English language. The hustle and bustle of Brick Lane, once a Tudor centre of brick making, became synonymous with all things Jewish. Solomon Belernof, whose Lithuanian family settled in Langdale Street in 1903, later recalled the Jewish East End at its height:

> Every other Saturday, Dad took us to Schewzik's (Benjamin Schewzik, 86 Brick Lane). These were the original Russian Vapour Baths, used by everybody in the East End throughout the week. Wednesdays were reserved for women, and Mum also went there with my sisters once a fortnight. When we got there, Dad paid his few coppers (half price for me) and was given a key to one of the clothes lockers . . . On the corner of Old Montague Street, where I was born, was the original Blooms'. This was, at first, just a little shop, specialising in selling salt-beef sandwiches for ten pence each . . . Blooms' always had the best beef (or perhaps the trick lay in the pickling brine) and certainly had the most enormous fillings. Business prospered, and in the early [19]30s the shop

was demolished and a brand new restaurant was built in its place . . .
This became the eating centre for anybody with money, and was
crowded every Saturday night.[3]

As before, and since, in the immigrant's experience of Britain, hostility
to an 'alien' culture came at both an official and a popular level. Concerned
by the rapid influx of immigrants from Eastern Europe, the government
passed the 1905 Aliens Act to restrict the numbers of new arrivals in
London. Meanwhile, members of the local non-Jewish community formed
the anti-Semitic British Brothers League in 1901. Anti-Semitism remained
a constant in the East End throughout the early decades of the twentieth
century, reaching boiling point in the 1930s in the wake of an economic
recession that caused a backlash against 'foreigners' supposedly taking
homes and jobs away from others. This was the era of the 'Battle of Cable
Street' when, on 4 October 1936, an army of Jewish residents and anti-
fascists fought the police to prevent a march by Oswald Mosley's
Blackshirts through the streets of the East End.

As the Jewish community became more established, however, and as
many of its members 'made good', so the next milestone along the immigrants' path in London was reached: gradual dispersal through the suburbs.
New waves of incomers continued to pile into the East End in the first
decades of the twentieth century, but as they did so longer-standing
members of the community were both pushed and pulled away from the
poorer areas to settle elsewhere. Solomon Sugar affords a typical example
of this process. Like so many others, he had come to England from Poland
in the 1880s – the exact date is uncertain – and settled in Fashion Street,
Spitalfields, alongside other Polish families such as the Leibovitches,
Schneiders, Weinbergs and Abrahams. Solomon was a tailor, making
clothes for merchants who then sold them in local markets or in the
shops of the West End. He was also a hard worker. By the time of the
1911 population census, twenty years after he had first made his appearance in British records, the family had moved to Balaam Street, Plaistow
– just down the road from the green space of Plaistow Park – and were
running their own tailoring business. They continued to prosper; a century
later, Solomon's great-grandson Alan sits in the House of Lords.

It was at this time that Jewish communities started to build up in
Edgware, Finchley, Hampstead Garden Suburb, Hendon and, of course,

Golders Green. Today Golders Green has a clutch of kosher butchers and bakers offering bagels and challah loaves for sale. Many houses bear a distinctive mezuzah next to their front door, and every Hanukkah an enormous menorah is lit outside Golders Green tube station.

Nineteenth-century Southall was famed for three things: its market (which dated back to the seventeenth century), its nascent industry (brick making, pottery and margarine) and its County Lunatic Asylum. In the course of the twentieth century agriculture disappeared, the County Lunatic Asylum became a hospital but local industry continued to expand; and in the 1950s the first South Asian migrants arrived in the area. The popular legend – which like most popular legends has been challenged – is that the personnel officer at Woolf's Rubber Company, finding himself short of workers prepared to face the heat generated by the factory, and having once officered and been impressed by the men of a Sikh regiment, decided to encourage recruitment from the Punjab. Whether that is true or not, it is certainly the case that by the 1960s the factory workforce was predominantly Asian, and the India Workers' Association had been formed to support people arriving in the area. As nearby Heathrow Airport expanded in the 1970s and 1980s, creating further employment in the area, so yet more Asian people moved to Southall, new housing began to encroach on such open fields and market gardens as there still were, and the suburb acquired the look and feel it has today. Over half of Southall's population now are ultimately Indian or Pakistani in origin, the signage on the main railway station is in both English and Punjabi, and the suburb is host to ten Sikh gurdwaras (including one of the largest in the world outside India), two Hindu temples and three mosques.

As with so many ethnic groups, there is a much longer history of Asian settlement in London than their comparatively recent presence in Southall might suggest. During the days of the Raj, for example, a South Asian community flourished in and around the capital, many of them scholars, traders and diplomats. At their centre was the remarkable Dadabhai Naoroji, a partner in Cama & Co, which opened an English branch in 1855, making it the first Indian company to be established in England. He went on to become professor of Gujarati at University College, London,

Southall, 9 April 2009.

and ultimately, in 1892, Member of Parliament for Finsbury Central. He was also instrumental in setting up institutions to promote Indian culture, such as the London Indian Society, East Indian Association and the London Zoroastrian Society. Victorian London was also home to the 'lascars', Asian sailors in the merchant navy, of whom there were a fair number crammed into the East End.

That said, though, Asian immigration to London only really became marked in the post-Second World War period. From the 1950s onwards, Sylhetis from East Pakistan were moving to Brick Lane in the East End to join a community that had its roots in the interwar period. Many more arrived in 1961–2 to beat the curb on immigration that the Commonwealth Immigration Act was about to impose; and a further migration occurred in the 1970s in the wake of East Pakistan's war of independence with West Pakistan, which led to the formation of Bangladesh. Now an area that had once been home to Huguenot weavers and Jewish peddlers was becoming known as 'Banglatown'. Many of the new arrivals sought work in the area's traditional textile industry, but as that declined many started

456

up restaurants. By 1991 there were nearly 40,000 Bangladeshis living in and around Spitalfields. Others from the Indian subcontinent arrived to take up invitations to work with London Transport (in the 1950s) and with the National Health Service (in the 1960s). By the time that the 2001 census was compiled, some 350,000 Londoners described themselves as coming from the Indian subcontinent – the largest of all the capital's ethnic minority groups.

Soho's Chinatown has to be one of the most distinctive and instantly recognisable areas in the whole of London. Gerrard Street, created in the 1670s and 1680s by the notorious Nicholas Barbon on land belonging to Charles, Lord Gerrard, now boasts a street sign in both English and Chinese. A pagoda stands in Newport Place. Chinese lions adorn Wardour Street and Chinese restaurants and supermarkets are to be found everywhere. Every Chinese New Year since around 1973, celebrations have been held throughout the area, with dancing dragons, lions, firecrackers and music.

In fact, Chinatown is of fairly recent origin, but the Chinese presence in London is, like south Asian settlement in the capital, of long-standing

An Edwardian photograph of Chinese graves in the East London cemetery.

and similar origin. Like the lascars from India and other parts of south Asia, early Chinese settlers tended to be sailors congregated initially in the areas around the docks. Like the lascars, too, they were never that big a community: it has been estimated that there were perhaps 500 or so in the capital towards the end of the nineteenth century, concentrated in Limehouse. However, such was the popular fascination with them – as with various immigrant communities in Victorian times – that it must have seemed to contemporaries that there were many more and that the opium dens that intrigued such writers as Charles Dickens and Arthur Conan Doyle clustered thickly on every street corner – even though, in reality, there were only a handful.

The Chinese in London attracted tourists to make the trek across town from the West End to Pennyfield and the streets around, so that by the time the Chinese writer Chiang Yee visited the capital in the 1930s he found that many Londoners were quite familiar with – admittedly limited – aspects of Chinese culture:

> I suppose most people who know anything about Chinese food have heard the expression 'Chop Suey'. Since I came to London, I have frequently invited my English friends to a Chinese meal. They generally choose 'Chop Suey' from the menu – as soon as they get it, they ask what it is made of. I simply answer – 'made of all things'. All Chinese cooks and waiters know their English visitors like this dish.[4]

Inevitably, though, the community also attracted hostile locals who resented the presence of a very different culture from their own. The first Chinese laundry to open in Poplar in 1901, for example, was stoned by crowds.

The Chinese remained few in number throughout the first half of the twentieth century. Nevertheless, they continued to figure prominently in sensationalist literature, notably in Arthur Henry Ward's *The Mystery of Dr Fu Manchu* (1913), in which the leader of the secret society the Si-Fan gets up to no good in Limehouse. In fact, so prominently did they figure in novels of the interwar years that both P. G. Wodehouse and George Orwell were driven to mock writers who made such easy money out of such ridiculous stereotypes. The days of Limehouse, however, were to be of limited duration. Extensive bombing of the area during the Second World War drove the community westwards and into Soho, where the

*Soho's Chinatown celebrating both its Chinese heritage and
the Queen's Diamond Jubilee.*

first Chinese restaurants had opened by 1920 and which in the course of
the 1950s was to become the new Chinatown.

Two factors transformed the Chinese presence in London after the
Second World War: land reform in Hong Kong, which drove many people
overseas in search of a more stable livelihood; and the British military,
whose experience of Chinese cuisine during the war, or while on National
Service, had created a hunger for Chinese food. Then, during the Vietnam
War of the 1960s and 1970s, a wave of Vietnamese immigrants arrived,
and the complicated settlement patterns that the Jewish community had
established for itself started to be repeated. Newcomers were often
attracted to Soho, but they might well also opt for Lewisham, Lambeth
or Hackney; and with economic prosperity in the 1980s came a move of
many professionals both to the north of town, in Colindale, and to the
south, in Croydon.

This tendency of new communities to disperse more widely across the
capital over time can be seen again and again. When Kenyan Asians fled

the victimisation of President Kenyatta's 'Africanisation' policy between 1965 and 1967, many of them ended up in the outer suburbs, particularly in areas where there was already a strong Asian community, such as Southall, but also further afield towards Neasden, as well as to the south in Norwood and Croydon. A large proportion of the 28,000 Ugandan Asians expelled in 1972 by President Idi Amin ended up in or near Wembley. In the early days of the Ghanaian community in London, many could be found in Hendon, Hounslow and Walthamstow, while Nigerians opted for Dalston, Hackney and Peckham (which acquired the nickname 'Little Lagos' or 'Yorubaland'). However, as the decades passed, so many moved on. Today, for example, there remains a strong Jewish presence in Golders Green, Finchley and elsewhere throughout the borough of Barnet; but, according to a survey undertaken by the Greater London Authority in 2001, people of Jewish ancestry may equally choose to live in Harrow, Redbridge, Camden or Hackney. Ghanaians can be found as far apart as Southwark and Brent. Many Lebanese congregate in the Edgware Road, but many also live in Queensway, Bayswater and Kensington.

<hr />

After the Second World War, as Britain struggled to rebuild itself, it looked to the Commonwealth to supplement its labour force of bus and train drivers, health-care workers, builders and others, passing the 1948 British Nationality Act to entice would-be immigrants with the promise of British citizenship. On 22 June 1948 the first group of predominantly male Caribbean settlers arrived at Tilbury Docks aboard the SS *Empire Windrush*, to be ushered to temporary accommodation in the deep shelter at Clapham South tube station. This was under a mile away from the Coldharbour Lane Employment Exchange in Brixton, where many of them went to find work, and where a handful of black people already lived, and it was in and around this area that many chose to settle, joined in time by their families to create small, tight-knit communities.

That initial group was small in number – only 492 – but from the mid 1950s the numbers arriving in London from the Caribbean started to escalate. Eleven hundred people arrived on the SS *Auriga* alone in 1955, just a few of an estimated 27,500 who came to Britain that year. In 1960 the figure was 50,000; the following year it was 66,300. Many moved to

Two Afro-Caribbean men walking along Latimer Road in 1957.
Racial tensions in the area spilled over into a full-blown riot in 1958.

the Brixton and Clapham area. Others rented accommodation in Harlesden, Notting Hill, North Kensington, parts of Camden, Tottenham and Edmonton, and, to the south, in Peckham, Streatham and Lewisham. Often it was the cheapness of the rents that appealed, often it was the proximity of a particular area to employment prospects (termini, depots and so on), and often both factors were in play at the same time. All too often where the new immigrants ended up having to live is a virtual mirror image of the most run-down of London's post-war inner suburbs.

Over time, tensions with long-standing communities boiled over, particularly in socially deprived North Kensington; and in the summer of 1958, following a spate of attacks on black men, hostility turned to full-scale rioting in Notting Hill:

> Within half an hour the mob which had by now swelled to uncontrollable numbers had broken scores of windows and set upon two negroes who were lucky to escape with cuts and bruises. Women from the top floor windows laughed as they called down to the thousand strong

461

crowd, 'Go on boys, get yourself some blacks.' As the crowds swung into Blenheim Crescent milk bottles rained down from tenement roofs where coloured men were sheltering . . . All through the evening, gangs of hooligans from all over London came to join in. They came on foot, by train, bus, motorbike, car and lorry, shouting, 'Alright boys, we're here.' Those on motorbikes and in cars toured the district looking for coloured people.[5]

The Notting Hill riots became the latest in a series of flare-ups between London's established population and its newcomers that, depressingly, stretches back centuries. During the Peasant's Revolt of 1381, for example, in addition to storming the hated John of Gaunt's Savoy Palace on the Strand, the mob attacked and killed over a hundred Flemings and Lombards. On 1 May 1517 the City witnessed a race riot in which a crowd of perhaps a thousand attacked houses and shops belonging to foreigners, one of the rabble-rousers vociferously stating, according to *Hall's Chronicle*, that 'this land was given to Englishmen, and as birds would defend their nests, so ought Englishmen to cherish and defend themselves, and to hurt and grieve aliens for the Commonweal'.[6] During the anti-Catholic Gordon Riots of 1780, foreign embassies were attacked.

Brixton, too, came to experience its fair share of local tensions. By 1958, along with neighbouring Stockwell, it was home to some of the most run-down housing stock in the inner suburbs and to one in five of the capital's West Indian population. Measures were then taken to deal with the worst of the area's housing, leading in the 1960s and 1970s to the demolition of many old Victorian streets and their replacement by such new estates as Myatts Field North and Angell Town, with its concrete blocks connected by high-level bridges. However, these estates acquired their own problems over time, falling prey to many of the problems that bedevilled so many post-war developments: poverty, vandalism, drugs and crime. At the same time, relations with the police were frequently strained. In 1981, 1985 and 1995 confrontations descended into riots, in which many were injured.

Yet increasingly from the 1980s onwards Brixton also saw improvements. The worst of post-war housing was refurbished or replaced. New urban schemes were introduced, and the area became ever more cosmopolitan. The 2001 census returns for Brixton Hill reveal an area with high white

Brixton market today.

British and black populations (together accounting for around 90 per cent of the total, of which white British account for nearly two-thirds), but also Asians, Chinese, Americans, Australians and Europeans from as far apart as Portugal (124 people) and Finland (6).

In many ways, the changing face of Brixton has been reflected in the changing nature of Brixton Market. When it was founded, in around 1870, Brixton had only recently become substantially built up (Angell Town, for example, was laid out in the 1850s), and the area still retained many of its old open spaces and market gardens. The market gradually spread through the area between Atlantic Road and Brixton Road, and Electric Avenue was laid out in the 1880s, becoming in 1888 the first shopping street to be lit by electricity and with a protective iron and glass canopy for shoppers that survived until the 1980s.

By the mid 1920s Brixton had acquired department stores, shops, pubs, cinemas and a theatre, but it was also beginning to experience tougher times: some of its grand houses were demolished to make way for flats; others became down-at-heel boarding houses. By 1952 the market itself was threatened with closure. It survived, however, to be gradually transformed from a market selling the standard range of meat, fish, fruit and vegetables to one that also included items that to many of Brixton's older and long-standing residents must have seemed very exotic indeed: yams, plantains and black beans. Today, Brixton Market sells everything from food to mobile phones, and its cuisine ranges from Caribbean to Italian and from Thai to Japanese. It remains a vital and very varied hub of the community.

NINETEEN

HAMPTON

The Story of a London Suburb

Modern Hampton lies on the outer edge of the borough of Richmond upon Thames. Its southern border is defined by the River Thames, across which a centuries-old ferry service runs from beneath the shadow of the Bell Inn and Hampton Church to Molesey on the opposite bank, in the Surrey County Council borough of Elmbridge. To the east is the royal borough of Kingston upon Thames. Westwards lies Sunbury, formerly part of Middlesex and excluded, after much horse-trading, from becoming a London borough when the GLC was established in 1965. Sunbury now forms part of Spelthorne and is technically counted as belonging to Surrey. Hampton, in other words, clings on to London by its fingertips, the outermost edge of an outermost borough.

There are three elements to Hampton. First there is the 'village', which constitutes the ancient heart of the parish and which is situated to the south bordering the river. It consists of a triangle of three roads (Church Street, High Street and Thames Street) by St Mary's church, and also a more recent shopping and residential district along and around Station Road. Then there is the northern half of the parish beyond Broad Lane and boxed in by Uxbridge Road. This contains three secondary schools situated along Hanworth Road – Hampton Academy, Hampton Independent School for boys, and Lady Eleanor Holles girls' school – jostling with residential streets from the 1930s, along with new developments from the 1970s and a shopping centre in the 'nursery lands'. Finally there is Hampton Hill, covering the northern stretch of the High Street as it heads towards Teddington to the east, Fulwell and ultimately Twickenham further north. Around 27,500 people live here today, spread fairly evenly across the three communities in 12,500 houses. Some have lived in Hampton for years; others have arrived more recently, attracted perhaps by the suburb's open spaces and parks, or by its schools, or by its mix of housing (the recent redevelopment around Station Road, for example, has proved popular), or by the fact that it takes only about forty minutes by train to reach central London, or by a mixture of these considerations. It's quite a 'young' place: the 2001 census shows that many of Hampton's residents are in their thirties and forties, a fair proportion of them lower or middle managers. Once, as a child, I too lived in Hampton.

Of the many major changes that have occurred in Hampton, the redevelopment of the 'nursery lands' is perhaps the most recent. These were once part of the Old Farm House estate, which at its height consisted of a hundred acres of land. After 1862, parcels of the estate were gradually sold off for redevelopment, but a fair amount of open land remained, which by 1900 was home to around 32 nurseries and 600 greenhouses. These remained in operation up to and through the Second World War, when their usefulness in a time of food shortages was particularly welcome. However, as cheap food flooded in after the war, so the nurseries declined and by the 1970s most were derelict. Bit by bit the land was sold off to be turned into the Nurserylands housing development – now one of the most heavily populated parts of Hampton – and also a shopping centre. Only Buckingham Field remained, claimed recently by local residents as a village green. As for the Old Farm House itself, this hung on until the 1960s and was then demolished.

Previously Hampton had another large estate, Manor House, owned by the Earl of Carlisle, but this was built over rather earlier, between the 1890s and 1930s, yielding the majority of the terraced streets and semi-detached houses to be found south of the Nurserylands estates, down Percy Road and across Old Farm Road towards Broad Lane. First to be developed was the area adjacent to Station Road, including Ormond Avenue, where I grew up, Ormond Drive, Ormond Crescent and Gloucester Road, all of which feature on the earliest twentieth-century Ordnance Survey maps. Many of the first houses to be built here were large, grand affairs. Scattered somewhat randomly along the newly laid-out streets they attracted affluent professionals, whose status demanded detached houses with sizable gardens but whose income would not run to one of the grand Georgian mansions or estates that had dominated Hampton's landscape for so many decades. According to the 1911 census,

No. 14 Ormond Avenue, for example, was home to Charles James Goldstone, a 39-year-old stockbroker. He lived in some luxury, able to afford three live-in servants to cook, clean and look after his children. His neighbours included Henry Rugg, an insurance official; James Potter, a managing director; and Nicholas Collier, a doctor.

Once these new houses were built, Hampton's population, which stood at 6,813 living in around 1,350 houses in 1901, rose sharply to 13,061 living in around 3,200 houses in 1931. A shopping area developed along Priory Road, complete with a post office (now gone) and a doctor's surgery (still there). In the 1920s and 1930s yet more shops arrived, including a bakery, greengrocer's and butcher's – and also a bank – all scattered along Ashley Road, Station Approach and Milton Road. Many are still there today. Hampton's acknowledgement that the car was rapidly becoming king of the road took the form of introducing no fewer than three petrol stations to the vicinity to serve a new generation of suburban commuters, many of whose newly built semi-detached houses now came complete with garages. All the petrol stations have now gone. As for Manor House itself, this was demolished in 1937 to make way for more houses to the west.

Of all these various roads it is Station Road that has perhaps played the most important part in Hampton's recent history. Known before 1900 as New Street, it had previously gone under a variety of names since at least the seventeenth century, including 'Road to Hanworth', 'Road to Four Hills', 'Road to Warfield' and even 'Smoaky Road'. At the start of the nineteenth century it contained a few houses and at least two pubs, but then came further development – more houses, some shops and a police station – and then came the railway. With the opening of Hampton railway station in 1864 as part of the London and South Western Railway network, this tiny village was at last formally linked with central London, rather than informally linked by coach routes, and expansion duly followed. New Street became ever more built up, and in the late 1880s and early 1890s new streets of Victorian terraces appeared, Belgrave Road, Avenue Road, Varna Road and Plevna Road among them. Many were occupied by market gardeners or by reasonably well-off workers engaged in light industry or local trades. In 1891, for example, No. 6 River Hill Cottages, Plevna Street, was occupied by William Thomas Parker, a ferryman, who lived there with his wife Lydia and their four children, the youngest of

whom, Charles, had only recently been born. New Street was now the
heart of a thriving Victorian suburb.

One of the principal reasons why the decision was taken to site a
railway station at Hampton rather than at any other village nearby was
that it had recently acquired a very important asset and one that marked
it apart from its more workaday neighbours: a waterworks. In 1852 the
Metropolis Water Act had prohibited the removal of any water from
the tidal stretch of the Thames. London's water companies were therefore forced to look elsewhere for supplies, and in 1855 the Southwark
and Vauxhall, Grand Junction and West Middlesex Water companies
decided that Hampton was the perfect location for a new enterprise,
lying as it did just upstream from non-tidal Teddington. Reservoirs
and filter beds were therefore installed between Thames Street and New
Street, as well as at further sites along both sides of the Thames on
the roads towards Sunbury, turning the southern half of the village
into an industrial hive of activity. Establishing a waterworks meant
creating new jobs, and locals and incomers benefited alike, although
the incomers had temporarily to make do with shacks and hovels in
'new Hampton', later to be known as Hampton Hill. In the context

Hampton from the river.

of all this hustle and bustle, building a railway station here must have seemed entirely logical.

It wasn't only the waterworks, however, that brought the railway to Hampton. The village also happened to lie very close to a major Victorian tourist attraction, Hampton Court; and while it was true that Hampton Court had had its own railway station since 1849, it was also true that the palace could be reached very easily from Hampton via its historic riverside and tempting tea rooms. Then there was the appeal of horse racing at Kempton Park and Sandown Park, not to mention the 'Hampton races', as Charles Dickens refers to them in *Nicholas Nickleby* (1838–9), on Molesey Hurst just across the Thames (the racetrack is still visible on Ordnance Survey maps into the 1900s). When James Thorne described Hampton in his *Environs of London* of 1876 he mentioned that the village was also very popular with anglers ('Hampton may be considered the headquarters of the Thames Angling Preservation Society'). Later it was to gain a football club (formed in 1921), which acquired grounds off Station Road in 1959, and, for the more aquatically minded there was Hampton Lido – now Hampton Heated Outdoor Pool – which was constructed next to Bushy Park in 1922, and remains one of London's last such open-air ventures. Hampton was not just a centre of industry, then, it was also a centre of entertainment and relaxation.

With the arrival of the waterworks and the station, by 1901 Hampton's population had nearly doubled from 3,915 people living in 805 houses in 1871. Now the first of the streets on Manor House estate were laid out, older roads were widened, and electric trams introduced, connecting Hampton to Twickenham, Richmond and Kingston. New Street became Station Road and as such rose to be the commercial heart of Hampton, with various pubs and a range of shops offering food, ironmongery, books and even toys.

As the population started to boom, so other industries arrived in the area, even if none rivalled the scale of the waterworks. I can recall a candle factory near the river, not least because it burned down in a spectacular way in the 1970s, causing considerable alarm to a small child who had recently learned about the Great Fire of London. Then there was Saft Ltd, which made batteries, not to mention an electric blanket factory in the High Street. All have long gone, though the electric blanket building still just about stands and other industrial buildings have been turned into business parks, one of which is the Hampton Business Centre off the High Street. As for the various buildings that once belonged to the water companies, these still stand, many of them now luxury residential apartments and flats. The filter beds adjoining Station Road were decommissioned in the 1990s and then filled in and converted into a pleasant green space (complete with children's playground) with modern townhouses built around the site. Hampton's industrial age was short-lived.

❖ ❖ ❖

New Street may have become the centre of Victorian Hampton, but before that the heart of the village lay some way away in that triangle formed by High Street, Church Street and Thames Street. Here, in 1851, 3,134 peopled lived, crammed into a mere 540 houses. Even within this ancient triangle, development was relatively recent. Just fifty years before, when the first census had been taken, there had been only 141 houses and 1,722 residents. It was thanks to the granting of an enclosure award in 1811 that created common land out of which 'new Hampton', or Hampton Hill as it became known, was formed that the upper end of the High Street acquired the houses and shops that took it to its 1851 level.

Before 1801, that tiny nucleus of Hampton was a village standing on a road that led to Hampton Hill and onwards towards Teddington and Twickenham, and adjoining Church Lane, where the oldest houses, shops and businesses could be found. As late as the 1970s and early 1980s their descendants still clung to the area: Stacey's butchers; a chemist's shop with glass dispensary jars in its windows; the Hampton Pantry, which sold dried store provisions; fresh meat and dairy products from Job's Dairy over in Hanworth; and Townsends newsagents. All, however, have now been converted into domestic dwellings. Some of Hampton's Georgian properties still stand here, and there are even one or two older houses. Penn's Place, for example, tucked away by St Mary's church, probably dates back to the early sixteenth century; it was reputedly once the home of Edward VI's nurse, Sybil Penn.

Hugging the river along Thames Street are some of the grandest properties to have survived from the eighteenth century. This was the period when Hampton was home to such luminaries as the actor David Garrick,

Garrick's Villa.

who rented what is now known as Garrick's Villa (then Hampton House) in 1754 to serve as his country house, bought it the following year and then enlarged it, adding a new front and building a temple to Shakespeare. The temple contained a statue of the great playwright, for which Garrick himself, either for reasons of economy or lack of modesty, stood as model; and the house became a popular haunt for London society. Here Garrick would host night fetes in which he decorated his grounds with thousands of coloured lamps, and here on one occasion Horace Walpole recalled meeting a whole range of luminaries who included 'the Duke of Grafton, Lord and Lady Rochford, Lady Holderness, the Crooked Mostyn, and Dabreu the Spanish minister; two regents, of which one is lord chamberlain, the other groom of the stole; and the wife of a secretary of state'[1]. On Samuel Johnson's first visit to the house, Garrick asked him how he liked it. 'Ah, David!' Johnson replied, 'it is the leaving of such places that makes a death-bed terrible.' Not all local residents, though, were quite so reputable. Thames Street was also home in the 1820s to Henry Fauntleroy, the last man in England to be hanged for forgery.

To the west and towards the heart of Hampton is Rosehill, still standing today only because it was bought by the Unitary District Council in 1902 and converted to provide it with offices and a community library. Originally it belonged to a friend of David Garrick's, the tenor John Beard, who had once performed at Covent Garden and was married to the daughter of its manager, John Rich (responsible for the first production of John Gay's *The Beggar's Opera*). Many other Georgian mansions, however, have disappeared. Hill House, Rose Villa, Castle House (now the site of Castle business village) and Warfield House, all still clearly marked on the 1894 Ordnance Survey map, were demolished to make way for housing and shops in the course of the twentieth century. The Elms, a grand, originally seventeenth-century affair, was burnt down by suffragettes in 1913. Beveree House is one of the few survivors, hidden away off the High Street and now part of Twickenham Preparatory School.

Before Georgian gentrification, Hampton was little more than three principal open fields, originally named West Field (on some of which the waterworks were later built), East Field (which became part of Bushy Park) and Oldfield (from which today's Oldfield Road dervies its name): farmland in which stood one or two substantial houses – Manor House and Old Farm, for example – gaining such lustre as it had from its proximity to Cardinal Wolsey's, and then Henry VIII's, palace at Hampton Court and the royal hunting ground of Bushy Park, which still forms Hampton's eastern border.

In 1500 the population probably stood at around 300. Before that, it's hard to say. We do know, however, that for much of the Middle Ages the manor of Hampton was owned by the Knights Hospitaller of the Order of St John of Jerusalem, an ancient Crusading order whose prior, Terrice de Nussa, bought extensive lands in 1237 for 1,000 marks (Cardinal Wolsey was to purchase the estate in 1514 to accommodate his grand plans for Hampton Court). There may conceivably have been a small religious house here – we know from a brief 1338 description of the 'camera' of Hampton that there was a dovecot, garden and 840 acres of land, and that whoever lived here claimed £30.7s.2d in expenses to run the entire estate.

Some 250 years earlier, when the Domesday Survey of 1086 was prepared, the manor of Hampton (including Teddington) was part of the Hundred of Hounslow, and was held by Walter de Saint-Valery, one of William I's supporters from Normandy, whose family continued to hold the manor until around 1219 when they paid the price for backing the wrong side in the struggle against King John and then his son Henry III. It seems to have been a thriving rural community in the eleventh century, with thirty-five hides supporting twenty-five plough teams, and with around forty-five villeins working on the estate's meadows and pastures – part of a community that may have numbered perhaps 200. We know nothing more about them, however, not even their names. We can assume that all most of them can have hoped for was that their new Norman overlords would treat them kindly, and it's hard to believe that their horizons spread much further than the fields in which they worked. Few if any would ever have been to the walled City of London, little more than thirteen miles downstream as the crow flies. Indeed, the chances are that most of them had never even heard of it, though perhaps some had been told about the major settlement at Kingston and the Anglo-Saxon coronation stone that stood there. Their sole concern was the 'farmstead or estate in a river bend' from which Hampton derived its name.

This is the place where I grew up, and here I witnessed the latest events in Hampton's long history. Some of the changes I saw were of entirely local interest: the loss of shops on the High Street, the building of the Nurserylands housing estates, the redevelopment of Station Road. Some were reminders of Hampton's role in the wider story of London's development: the waterworks, the railway station, the Georgian houses that had once been fashionable country retreats for rich and famous Londoners. All fascinated me then, and they fascinate me still.

The story of Hampton is the history of many other London suburbs. At the same time, the story of Hampton is wholly unique.

LONDON'S BOROUGHS: A HISTORICAL GAZETTEER

BARKING & DAGENHAM

When established in 1965 the borough was initially known simply as Barking; the Dagenham element was not added until 1980. Both constituent parts have a long history. Barking was the site of one of the most powerful religious houses in early medieval England, Barking Abbey. Mentioned in the Domesday Book, and a major landowner in the immediate area and beyond, the abbey continued to increase its vast estate until it was suppressed in the sixteenth century. Some measure of its importance is reflected in the status of its heads of house, who included three queens, two princesses and the sister of Thomas Becket. Only fragmentary remains survive today. Dagenham is not mentioned in the Domesday Book, but its name does appear in a number of earlier Anglo-Saxon charters.

Hainault Forest was an important feature of the borough until its destruction in the nineteenth century. The name Marks Gate, for example, signifies a former entrance to the forest. It was a medieval manor, and the remains of the moat around the old manor house can still be seen today. Chadwell Heath, and its early medieval settlement at Chadwell, was once a notorious haven for the highwaymen who operated from the cover of the forest.

The Thames shoreline also played a significant role in the borough's development. Saltwater fishing was vital to the area's economy from medieval times, and when Daniel Defoe visited in 1722 he encountered a thriving port that supplied the London markets. The fishing fleet continued to grow until the 1850s, when the arrival of the railways meant that fresh fish could easily be delivered from the east-coast ports each day. A further crushing blow came in 1863, when the fleet was caught in a terrible storm off the Dutch coast and sixty men lost their lives.

The marshland around the Thames was formerly an important source of reeds for thatched roofs and it was also home to oyster beds. From the 1200s onwards, various attempts were made to embank the Thames to allow cattle to graze on the lowlands abutting it, but the embankments created proved difficult to maintain. In 1621 Dagenham and Hornchurch marshes were severely flooded, and a new barrier was therefore constructed. It was subsequently allowed to fall into disrepair, and after another flood in 1707 a new project was undertaken to dam the breach in the banks. This was completed in 1721 and in the process an extensive inland lake (Dagenham Breach) was created, which became a fishing and recreational spot until the beginning of the last century.

At the turn of the nineteenth century, Barking and Dagenham were still largely rural, home to woodland and farming, and while the population did rise slowly during the Victorian period, the area remained largely unchanged until the 1920s and 1930s. In the interwar period, however, large swathes of housing were built to meet the demands of the slum clearances that were taking place in inner London. The most well-known development is the Becontree Estate, its name derived from that of the ancient Essex hundred that had its meeting place on Becontree Heath; at the time of its completion, it was the largest public housing estate in the world, providing nearly 27,000 homes. When construction started there were comparatively few employment opportunities in the area, but the situation was transformed by the decision of Ford Motor Company to move to Dagenham in 1931. Ford became the borough's dominant employer, though in the 1960s it found itself at the centre of strike action, some brought about by women at the plant demanding equal treatment to male employees. By the 1970s and 1980s the Ford plant was struggling, and car production there halted in 2002.

Valence House, the only surviving medieval house in Dagenham, is now the borough's museum.

BARNET

In 1965 there was much discussion over what to call the new London borough that would incorporate the municipal boroughs of Finchley and

Hendon, and the urban districts of Barnet, Friern Barnet and East Barnet. Northgate and Northern Heights were mooted, but Barnet was eventually settled on.

The name derives from an ancient settlement, recorded as early as 1070, and literally meaning a 'clearing in the forest made by fire'. There were three manors in Barnet: Chipping Barnet, East Barnet and Friern Barnet. Chipping Barnet, or High Barnet, held its own market charter from 1199, granted by King John to the abbot of St Albans, to whom the manor belonged. Friern Barnet's name refers to the manor held by the brothers (friars) of the Knights of St John of Jerusalem. The sixteenth-century manor house, built on the site of the old medieval manor house, was given to Sir Walter Raleigh by Elizabeth I, who enjoyed hunting in the surrounding woodlands. In the seventeenth century, Barnet was celebrated for its fresh air and a spa, enjoyed by the likes of diarist Samuel Pepys, which grew up around a mineral well on Barnet Common. At the turn of the nineteenth century, Barnet was still some eight to nine miles from the limits of built-up London, but in the 1860s railway lines connected the area to the rapidly expanding city. Communities at New Barnet and Barnet Vale developed in the late nineteenth century.

To the west of Barnet is Edgware. The settlement is first mentioned in a charter dating from around 978 (the '-ware' element denotes a weir or fishing enclosure). In medieval times it was a rest stop for pilgrims on their way to the shrine at St Albans and it became a market town and important coaching centre in the seventeenth century. Further down the pilgrim's route – the modern Edgware Road and A5 – is Burnt Oak, which only acquired its name in the mid eighteenth century.

Hendon's strategic position on the top of a prominent hill ensured its early settlement: there is evidence of Roman occupation, and the manor of Handone (which included nearby Mill Hill) was recorded in the Domesday Survey. Its extensive woodland supplied fuel to London's tradesmen until coal supplanted wood in the sixteenth century, at which point trees gave way to hay farms. Hendon, along with neighbouring Golders Green, became a developed London suburb at the beginning of the twentieth century. Hendon Aerodrome grew up between the wars, and the area also became home to the Police College, which began training cadets in 1935.

Mill Hill is first mentioned in records in 1547, when it was clearly – as its name suggests – the location of a windmill. Situated on an important northbound route out of London, known as the Ridgeway, the village attracted travellers, and in the eighteenth century acquired a number of large houses and a thriving hospitality trade. The area also became associated with religious Nonconformists and free thinkers. Quakers met on the Ridgeway in the late 1600s and early 1700s. In 1807, Mill Hill School was established at Ridgeway House to educate the children of Nonconformists. Mill Hill was home to the abolitionist William Wilberforce in his later life.

Much of the rest of the borough was formerly woodland and open spaces, as is suggested by place names such as Finchley, meaning 'woodland clearing frequented by finches', and Hadley, meaning a 'heath clearing'. Finchley, whose common was the haunt of highwaymen and therefore a no-go area for many eighteenth-century Londoners, became the borough's most rapidly developing area in the nineteenth century. Good transport links with the city in the form of coach routes and later the railways meant that in a matter of decades it was transformed from an area of arable land dotted with rural hamlets to a thriving suburb, home to many of London's merchant and professional classes.

Totteridge ('Tata's Ridge) marks another apex in the 'northern heights' – some 400 feet above the old heart of London. For many centuries the manor of Totteridge was in the possession of the bishops of Ely. It attracted large houses and country retreats, a tradition that was kept up into the twentieth century with the building of large suburban houses along Totteridge Common. Restrained development has ensured that the area still has a strongly rural feel.

BEXLEY

The borough was formed in 1965 by the union of the municipal boroughs of Bexley and Erith with the urban districts of Crayford and part of Chislehurst and Sidcup. Originally part of north-west Kent, Bexley is one of the classic suburban areas of London, a construct of late nineteenth-century and twentieth-century metropolitan sprawl. Before then, the area was largely rural and undeveloped. Nevertheless, pockets of settlement can be traced back to Anglo-Saxon times. Bexley itself – the name meaning a 'woodland clearing where box trees grow' – dates back to at least the ninth century, while settlements had been established at Crayford by the sixth and Erith by the seventh century. Foots Cray and North Cray are also ancient settlements in the borough, both named in the Domesday Book. Other areas of the borough can be traced back to the Middle Ages, including Bostall, East Wickham, Sidcup and Welling. Slade Green and Northumberland Heath (a popular suburb in the late nineteenth century) have much later roots, their development dating from the sixteenth century.

One of the most important medieval foundations in the area was Lesnes Abbey, established in 1178. The community of Augustinian monks there farmed the land surrounding the abbey, cultivating crops and grazing animals, and they made a concerted effort to drain the surrounding marshes. In the late sixteenth century, after the abbey had been dissolved during the reign of Henry VIII, some of its lands were used as a testing ground for the Royal Arsenal, because the marshes deadened the impact of the explosions. The area's military connections inevitably had an impact on its development in the eighteenth and nineteenth centuries, and towns and villages became populated by workers in the munitions factories connected to the Royal Arsenal. An armaments factory was opened in the early nineteenth century, and then taken over by Vickers in 1897; by the end of the First World War, Vickers was employing 14,000 workers in the region and had built the Crayford Garden Suburb to house many of its staff. Such military links were not without their dangers. During the Second World War, the area was heavily bombed and sustained a large number of casualties, being badly affected by V1 and V2 bombs in 1944.

In the seventeenth century, the development of the London–Dover road stimulated the growth of Bexleyheath and Welling, but the area retained its rural peace and quiet, home to large country houses like Danson House and park (eighteenth century) and the Red House (nine-teenth century). Development gathered pace, however, with the coming of the railways in the 1860s and the opening of such stations as Bexleyheath in 1895. Belvedere, which was originally the name of an eighteenth-century mansion, gradually became built up, as did Barnehurst, built on what had once been woodland. The establishment in 1865 of Crossness sewage works (to cope with London's sewage) near Erith, a seventeenth-century river port, turned it into an industrial town in Victorian times.

Even so, large open spaces and marshland still existed at the end of Queen Victoria's reign, and it was only in the course of the twentieth century that they succumbed to residential development. One of the new towns of the 1960s – Thamesmead – was developed from 1967 on the lowland marshes of Erith and Plumstead. It was named by a local resident, Anthony Walton, who won £20 for his suggestion, and the first family to move in were the Gooches. Later, after the abolition of the GLC in 1986, it was to become the first residential estate in the country to be run by a private company controlled entirely by residents.

BRENT

The borough was formed in 1965 from the municipal boroughs of Wembley and Willesden. Its name is unusual in that it does not derive from a major settlement site within the borough, but from the river that runs through it. The River Brent was first recorded as such in the tenth century, although the name is Celtic, meaning 'holy one', suggesting it was perhaps a place of worship in ancient times. The borough contains a number of settlements that can boast a long history. Harlesden, Kingsbury and Willesden were all recorded in the Domesday Book. Other medieval and Tudor settlements include Alperton, Brondesbury, Church End, Cricklewood, Dollis Hill, Kensal Green, Kilburn, Neasden, Preston, Sudbury, Tokyngton, Uxendon and Wembley. Many of these remained little more than small villages until the coming of the railways in the nineteenth century.

There was certainly a settlement at Wembley ('Wemba's woodland clearing') in the ninth century. However, the Wembley Park area was a private wooded park until 1889, when the Metropolitan Railway Company bought it for leisure purposes. It was then chosen as the site of the British Empire exhibition of 1924–5, for which the first Wembley Stadium was built. A new stadium replaced it in 2007. It remains a major venue for football and rugby matches, as well as live concerts. Wembley acquired Victorian housing, but much of its present appearance dates from the 1920s and 1930s.

Kilburn is another historically significant area, with its roots in a small priory of nuns that was founded there in the twelfth century. After the priory was dissolved in the sixteenth century, part of it became the site of the Bell Inn, a useful stopping-off place for those travelling along the ancient trackway first paved in Roman times and later known as Watling Street (now the A5). Kilburn's appeal was boosted in the eighteenth century by the discovery of a chalybeate spring (commemorated today on a plaque at the corner of Kilburn High Road and Belsize Road), which led to the creation of a spa and gardens to promote the healing qualities of the water. Nevertheless, the area did not become greatly developed until the nineteenth century. Its large Irish population won for it the nickname 'County Kilburn'.

Two forms of transport had a major impact on the development of today's borough of Brent. The first was the Grand Junction Canal, which cut its way through the area in the first decade of the nineteenth century, creating thriving settlements at Alperton and Kensal Green. These two hamlets not only handled barges loaded with coal, iron, gravel and sand, but also acquired their own brickworks. At the same time, they became popular with visitors, who were also drawn to the area by the foundation of Kensal Green cemetery. Kingsbury was affected, too, especially when the Welsh Harp Reservoir (named after a local pub) was constructed there in the 1830s as a water supply for the canal. It similarly became a popular recreation spot.

The second transport revolution to come to Brent was the railway. In 1866, Willesden Junction station was opened, replacing an earlier nearby station established by the London and Birmingham Railway Company and encouraging the development of Stonebridge as a new residential area, popular with professional men working in the City of London. Stonebridge Park was a particularly favoured estate filled with smart new villas. The arrival of the Metropolitan Railway Company (now part of the London Underground system) led to the development of many of what had previously been small rural hamlets and villages into sizable suburbs, from Church End to Neasden, Harlesden and Kensal Green.

In the early twentieth century, the area hosted a short-lived Royal Agricultural Show Ground, which was later to be covered by Park Royal station and various industrial concerns. Therefter, remaining pockets of green were swiftly built up, and various council estates erected.

Brent Cross Shopping Centre, incidentally, is not in Brent but in Barnet.

BROMLEY

Bromley is the largest and greenest of all the London boroughs, as most of it falls within the Metropolitan Green Belt. It was formed from the municipal boroughs of Bromley and Beckenham, with the urban districts of Penge, Orpington and Chislehurst (from the Chislehurst and Sidcup urban district). Much of the borough was taken – amid considerable opposition – from the county of Kent. The village of Knockholt campaigned successfully to be restored to Kent's Sevenoaks rural district in 1969.

The borough is rich in early history and many of its towns and villages can be traced back to the Anglo-Saxon period and the Domesday Survey. Bromley itself was identified in Domesday, along with Beckenham, Chelsfield, Cudham, Orpington, Ruxley, St Mary Cray, St Paul's Cray and West Wickham. Although not mentioned in Domesday, Chislehurst, Mottingham and Penge have Anglo-Saxon roots, and Bickley, Downe, Elmers End, Farnborough and Hayes all originated in the Middle Ages. The bishops of Rochester had a palace in Bromley, first built some time around 1100, and the settlement became an important centre in 1205 when the bishop was granted a market in the town (which continues to the present day). The palace was rebuilt and restructured a number of times in its history, its final incarnation constructed in 1774. It was sold in 1845, and after having a number of uses, including as a girls' finishing school, became part of Bromley's Civic Centre.

The rural nature of the borough began to change with the coming of the canals and railways. Penge became developed after the Croydon Canal was opened in 1809, and its popularity was enhanced after 1854 when the Crystal Palace was relocated to the area from Hyde Park. Shortlands, New Bromley and Bromley Park, Mottingham and Orpington were all transformed by the railways. That said, not every settlement to be served by the railways automatically expanded as a result. In the case of Chislehurst, for example, the arrival of the railway in 1865 had less impact than the arrival of the exiled Emperor Napoleon III at Camden Place in 1870. His presence boosted the reputation of the area, making it fashionable with city workers and businessmen. The railway network continued to expand, and the borough is well served by overland trains. The underground railway system, on the other hand, never reached the Bromley area, which remains the only Greater London borough not to have a London Underground station.

Aspects of Biggin Hill's development were similarly unusual. While many areas of Bromley attracted second home owners who were gentry or City magnates, Biggin Hill became one of the first places where the less affluent could acquire a rural weekend retreat relatively cheaply, a small plot on the Aperfield Estate being available for just £10. Those who bought there erected self-built homes of varying standards, and became known as 'plotlanders'. In time they were joined by an aerodrome that was to prove its worth during the Second World War.

Other new residential centres sprang up in the early twentieth century, such as Park Langley in Beckenham, where building began around 1910. A few years later came Petts Wood, perhaps one of the most successful of the interwar London suburbs, thanks to the planning and development skills of Basil Scruby. Petts Wood station opened in 1928 to serve the new community, and Scruby made meticulous plans for such features as a recreation ground and sports club. Unfortunately, he was unable to complete his plans for the area, and the second phase of building from 1933 gave rise to less high-quality, more densely packed houses to the west of the railway line. This inevitably led to a degree of local rivalry and snobbery.

CAMDEN

Named after Camden Town, the borough includes the metropolitan boroughs of Hampstead, Holborn and St Pancras. Some of its constituent parts are ancient, but others are rather more recent, the medieval manors of Bloomsbury, Hampstead, Holborn, Kentish Town and St Pancras being joined in time by the eighteenth- and nineteenth-century settlements of Camden Town, Dartmouth Park and Gospel Oak.

To the south of the borough, Bloomsbury Square, originally called Southampton Square, was laid out in the 1660s by Thomas Wriothesley, fourth Earl of Southampton, and it set the tone for many other London squares, with its tall town houses designed for the gentry. It retained its fashionable status in the eighteenth century, and in the twentieth century became closely linked with such writers and artists as Virginia Woolf, Vanessa and Clive Bell, and E. M. Forster, various of whom lived in the area. The intellectual nature of the area, however, was established as early as the fourteenth century when the legal quarter of London (including Gray's Inn and Lincoln's Inn) developed around Holborn. In 1753 the British Museum was founded, following the bequest of Sir Hans Sloane's collection of over 71,000 objects, and it opened its doors to the viewing public in 1759. The current quadrangular building and round reading room were completed in the 1840s and 1850s. University College was established in Gower Street in 1826.

Camden Town was developed in the 1790s by Charles Pratt, the first Earl of Camden, in what had previously been a quiet country area, dotted with farms and two coaching inns (the Mother Red Cap and the Southampton), and prone to the depredations of highwaymen. By the time of the first census in 1801, it had already attracted a large population and this continued to rise until the middle of the nineteenth century. However, whereas other areas of London generally expanded when the railways came, Camden's population momentarily slowed, principally because so much of it was destroyed to make way for the new lines and stations. The railways nevertheless did some good, since they led to considerable slum clearance in the Holborn and St Pancras areas. The notorious Agar Town, for example, was demolished in the 1860s and replaced by the Midland Grand Hotel and terminus. The various railway stations made Camden a target for German raids during the Second World War, and much damage was done, particularly around Mornington Crescent. Since then, the area has enjoyed something of a renaissance, acquiring a cosmopolitan and somewhat bohemian atmosphere. In the 1970s the conversion of Camden Lock's wharves and warehouses on the Regent's Canal into craft markets made it a major tourist attraction and centre for creativity.

Kentish Town's development began much earlier, when a clearing was made in the great forest of Middlesex for a small hamlet that became known in time for its farms, hayfields and clean water. Kentish Town also proved popular with those wanting a substantial country house close to town and in the eighteenth century was home to the fashionable Assembly Rooms, where balls were regularly held. To that extent it was not too dissimilar in tone from the high ground of Hampstead, also considered a rural retreat from the bustle of the City of London – and also a place of safety where Londoners fled in 1524 to avoid the threat of flooding by the Thames, and in 1665 to escape the plague (though 260 people in 100 houses in Hampstead nevertheless perished). Kentish Town started to become heavily built up in the 1840s, but the core of Hampstead managed to retain its village atmosphere and many of its old buildings, even though the surrounding area went the same way as Kentish Town.

CROYDON

Previously the county borough of Croydon and the urban district of Coulsdon and Purley, Croydon boasts the largest population of any of the London boroughs. The town of Croydon itself is of ancient origin, mentioned in the Domesday Book (when it had a church, mill and farm-land), certainly in existence in the Anglo-Saxon period, and very probably settled in prehistoric times (its name means 'valley where saffron grows'; saffron may have been introduced to the area by the Romans, who used it for dyeing). Croydon Palace was the summer home of the archbishops of Canterbury, and was also the setting for a number of key events in English history. In the fifteenth century King James I of Scotland was imprisoned in the palace before being moved to the Tower of London, and in the Tudor period numerous meetings of the Privy Council were held there. By the eighteenth century the building had become sadly dilapidated and the local area was regarded as less than salubrious. The palace was sold in 1781 and became a calico printing factory. The arch-bishopric nevertheless kept its links with the area, moving its summer residence to nearby Addington Palace from 1807.

Many of the borough's main settlements are similarly ancient, with evidence of settlement as early as the Bronze Age. It is also likely that there was Roman settlement in the area, especially along the Roman road that linked London to Portslade (Brighton). Some places can certainly trace their roots back to at least the Anglo-Saxon period, such as Selsdon, Coulsdon and Sanderstead. Addington, like Croydon, was also identified in the Domesday Survey. Other places have medieval roots, including Addiscombe, Kenley, Norbury, Selhurst, Shirley, South Norwood and Waddon. Several contain in their names reminders of the extensive wood-land that once covered much of the borough.

The borough was one of the first areas to welcome in the age of the train. In 1801 the Surrey Iron Railway was authorised by Parliament to create a horse-drawn freight line between Croydon and Wandsworth – a distance of some nine miles. A couple of decades or so later, in 1835, parliamentary authorisation was given to the London and Croydon Railway Company, which went on to buy the rival Croydon Canal (opened in 1809 and a financial failure) before opening a new railway line in 1839 and then merging six years later with other railway companies to extend the railway to the south coast.

Croydon was also at the forefront of aviation from the First World War until the end of the 1950s, maintaining for a while the largest airport in the London area. In 1915 an airfield was opened at Beddington as part of the air defence of London against Zeppelin attacks. Around the same time the National Aircraft Factory was built at Waddon, with a flying ground for testing new aircraft. At the end of the war the airfield was combined with the Waddon airfield to form Croydon Aerodrome, which became the customs airport for London in 1920. As air travel became more popular, a new terminal, hotel and airfield were built in 1928, making Croydon Airport world-renowned. The location of the new airport, and the opening of Purley Way, encouraged a great number of factories to be built there in the 1930s. For a while the airport was home to British Airways and Imperial Airways, but by the turn of the 1950s and the advent of new, larger aeroplanes, it proved too small to cope and was superseded by Heathrow and Gatwick airports. It closed in 1959.

Over the years, a number of applications have been made to give Croydon city status; all have failed.

EALING

In 1965, the three municipal boroughs of Ealing, Southall and Acton were amalgamated to create the new borough of Ealing. These in turn had once been part of a number of different Anglo-Saxon and medieval manors, namely Acton, Ealing, Northolt, Southall, Greenford and Hanwell.

A seventh-century Anglo-Saxon charter makes reference to Gillingas ('the settlement of a man named Gilla'), an early incarnation of Ealing. Though this may be the earliest written record of settlement within the borough, excavations at Hanwell have revealed a Saxon settlement that is perhaps even older. In 1086, Hanwell was recorded as an independent manor in the Domesday Survey. Northolt and Greenford, the latter the property of Westminster Abbey, are also mentioned, while Ealing and Acton were merely part of larger manors, as was Southall, which fell within the manor of Hayes and formed part of the Archbishop of Canterbury's estates.

The parish of Northolt in the Middle Ages contained a village and several hamlets, much of the land being given over to open-field arable farming and (according to fourteenth-century records) sheep. At this time the northern half of Acton was heavily wooded (the name derives from the Old English for oak) and was an important source of firewood for the City of London. In addition, it was starting to prove popular with Londoners looking to buy estates in the vicinity, and by the sixteenth century had become a summer retreat for the capital's high society. The Acton Wells spa in the eighteenth century confirmed the popularity of the area with city dwellers.

Perivale, known throughout the Middle Ages as Little Greenford, acquired its now familiar name (meaning 'pear tree valley') in the 1500s. It contains the remains of at least two moated manor houses, though the parish itself was very sparsely populated until the twentieth century. The area was known for its high-quality wheat until the early nineteenth century when, in response to London's demand for hay for its many horses, production switched to growing grass, which was then transported along the Grand Junction Canal.

Like Perivale, Ealing at this time consisted predominantly of fields and open countryside. The Uxbridge Road, which traversed the parish, was an important coaching route, and Ealing was a popular resting spot. The area around Ealing village became a fashionable residential district in the eighteenth and early nineteenth centuries, celebrated residents including the novelist Henry Fielding and John Quincy Adams, later president of the United States. The replacement of coaches by railway engines in the mid nineteenth century meant the inevitable encroachment of the city suburbs, but Ealing fought hard to maintain the status quo – trams and workmen's trains were discouraged or barred from the district – and it styled itself the queen of the suburbs. In Acton, meanwhile, England's first garden suburb was created at Bedford Park attracting upper-middle-class householders intermingled with a dash of artists and literary men. Middle-class housing spread across Ealing and Hanwell in the pre-First World World Edwardian housing boom; this was the period when most of Ealing's surviving open spaces were built upon.

It wasn't until well into the twentieth century that other areas of the borough, including Acton, Northolt and Perivale, began to catch up. Northolt grew rapidly in the 1920s, while in Acton the same decade brought a wealth of industrial development, with manufacturers of every description setting up in the district. On the other side of perennially genteel Ealing, factories began appearing in Perivale in the 1930s and J. Lyons and Company went into production in neighbouring Greenford in the 1920s. For its part, Southall, which had a manufacturing history that extended back to Victorian times, flourished in the post-war period, attracting a large South Asian community there from the 1950s onwards.

The borough is now a melting pot of cultures and social classes, and a bustling suburban area, renowned for its large Irish, Polish and Asian communities.

ENFIELD

Enfield is the most northerly of London's boroughs, formed in 1965 from the municipal boroughs of Enfield, Edmonton and Southgate. Enfield and Edmonton can both trace their histories back to the Domesday Book and beyond. Indeed, Enfield was a small settlement that grew up along the Roman Ermine Street, which connected London to York. Roman artefacts have also been found in Edmonton and Bush Hill Park, which was the site of an Iron Age settlement dating to around 1200 BC.

In the Domesday Book, Enfield was recorded as a sizable habitation with a mill, fish ponds, and pasture for 2,000 pigs. It also had a park – a forested hunting ground formed from land that was deemed too intractable to cultivate. The enclosed Enfield Chase attracted wealthy Londoners, who first went there to hunt and then over time built homes where they could retreat from the crowded confines of the city. The

Crown acquired the Chase in 1399 and it became a royal hunting ground until 1777 when it was enclosed by a special Act of Parliament, apart from 152 acres that the Crown granted to the surveyor; the mansion he built for himself is now the clubhouse of the Hadley Wood Golf Club. As for the town of Enfield, it was given a boost in 1303 when Edward I awarded it a market charter (the weekly market continues to the present day), but its fortunes turned later in the fourteenth century when it was devastated by the Black Death. Enfield was also hit by the plague in the seventeenth century.

To the south, the lands of Edmonton were given to St Albans Abbey in the eighth century, and the area became an important strategic point during the Danish invasions of the ninth century. Like Enfield, Edmonton had a mill at the time of the Norman Conquest, and the Domesday Survey also reveals that there were eighty-seven inhabitants who had land or ploughs there. Much of the area consisted of meadow and woodland. A parish church was first built at Edmonton about 1140, and parts of the original fabric of the building have survived.

While Enfield suffered pestilence in the seventeenth century, Edmonton was struck by another plague of sorts that seemed to be sweeping the country in the same period: witchcraft. Elizabeth Sawyer, wife of an Edmonton labourer, was found guilty of killing by witchcraft and hanged at Tyburn. She was immortalised in not one but two Jacobean plays, *The Witch of Edmonton* and *The Merry Devil of Edmonton*.

In the early eighteenth century, Daniel Defoe noted that Edmonton was becoming quite a sizable community of the 'middle sort of mankind'. By the 1780s, a regular stagecoach service was transporting her newly prosperous residents and those of neighbouring Enfield into the City. The real impetus for growth, however, came in the middle of the nineteenth century when the railway began carrying passengers from Enfield and Edmonton to the city via Stratford. As with the stagecoaches, railway fares were initially beyond the reach of London's labourers, but in 1875 the Great Eastern Railway began running workmen's trains from Edmonton to Liverpool Street, opening up the area for a new wave of suburban development.

Southgate started out life as a hamlet that grew up at the south gate to Enfield Chase. It was known for its elegant mansions, and was at one time home to Sir John Moore, Lord Mayor of London in 1681. In 1881 it was combined with Winchmore Hill, Palmers Green and Bowes to form its own district separate from Edmonton. Before the First World War, Winchmore Hill was home to Herbert Goulden, brother of Emmeline Pankhurst, and the area became a centre for the suffragette movement. Palmers Green for its part was little more than a collection of cottages on Green Lanes until the railway came. It became extensively built up after the turn of the twentieth century. In 1933 the London Underground was extended to Southgate, and in the same year it became a municipal borough and received a royal charter.

The borough is perhaps most famous for its armaments production, such as the (until 1957) army standard-issue Lee-Enfield rifle and machine guns. Another claim to fame is that Barclays Bank in Enfield witnessed the installation of the world's first ATM in 1967.

GREENWICH

The borough was formed in 1965 from the metropolitan boroughs of Greenwich and Woolwich, becoming a royal borough in 2012.

A number of places in the borough were identified in the Domesday Survey. Greenwich itself first appears in written records in the tenth century (the name means 'green harbour or trading settlement') and achieved a measure of notoriety in the early eleventh century when a Viking army camped there; it proceeded to take the Archbishop of Canterbury hostage and then killed him when a ransom was not forthcoming. Later, Greenwich became the site of a royal palace, built in 1426 and particularly favoured some decades later by Henry VIII; during Christmas 1518 three queens stayed there: Catherine of Aragon, Margaret, Queen of Scots, and Mary, Queen of France. The palace fell into a state of disrepair after the English Civil War and was replaced by the Royal Hospital for Seamen, which was founded in 1694. Royal patronage was also responsible for the Royal Observatory, founded in 1675 by Charles II on the site of a medieval tower built by Humphrey, Duke of Gloucester, in 1433. Thereafter royal interest in Greenwich and its large park waned, James II being the last monarch to use Greenwich. The park was opened to the public in the eighteenth century and

Greenwich acquired an attractive array of Georgian houses, many of which survived the coming of the railways in the latter part of the following century.

Another important royal centre in the borough was Eltham. Mentioned in the Domesday Book, when the manor was held by one of William Conqueror's leading supporters, Odo, Bishop of Bayeux, it later came into the hands of Edward, Prince of Wales, son of Edward I, and was then extended by Edward II. In time, however, its popularity was eclipsed by the nearby palace at Greenwich and it gradually became very dilapidated. The village that grew up around it was transformed first by the railways and then, in the interwar period, by the building of the Eltham bypass.

Woolwich might not have been home to royalty, as Greenwich and Eltham were, but it was nevertheless favoured by them. It first appears in written records in 918, the name reflecting the importance of the wool trade to the area. It also marked an important Thames crossing point, and the first record of a ferry there dates from 1308. It was to be followed by a ferry established by the army in 1810 from the Woolwich Arsenal to Duvals Wharf and by the Woolwich Free Ferry, established in the 1880s. However, its transformation came with the foundation of the royal dockyard by Henry VIII in 1512 in order to build his flagship the *Great Harry* (probably destroyed by fire in 1554). The docks remained open until 1869, by which time quite a lot of industry had built up in the area – stoneware and glass in the seventeenth century, followed by the Royal Arsenal, which at its peak in the Second World War employed up to 40,000 workers.

Plumstead ('place where plum trees grow'), Charlton ('farmstead of the freemen') and Kidbrooke ('brook frequented by kites') are all early settlements transformed by suburbanisation. The little village of Plumstead was by the late nineteenth century providing housing for workers at Woolwich Arsenal. For its part, Charlton acquired the elegant Jacobean Charlton House, built for the tutor to James I's son, but by Victorian times was heavily industrialised; while the farming community at Kidbrooke gave way to Victorian housing to the north and extensive interwar development before becoming dominated by the Ferrier Estate in the 1970s.

HACKNEY

The borough was formed in 1965 from the metropolitan boroughs of Hackney, Shoreditch and Stoke Newington. Like its neighbour Tower Hamlets, it has had a very mixed history. Originally comprising marshes and arable fields, it was a fashionable residential area on the outskirts of built-up London in the sixteenth and seventeenth centuries, but then became increasingly industrialised and poverty-stricken by the late nineteenth century.

The names of several of the original settlements that now make up the borough, including Dalston, Homerton, Clapton, Hoxton and Stoke Newington, carry the Old English suffix *tūn*, indicating they were farmsteads or estates. Many were named for an early landholder, for example Homerton, which means 'farmstead of a woman called Hūnburh'. Hoxton, Stoke Newington and Haggerston are recorded in the Domesday Survey, while Shoreditch – the name harks back to a long-forgotten ditch leading to the river – and Stamford Hill first appear in the records in the twelfth and thirteenth centuries. During the Middle Ages, much of the land in the area belonged to the religious order of St John, while the manor of Stoke Newington was the property of the prebendary of St Paul's Cathedral. In the thirteenth century, wealthy London tradesmen began acquiring estates in Hackney. After the Dissolution of the Monasteries, the church's land, with the exception of the prebendary's holdings, was divided up and passed into the hands of the nobility. The area became a favoured retreat from the bustle of the City of London and the site of many grand houses of the Tudor and Stuart periods. The citizens of Hackney and Stoke Newington now counted aristocrats and courtiers among their numbers. Thanks to its location outside the highly regulated City of London, the area also became home to some of the first Elizabethan theatres, namely The Curtain in Shoreditch and The Theatre, which staged the first production of Shakespeare's *Romeo and Juliet*.

The area wasn't entirely given over to housing and entertainment for London's upper classes; its market gardens and nurseries supplied fruit and vegetables to the City from the sixteenth century onwards. By the early seventeenth century the villages of Hoxton and Stoke Newington were hugging the outer limits of the City, while other settlements remained detached – indeed Hackney remained largely rural right up until the early 1800s. In the second half of the seventeenth century, the area became a place of refuge, first for London citizens fleeing the devastation of the Great Fire in 1666 and then for Protestant refugees fleeing persecution in France and Germany. So began a tradition of immigration to the area that was continued in the nineteenth century when Jewish refugees arrived from Russia and Eastern Europe and which has persisted to the present day.

The 1700s saw coffee houses and fashionable private ladies' academies in Hackney, horse racing on Hackney Downs and bowling at Stoke Newington for City businessmen and their ladies, but the character of the area began to change as new, heavier industries such as chemicals and paint manufacturing were established. Shoreditch was rapidly becoming industrialised by the turn of the nineteenth century, driving the moneyed classes away and drawing in labourers to the area. By the 1860s, early plastic – parkesine – was being manufactured in Hackney Wick. Another local firm, confectionary and jam makers Clarke, Nickolls & Coombs, became the district's leading employer at the turn of the twentieth century. The clothing industry became an essential part of Hackney life, while Stoke Newington supplied the building trade with bricks and tiles. By 1904, Hackney had an estimated 374 factories and well over 800 workshops. Industrialisation was coupled with rapid housing development, much of it thrown up quickly and cheaply. In Charles Booth's 1898 survey of poverty in the capital, Hoxton's streets were classed as some of the poorest. Areas of Hackney, Homerton and Haggerston fared little better. In the 1890s, the Boundary Street area of Shoreditch was the site for the newly formed London County Council's first major slum clearance and rehousing project, in the course of which the Old Nichols rookery was cleared away and replaced by a central open area (Arnold Circus), from which seven tree-lined roads radiated. Social deprivation nevertheless persisted in the borough into the twentieth century, though the last few decades have witnessed the typical inner-London mix of regeneration schemes and large-scale housing estates.

HAMMERSMITH & FULHAM

The London borough of Hammersmith was formed in 1965 out of the metropolitan boroughs of Hammersmith and Fulham. The borough council added Fulham to its name in 1979.

While twentieth-century nomenclature would seem to suggest the dominance of Hammersmith over its neighbour, for nearly a millennium Hammersmith was merely an outpost belonging to the large manor of Fulham. Part of the Bishop of London's estates since the eighth century, the manor encompassed Fulham, Hammersmith, Ealing, Acton and Brentford as well as lands to the north of London at Hornsey and Finchley. The bishops' country and summer residence was at Fulham Palace, rebuilt in the sixteenth century. In the 1550s, the occupant was the powerful Bishop Edmund Bonner, who was closely involved in the persecution of Protestants during the reign of Mary I. Over time the bishops' lands were greatly reduced; after the Civil War even Fulham Palace passed from their ownership for a while.

The Hammersmith area, which takes its name from an old hammer forge or smithy, was in early times primarily arable and grazing land. At the northern end of the district, the Wormholt, from Old English meaning 'snake-infested thicket or wood', was cleared in the twelfth century to form what is now Wormwood Scrubs – in the early nineteenth century a place for pasturage, military exercises, highway robbery and duelling. In the late Middle Ages, rich City merchants and officials began eyeing estates in Hammersmith and the area acquired a number of mansions and villas over the following centuries. However, the establishment around the year 1500 of a leprosy hospital is proof that Hammersmith was regarded at that point as being well outside London and even in the 1600s it was home to only a relatively small number of residents. Hammersmith's strong association with Nonconformity began when Parliamentarian soldiers founded a religious community off the Broadway in the 1640s. Forty years later, Huguenot refugees established a chapel in Hammersmith and a Presbyterian meeting house opened on the Broadway in 1724. Baptist and Methodist chapels later joined them.

The bend in the Thames at Fulham provided ample shoreline from which to fish, an important source of income for local people right up until the early nineteenth century, and also a spur for the creation of a basket-making trade. Industry began appearing in Hammersmith and Fulham in the 1600s with potteries and later carpet factories in Fulham, a saltpetre factory at Sands End, and breweries at Walham Green and Hammersmith Creek. Meanwhile, fruit nurseries and market gardens began to replace traditional farms to meet the demand for fresh food in the capital, which was growing ever closer.

Daniel Defoe described Hammersmith in the 1720s as 'a well-to-do village which seems inclined to grow into a city'. Its importance grew after the opening of the Thames's first suspension bridge, connecting Hammersmith with Barnes, in the 1820s. Both Hammersmith and Fulham grew rapidly in the second half of the nineteenth century, their combined population mushrooming to nearly a quarter of a million inhabitants by 1901.

Other areas of the borough include Shepherd's Bush, for most of its history a village green with a handful of cottages and surrounded by farmland and market gardens, and Parsons Green, a small community that grew up around the Fulham parsonage at the west end of the green and which in the eighteenth century attracted well-heeled residents who built a number of grand houses. Ravenscourt Park was originally the manor of Paddingswick. The large fourteenth-century moated house there was rebuilt in the 1700s and renamed Ravenscourt by its new owner Thomas Corbett, Secretary to the Admiralty, whose coat of arms depicted a raven (inspired by the French word for the bird from which his surname derived). George Scott, who purchased the house in 1812 and was its last private owner, encouraged house building in and around the estate, and at the end of the century his family sold it to the Metropolitan Board of Works. The house became a municipal library, but was destroyed during the Second World War.

The borough played host to the first London Olympiad in 1908, building the stadium at short notice in White City. The area also hosted the Franco-British Exhibition, which attracted more attention than the games. However, the sites in White City were not developed after the two events, and it was not until the 1960s that the BBC moved in and opened the Television Centre. The redevelopment of the White City area has only recently been completed, with the opening of the major shopping centre Westfield London, along with improved transport links, in 2008. The borough is also home to three of the country's top football clubs: Chelsea, Fulham and Queens Park Rangers.

HARINGEY

The borough was formed in 1965 from the municipal boroughs of Hornsey, Wood Green and Tottenham. Among the first written mentions of the area is an account in the *Anglo-Saxon Chronicle* for 896 of the pursuit of Danish forces along the River Lea by King Alfred's men. Yet there are traces of far earlier settlement, and various Roman finds have been made. Two of the most prominent places in the borough were identified in the Domesday Book – the manors of Harringay (whose name was altered to Hornsey over time) and Tottenham.

Harringay was a largely rural area until the eighteenth century. Much of the land was covered with ancient woods, remnants of which are still to be found at Highgate Woods, Queen's Wood, and Coldfall Wood, though slowly areas of forest were cleared to make way for grassland. In the Middle Ages, the Bishop of London held the manor of Harringay/ Hornsey, though in the twelfth century the bishop gave to the Augustinian priory of St Mary at Clerkenwell the area that is now Muswell Hill, named for its ancient mossy spring or well and used by the nuns as a dairy farm. The Bishop of London also set up a toll gate to collect a fee from travellers passing over his estates via the Great North Road, giving rise to the name of Highgate. In time the wooded high ground of Highgate and Muswell Hill proved popular places for the well-to-do. Grand mansions began appearing at Highgate in the sixteenth and seventeenth centuries and mansion building spread to Muswell Hill in the eighteenth century.

Highgate gained its most famous landmark – and subsequently some of its most famous residents of the permanent variety – with the opening of Highgate cemetery in 1839. Muswell Hill acquired its own landmark, the Alexandra Palace, in 1873, a special railway line being created to bring day-trippers to the 'Ally Pally' (on 26 August 1936 the setting for the first television transmission from the BBC studios established there). Overall, though, the area was never particularly well served by the railway. Hornsey railway station, the first stop on the Great Northern line out of King's Cross, opened in 1850 serving Hornsey and Crouch End. However, the northern and western parts of the district were largely undisturbed by the steam age until the Hampstead Railway through Highgate (now London Underground's Northern Line) opened in 1907. In the twentieth century, Harringay became well known for its greyhound racing stadium, which opened in 1927.

In the manor and parish of Tottenham, the village and several hamlets grew up along an old Roman road (known as Tottenham Street in the medieval period). To the east, the marshlands of the River Lea provided rich pasture and grazing land. The Elizabethan manor house Bruce Castle was built by a branch of the powerful Scottish family that also produced the famed King of Scotland, Robert Bruce. The house is now the borough museum. The railway came to Tottenham in 1840, but the growth of the area as a London suburb really took off in the 1870s. The Northumberland Park neighbourhood of east Tottenham, which started to be laid out and developed in the 1850s, took its name from an association with the Dukes of Northumberland. Their celebrated antecedent Sir Henry Percy, known as Hotspur, also gave his name to the Tottenham Hotspur Football Club, founded in the 1880s.

Today, though it only covers a small eleven square miles, Haringey is one of the most diverse of the London boroughs, in both its geography and demographics. It contains some of the most prosperous places in the country, including Highgate, Muswell Hill and Crouch End, but in the east end of the borough are some of London's most deprived areas.

HARROW

The borough is the only one in Greater London whose boundaries were not changed in 1965; instead it retained those established when the urban district of Harrow was created in 1934.

In early times much of Harrow was woodland, with the lower areas of the borough covered in dense forest and light woodland and heath land on the various hills. Signs of industry in the Roman period, including a pottery at Brockley Hill in Stanmore and tile kilns at Canons Park, indicate early settlement in the area. In Saxon times, most of the land in the borough passed into ecclesiastical hands. The Mercian king Offa gave lands at Great Stanmore to St Albans Abbey in Hertfordshire and the large Harrow estate was the possession of the archbishops of Canterbury.

Harrow is recorded in the Domesday Survey as the largest manor in Middlesex. During the Middle Ages there were a handful of centres of settlement there, the largest of which was to become Harrow-on-the-Hill, whose parish church of St Mary's was begun in 1087 (it gained its famous spire in 1450) and which also hosted a medieval market. In 1545, the manor was appropriated by the Crown and was never returned to the church. A few years later came the founding of Sir John Lyon's free grammar school for local boys, which became the famous Harrow School. By the 1600s, Harrow-on-the-Hill was becoming a popular City retreat.

The settlement at Pinner – originally focused on the south-west side of Nower Hill (both names mean a 'flat-topped hill') – is first mentioned in the thirteenth century. It was an important village in the Harrow estate, with its own church and market (granted by Edward III in 1336). Clearance of the forests south and west of the village began in the twelfth and thirteenth centuries, though the archbishops' hunting enclosure at Pinner Park remained woodland for most of the Middle Ages. Pinner became an independent Anglican parish in 1766, by which time it had acquired an attractive collection of half-timbered sixteenth- and seventeenth-century houses and elegant Georgian dwellings.

The Weald, later known as Harrow Weald, was, as its name suggests, formerly a large area of forest, though a number of small tenements of arable land existed as early as the thirteenth century. Clearance of the woodland began from the southern end where the Harrow Weald settlement was established. In the eighteenth century it was home to the famous wealthy miser Daniel Dancer, who is said to have refused to incur the expense of cultivating his property, Waldo's Farm, fashioned clothes from hay and needlessly limited his sustenance to one meagre meal a day. Hatch End formed the boundary between the Weald and Pinner, its name denoting the hatch gate that gave access to Pinner's deer park. The Weald sarsen stone which marked the boundary between Harrow Weald and the other areas of the Harrow estate gave its name to the Wealdstone district.

At the time of Domesday, the Great Stanmore estate had been temporarily appropriated by William the Conqueror's half-brother Robert, Count of Mortain, but it was later returned to the Abbey of St Albans. The estate included Stanmore, the main settlement in the north-east of the present borough. Great Stanmore was united with Little Stanmore, which included the Canons estate, in the 1700s when the heavily wooded hillsides were being cleared. By then, like Harrow before it, Stanmore was attracting East India Company and London merchants, drawn by the convenience of the Edgware Road to build houses and grand mansions on the Canons estate. For its part, Bushey Heath was an extensive common and recognised in the 1500s as a dangerous area where robbery was rife. It was enclosed in 1809.

In the early 1800s, most of the region was still wooded or agricultural land, but in the late nineteenth and early twentieth century the London and North Western and Metropolitan District Railway lines began snaking their way across Harrow and Stanmore. Stations appeared at Harrow, Hatch End, Stanmore, Harrow-on-the-Hill, Harrow and Wealdstone, South Harrow and Rayner's Lane, each giving rise to suburban housing development. In the 1920s and 1930s, the area was publicised as part of Metroland and new housing grew up accordingly. The Air Ministry purchased Bentley Priory in Stanmore in 1926, which famously became the headquarters of the Royal Air Force's Fighter Command during the Battle of Britain.

HAVERING

The borough approximates roughly to the royal liberty of Havering, which was abolished in 1892. In 1965 it was re-created by combining the municipal borough of Romford and the urban district of Hornchurch. Lying at the far eastern extremity of Greater London, it is a mainly suburban borough with large areas of open space.

Evidence of Neolithic, Iron Age, Bronze Age and Roman settlements have been found in the area, and the Roman station of Durolitum appears to have been located within the vicinity of Romford (according to a Roman road book, *The Antonine Itinerary*). The royal roots of Havering can be traced back to the Anglo-Saxon period, when Havering Palace, and the surrounding land, was owned by the Crown. This was reputedly the main residence of Edward the Confessor and has been linked to a legend in which Edward the Confessor had a mystical ring returned to him there by St John the Apostle. The palace was then used by nearly every sovereign up to Stuart times. Towards the end of the Middle Ages, in 1465, came the creation of the royal liberty of Havering, taking in the parishes of Havering-atte-Bower, Hornchurch (so named after the appearance of the gables on the church) and Romford. At the time of Domesday these had formed the large manor of Havering. In the north, the woodlands were slowly cleared over time while the southern portion of the manor was dominated by the common marshlands at Hornchurch. Between were areas of mixed farming, though by the eighteenth century Havering was specialising in the growing of corn, and market gardens had appeared at Hornchurch.

Various trades have been pursued in the area over the centuries. In 1247 Henry III granted Romford a market charter, and the market, which became one of the largest in Essex, achieved a reputation for its locally produced leatherwear. In the eighteenth century the town was famed for its manufacture of leather breeches. Romford also became a significant coaching town, thanks to its location on the main road to London, and Ind Coope & Co's brewery was established there in 1799. In the eighteenth and nineteenth centuries, clay and gravel quarrying was carried out at South Ockendon, while ships at Rainham were exporting wool to Calais in the late fifteenth century, and it has been suggested that ships were actually built there too in the sixteenth century.

The suburbanisation of the borough occurred in two distinct waves: late Victorian and Edwardian, and interwar. Prosperous Londoners had been buying estates in Upminster since the mid seventeenth century, but it was the building of the railway line running through Havering to Liverpool Street that was responsible for the Victorian middle-class garden suburbs of Upminster, Emerson Park and Gidea Park. Interwar development was spurred on by the electrification of the underground railway line and its extension to Elm Park and Upminster Bridge. A number of important institutions opened in the same period, including Romford's Royal Liberty School at Hare Hall (dating back to 1768–9) in 1921, and Gidea Park College in the same decade. In 1939 St George's hospital, originally a home for the elderly known as Suttons Institution, opened in Hornchurch, which by now had a population of over 28,000.

During the First World War, Gidea Hall was used by the Army and the military airfield at RAF Hornchurch was deployed to defend London from Zeppelin raids. During the Second World War, Hornchurch became a base for the fighter squadrons that played a significant part in the Battle of France and the Battle of Britain. Dagenham Park was also used by the Army, and Harold Wood Hospital (opened originally in 1909 as the Grange Convalescent Home for Children) was used as an emergency hospital. Romford (which had become a municipal borough in 1937, with a new town hall) suffered heavy bombing between 1940 and 1945. Post-war developments included the establishment by the Ford Motor Company of a depot in South Ockendon, a new shopping precinct at Romford in 1972 and a new theatre at Hornchurch in 1975. More recently, the Royal Society for the Protection of Birds purchased 870 acres of Rainham Marshes, formerly a military firing range.

HILLINGDON

In the 1960s, when plans for borough restructuring were underway, Hillingdon was originally going to be named Uxbridge. It was formed out of the municipal borough of Uxbridge, and the urban districts of Hayes and Harlington, Ruislip and Northwood, and Yiewsley and West Drayton. It is the westernmost borough of Greater London, and is itself split between North and South Hillingdon. It is one of the less densely populated of London's boroughs.

Palaeolithic flint tools have been found in the Hayes area and evidence of an Early Iron Age settlement discovered north-east of Heathrow. Roman finds include sepulchres and indications of farming estates. There is little evidence of settlement in the North Ruislip area before the late Saxon period. At the time it was dense woodland; indeed, as late as 1289, 25 per cent of the annual income of the lords of Ruislip manor came from the selling of wood, some of which in the thirteenth century went to such royal buildings as the Tower of London and Windsor Castle. Early settlement at Ruislip appears to have been centred on the ancient Bath Road, which bisected the parish.

The Domesday Book records manors at Colham and Hillingdon. Arable farming took place here in the Middle Ages, along with some pig and dairy farming, though by the seventeenth century much of the area had been turned over to grassland to produce hay for the city. In the 1800s, orchards appeared, as did market gardens, and though the development of Heathrow Airport inevitably led to a decrease in their number, they continued to supply London markets into the 1960s. The small agricultural Uxbridge Show was started in 1909 and developed into what became the annual Middlesex Show. Between the 1930s and 1950s the largest cut-flower firm in the country was based in Uxbridge.

Uxbridge itself grew up at a strategic crossing over the River Colne on the main trade route from Middlesex to Buckinghamshire, a bridge there recorded as being in a ruinous state in 1377 (it was repaired many times subsequently). From the twelfth century the village of Uxbridge was a commercial centre, granted a weekly market around 1189 and from the thirteenth century it hosted fairs on St Margaret's Day and at Michaelmas. Its prosperity was also aided by watermills, of which there were some thirteen along the Colne and Frays rivers in the sixteenth century. During Mary's reign several 'heretics' were burned here in the 1550s, while in the following century Uxbridge's convenient location between the Royalist headquarters in Oxford and Parliamentarian London resulted in peace treaty negotiations being held there. However, when the Great Western Railway decided to open its first outer-London station at West Drayton in 1838, Uxbridge and its various coaching inns were eclipsed. Transport links greatly improved during the early twentieth century, and Underground extensions to Uxbridge (the Metropolitan Line in 1904 and the Piccadilly Line in 1933) led to further suburban development. Cricket is mentioned as having been played on Uxbridge Moor in 1735, and Uxbridge duly became home to the oldest cricket club in Middlesex.

Sparsely settled for most of its history, with much of the area given over to farmland, Northwood's expansion only really came in the aftermath of the opening of Northwood station in 1887. There are, however, references to tile kilns in the area in the late fourteenth century and brick-making was an important local industry from the sixteenth century onwards. An extension to the Grand Junction Canal helped stimulate the trade, but by the beginning of the twentieth century the brickfields and the secondary industry of gravel and sand extraction were in decline. Twentieth-century industry was also to be found in Hayes, notable firms there including EMI and Heinz.

HOUNSLOW

The borough was formed in 1965 by the merger of three urban districts: Brentford and Chiswick, Feltham, and Heston and Isleworth.

At the time of the Roman invasion of Britain, Bedfont and Brentford were the main areas of settlement in the district, and Brentford became a significant Roman-British site. Various villages then grew up around the Roman road that ran to Silchester via Staines. A simple rectangular hut, excavated on the High Street, provides the only evidence of later Saxon settlement in Brentford, but a letter from the Bishop of London in 705 records a meeting there between the Kings of Wessex and Essex and in 790 King Offa of Mercia held a council there. Its strategic importance as a river crossing was demonstrated in 1016 when King Edmund Ironside and King Canute fought a battle there. Chiswick and Isleworth were also Anglo-Saxon settlements on the river, Chiswick's name probably meaning 'cheese farm' and Isleworth being a settlement belonging to a man named Gislhere.

Throughout this period and for a long time after the area was dominated by Hounslow Heath, though by the time of the Domesday Book a handful of villages had begun to appear on or around the heathland, including Feltham, Isleworth, Hanworth, Hounslow and Cranford. In 1545 the estimated extent of the heath was over 4,000 acres and an attempt was made to enclose it and apportion it among the various neighbouring parishes. This process, however, was not completed until the eighteenth century. The heath was primarily used for pasture, though it was also popular with sportsmen: James I is known to have hawked on the heath; William III had a hunting lodge at Hounslow manor house; and prize-fighting and duelling are also known to have taken place. Arable farming was conducted beyond the heath at Cranford, where there were four fields in the seventeenth century, and there were open fields at Heston and Isleworth until the fifteenth century, when early enclosures began around the monastery at Syon, which moved here in 1431 a few years after it had been founded by Henry V at Twickenham. But over time there was a gradual transition to orchards and market gardens in many places – for example, in Brentford, where by the late sixteenth century they were taking over from grassland, and in Chiswick, where by 1746 most of the parish comprised market gardens and orchards. Chiswick was also home to Fromows nursery gardens between 1829 and the 1970s. Isleworth had dozens of market gardens in the 1830s, and in 1837–8 terraced houses were built specifically for those who worked in the gardens.

Fishing was an important early feature of the borough. It was first recorded in Brentford in 996, and in 1257 Henry III commanded the Bailiff of Brentford to supply fish for the royal kitchen. In 1181 St Paul's Cathedral charged five shillings a year for fishing at Chiswick or for every tenth fish caught. In time, though, more substantial industries started to be built up. It is likely that the paper mill built within the Osterley Park estate in 1575 was one of the first of its kind in the country. A survey of Brentford in 1792 shows that a soap works, lime kilns and a leather tanner were operating there, among other businesses. The Chiswick Press, specialising in high-quality, affordable small books, was founded in 1809 by Charles Whittingham. In 1820, Messers J. & G. Barlow won the contract to light (by gas) the Turnpike Road from Kensington to Hounslow. The small gasworks that they built on the riverside was absorbed into the Brentford Gas Company in 1821, which supplied most of the parish of Chiswick by 1859. As for the town of Hounslow, its location at the beginning of the Great South-West Road (now the A30) ensured its development, but it was not until Heathrow Airport was established that it started to experience expansion on a major scale. Other areas of the borough closer to the river, such as Chiswick, were transformed rather earlier when the railways arrived, and many of Chiswick's grander houses, such as Sutton Court, were demolished in the late nineteenth century and early twentieth century to make way for denser developments of houses and flats.

ISLINGTON

Formed in 1965 by bringing together the metropolitan boroughs of Islington and Finsbury, the modern borough is one of the capital's smallest. It is also crowded, bustling and multi-faceted.

A Roman road from Cripplegate, in the City, to St Albans probably ran through the area, but the earliest recorded settlements at Islington and Tollington (near the area now associated with Arsenal football club) date from around 1000. In the Middle Ages the area was scattered with a number of manors that have become familiar names – not only Islington, but also Barnsbury, Canonbury and Highbury. Much of the land was divided among the religious houses of London. Tollington was part of the lands of the priories of St John of Jerusalem and St Mary, Clerkenwell; the canons of St Paul's held lands in Islington; and the manor of Barnsbury was in the possession of the Bishop of London. The bishop's tenants were the de Berners family (originally from Normandy) who gave their name to the manor and held sway in Islington well into the thirteenth century. It was a Ralph de Berners who granted land in Islington to the canons of St Bartholomew's Priory at Smithfield probably in the twelfth century, and by the 1300s the area was known as Canonesbury. The manor of Highbury was known originally as Newenton Barwe, indicating its connection to the neighbouring parish of Stoke Newington, but by 1375 its position on the higher ground above Barnsbury and Canonbury had given rise to its current name.

The various manors were a mix of arable, meadow and grazing land, though Highbury was mainly arable. By the eighteenth century, dairy farming was popular and Islington was responsible for much of London's milk supply well into the nineteenth century. There were woodlands at Tollington and Barnsbury at the time of Domesday, but these seem to have disappeared during the Middle Ages. Nevertheless, in the sixteenth century some tenements at Holloway still contained mature trees, and Highbury contained some woodland, though it was being rapidly encroached upon. By 1710, only twenty-five acres remained.

Clerkenwell lay just north of the old City of London walls and was home to a number of religious houses, including the Charterhouse and the priories of St Mary and St John of Jerusalem. Medieval clerks or scholars drew water from the ancient wells which gave the district its name, and an account from 1174 describes summer-evening gatherings of students and youths at these early watering holes. By 1430 the religious houses were piping fresher water down from Barnsbury and Islington. In the sixteenth century the religious houses were suppressed. Then, as the capital grew beyond the bounds of the City walls, Clerkenwell became one of its first residential suburbs. The year 1665 saw the opening of the dissenters' cemetery at Bunhill Fields, where John Bunyan, Daniel Defoe and William Blake are buried. After the Great Fire, Clerkenwell began to acquire some local industry and continued to do so through the eighteenth and nineteenth centuries.

Similarly Islington, which had grown into a prosperous residential suburb around the turn of the nineteenth century, began to experience industrial development as factories for printers' ink, India rubber, varnish, white lead and other noxious products began to spread across the area and into Holloway. In the process the 'merry Islington' of earlier times – home to pleasure gardens and fine houses – became overcrowded, with run-down housing and slums. By the turn of the twentieth century it had the largest population and worst overcrowding of all the newly formed metropolitan boroughs. To the north, Holloway (the name means 'hollow road' and refers to the low-lying section of the Great North Road between Highgate and Islington) underwent a similar transformation, becoming heavily built up by the 1860s. Tufnell Park, too, exchanged its manor house (on the junction of Tufnell Park and Holloway Roads) for intensive Victorian housing. The borough's Holloway Prison was opened in 1852, its gateway modelled on that of Warwick Castle. Since 1902 it has been the country's main women's prison, Mrs Pankhurst and other suffragettes being held there in the early 1900s.

Islington experienced a decline in the early decades of the twentieth century, but regeneration of the borough's most run-down areas and restoration of its Georgian and Victorian housing stock has led to a revival in prosperity in recent times. By 2001, it was once again one of London's most populous boroughs.

KENSINGTON & CHELSEA

In 1965 it was initially decided that the new borough should be called simply the Royal Borough of Kensington, perpetuating Kensington's royal-borough status, but neighbouring inhabitants were unimpressed, and so Chelsea was duly joined to the name. Today Kensington and Chelsea is one of the two wealthiest boroughs in the country; it is also its most densely populated.

A manor at Kensington is recorded in the Domesday Survey. Its lords were the de Vere family (made Earls of Oxford in 1155), who held the land until the sixteenth century. Their manor house and the manor court were situated in the area now known as Earl's Court. In time, a small settlement established itself around Kensington's parish church of St Mary Abbots (the church was first recorded in 1242), while a village grew up around the church of All Saints in Chelsea (a church certainly existed in Chelsea by the end of the eighth century, and Offa, King of the Mercians, held a synod in Chelsea in around 787). At the northern end of the present borough the manor of Notting Barns was also held by the de Veres until the Wars of the Roses, when Edward IV had the twelfth Earl executed for supporting the Lancastrian side and the manor was forfeited.

The first connection between the borough and royalty was forged by

Henry VIII, who bought the manor of Chelsea in the 1530s. He built the manor house which then became home to the young princess Elizabeth and Lady Jane Grey, both of whom would be queen (briefly, in the case of Lady Jane Grey). Chelsea also attracted several high-ranking nobles in the Tudor period, earning it the epithet 'Village of Palaces'. In the early seventeenth century, grand aristocratic houses also began appearing in Kensington. The magnificent Holland House was one such, built by Sir Walter Cope (James I's Chamberlain of the Exchequer) around 1604 and then forfeited by his son-in-law Lord Holland in 1648 for making the mistake of picking the wrong side in the Civil War. Holland House was appropriated as temporary headquarters for the Parliamentarians before being returned to the Hollands at the Restoration. Later in the century, in 1689, William III, seeking a new rural residence that would help relieve his asthma, settled on Nottingham House, at the time in open countryside, and remodelled it into Kensington Palace. The palace remained a favoured residence of the monarchy until George II's day. Royal patronage also remodelled the village of Kensington, attracting new shops and various craftsmen. It began to look a bit like the fashionable West End.

The area nevertheless retained a strongly rural feel. Chelsea, Brompton and Kensington were all known for their market gardens in the seventeenth century. In Chelsea, the Physic Garden, the oldest surviving in the world, was founded in 1673, while Brompton Park Nursery opened in 1681. In the nineteenth century, though, the West End and points further west converged. In 1800 Kensington was home to under 10,000 people; by the end of Queen Victoria's reign over 175,000 people lived there. Profits from the highly successful Great Exhibition of 1851, held in Hyde Park, went to develop land at 'Albertopolis', the area of South Kensington which now forms the capital's main museum district. Kensington may have lost a degree of its former royal shine when the palace was given over to minor royals, but it was nevertheless referred to in the nineteenth century as 'The Old Court Suburb' and retained an air of exclusivity. Chelsea was similarly home to the well-to-do, even if it did not have quite the cachet of Kensington. Further north the picture was more mixed: Notting Hill had its fine houses, but it also contained slums, particularly in the 'Piggeries and Potteries' area of Notting Dale.

Both Kensington and Chelsea preserved their genteel image into the twentieth century. The borough was quite heavily bombed during the Second World War, resulting in 800 deaths and the destruction of Chelsea Old Church, Sloane Square station, Holland House and many other buildings. Despite the gentrification of such areas as Notting Hill, however, the contrast between the well-to-do and the more deprived areas of the borough remains marked.

KINGSTON UPON THAMES

The royal borough is the oldest of the three royal boroughs in England, retaining its status when the municipal borough of Kingston upon Thames merged in 1965 with the boroughs of Malden and Coombe, and Surbiton.

The borough is dominated by the ancient town of Kingston upon Thames, which, according to legend, was the site of the coronation of seven Anglo-Saxon kings. The manor of Kingston was the possession of the king until it passed by charter in 1200 to freemen of the borough. Home to five watermills at the time of the Domesday Survey, it was a significant market town in the Middle Ages and the site of a very important river crossing (the bridge at Kingston is first recorded in the early thirteenth century). The water-hungry industries of malting and brewing as well as tanning are recorded there by the sixteenth and seventeenth centuries, and by the mid nineteenth century the town was home to a substantial population of 8,000. The river afforded entertainment and leisure as well as serving local industry, and the Kingston Rowing Club was formed in 1858 (the regatta actually dates from a year earlier).

The gentle undulation of the south-western boundary of Greater London is noticeably disturbed by a detour around Chessington parish, a long finger of territory that stretches out into Surrey. Chessington was recorded in Domesday and the manor of Chessington together with that of Malden were given to Merton College, Oxford, upon its foundation in the thirteenth century. The estate became known as Chessington Park. There was farmland at Chessington, but much of the parish was woodland – some of it preserved to the present day. The village's grandest house, Chessington Hall, is associated with the musicologist Charles Burney and his daughter Fanny Burney, who is thought to have written much of her novel *Cecilia* while staying at the house. In the 1880s, Chessington was described as a quiet, secluded village, undisturbed by the railways and suburban development. However, the Hall was demolished in the 1960s to make way for housing. Chessington Zoo opened in 1931.

Norbiton and Surbiton both appear in records about 1200, their names distinguishing between the northern and southern farms of the royal manor at Kingston. In addition to farming, there were fish ponds at Surbiton and there was also a local brick-making industry. Surbiton Common witnessed one of the last gasps of the Royalist cause during the Civil War when in 1648 troops loyal to King Charles under the command of the Earl of Holland were swiftly and thoroughly beaten in a skirmish. Several officers were captured or killed and Royalist hopes of raising a rebellion in Surrey were dashed. In the mid nineteenth century the railway was originally routed through Surbiton to protect coaching traffic at Kingston, and as a result what had been a hamlet since the twelfth century grew by 1880 into a suburb of 10,000 residents. It became celebrated for its wide, tree-lined streets and riverside promenade, and home to a prosperous population.

Coombe ('valley') and Tolworth ('enclosed settlement of a man named Tala') are both mentioned in Domesday. The manor of Coombe was granted to Merton Abbey in 1423, which also held lands in Tolworth, while ownership of the manor of Tolworth passed through many hands, including those of the earls of Kent and Westmorland, in the Middle Ages. Like Surbiton, Tolworth remained a small settlement until the late nineteenth century when the streets became lined with villas. Agriculture defined the district of Motspur Park in the 1620s when it was recorded as Motes Firs Ferm, and farming continued at Berrylands into the twentieth century, though the district gradually became residential.

LAMBETH

The precise limits of the current borough proved a bone of contention in 1965, when it was debated whether the metropolitan boroughs of Lambeth and Southwark should merge. Eventually, however, it was decided that Lambeth should merge with part of the metropolitan borough of

Wandsworth. The borough extends from the riverbank and the railway terminus at Waterloo down through Vauxhall, Clapham and Brixton to Streatham and West Norwood at its southern extremity.

At its medieval heart, Lambeth was the residence of the bishops of London, who kept a watchful eye on the palaces of Westminster and Whitehall across the river. A ferry to Westminster existed in Roman times and a horse ferry linked Lambeth with Westminster from as early as the twelfth century. The boatmen made their home on the Lambeth shore. Much of the area's marshland was drained in the thirteenth century, though flooding remained a danger. The main settlement was Water Lambeth – home to the Dukes of Norfolk, who controlled much of the area until they sold it in the mid sixteenth century. From this point, Lambeth became increasingly industrial, acquiring Dutch-style potteries and then London's first sawmill, set up here during the Commonwealth and so novel that it warranted a visit from Oliver Cromwell, then Lord Protector. The remainder of Lambeth Marsh was drained in the eighteenth century, creating the area around Lower Marsh. The botanist William Curtis established the London Botanic Garden at Lambeth Marsh in 1779 but, owing to smoke pollution, decided to move the plants to a larger garden in Brompton in 1789. The Prince Regent opened a new bridge across the Thames in 1817, naming it Waterloo in honour of the recent victory over Napoleon, and the railway terminus that derived its name from the bridge was later built on the site of the former botanic gardens. During the course of the century, many people seeking to escape rural poverty came to settle in Lambeth, which degenerated into a slum area.

Further south, the Domesday Survey described settlements at Kennington, Brixton and Streatham. In the Middle Ages Kennington was the site of a royal palace, but much of the area remained open land until the late nineteenth century, one notable green space being St George's Fields (today's St George's Circus preserves the name). The road south from Kennington led next to Brixton, whose Saxon name suggests that a stone once stood here that marked the meeting place of the Saxon hundred court. Seventeenth-century justice saw the setting up of a gallows at Brixton to dispose of highwaymen who preyed on the Croydon road. In 1818 a Surrey house of correction was established in the neighbourhood (with another at Guildford), which after various vicissitudes became Brixton Prison. Brixton itself started to evolve in the early nineteenth century, becoming ever more densely built up after the coming of the railways.

Further down the main road, Streatham was dominated by its common, which once encompassed a far greater area. Much of the parish remained arable land (some given over to pasture) right into the nineteenth century, but the village also proved popular with City merchants, particularly when a spring was discovered in Streatham Common in the 1650s; the spa that grew up around it remained a fashionable attraction until the late eighteenth century.

On the main road to Tooting the manor of Stockwell was certainly in existence by the twelfth century, although it is not mentioned in the Domesday Book. As its name suggests, it was once wooded ('stock' means a tree trunk), but by the seventeenth century it was being cleared to make way for fields. Clapham is mentioned in Domesday, and grew up around the site of St Paul's church. It remained a small village until the seventeenth century, when it started to prove an attractive country retreat for Londoners. One early prominent citizen was Dr Henry Atkins, physician to James I, who purchased the manor of Clapham for £6,000 in the early seventeenth century. Dominating the area is Clapham Common, which was drained in the early seventeenth century. Fairs were regularly held there until the 1870s, the same decade that it was preserved for posterity by being purchased by the Metropolitan Board of Works.

Much of the Lambeth area was primarily agricultural until the nineteenth century, but there were industrial parts to it as well. Vauxhall was one such (it took its name from the hall belonging to Falkes de Bréauté, regarded variously as a loyal supporter of King John or an 'evil robber'). While it became famous in the seventeenth and eighteenth centuries for its pleasure gardens, it was also home to a distillery and glassworks, among other businesses. In the nineteenth century other areas of the borough also acquired commercial enterprises, as well as becoming increasingly built up. A street market developed at Brixton in the 1870s, for example, and the capital's first purpose-built department store opened its doors there in 1877. Streatham High Street also became a commercial centre from the 1870s onwards.

Heavy bombing during the Second World War led to major redevelopment as well as slum clearance, and by 1981 nearly half the borough's households resided in council-built housing.

LEWISHAM

The borough was created in 1965 by amalgamating the metropolitan boroughs of Deptford and Lewisham, an area that had been part of Kent until the creation of the County of London in 1889. It stretches from the old waterfront community at Deptford to the heights of Sydenham Hill and Crystal Palace, taking in Brockley, Lewisham, Hither Green, Lee, Downham, Catford, Bellingham and Forest Hill in between.

Deptford, so-called after a deep ford over the River Ravensbourne, was originally a small fishing village. Henry VIII created the royal dock here in the early 1500s where initially much of the English navy was built and repaired. This attracted the development of private docks, and Deptford became a centre for shipbuilding and the loading of cargo. In the 1830s the area was traversed by London's first suburban railway line, from London Bridge to Greenwich. To the west of Deptford is New Cross on the former Surrey–Kent border, where the old Watling Street from Canterbury and Dartford joined the road coming up from Lewisham on their way towards London.

To the south, the borough consisted of valleys along the Ravensbourne flanked by wooded hills and heathland. The area is not associated with particularly ancient occupation, but there were certainly Saxon communities at Bellingham and Lewisham: a daughter or niece of Alfred the Great gave her lands at Lewisham to the Abbey of St Peter in Ghent, who still possessed them at the time of Domesday and for a considerable time afterwards (a priory was also established locally). With eleven mills recorded in Domesday, Lewisham was clearly already a place of industry, but with its low and mostly flat land, watered by the Ravensbourne and its feeders, it was, like Lee (also recorded in Domesday), mostly composed of rich meadow and pasture land. During the Wars of the Roses, lands at Lee and Lewisham came into the possession of Richard Woodville, made Earl Rivers and Constable of England after Edward IV married his daughter Elizabeth. They passed in time to Elizabeth's son Sir Thomas Grey.

To the south lies Hither Green, known in the medieval period as Rumbergh, meaning 'wide hill or barrow'. At Brockley, on the west side of the borough, the area was heavily wooded until the eighteenth century; and in the sixteenth century the timber from the woods on top of Sydenham Hill was ordered by Elizabeth I to be reserved for shipbuilding.

Above Lewisham to the north-east sits Blackheath, traditionally an area where people gathered – invading Danes, royal armies, bands of rebels. It was also a place where the London citizenry greeted returning kings and where royal parties met foreign dignitaries as they approached the capital. In 1540, Henry VIII rode out to meet his fourth bride, Anne of Cleves, on Blackheath. He was not impressed, and the marriage was a short one. In the seventeenth and eighteenth centuries, Blackheath was a notorious highwaymen's haunt. More usefully, the lonely high ground was also given over to a number of windmills.

In the same period the village of Lewisham was starting to expand and by the end of the eighteenth century it had become a bustling area, home to a number of well-to-do London merchants. Once the railways came, existing villages grew and new residential developments took shape in areas such as Blackheath Park, Blackheath Vale, Ladywell and Sydenham Hill. Catford, an old ford on the River Ravensbourne, was typical in this regard: a small rural hamlet, it was transformed after the 1850s when the suburban railways were extended across the district. Gradually, new parks were laid out in the area and the Ladywell Recreation Ground was purchased for the parish in 1889. In the twentieth century some open spaces succumbed to new development, such as the London County Council housing estate at Downham.

MERTON

The borough was formed in 1965 from the municipal boroughs of Mitcham and Wimbledon, and the urban district of Merton and Morden.

That Wimbledon was home to early man is indicated by the discovery of Palaeolithic flint tools and Mesolithic implements such as stone knives in the area. A pre-Roman hill fort, misleadingly known as Caesar's Camp, lies on the high ground of what is now Wimbledon Common and a pre-Roman track crossed the area. The name Wimbledon originated in the Saxon period as Wunemannedune, 'the hill of the man called Wynnmann', and the common at Wymbyldon was recorded in 1490. The area came to the notice of the City in the 1540s, when Henry VIII granted the manor of Wimbledon to his sixth and final wife, Katherine Parr. Soon well-to-do residents, including Elizabethan statesman Sir Thomas Cecil, were making their home in the area. Cecil's house, Wimbledon House, was destroyed by an accidental explosion of gunpowder in 1628 but was subsequently rebuilt and was, by all accounts, a grand affair; decorated with frescos, it was said to rival the nearby royal palace at Nonsuch. Wimbledon's ancient common was safeguarded by an Act of Parliament in 1871, and a few decades later in 1907 Wimbledon Park was opened. South of these lie a built-up area that grew around the junction of the London and South-Western and London, Brighton and South Coast railways.

To the south of Wimbledon are the old Surrey parishes of Mitcham, Merton and Morden. Of these, Merton was the largest community at the time of the Norman Conquest. Situated where the Roman road from London to Chichester crossed the river, it was a natural stop-over point for early travellers. In the Domesday Book it was recorded as being the property of the king, and its famous priory was founded during the reign of his son Henry I. Some 300 years later, it would witness the coronation of his namesake, Henry VI, the first English king since the Conquest not to be crowned at Westminster Abbey. In the course of the eighteenth century, its location on the river made it attractive to dye works, mills and metalworking. In late Victorian times, two of Britain's best-known Arts and Crafts manufacturers, William Morris and the Liberty Company, established works at Merton Abbey Mills, where they produced hand-printed fabrics as well as furnishings and stained glass. Around the same time, City businessman John Innes developed the residential garden suburb of Merton Park on former agricultural land. Collier's Wood also had an industrial heritage, being an important source of charcoal in the Middle Ages.

While Merton's suburban transformation began in the nineteenth century, Morden remained largely pasture land until the 1920s when the London Underground established a station there. Raynes Park was similarly transformed by the railway when a station opened there in 1871; its name derives from Edward Rayne, who was a former landowner in the area.

The River Wandle separates Merton and Morden from their neighbour Mitcham to the east. Roman graves at Mitcham point to an early settlement, and it was also an important place of burial in the Saxon period.

The lands at Mitcham were granted to Chertsey Abbey in 727 and it is recorded in the Domesday Book. In the sixteenth and seventeenth centuries Mitcham was home to such luminaries as Sir Walter Raleigh and Sir Julius Caesar (Master of the Rolls) and it is known that Sir Julius entertained Elizabeth I there at very considerable personal expense. Nevertheless, most of the parish remained pasture land, while the extensive physic gardens founded in the 1700s grew medicinal herbs that were still famous in the late Victorian era. It was not until the railways and tramways began criss-crossing the area in the mid nineteenth century that the population of the area rose sharply.

NEWHAM

Newham is one of the most culturally diverse of all the London boroughs, formed in 1965 from the two Essex county boroughs of East Ham and West Ham, along with North Woolwich and a small part of the municipal borough of Barking.

'Hame' – meaning 'area of land bounded by marsh or water' – is recorded as one large estate in the Domesday Survey, though by the twelfth century both East and West Ham had emerged. The area was extensively farmed, much of the once-extensive woodland at East Ham having been cleared by the thirteenth century, and it's clear that by the following century the soil had been overworked and was declining in fertility. In the later Middle Ages, livestock rearing became increasingly important, meat being butchered for sale in the City. The area was also home to the abbey of Stratford Langthorne, also known as West Ham Abbey, founded in 1135. The fact that this was a Cistercian house, and that the Cistercians favoured remote sites, suggests that at this time West Ham would have been sparsely populated. The abbey, one of the largest of all Cistercian foundations, was dissolved in the sixteenth century. A number of grain mills lay on the branches of the River Lea that form the borough's western border and the ancient dividing line between the counties of Middlesex and Essex (eight were recorded in Domesday). In the Elizabethan period, gunpowder mills were opened, and in the following century calico printing also became an important local industry.

At this time, West Ham parish was more populous and industrialised than its eastern neighbour, with Plaistow the largest village in the area, home to agriculture and also silk weaving and leather working. In the 1760s an important botanical garden was established at Upton House in West Ham by Dr John Fothergill, physician and friend to American diplomat and scientist Benjamin Franklin during his many years in London. There Dr Fothergill experimented with exotic plants for both medicine and food. In East Ham, meanwhile, less exotic crops such as potatoes and turnips were being grown, forming the basis of what was to become a flourishing vegetable-growing industry. East Ham also attracted its own luminaries. In 1809 the celebrated prison reformer Elizabeth Fry took up residence at Plashet House; her daughter Katherine wrote one of the borough's first comprehensive local histories.

The more familiar industrialised landscape of West and East Ham really began to take shape in the mid nineteenth century. The 1850s was a boom time for West Ham, with the establishment of the industrial estate at Canning Town, the rubber works of S. W. Silver & Co on the waterfront at Silvertown, and the opening in 1855 of the Royal Victoria Dock. East Ham began to catch up, with the opening of Beckton Gas Light and Coke Company in 1870 and the Royal Albert Dock in 1880. At the outbreak of the Second World War, nearly 48,000 residents were evacuated in anticipation of the heavy bombing that devastated much of the area. Many opted not to return, and in the early 1950s West Ham's population was only half what it had been in 1939. In the 1960s and 1970s the area suffered industrial decline, notably at Stratford and in the docks, but in 1981 the Dockland Development Corporation began the task of regeneration. In 1987 the borough's London City Airport opened on former dockland.

REDBRIDGE

The municipal boroughs of Ilford, Wanstead and Woodford merged in 1965 and joined with parts of Dagenham and the urban district of Chigwell to form the London borough of Redbridge. The name was not derived from an existing administrative district but from a red-brick bridge over the River Roding that had been demolished in the 1920s.

The administrative centre of the borough is at Ilford, a site that has been occupied since ancient times. It grew up along the Great Essex Road from London to Colchester, its name indicating the place where the road crossed the River Roding (once known as the River Hyle), which flows through Barking to the Thames. There was a stone bridge at Ilford from at least the early fourteenth century, and Ilford itself is first mentioned by name in a tenth-century Saxon charter. The area was part of the ancient parish of Barking, and the manor of Ilford is recorded in Domesday. In the Middle Ages there was a village there with a small network of roads connecting it with Barking and various hamlets and farms, including Little Heath and Barkingside, along the edges of Hainault Forest. Ilford was home to the medieval Hospital and Chapel of St Mary, which was founded in the twelfth century by Adeliza, sister to one of Henry I's justices, and supported by landholdings in the area. Unusually, the hospital survived the Dissolution and continued into the twentieth century. The village grew in the eighteenth century as a number of fine houses were built in the district, and a twice-daily stagecoach to London started to operate. The Eastern Counties Railway came through Ilford in 1839, adding further links with the city and ultimately instigating its rapid growth into a town and suburb between 1880 and 1910.

Wanstead was a Roman settlement and at the time of Domesday contained two manors, which comprised woodland for 450 swine, a number of small forest hamlets, and a saltpan and mill at Aldersbrook. Clerkenwell Priory acquired the mill in the twelfth century. Though small farms and areas of arable land grew up and part of the lower forest was heath used to pasture sheep and cattle, most of Wanstead remained woodland right up into the nineteenth century. In 1499 Henry VII acquired Wanstead Park, and a few years later it was enclosed, the medieval hall that stood there serving as a hunting lodge. From 1549 the estate belonged to Lord Richard Rich, who rebuilt the manor house and made Wanstead his country residence. Later, Robert Dudley, a favourite of Elizabeth I, bought Wanstead and it became a fashionable place of recreation for the capital's elite. Dudley entertained Elizabeth here, and her successor James I visited on multiple occasions. Royal connections continued into the eighteenth and nineteenth centuries, when Wanstead House provided refuge to Louis Joseph, the Prince de Condé, who had fled revolution in France. The future Louis XVIII of France also stayed here.

To the north, the neighbouring district of Woodford is also recorded in Domesday – a cluster of hamlets that grew up along the High Road. Later a village was established at Woodford Bridge, at a ford on the Roding. In the fifteenth century the wooded landscape attracted wealthy Londoners to the area, and they duly began to build mansions here. It also proved a popular summertime retreat, and renting accommodation could be an expensive affair, prices being close to those of London. The Woodford loop of the Great Eastern Railway opened in 1862, bringing the middle classes to the area. However, Wanstead was never extensively developed and much of what was built was influenced by the garden-suburb ethos. Patches of the ancient woodlands are still enjoyed by the borough's modern residents.

Cranbrook and Snaresbrook both derive their name from the borough's many watercourses. The manor of Cranbrook ('brook frequented by cranes') is first mentioned in the thirteenth century and the area is named for the Cran Brook, which rises in Barkingside. Snaresbrook, originally Sayesbrook, and so possibly named after a person, is a tributary of the Roding, which rises north-west of Wanstead and gives its name to the local district. Parts of the ancient Epping Forest also survive at Snaresbrook.

RICHMOND UPON THAMES

The borough was formed by merging the municipal boroughs of Twickenham, Richmond and Barnes in 1965, and it is the only London borough to straddle both sides of the River Thames. Famed for its royal links and rich history, it includes some of the more exclusive suburban areas of London, as well as the green spaces of Kew Gardens, Richmond Park, Bushy Park and Hampton Court Park.

The Saxons called the area at Richmond *Shene*, and it was known as Sheen until the sixteenth century. The first record of a settlement there dates from 950, and at the time of the Domesday Survey it was part of the royal manor of Kingston. In the 1290s a separate manor of Sheen was granted to Edward, Prince of Wales, and as King Edward II he went on to establish his court there. The manor house was later home to Edward's widow Isabella, the notorious She-Wolf of France. After her death in

1358, their son Edward III made it into a royal palace. Sheen Palace was destroyed on the orders of Richard II, devastated by the death of his wife Anne there in 1394, but in the early fifteenth century Henry V rebuilt it and confirmed royal interest in the area by founding three religious houses, including a Carthusian monastery, Sheen Priory.

The palace was badly damaged by fire in 1497, but was then rebuilt by Henry VII, who rechristened it with the name of his Yorkshire earldom Richmond in 1501. His son Henry VIII staged lavish entertainments there, and at the Dissolution of the Monasteries gave Sheen Priory to his brother-in-law Edward Seymour (later Lord Protector to Henry's son Edward VI), who made it into a private residence. After Seymour's fall from grace in 1549, the lord protectorship and base of power shifted to John Dudley at Kew. Richmond Palace recovered its pre-eminence later in the Elizabethan period, and the entire court retreated there in 1588 when the country was threatened by the Spanish Armada. Elizabeth I died at the palace in 1603. Charles I's reign saw the establishment of the Richmond Park hunting preserve in 1635, but after the Civil War Richmond's royal heritage came to an end, and Parliament ordered the demolition of the palace in 1650. Richmond itself, though, became a fashionable summer resort, its fortunes restored with the discovery of a chalybeate spring there in the 1670s. It has remained popular with prosperous Londoners ever since.

Neighbouring Kew was the site of an old ford across the Thames, first recorded in a 1313 survey of Sheen Manor; it was home to a thriving fishing industry, and a ferry was recorded in 1483 when its profitability attracted the attention of the taxman. Its proximity to Richmond made it attractive to courtiers in the sixteenth and seventeenth centuries, and also to the monarchy, and in time it became a royal centre in its own right, the Dutch House there being leased by George II's wife Queen Caroline in 1728 and being used by George III as a family home towards the end of the century. By this time the village of Kew had acquired some elegant houses, and it continued to expand throughout the nineteenth century.

To the east of Richmond, nestled in a sharp river bend, lies Barnes. In Saxon times it was united with Mortlake, but a separate manor was hived off in 939 which Saxon king Athelstan granted to the Dean and Chapter of St Paul's. The church of St Mary is first mentioned in an 1181 survey of the cathedral's estate, though the church was probably begun earlier at the beginning of the twelfth century. In the sixteenth century Barnes was home to Elizabeth I's private secretary and spymaster Sir Francis Walsingham, who owned Barn Elms manor house. Like Mortlake, Barnes became known for its market gardens, which supplied the capital, while Mortlake also acquired a tapestry works, established by James I in 1619; the fine work of its Flemish weavers adorned the royal collection. The railway came to Barnes and Mortlake in 1846, at which point they started their transformation into commuter villages.

Twickenham, on the north side of the Thames, is of very ancient origin. Traces of a Roman villa and a Roman farm have been unearthed in the district, and it is mentioned in a grant of land dating from 704. During the Middle Ages, along with Whitton and Isleworth, it formed part of a large manor. It was probably the site of an early ferry, though the first record of the crossing dates from the fifteenth century. The area also had royal connections. It was home to Elizabethan courtier Francis Bacon from 1580 – the queen dined with him at his lodge in 1592 – and the manor of Twickenham was given to Henrietta Maria of France on her marriage to Charles I in 1625. Twickenham's significance as a river crossing grew in 1777 with the construction of Richmond Bridge – now the oldest surviving Thames bridge – and again in 1848 as the site of the first railway bridge across the river. In the twentieth century, by which time Twickenham was becoming increasingly built up, it became home to the Twickenham Film Studio, which opened in 1913.

SOUTHWARK

The London borough of Southwark was formed in 1965 when the metropolitan boroughs of Southwark, Bermondsey and Camberwell were merged.

Southwark was originally a Roman settlement where two important roads, Stane Street and Watling Street, converged as they approached the river and the bridge that crossed it. It declined at the end of the Roman occupation but re-emerged in the ninth century as a fortified burgh, which became significant enough to be minting coins during the reign of Æthelred II (978–1016). It was devastated by William the Conqueror

when he invaded England in 1066, but then revived, and a new stone
bridge was built across the Thames in 1176. Because it lay beyond the City
of London, it became regarded as the City's playground and from at least
the fourteenth century, if not earlier, Southwark was renowned for its
stews, or brothels. In the Elizabethan period, theatres were established in
the area, again because the area was free from the jurisdiction of the City.
It was a lively, bustling area, full of houses and shops. It also boasted
fashionable residences, including Edward II's moated house the Rosary
at Horsleydown, built in the 1320s. Local industries included milling and
brewing, both benefiting from Southwark's waterfront location.

Rotherhithe, meanwhile, had by the twelfth century become a landing
place on the river for cattle on their way to London's Eastcheap meat
market, and docks came to dominate the area, though Edward III had a
palace there and Henry IV stayed in Rotherhithe, hoping that the fresh
air would cure his leprosy. Bermondsey is also of early date, being first
mentioned in an eighth-century charter, and again in the Domesday Book,
along with Camberwell. Bermondsey Abbey, an important Cluniac priory,
was founded in 1082 and later granted land in Rotherhithe, Dulwich,
Southwark and Whaddon. Medieval Bermondsey was home to a thriving
leather industry, which continued until the nineteenth century; and the
area was also known for its food production (in 1811 a local factory produced
Britain's first tinned food). Rotherhithe's Howland Dock opened in 1699,
and its successor the Greenland Dock, the first wet dock on the south
side of the Thames, was the base for London's whaling fleet until the mid
nineteenth century. Yet although this stretch of the Thames became ever
more busy, and some areas declined into slums, both Bermondsey and
Rotherhithe retained green spaces well into the nineteenth century,
Bermondsey even boasting a spa in Georgian times.

Further south, urbanisation was relatively late. Camberwell, for example,
which in 1086 was a small village with a church, surrounded by woodland,
remained largely rural until the 1830s. An annual fair was held on the village
green until the 1850s. Walworth and Peckham, also identified in the
Domesday Book, followed a similar path. Walworth is probably the oldest
settlement in the borough, its name suggesting that it was an enclosed
Celtic settlement which survived into Saxon times. Peckham refers to a
farm or homestead by a hill (probably Telegraph Hill). It was an important
market-gardening area until the last of its gardens gave way to suburban

housing in the late nineteenth century, though common land at Peckham Rye was preserved to form a haven of urban greenery. Rather later in date are Herne Hill and Denmark Hill, first recorded in 1789 and 1816. They were prosperous residential areas until the district was transformed in the mid nineteenth century by the construction of a web of railway lines that provided cheap and easy access to the city. Soon the two hills were covered in developments of small suburban houses. Right to the south, Dulwich, first recorded in the tenth century, its name meaning 'marshy meadow where dill is grown', was an attractive area of farmland and woods where Charles I hunted and by the eighteenth century a fashionable spa. It attracted wealthier residents, as did Alleyn's College (later Dulwich College), founded in the early seventeenth century. In the nineteenth century, tourists came to visit both Dulwich's picture gallery and its rural beauty. Intensive building came in the wake of the arrival of the railways in the 1850s.

SUTTON

The borough was formed in 1965 by merging the municipal boroughs of Sutton and Cheam, and Beddington and Wallington, and the urban district of Carshalton. It sits on a slope of the North Downs, the ridge of chalk hills extending along London's southern fringe.

Sutton ('south farmstead'), the ancient Surrey parish from which the borough takes its name, was a manor recorded in Domesday which belonged to the abbey at Chertsey until the Dissolution. For centuries the small village was quiet and unremarkable, but in the eighteenth century new roads from London to Epsom and to Brighton and the south coast brought travellers to the area and coaching inns to serve them. In the following century, Sutton became a railway junction, at which point the village grew rapidly. By the early twentieth century it was a town of suburban villas and modest houses, though the northern part of the parish remained largely agricultural.

Cheam is also recorded in Domesday and in the Middle Ages was divided into the manors of East Cheam and West Cheam, the former belonging to the Archbishop of Canterbury and the latter to the priory of Christchurch at Canterbury. A church is mentioned in Domesday. It was rebuilt on a new site just north of the original structure in 1864; a number of its post-Reformation clergy went on to become bishops. After the Dissolution of the Monasteries the two manors were taken and united by Henry VIII, who went on to build Nonsuch Palace near Cheam with stone cannibalised from Merton Abbey. The magnificent palace remained a regular royal residence until the time of Charles II. Incidentally, the town of 'East Cheam', made famous in the 1960s by comic actor Tony Hancock, although it has genuine medieval credentials, was entirely fictitious.

The origin of the name Carshalton, meaning 'farmstead where watercress grows by a river spring', alludes to the head springs of the River Wandle, which meets the Thames at Wandsworth. Such an abundant water supply clearly attracted early man and there is evidence of a prehistoric settlement here. Later, Hackbridge was to be built across the Wandle headstream near Carshalton, becoming the site of a number of powder mills from the seventeenth century. At the time of Edward the Confessor there were five manors in Carshalton, but after the Norman Conquest these were consolidated into one held by Geoffrey de Mandeville, one of William the Conqueror's wealthiest barons. By the eighteenth century Carshalton was home to a number of grand mansions, most notably Carshalton House, which in its long history has been a private home, a military college, a boarding school and a convent. The first railway line came to Carshalton in 1847, though the suburbanisation of the area did not really begin until the 1890s.

Both Beddington and Wallington are recorded in the Domesday Book, and both have more ancient roots. A Roman villa has been unearthed at Beddington, while Wallington's name indicates a Celtic settlement that survived Saxon colonisation of the area. The manor of Beddington was acquired by the Carew family in 1363, who held it until the nineteenth century. One scion of the family, Nicholas Carew, was briefly a favourite of Henry VIII and had a hand in the downfall of his second queen, Anne Boleyn, before falling foul of the king and being beheaded in 1539. For much of Beddington's history, the area was dominated by arable fields and grassland, though it was also known for the growing of medicinal herbs such as lavender.

The rural atmosphere persisted until the early twentieth century, at which point housing increasingly began to colonise the agricultural land and open spaces. Carshalton Beeches and Carshalton-on-the-Hill developed south of the old village. A major London County Council project at St Helier, named after LCC alderman Lady St Helier, was built between 1928 and 1936. The ambitious development included churches, schools, shops and a cinema and a mixture of houses and flats designed to house 40,000 residents.

TOWER HAMLETS

Tower Hamlets takes in much of the traditional East End and includes the old docklands of London. The 'Tower' of the borough name acknowledges the long association of the area with the Tower division of Middlesex, the Tower of London and its Constable; and the borough formed in 1965 also includes the metropolitan boroughs of Bethnal Green, Poplar and Stepney. The area became synonymous with poverty, overcrowding, disease and criminality during the late nineteenth century, as the area was inundated with people displaced by new building and industrialisation. Earlier, however, it had been a landscape of small villages, farmland and marshes.

Stepney is one of the oldest of the many familiar neighbourhoods of the East End. Meaning originally 'the wharf or landing place of a man called Stybba', and mentioned in the Domesday Book, the Bishop of London's manor and ancient parish of Stepney included all the land of the present-day borough and Hackney beyond. Many local place names emerged in the medieval period. Some, such as Ratcliff, meaning 'red bank or cliff', and Blackwall, meaning 'artificial bank for holding back the river', point to the area's proximity to the Thames. Others refer to their location in reference to the City of London – the medieval settlement of Mylesende was one mile distant from the City's Aldgate. At the area's eastern extremity was the River Lea, which formed the boundary between the ancient counties of Essex and Middlesex and later the County of London. Along its southern edge there was marsh and reclaimed land that was prone to flooding, and much of the ancient parish sat less than twenty feet above sea level. The manor of Stepney was surrendered to the Crown in 1550 and was granted first (along with the manor of Hackney) to Sir Thomas Wentworth, a courtier of Henry VIII, and his son Edward VI, and later to Elizabeth I's chief adviser Lord Burghley (linked to

Wentworth by marriage). During the English Civil War of the mid seventeenth century the estate was sequestered from the Royalist Earls of Cleveland (descendants of Baron Wentworth). It was returned to the family at the Restoration, but was then at the centre of legal wrangling after they become heavily indebted.

Arable farming formed the basis of the medieval economy of the area. Tenants on the marshland managed to maintain some arable fields until fifteenth-century floods chased them off. Consequently, much of the Isle of Dogs was given over to sheep grazing. Domesday records four flour mills in the district and in the following centuries there were mills at Shadwell, East Smithfield, Bow, Wapping and Old Ford. Domesday woodlands supported 500 pigs and stretched eastward from Bethnal Green, though much had been cleared by the fourteenth century. At Limehouse, the kilns which gave their name to the district produced valuable lime for use in building, agriculture, bleaching and curing leather. Shipbuilding was taking place at Ratcliff on the river from at least the fourteenth century. Some London merchants and traders who did business with European ports made their home in the waterfront hamlets, and they were joined in time by the craftsmen and other labourers needed to support a growing community. The area near the river and beyond developed further as it attracted foreign migrants – notably Huguenot weavers, who sought refuge in Bethnal Green and Spitalfields – and then as the docks became industrialised many sought employment there.

The docks were primary targets for German air raids in the Second World War, causing the deaths of over 2,000 residents in the borough area. Tower Hamlets remained in a deprived state after the war, despite some new building, and things were made worse by the closing of many of the docks by the 1980s. Regeneration schemes have included the development at Canary Wharf and, more recently, that at the Olympic Park. Nevertheless, many parts of the borough remain severely deprived.

WALTHAM FOREST

The borough of Waltham Forest is an amalgamation of the municipal boroughs of Chingford, Leyton and Walthamstow, and took its name in

1965 from the original name of what is now Epping Forest. The area remains one of London's greenest boroughs, dominated by the forest and open spaces, which together constitute a fifth of the borough. It is rich in pre-Conquest history, with evidence of early hunting and habitation at Leyton and Bronze Age dwellings at Walthamstow. Roman building foundations and a cemetery have also been found at Leyton.

There were two manors in Walthamstow at the time of Domesday, those of Walthamstow and Higham. Substantial areas of woodland had already been cleared by this point to make way for cultivation, though the area remained part of the royal forest. Deer and their royal pursuers had free rein over woodland and farmland alike, though hunting was temporarily halted and the forest nearly sold off during the Interregnum that followed the English Civil War. In the same century, large houses for London's officials and merchants began appearing in Walthamstow, its oldest surviving domestic building, now known as the Ancient House, being built towards the end of the Middle Ages. A well-subscribed coach service ran to the city for much of the nineteenth century, eventually superseded by the railway. The Upper Walthamstow residential district developed in the late nineteenth century. The much-loved Walthamstow greyhound stadium was established in 1931.

The name Chingford points to an early ford across the River Lea, perhaps on the old road to Edmonton. Early farmers worked small clearings in the woodland, and the fertile land by the Lea provided meadows and pasturing for their animals. The Domesday Survey records two manors at Chingford: the manor Chingford St Pauls, which the Dean and Chapter of St Pauls in the City had acquired in the eleventh century; and the manor which came to be known as Chingford Earls. Between them there were six fisheries using the River Lea. More forest in Chingford parish was cleared for settlement in the twelfth and thirteenth centuries. Henry VIII acquired both manors in the 1540s, and in 1543 built what came to be known as Queen Elizabeth's Hunting Lodge (originally the Great Standing), from which to view the hunt (it was made into the Epping Forest Museum in 1895). The natural boundaries of river and forest meant that Chingford parish remained somewhat isolated and undisturbed by the growing city to the south: in the seventeenth century it consisted of little more than a scattering of small villages, including those at Chingford Hatch and Chingford Green.

However, the railway (via Walthamstow) arrived in Chingford in 1873 and in the 1880s Chingford played host to day-trippers from the metropolis planning to spend a day in Epping Forest. Rapid growth came during the interwar period, and Chingford Mount and South Chingford also developed south of the town.

Leyton, anciently the farmstead on the River Lea, is recorded in the Domesday Book as Leintune, at which time it was divided into six estates. On early maps it is sometimes referred to as Low Leyton. Away from the river, the medieval Leyton atte Stone, now Leytonstone, grew up around what was probably a milestone on the old Roman Road from London to Waltham and Epping Forest. For much of its history the north of the parish remained largely wooded, while some areas of marshland were used for grazing and others for hay production; there is also evidence of some early open-field cultivation. In the nineteenth century Leyton, like Chingford, proved popular with day-trippers attracted to the area by its woodland, and it also became known for its local sports: it was home to the Leyton Orient football club and Essex County Cricket Club from 1881 and 1886 respectively. During the First World War Leyton suffered heavily from airship raids and nearly 1,300 homes were damaged.

WANDSWORTH

One of the inner London boroughs, it was formed in 1965 by the amalgamation of the metropolitan boroughs of Battersea and Wandsworth, with the exception of Clapham and most of Streatham, which became part of Lambeth.

Many of the familiar districts of the borough are listed in Domesday – Wandsworth, Tooting, Putney, Balham and Battersea – at which time it was a relatively populous area. A Roman farming community had flourished at the Putney river crossing, and various sites including Balham and Tooting had emerged as Anglo-Saxon settlements. By 1086, Tooting was divided into three manors, the two largest of which became Tooting Bec, so called owing to its association with the Abbey of Bec in Normandy, and Tooting Graveney, the manor of the Abbey of Chertsey which in the twelfth century was owned by one Haimo de Gravenel. Balham was a small settlement of perhaps only twenty people, held by a Norman lord who gave the manor to Bermondsey Abbey in 1103. Battersea, by contrast, had a population of over 300 people, seven watermills and land for seventeen plough teams. Putney and Roehampton formed part of the Archbishop of Canterbury's manor of Mortlake, which drew some of its revenue from the levying of tolls on those crossing the river.

During the Middle Ages, most of the borough was in cultivation under various systems of open fields. The North Field and South Field (now the district of Southfields) in Wandsworth are recorded during this period. There was also common and heath land: the West Common at Putney, Roehampton and Wimbledon, and the East Common in what is now Battersea and Wandsworth. Some areas of common and woodland were also brought under enclosed cultivation, forming early market gardens. Putney Park was created in the fourteenth century to supply venison to the house of the Archbishop at Mortlake.

In the fifteenth century, prosperous Londoners began to look to Wandsworth and Putney as areas in which to buy estates and invest their money. This led to further enclosures, and woodland was cut down and turned over to more profitable uses. By the mid sixteenth century, Roehampton's open fields were all enclosed and Putney had acquired a number of well-to-do residents. Wandsworth village was also growing, and a new stone bridge over the Wandle was bringing increased traffic to the area. Dutch craftsmen settled in the area in the late 1500s and in the following century Wandsworth gave refuge to French Huguenots, the two groups bringing with them valuable skills in cloth weaving, dyeing, printing, metal and leather working and various other enterprises. Wandsworth now began to emerge as an important industrial area. Industry also spread to such waterfront areas as Battersea, where fishing and transport formed a large part of the local economy, too.

The prosperity and prestige of Roehampton and Putney continued to grow throughout the seventeenth century, and the two settlements attracted ever-grander houses and wealthy inhabitants. Putney even went so far as to pave its high street at great expense in 1656. One of England's first great Palladian mansions, Roehampton House, was built in 1712 and some of Georgian Britain's finest architects, such as Sir John Soane and

James Gibbs, undertook commissions in the district. Roehampton housed many MPs, including Pitt the Younger, and George III regularly held military reviews on Putney Heath.

The plague of 1665 dealt a heavy blow to Battersea and Wandsworth, killing nearly 20 per cent of the local population. Nevertheless, industrial growth continued and by 1687 Wandsworth gunpowder mills were the second largest in the country. The largest of the land enclosures took place after 1750, and in the early nineteenth century areas of the borough began to gain value as building land. The usual ribbon development took place along thoroughfares and around areas of common land, followed by the creation of new roads and full-scale residential estates. Building became an important local industry as the area was developed into middle- and working-class suburbs. The arrival of the railways did much to lessen the exclusive atmosphere of Putney and Roehampton in the course of the later nineteenth century, and large houses were increasingly given over to institutional ownership.

In the twentieth century the borough suffered the suburban decline typical of many of London's inner suburbs. A number of major housing schemes were embarked upon after the Second World War, including those at Roehampton, but swathes of rehabilitated Victorian and Edwardian housing survive throughout the borough.

WESTMINSTER

Westminster has always been at the political heart of not only London, but also England. While it is a London borough, it was awarded city status in 1965, after the metropolitan borough of Westminster was amalgamated with the metropolitan boroughs of St Marylebone and Paddington.

Westminster originally denoted the great west monastery of St Peter founded by Edward the Confessor on Thorney Island, where two streams of the River Tyburn flowed into the Thames. William the Conqueror chose the abbey as the venue for his coronation on Christmas Day 1066, and his son William II built the great Westminster Hall in 1097. For a thousand years this area has been the main seat of government for England

and later the United Kingdom. The borough not only includes this ancient seat of power, but also reflects the many stages in the capital's development, containing some of London's earliest suburbs, in the West End (St James's, Soho, Mayfair), and later developments of the eighteenth and nineteenth centuries (Marylebone, Paddington, St John's Wood, Bayswater, Pimlico, Belgravia).

London grew west from the boundaries of the City into areas we now know as Soho, St James's and Mayfair in the seventeenth and early eighteenth centuries. Before this there were few roads, almost no houses, and the church of St Martin-in-the-Fields, first recorded in 1222 when it was the subject for dispute between the Abbot of Westminster and the Bishop of London, sat as the name indicates in the middle of arable fields. There were the fields of St Martin, St Giles and St James, which in the medieval period mostly belonged to the religious houses, including Westminster Abbey and the Convent of Abingdon, and the Hospital of St James, located on the site of the current palace. Henry VIII acquired St James's in the 1530s. The hospital made way for his palace and part of the fields was enclosed and turned into meadow land. Eventually Soho, St James's and then Mayfair acquired squares and streets of fashionable houses.

The inexorable growth of London continued across Westminster, taking in Marylebone and Bayswater to the west and to the north Paddington, Maida Vale and St John's Wood. The estate of Paddington was held by Westminster Abbey until the Reformation when it passed to the Bishop of London, who held the estate until it was given to the Ecclesiastical Commissioners in 1868. Bayswater, its name deriving from the medieval 'Bayards Watering' where horses were rested and were given water at a crossing of the Westbourne Brook, was only a small hamlet in the seventeenth century. At Paddington, extensive woodlands that had been there in the fourteenth century had been reduced to mere dozens of acres by the eighteenth century. At that time there were common fields at Westbourne, but the Paddington estate was mostly pasture and meadow, which supplied hay to London. There were nurseries and market gardens at Marylebone and Paddington as well as dairy herds. By the early nineteenth century, much of the area was still semi-rural, though streets filled with new houses soon brought the unbroken march of development up to Maida Vale and St John's Wood. To the south of Hyde Park the aristocratic estates were also developed. At Belgravia in the 1820s, some of London's finest squares appeared in what had once been a swamp and where just forty years before one of the first experiments with ballooning had been made. Further south, Pimlico had once contained osier beds where willow was grown. By the mid nineteenth century, both were residential neighbourhoods.

LONDON'S POSTCODES

In 1856, to cope with the estimated 100 million items or so of post sent to and within the capital each year, Sir Rowland Hill devised the London postal district. It adopted a twelve-mile radius from the central post office at St Martin's le Grand, and stretched from Waltham Cross in the north to Carshalton in the south, and from Southall in the west to Romford in the east. The area as a whole was divided into ten regions, each given a new London suffix – EC, WC, N, NE, E, SE, S, SW, W and NW. It took some two years to implement the new system fully, and then ten years later in 1868 various refinements were made: NE was abolished and the area merged with E, while S was dropped and the area split between SW and SE. At the same time, the boundary in the east was brought back, removing areas such as Great Ilford.

A further refinement was introduced in 1917 when, to ensure greater efficiency at a time of war, area numbers were introduced, 1 being allocated to the head office in each district and the other numbers then being distributed alphabetically according to the name of location of each area post office (SE2 is Abbey Wood, SE3 is Blackheath, SE4 is Brockley, SE5 is Camberwell, and so on). Some particularly heavily populated districts were later subdivided further.

Keeping up with the changes to the boundaries of Greater London proved quite a task for the Post Office, and was something it never quite achieved. The changes implemented in 1917, for example, substantial though they were, did not actually match the boundaries of the London County Council. The creation of the GLC in 1965, similarly, did not lead to seismic change in London's postal districts, principally because it was deemed that such change would be prohibitively expensive. The new area included in Greater London therefore made use of twelve different postcodes for the new areas: EN (Enfield), HA (Harrow), UB (Uxbridge), and so on. London's postal district today covers most of Greater London, but excludes Barking and Dagenham, Havering,

Hillingdon and Sutton. Strangely, it does include one place outside Greater London: Sewardstone in Essex.

Postcodes have become something of a social badge. People in north-west London are very aware of the different nuances of neighbouring NW6 and NW10, just as those in SW1 feel their postcode makes a very different statement from SW3. Among teen gangs, postcodes have even achieved tribal status on occasion.

APPENDIX 3

LONDON'S POPULATION, 1801–2011

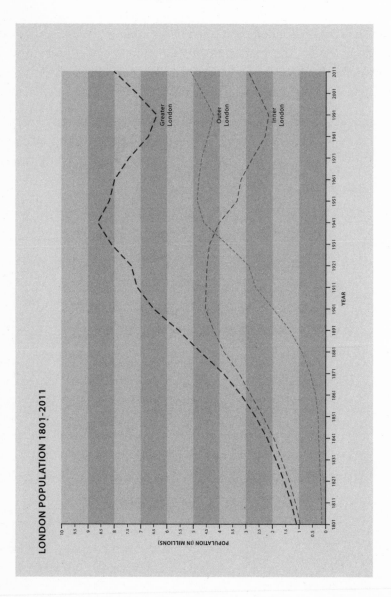

GREATER LONDON
IN THE 1830s

'The Environs of London', published in 1832, shows the Greater London area as it was in the years immediately preceding the coming of the railways. At the time, the centre was still quite contained, while the outer areas remained a patchwork of villages, farms, woodland and marsh.

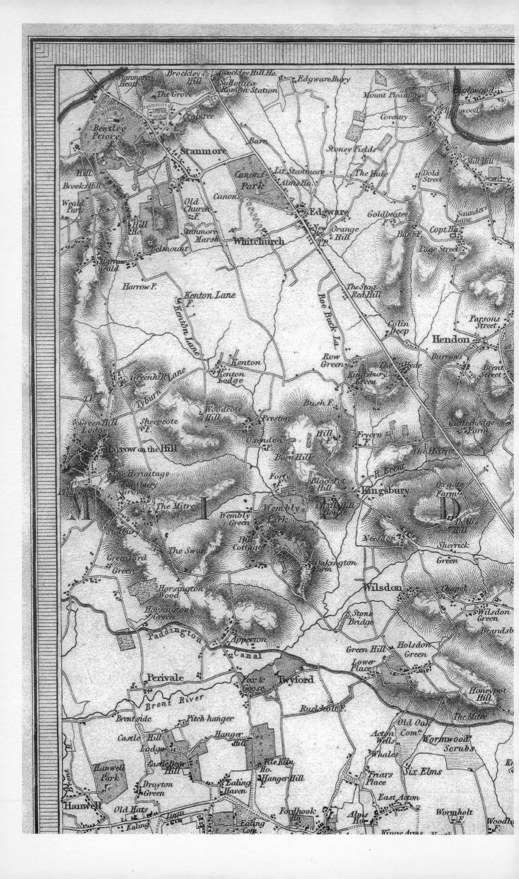

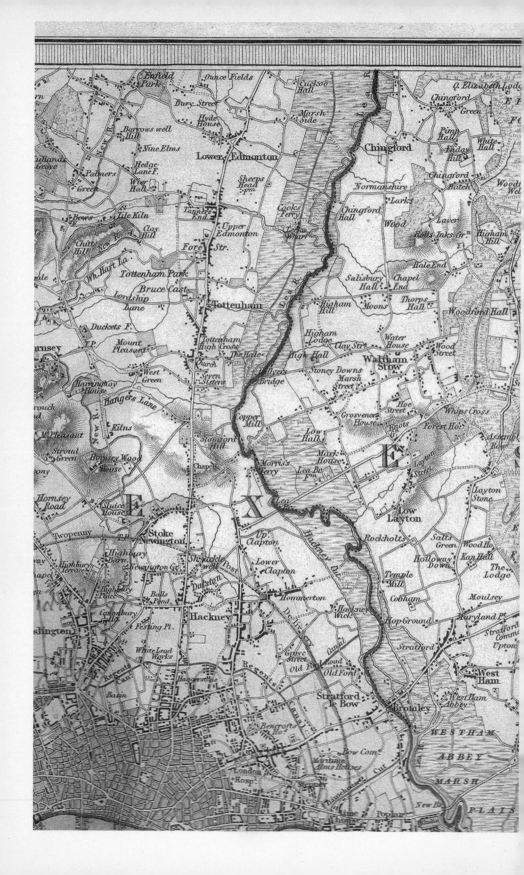

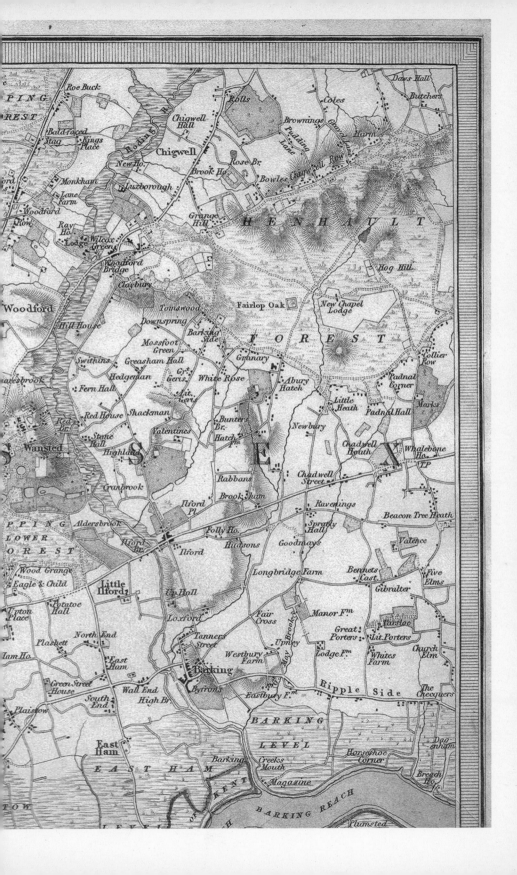

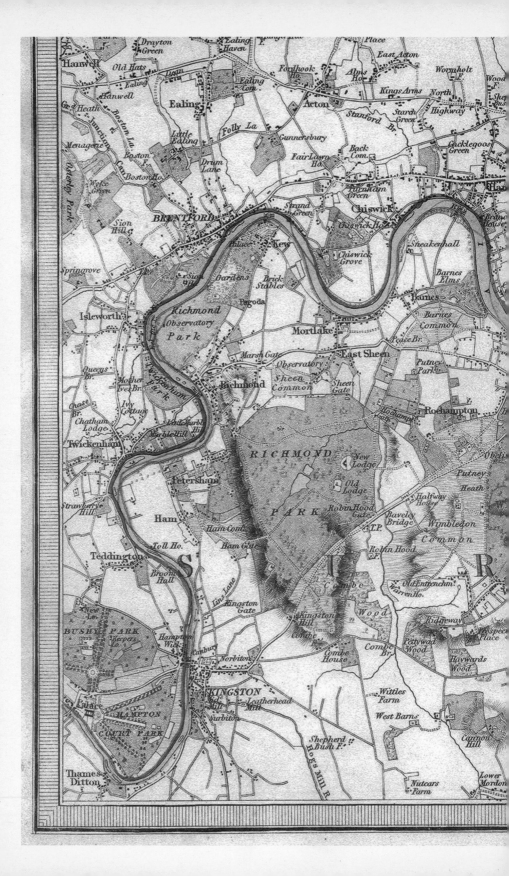

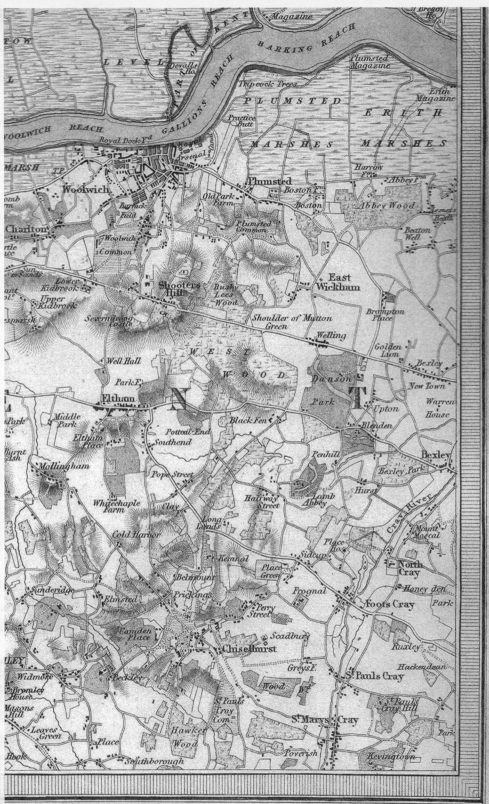

Drawn & Engraved by H. Waters.

A wealth of material exists about the history of London's thirty-two boroughs and their constituent towns, villages and parishes. If you want to find out more about a particular area, one of the best places to start is the Victoria County History (VCH) series for Middlesex, Surrey, Essex, Hertfordshire and Kent, and also (for places closer to the centre) the Survey of London (see www.british-history.ac.uk). Various detailed local and pictorial histories are also available. The relevant volumes of the Buildings of England series (Yale University Press) are invaluable for an understanding of local architectural history.

Each London borough has its own archive service or local study centre, and a major collection of records for the various representative bodies (Metropolitan Board of Works, London County Council, Greater London Council and the Greater London Authority) is housed at the London Metropolitan Archives. In addition, the Museum of London and various local museums not only contain displays that pertain to London life but also house invaluable documents. The National Archives at Kew (www.nationalarchives.gov.uk) are awash with material relating to the history of the London area, from the Domesday Book (1085) to the Lloyd George Domesday (1910) and beyond. Many of these rich archival collections are listed in the holdings of AIM25, a major online project designed to bring together all the disparate sources for the region bounded by the M25.

Other useful online resources include booth.lse.ac.uk (for Booth's poverty maps), www.oldbaileyonline.org (for records of trials at the Old Bailey), www.oxforddnb.com (for biographies of eminent Londoners) and www.ukcensusonline.com (for census returns).

The following bibliography is inevitably highly selective and does not list individually the various resources referred to above.

B. Abel-Smith, *The Hospitals, 1800–1948: A Study in Social Administration in England and Wales* (2000)
P. Ackroyd, *London: The Biography* (2000)

Anonymous, *14 Stanhope Gate, Fashionably Situated in Mayfair: The Story of a Georgian House* (1947)

C. Arnold, *City of Sin: London and Its Vices* (2010)

C. Arnold, *Necropolis: London and Its Dead* (2006)

G. M. Ayres, *England's First State Hospitals and the Metropolitan Asylums Board* (1971)

C. Barron, *London in the Later Middle Ages* (2004)

N. Barton, *The Lost Rivers of London* (1992)

W. Besant, *London South of the Thames* (1912)

R. Byrne, *Prisons and Punishments of London* (1989)

J. Carey, *The Intellectuals and the Masses* (1992)

G. Clegg, *Clapham Past* (1998)

H. Conway, *People's Parks: The Design and Development of Victorian Parks in Britain* (1991)

E. Course, *London Railways: Then and Now* (1987)

H. Cunningham, *The Invention of Childhood* (2006)

P. Cunningham and H. B. Wheatley, *London Past and Present: Its History, Associations and Traditions* (2011)

J. R. Day and J. Reed, *The Story of London's Underground* (2010)

D. Defoe, *A Tour thro' London about the Year 1725*, ed. Sir M. M. Beeton and E. Beresford Chancellor (1929)

——, *A Tour through the Whole Island of Great Britain* (1726)

J. Dent, *The Quest for Nonsuch* (1962)

C. Dickens, *Dickens's Dictionary of London: An Unconventional Handbook* (1879)

W. A. Drew, *Glimpses and Gatherings during a Voyage and Visit to London and the Great Exhibition in the Summer of 1851* (1852)

A. E. Dyson and J. Lovelock, *Education and Democracy* (1975)

E. Ekwall, *Two Early London Subsidy Rolls* (1951)

F. Engels, *The Condition of the Working Class in England in 1844* (1885)

J. Evelyn, *Fumifugium, or the Inconvenience of the Air and Smoke of London Dissipated* (1772)

J. Flanders, *The Victorian House* (2003)

J. Francis, *A History of the English Railway* (1851)

A. G. Gardiner, *The Life of Sir William Harcourt* (1923)

J. Gardiner, *The Blitz* (2010)

D. Gerhold, *Putney and Roehampton Past* (1994)

I. G. Gibbon and R. W. Bell, *History of the London County Council 1889–1939* (1939)

J. Gough Nichols (ed.), *The Diary of Henry Machyn: Citizen and Merchant-Taylor of London, from AD 1550 to AD 1563* (1848)

S. Halliday, *The Great Stink of London: Sir Joseph Bazalgette and the Cleansing of the Victorian Metropolis* (1990)

L. Hanley, *Estates: An Intimate History* (2012)

C. Hibbert, *London: The Biography of a City* (1980)

H. Hobhouse, *Thomas Cubitt: Master Builder* (1995)

A. Hope, *Londoners' Larder* (1990)

R. Imrie, L. Lees and M. Raco (ed.), *Regenerating London: Governance, Sustainability and Community in a Global City* (2009)

S. Inwood, *A History of London* (2000)

A. A. Jackson, *London's Local Railways* (1999)

——, *London's Termini* (1985)

——, *Semi-Detached London* (1991)

W. E. Jackson, *Achievement: A Short History of the London County Council* (1965)

R. Jenkins, *The First London Olympics 1908* (2008)

H. L. Jephson, *The Sanitary Evolution of London* (1907)

J. Kimber and F. Serjeant, *The Changing Face of Hammersmith and Fulham* (2002)

J. E. Lewis, *London: The Autobiography* (2008, pbk edn 2009)

W. S. Lewis (ed.), *Horace Walpole's Correspondence*, vol. 11 (1944)

F. Linnane, *London's Underworld: Three Centuries of Vice and Crime* (2004)

——, *London: The Wicked City: A Thousand Years of Vice in the Capital* (2003)

P. Loobey, *Battersea Past* (2002)

London County Council, *Administrative County of London Development Plan* (1955)

——, *London Housing* (1937)

D. Lysons, *The Environs of London: Being an Historical Account of the Towns, Villages, and Hamlets, within Twelve Miles of that Capital, Interspersed with Biographical Anecdotes* (1792–6)

J. Marriott, *Beyond the Tower: A History of East London* (2011)

B. Marshall, *Building London: The Making of a Modern Metropolis* (2007)

W. Matthews, *Hydraulia* (1835)

H. Mayhew, *London Labour and the London Poor* (1851)

V. C. Medvei and J. L. Thornton (eds), *The Royal Hospital of Saint Bartholomew, 1123–1973* (1974)

H. Meller and B. Parsons, *London Cemeteries: An Illustrated Guide and Gazetteer* (2011)

J. Middleton, *A View of the Agriculture of Middlesex* (1798)

M. Middleton, *Cities in Transition: The Regeneration of Britain's Inner Cities* (1991)

M. Miller and A. Stuart Gray, *Hampstead Garden Suburb* (1992)

A. D. Mills, *A Dictionary of London Place Names* (2001).

Geoffrey of Monmouth, *De Gestis Britonum*, ed. M. D. Reeve, trans. N. Wright (2007)

R. Morris, *The Verderers and Courts of Waltham Forest in the County of Essex 1250–2000* (2004)

J. J. Park, *The Topography and Natural History of Hampstead* (1818)

M. and C. Phillips, *Notting Hill in the Sixties* (1991)

R. Porter, *English Society in the Eighteenth Century* (1982)

——, *London: A Social History* (1994)

H. Quigley and I. Goldie, *Housing and Slum Clearance in London* (1934)

W. Ramsey (ed.), *The Blitz Then and Now*, vols 1–3 (1987–90)

S. Reynolds, W. de Boer and G. MacNiocaill (eds), *Elenctius Fontium Historiae Urbanae* (1988)

J. Richardson, *Covent Garden Past* (1995)

——, *Islington Past* (1998)

H. T. Riley (ed.), *Chronicles of the Mayors and Sheriffs of London: 1188–1274* (1863)

—— , *Liber Custumarum*, Rolls Series, No. 12, Vol. 2 (1860)

W. Robson, *The Government and Misgovernment of London* (1948)

T. Rowley, *The English Landscape in the Twentieth Century* (2006)

F. Rule, *London's Docklands: A History of the Lost Quarter* (2009)

A. Saint (ed.), *Politics and the People of London: The London County Council 1889–1965* (1989)

J. Schofield, *Medieval London Houses* (1995)

A. Scull, *The Most Solitary of Afflications: Madness and Society in Britain 1700–1900* (1993)

F. H. W. Sheppard, *Survey of London*, vol. 39: *The Grosvenor Estate in*

Mayfair, Part 1 (General History) (1977)

J. Simmie (ed.), *Planning London* (1994)

G. Simms, *Horrible London* (1889)

F. Smallwood, *Greater London: The Politics of Metropolitan Reform* (1965)

J. Stow, *A Survey of London Written in the Year 1598* (2005)

J. Strype, *A Survey of the Cities of London and Westminster* (1720)

R. Tames, *Barking Past* (2002)

——, *Clerkenwell and Finsbury Past* (1999)

S. Taylor (ed.), *The Moving Metropolis: A History of London's Transport since 1800* (2001)

E. M. Thompson (ed.), *Robertus de Avesbury de Gestis Mirabilibus Regis Edwardi Tertii*, Rolls Series 93 (1889)

W. Thornbury and E. Walford, *Old and New London: A Narrative of its History, its people and its places*, 6 vols (1873–8)

A. Thornley (ed.), *The Crisis of London* (1992)

B. Thorpe (ed. and trans.), *The Anglo-Saxon Chronicle* (1861)

P. Thurmond Smith, *Policing Victorian London* (1985)

G. Tindall, *The Fields Beneath: The History of One London Village* (1977)

K. Waddington, *Charity and the London Hospitals, 1850–98* (2000)

E. Walford, *Greater London: A Narrative of Its History, Its People and Its Places* (1882)

——, *Old and New London* (1878)

R. Ward, *London's New River* (2003)

F. Warren, *Addington: A History* (1984)

B. Weinred and C. Hibbert, *The London Encyclopaedia* (1983)

J. White, *London in the Eighteenth Century* (2012)

——, *London in the Nineteenth Century* (2007)

——, *London in the Twentieth Century* (2001)

A. N. Wilson, *The Victorians* (2002)

C. Wolmar, *Fire & Steam* (2007)

D. Wragg, *Commuter City: How the Railways Shaped London* (2010)

P. Ziegler, *London at War 1939–45* (2002)

NOTES

Introduction

1. J. Stow, *A Survey of London Written in the Year 1598* (2005); P. Ackroyd, *London: The Biography* (2000); J. White, *London in the Twentieth Century* (2001); J. White, *London in the Nineteenth Century* (2007); J. White, *London in the Eighteenth Century* (2012).
2. J. E. Lewis, *London: The Autobiography*, pbk edn (2009).
3. W. fitz Stephen, *A Description of London*, trans. H. E. Butler, Historical Association Leaflets, 93–4 (1934).
4. J. Gough Nichols (ed.), *The Diary of Henry Machyn: Citizen and Merchant-Taylor of London, from A.D. 1550 to A.D. 1563* (1848).
5. J. Stow, *A Survey of London*, www.british-history.ac.uk.
6. J. Strype, *A Survey of the Cities of London and Westminster* (1720).
7. D. Lysons, *The Environs of London: Being an Historical Account of the Towns, Villages, and Hamlets, within Twelve Miles of that Capital, Interspersed with Biographical Anecdotes* (1792–6).
8. E. Walford, *Greater London: A Narrative of its History, its People and its Places* (1882), vol. 1, p. 5.

1: A Tale of Two Cities

1. Geoffrey of Monmouth, *De Gestis Britonum*, ed. M. D. Reeve, trans. N. Wright (2007), p. 66.
2. For more information about London place names, see A. D. Mills, *A Dictionary of London Place Names* (2001).
3. Quoted in J. E. Lewis, *London: The Autobiography*, pbk edn (2009), p. 10.
4. S. Sturluson, *Heimskringla or the Chronicles of the Kings of Norway*, 'The Saga of Olaf Haraldson', Part 1, Online Medieval and Classical Library, http://omacl/org/Heimskringla/haraldson1.

2: From the Battle of Hastings to the Battle of Barnet

1. B. Thorpe (ed. and trans.), *The Anglo-Saxon Chronicle* (1861), vol. 2, p. 186.

549

2. C. Barron, *London in the Later Middle Ages* (2004), p. 121.

3. S. Reynolds, W. de Boer and G. MacNiocaill (eds), *Elenctius Fontium Historiae Urbanae* (1988), p. 80, and H. T. Riley (ed. and trans.), *Liber Custumarum*, Rolls Series, No. 12, vol. 2 (1860), pp. 2–15.

4. J. Schofield, *Medieval London Houses* (1995), pp. 210–12.

5. Quoted in W. Thornbury, *Old and New London* (1878), Vol. 3, ch. 16.

6. J. Stow, *A Survey of London*, 'Liberties of the Dutchie of Lancaster without Temple Barre'. www.british-history.ac.uk.

7. H. T. Riley (ed. and trans.), *Liber Custumarum*, Rolls Series, No. 12, Vol. 2 (1860), pp. 2–15.

8. You can confirm this picture for yourself: the miracle of modern technology has produced a digitised and indexed version of the Domesday Book, now available online via the National Archives website, www.nationalarchives.gov.uk. Type in a place name from any of the modern London boroughs, and chances are you will find a corresponding entry for its eleventh-century forebear among the hundred or so that appear, revealing the names of the handful of landowners, the composition of the manor, and the fact that it was mainly covered in grassland, crops or trees.

9. Calendar of Close Rolls (1364–8), p. 395.

10. H. T. Riley (ed. and trans.), *Chronicles of the Mayors and Sheriffs of London: 1188–1274* (1863), pp. 61–74.

11. E. Ekwall, *Two Early London Subsidy Rolls* (1951), pp. 142, 144, 262 and 328.

12. E. M. Thompson (ed. and trans.), *Robertus de Avesbury de Gestis Mirabilibus Regis Edwardi Tertii*, Rolls Series, No. 93 (1889), pp. 406–7.

13. Quoted in J. E. Lewis, *London: The Autobiography*, pbk edn (2009), p. 104.

14. Calendar of Husting Wills, vol. 2 (1890), p. 346.

15. London Metropolitan Archives, Commissary Court Will, register 5, folio 210v.

16. The National Archives, PROB 2/486.

17. D. Keene, 'Medieval London and Its Region', *London Journal*, 14 (1989), p. 103.

18. Ibid., p. 104.

19. F. J. Fisher, 'The Development of the London Food Market, 1540–1640', *Economic History Review*, 5:2 (April 1935), p. 62.

20. Ibid., p. 60.
21. Ibid., p. 54.
22. J. A. Galloway and M. Murphy, 'Feeding the City: Medieval London and its Agrarian Hinterland', *London Journal*, 16 (1991), p. 9.
23. J. A. Galloway, D. Keene and M. Murphy, 'Fuelling the City: Production and Distribution of Firewood and Fuel in London's Region, 1290–1400', *Economic History Review*, xlix, 3 (1996), pp. 453 and 463.
24. Ibid., p. 465.
25. J. Stow, *A Survey of London*. www.british-history.ac.uk.

3: 'The Monstrous Growth'

1. J. Dent, *The Quest for Nonsuch* (1962), pp. 42, 79.
2. T. More, *Utopia* (1516), Book 1.
3. Quoted in V. C. Medvei and J. L. Thornton (eds), *The Royal Hospital of Saint Bartholomew, 1123–1973* (1974), p. 23.
4. J. Stow, *A Survey of London*. www.british-history.ac.uk.
5. Ibid.
6. Quoted in R. Porter, *London: A Social History* (1994), p. 82.
7. Baron Waldstein, *The Diary of Baron Waldstein*, trans. G. W. Groos (1981), quoted in J. E. Lewis, *London: The Autobiography*, pbk edn (2009), p. 145.
8. Quoted in Ben Weinreb and Christopher Hibbert (eds), *The London Encyclopaedia* (1983), p. 202.

4: The Industrial East, the Fashionable West

1. A. Young, *A Six Weeks' Tour through the Southern Counties of England and Wales* (1759), p. 75.
2. D. Defoe, *Tour through the Whole Island of Great Britain* (1726), Letter VI.
3. Quoted in R. Porter, *English Society in the Eighteenth Century* (1982), p. 46.
4. Cited in J. D. Pelzer, 'The Coffee Houses of Augustan London', *History Today*, 32:10 (October 1982).
5. Quoted in *14 Stanhope Gate* (1947), pp. 11–12.
6. D. Defoe, *A Tour thro' London about the Year 1725*, ed. Sir M. M. Beeton and E. Beresford Chancellor (1929), pp. 97–8.

7. F. H. W. Sheppard, *Survey of London*, vol. 39: *The Grosvenor Estate in Mayfair, Part 1 (General History)* (1977), p. 6.
8. W. S. Lewis (ed.), *Horace Walpole's Correspondence*, vol. 11 (1944), p. 287.

5: In Search of 'Healthful Air'

1. D. Defoe, *A Tour thro' London about the Year 1725*, ed. Sir M. M. Beeton and E. Beresford Chancellor (1929), p. 98.
2. D. Defoe, *A Journal of the Plague Year* (1722), p. 117.
3. Ibid., pp. 21–2.
4. T. Smollett, *Humphry Clinker* (1771), letter to Dr Lewis.
5. R. Percy, J. Limbird and J. Timbs, *The Mirror of Literature, Amusement & Instruction* (1828), vol. 10, p. 210.
6. D. Defoe, *Tour through the Whole Island of Great Britain* (1726), Letter VI.
7. Quoted in R. Porter, *London: A Social History* (1994), p. 145.
8. R. Anderson (ed.), *The Works of the British Poets* (1795), vol. 10, p. 464.
9. Quoted in J. White, *London in the Eighteenth Century* (2012), p. 35.
10. W. H. Quarrel and M. Hare (eds), *Travels of Zacharias Conrad von Uffenbach* (1934), p. 120.
11. D. Defoe, *Tour through the Whole Island of Great Britain* (1726), Letter VI.
12. J. J. Park, *The Topography & Natural History of Hampstead* (1818), p. 242.
13. J. Hawkins, *A General History of the Science & Practice of Music* (1776), p. 888.
14. J. Boswell, *Boswell's Life of Johnson* (1851), pp. 599–600.
15. M. Grosely, *Tour to London* (1772), cited in E. Walford's *Old & New London* (1893), vol. 6, pp. 452–3.

6: The Welfare of the People

1. Victoria County History, vol. 10, *A History of the County of Essex* (2001), p. 106.
2. R. Morris, *The Verderers and Courts of Waltham Forest in the County of Essex 1250–2000* (2004).
3. R. Porter, *English Society in the Eighteenth Century* (1982), p. 46.
4. J. Stow, *A Survey of London*, p. 116.

5. A. Pope, *The Dunciad* (1728), Book II.

6. Quoted in C. Hibbert, *London: The Biography of a City* (1980), pp. 163–4.

7 : 'The March of Bricks and Mortar'

1. Quoted in R. Porter, *London: A Social History* (1994), p. 248.

2. C. Dickens, *Oliver Twist* (1838), ch. 50.

3. C. Dickens, *Sketches by Boz* (1836), ch. 22.

4. F. Engels, *The Condition of the Working Class in England in 1844* (1885), ch.2

5. Quoted in J. E. Lewis, *London: The Autobiography*, pbk edn (2009), p. 271.

6. Quoted in R. Porter, *London: A Social History* (1994), p. 263.

7. Quoted in A. N. Wilson, *The Victorians* (2002), pp. 382–3.

8. *Illustrated London News*, 18 September 1852.

9. Quoted in R. Porter, *London: A Social History* (1994), p. 267.

8: 'The Ringing Grooves of Change'

1. Quoted in C. Wolmar, *Fire & Steam* (2007), p. 58.

2. C. Dickens, *Dombey and Son* (1848), ch. 6.

3. London and Birmingham Railway Company prospectus.

4. *Birmingham Daily Post*, 2 December 1858, Issue 258, p. 4.

5. Metropolitan Board of Works Minutes (1862), p. 476.

6. 'Into Hades', *The Times*, 10 January 1863, quoted in J. E. Lewis, *London: The Autobiography*, pbk edn (2009), pp. 324–5.

7. C. Dickens, *Dombey and Son* (1848), ch. 15.

8. M. Robbins, 'A Middlesex Diary', *Transactions of the London & Middlesex Archaeological Society*, vol. XI, Part II, quoted in W. G. Hoskins, *The Making of the English Landscape* (1955), pp. 207–8.

9. *Building News* (1890), quoted in R. Porter, *London: A Social History* (1994), p. 280.

10. D. H. Laurence (ed.), *George Bernard Shaw: Collected Letters, 1911–25* (1985), p. 367, quoted in J. Carey, *The Intellectuals and the Masses* (1992), p. 48.

11. Quoted in C. Wolmar, *Fire & Steam* (2007), p. 85.

12. *Illustrated London News*, 6 June 1857, Issue 862, p. 556.

13. Ibid., p. 535.

14. Ibid., p. 556.

15. Quoted in J. E. Lewis, *London: The Autobiography*, pbk edn (2009), p. 239.

16. *Illustrated London News*, 1 April 1843, Issue 40, p. 226.

17. W. A. Drew, *Glimpses and Gatherings during a Voyage and Visit to London and the Great Exhibition in the Summer of 1851* (1852).

9: A Tale of Several Suburbs

1. Quoted in J. Carey, *The Intellectuals and the Masses* (1992), p. 46.

2. C. L. Graves, *Life and Letters of Sir George Grove*, quoted in 'Parishes: Battersea with Penge', in H. E. Malden (ed.) *A History of the County of Surrey*, vol. 4 (1912), pp. 8–17.

3. H. E. Malden (ed.), *A History of the County of Surrey* (1912), vol. 4, pp. 8–17.

4. 'The Incorporation of West Ham', *The Times*, 1 November 1886, p. 12.

5. 'Finchley: Introduction', in *A History of the County of Middlesex*, vol. 6 (1980).

6. See J. Flanders, *The Victorian House* (2003), p. 92.

7. 'Finchley: Introduction', in *A History of the County of Middlesex*, vol. 6 (1980).

8. Quoted in R. Tames, *London: A Cultural History* (2006), p. 251.

9. Booth notebooks, B360, p. 141.

10. Ibid., B361, pp. 239–41.

10: Feeling the Strain

1. Quoted in J. White, *London in the Nineteenth Century* (2007), p. 30.

2. Quoted in A. Morrison, *A Child of the Jago* (ed. P. Miles, 2012), p.176.

3. A. Morrison, *A Child of the Jago* (ed. P. Miles, 2012), pp. 11–12.

4. http://booth.lse.ac.uk.

5. Booth notebooks, B372, pp. 69–71.

6. Ibid., B365, p. 45.

7. G. Gissing, *New Grub Street* (2007 edn), p. 163.

8. W. Besant, *London South of the Thames* (1912), p. 127.

9. *The Times*, 3 August 1846.

10. Quoted in H. L. Jephson, *The Sanitary Evolution of London* (1907), p. 70.

11. Quoted in S. E. Finer, *The Life and Times of Sir Edwin Chadwich* (1980), p. 334.

12. Quoted in W. Matthews, *Hydraulia* (1835), p. 372.
13. Quoted in J. E. Lewis, *London: The Autobiography*, pbk edn (2009), p. 301.
14. C. Dickens, *Dickens's Dictionary of London: An Unconventional Handbook* (1879).

11: Essential Services
1. Quoted in H. Cunningham, *The Invention of Childhood* (2006), p. 147.
2. A. Trollope, *Autobiography* (1883), ch. 1.
3. Quoted in A. E. Dyson and J. Lovelock, *Education and Democracy* (1975); see also www.educationengland.org.uk.
4. Letter from Charles Dickens to Angela Burdett-Coutts, 16 September 1843, quoted in J. White, *London in the Nineteenth Century* (2007), pp. 427–8.
5. H. Mayhew, 'Of the children street-sellers of London', in *London Labour and the London Poor* (1851), vol. 1.
6. G. Sims, *Horrible London* (1889), ch. 4.
7. G. M. Ayers, *England's First State Hospitals and the Metropolitan Asylums Board* (1971).
8. House of Commons, Report of the Select Commission on Criminal and Pauper Lunatics 1807, quoted in A. Scull, *The Most Solitary of Afflictions: Madness and Society in Britain 1700–1900* (1993).
9. www.oldbaileyonline.org.
10. www.oldbaileyonline.org.
11. www.oldbaileyonline.org.
12. A. D. Mills, *A Dictionary of London Place Names* (2010), p. 278.
13. C. Dickens, *Our Mutual Friend* (1864–5), ch. 8.
14. D. Defoe, *A Journal of the Plague Year* (1722).
15. *Punch*, July–December 1849.

12: A Government for the Metropolis
1. P. B. Shelley, *Peter Bell the Third, by Miching Mallecho, Esq.* (1839).
2. E. Walford, *Greater London* (1882), p. 2.
3. J. S. Mill, *Considerations on Representative Government* (1861), ch. 15.
4. A. G. Gardiner, *The Life of Sir William Harcourt* (1923), vol. 1, p. 501.
5. Hansard, Parl. Debs. (series 3), vol. 287, cols 40–70 (8 April 1884).
6. *Oxford Dictionary of National Biography* (2004).

7. A. G. Gardiner, *The Life of Sir William Harcourt* (1923), vol. 1, pp. 501–3.

8. Hansard, 19 March 1888.

9. Fabian Society Tract 8, pp. 12–13.

10. Speech of Lord Rosebery on re-election as chairman of the council, 7 November 1889, quoted in I. G. Gibbon and R. W. Bell, *History of the London County Council, 1889–1939* (1939).

11. I. G. Gibbon and R. W. Bell, *History of the London County Council*, p. 76.

12. R. Porter, *London: A Social History* (1994), p. 289.

13. *The Times*, 19 April 1905, p. 12.

14. Ibid., 6 February 1892, p. 7.

15. Ibid., 24 November 1892, p. 14.

16. Quoted in W. A. Robson, *The Government and Misgovernment of London* (1948), p. 88.

17. *The Times*, 17 November 1893, p. 12.

18. Ibid., 18 March 1889.

13: 'Breathing Places for the Metropolis'

1. J. Middleton, *A View of the Agriculture of Middlesex* (1798), p. 100.

2. Ibid., p. 101.

3. J. Loudon *Hints on Breathing Spaces for the Metropolis* (1829). See www.gardenvisit.com/landscape_architecture.

4. Ibid.

5. W. Thornbury and E. Walford, *Old and New London* (1893), p. 228.

6. C. Dickens, *Sketches by Boz* (1836), ch. 12.

7. E. Walford, *Old and New London*, Vol. 6 (1878), pp. 224–36.

8. E. Walford, *Greater London: A Narrative of Its History, Its People and Its Places* (1885) pp. 3–4.

9. Quoted in J. E. Lewis, *London: The Autobiography*, pbk edn (2009), p. 287.

10. Booth notebooks, B346, p. 23.

11. Ibid., B371, p. 237.

14: From Metropolis to Metroland

1. See A. A. Jackson, *Semi-Detached London* (1973).

2. W. R. Powell (ed.), *A History of the County of Essex* (1973), vol. 6.

3. E. Nesbit, *The Railway Children* (1906), ch. 1.

4. http://www.acepilots.com/wwi/zeppelin.html.

5. H. Quigley and I. Goldie, *Housing and Slum Clearance in London* (1934), p. 116.

6. London County Council, *London Housing* (1937), p. 74.

7. J. Betjeman, 'The Metropolitan Railway' (1954).

8. Quoted in J. E. Lewis: *London: The Autobiography*, pbk edn (2009), pp. 385–6.

9. P. G. Wodehouse, 'Uncle Fred Flits By', in *Young Men in Spats* (1936).

10. J. B. Priestley, *English Journey* (1934), p. 325, quoted in J. White, *London in the Twentieth Century* (2001), p. 30.

11. See J. White, *London in the Twentieth Century* (2001), p. 221.

12. G. Orwell, *Keep the Aspidistra Flying* (1989 edn), p. 231.

15: Wartime Destruction, Peacetime Reconstruction

1. Anonymous schoolgirl, 'Children Evacuated', from *North London Collegiate School Magazine*, December 1939, quoted in J. E. Lewis, *London: The Autobiography*, pbk edn (2009), pp. 405–6.

2. Len Jones, 'The Blitz', from Peter Stansky, *The First Day of the Blitz* (2007), quoted in J. E. Lewis, *London: The Autobiography*, pbk edn (2009), pp. 409–10.

3. www.raf.mod.uk/history/campaign_diaries.cfm.

4. Virginia Woolf, 'The Blitz', from *A Writer's Diary* (*c.* 1954), ed. Leonard Woolf, quoted in J. E. Lewis, *London: The Autobiography*, pbk edn (2009), pp. 410–12.

5. LCC Bomb Census Maps, p. 8.

6. Vera Hodgson, 'Doodlebugs', from *Few Eggs and NO Oranges: The Diaries of Vera Hodgson, 1940–45* (1999), quoted in J. E. Lewis, *London: The Autobiography*, p. 416.

7. 'The Blitz', CBS broadcast, 13 September 1940, quoted in J. E. Lewis, *London: The Autobiography*, p. 413.

8. James Lees-Milne, 'VE Day', from *Diaries, 1942–54*, abridged by Michael Bloch (2007), quoted in J. E. Lewis, *London: The Autobiography*, p. 338.

9. M. and C. Phillips, *Notting Hill in the Sixties* (1991), p. 22.

10. *New Yorker*, vol. 29, pt 3 (1953), p. 108.

11. *Administrative County of London Development Plan* (1955).

12. J. Evelyn, *Fumifugium, or the Inconvenience of the Air and Smoke of London Dissipated* (1661), p. 1.

16: Second Thoughts

1. L. Hanley, *Estates: An Intimate History*, (new edn 2012), p. 126.
2. Hansard, 28 February 1984.
3. Quoted in *Daily Mail*, 22 August 2007.
4. Quoted in T. Rowley, *The English Landscape in the Twentieth Century* (2006), p. 68.
5. www.civilservant.org.uk/numbers.pdf.
6. http://www.guardian.co.uk/data.

17: Who is in Charge?

1. Royal Commission on London Government, 1921.
2. Minutes of Evidence, Royal Commission on London Government, p. 51, quoted in W. A. Robson, *The Government and Misgovernment of London* (1948), p. 298.
3. Wal Hannington, 'The Hunger Marchers in Hyde Park', from *Unemployed Struggles, 1919–1936* (1977), quoted in J. E. Lewis, *London: The Autobiography* (2008), p. 318.
4. Terms of reference for the Royal Commission on Local Government in Greater London.

18: The People of the Suburbs

1. Joseph Addison, *The Spectator*, 12 June 1712, quoted in J. White, *London in the Eighteenth Century* (2012), pp. 2–3.
2. *London: North*, vol. 4, Buildings of England, B. Cherry and N. Pevsner (2002).
3. Quoted in J. E. Lewis, *London: The Autobiography*, pbk edn (2009), pp. 375–9.
4. C. Yee, *The Silent Traveller in London* (1938), introduction.
5. Quoted in J. E. Lewis, *London: The Autobiography*, pbk edn (2009), pp. 341–2.
6. Quoted in Graham Noble, '"Evil May Day": Re-examining the Race Riot of 1517', *History Review* (2008).

19: Hampton

1. H. Walpole letter to Richard Bentley, 15 August 1755.

PICTURE ACKNOWLEDGEMENTS

Black and white illustrations are reproduced by kind permission of:

The Advertising Archives: 346; Alamy: 41 (© Timewatch Images), 209 (© Classic Image), 232 (© Paris Pierce), 338 (© Lordprice Collection), 364 (© Interfoto), 384 (© Trinity Mirror/Mirrorpix); The Art Archive: 229; Bridgeman Art Library: 17 (Ken Welsh), 66, 167, 236 (The Stapleton Collection), 185, 201, 233, 239 (Private Collection), 140 (© Look and Learn/Peter Jackson Collection), 182 (Science Museum, London, UK); Corbis: 410 (© Gideon Mendel), 456 (© Eleanor Bentall); Getty Images: 243, 255 (Nick Wild), 358, 369, 375, 391 (Popperfoto), 387, 403, 407, 432, 435, 441, 442; Heritage Images: 77, 110, (City of London), 132 (© Museum of London); Mary Evans Picture Library: 57, 216, 225, 265, 287 & 452 (Peter Higginbotham Collection), 312, 326 (© Illustrated London News Ltd), 328, 334 (Bruce Castle Museum), 350, 366 (Vanessa Wagstaff Collection); © Museum of London: 258, 394, 461 (© Roger Mayne).

Colour illustrations are reproduced by kind permission of:

Inset One
Page 1, © Museum of London/Heritage-Images; page 2–3, O'Shea Gallery, London/The Bridgeman Art Library; page 4 (top), © Tyne & Wear Archives & Museums/The Bridgeman Art Library, page 4 (bottom) © Museum of London/The Bridgeman Art Library; page 5 (top), The Stapleton Collection/The Bridgeman Art Library; page 5 (bottom), City of London/Heritage-Images; page 6 (top), © Guildhall Art Gallery, City of London/The Bridgeman Art Library; page 6 (bottom), City of London Libraries & Guildhall Art Gallery/Heritage-Images; page 7 (top), City of London/Heritage-Images; page 7 (bottom), National Railway Museum, York, North Yorkshire/The Bridgeman Art Library; page 8, Mary Evans Picture Library.

Inset Two

Page 1, Mary Evans Picture Library; page 2–3, © Museum of London/ The Bridgeman Art Library; page 4 (top), The Art Archive/Museum of London; page 4 (bottom), The Bridgeman Art Library; page 5 (top), The Art Archive/Amoret Tanner Collection; page 5 (bottom), Mary Evans Picture Library; page 8, Tobi Corney/Getty Images.

Maps © Darren Bennett

INDEX

Page numbers in *italics* denote illustrations